Selected Essays of
Gottfried Haberler

Selected Essays of
Gottfried Haberler

Edited by
Anthony Y. C. Koo

The MIT Press
Cambridge, Massachusetts
London, England

This book was set in Palatino by Asco Trade Typesetting Ltd., Hong Kong, and printed and bound by Halliday Lithograph in the United States of America

Library of Congress Cataloging in Publication Data

Haberler, Gottfried, 1900–
  Selected essays of Gottfried Haberler.

  Bibliography: p.
  Includes index.
  1. Economics—Addresses, essays, lectures.   I. Koo, Anthony Y. C., 1918– .   II. Title.
HB171.H12   1985   330   85-68
ISBN 0-262-11105-5

This volume is respectfully and lovingly dedicated to Professor Haberler, whose wisdom and kindness have helped and inspired generations of students, and to Mrs. Friedl Haberler, whose eternal charm and vivacity have warmed so many hearts.

Contents

II International Finance

III Inflation and Business Cycles

Editor's Preface

The selection of essays by Gottfried Haberler has been a challenging task. His contributions, numbered in hundreds, span more than half a century and cover a broad spectrum of fields in economics. The page constraint of a single volume necessitated leaving out many worthy ones. The selected essays are arranged into five sections of closely related topics, and within each section they are arranged chronologically. The grouping by topics has not been easy; several essays properly belong to more than one heading or in sections of their own. The final decision in a few cases has to be arbitrary.

Four articles in the volume are translated from German and appear in English for the first time. One of them, "Critical Notes on Schumpeter's Theory of Money— The Doctrine of the 'Objective' Exchange of Money" is Haberler's maiden article. He later developed the idea into a book on the theory of index number, *Den Sinn der Indexzahlen*, 1927. The author has gone over the translation to ensure accuracy.

There are no substantive changes in the text except for minor typographical and mechanical corrections, updating forthcoming references, and insertion of first names to a few authors mentioned in Harberler's early papers. Postscripts have been inserted after several essays by Haberler himself to reflect his current (1984) thinking, and a bibliography of his works is included.

I am grateful to Herbert K. Zassenhaus for this translations, and my thanks to Robert E. Baldwin, Lawrence H. Officer, Thomas D. Willett and, above all, Gottfried Haberler for advice on selection.

I International Trade

1

The Theory of Comparative Costs and Its Use in the Defense of Free Trade[1]

Motto: As I read it, protection might procure economic advnatage in certain cases, if there was a Government wise enough to confine itself to them; but this condition is very unlikely to be fulfilled—F. Y. Edgeworth.
Free Trade, like Honesty, still remains the best policy—J. S. Nicholson.

The principal argument for free trade, to which most other arguments must be subordinate, or next to which their significance vanishes, is and has always been the doctrine of the international division of labor. With free trade, so runs this argument, every country produces those goods for whose production it is, for whatever reason, especially well adapted, or—to put it differently—every good will be produced where the conditions for its production are especially favorable. That this is true—at least in the long run—when there is also free movement of the factors of production, that is, first of all freedom of migration, can hardly be contested. Labor and other factors will then move where conditions of production are most favorable and where therefore they earn and are paid most. Thus, the largest possible total output is assured.

One must of course not be satisfied with this statement. For, first, freedom of migration does not exist, has never existed and will probably never exist, not even if free trade were ever the rule. And, secondly, such a situation of absolute mobility for men and goods may bring with it prospects that are not wholly desirable. One could imagine the agglomeration of a large part of mankind in the Ruhr District, in Upper Silesia and in other centers of industry, and the desertion of large areas such as, e.g., the Alps. No need to be a nationalist to consider such a state of affairs less than desirable.

However, there is good reason for believing that things will not come to this pass. But I leave this question open because it can be shown that free trade is advantageous, *for all participants*, even when there is *no mobility at all* and people are rigidly tied to their countries. The English classics, the founders of the free trade doctrine,

Weltwirtschaftliches Archiv, 32: 349–370. (1930 II). Translated from German. Reprinted with permission.

did indeed make immobility of all factors of production, especially of labor, the *defining characteristic of international trade* by which it was distinguished from *internal trade*. Thus they not only did not neglect this case—as has again and again been argued; they built up the free trade doctrine precisely on this assumption. This is, however, not generally recognized; on the contrary, one can hear again and again that free trade would be well and good if only it were accompanied by free mobility. Without it, it would disadvantage the countries which nature had niggardly endowed and which work in less favorable conditions of production than others. The proof that free trade is advantageous even for such less favorably equipped countries is, it is now well known, furnished by the theory of comparative costs which is indeed nothing but an exact formulation of the theorem of the international division of labor.

1. The Classical Theory of Comparative Costs and the Monetary Mechanism

The theory of comparative costs originated probably with Ricardo,[2] and was developed on the basis of the classical labor theory of value. I may be permitted briefly to recapitulate the theorem and its foundation. The labor theory of value says that labor cost determines the value of commodities. Commodities are exchanged against one another in the market in proportion to the quantities of labor contained in them. (We shall work with the labor theory of value in this general and easily understood form and we can dispense with any further proof or critique because it will turn out that the doctrine of comparative costs in independent of this formulation.) Taking this as a base, the proposition that with free trade goods will be produced where the conditions of production are most favorable, may be put more precisely: they will be produced where costs—i.e., the exertions of labor—are least. Thus, for any international exchange of goods to occur, there have to be *differences in the (labor) costs of production* of the several goods in different countries. The law of labor value requires, however, free mobility of labor. This is not the case in international transactions; it becomes necessary to distinguish between *absolute* and *comparative differences in costs*.

An absolute cost differential exists when a certain country can produce a certain good with a smaller labor effort than another country. If, for instance, in country I good A costs 10 and good B 20 units of labor, while in country II good A requires 20 and good B 10 units of labor, then I has an absolute cost advantage in A and II in B. In this case, country I will specialize in A and II in B, and there will be a rise in total output by 50 percent.

The case of a *comparative* cost differential is characterized by one country having a cost advantage in both branches of production, that is, is able to produce both goods with a smaller labor effort per unit of output than the other country, but that the advantage, the cost differential, is not equal in the two branches of production, being relatively larger in one than in the other. Ricardo illustrates this by the following celebrated example: In England a unit of cloth costs 100 hours of labor and a unit of wine 120 hours; in Portugal a unit of cloth costs 90 hours and a unit of wine 80 hours of labor.

Thus, Portugal has an absolute advantage in both branches of production. But the advantage is larger in wine; it has there a comparative advantage because the cost differential in that product is larger: 80/120 < 90/100. In this case it is advantageous for both countries to specialize: Portugal will produce only wine—where it has a comparative advantage—and England only cloth, i.e., the good in which its disadvantage is relatively small. That both countries profit from this division of labor is clear from the following reasoning: The exchange ratio between cloth and wine, before the opening of international trade, was 1W : 1.2C in England and 1W : 0.89C in Portugal. It is therefore of advantage to England to offer less than 1.2C for a unit of wine, and for Portugal to obtain more than 0.89C for a unit of wine. Any price of wine in terns of cloth between 1.2 and 0.89 brings advantage to both countries. Where in this range the exchange ratio will settle, cannot be determined solely on the basis of cost data. Other determinants, namely, the demand functions, must be drawn on. This elaboration of the theory was performed by J. S. Mill.

Much misunderstanding arose because the classics often neglected to give realistic color to these numerical examples by translating the comparative cost differentials into absolute price differences, or because they offered instructions for this translation in other parts of their works and often took it for granted, leaving the solution to the reader.[3] Trade proximately is determined by absolute money costs and prices, and not by comparative labor costs, and it is therefore necessary to show how comparative cost differentials translate into absolute money cost and price differences. The mechanism through which this transformation operates is now well known and may be recalled by means of a simple numerical example:

Table 1.1
Output and costs of 10 days labor in the U.S. and in Germany[4]

Country	Wages (in $)		Output	Supply Price/Unit ($)
	per day	total		
U.S.	1.5	15	20 units wheat	0.75
	1.5	15	20 units linen	0.75
Germany	1.0	10	10 units wheat	1.00
	1.0	10	15 units linen	0.67

It will be seen that the translation of the labor costs into money prices makes no difficulties. Money wages have, it is true, been set arbitrarily but only within certain limits which are set by the comparative costs. If, that is, one were to set money wages in the United States, not at $1.50 but at $2.00, or twice those in Germany, the supply prices would become $1.00 each instead of $0.75, and the trade would flow in only *one* direction, namely, from Germany to the United States, the American balance of payments would turn passive, and the well known balance of payments adjustments mechanism would begin to operate: the exchange rate would rise against Germany, gold flow out from the United States and *money wages there would fall* and thus be brought back in line with cost differentials. By the same argument it can be shown that the difference between money wages in the two countries has also a lower limit. American wages, just as they cannot exceed $2, cannot fall below $1.33, because otherwise trade would flow entirely in the other direction, from the United States to Germany. Where in this range the *ratio between wages* in the two countries will settle, can again be determined only with the help of the demand functions—supply functions are given by the assumption of constant costs. The *limits* of this range are, however, unambiguously fixed by the cost data.

2. Pareto's Objection and the Assumption of Variable Costs

Innumerable objections to this theory have been raised. We propose to select those that do not originate in mere misunderstands.[5]

Above all, there is the following matter which still requires clarification even though it had already been touched upon by Bastable[6]; it has been stressed by Pareto,[7] has since repeatedly been "rediscovered" in the literature[8] and used in an assault on the theory of comparative costs. Pareto has in fact shown that it is not true that a *complete* division of labor in the direction of comparative costs—in the sense that each country produces only *one* good (we are still with the simplified two-country example) always leads to a larger output of both goods. That this is so one can understand, without following Pareto into his numerical examples and mathematical deduction, by focusing on the following case: Suppose there is one "large"[9] and one very "small" country, say, the United States and Luxembourg. If then the division of labor becomes complete, it is probable that the output of the good in which the "small" country specializes will be smaller than before, because naturally the "small" country, even with its comparative advantage, cannot produce as much as the "large" country did before. But this can be accepted as an argument against the comparative cost theory only if we stick too narrow mindedly to the numerical examples of the classics. What, in this case really follows from a reasonable interpretation of comparative cost theory is, not a *complete* but only a *partial* division of labor: the "small" country will indeed completely specialize on the good in which it has a comparative advantage; but in the "large" country there will occur only a *shift* of production, that is a reduction in output of the good producible only at comparatively higher cost, in favor of the other one.

However, it can happen that the division of labor is pushed beyond what is in accord with the postulate that full specialization results in larger outputs of both goods than before. It is possible that demand functions are such that, with the new price ratio which follows full division of labor, demand for the cheaper good will, in one or both of the participant economies, rise strongly enough to increase output at the expense of the other good. This does not, however, yield an argument against free trade. For the output reduction of the one good will be overcompensated by the output expansion of the other—in the evaluation, that is, of both economies as manifested by the direction of their demand.

There is another gap in our deduction, in that we have so far assumed *constant costs*. This assumption is easy to eliminate. We may well assume *rising costs*; but then we shall have to interpret the numbers in our examples as *marginal* costs. *Falling costs* (or rising returns) pose greater difficulties. Frank D. Graham has shown, in his interesting article "Some Aspects of Protection Further Considered" [10], that there are serious complications if one assumes that one of the two branches of production is ruled by rising, and the other by falling, costs. Knight has, it is true, pointed out in his essay "Some Fallacies in the Interpretation of Social Costs," [11] that Graham's conclusions require qualification. But, as appears from Graham's reply and Knight's rejoinder, [12] the latter did not entirely succeed in refuting Graham. And Graham's opinion that in cases of falling costs there are at times advantages to import duties, does seem to contain a grain of truth. I would not like here to follow this up because it would be necessary first to clear up a few disputed questions on the analysis of the laws of return. [13] Let me note only that the recommendation of tariffs in the cases of increasing returns as a consequence of external economies, seems to me to be no more than an exact formulation of the infant industry argument for tariffs.

3. The Elimination of the Labor Theory of Values from the Theory of Comparative Costs

It is a weighty objection, raised also already by Pareto [14] and repeated by many others [15], that the theory rests on the antiquated labor theory of value and that it must share this latter's fate.

The theory of comparative costs was developed on the basis of the labor theory of value, and all theorists who accepted it have indeed assumed that it rests also *logically* on the labor theory of value. For the authors who reject the labor theory of value, the theory of comparative costs founders on the same cliffs as the former, that is, on the fact that there simply exists no units of real cost, neither in the shape of

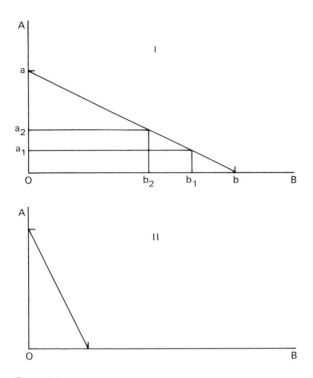

Figure 1.1
Comparative costs for goods A and B in countries I and II.

days of labor nor in any other shape that would permit the reduction of qualitatively different types of labor for a common denominator. Neither would the expedient of speaking of comparative advantage instead of comparative costs be a way out. Bastable[16] began this exercise without himself wishing to distance himself from the labor theory of value. A certain contradiction may be found even in Marshall when, in Appendix H of his book *Money, Credit and Commerce*,[17] he pays attention to the theory of comparative costs even though his general theory of value and also his theory of foreign trade follow other directions. Accepting the doctrine of comparative costs he lands on a branch of the tree of theory which he himself had sawed off years ago—as Mason[18] remarks jokingly.

Fortunately, however, it is possible to reformulate the theory in such a way that its analytical value and all conclusions drawn from it are preserved, rendering it at the same time entirely independent of the labor theory of value. This may most readily be shown in a diagrammatic presentation of our theorem.

Let us start from very simple assumptions. There are constant costs and in country I one unit of good A per unit of labor and two units of good B per unit of labor can be produced. Given the stock of means of production—that is, the quantity of labor—all possible combinations of producible outputs of A and B are determined and may be represented by a straight line in a system of coordinates which shows quantities of A on one and quantities of B on the other axis. Alternatively, we can produce Ob of B and no A, Ob_1 of B and Oa_1 of A, or Ob_2 of B and Oa_2 of A or, ..., Oa of A and no B. In country II, the slope of the straight line will be different. The slope represents the rate of substitution of the two goods: in country I, instead of a unit of A that is not produced, two units of B can be produced. The rate of substitution in country II is the reverse.

The *rate of substitution* determines the rate of exchange of the two goods, and this is all that is required for the deduction of the conclusions drawn from the theory of comparative costs. It should be clear by now that we need not make use of the labor value hypothesis at all. We are perfectly at liberty to assume that there are many means of production which cooperate in the production of goods A and B in different mixes, different according to type and volume of output. So long as at least *one* means of production is common to both branches of output—and that is sure to be the case with the factor labor—so long there will always be a rate of substitution, albeit not necessarily a constant one. Applying the cost concept of the Austrian School[20] we may say that as the cost of a unit of A the quantity of B that one must go without in order to procure a unit of A. And a unit of good B costs so many units of A as must be foregone to produce an additional unit of B.

One could therefore use up the whole stock of means of production for the producing of B and obtain the quantity Ob, or one may wish to obtain, apart from B also a small quantity bb_1 of B. Should one desire a further unit of A, the production of B would again have to be reduced and so on progressively one obtains the whole of the curve of substitution. The farther the production of A is expanded, the larger are the quantities of B that one has to do without in order to obtain yet another unit of A: There is a law of diminishing returns for A in terms of B and for B in terms of A. This is expressed in the concavity towards O of the substitution curve. Thus, the substitution curve represents, by the distances of any of its points from the two axes, all combinations of quantities of goods A and B that can be optimally produced by the use of a given stock of means of production. The ratios in which the different means of production are employed may be constant or variable from combination to combination. On this, as a technical matter, we need not make any assumptions.

Which of the possible combinations will be the one actually selected will depend on the demand functions, and the price of, or more exactly, the exchange ratio between, the two goods is represented by the slope of the tangent to the curve of substitution at the point representing the combination selected; in other words, the price equals the marginal rate of substitution.[21] This curve may, as needed, be thought of as a long or a short run curve, depending on whether one wishes to

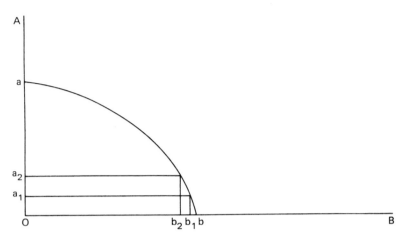

Figure 1.2
Substitution curve for the quantities of goods A and B that are optimally produced by a
given means of production.

consider, after a change in demand, all processes of adjustment, and depending on
the time one gives to fixed capital to be adjusted and put into the most adequate
shape.[22] It will probably be flatter in the long run that in the short run.

In the manner thus indicated we succeed easily in making our theorem independent of the labor theory of value. Let this exposition of the possibility to do without
the labor hypothesis suffice. What follows will, for simplicity's sake, retain the fiction
of a uniform homogeneous factor of production ("resources in general"); it will, that
is, be set out on the basis of the labor theory of value.

4. Extension of the Theory to the Case of Many Branches of Production

We must now address a further objection to the theory of comparative costs in the
form that Ricardo gave to it and which it has retained since. That is the assertion that
this theory is applicable only to the simplified case in which there are only two
branches of production. In his essay "1st eine Modernisierung der Aussenhandelstheorie erforderlich?" ("Is a Modernization of Foreign Trade Theory Necessary?"),[23]
Ohlin, complaining that the classics always considered only two goods and two
countries, maintains that the introduction of more than two goods would lead to
different results because then demand circumstances would also have to be allowed
for "if one wants to know something about the character of the exchange of
commodities."[24] "That England can produce a certain good relatively more cheaply
than Germany or Portugal, while one of these latter two can produce another good
relatively more cheaply than England, can—leaving aside costs measured in

money—be maintained only when *two* goods are considered. If one takes on three or more goods, then there is no more sense in the proposition that one country produces one good, another certain others, relatively more cheaply, measured in days of labor. Ricardo's theory of comparative costs, by itself admirable, turns out to have less analytical value than has generally been presumed." [25] This objection can, however, be refuted so easily that it is surprising to see it raised by an economist of the stature of Ohlin. The generalization of the two-goods examples and the extension of the theory to any number of branches of production is quite simple. All that is needed is to regard the two commodities as representative or as averages of a number of goods with similar cost conditions. We can then formulate the theory as follows: *Country I possesses a comparative advantage as against country II in all export goods compared with all import goods* (the same holds, of course, *vice versa* for country II). The proof is easy. We denote by $a_1, b_1, c_1, \ldots$ and $a_2, b_2, c_2, \ldots$ the numbers of work days necessary to produce in country I or, respectively, in country II one unit of goods A, B, C. Let $p_{a1}, p_{b1}, p_{c1}, \ldots$ and $p_{a2}, p_{b2}, p_{c2}, \ldots$ be the (money) supply prices (money costs) of A, B, C, ... and l_1 and l_2 the money wages in countries I and II. Then there hold the equations $p_{a1} = a_1 l_1$, $p_{b1} = b_1 l_1$ and $p_{a2} = a_2 l_2$, $p_{b2} = b_2 l_2 \ldots$. Further, if w stands for the number of currency units of country II which can be exchanged for a unit of currency of country I (rate of exchange), we can say: for each export good of country I we have the inequality $a_1 l_1 w < a_2 l_2$ and for each import good $b_1 l_1 w > b_2 l_2$. Thus, for export goods $a_1/a_2 < l_2/l_1 w$, and for import goods $b_1/b_2 > l_2/l_1 w$ and thus: $a_1/a_2 < b_1/b_2$; q.e.d. Now order the various goods in the sequence of the comparative advantage of country I as against country II: A, B, C, D, E, F, G, H, I, K, ... that this so that

$$\frac{a_1}{a_2} < \frac{b_1}{b_2} < \frac{c_1}{c_2} < \frac{d_1}{d_2} < \frac{e_1}{e_2} < \frac{f_1}{f_2} < \frac{g_1}{g_2} < \frac{h_1}{h_2} < \frac{i_1}{i_2} \ldots$$

Then the line that separates export from import goods must be drawn in such a way that all export goods are placed before it and the import goods are following it (so long as we assume constant costs and neglect transport costs, there are only export and import goods—setting aside imperfect division of labor in the sense previously explained, which can occur only with a "marginal goods"). It is therefore impossible that, e.g., country I exports goods A and C and imports B.

The *precise* position of the dividing line cannot be determined if only cost conditions are given. We can say only that it must be drawn such that every export good holds a comparative advantage over every import good. To fix the precise position of the dividing line we require, as a further element of determination, the proposition that exports and imports must balance (allowing for invisible items in the balance of payments). Assume, the line, which is numerically determined by the ratio $l_2/l_1 w$, is located between E and F; goods A to E are exported and the rest imported, and $e_1/e_2 < l_2/l_1 w < f_1/f_2$. Assume further the balance of payments is brought to equilibrium by, say, a loan from country I to country II. Then the play of the well-known monetary mechanism is set off: gold flows from country I, prices and wages fall while rising in country II, the ratio l_2/l_1 increases and the dividing line is pushed down: further goods, say F and G, change from imports to exports.[26]

5. The Alleged Disadvantages of Unilateral Free Trade

Using this scheme it is easy to deal with an argument for protective tariffs, whose significance for international trade policy can hardly be overestimated and which it is difficult to refute by other methods. Again and again, it has been argued—even by people who count as free traders—that *unilateral* free trade is damaging. General free trade is said to be most desirable, but when a country is surrounded by countries with tariffs, it will damage itself by retaining free trade itself—disregarding tactical considerations and all tariffs adopted as negotiating chips. This free trade oasis, it is argued, would turn into a battle ground of foreign competitors and it would be exposed unarmed against the attack of tariff-protected foreigners. There is hardly a tariff argument that enjoys as general consent as this. Nevertheless, it is wrong and without foundation. It can be shown that, if the free trade position remains well founded it must hold also in the case of unilateral free trade. This is so because *the existence* of tariffs abroad—considerations of trade policy tactics aside—does *not change* the position as explained by our scheme.

Start again from our sequence A, B, C, D, E, F, G, ... and assume the dividing line falls between F and G. Now let the rest of the world impose a prohibitive tariff on A; consequently, A is eliminated from the export list of country I and from international trade altogether.[27] What happens now we know: the "mechanism" which keeps the balance of payments in equilibrium is activated, the dividing line is lowered and imports of G are blocked or perhaps G is even exported (in country I there will be a re-ordering of production from A to G and in country II, which now itself produces A, from G towards A).

The protectionist measure of country II, which limits the international division of labor between the two countries, damages both countries by diminishing the national product of both of them. This follows from a simple reflection. What can be calculated from the numerical examples used earlier for any two branches of production, holds true of course also for any pair of production branches above and below the dividing line in our sequence: that is, that the division of labor in the direction of comparative costs leads to a larger output of both goods, and that this gain is distributed between the two countries in a proportion determined in detail by the demand functions concerned. And any policy measure that eliminates such a pair of exchanges and shortens both sides of the balance of trade,[28] reduces the division of labor and the national product of *both* countries.[29]

If, now, country I does not leave matters with this restriction of the division of labor through the tariff of country II, but itself *responds with tariffs*, say on good L, whereby this good disappears from international trade, then the "mechanism" will again be activated, the line of division rises and there results a further shortening of both sides of the balance of trade. This additional restriction of the division of labor between the two countries spells further damage to both countries, additional to the damage from country II's tariff. It follows that it is in the interest of the country to retain free trade even when all countries around it impose tariff duties. *Unilateral* free trade is thus—tactical considerations aside—thoroughly desirable and preferable to a generalized tariff regimen.

6. Immobility of the Means of Production and Adjustment Losses

But now it will be argued against this deduction, and against the whole of our theory, that it does not hold water because it is based on the unrealistic proposition that the means of production are freely mobile, so that they can be withdrawn, say, from wheat production and applied to the production of linen.[30] That would, however, be possible only in part, for by and large means of production are firmly attached and cannot, or only with considerable cost, be withdrawn from their employment and shifted. Think of machinery, buildings, many intermediate products which, designed for a specific branch of production, can only in exceptional cases be employed elsewhere, or will, in an improvised new employment, produce less and thus suffer a loss in value. Any removal of duties which requires a shift in production must therefore be accompanied by sizeable frictional losses. The enormous reorganization of industrial and agricultural production which, e.g., a paneuropean tariff would entail, would be associated with a destruction of capital so catastrophic that the question would be raised whether the enhancement of output that could be expected in the long run, would not be purchased too dearly.[31] For what do we benefit today from the advantages to be expected only after the adjustment process has run its course? "In the long run we are all dead!", as Keynes once put it drastically. But this objection, however, convincing it may sound,[32] hides a serious fallacy, and we shall see that the alleged frictional losses will have to be cut back considerably so that nothing, or very little, is left of them.

We can distinguish *two cases of immobility* of the means of production. Either *all* means of production which contribute to a branch of production are immobile (more precisely: unemployable in other applications; specific means of production in Wieser's meaning), or only *a part* of them is bound to one branch, e.g., factory buildings, while another part, e.g., labor, is mobile and shiftable elsewhere, thus rendering the immobile part inactive and valueless.

Consider, briefly, the first case, the *absolute immobility of the whole of the productive combination,*[33] which will, to be sure, never be fully realized. Assume in our example (p. 5) of the German linen industry and the American wheat production, it were true that, for whatever reason, the German wheat farmers were tied to the soil with all their possessions. If, in these conditions, cheap American wheat enters the country, the German wheat farmers must reduce their demands and be content with an exchange ratio corresponding to that in America (1W = 1L, instead of 1W = 1.5L), because otherwise they would be unable to sell. There is perhaps no need to work through the example in detail; this was in part done in the writings of Cairnes,[34] Bastable and Taussing on the occasion of presenting the doctrine of *non-competing groups.* No diminuition of total output follows from this, for the wheat farmers have no alternative to continuing working, albeit perhaps for a sharply reduced compensation. (If this compensation becomes so small that they emigrate or are unable to keep their means of production, then case II—partial mobility of factors of production—sets in; we shall deal with it presently). What does follow is a possibly radical shift in the distribution of gains in disfavor of the immobile factors that are exposed to the foreign competition which enjoys a comparative advantage. If it is then desired to prevent this shift for whatever reason, say, to protect agriculture as a class supportive of political or social structures, then a tariff is appropriate. Only, one must be clear that one aims at a goal of redistribution in favor of certain groups, and not of enhancing national output. Since the assumption of immobility is in reality never fully applicable because some factors of production are always capable of alternative employment, the goal of a shift in distribution can always be achieved at the expense of total output. (Whether one would speak then of an economic or an extra-economic purpose is a question of convention, which need not detain us.)

The same holds for the question whether one wishes to consider the manner of distribution of the social product as a determinant of its magnitude—as, e.g., Pigou[35] does—so that a distributive shift of national income *ipso facto* means a change in its size—not *causes* it; this is not the point here.

The second case of immobility, if only a part of the means of production employed in a given branch of production is immobile while others can be withdrawn and employed elsewhere, is more important. Here it may happen that the mobile factor leaves the productive combination and thus idles the immobile one, and that the impression is created of unused factors which could be economically reactivated by a tariff. Schüller constructs his theory of protection on this assumption. The free traders are wrong, he says, in maintaining that tariffs always cause only a shift in composition and never an increase in total output, for in any economy there are unutilized means of production. "In no country are natural economic forces—fertile soil, deposits of coal, ore and minerals, water power—fully made use of; rather, they are in all countries available for an expansion of branches of production for which they are needed." [36] And tariffs, by causing such unused means of production to be employed, can increase total output of the economy. An analysis of a typical case will convince us that we have here to do with a serious fallacy.[37]

Assume we are faced with a coal mine connected with an iron works. Suppose then coal seams are discovered abroad, coal and iron are imported at falling prices and the domestic enterprise is threatened. What will happen? The remuneration of the mobile factors of production—labor and variable capital—cannot be reduced below the market level, for these mobile factors would leave the enterprise. There is no alternative to accept a smaller profit and to write off the value of the fixed capital that cannot be withdrawn and employed elsewhere (coal deposits, buildings, etc.) As long, however, as the circulating capital—that is, the sums needed to pay for wages, materials, repairs, etc.—brings interest, the enterprise will continue to operate. And so long as this happens, there will be no decline in the social product—production continues unabated—there has only been a distributive shift in favor of the consumers of the cheapened product. Now assume that the product price falls further as a result of sharper competition, or that costs rise because parts of the fixed capital are being used up and in need of replacement. The consequence is that even the circulating capital, monthly expenses of, say, $100,000, cannot be retrieved. The enterprise will be shut down, the laborers go somewhere else, the circulating capital will be employed elsewhere, buildings stand empty and the coal deposits are not worked any longer. Are we not now confronted with a destruction of capital which could be prevented by a tariff? Cannot now a reduction of the social product be prevented by a suitable intervention? A simple reflection shows that these questions must be answered in the negative, that on the contrary introducing a tariff would bring about an effective loss of social output. Indeed, that the factors of production—labor and materials—which need to be employed every month represent a value of $100,000 and will not accept a reduction of their remuneration (otherwise the enterprise would not be shut down). These factors earn $100,000 elsewhere because then they can produce $100,000 worth of goods. It would, therefore, be unreasonable to draw them out of the employment where they produce $100,000 and put them to work where they can produce only less.

Thus, that there are unused means of production should not surprise us. Indeed, a situation where that were not so—where every spot of land were cultivated, every antiquated plant working, and every, even the poorest, deposit of coal were mined—such a situation is hard to imagine. It should, at any rate, be taken only as sign of *severest poverty* and not as a symptom of flowering wealth.

It does not make the slightest difference whether these unemployed factors of production are elements of nature—uncultivated fields, a deposit of coal—or whether they have been produced by man—a factory or an antiquated machine— even though the innocent observer will, in these latter cases, have more the impression of a loss and a destruction of capital. These inactive means of production are in truth no witnesses of a destruction of capital, of a loss which must be set against the advantages of the division of labor, but rather they are the milestones of economic progress induced by the international division of labor. If there is a loss, it is purely private (shift in distribution), and *misguided* was perhaps the *initial investment*, which later turned out to have been uneconomic (leaving open the question whether this was predictable and whether somebody was therefore at fault or not) but not the later closing of the enterprise.

True losses of friction and adjustment are of a quite different character, have nothing to do with works that have become unprofitable, and are of very much smaller dimension. Our demonstration has proceeded on the assumption of a faultless operation of the price mechanism, especially in respect of the specific, immobile factors or production that are tied to a production process. As to the material production factors, one can probably assume such working of the price mechanism. For the owner of such physical means of production will, in case of need as he cannot employ it elsewhere, be content with a very small remuneration: he will write it off to zero before leaving it unemployed. But there is a very important factor of production for which this does not hold, which will refuse its services long before its remuneration has fallen to zero: that is the factor labor. Here the price mechanism is partially put out of operation, and genuine losses of friction in the form of strikes and unemployment may occur.

However, the danger in this case is not as great as might appear at first sight, because labor is in fact no specific factor of production tied to specific employment; rather it is the most mobile and most versatile factor. To be sure, in the short run the elimination of free competition by labor organizations results in losses, which will appear in the form of unemployment, strikes and dismissals. But unemployment is a short run phenomenon also in countries where it has become permanent. For even where the number of the unemployed remains constant, the composition of unemployment changes. In general, it is therefore probably correct to say that the transitory damage from unemployment caused by the reorganization of production will not outweigh the permanent advantages of the international division of labor; moreover, it can be reduced by domestic policies. But there is no denying that marginal cases are conceivable, in which transitional losses outweigh permanent advantages. Since, however, these *are* marginal cases, difficult to diagnose, they are not appropriate for government intervention.

Postscript to Comparative Cost Paper

The problems discussed in this paper have been developed in my book *The Theory of International Trade* (English edition, New York, 1936; original German edition,

Berlin, 1933), in *A Survey of International Trade Theory* (first edition, Princeton, 1955; second revised edition, Princeton, 1961) [Chapter 4], in "Some Problems in the Pure Theory of International Trade" (*The Economic Journal*, June 1953) [Chapter 3], and in "Survey of Circumstances Affecting the Location of Production and International Trade as Analyzed in the Theoretical Literature [Chapter 5].

Notes

1. A paper read on March 7, 1930, in the *Nationalökonomische Gesellschaft* (Economic Society) at Vienna.

2. See the celebrated Chapter VII in David Ricardo's *Principles of Political Economy and Taxation*. Whether priority should not be granted to Col. Torrense is debated. See J. W. Angell, *The Theory of International Prices. History, Criticism and Restatement*, Harvard Economic Studies, 28: 54 ff. (Cambridge, 1926); Luigi Einaudi, "James Pennington or James Mill. An Early Correction of Ricardo," *The Quarterly Journal of Economics*, 44: 164ff. (1929–30); and the reply of P. Sraffa, "An Alleged Correction of Ricardo," ibid., pp. 539 ff.

3. For evidence that also trained economists fall victim to such misunderstandings, see J. W. Angell, op. cit., 372 ff. and my criticism: "The Theory of Comparative Cost Once More," *The Quarterly Journal of Economics*, 43:376 ff. (1928–29). Also L. Sommer, "Freihandel und Schutzzoll in ihrem Zusammenhang mit Geldtheorie und Währungspolitik," ("Free Trade and Protection in Their Connection with the Theory of Money and Foreign Exchange Policy"), *Weltwirtschaftliches Archiv.* XXIV : 33 ff. (1926 II).

4. The numerical example comes from the book by F. W. Taussig, *International Trade*, (New York, 1927), p. 45.

5. See the objections presented by E. Kellenberger in his essay "Zur Theorie von Freihandel und Schutzzoll" ("On the Theory of Free Trade and Protection"), *Weltwirtschaftliches Archiv.* VII:1 ff. (1916 I).

6. C. F. Bastable, *The Theory of International Trade with Some Applications to Economic Policy*, 4th ed. (London, 1903).

7. V. Pareto, *Manuel d'economie politique*, Trad. sur 1'edition italienne par A. Bonnet, 2e ed. (Paris, 1927), pp. 397 ff.

8. The last time by Arthur F. Burns, "A Note on Comparative Costs," *The Quarterly Journal of Economics*, 42:495 ff. (1927–28). See also my remarks ("The Theory of Comparative Costs," op. cit., p. 380); also F. D. Graham, "The Theory of International Values Re-examined," *The Quarterly Journal of Economics*, 39:54. ff. (1923–24).

9. Apologies for the rather inprecise expressions here and elsewhere. What matters is, of course, productive capacity and not the size of a country. A fully exact form of expression has often in our science been taken as pedantic, if it does not even bring the author under suspicion of being a gray theorist far from all life.

10. F. D. Graham, "Some Aspects of Protection Further Considered," *The Quarterly Journal of Economics*, 37 : 199 ff. (1922–23).

11. F. H. Knight, "Some Fallacies in the Interpretation of Social Cost," ibid., 38:582 ff. (1923–24).

12. F. D. Graham, "Some Fallacies in the Interpretation of Social Cost. A Reply," ibid., 39:324 ff. (1924–25).

13. The question, that is, whether decreasing costs are compatible with free competition. Only when decreasing costs result from the so-called *external* economics is this at all conceivable. On this see "Increasing Returns and the Representative Firm," a symposium by D. H. Robertson, P. Sraffa, and G. F. Shove, *The Economic Journal*, 40(157): 24 ff. (London, 1930) and the literature there cited.

14. V. Pareto, op. cit., p. 507 fn.

15. Extensively by E. S. Mason, "The Doctrine of Comparative Costs," *The Quarterly Journal of Economics*, 41:63 ff. (1926–27).

16. C. F. Bastable, op. cit.

17. A. Marshall, *Money, Credit and Commerce* (London, 1923), Appendix H.

18. E. S. Mason, op. cit., p. 86.

19. Country I has an absolute advantage over country II in both branches of production and a larger (comparative) advantage in B.

20. See F. Friedrich von Wieser, "Cost-Utility Forgone," in *Theorie der gesellschaftlichen Wirtschaft* (*Theory of Social Economics*), Grundriss der Sozialökonomik, Abt. I, pp. 125 ff. Tübingen 1914. Here I have used a rather unpretentious formulation which eliminates utility and simply expresses good A as the cost of good B. This formulation originated with F. H. Knight, who develops it—apparently without realizing that he thus in fact uses the concept of the Austrian school—in his excellent article "A Suggestion for Simplifying the Statement of the General Theory of Price," *The Journal of Political Economy*, 36:353 ff. (Chicago, 1926). Knight sets out from the celebrated beaver—deer case of Adam Smith and says: "The cost of beaver is deer and the costs of deer is beaver." (ibid., p. 359). The Austrian cost concept had been used already in American literature: D. I. Green defends it against the attacks from McVane in his essay, "Pain Cost and Opportunity Cost," *The Quarterly Journal of Economics*, 8:218 ff. (Boston, 1894). See also H. J. Davenport, *Value and Distribution. A Critical and Constructive Study* (Chicago, 1908), especially chapter 7.

21. See F. H. Knight, "A Suggestion for Simplifying the Statement . . . ," op. cit., p. 359, "The number of units any commodity B which exchange in the market for one unit of any other commodity A must be the number of units of B which are sacrificed in production in adding the last unit of A to the total produced." (In italics in the original.)

22. Strictly speaking, there are not *one* long run and *one* short run, but many runs.

23. Bertil Ohlin, "Ist eine Modernisierung der Aussenhandelstheorie erforderlich?" ("Is a Modernization of Foreign Trade Theory Necessary?"), *Weltwirtschaftliches Archiv*. XXVI: 97 ff. (1927 II). See also F. D. Graham, *The Theory of International Values Re-examined*, op. cit.

24. Bertil Ohlin, op. cit., 110 ff. Demand conditions must be taken into account even when there are only two goods, as we have seen already, not only to determine the exact exchange ratio, but also to establish whether there can at all be a *complete* division of labor.

25. Ibid., p. 112.

26. Perhaps it sounds strange that an imported good turns at once into an export. If we allow for transportation costs and tariffs, there is a third type of goods which is neither exported nor imported but produced in both countries—nontraded goods—and before an import turns into exported goods, it enters the ranks of nontraded goods and is exported only when the price difference exceeds the transport costs. It is clear, however, that this minor modification does not alter the essence of the matter and leaves all conclusions from it untouched.

27. If we wish not to make the assumption of constant costs, we could merely let the same commodity appear several times in the sequence $A_1, A_2, A_3, \ldots$ every time with that partial quantity that can be produced at the corresponding cost. It is clear that this creates no difficulty of principle and does not touch the results. Therefore we neglect this complication.

28. In a scientific paper we need not pay attention to the totally dilettante but very popular conception that such a country, which hangs on to unilateral free trade, would be inundated by imports, could only import and no longer export.

29. We neglect here two *restrictions*, i.e., that it is conceivable—within very narrow limits that need not be discussed here—that the disadvantage connected with the limitation of the division of labor may be offset by (a) tariff revenues and (b) by the possible shift of the *real term of trade* in favor of the country which imposes the tariff.

30. A theoretically trained reader will notice at once that this objection totally misses the point, because the immobility of some or all means of production will be reflected in the shape of the substitution curve, and that therefore our theory already allows for it. It is nevertheless useful to follow this point up.

31. See, e.g., P. Kaufmann, "Paneuropäische Wirtschaftsfragen" (" Pan-European Economic Questions"); Der *Oesterreichische Volkswirt*, Vienna, (1925/26), pp. 372 ff. This essay is most instructive, because it contains in its purest form the fallacy exposed in the text, apart from many interesting and poignant remarkes. Similarly, F. Eulenberg, "Gegen die Idee einer europäischen Zollunion" ("Against the Idea of a European Customs Union"), in *Europäische Zollunion*, H. Heimann, ed., (Berlin, 1926), 109 ff.

32. As it is indeed presented, in more refined form, by leading economists. The fundamental argument of R. Schüller's theory of protection (*Schutzzoll und Freihandel. Die Voraussetzungen und Grenzen ihrer Berechtigung* [*Protection and Free Trade. The Assumptions and Limits of Their Justification*], Vienna and Leipzig, 1905) is, as we shall see, a species of this idea (see especially pp. 83 ff.)

33. This assumption implies a very special shape of the substitution curve. If the factors of both production branches are absolutely specific, the curve contracts to a point, for none of the two branches can be expanded at the expense of the other.

34. J. E. Cairnes, *Some Leading Principles of Political Economy* (London, 1874).

35. A. C. Pigou, *The Economics of Welfare*, 3rd ed. (London, 1929).

36. R. Schüller, op. cit., p. 78.

37. See also the very appropriate critique by G. MacKenroth in his fine article "Zollpolitik und Produktionsmittelversorgung" ("Tariff Policy and Supply of Resources"), *Weltwirtschaftliches Archiv*, XXIX: 89 ff. (1929 I).

2   Real Cost, Money Cost and Comparative Advantage

Trade is proximately governed by money prices and money costs, including transportation costs and other transportation charges, all in terms of money.

International comparisons of money costs and prices imply exchange rates between various currencies. Under a system of freely convertible currencies and uniform, consistent and stable exchange rates, the currency factor does not cause any difficulties. However, under the system of inconvertible or only partially convertible currencies, multiple exchange rates (of which the coexistence of official and unofficial rates is but one example), of clearing and payments arrangements and barter deals, the picture becomes extremely complicated and obscure and serious analytical difficulties arise already on the monetary level, i.e., it is no longer easy to define the meaning or to test the validity of the proposition that money prices and money cost govern trade.

Even in the absence of these complications (i.e., assuming uniform and stable exchange rates), it would not be correct to interpret that statement, as it is often done, to mean that each country will export those goods which in terms of money it produces more cheaply in the absence of trade.

First we should have to define: "produces more cheaply" in terms of some "real" *numéraire*, i.e., in terms of some commodity. For if we defined it in terms of money it might happen that before trade *all* commodities are cheaper in one country than in the other. Or better still, we ought to say that for purposes of international comparison the equilibrium rate of exchange must be used, i.e., that rate which will assure equilibrium in the balance of payments when trade is opened.

Second, even in that sense the statement need not be generally true. If in the absence of trade, production in some lines is not at that level which permits the utilization of plants of optimum size and trade therefore enables the participating countries to reap the advantages of large-scale production, pre-trade costs and prices

Proceedings of a Round Table Discussion, International Economic Association, Monaco, Sept. 1950. Extracts from *International Social Science Bulletin*. © Unesco 1951. Reproduced by permission of Unesco.

give no certain clue concerning the question where the combined production will be located. The outcome will depend on the shape of the cost curve in conjunction with the shape of the demand curve and not merely on the comparative level of the intersection of marginal cost and marginal revenue in each country before trade. It depends, in other words, on total, not on marginal properties and conditions. (These cases are, of course, incompatible with perfect competition.)

It would be an overstatement to pretend that modern theory can handle all those problems satisfactorily. As soon as there are elements of bilateral monopoly or oligopoly, serious difficulties arise which modern theory has not been able to master completely. But to the extent, the large extent I hope we may say, to which modern theory is able to deal with these problems, it does so without recourse to the notion of real cost, which has played such a prominent role in the theory of international trade.

What is the use of the real cost theory? Is it a worthless relic from the past which ought to be discarded? Or has it still a live function?

Real cost theory always had two functions (which the earlier theorists hardly distinguished), namely, an analytic and explanatory function on the one hand and a welfare or policy function on the other. It was supposed to explain why trade is what it is and why trade is desirable from the "economic point of view".

There is a certain tendency in the literature to abandon real cost theory as an explanatory device but to claim importance or usefulness for it as an instrument of welfare analysis.

I do not believe that this is a possible position. The theory cannot be useful for welfare analysis unless it also has some explanatory value. If its explanatory value is limited in the sense that it describes only tendencies and holds only approximately (except under ideal conditions), then the same limitations apply to the welfare implications. And if it can be entirely dispensed with as an explanatory device, the same must be true, one should think, in the welfare field.

The real cost theory originated as a labour theory of value, more specifically as a labour time theory. This theory is, however, so obviously impossible that right from the beginning all sorts of qualifications had to be made.

Two interpretations or variants emerged: The one may be called the real cost theory proper, the Marshall-Viner line, the other is the opportunity cost theory first propounded by the Austrians and in our times by F. H. Knight and F. H. Graham.

The first variant holds that relative prices are roughly and approximately proportional to the subjective cost (disutility of labor and abstinence associated with the production of the various commodities). It is powerfully supported (with important qualifications) by J. Viner. (See his *Studies in the Theory of International Trade*.)

With all respect to the theoretical acumen of this eminent scholar and his most distinguished theoretical ancestry, I must say that the defects of that theory seem to me so serious as to make the whole approach futile. In contrast to the opportunity cost theory I cannot even see a possibility of regarding the real cost theory as a first approximation to a general equilibrium approach; in other words I cannot see how it can be looked upon as a special case of a more satisfactory general theory, i.e., a case which would be realised under certain simplified, though not palpably absurd conditions.[1]

The opportunity cost theory asserts that relative prices are proportional to the marginal opportunity cost, i.e., to the rate at which various commodities can be transformed into one another. If this is true (and if we assume increasing marginal opportunity cost, i.e., if we rule out increasing returns) important welfare and policy conclusions follow. Free trade then assures "optimum allocation" of world resources and maximization of world income.

It does not follow, however, that free trade would be the best national policy for each country, except if each country were confronted with perfectly elastic demand and supply schedules.

If that condition is not fulfilled and assuming the rest of the world to act competitively, it would pay any country to equalize by suitable policies the marginal rate of substitution between export and import goods at home with the revenue (marginal rather than average terms of trade) abroad. (The practical limitations of a rational policy along these lines are extremely severe. They are due to administrative difficulties and to the certainty of retaliation. These matters cannot be discussed in the present paper.)

Moreover interference with the free flow of trade for the purpose of changing the income distribution in some desired way is logically defensible. (It is true that it would be better to bring about a desired change in income distribution by taxes and subsidies rather than by trade policy. Practical difficulties are again severe, even if we assume agreement in principle about the desired changes in income distribution and the means to be adopted. But they cannot be discussed here.)

The equality of relative prices and the marginal rate of substitution (or transformation) is, however, subject to important conditions. It holds only, (a) if there are no monopolistic elements in the labour and product markets; (b) if people are indifferent with respect to place of employment and kind of job; (c) if prices are not rigid; (d) if there are no external economies or diseconomies.

Condition (b) needs some explanation. It does *not* imply perfect mobility of labour. If it did, the theory would indeed be useless. Labour (or any other factor) can be completely immobile and broken up into watertight non-competing groups— the theory would still hold if the price of each factor (and kind of labour) is flexible and the supply inelastic. On the other hand inelasticity of the total supply of labour with respect to price is *not* required.

These restrictions on the validity of the theory are serious and have very important welfare implications. Whenever any one of the enumerated conditions does not hold, free trade no longer ensures "optimum" allocation of world resources and, as a corollary, it follows that there exists some sort of interference with the free flow of goods and services which would improve the situation.

This may seem very protectionist and may seem to give aid and comfort to the mercantilists and to the defenders of present-day protectionist policies. This is, however, not so, although it is true that the naive, simon-pure free trade—liberal position is, in fact, scientifically indefensible.[2]

The implications of the above considerations for the free trade doctrine are less damaging than may appear at first sight for the following reasons:

(1) Some exceptions to the free trade rule are apparent and not real. Suppose, e.g., that people have a preference for working in industry A as compared with B, because work in A is more agreeable or less expensive in terms of living cost (A may be, for example, work in the country or in small towns as against work in big cities or industrial centres).

If, then, wages are uniformly higher in B than in A in order to overcome people's aversion to work there and to compensate them for the inconveniences or costs connected with A employment, the price ratio of A-output to B-output will not correspond to the opportunity-cost of A and B. And if, say, B is an import article, it would seem that protection given to the B-industry will improve the allocations of resources and increase national income.[3]

This is, however, correct only if we define national income (and economic welfare) narrowly in terms of output of A and B only. If, as we obviously should, we make allowance for the comparative disutility of labour, *the contradiction vanishes.*[4]

(2) Another apparent deviation from the ideal case occurs if voluntary unemployment exists.

Suppose commodity B is imported cheaply from abroad. If wages in B are rigid, unemployment will result; labour will go into unemployment rather than into employment in A. If the wage rigidity is due to union dictate (or to minimum wage legislation or simply to tradition and custom), i.e., if the unemployment is involuntary on the part of the individual workers, there will be a net loss to the economy.[5] Now suppose that the unemployment is due to the fact that the workers concerned were on the margin of indifference between working and not working. The utility of income just compensates them for the disutility of work and they prefer to go idle if their wage is cut further. They are then voluntarily unemployed and if the disutility of labour is taken into account in addition to output in the calculation of national income (or "economic welfare"), unemployment does not imply a loss in economic welfare.[6]

(3) Some of the deviations are temporary, e.g., those resulting from shortrun rigidity of wages and prices, and short-run immobility of labour, which give rise to short run ("frictional") unemployment.

(4) I would not deny, however, that there exist many genuine and persistent deviations from the ideal conditions postulated by the free trade theory (apart from those various and temporary ones enumerated above). In all those cases interference with the free flow of goods and services, in other words deviations from the *laisser-faire* policy are, in principle, defensible. But it by no means follows that simple protectionist devices are the measures that are called for. The opposite (i.e., import subsidies rather than duties) may be indicated and many conditions (e.g., monopolistic restriction) would require treatment at the source rather than restrictions on imports. It all depends upon the details of the situation.[7]

Along those lines a very good case can be made for liberal trade policies. The arguments used must be different, however, from those usually put forward. They cannot be that we live in the best of all possible worlds and that there is no scope for economic improvements. This position is untenable. The case for liberal trade policies should be based on the fact that although the ideal conditions postulated by competitive theory and the free trade doctrine are never realized, there is at least a rough approximation. Furthermore, the deviations from the ideal conditions are so complicated and variegated, so difficult to diagnose and to correct, that it is extremely difficult, if not impossible, to improve upon the outcome of the market mechanism. Especially in the present period which is characterized by a multiplicity of haphazard interventions of all kinds, tariffs, quotas, exchange controls, multiple exchange rates of official and unofficial character, etc., etc., the underlying comparative cost situation is so completely obscured that a rational policy is well-nigh impossible.[8] There can be no doubt that the unhampered price mechanism with all its imperfections would constitute a great improvement over the trade system which is currently *en vogue* almost everywhere in the world.

Summarizing, we may say that a fully elaborated general equilibrium theory contains the comparative cost theory as a special case. Or, putting it the other way round, a fully completed comparative cost theory merges into a full-fledged general equilibrium theory. This is true of explanatory theory as well as of its welfare complement.[9] The comparative cost theory in terms of opportunity cost is a close and most useful approximation to a more general equilibrium approach.

It must not be overlooked, however, that even the so-called "general" equilibrium theory (and *a fortiori* the approximation thereto) is subject to severe limitations: problems of oligopoly and bilateral monopoly have not yet been fully solved.[10]

This is probably a more serious limitation than the fact that the theory is almost entirely static and can deal with economic change only by comparative methods.

Concluding Remarks[11]

Introduction

The purposes of the International Economic Association are purely scientific. Nevertheless it has chosen for its first round table discussion a subject which is not only highly practical but also highly controversial and charged with political emotions. This fact calls for a few words of comment.

There is, in reality, no contradiction or incongruence. What is scientific is the unemotional, objective and systematic method of dealing with a subject. It does not follow that the scientist must dwell in an ivory tower, that he must be concerned exclusively with academic subjects, although he may choose (and should be granted the right by society) to busy himself with highly abstract matters which seem to have no relation whatever with the practical problems of the day. (Let us not forget that it is very difficult, if not impossible, to be sure that a highly abstract theory may not acquire great practical importance in the future. Examples would not be hard to find.)

It is, however, a fact that the social sciences and economics in particular have often been stimulated to activity and discoveries by confrontation with pressing practical problems. The theory of international trade offers many illustrations—witness the extensive discussions caused by the monetary disorders during and after the Napoleonic wars or 100 years later by similar disorders after World War I and by the German reparations ·problem—discussions which, although they were not on a uniformly high scientific level, undoubtedly led to a permanent enrichment of economic science. I believe there can be no doubt that the same will be true of the discussions engendered by the events after World War II, although it will take time and much patient work to separate the chaff from the wheat and to assimilate and consolidate the new accretions to the stock of scientific knowledge.

I think it fair to say that the discussions which are summarized in the preceding pages were conducted in a scientific spirit and contributed to such a consolidation and assimilation.

In the following paragraphs I select what seem to me the most important problems that were raised and comment on them in the light of the discussion.[12]

Short Run and Long Run Disequilibria in the Balance of Payments

The overriding problem of the discussion was the nature and explanation of and possible cures for the long lasting lack of balance in the international accounts of many countries—a condition that is popularly known as the dollar shortage. I believe that there was general agreement about the meaning of that by no means unambiguous term. By "dollar shortage" is meant a lack of balance which may manifest itself in three ways; (a) as an actual loss of gold or dollar reserves; (b) as a potential loss which does not materialize because a country receives American aid in some form (e.g., ERP); or (c) one which does not materialize because the country employs more or less drastic measures of control (quotas, exchange restrictions, etc.) to hold down imports and to stimulate and direct exports.

There was, naturally, open or implied disagreement about the causes of those conditions and about suitable or desirable remedies.

As to the causes, there are broadly speaking two schools of thought. Let me call the two groups "optimists" and "pessimists", respectively. The pessimist speaks of a chronic dollar shortage which he attributes to far-reaching, long-run structural changes. This reasoning is usually applied to Western European (ERP) countries, although there is an "overseas variety" which is popular in underdeveloped countries. The European pessimists (and their many American supporters) point to the undeniable fact that Europe suffered grievously during the war; that she lost her export markets in many parts of the world, that investment income from abroad is permanently down by about one billion dollars a year, etc. But they also insist that these difficulties, although they have been enormously aggravated by the war, really started to make themselves felt long before: Europe and the United Kingdom in particular had started to lose ground even before the first war. The industrialization of backward countries has reduced international demand for industrial products and the competition by U.S. industry has increased all the time and became overpowering during the second world war.

The optimistic school, to which the present writer belongs, offers a more cheerful interpretation. The optimist does not, of course, deny that the countries of Western Europe have been specially hard hit by a series of calamities: The first world war, the great depression, the second world war. But he emphatically denies that a victim of a series of accidents is for that reason a chronic invalid.[13] He will point to the fact that after the first as well as after the second world war there was a rapid improvement, and he sees no reason why this improvement should not lead to complete recovery provided proper policies are pursued and the recovery is not interrupted by a new disaster.

Optimists and pessimists agree on one thing: A deficit in the balance of payments can be eliminated only by an increase in exports of goods and services and/or a decrease in imports. This implies that the removal of a deficit necessitates a corresponding reduction of domestic consumption and investment. Such a reduction may be economically difficult or socially and politically intolerable. Opinions can legitimately differ on what should in a concrete case be regarded as economically, socially or politically tolerable.

The optimist will compare the magnitude of the deficit with the national income of the country concerned. At the present time he will find that for most ERP countries American aid is hardly more than, say, two per cent of their national income and he will conclude that a reduction of consumption and investment in that order of magnitude cannot be regarded as intolerable. He will also be optimistic as regards the possibility of bringing about a balance-of-payments adjustment of that order of magnitude by liberal policies. He is confident that if four conditions are fulfilled the balance of payments will equilibrate itself: (a) inflation, open or suppressed, has to be discontinued; (b) realistic exchange rates have to be set; (c) surplus countries (primarily the U.S.) must avoid severe depression; and (d) these same countries must not hamper adjustment by tightening restrictions on imports.

The pessimist will, first, question the usefulness of comparing such overall magnitudes as national income and size of deficit. He will insist that a reduction of the national income by a few per cent may well be intolerable if the decrease is very unequally distributed. (The optimist may well accept this proposition, but will point out that it is a matter of domestic policies of the deficit countries to make sure that the reduction is equitably distributed.) A more important source of disagreement is that the pessimist will, secondly, assert that trade flows do not easily adjust themselves. During the discussions about the German reparations problem in the 1920's, Keynes compared trade with a sticky mass and said it was a mistake if classical and neo-classical economists (who in general take the optimistic view with respect to the problem here under discussion) applied a theory of "liquids" to international trade, because trade was not a fluid but, if not rigid, at least a very sticky mass. He was the first to question the optimistic assumption of highly elastic international demand. On several other occasions, however, he was optimistic in these matters, e.g., when he recommended currency depreciation in 1930 and especially in his famous posthumous article on the prospects of the American balance of payments (*Economic Journal*, June 1946). In this latter case he expressed confidence that "the classical medicine" would work, if given a chance. By "classical medicine" he meant something like the four conditions enumerated above.

It will be remembered that Keynes wrote that article in defence of the provisions of the British-American Loan Agreement, which stipulated immediate convertibility of sterling. Superficially, it would seem that subsequent events have proved that Keynes' optimism was entirely unfounded.

It is true that Keynes' forecast, implied in the loan agreement which he had negotiated, that the loan would be sufficient to enable Great Britain to make sterling immediately convertible, turned out to be entirely wrong. But I submit that what was wrong was not Keynes' theory, i.e., the proposition that "the classical medicine would work", but his judgment that the necessary conditions for the efficacy of the classical medicine were already fulfilled: inflationary pressure continued unabated (Britain was still living in the Daltonian era) and sterling was grossly overvalued.

Later events, the effects of Sir Stafford Cripps' policy of disinflation, and especially developments since devaluation of sterling in September 1949, have, it seems to me, clearly demonstrated that Keynes' optimism with respect to the efficacy of classical policies was not entirely unjustified. There can be no doubt that the great improvement in the balance of payments of the sterling area and other soft currency countries between the autumn of 1949 and the outbreak of the war in Korea is largely due to the re-alignment of currencies which was initiated by the devaluation of sterling. The recovery of the American economy from the slight recession (which had lasted about a year, from the summer of 1948 to the summer of 1949) has, of course, also contributed to the passing of the dollar shortage. The major credit must, however, be given to devaluation and disinflation.

The boom which was started by the outbreak of the Korean war has led to a further alleviation of the dollar crisis. In fact, nobody can now seriously maintain that there is a dollar shortage, in the sense that there are difficulties of selling in the U.S. market. Our optimist and pessimist should be able to agree on that. But they will also agree that in another sense the dollar shortage will probably soon become more serious: many countries will find that they have fewer dollars than they require to maintain the standard of living to which they are accustomed and which they need to maintain social order and political stability. In other words, they will find it difficult to make both ends meet when defence expenditures rise sharply. The difficulty will be aggravated by the deterioration of the terms of trade, which has already taken place and is due partly to depreciation and even more so to the war boom.

In this sense, and only in this sense, the optimist admits the possibility of a dollar shortage. The optimist should, however, make one point quite clear (in fact this may be regarded as a qualification of his position, which would reduce the area of disagreement with the pessimist and restrict the disagreement between the two schools to a question of fact and judgment about fact): When comparing the size of the deficit in the balance of payments with the national income in order to judge whether the reduction in national expenditure can be regarded as tolerable, allowance should be made for the possibility that the elimination of the deficit may deteriorate the terms of trade.[14] In the judgment of the optimist, however, this secondary burden will rarely amount to very mush[15] and for that reason he is apt to play it down. This may be justified but the secondary burden should not be entirely ignored.[16]

The Problem of Discrimination in International Trade

Optimists and pessimists are likely to disagree about the much debated problem of discrimination. The pessimist takes a "dim" view of the efficacy of orthodox methods—Lord Keynes' "classical medicine"—of correcting a deficit. He cannot very well deny that some sort of a stable equilibrium would emerge, if the deficit countries run out of gold and dollar reserves (including ERP funds, IMF drawing rights, etc.) provided they stop inflation and let their currencies depreciate to the equilibrium level. But he will insist that such a policy will be accompanied by a severe deterioration of the terms of trade, which the deficit countries can ill afford. He therefore insists that if the gap in the balance of payments is to be closed, the deficit countries should be allowed to do it by discriminatory methods, i.e., by collectively imposing import restrictions on dollar goods from which imports from other deficit countries would be exempted.

The optimist on the other hand, as was pointed out above, is inclined to minimize the quantitative importance of changes in the terms of trade which are at all likely to be induced by the transfer mechanism. (That does not imply a neglect or under-estimate of changes in the terms of trade produced by other factors, e.g., severe depressions or war booms.)

The problem of discrimination is very complex and has many different angles. It can be discussed from the point of view of economic theory, but political and psychological reactions to, as well as severe administrative difficulties and limi-tations of, a policy of discrimination are of first importance and must not be overlooked.

Not more can be done in so short a space than give a brief outline of the most important aspects of the problem.

From the purely economic point of view it has been generally recognized by classical and neo-classical writers (most of whom belonged to the school of optimists in our sense) at least since J. S. Mill that, by skilful discrimination, any country or group of countries can turn the terms of trade in its favour and derive some benefit, especially when foreign demand is perfectly elastic, and *provided* there is no retaliation in kind. The terms-of-trade argument for protective tariffs (and any kind of protection implies discrimination between foreign and domestic producers) has always been a "theoretically respectable" argument.

A rational application of this principle is, however, subject to such severe limitations and difficulties that it must be doubted whether it has ever applied on a large scale.

First, retaliation must not be excluded. Secondly, even if there is no danger of retaliation, protection must not be overdone. Advocates of a policy of discrimi-nation frequently argue as though any improvement in the terms of trade were desirable, irrespective of the contraction in the volume of trade which it implies. That this is not so follows from the fact that, if it were true, the consequence would be that trade should be restricted to an infinitesimal amount. (The other extreme argument also encountered, namely, that the volume of trade should be maintained, is of course equally erroneous.)

The "optimum degree" of discrimination and optimum term of trade depend on the elasticities of international demand and supply. Hence those who are in charge of policy must know what they are doing and must be reasonably well informed about the relevant elasticities. This implies that they must not be unduly influenced by those whose particular interests are at stake; the interests of the protected industries and of the community go parallel only a part of the way (how far, depends on the relevant elasticities), and there can be no doubt that in actual practice protection has in most cases gone far beyond what can be justified by the theory here under consideration.[17]

Thirdly, it should not be forgotten that even if protection and discrimination benefit those who practice it (if it is not overdone), it does so at the expense of the rest of the world and it can be shown that for the world as a whole the losses are greater than the gains. The more careful advocates of discrimination recognize that, but they justify their policy on the ground that they recommend discrimination for the relatively poor non-dollar world against the relatively rich dollar countries. This argument is, however, very weak when applied to the ERP countries; because there are obviously much poorer countries in the world, some of them even in the dollar area (e.g., certain Latin American countries).

Fourthly, a single country, even one of the economic weight of Great Britain, cannot, when acting in isolation, have much influence on its terms of trade unless it is able to drive hard bargains with individual countries, e.g., by means of a policy of bulk purchases, that is by applying what has been called "discrimination to the second or third degree". Such a policy is, however, highly objectionable and can hardly be applied without evoking retaliation except from weak and defenceless countries.

The only alternative would be the banding together of a number of countries for a common policy. But in view of the inherent economic and administrative difficulties of a rational policy of discrimination and the almost insuperable complexities of international cooperation (which rise with the square or cube of the number of countries involved) a rational policy of this kind on an international basis must be ruled out as Utopian.

One of the difficulties about discrimination which has given rise to much confusion is that its precise meaning is not always clear. It has been argued that if more than two countries are involved the elimination of a disequilibrium in the balance of payments will always involve discrimination. Suppose we have three countries, A, B, C. Country A has a surplus, countries B and C a deficit. Take the most straightforward case that equilibrium is restored by joint depreciation of the B and C currencies against the A currency.[18] Now a currency depreciation of, say, 10 per cent is analytically equivalent to a combination of a uniform *ad valorem* import duty of 10 per cent and a uniform export subsidy of 10 per cent.[19] Hence joint depreciation by B and C is equivalent to B and C levying a duty of 10 per cent on imports from A but not on imports from one another, and granting a subsidy of 10 per cent on exports to A but not on exports to one another.

Therefore, so the argument goes, even the orthodox method of currency depreciation involves discrimination and there is no point in objecting to discriminatory methods.

This reasoning is, however, entirely fallacious. It obliterates the distinction between discrimination and non-discrimination altogether. If this argument were valid a perfectly free trade equilibrium would be discriminatory, because any equilibrium can be conceived as having arisen from a pre-existing disequilibrium by joint depreciation of the deficit countries. The argument overlooks the economic rationale of using non-discriminatory methods (e.g., devaluation or, for that matter, the equivalent tariff-*cum*-subsidy scheme) in preference to discriminatory methods (e.g., tariffs without subsidies or quotas), which is that the non-discriminatory policies "ensure that the equality of relative prices of international goods is maintained as between different countries."[20] This equality is a condition for maximizing world income.

While thus, the above argument against the postulate of non-discrimination can be categorically dismissed as fallacious, it cannot be denied that the very meaning of discrimination, and hence the meaning and rationale of the postulate that discriminatory policies should be avoided, becomes blurred in the case of quotas and exchange control.

Historically the case against discrimination has been developed in respect of tariff protection, where its meaning and reationale is fairly well and unambiguously established. It is identical with the case for the unconditional most-favoured-nation clause.[21]

How to apply the principle of non-discrimination to the administration of quotas and exchange control is an almost insoluble problem. The formula which is usually applied stipulates that quotas on imports should be distributed among various importing countries in proportion to the imports from those countries in a given base period which is regarded as normal. For obvious reasons this is a very unsatisfactory solution which becomes inapplicable if the year of application is separated from the base year (the "normal" year) by a period of economic upheaval. A simple example will show that the distribution of quotas and exchange licences according to that formula cannot be regarded as a non-discriminatory policy. Suppose again we have three countries, the U.S., France and Great Britain. Now suppose the two latter develop a deficit (either because they underwent an inflation or because the U.S. suffered from deflation or because of a shift of international demand). It has been pointed out by many writers that if the deficit countries use quotas to redress their balance and apply them according to the usual formula, they will have to reduce the total volume of trade much more than if they were allowed to apply the quotas only to the surplus countries. This is perfectly true. But it is not an argument against the principle of non-discrimination, because the so-called "non-discriminatory" quota method is not in the spirit of the most-favoured-nation, i.e., the non-discrimination principle. This can easily be seen if we compare the operation of that formula with the operation of a truly non-discriminatory policy, as for example depreciation. If France and Britain jointly depreciate their currency as against the dollar,[22] trade between them will not suffer as much as in the case of the pseudo non-discriminatory quota restriction.[23] What constitutes a non-discriminatory administration of quota and exchange control is almost impossible to say.[24] This is in keeping with the fact that one of the reasons for the increased use of quantitative trade restrictions (quotas and exchange control) is precisely the fact that it enables the country which applies them to evade most-favoured-nation promises.

The upshot of this whole discussion is that the case for and against discrimination raises very complex problems and deserves careful study. I believe that on the whole a very good case can be made for the classical principle of equal treatment, non-discrimination and the most-favoured-nation rule which has been one of the pillars of American foreign economic policy for a long time. But it must not be taken as a self-evident dogma.

If the optimistic view with respect to the efficacy of the traditional methods of securing international equilibrium, i.e., of Lord Keynes' "classical medicine", is approximately correct, it is not hard to prove that discriminatory policies in the long run do not pay. They can do, and in many cases actually have done, a great deal of harm and, unless Utopian assumptions with respect to administrative efficiency, effective international co-operation and absence of retaliation are made, an aggressive policy of discrimination cannot possibly do much good.

Non-discrimination like honesty still remains the best policy.

[A brief section on stable versus fluctuating exchanges is not included.]

Notes

1. It could be easily demonstrated that Viner's own admission of defects of the "real cost theory" makes the theory appear useless. But I refrain from going into that matter, because it seems that Viner is ready to substitute a modern general equilibrium theory for the real cost doctrine. I am ready to make the same substitution for the opportunity cost theory. But I assert that the opportunity cost theory is a convenient approach, a first approximation to a general equilibrium theory, while the real cost theory is not.

2. Some may object to the word "scientific" in connection with welfare and policy questions. Let me say, therefore, that in my opinion science should not and cannot pronounce value judgements. But that does not make welfare economics impossible. It only means that the

underlying value judgements should be made explicy; or in modern jargon: an arbitrary "welfare function" has to be defined. The rest is then entirely "scientific".

3. This was actually the argument for protection used by M. Manoilesco and effectively criticized by Ohlin and Viner.

4. We have here another case stressed by Viner in defence of the real cost theory. The "true real cost" of producing B is greater than its opportunity cost, because of the special inconvenience (disutility) associated with employment in B. This may be readily granted but there is no difficulty, as we have seen, in making allowance for this fact within the framework of the opportunity cost theory. It is not necessary to adopt an untenable real cost theory.

It should be observed that if the wage differential is imposed by, say, union action and does not correspond to the preference of individuals, the situation would be different from the welfare point of view. In that case the price ratio would correspond to the "real cost ratio".

5. This has to be qualified: If B is imported at very favourable terms, the loss through unemployment may be offset by availability at low prices of B. (The offset does not concern the unemployed themselves, but the economy as a whole. I here exclude the question of changes in the income distribution. For details see my paper in *Economic Journal*, June 1950.) [Chapter 3 in this volume]

6. It should again be observed that this argument does not imply a denial of the obvious fact that the reduction in income of those concerned is painful to them. But the redistribution of income is a separate matter which is not considered here. It could, however, be taken into consideration by introducing a value judgment *ad hoc*.

7. Speaking of monopolistic restrictions in the labour and especially in the commodity markets, it should be remembered that the easiest and most effective measure against many (perhaps most) monopolies is free trade.

8. This has been very forcefully demonstrated by A. Henderson in his article "The Restriction of Foreign Trade" (Manchester School, January 1949).

9. The latter is by no means completely separate from the former, but consists of the former plus certain value postulates. The systematic formulation and cataloguing of these value postulates ("possible welfare function") has been far advanced but not yet quite achieved in the recent literature on welfare economics. (See esp. the works by Bergson, Hicks, Little, Reder, Samuelson and Scitovsky.)

10. As William Fellner points out the "Theory of Games" developed by Neumann and Morgenstern "has not so far been presented in a form in which economists could find it directly applicable to their problems". (See Fellner, *Competition among the Few*, New York, 1949, p. 41.) Despite exuberant claims and enthusiastic reviews the theory has not yet been applied to any economic problem as far as I am aware, except the Böhm-Bawerkian horse-market!

11. Written *ex-post* by Professor Haberler.

12. Since the above summary is not a verbatim record, I refrain from attributing views which I criticize or adopt to any particular speaker.

13. This is the striking formulation of Professor H. S. Ellis, "The Dollar Shortage in Theory and Fact", *Canadian Journal of Economics and Political Science*, August 1948.

14. That deterioration has been called the secondary or transfer burden in the case of reparations. In the case of ERP it may be termed the secondary burden of getting along without U.S. aid.

15. Moreover it is very easy to exaggerate the importance of a *given* deterioration in the terms of trade. Even for a country like Great Britain the volume of trade is a small fraction of its national income. Many of the so-called underdeveloped countries on the other hand depend much more on international trade for their economic welfare than the highly industrialized countries.

16. It should be noted that what matters is "factoral" not "commodity" terms of trade, although for most short-term purposes the latter can probably be taken as reflecting also the former. However, the following situation is conceivable: Suppose a deficit country is confronted with a large world market for its principal exports and imports: in other words, the commodity terms of trade are fixed. But suppose the country can produce additional export goods or import goods only at sharply rising cost (in terms of domestic goods and "effort"). Then although its commodity terms of trade remain constant "the terms of trade in terms of factors of production" would sharply deteriorate. But that is probably only a theoretical case.

17. F. Y. Edgeworth in a famous passage has well expressed the view which our "optimistic" economists are likely to take: "Thus the direct use of the theory is likely to be small. But it is to be feared that its abuse will be considerable. It affords to unscrupulous advocates of vulgar Protection a peculiarly specious pretext for introducing the thin edge of the fiscal wedge. Mr. Bickerdike may be compared to a scientist who, by a new analysis, has discovered that strychnine may be administered in small doses with prospect of advantage in one or two more cases than was previously known; the result of this discovery may be to render the drug more easily procurable by those whose intention or at least whose practice is not medicinal. ... Let us admire the skill of the analyst, but label the subject of his investigation POISON"; "Mr. Bickerdike's Theory of Incipient Taxes and Customs Duties"; *Economic Journal*, 1908. Reprinted in *Papres Relating to Political Economy*, Vol. II, pp. 365–66.

18. Precisely the same argument would hold in case of internal deflation in B and C compared with A (gold standard technique).

19. The equivalence holds only under ideal conditions. But that need not disturb us here.

20. In the formulation of Professor A. Henderson in his excellent article, "The Restriction of Trade" (The Manchester School, January 1949, p. 191).

21. Even in this area there are difficulties and apparent inconsistencies. For example, the exemption of customs unions, i.e., of 100 per cent preferential regimes from the most-favoured-nation clause is hard to reconcile with the objections raised on the basis of most-favoured-nation pledges against, say, the British Impreial preferences which amount to about 30 per cent. This apparent inconsistency has been vividly illuminated by contrasting the position of Jamaica and Puerto Rico. The latter grants 100 per cent preference to American imports because it has a customs union with the U.S. which according to the official American theory is unobjectionable. The former grants a preference of something like 30 per cent to Empire goods which is held to be in contradiction with the most-favoured-nation principle. Evidently the discriminatory treatment of different degrees of discrimination requires a good deal of explanation and justification. I think a fairly good case can be made for it. But this is not the place to attempt it.

22. Unless the deficit countries could maintain convertibility between themselves before their joint depreciation, it is unlikely that equal devaluation aganist the dollar will restore equilibrium. Even if they had maintained convertibility it is possible that they may be affected differently by the introduction of dollar convertibility and, hence, should depreciate in different degrees. But all that does not change our argument.

23. To this reasoning it could be objected that it compares the pseudo non-discriminatory quota case with a case which is not only non-discriminatory but also non-protectionist, and that a protectionist although non-discriminatory method (e.g., application by France and Great Britain in our example of general, i.e., non-discriminatory tariffs) would also result in a greater loss of trade than a discriminatory tariff on U.S. imports only. This is quite true. But the moral is that for the sole purpose of eliminating a balance of payments deficit, the protectionist method should not be used. The non-protectionist (and non-discriminatory) method of devaluation will reduce trade less than a discriminatory tariff.

24. The auction system under which import licences for individual commodities or payment licences are auctioned to the highest bidder without regard to the origin of the import might be regarded as a non-discriminatory system.

3

Some Problems in the Pure Theory of International Trade[1]

1

The present article discusses certain elaborations and applications of the now familiar and widely used presentation of the theory of comparative cost in terms of opportunity cost. It is largely an essay in welfare economics. I shall, however, not discuss the issue of real or labor cost versus opportunity cost, because it would not serve any useful purpose. For as Samuelson once said, "the doctrine of opportunity cost, properly stated, in no way contradicts the so-called pain cost theory of value. In fact, when stated with full qualifications, the doctrine of opportunity cost inevitably degenerates into the conditions of general equilibrium.[2] The issue seems to me no longer a live one, and its discussion can therefore be appropriately relegated to a footnote.[3]

2

As is usual in such discussions, I shall use a two-country, two-commodity approach. One country may stand for the rest of the world, and the external terms of trade will be assumed to be given. This does not mean that what will be said applies only to a country of so negligible a size in the world economy that it literally cannot by its action influence its terms of trade. It only means that the country is supposed to act competitively and that the possibilities of monopolistic doctoring of the terms of trade and oligopolistic or bilateralistic complications will not be discussed in the present paper. Dynamic aspects will also be ignored.

Let us now start with the familiar diagram (Figure 3.1) showing a production opportunity curve AB, which represents the maximum combinations of A and B that can be produced. The curve is drawn under the assumption of constant (inelastic)

Economics Journal LX: 223–240 (June, 1950). Reprinted in *Readings in International Economics*, R. E. Caves and H. G. Johnson, eds. (Homewood: Richard D. Irwin, 1968), 215–229. Reprinted with permission.

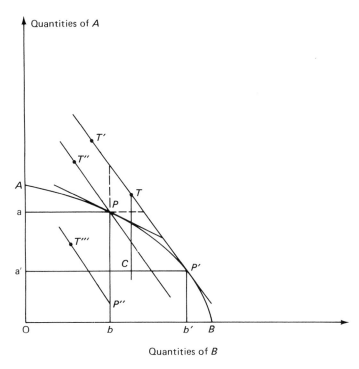

Figure 3.1
Production opportunity curve for goods *A* and *B*.

supply of factors of production and of perfect competition in the factor and product markets.[4] The curve is drawn concave towards the origin signifying increasing opportunity cost of *A* in *B* and of *B* in *A*. Assume that in the absence of trade production takes place at point *P*, output (national income) being *Oa* of *A* and *Ob* of *B*. The tangent to the curve at *P* has then a double meaning: Its slope indicates (1) the exchange ratio between *A* and *B*, one unit of *A* being exchanged for two units of *B* (this is, of course, the reciprocal of the money price ratio and of the ratio of marginal money cost of *A* and *B*) and (2) the marginal transformation ratio: for one unit of *A* that is given up, two units of *B* can be produced.

It is very important to keep these two meanings apart, for only under special conditions will the two ratios be identical. These conditions are, roughly speaking, competition, indifference of factors with respect to the industry in which they are employed, and absence of external economies and diseconomies. If any one of these two conditions is not fulfilled, the exchange ratio (price ratio) and transformation ratio will diverge from one another and, as we shall see presently, very important welfare consequences flow from this divergence [or "distortions" as they are called in recent writings].

Assume now that trade is opened and the international-trade ratio is given by the slope of line $P'T$. That is to say, abroad one B buys about two As; while at home one B can be exchanged for only half an A. Our country will therefore specialise in B. Commodity A, which is cheap abroad, will be imported, while B, which is cheap at home, will be exported. The production point will travel from P to P', where the marginal transformation ratio is equal to the new exchange ratio, and by trade the country will then move to, say, T, exporting $P'C$ of B in exchange for CT of A.

How is the precise location of T on the line TP' determined? For our purposes it will be sufficient to answer: by demand conditions. Some writers prefer to say that the location of T is determined by the point of tangency of the trade line with an indifference curve. It must not be forgotten, however, that a shift in production will usually be accompanied by a redistribution of income. This precludes the uncritical application of community indifference curves, either as an explanatory device (we cannot say "the community" will choose the most preferred point on the trade line, because "the community" does not do any choosing except in a centrally planned economy) or as a criterion of welfare (we cannot simply say any point T on the trade line is "better" than P, on the ground that it obviously lies on a higher indifference curve). Things are not as simple as that. But we shall not pursue this matter any further, and the reader who wishes to think in terms of indifference curves may do so for the purposes of the present paper.[5]

But that point T is "superior," i.e., represents larger "national income" or "economic welfare" than point P, can be established without making use of indifference curves. If T is above and to the right of P, a larger quantity of A and B is available after trade than before, and it is natural to call this a superior position. If T were, as it may well be, above P but to the left of it, say at T', there would be consumed after trade more of A but less of B. In what sense, then, can T' be said to be a "better" position than P? I reject the anthropomorphic argument to the effect that the society could have chosen T, which is superior to P, and since it actually chose T', this, *a fortiori*, must be better than P. This argument is unsatisfactory, at least for an individualistically organised economy. In such an economy what is to be regarded as a better position, a larger national income or superior welfare position must be defined in terms of individual incomes or welfare positions. Modern welfare economics has, however, shown that in the following sense the situation after trade can be said to be better than before: if income were appropriately redistributed, every individual could be made better off than before.[6] It is not necessary that income will actually be redistributed so that everybody will in fact be better off; there will practically always be some individuals who are worse off than before. But it is sufficient that everybody *could* be better off. That is the definition of what is meant by saying that one situation is better and constitutes a larger national income than another.[7]

3

What we have stated above is an ideal case which underlies much of the free-trade reasoning. Everybody knows, of course, that it is an idealised case which is never completely realised in actual practice. There are many types of frictions and deviations from the ideal conditions ["distortions"] caused by monopolistic and oligopolistic imperfections of the market, external economies and diseconomies, price and wage rigidities, lack of information, irreversibilities of the various curves involved, etc. Each of these conditions *may* operate in such a way as to make certain deviations from the free-trade policy rational on purely economic grounds.[8] But these imperfections may just as well be such as to strengthen the economic case for free trade. A mere enumeration of possible imperfections and deviations from the ideal case does not prove more than the possibility that certain controls might be beneficial (provided of course that they are efficiently administered—which amounts to assuming quite a lot). On this practically all economists agree. In order to prove that the restriction of international trade (rather than the opposite) is justified, it is necessary to show that these imperfections are persistent (in other words that there is not even a tendency for the ideal situation to work itself out) and that they persistently operate in such a direction as to weaken (rather than to strengthen) the case for free trade.[9]

I shall now illustrate this by discussing with the aid of our diagrammatic apparatus a few cases of real and imaginary deviations from the ideal type.

It is often said that perfect mobility of factors within each country is a necessary condition for the ideal classical model. The old classical assumption of international immobility versus national mobility of labor[10] is undoubtedly responsible for this misconception.[11] It can be easily shown, however, that what really causes trouble and may make trade detrimental and justify protection is rigidity of factor prices, which may or may not be associated with immobility of factors.

If perfect mobility of factors between industries were required, the theory of comparative cost would indeed be useless. For it is obvious that land and other natural resources as well as man-made factors of production, such as fixed capital, are in fact immobile locally and occupationally. So is labor to a large degree, at least in the short run. In order to bring the basic principles out quite clearly, let us make the extreme assumption that there is no factor mobility whatsoever. (This assumption is, of course, even more unrealistic than the opposite extreme of perfect mobility. In any real economy there is a large amount of mobility, even if labor [were] occupationally almost entirely immobile, through the possibility of redirecting intermediate goods such as iron and steel and other materials and fuels, certain types of machinery, transportation services, etc., from one industry to the other.)

Under this highly unrealistic assumption the production opportunity or transformation curve shrinks to the broken line, aPb[12] (Figure 3.1). If all factors are in inelastic supply (implying that their prices are perfectly flexible), production will take place at point P. Assume that before trade the exchange ratio between A and B is the same as before, i.e., is given by the slope of the straight line drawn through P. (It is true we cannot now say that it is equal to the marginal rate of transformation, because there is none if there is a kink at P. But we need not discuss here how the exchange rate is determined. If we permit ourselves the use of community indifference curves, we would say that the slope of the indifference curve going through P determines the exchange ratio between A and B.)

Now assume foreign trade is opened at the rate shown by the trade line TP'. The production point will stay where it was, but the country will import a certain amount of A in exchange for B and move to, say, T''.

T'' is certainly inferior to T or T', and its superiority over P is not so obvious as that of T. Still it can be shown that with trade the country is better off than without in exactly the same sense as in the case of T': By redistributing income it would be possible to make everybody better off, although in fact the A-producers will be worse off and the B-producers better off than before.[13]

Now let us introduce in addition to immobility of the factors complete rigidity of factor prices. A-producers are, say, organised and their union does not permit any reduction of their members' real wage in the face of falling demand and a lower price of A. In that case, production of A will fall, and some (or all) A-producers will become unemployed. Production will fall to, say, P'', and the trading point may be T''', which is clearly inferior to P. Conversely, if by a tariff or some other protective device the *status quo ante* is restored, the result is a definite improvement. Protection thus may become highly beneficial.[14]

A number of questions remain to be answered. First, how is point P'' determined? Why is it not higher up or lower down? We may say that the extent to which production will fall depends on the shape of the marginal-cost curve. Production will fall to that point where marginal cost has fallen to the price level at which A is being imported. If the production function is homogeneous and all factor prices are rigid, constant costs will prevail and production of A will cease altogether. We need not, however, make such extreme assumptions. If the production function is not homogeneous or if some factor prices are not rigid (the price of land and of fixed capital equipment are likely to fall, in other words, these factors are likely to be in inelastic demand—barring dynamic complication, e.g., expectations that the price change will not last) or if inefficient workers will be dismissed first or if efficiency all around goes up, as is likely to be the case when unemployment rises—in all these cases marginal cost will fall when output is reduced, and P'' will not move all the way down.

A second question is whether T''' is necessarily inferior to P. The answer is no, not necessarily, not even if production of A ceases altogether. Suppose that the international terms if trade are extremely favorable, that is to say, that the trade line is very steep, for example, bT'' (not drawn in the diagram). Then it would be possible to reach T'' or a still more favorable point beyond T'' on the line bT''. This is really obvious: If any commodity can be obtained from abroad almost without cost, it would be better to discontinue production altogether, even though it involves a lot of unemployment.[15]

What we have proved is the *possibility* of an unfavorable outcome, not its necessity. This possibility is, naturally, the greater the lower the production point (i.e., the greater unemployment) and the less favorable (i.e., the less steep) the trade line.

A third question concerns the implied change from the assumption of inelastic to that of perfectly elastic factor supply. For absolute rigidity of factor prices is equivalent to perfect elasticity of factor supply, while previously we assumed (for simplicity) inelastic factor supply.

Two kinds of supply curves of labor must be carefully distinguished: (*a*) The supply curve of the individual worker reflecting his subjective preferences for work (or income) as against leisure, and the market supply obtained by adding all individual supply curves; (*b*) the market supply curve as determined by union policy (or minimum-wage legislation or some other collective regulation). I suggest that failure to distinguish between these two meanings of labor supply has confused the discussion about voluntary versus involuntary unemployment. What is really meant by involuntary unemployment is an excess of supply in sense (*a*) over actual demand, more people wishing to work at the current wage than can be employed. This is quite compatible with supply in sense (*b*) being equal to demand.[16]

There would be complications from the point of view of the welfare interpretation, if contrary to our assumption the supply curve in the sense (*a*), i.e., the subjective, individual supply curve of labor, were not inelastic. Although it is impossibly unrealistic, let us assume that labor supply in that sense is entirely elastic. (Assume, for example, that people have income from other sources and don't care for work below a certain wage-level.) In that case the resulting unemployment would have to be called voluntary. Point T''' need then not be called inferior to P. If namely, economic welfare is then defined not only in terms of products A and B, but also interpreted to make allowance for "irksomeness" of labor, the reduction in commodity supply implied by T''' as compared with P would be offset by more leisure.[17]

4

We have proved for the extreme case of factor immobility and factor price rigidity that trade may be very detrimental. It should be observed that no adverse

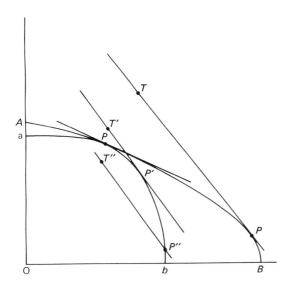

Figure 3.2
Comparison of transformation curves for goods A and B for the three cases, T, T', and T''

multiplier effects depending upon a temporary excess of imports over exports are involved. The balance of payments is in equilibrium all the time. The detrimental effect of trade, the failure to reach an optimum, is entirely due to the fact that a static optimum condition is not fulfilled: the equality between the price ratio and the marginal substitution ratio is not preserved.[18] The exchange ratio (reciprocal of money-price ratio) is given by the slope of $P''T'''$, while the ratio of marginal transformation is given by the slope of Pb (as was explained above, aPb can be regarded as a degenerate transformation curve). Thus, because the price mechanism does not function properly, the price line cuts the transformation curve instead of being tangential to it.[19]

It will be instructive to apply now the argument to a less extreme case in which only some, not all, factors are immobile and only some factor prices are rigid.

In Figure 3.2, we compare three cases, T, T' and T''. We have two transformation curves. The outer one APB is drawn under the assumption that most factors can be shifted and that the price system functions competitively. It thus portrays the "ideal" case. If P is the situation before trade, the country moves by production from P to p, and from there by trade to T.

Now let us start from the same initial position P, but assume that a number of factors are immobile. The reason for the immobility may be technological or unwillingness to move. Then we get a more sharply curved transformation line, aPb, inside *APB*. This curve might well be regarded as a short-run curve, inasmuch as in the short run factor mobility is in all probability much less than in the long run. We assume, however, that factor prices are still in inelastic supply, and that competition prevails, all prices including wages being perfectly flexible.

This case is then, in principle, no different from the preceding one. The country will move by production from P to p', and from there to T' by trade. T' is inferior to T, but superior to P. The inferiority of T' compared with T is due to the fact that owing to the reduced mobility of factors or, in other words, due to the lower adaptability of production, the output of B cannot be expanded so much as previously when the output of A is reduced. It should be also observed that when the production of A contracts, it is quite likely that certain factors of production will become idle; but only after their prices (imputed value) have fallen to zero. Suppose A is wheat growing, then marginal pieces of land will be abandoned. (On the other hand, in the B industry extra marginal factors may be drawn into employment.) The existence of unused free goods, extra marginal land, machinery, buildings, mineral deposits or even labor does, however, not constitute unemployment, although its emergence may constitute extreme hardship for the owners of the factors which have become worthless. The hardship is, of course, especially conspicuous in the case of labor, but is not necessarily confined to it. In the case of labor there is the further complication that its supply is surely not inelastic at low wages. Therefore labor will become unemployed long before its price has fallen to zero. But we come to this point presently.

The third case is distinguished from the second by the fact that in addition to immobility we assume price rigidity for some factors. We ought, then, to draw a third transformation curve more sharply curved than, and inside, the second one. But for simplicity I use the curve *aPb* again. It, thus, illustrates two alternatives cases.

If the price mechanism does not work competitively, if certain factors used in the production of A cannot shift to industy B *and* refuse to accept a price cut, but choose to become unemployed, the price line will cease to be tangent to the transformation curve. The country will move by production from P to (say) p'', and by trade from p'' to, say, T''.

T'' is inferior to P, and trade is therefore detrimental. What was said in the preceding section concerning the precise location of p'' and the possibility of T'' being superior to P applies also to the present case.

Why the two cases (the case of mere immobility and the case of price rigidity) lead to different results can be explained as follows. In the "ideal" case we have the following equilibrium conditions: the money prices of A and of B are equal to their respective marginal cost. Each factor is remunerated according to its marginal productivity, and all factors that are willing and able to move receive the same remuneration in both industries.

Now suppose that output of A is reduced by one unit. A marginal cost's worth of factors is thereby set free. But these factors produce the same value in industry B. It follows that the price ratio is equal to the marginal rate of transformation.[20] No factor released from industry A becomes unemployed unless its price has fallen to zero, i.e., unless its marginal productivity has vanished. Hence the existence or emergence of unutilised extramarginal factors does not affect the equality of the price and substitution ratio.

In the other case where some factor prices are rigid, factors become unemployed before their price has fallen to zero. Hence, when the production of A is curtailed by one unit, the production of B is expanded by less than the corresponding value because some of the factors go into unemployment rather than into employment in B. Therefore, the price ratio is not equal to the marginal rate of transformation. Expressed differently, the ratio of private marginal cost of A and B does not reflect the social ratio of marginal substitution, or, shorter, private and social cost deviate from one another.[21]

We have established the possibility (though not necessity) of detrimental effects of trade in case of rigid prices and of beneficial effects of protection in the case of unemployment. It should be remembered that unfavorable multiplier reactions are excluded and changes on the income distribution ignored.

How important is the case here analysed? Is It a theoretical curiosum or a matter of practical importance?

It is dangerous to jump from such an abstract model to practical application, and there is room in an article not even for a sketch of how to fill the gap. Still I venture to say that, at least in the short run, it is a matter of serious practical concern. However, even in the short run certain qualifications would have to be made, protection would not be more than a *pis aller* ["second best" it is now called] and rational policy should not be concerned entirely with short-term considerations. But we cannot pursue these thoughts any farther at this point.

5

In this section two other cases will be briefly analysed which give rise to a deviation of price ratio from the marginal rate of transformation. Unemployment is not involved in either case.

The first case is the much-discussed case of external economies or diseconomies.[22] It is usually thought to be connected with the case of decreasing cost. Decreasing cost may be due to external economies. The assumption of external economies is, then, a way of making decreasing cost compatible with competition.

External economies (or diseconomies for that matter) need, however, not be associated with decreasing cost. Social as well as private costs may be increasing,

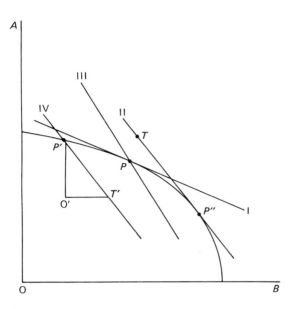

Figure 3.3
Effect of an external economy on the costs of commodities *A* and *B*.

and the underlying situation may therefore be quite stable and still there may be a deviation between social and private cost due to external economies or diseconomies, i.e., due to certain cost-raising or cost-reducing factors which would come into play if one industry expanded and the other contracted—factors which for some reason or other are not, or not sufficiently, allowed for in private cost calculations.

This situation is depicted in Figure 3.3. Production initially takes place at *P*. The true, social ratio of transformation is given by the slope of the transformation curve (line I). The international exchange ratio (again for simplicity assumed to be fixed) is given by the slope of line II. Commodity *A* being cheaper abroad ought to be imported in exchange for *B*. The country should move to *P″* by production, and thence to (say) *T* by trade.

But now we assume that the ratio of private marginal cost of *A* and *B* and hence the domestic price ratio does not correspond to the true social-transformation ratio. Suppose it is given by the slope of line III. The exchange ratio overvalues *B* and undervalues *A*. This is due to external economies which could be realised and would lower the cost of production of *B*, if the *B* industry were expanded. These economies are, however, not recognised by *B* producers or for some other reasons fail to induce them to expand production.[23]

If the discrepancy between private and social cost is as large as assumed in Figure 3.3, the country will show a comparative price advantage in the "wrong" commo-

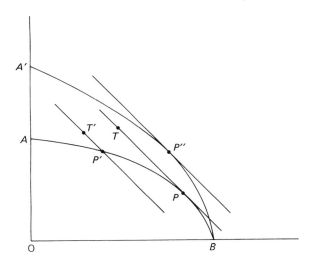

Figure 3.4
Diagram of the infant-industry argument for protection.

dity. According to line III, B is cheaper abroad. Hence B will be imported and A exported. The production point will move to the left, to say p′, where the ratio of private marginal cost (slope of line IV) becomes equal to the international price ratio (slope of line II). p′o′ of A is exported and o′T′ imported. The new trading point, T′, is inferior to P. This is, I believe, a correct representation of what Graham really meant.[24]

It is one thing, however, and an easy one at that, to point out the possible consequences of a divergence of private and social cost and to cite instances in which such a divergence is likely to arise. It is an entirely different and infinitely more difficult task first to demonstrate that such discrepancies do in fact occur frequently, persistently and on a large scale and to indicate concretely how these cases can be recognised and evaluated.

Most economists who have given serious thought to these problems have reached the conclusion that roughly, and as a rule, the ratios of private money costs do reflect the true social real cost ratios. Practically all economists recognise that there are exceptions to the rule, but they would insist that the burden of proof is on those who maintain that the exceptions are numerous, persistent, large, and, last but not least, practically recognisable and calculable.[25]

The theory of external economies is related to the reasoning underlying the infant-industry argument for protection, but the two are not identical.[26] The essence of the latter can, I think, be described with the help of our diagrammatic apparatus, as shown in Figure 3.4. We start this time with a situation where trade takes place, the production point being P, the trading point T. Suppose now that by means of an import tariff on A, production is shifted from P to P' and the new trading point is at T'.[27] The new situation is inferior to T, which represents the fact that, with the assumptions made, protection is necessarily detrimental.[28]

The essence of the infant-industry argument is that a movement on the transformation curve will bring about an irreversible shift of the curve itself. Concretely, if the A-industry is protected and expands, methods of production will gradually be perfected, skills will be acquired, and so the short-run curve AB will assume the long-run shape $A'B$. The production point will shift to P''. In the new situation trade may or may not take place, and the country may export either A or B, i.e., the trading point may be on either side of P'' depending upon "demand conditions."[29]

Again, it is an easy thing to state the assumptions, to derive the conclusions and to recognise that in principle the possibility must not be ignored that deliberate movement on the production-opportunity curve may shift the curve itself. But it should also be remembered that, in principle, the shifts may be in either direction; there may be external diseconomies as well as economies, and the possibility of favorable shifts in production-opportunity curve is not confined to import commodities. Improvements may just as well be realisable in the export industries, in which case the opposite of a trade restriction would be indicated. In other words, the argument may cut either way, and it is a little suspicious that the argument is practically always used in one direction, that is to say for the justification of protection rather than of freer trade.

To go beyond the statement of possibilities, to generalise about the overall importance of the infant-industry effect, and to evaluate it in concrete cases is an extremely difficult task which requires not only theoretical acumen, but intimate empirical knowledge of industrial development and, above all, historical perspective. Most leading economists, beginning from J. S. Mill, Marshall, Taussig to Pigou and Viner, accept the principle [of infant industry protection]. But those who made empirical studies, like Marshall and Taussig, became in the course of their studies somewhat sceptical with respect to the scope of the principle, and even more so concerning the chances of a rational application. It is to be hoped that the rapidly growing literature on the problem of developing underdeveloped countries will eventually add to our knowledge of these matters. But that is beyond the scope of the present paper.

Notes

1. The author has elaborated the argument of the present paper in a reply to a critic: "Welfare and Freer Trade—A Rejoinder" (*The Economic Journal*, Vol. 61, No. 244 [December, 1951], pp. 777–84). The present reprint contains a few additional remarks in square brackets.

2. "Welfare Economics and International Trade," *American Economic Review*, Vol. 28 (1938), p. 263.

3. Ten years later Samuelson seems to have forgotten what he had written in 1938. In June, 1948, in the *Economic Journal* he said: "Professor Viner has steadfastly maintained the more general equilibrium approach of Walras, Pareto and Marshall against his opponents Knight Haberler and Robbins. And one by one they have either had to maintain an empirically gratuitous position (that all factors must be perfectly inelastic in total supply and indifferent between different uses) or else have had to reformulate the opportunity cost doctrine so that it becomes not only a rather awkward mumbo-jumbo but loses all novelty and distinctiveness as well" (p.182).

It could be easily shown that Böhm-Bawerk himself had already in 1894 (see his article "Der letzte Massstab des Güterwertes"–1894, Reprinted in *Gesammette schriften von Böhn-Bawerk*, F. X. Weiss (ed.) (Vienna, 1924), especially pp. 428 *et seq.*) extensively, though perhaps not quite satisfactorily in all details, discussed the simplifying assumptions stated in parenthesis above which Samuelson chooses to call a "gratuitous position." These assumptions can, therefore, hardly be characterised as subsequent concessions grudgingly made "one by one."

Viner himself admits that the opportunity-cost approach (in the narrow, unqualified sense) is superior to the real-cost approach "in the case of land use" where "real costs are absent or unimportant" (*Studies*, p. 520). He speaks of a "genuine contribution" of the opportunity-cost technique "to the treatment of land-use costs." Surely, what holds of land also holds of other factors to some extent even of labor (*ibid.*, p. 525). He insists that "the opportunity-cost form of the income approach has no obvious advantage as compared to an outright income approach" (*ibid.*, p. 520).

Now I never regarded the opportunity-cost theory as anything but an "outright" income approach, in fact nothing but a somewhat simplified general equilibrium approach; and it does not require excessive generosity and tortuous interpretations to see that this is also the attitude of the other (including the original) propounders of the theory. Everybody seems to be agreed, in principle, on which factors have to be taken into consideration as determinants of income or, better, of economic welfare. But not being sufficiently skilful mathematicians, most of us resort to simplifications and allow for factors from which we abstract in our simplified models by means of somewhat vague verbal qualifications. Without pursuing this matter farther, I would still say that the simplifications made in the (unqualified) opportunity-cost approach are empirically much less absurd than those resorted to by any real-cost or pain-cost doctrine; the opportunity-cost approach is more fertile, because it can be readily extended into a general equilibrium system. It is therefore not surprising that the opportunity-cost approach has gained more and more popularity, and that it is used even by those who, in principle, attack it. (See, e.g., Samuelson in the very article from which the passage cited above is taken, and Stolper and Samuelson, "Protection and Real Wages," *Review of Economic Statistics* [*Studies*—Ed.], 1941.)

4. The assumption of inelastic factor supply is made for convenience, but is strictly speaking not necessary. How the production-opportunity curve is to be derived from the production functions of the two commodities is shown in W. F. Stolper and P. A. Samuelson, "Protection and Real Wages," *Review of Economic Statistics* [*Studies*—Ed.], 1941, reprinted in *Readings in the Theory of International Trade*, Philadelphia, 1949. Stolper and Samuelson, too, assume inelastic factor supply. If they did not, they would need two additional dimensions, and their box diagrms would not work.

5. T. de Scitovszky, in his article " A Reconsideration of the Theory of Tariffs" (*Review of Economic Studies*, 1942, reprinted in *Readings in the Theory of International Trade*) has made the only serious attempt, as far as I know, at constructing community indifference curves, taking into account changes in the income distribution. His solution of the problem is, however, not entirely satisfactory in my opinion.

6. See especially Samuelson's formulation in "The Gains from International Trade" (*Canadian Journal of Economics and Political Science*, 1939, reprinted in *Readings in the Theory of International Trade*). ["Redistribution of income" must be broadly interpreted. It does not necessarily mean that the *actual* combination of goods produced and consumed under free trade can be so redistributed as to compensate all losers for their loss without taking away all the gains from the gainers. If gainers and losers have different tastes, compensation would require that the collection of goods be changed. That this change is in fact possible can elegantly be demonstrated with the help of Samuelson's "utility possibility curves." (See R. E. Baldwin, "The New Welfare Economics and Gains in International Trade," *Quarterly Journal of Economics*, June, 1952; and Paul A. Samuelson, "The Gains from Trade Once More," *Economic Journal*, December, 1962.]

7. It should be clearly realised that such a statement necessarily implies a value judgment on the part of the scientist, and in that sense is not entirely objective. But it seems to me that the formula in the text expresses clearly what we have in mind, when we say that trade (under certain assumptions) or something else, say technological advance (again under certain assumptions) increases national income and economic welfare. There are, of course, other alternative or supplementary valuations possible: for example, certain value postulates with respect to inequality of income distribution could be introduced. Moreover, it may be questioned whether a situation in which more goods are available for everybody is under all circumstances to be regarded as a better situation. But we need not go into these questions in the present paper. [Some critics have objected to the compensation criterion. It is not enough, they say, to show that every loser *could be* compensated for his loss. In order to demonstrate that one position is "better" than the other, it must be shown that the losers *actually* have been so compensated. Everybody is, of course, free to proclaim any value judgment he likes. But *actual* compensation as a criterion has implications which are hardly acceptable. Everybody prefers prosperity to depression despite the fact that there are always some deserving persons—the proverbial widows and orphans, pensioners, Oxford dons, etc.—who are worse off in prosperity than in depressions. Must we hold off our judgment that prosperity is better than depression until we have made sure that every deserving loser has been actually compensated?]

8. The above list is not meant to be a complete catalogue of cases in which a certain amount of control can be justified. For example, protection for the purpose of improving the terms or for changing the income distribution will not be discussed in the present paper.

9. Thomas Balogh does not betray any awareness of the complexity of these issues, and seems to believe that he has proved something by a loose and inexact enumeration of possible deviations from the competitive ideal. "The Concept of a Dollar Shortage," *The Manchester School*, May 1949, p. 188.

10. Ohlin makes the same assumption as the early classical writers for his "region." His interregional trade is the same as classical international trade, for regions are characterised by internal-factor mobility. See his *Interregional and International Trade*.

11. See, e.g., Thomas Balogh, *op. cit.* This paper is a convenient and inexhaustible store of fallacies and misconceptions in this field. He says "there must be free internal mobility of factors" (p. 188).

12. It could be objected that in this case there is, by assumption, no transformation possible. This is quite true; still it is useful to regard the broken line, *aPb*, as a degenerate transformation curve.

13. The redistribution of income will, naturally, be much more drastic than in the case of mobility of factors. In fact, it may socially be intolerable.

On the other hand, it is perhaps worth pointing out that the distributional aspect may be absent: Suppose *A* and *B* are in joint supply (although without any possibility of changing their proportion). Then it would be impossible to distinguish between *A*-and *B*-producers.

In terms of indifference curves it is clear that T'' is superior to P.

14. If we make, however, the by no means unreasonable assumption that in the meantime wages of the *B*-producers have become rigid at the new real wage-level, a tariff will not carry us back from T''' to P. While production of *A* will expand, production of *B* will shrink, and we shall arrive at a point to the left and probably below P.

15. Of course, under the extreme assumption made with respect to complete factor immobility, it would be still better to let production of *A* continue *and* to import additional amounts. But that would require either flexibility of wage-rates of *A*-workers or an arrangement by which some of the gains made by *B*-producers through cheap imports of *A* can be transferred to the *A*-producers so as to maintain their real wage.

16. We may put the distinction in the following way: from the point of view of the preference of the individual workers, that is to say, from the welfare standpoint, unemployment is involuntary; but from the point of view of the union it is voluntary, because the union voluntarily withholds labor supply at a lower wage. This does, however, not necessarily mean that the unions act against the wish of their members, not even of their unemployed members.

I think that our construction is in accord with, in fact gives life to, Prof. T. Haavelmo's forbiddingly abstract scheme: "The Notion of Involuntary Economic Decisions" (*Econometrica*, Vol. 18, No. 1 [January, 1950], pp. 1 *et seq.*). Haavelmo is troubled, as any theorist who values precision and clarity may well be, by the problem of how to interpret and to reconcile with accepted theoretical notions the concept of "involuntary" decisions and "involuntary" unemployment. He reaches the sensible conclusion that "the concept of involuntary decisions is related to the comparison of alternative economic systems, and not to the decisions within a given system" (*loc. cit.*, p. 2).

Applied to our case we would have to say, that in a system not characterised by wage rigidities employment would be larger, and the difference in the amount of unemployment between the two systems is "involuntary unemployment."

17. It is a terminological question whether in this case we should distinguish between national income and economic welfare, the former being defined in terms of products only, while the latter makes also allowance for disutility of labor and similar factors. It may be also observed that the case takes on another complexion, if labor supply becomes very elastic (as is likely to be the case) at a very low wage-level. It then would sound rather artificial, if not callous, to say that those workers who do not care for work at a very low wage "don't care" for work and "prefer leisure." But we cannot pursue this matter at this point.

18. This is an optimum condition, because we assumed, for simplicity, the terms of trade as given. If that assumption were dropped we would have to substitute for the international price ratio what might be called the "marginal terms of trade."

19. We may also say the ratio of private marginal cost, which determines, and is equal to, the price ratio (since the commodity markets are assumed to be competitive), does not reflect the social ratio of marginal substitution.

20. This is, of course, true only if, as we assumed, the wage of those factors which can move is the same in both industries. Suppose factors can move freely, but that there exists a definite wage differential, wage-rates in one industry being, say, 20% higher than in the other; then the price ratio would not be equal to the marginal ratio of substitution. This is true whatever the cause for the existence of the wage differential. The welfare implications are, however, different according as to whether the wage differential is based: (a) on preferences of the workers (e.g., the one type of work being more disagreeable than the other) or (b) on an arbitrary regulation. (See Viner's critique of Mihail Manoïlesco's "The Theory of Protection and International Trade" in *Journal of Political Economy*, 1932, p. 121, and my *Theory of International Trade*, p. 197. This case could be analysed with the help of our diagrammatic apparatus. In fact Figure 3.3 could be used without any change to portray this case.

21. In Pigou's terminology: Private and social marginal net product do not coincide.

The reader should remember that we have assumed inelastic supply of labor as far as the individual workers are concerned (as distinguished from the market supply as determined by collective action). This implies that our welfare scheme includes only alternative product cost and ignores other elements, e.g., possible differences in the "irksomeness of labor" in the two lines of employment. In other words, economic welfare (national income) is defined in terms of products A and B only. We could, of course, introduce in addition to that disutility of labor. If the rigidity of factor prices, i.e., elasticity of factor supply, were due to individual preference rather than to collective regulation, that is to say, if individuals preferred to go idle rather than to work below a certain wage, case 3 (T'') would not involve a welfare loss as compared with case 2 (T'), because the loss in terms of product would be voluntary: a certain amount of product would be voluntarily foregone in exchange either for more leisure or in order to avoid subjective or material cost of working.

To avoid misunderstanding, it should be emphasised that this construction does not neglect or minimise the hardship imposed on the owners of the factors whose income has fallen. These hardships may be severe, they may be socially intolerable. Compare what was said above concerning the neglect of income redistribution in the global welfare calculation. It is, of course, always possible to introduce additional value postulates concerning income distribution.

22. The literature is fairly voluminous. See especially the famous controversy between F. P. Graham and F. H. Knight. Graham, "Some Aspects of Protection Further Considered" (*Quarterly Journal of Economics*, Vol. 37 (1923), p. 199 *et seq.*); Knight, "Some Fallacies in the Interpretation of Social Cost" (*ibid.*, Vol. 38 (1924), p. 582; Reply and Rejoinder, *ibid.*, Vol. 39). J. Viner has an illuminating review of the whole issue in his *Studies* (pp. 475–81). J. Tinbergen, *International Economic Co-operation* (Amsterdam-New York, 1945) devotes Appendix I, "Professor Graham's Case for Protection" (pp. 182–99) to a penetrating diagrammatic analysis of the subject.

On the broader issues about external and internal economies, private *vs.* social cost, the *locus classicus* is still Marshall's *Principles* and *Industry and Trade* and Pigou's *Economics of Welfare*. [As indicated earlier, the following analysis applies also to the case of differential wage rates, "the Manoïlesco case" which has received much attention recently. (See E. Hagen, "An Economic Justification of Protection," *Quarterly Journal of Economics*, Vol. 72, November 1958, and J. Bhagwati and V. K. Ramaswami, "Domestic Distortions, Tariffs and the Theory of Optimum Subsidy," *Journal of Political Economy*, Vol. 71, February 1963. As pointed out by Hagen, this distortion, unlike the one treated above in my text, does not only shift the production point on the transformation curve away from the optimum but also pushes the transformation curve itself inward (towards the origin).

A point which seems to have been neglected in the literature cited is that wage differentials produced by trade union action do not always correspond to the Manoïlesco-Hagen-Bhagwati theory. Thus, if the union pursues a strict policy of closed shop, it creates two noncompeting groups. This changes the transformation curve, but does not justify protection on Manoïlesco grounds although it may create unemployment if the wage is set too high. Only if the union enforces a higher wage in industry while leaving entry of workers into industry from agriculture free do we have the Manoïlesco case.]

23. There is not enough space here for a thorough discussion of why this may be so. But let me say that it would be gratuitous simply to assume ignorance. The reason may be that investments would have to be made the fruits of which cannot be appropriated by private individuals (e.g., investment in the skill of the working population). On that point the literature mentioned above should be consulted. [In modern terminology we would now say "investment in human capital" is required and since in a nonslave economy it is not possible to "mortgage human beings" (Rosenstein-Rodan), private initiative often fails.]

It may be also noted, in parenthesis, that the existence of external economies involves a misallocation of resources in the absence of international trade. *P* would not be the optimum point. If I may be allowed to use briefly and inexactly community indifference curves, this could be demonstrated by pointing out that *P* is determined by the condition that an indifference line be tangent to line III, while the optimum point would be located at that point where an indifference curve is tangent to the transformation curve, that is somewhere to the right of *P*.

24. If the discrepancy between the social and the private cost ratio is less extreme, i.e., if line III is steeper than line I, but less steep than line II, the country would specialise in the "right" direction but not sufficiently. It would after trade be better off than before, but it would not reach the optimum point *T*. In that case an export or import subsidy (rather than a tariff) would be indicated. [It should be added that if line III is less steep than line I, i.e., if it cuts the transformation curve at *P* "from below" (which implies that the external economies are in the *A*, the import competing industry, rather than in *B*, the export industry)—then the free trade production point will be located on the transformation curve beyond and below the optimum point *P*. The country will "overtrade" (rather than "undertrade") and an import *duty* will be indicated to bring production and trade to the optimum position, not a *subsidy* as in the case of "undertrading" discussed in the first paragraph of this footnote. This clears up, I believe, a point which bothered Bhagwati and Ramaswami, *loc. cit.*, p. 47. (The analysis has been considerably sharpened and generalized by H. G. Johnson in "Optimal Trade Intervention in the Presence of Domestic Distortions," *Trade, Growth and the Balance of Payments*, Chicago, 1965.)]

It is not, however, a literal rendering of what Graham said. Such a literal interpretation is not attempted. It presents considerable difficulties, because Graham was not too clear and seems to have changed his position in the course of the controversy. Cf. the literature quoted above, especially Viner and Tinbergen.

25. We may again turn to Dr. Balogh's convenient store of all sorts of confusions to find an exception which proves the rule. He says: "It is wholly illicit to assume that *money prices* are proportionate to *long run social real costs*. We know that private money costs are not proportionate to social real costs, and neither are prices proportionate to private money costs" (*loc. cit.*, pp. 189 and 190. Italics in original). Dr. Balogh is, of course, unable to give any proof; he just asserts and states impressions. I would not blame him for that, because such a statement as his could, in the nature of the case, not be proved within the frame of a few articles. But he accuses me of "invoking high authorities instead of proving" my contention that there is a rough correspondence between relative prices and real social cost. He seems to be not aware of the fact that the "high authorities," in fact practically all leading economists who have dealt with these matters, have, if not "proved" (such a theorem cannot be neatly proved like an arithmetical proposition), given plenty of reasons for accepting the contented proposition. They all treat deviations between private and social costs as exceptions to the rule of correspondence. This is, however, perfectly compatible with many shades of opinion about the relative importance or unimportance of these exceptions. Every leading economist who has dealt with these questions can be adduced (J. S. Mill Marshall, Pigou, Taussig, Knight, Viner, etc.). Even Friedrich List could be read by Dr. Balogh with considerable profit. List was of the opinion that a manufacturing industry that cannot be kept alive on 20–30% tariff can be regarded as unsuited for the country concerned. (*Das Nationale System der Politischen Ökonomie*, Edition Berliner, 1930, p. 326.) Protection of 20–30% *ad valorem* has to be regarded as very moderate nowadays.

Dr. Balogh makes a lot of special risks attaching to foreign trade as an argument for protection and discrimination. It is true that the ultra-protectionist and chauvinistic economic policies advocated by Dr. Balogh which most countries have been now pursuing for many years (without waiting for Dr. Balogh's recommendations) have enormously increased the risk of investment abroad and at home for the purpose of building up export industries. But surely this fact cuts the other way than Dr. Balogh thinks. It increases the importance of expanding rather than of restricting international trade.

26. On that I agree now with Viner (*Studies*, p. 482), while in my *Theory of International Trade* I held that Graham's case was but a variant of the infant industry argument for protection. However, in view of the vagueness which attaches to much of the discussion and in view of the fact that different shades of each theory can be found, there would be not much point in a historical investigation about the closeness of their interrelation.

27. The international terms are again assumed to be fixed. But that is not essential for the argument. The domestic terms of trade (internal price ratio including the tariff) is equal to the slope of the transformation curve at P', and the height of the tariff is given by the difference between the slope of the transformation curve and the slope of the trading line.

28. If we drop the assumption that foreign demand is infinitely elastic and assume instead that the terms of trade for the protected country improve, protection may be beneficial. This would be shown in our diagram by making the trading line steeper (not shown in the diagram). If it becomes sufficiently steep, T' may reach a position superior to T. In fact, as is well known, it can be shown that unless foreign demand is infinitely elastic there is always some tariff which makes T' superior to T.

29. In terms of indifference curves: depending upon whether an indifference curve is tangent to the trading line at P'' or to the left or right of it.

4 — A Survey of International Trade Theory

1. Introduction[1]

International economic transactions are defined as economic transactions, including financial transactions and capital movements, among independent countries or states. *Foreign* or *international trade*, on the other hand, is defined to mean the exchange among such states of goods and services only. Although the definitions—when framed in this manner—are not stated in purely economic terms and are encumbered by the vagueness of the concept "country" or "state," this need not concern the economist unduly; for we do have a fairly clear notion, at least with respect to recent times, of what is meant by independent "states."

There has been and continues to be much discussion in the economic literature regarding the manner in which foreign trade differs from domestic trade and whether a separate theory of international trade is possible or necessary. Why can we not simply make use of the general theory of production, prices, money, employment, etc., when dealing with foreign trade problems?

Strictly speaking, it is neither possible nor essential to draw a sharp distinction between the problems of foreign and domestic trade.[2] If we examine the alleged peculiarities of foreign trade, we find that we are dealing with differences in degree rather than with such basic differences of a qualitative nature as would warrant sharp theoretical divisions.

The classical economists regarded the international immobility of the factors of production as the most important distinguishing characteristic of international trade. Obviously, this fact alone does not really present us with any sharp distinctions. In the first place, complete mobility of the factors of production frequently does not exist in the domestic sphere either. Secondly, considerable movements of capital and labor often occur across national boundaries. As a matter of fact, both of these

Special Papers in International Finance, No. 1 (International Finance Section, Department of Economics, Princeton University, 1961). Revised edition. Copyright © 1961. Reprinted by permission of the International Finance Section of Princeton University.

situations were recognized by the classical writers, especially by John Stuart Mill and Bastable. From this it was then inferred, on the one hand, that where immobility of the factors of production existed *within* a country (Cairnes' "non-competing groups") the theory of international trade would be applicable, and, on the other, where there was capital and labor mobility at the international level, a separate theory of international trade would be superfluous.

It must be recognized, however, that particularly since 1914 national immobility of capital and labor has increased markedly as compared with the second half of the nineteenth century. This development carries with it considerable economic significance. It is therefore not surprising that even modern writers who are not steeped in the classical tradition repeatedly emphasize this immobility and cite it, for example, as one explanation for the fact that the adjustment process in the balance of payments often functions less smoothly at the international than at the interregional level.

The second most frequently cited distinguishing characteristic of foreign trade is the existence of independent monetary systems. Differences in currency systems usually do coincide with political boundaries, but here too we are often merely dealing with differences in degree. The existence of such independent currency systems may in itself be of varying significance. Under the gold standard, for example, the existence of different currency units is no more than an unimportant technical detail. But variations in currencies which result in independent and different monetary and credit policies and so influence the international movement of capital are of great significance.

A third characteristic often mentioned is the fact that the existence of political boundaries carries with it controls and regulations of international trade and payments, in the form of customs duties, quotas, exchange control, foreign trade monopolies, the more subtle measures of control referred to as "administrative protectionism," and so forth, which do not generally exist in the domestic trade area.

The importance of this factor is obvious, but it is clear that this too does not contribute more than a difference in degree, because on the one hand international trade is sometimes free, and on the other hand there often exist restrictions, though usually milder ones, on trade between regions of the same country.

Fourthly, many authors see the existence of greater geographical distances and the resulting increases in transport costs as the distinguishing characteristic of international trade. Quite clearly, this too is at best only a difference in degree. The implications of geographic distance and transportation cost have not been entirely neglected by international trade theory, but they have been more systematically explored by location theory, The logical relation between trade theory and location theory will be briefly discussed below. (See p. 58.)

The theory of international trade deals with the consequences of all of these alleged differentiating factors. It is therefore not necessary to concern ourselves, especially in a short account such as this, with the question as to which of the enumerated factors is the "essential" distinguishing characteristic of foreign trade.

International trade theory has never been satisfied merely with explaining, but has always aimed at *evaluation* and policy recommendation. Quite frequently concern with problems of economic policy has given rise to innovation and improvement in the theory itself.

Pre-classical writers, particularly the mercantilists, were strongly policy oriented. Classical theory not only served to explain the trade taking place but at the same time also provided the economic justification for free trade ideas. The newer "neo-classical" theory also generally leaned toward the free trade side, but as time went on more and more exceptions to the free trade rules were recognized so that by now, for many theorists, the position of "rules" and "exceptions" seems to be reversed.

A clear separation of explanation and evaluation, of theory and policy recommendation, frequently has been demanded and attempted. Typical of this trend is Ohlin's criticism of the classical theory on the ground that it intermingles in an unacceptable manner "normative considerations" and "objective analysis." That his demand for not just a clear distinction between political evaluation and theoretical explanation, but for actual separation of these two areas by putting them into separate books or chapters, is easier postulated than accomplished is demonstrated by Ohlin himself. Thus, in an early passage of his celebrated treatise,[3] in the midst of "objective theory," he proves in typical manner that interregional trade and division of labor results in an increased social product without making it clear that this statement implies a value judgment on his part and is not merely "objective analysis."[4]

The right attitude, I submit, is that one need not shy away from the application of theory to problems of economic policy as long as one recognizes the nature of the value judgments implied. This is the point of view which emerges with increasing clarity in modern welfare economics. In this respect also, theory of international trade has done valuable pioneering work for modern theory generally. (For further comments on the issue of analysis versus policy, see Section 6 below.)

A distinction is commonly made between the "monetary" and "pure" (or "equilibrium") theory of international trade. The former deals with the methods of adjustment in the balance of payments and with the determination of exchange rates. The latter abstracts from the monetary mechanism and attempts to describe the conditions of equilibrium in "real" magnitudes. How the two types of theories are interlocked has by no means been fully explained. Similarly, in economic theory in general the logical integration of monetary theory, macroeconomic employment theory, and the theory of business fluctuations on the one hand, and of price and value theory on the other, continues to present us with many unsolved problems.

The monetary theory of foreign trade is in part a dynamic theory and is closely related to business cycle theory and to the modern theory of the determination of income and employment levels associated for many with the name of Keynes. The pure theory of international trade, however, is a part of general value and price theory. Furthermore, the classical theory of "comparative costs," and the more modern version which succeeded and elaborated it, are static general equilibrium theories. Partial equilibrium analysis also may be applied to the problems of international economic transactions. The attempt to assess the effect of a customs duty on one commodity on the particular industry concerned (not on the economy as a whole) would be an example of this. There exist only rudiments of truly dynamic analysis in the field of non-monetary trade theory.

The non-monetary theory of international trade occasionally has been identified as a type of *location theory*, for example, by Ohlin. This is correct in a formal sense, since it is one of the major goals of the theory of foreign trade to explain the international division of labor, or, in other words, the geographical location of the various lines of production. It must be recognized, however, that a different type of location theory, independent of trade theory, has grown up and has reached a high level of refinement. The logical relationship of these two related theories, trade theory and location theory, can be characterized in the following manner: The traditional theory of international trade is at a higher level of abstraction; it treats the separate countries or regions as spaceless points (markets) and abstracts (with occasional exceptions) from the spatial characteristics of the domestic markets and from intraregional transportation costs. Location theory, on the other hand, emphasizes the space factor and operates "closer to reality." For the very reason that it is less abstract, however, this theory has as yet been unable to develop a comprehensive general equilibrium system. It is still largely partial equilibrium analysis. Lösch and Isard have gone further than anyone else in the direction of setting up a general equilibrium system of location. Only when this theory succeeds in developing a system of general equilibrium will the theory of international trade become merely a special case within such a general framework. It would seem advisable to approach this goal from both directions, by giving more consideration to the space factor and transportation cost in trade theory and by generalizing location theory into a fully interdependent system.[5]

2. The Classical Theory of Comparative Costs and International Values— from Hume to Marshall

No attempt will be made here to give an account of the *pre-classical theories*, commonly characterized as mercantilistic. The reason for this is not that the pre-classical literature is without interest to us, nor, as has been claimed so frequently, that one cannot speak of a theory of mercantilism as distinguished from mercantilistic policies. Pre-classical theories offer a great deal that is of interest, and the transition to the classical system is by no means as sudden as brief treatises on the history of doctrines often present it to be. The mercantilists did much indispensable pioneering work for the classical writers. But it is not surprising that most of the mercantilist literature is at a low scientific level compared with the classical writings, and deals to a great extent with economic policy matters rather than with problems of theory.[6]

The pre-classical literature of mercantilism must be divided into strongly divergent national groups and periods. For this reason no short summary of this material is feasible without doing grave injustice to it. We shall, therefore, begin our sketch of the history of doctrines with the classical writers; their work in the area of international trade theory, more than in other fields of economics, forms the basis of modern economic theorizing.

The brightest and best known stars on the firmament of the classical theory of international trade are David Hume, Adam Smith, Henry Thornton, David Ricardo, and John Stuart Mill. Grouped around them are numerous less influential, though in part highly original writers, such as Torrens, Malthus, Blake, Wheatly, Longfield, and Senior.

Hume's contribution to the theory of international trade (*Political Discourses*, 1752) is without question more significant and more original than the work of Smith (*The Wealth of Nations*, 1776), although the latter's influence on economic theory and practice proved much greater. Hume deals primarily with the international monetary mechanism. He not only refutes some mercantilistic errors but also develops the functional relationship, based on quantity theory of money considerations, between the circulation of money, prices, and the balance of payments. In this connection it is interesting to note that he does not overlook dynamic elements. Thus, he admits that during the period of transition from one equilibrium to another, following a disturbance in a previous equilibrium situation, an increase or decrease of the quantity of money may well have a temporary influence on the volume of production. This notion later assumed great importance in the work of Malthus and, more recently, in Keynesian theory.

Adam Smith's description of the balance of payments adjustment mechanism hardly goes beyond Hume's theory. However, Smith's refutation of the errors of the mercantilists, as well as his presentation of the advantages of free international movements and the division of labor, is much more detailed and better illustrated with historical examples than are the concise presentations of Hume. This probably explains, to a large extent, the greater subsequent influence of A. Smith.

Henry Thornton dealt primarily with the international monetary mechanism. Together with Hume, he was one of the originators of that version of the classical *transfer theory* which stresses the role of shifts in international price levels as against those transfer theorists who deny the necessity of price shifts and emphasize instead changes in incomes, purchasing power, and (more recently in Keynesian theory) levels of employment. Malthus, John Stuart Mill, and, subsequently, Taussig, and Keynes (in the debate over the German reparations problem), all belong to the school of Hume and Thornton. The other type of transfer theory, originating with Ricardo and Wheatly, which of late has frequently been called the "modern" theory (Iversen), emphasizes changes in "income" and "buying power" (of course, these words make their appearance only much later) and does not consider price shifts as always necessary for transfers. This version was stressed particularly by Wicksell and more recently, by Ohlin, as well as in the theories based on Keynes' *General Theory of Employment, Interest and Money.*

The pure theory of international trade begins with Ricardo's Theory of Comparative Costs, set forth in Chapter VII of the first (1817) edition of his *Principles.* Parenthetically, it is to be noted that the theorem had already been formulated by Torrens in 1815, who, however, does not seem to have been fully aware of the implications of his idea.[7] According to this theory, under free trade each country will specialize in the production of those goods which it can produce relatively cheaply and import those goods for the production of which foreign countries possess a comparative advantage. Based on the labor theory of value, the theory assumed complete mobility of the factors of production internally and complete immobility internationally. In the strict sense, the labor theory of value assumes that the factor "labor" is the sole means of production. For it, the existence of several factors of production, used in different and varying proportions, results in insoluble complications. (See Section 3, below.)

The theory is best illustrated with the aid of Ricardo's famous example: In England a gallon of wine costs 120 and a yard of cloth 100 hours of work, while in Portugal the real cost (labor cost) of wine and cloth amounts to 80 and 90 hours of work respectively. Portugal thus has an absolute advantage over England in the production of either commodity, but a comparatively greater one in the production of wine, since $80/120 < 90/100$. Without trade the internal ratio of the prices of wine and cloth (as expressed in labor, in terms of some "numéraire," or in terms of money) would be proportional to their costs of production, that is, $120:100$ in England and $80:90$ (or $88.8:100$) in Portugal. Thus, cloth is comparatively cheap in England and wine is comparatively cheap in Portugal. After trade is opened between the two countries, England will export cloth and import wine. Ignoring transport costs, an equilibrium price ("real exchange ratio" or "terms of trade") will result which will lie between the limits of $120:100$ and $88.8:100$. Let us assume, for example, that the equilibrium ratio of exchange is $100:100$. If England now specializes in the production of cloth and transfers labor from agriculture into industry, it can produce 1.2

units of cloth for each unit of wine which it no longer produces. These units of cloth could now be exchanged for 1.2 units of imported wine from Portugal—with a resulting net gain of .2 unit of wine for each unit of cloth exported; alternatively, the same quantity of goods produced before trade occurred could now be procured at lower total real costs.

Ricardo's presentation of this theory is extremely compact. He eliminates only few of the numerous simplifying assumptions, most of which are implied in his analysis and are not stated explicitly. A good part of the later theory of international trade has been devoted to the task of stating explicitly and then dropping one by one these simplifying assumptions so as to render the theory of comparative costs more precise and more generally applicable.

Ricardo himself demonstrated how labor costs could be translated into money costs and money prices. To do so, it is necessary to make assumptions about money wages in the two countries and the rate of exchange, and to introduce a condition concerning equilibrium in the balance of payments. In the event of disequilibrium in the balance of payments, money will flow from the deficit to the surplus country, resulting in a change in prices and money incomes in both countries until equilibrium is reestablished.

Thus an integration of the "monetary" and the "real" theory, is, in fact, accomplished although under the much simplified static assumption of "neutral money," in other words, under the assumption that money either does not affect the real magnitudes in the economy at all or does so only temporarily and superficially. It must not be overlooked, however, that the classical writers did not, in effect, make such assumptions in their writings on problems of domestic money and credit policy.

The assumption of constant costs can easily be replaced by a more realistic one of increasing marginal costs. On the other hand, the existence of decreasing costs involves complications of which the classical writers were not fully aware. The difficulties inherent in this situation were overcome only gradually in the course of the development of neo-classical theory.

In the two-commodity case constant comparative costs merely set the limits between which the ratio of international interchange ("barter terms of trade") will fall. Their exact location will be determined by the interplay of the forces of demand and supply. This extremely important addition to the comparative cost doctrine, known as the *theory of international values*, was introduced by John Stuart Mill, although hints of this can also be found in the earlier literature. Mill developed the theory of the demand of a country for the products of other countries expressed in terms of the units of its own exports. In this context, he employed the concept of demand elasticity which has become so important in modern times without, however, actually using the words themselves. Moreover, he also mentioned certain

analytical complications (multiple equilibria), as well as economic policy consequences, which could result under conditions of inelastic demand and supply
schedules.

The theory of international values was further systematically developed by
Marshall with the aid of graphic and analytical methods. Marshall introduced the so-
called *reciprocal demand and supply curves.* "Reciprocal" means here that the demand
curve of country A for the products of country B is simultaneously A's supply curve
of its own exports. These types of demand and supply curves should not be
confused with: (a) ordinary demand and supply curves which relate functionally the
quantity of *one* commodity supplied and demanded to its *money* price; (b) the so-
called export-supply or import-demand curves which present the quantity of
exports or imports of *one* commodity as a function of the market price (the b-curves
are derived from the a-curves, by subtracting at each price the abscissa of one curve
from that of the other, since supply of exports = total supply minus domestic
demand, and demand for imports = total demand minus domestic supply); (c)
supply curves for total exports or demand curves for total imports, which show the
volume of imports and exports as a function of (average) export and import money
prices, respectively. The curves mentioned in (c) have recently been employed
frequently in connection with the theory of currency devaluation and its influence
on the balance of payments (see Section 5 below). They can be regarded as an
average or summation of the curves mentioned in (b).

While (a), (b), and (c) are tools for *partial* equilibrium analysis, Marshall's more
complex curves attempt to represent a *general* equilibrium in international trade.
Each point along such a curve is in effect a possible point of equilibrium and each
movement along the curve pre-supposes that the economy of the country concerned
has adapted itself to the new equilibrium situation. Edgeworth very aptly compared
Marshall's curves with the hands of a watch which are moved by a mechanism lying
below the watch face. "A movement along a supply-and-demand curve of international trade should be considered as attended with rearrangements of internal trade;
as the movement of the hand of a clock corresponds to considerable unseen
movements of the machinery." [8]

Following the tradition of the classical writers, Marshall's model deals with *two
countries* and *two commodities.* However, exports and imports are assumed to be
composed of a large number of different commodities. The units he deals with are
"representative commodity bales," chosen in such a way that each bale contains a
constant quantity of labor or means of production in general. The commodity
composition of the bales changes not only when the curves shift "autonomously,"
that is, as the result of technological innovations, but also in consequence of
equilibrating adjustments, individual commodities shifting from the import to the
export side and *vice versa.* These constructions still betray the influence of the labor

theory of value and of the "real costs theory"; they are far from precise and obscure highly complex index number and aggregation problems.

A number of writers have attempted to extend the classical theory of comparative costs to the situation in which there are *several countries* and *several commodities*. The most important of these were Mangoldt (whose theory has been made familiar in the English literature through the summary given by Edgeworth and Viner), and more recently, F. D. Graham and August Lösch. The latter's position, however, is primarily a critical one with respect to the classical theory. Graham too, of course, has been critical of what he calls the "classical theory," but he is better characterized as "ultra-classical" than "anti-classical."

Under the assumption of constant cost, it is not difficult to imagine that all goods that could enter into the international trade between two countries are listed in the order of their comparative advantage to one of the countries. It can then be shown that in equilibrium exports and imports must be divided in such a way that each country will possess a comparative advantage with respect to all its exports and a comparative disadvantage with respect to all its imports. It is true that in this case, in contrast to the two-commodity model, the composition of exports and imports can no longer be determined purely on the basis of the cost data alone.[9] If we assume, for example, that foreign demand for a country's exports increases, we would find that this leads generally not merely to an improvement in the international terms of trade but also to a change in the composition of imports and exports as well. Certain commodities which were previously exported will now be imported or, if we take account of transport costs, goods which previously did not enter foreign trade but whose price was close to the import point, will now be imported. By import point we mean here that price above which it becomes profitable to import the commodity involved, analogous to the gold import point in the theory of foreign exchange rates. The export point, on the other hand, is that price below which the commodity involved will be exported. The spread between export and import points is determined by transport costs in the broadest sense of the term.

3. Modern Developments of the Pure Theory

One of the major objections to the classical theory has always been that it assumes labor to be the sole and universal factor of production and endows it with complete mobility. This is a fatal defect for it is after all perfectly clear that there are not one but many factors of production and that many of these are quite immobile in space or amenable only to *specific* uses, that is, can be utilized in only a limited number of ways. Even the factor "labor" is neither homogeneous nor mobile as between occupations or localities, particularly in the short run. One method frequently used to overcome this difficulty has been to speak not of labor but of "productive resources" in general. This may be acceptable as a shorthand form of expression, if based on a satisfactory theory, but not as a solution of the problem.

Among modern theorists, Taussig and Viner are the only ones who couch their arguments in terms of a *"real cost theory"* of value, but not a simple labor time theory. By real costs the classical writers meant, in Viner's words (*Studies*, p. 492), "all subjective costs directly associated with production. The irksomeness of labor, whether in comparison with leisure or with some other kind of labor, and the 'abstinence' associated with voluntary postponement of consumption ["capital cost"] were for them the important real costs." Defined in this manner, Viner feels that he is able to show that, as a rule, money costs and prices tend to be proportional to real costs. He concedes, however, that there are certain kinds of costs—he speaks of land costs as an example—which do not involve subjective cost. In order to vindicate the real cost theory it must be assumed either that all inputs involve subjective cost (disutility) and that their prices (remuneration of different kinds of labor) are proportional to the disutility involved, or that the proportion in which different types of labor and other inputs are used are at least approximately the same in different industries. Neither one of these alternatives can be regarded as representative of the real world and it is therefore not surprising that the real cost interpretation of the classical trade theory has found so little support in modern literature.

Instead of the artificial assumptions underlying a "real cost theory," it is now the general practice to apply either the concept of opportunity costs or the modern theory of general equilibrium to the problem of international trade. Basically there is no contradiction between these two methods. The doctrine of opportunity costs, when carried sufficiently far beyond the initial simplifying assumptions and elaborated more fully merges into the theory of general equilibrium. The former theory can thus be looked upon as a somewhat simplified version of the latter, designed for easy presentation and practical use.[10]

The Ricardian example of trade between England and Portugal can be interpreted in terms of the theory of opportunity cost without wrecking Ricardo's reasoning and objectives. The explanatory function of the labor theory of value is to determine the price ratio, or, put in reciprocal terms, the exchange ratio between the two commodities. It also has the purpose of showing that the two commodities can be substituted for each other in proportion to their costs by means of a shift in production; that is, by a transfer of the means of production (labor). If it were possible to show, without making the unacceptable assumptions of the labor theory of value, that the exchange ratio (price ratio) in the market and the rate of substitution coincide, the conclusions of the classical writers regarding the advantages of international trade would remain intact. And it can indeed be proved that, under certain "ideal" conditions, even if we assume the existence of a large number of more or less immobile and specific factors of production, the exchange ratio between any two commodities will be equal to the marginal rate of substitution between them. These required conditions are identical with those which usually underlie general equilibrium theory: free competition in all commodity and product markets as well as the absence of so-called "external economies." Under such conditions, commodity prices equal "private" marginal costs expressed in monetary terms; the price of each factor of production is equal to the money value of its marginal product; and the ratio of "private" marginal costs of any two commodities is equal to their "social" rate of substitution or transformation.

These conditions will of course only be approximated and will at best be satisfied only in the long run. They are not satisfied, for example, if commodity and factor prices (wages for example) are determined monopolistically, are fixed by the government, or are otherwise inflexible. Parenthetically, it is to be noted that rigid prices should not be identified with monopoly prices, for only in certain cases—kinked demand curve—is the monopoly price a rigid price.

Assuming "ideal" conditions as defined, a general equilibrium will result under free trade, ignoring transport costs, in which the international terms of trade are equal to the social rate of substitution between the two commodities in each of the two countries. These conditions correspond to the optimum requirements of modern welfare economics. "Optimum" is not used in an absolute sense but in the same ("Paretian") sense in which free competition is said to result in an optimum allocation of the factors of production as compared with monopoly. (Modern theorists like to speak in this case of "efficient" production, meaning thereby that if those conditions are not fulfilled it is always possible to produce more of some commodities without reducing the output of any other, or to produce the same output with a smaller input.)

It can further be shown that deviations from the competitive ideal, or the existence of external economies, result in a deviation of the free trade position from the obtainable optimum in the sense explained. This provides us with a theoretically valid argument justifying certain departures from a free trade policy. To mention merely one example, let us assume that a certain industry is exposed to foreign competition. If wages are rigid and workers become unemployed instead of accepting a wage cut or of being transferred to other industries, the prerequisites for free trade no longer exist. In such a case, a certain amount of protection *may* be economically justified.

For the standard case involving two countries and two commodities all of this can easily be demonstrated with the aid of graphic methods. Our major analytical tool is the so-called substitution, production possibility, or transformation curve. This curve shows the largest possible alternative combinations of the two commodities which can be produced with the available factors of production, or more precisely, the maximum amount of one commodity for each preassigned amount of the other.

Assuming that there are only two inputs, the transformation curve can be derived from the production functions for the two commodities (see Samuelson and Stolper). Such a derivation makes the theory of international trade an integral part of the general theory of production.

Another frequently used concept is that of a community *indifference curve*, first introduced into the theory of international trade by Edgeworth. More recently Kaldor, Leontief, Lerner, and Scitovsky have employed this tool of analysis. Through it the theory of international trade is closely linked to utility and consumption theory. It is important to note, however, that strictly speaking it is not acceptable—although it is often done even by first-rate theorists—to apply simple indifference curve analysis as a tool for purposes of explanation or of evaluation with respect to individualistically organized economies as if it were nothing but a somewhat more complicated replica of a single firm or household.

We are dealing here with the old problem of social or collective utility. Although attempts have been made to grapple with the problem of drawing indifference curves for a community or society rather than an individual (Scitovsky and Stolper), we are still far from a satisfactory solution. The literature of modern welfare economics is, however, beginning to show the first signs of a successful clarification of the problems involved here.[11]

Pareto attempted to apply the methods of the Lausanne school to international trade problems, but he did not get beyond a more or less formal equation system which can hardly be used for purposes of analysis. Yntema in 1932, on the other hand, produced an excellent mathematical reformulation of the classical theory, particularly of the balance of payments mechanism. Twelve years later Mosak, using more modern methods of analysis, based on the Hicksian theory of general equilibrium, further generalized and refined Yntema's work. More recently attempts at synthesizing, summarizing, and simplifying certain areas of trade theory have been made by Meade (*A Geometry of International Trade*), Harry Johnson (*International Trade and Economic Growth* and *Economic Journal*, March 1960) and R. A. Mundell (*American Economic Review*, March 1960 and *Quarterly Journal of Economics*, May 1960).

Ohlin, in the tradition of the Swedish school (Wicksell, Cassel, Heckscher), also attempted to apply general equilibrium methods in international trade. His work, however, differs from that of Yntema and Mosak and the other authors just mentioned because he regards his theory not as a generalization and amplification of the classical theory, but as a radically different approach. However, his disagreement with classical theory is, in reality, mainly with the labor theory of value and with the alleged intermingling of normative with explanatory considerations, as noted earlier.

Ohlin begins by setting up a model of two "regions" which, however, do not differ from the "countries" in the classical theory for he defines regions as areas within which factors move freely while they cannot cross regional boundaries.[12] From the start he assumes the existence of many commodities and many factors of production. He also posits an certain rate of exchange, since without such a rate prices in the various countries could not be compared. Each region will now specialize in the production of those commodities which it can produce more cheaply in terms of money, but not necessarily in terms of labor or other real units. Ohlin then discusses the circumstances which determine the comparative costs of production in money terms, that is, relative price structures. He considers the most important determinant to be the differential endowment of various regions (countries) with factors of production, taking into account not only different amounts of such factors of production as land, climate, natural resources, but also differences in the quantities and qualities of capital and labor, the influence of social institutions, and so forth.

Even assuming that two countries are equally endowed—both absolutely and relatively—with all kinds of factors of production, their price systems could still differ and thus render an exchange of goods between these two countries both possible and profitable. This would be the case if the structure of demand in the two countries were not identical and this might result either from a different distribution of income or from a different pattern of tastes. Moreover, even if all prices were equal before trade, trade could still take place if the increase of the area of trade resulted in economies of scale through large-scale operations.

Ohlin discusses all of these and many additional circumstances not only in an abstract static sense but also from a historical and dynamic point of view. For example, he demonstrates how the supply of the factors of production and the structure of demand, as well as the underlying taste pattern, might be changed through the influence of international competition and trade and that it would therefore be incorrect simply to assume these data as given. Many examples from economic history and commercial geography lend a good deal of realism to his theory; but there is also a certain amount of vagueness, obscurity or even apparent (uneliminated although possibly eliminable) inconsistencies and contradictions. His imagination, intuition and vision outrun his capacity for systematic, precise, theoretical presentation—which is ture of every empirical scholar worth his salt.

An interesting problem which Ohlin studies, building on Heckscher, concerns the tendency toward the international equalization of the prices of factors of production under free trade—the so-called *Heckscher-Ohlin law of factor price equalization*. An example of this is the well known theorem that the exchange of goods between agricultural and industrial countries will tend to result in an increase in the previously relatively low level of land rents and a drop of the high level of industrial wages (relative to rents though not necessarily also in absolute terms) in the agricultural country. In the industrial country, on the other hand, the opposite change in factor prices occurs. Ohlin claims that actually only a *partial* equalization of factor prices will take place; excepting special cases, complete equalization of factor prices could occur only if the factors of production themselves were freely mobile internationally.

This problem has been assiduously discussed during the last ten years. Independently of each other, both Lerner and Samuelson came to the conclusion, to their own surprise, that under certain assumptions free trade in commodities will result in *complete* equalization of the prices, both absolute and relative, of all factors of production as between the trading countries. This proposition was further developed by Tinbergen, Meade, and Laursen. It would thus seem that free trade may be a complete and not merely a partial substitute for free international mobility of labor and other factors of production.

This conclusion is at variance with the old classical theory of international trade. It is implicit in the Ricardian theory of comparative cost that free trade equilibrium is perfectly compatible with large and lasting differences in real wage or per capita real income levels; in other words, factor prices are not equalized by free commodity movements except perhaps in special cases. It is necessary to stress this fact because some writers (especially G. Myrdal) have criticized classical trade theory on the ground that it predicts equalization (or at least a tendency towards equalization) of real income levels resulting from international trade, while in reality the statistical record shows, it is said, an increase rather than a decrease of inequality of per capita real income as between poor and rich, developed and underdeveloped, primary producing and industrial countries.

This is not the place to discuss whether and in what sense international income inequality has in fact increased. Suffice it to say that classical trade theory does not teach that international trade must necessarily operate so as to benefit the poor countries more than the rich.

Myrdal's strictures apply to the special theory associated with the names of Samuelson and Lerner to the effect that free commodity trade is a perfect substitute for free international factor movements, and not to classical or neo-classical trade theory in general.

But even if directed against this special theory, the criticism misses the point because it ignores the fact that according to that theory factor prices are equalized by free commodity trade only under very special assumptions. These assumptions go far beyond what we called above "ideal conditions" (free competition and absence of external economies); in fact, they are so restrictive and so unrepresentative of actual reality that the theory can be said to prove the opposite of what it seems to purport to say—namely, that there is no chance whatsoever that factor prices will ever be equalized by free commodity trade.[13]

Briefly stated, the assumptions under which free commodity trade equalizes factor prices are as follows: (1) free competition in all markets; (2) absence of transportation cost, hence equality of all commodity prices as between different countries or regions; (3) all commodities continue to be produced in both countries after free trade has begun, in other words, that specialization is incomplete[14], (4) the production functions in both countries are identical and homogeneous in the first degree, that is, a given uniform percentage change in the quantity of all inputs results in an equal percentage variation in the resulting output; (5) in addition, the production function must be such that one commodity is always labor intensive and the other always capital intensive whatever the relative supply of factors and the ratio of factor prices; (6) the factors of production are qualitatively the same in all countries, although they are available in different quantities; and (7) the number of factors is not greater than the number of commodities. In a two-commodity model, for example, there could be no equalization of factor prices (except by chance), if there were three or more factors.

Making these assumptions, the Lerner-Samuelson theory can be proved somewhat like this: If under free commodity trade all prices of the factors of production in the two countries were *not* equal, then all costs and commodity prices could not be equal. This follows from the assumption that all commodities are actually produced in both countries and that costs only depend on the *relative* quantity of the inputs and not on the scale of output—the assumption of homogeneity of the production functions. Under free trade, however, and ignoring transport costs, commodity prices in the two countries would have to be equal.

As Samuelson and, before him, Viner have emphasized, the fourth prerequisite, identical production functions, is anything but self-evident, for it implies not only identical technical knowledge, skills, and so forth, but also identical climates, physical and social conditions, and so on.[15]

We must thus conclude that the Lerner-Samuelson theory, though formally correct, rests on such restrictive and unrealistic assumptions that it can hardly be regarded as a valuable contribution to economic theory. Its elegance and pedagogic value, as well as its importance as a precise presentation of all the implied assumptions, are however in no way affected by this fact. Ohlin's more modest and somewhat unprecise contention, of which he himself admitted the possibility of exceptions, to the effect that trade will tend to bring about a partial equalization of factor prices would, however, seem to be valid as an empirical proposition.

We are confronted here with an example of a frequent dilemma in theoretical research.[16] If, on the one hand, we base our analysis on more or less realistic assumptions, we have to be content with rather uncertain and at best approximate results. If, on the other hand, we are looking for unambiguous results, we are forced to make highly specific, and, usually, not generally applicable assumptions, or, at any rate, assumptions that are difficult to prove.

The same general comment applies to a proposition developed by Stolper and Samuelson, later qualified by Metzler, dealing with the *influence of international trade on functional income distribution*.

Numerous classical and neo-classical writers, including Bastable, Wicksell, Taussig, and Viner, have dealt with the effect of international trade, and the results of a reduction in tariffs, on the income distribution in general and on the level of real wages in particular. For economic policy this problem is of great interest, for one of the most powerful protectionist arguments has always been that under free trade the wage levels in wealthy countries will be depressed by competition from poor countries with low wages. That this argument in its crude form is untenable and is disproved by the theory of comparative cost has been generally recognized. However, doubts arise as soon as one turns away from the simplified model of the classical world and assumes instead the existence of numerous, in part immobile, or highly specific or specialized factors of production. The results of older theorizing can be summarized as follows: The incomes of the owners of specific factors of production in the export industries are affected favorably by international trade; in the import industries they are affected unfavorably. Thus, in agricultural countries rents will increase under free trade while the opposite will occur in industrial countries. The same applies in the short run to "quasi-rents" (incomes from durable capital goods) and to the wages of specialized labor groups. The situation is more complicated for mobile factors of production, such as, for example, labor and capital in the long run.

Wicksell, Pigou, and Viner have pointed out that free trade may shift the distribution of incomes against wage earners if the export industries are less labor intensive than the import industries. It is even conceivable that labor's share in the social product falls more than the social product itself increases, with the result that labor income would fall in absolute terms. This, however, is regarded by them as improbable and, in any case, would only be a possible and not a necessary result.

Samuelson and Stolper on the other hand believe they can unambiguously demonstrate that the relatively scarce factor of production will suffer absolutely under free trade—not only relatively in the sense that its share in the larger product will decline. This would apply, for example, to the labor factor in a thinly populated country, such as the United States during the nineteenth century. Conversely, the classical writers found a strong supporting argument for free trade in the fact that in the densely populated older countries the distribution of income would, under free trade, be altered in favor of the workers at the expense of the landowners. Stolper and Samuelson affirm that their result contradicts the "traditional" theory.

This contention is, however, misleading. As stated by the two writers themselves, their unambiguous conclusion strictly holds only under the unrealistic and highly restrictive assumptions of two factors of production and the production of all commodities taking place in each of the two countries after trade has been opened—that is, incomplete specialization. The theory thus would not apply to what would seem to me a more realistic model with three or more factors of production, for example, a model with one factor specific for export industries, another specific for the import industries, plus two or more transferable ones.[17] What we called above the results of traditional theory would seem to be reasonable for this model.

Some of the issues here involved have recently been pushed beyond the area of theoretical speculation into the field of statistical measurement. In an econometric article that immediately acquired fame and caused a great deal of puzzlement, Leontief has put his input-output machinery to work and reached the conclusion, apparently to his own surprise, that United States exports are labor intensive and imports capital intensive. "... an average million dollars' worth of our exports embodies considerably less capital and somewhat more labor than would be required to replace from domestic production an equivalent amount of our competitive imports. America's participation in the international division of labor is based on its specialization on labor, rather than capital intensive lines of production. In other words this country resorts to foreign trade in order to economize its capital and dispose of its surplus labor, rather than *vice versa.*"[18]

These findings are *prima facie* astonishing because nobody doubts that compared with the rest of the world the United States is a capital-rich country in the sense that per worker more capital is used in the American economy than in almost all foreign countries. This holds for the economy as a whole as well as for most individual industries compared with similar industries abroad. One would therefore expect that America has a comparative advantage in, and exports the products of, those industries which use much of the abundant factor—capital—and imports the products of those industries that use much of the scarce factor—labor, except if by chance tastes are different compared with abroad so as to offset the influence of differences in factor endowment.

The factual findings themselves will not be called in question here, although some doubts have been raised in the literature on that score. A few observations will be offered on how Leontief's results can be reconciled with traditional theory, an issue hotly debated by Ellsworth, Valavanis-Vail, and others.

I suggest that the circumstance which some critics, especially Ellsworth, have overlooked, or whose far-reaching implications they have not sufficiently realized, is that Leontief operates not from a two-factor model (as a large part of the theoretical literature does) but from a many-factor model. Capital for him is not a catchall for everything that is not labor, but is defined as produced means of production, plant and equipment, buildings, goods in process and inventories. In addition to labor and capital there exists a variety of other factors, including "natural resources," "management," and "entrepreneurship." These other factors are so heterogeneous in quality and so difficult to identify and measure—the line between quantifiable inputs and "milieu" or "atmosphere" is not easy to draw—that Leontief has found it impossible as yet to include them in his statistical measurements.

The existence of factors other than those explicitly treated implies that the production functions, *in terms of labor and capital*, are not necessarily homogeneous and that the production functions are not the same in different countries. (Leontief's statistics refer exclusively to the United States.)

Leontief himself tries to reconcile his findings with the postulates of traditional theory, which he fully accepts, by assuming that American labor is so much more "productive" than foreign labor that, if labor supply is measured in "efficiency units" rather than man-years, the United States may well be rich in labor and poor in capital compared with the rest of the world.

It is important to be quite clear what is meant by high labor productivity in this context. It is not simply the fact that output per man-hour is high; this might be entirely due to the large capital stock and hence could not explain why the United States exports are labor intensive commodities. On the other hand, if the higher productivity of labor in the United States was simply the reflection of superior skill, better education, better discipline, reliability, and so on of the American worker, it would be capable of providing a logically acceptable answer to the problem. But as compared with other industrial countries this kind of superiority of United States labor is hardly sufficiently large—if it exists at all—to bear the whole burden of the explanation. The factor stressed most by Leontief is another one. American labor is superior because of the superiority of cooperating factors *other than capital*, namely: management, entrepreneurship, and natural resources. This surely helps to provide a theoretically acceptable reconciliation between the statistical findings and the postulates of traditional theory.

There is, however, still another explanation which overlaps and supplements Leontief's explanation. It could be that import competing industries in the United States are comparatively capital intensive because United States capital is a better substitute for foreign natural resources than United States labor. An extreme example cited by Leontief himself can serve as illustration. If the United States were to produce tea or coffee it would require great amounts of capital in the form of hot-houses to make up for the lack of suitable soil, climate and other natural resources which favor the production of these things in foreign countries.

The existence of other factors in addition to labor and capital destroys the symmetry which exists in theoretical two-factor models: From the fact that the United States exports labor intensive commodities it no longer follows that other countries export capital intensive commodities. In view of their different endowment with natural resources and other non-labor and non-capital factors what is, or would be, a capital intensive industry here—coffee production, for example—may well be a labor intensive industry aboard.

In general, we may say that with many factors of production, some of which are qualitatively incommensurable as between different countries, and with dissimilar production functions in different countries, no sweeping *a priori* generalizations concerning the composition of trade are possible.

4. The Terms of Trade

Of great importance in the recent theory, as well as in economic policy discussions, is the concept of "the barter terms of trade" or "the real ratio of international interchange," the "commodity terms of trade" for short. It has become customary to distinguish between several types of such terms of trade. If, in the Ricardian example, the terms of trade work out as one gallon of wine exchanging for 0.89 yards of cloth, the outcome is very advantageous for England. If one gallon of wine exchanges for 1.20 yards of cloth, then Portugal is highly favored. In such simple cases, where we are dealing with only two commodities and with constant costs, the terms of trade are easy to define and to compute. Moreover, the measure has a double meaning in such a case: (a) It refers to the *commodity terms of trade*, that is, the terms under which two commodities are exchanged; and (b) it refers to the *factoral terms of trade*, that is, the ratio at which English and Portuguese labor, or the factors of production generally, are exchanged for each other.

Once we consider many commodities, the possibility of a changing composition of exports and imports, and historical changes in cost, the terms of trade concept loses its precision. Moreover, (a) and (b) then may differ from each other and we are confronted with complicated problems of measurement involving the use of index numbers. Only the commodity terms of trade are readily measurable and currently computed in most countries, although in recent years several attempts have been made to evaluate statistically changes in factoral terms of trade of a few countries during a few selected periods. In contrast to the ready availability of the commodity terms of trade and the extreme paucity of information about the factoral terms of trade, many economists prefer the latter for purposes of analysis and evaluation. Thus, the factoral terms of trade form the basis for Marshall's theory, since his REPRESENTATIVE BUNDLES OR BALES OF COMMODITIES are chosen in such a manner that each contains a constant quantity of "productive resources" and Robertson calls the double factoral terms the "true" terms of trade.

The commodity terms of trade can be calculated by dividing the index of export prices by the index of import prices. But in order to find the factoral terms of trade, the index of export prices has to be multiplied by a productivity index indicating by how much the input of factors per unit of exports has changed. Let us assume that the export price index is 1.10, or, in other words, that the average price of export goods has risen by 10 percent. Let us further assume that the productivity index is

1.05, or, in other words, that output per unit of input, per hour of labor for example, has increased by 5 percent. Each unit of exports thus contains less labor and the index of export prices of the factors of production will be $1.10 \times 1.05 = 1.15$. In other words, the export price of the factors of production has increased by 15 percent over the base period, the price of a Marshallian bale expressed in money has gone up by 15 percent.

If we assume further that import prices remained unchanged, we would then have an improvement of 10 percent in the commodity terms of trade and of 15 percent in the *unilateral or single factoral terms of trade*, that is, one unit of labor exported buys 15 percent more import goods. If we multiply the import price index of 1.0 by the foreign productivity index of, say, 1.1 and divide the two corrected price indices by each other ($1.15 : 1.10 = 1.05$), we have the *bilateral or double factoral terms of trade*. That is to say, one hour of exported labor now buys 5 percent more foreign labor hours than in the base period.

The factoral terms of trade, either single or double, are extremely difficult to calculate in practice, because the concept of a "unit of productive factors," and thus that of a productivity index, is almost impossible to define operationally and to measure statistically. The mention above of units of labor hours was only for the purpose of elucidation, it was not meant to imply that we can ignore all the other factors of production or the existence of heterogeneous types rather than of a homogeneous quantity of labor factor.[19]

There is nonetheless a good reason why, in spite of all this, the concept of factoral terms of trade is still preferred by many economists. The interpretation of historical changes, especially those in the long run, depends to a large extent on the particular circumstances and causes which give rise to them. For example, it is customary for the so-called underdeveloped countries to complain that, apart from some temporary interruptions, the commodity terms of trade have shifted to their disadvantage since the 1870s. In other words, they assert that world prices of raw materials and agricultural products have fallen relative to those of finished products. Even assuming that the facts are correct, which we will not examine here, it does not follow at all that these countries are any worse off today or that they derive less advantage from international trade than previously, or that the changes which led to the alleged deterioration of their terms of trade have adversely affected them. This would depend on the nature of the causes of the deterioration in the trade terms.

Suppose that the commodity terms of trade have become less favorable for country A because, for some reason, B's demand for A's goods has decreased. This might happen because B's national income has temporarily or permanently fallen, or because B's import industries have either matured or are receiving greater protection than before, or because third countries are competing with A in B's market. In these cases a deterioration in the terms of trade is without question unfavorable for A.

Clearly, not only the commodity terms but also the single, and perhaps the double, factoral terms have shifted against A.

Another possibility would be that the productivity of A's export industries has increased and they are therefore able to supply their products more cheaply. In this case the change of the commodity terms of trade against A is evidently more favorable (or less unfavorable) than in the former case. If the unfavorable shift in the commodity terms of trade has not been greater than the increase in productivity (which, in turn, would depend on the elasticity of foreign demand) then A's situation is better than it was before the change occurred. This is precisely what is meant by saying that the (single) factoral terms of trade have not deteriorated. If would, of course, have been still better if a high elasticity of B's demand had prevented any deterioration of A's commodity terms of trade, entailing an improvement in the factoral terms of trade.

A fall in transport costs is a special case and this development has in fact played an important role in the historical example mentioned above. For example, lowering of freight costs between the La Plata harbors and Liverpool would make it possible for both the English and the Argentine terms of trade to improve simultaneously if each is calculated at the home port. This would evidently imply that terms of trade for both have worsened if calculated at the port of the other country.[20] It should be observed, that the contention concerning the deterioration of raw material prices so often mentioned today refers exclusively to the statistics of the British commodity terms of trade loco British ports of importation.

We see therefore that extreme care must be taken when evaluating a change in the terms of trade, and that a distinction must be made between a number of different cases. However, it does not seem necessary nor would it be sufficient, to handle all the various cases by simply substituting for the commodity terms of trade the concept of the *"factoral terms of trade"* with which it is so difficult to operate in actual practice.

It should also be noted that at least two other types of terms of trade (with some variations in detail) have been suggested in the literature which, in contrast to the factoral terms of trade, are more easily amenable to statistical measurement and have actually been calculated for England by Imlah. These are the *gross barter terms of trade* (Taussig) and *income terms of trade* (Dorrance and Staehle), also called "Export Gain from Trade" (Imlah). Viner, who in Chapter IX of his *Studies* gives the most thorough and comprehensive theoretical discussion of the various concepts of terms of trade in their relation to the gains from trade, has labelled a variant of the income terms of trade an index of "total gain from trade." He makes it clear, however, that he himself does not believe that measure of this type of terms of trade, or that of any other, can be regarded as an adequate and unequivocal indication of the gain which a country derives from trade or even of the amount or direction of change in such gains.

If we let $P_e(P_i)$ be the export- (import-) price index and $Q_e(Q_i)$ the export-(import-) quantity index, then the gross barter terms of trade is defined as Q_e/Q_i, the income terms of trade as $Q_e P_e/P_i$, while the commodity terms of trade is P_e/P_i.[21]

Neither an increase in the index of the gross barter terms of trade nor of that of the income terms of trade can be regarded as an indication that a country's position has improved or that its gains from trade have increased. In fact, both of these measures are inferior to, and a less reliable guide than, the simple commodity terms of trade, because each of them treats as equivalent cases that have to be judged differently, even if other things have remained unchanged. Let me first explain what is meant by the "other things" that are supposed to remain constant. For the present purpose we define them as (a) volume of employment (or volume of production),[22] and (b) the balance of payments. We shall then assume that full employment as well as equilibrium in the balance of payments is maintained.[23]

Thus the gross barter terms of trade indicate an improvement when the volume of exports rises (the volume of imports remaining the same) because the country pays reparations or because it exports capital. Obviously, these two cases have to be judged differently.

Similarly, the "income terms of trade" can lead to a wrong conclusion in cases where the commodity terms of trade give the right answer. Consider, for example, the following two cases. For simplicity, assume that import prices, quantities and value are unchanged and the value of exports and imports remain equal (the balance of trade and payments is in equilibrium). Now suppose, first, that export prices have risen by 10 percent and export quantities have fallen by 10 percent. Obviously, the country is better off (real national income is larger) than before, because it buys the same imports with smaller exports. The direction in the welfare change is correctly indicated by an improvement in the commodity terms of trade, while the income terms of trade ($Q_e P_e/P_e$) indicate no change (the rise in P_e cancels out the fall in Q_e).

Suppose, secondly, that export prices have fallen by 10 percent and export quantities have grown by 10 percent. The country is now worse off than before because for the same imports it must export (give away) larger quantities of goods. The commodity terms of trade indicate, correctly, a deterioration while the income terms of trade register no change. Thus the commodity terms of trade would seem to be a better indicator of the welfare implications of international trade. But it must not be assumed that every improvement in the commodity terms of trade signifies that the country is better off, and every deterioration that the country is worse off— even if there has been no change in productivity (production function) or in overall employment and output.

We have to distinguish between (a) changes in the terms of trade of a country which result from changes in foreign demand (shift, for any reason, in the foreign reciprocal demand or offer curve) and (b) changes resulting from a shift in the country's own reciprocal demand or offer curve.

Any improvement in the terms of trade which results from a change in foreign demand is favorable, provided full employment and production can be maintained.[24]

Similarly, a deterioration of the terms of trade resulting from a contraction of foreign demand leaves the country worse off than before.

On the other hand, a change in the terms of trade of a country resulting from a shift of the country's own offer curve cannot be unambiguously judged as good or bad according to the direction of the change, even if full employment is maintained continuously. Consider, for example, the case in which a country "improves" its terms of trade deliberately by restricting its imports (or exports) by means of tariffs or other measures of trade restriction, assuming, of course, that foreign demand is not perfectly elastic (in which case a restriction of imports would not improve the terms of trade) and that the import restrictions on the part of the country in question are not countered by retaliatory restrictions on the part of other countries.

It is generally agreed that up to a point—"the optimum tariff level"—such a policy will improve the country's economic welfare, the precise position of the optimum depending on certain elasticities.[25] But it is equally well known that beyond the optimum tariff point any further restriction of trade, although it will further "improve" the terms of trade, will nevertheless reduce economic welfare. Just as the optimum price of a monopolist, i.e., the price which maximizes the monopolist's income, is not the highest price the monopolist is able to charge, the optimum terms of trade which maximize national income are not the highest price of exports in terms of imports. In other words, the terms of trade should be optimized not maximized. This can also be expressed by saying that beyond a certain point the favorable effect on welfare resulting from better terms of trade is compensated and over-compensated by a fall in volume of trade.[26]

We have here a clear case where an "improvement" in the terms of trade marks a deterioration in economic welfare; and a "deterioration" in the terms of trade signifies an improvement in economic welfare.

5. The Balance of Payments Mechanism

1. The Balance of Payments and National Income

The theory of the adjustment mechanism of the balance of payments is as old as economic theory itself. Concerning the history of doctrines the reader is referred to the well known books by Angell, Iversen, Viner, and Wu.

Much like the monetary disturbances following the Napoleonic wars, the severe balance of payments crisis during the inflation period after World War I, and those caused by the "Great Depression" of 1929–1932 have all done much to stimulate theoretical thinking in this area. After World War II, prolonged balance of payments difficulties of most countries, excepting the United States, Switzerland and a few others—the so-called "structural Dollar shortage," which according to many writers had really started long before the war—have again given a strong impetus to further theoretical and empirical research in the mechanism of adjustment of the balance of payments. The "reverse Dollar problem," the Dollar "glut" or "surplus," which became clearly visible in 1958 has not yet given rise to further innovations and improvements in theoretical analysis. But it can probably be said, without exaggeration, that during the last thirty years the theory has advanced as much as during all of the 200 years which preceded them.

By the balance of payments of a country is meant the statistical record in balance-sheet form, of all its economic transactions during a certain period of time. Depending on the purpose, such a balance sheet may be drawn up in many different ways. In its usual form, the balance distinguishes between items on current and on capital account. The former lists all kinds of exports and imports of goods and services, interest and divide[n]d payments, private gifts, and so on. The capital balance, on the other hand, is subdivided into long- and short-term capital transfers—the import and export of all kinds of debt instruments as well as of corporate stocks—and imports and exports of monetary gold. Reparations and other unilateral transfers, such as Marshall aid, are best listed separately. This, however, is all purely a matter of convenience and no one particular arrangement of these accounts should be considered the "best" or the only "correct" one for every conceivable purpose.

By a *deficit* or *surplus* in the balance of payments is usually meant gold movements plus "accommodating" capital movements; that is, capital movements that are induced by balance of payments conditions and loans given or taken for the specific purpose of equalizing the payments balance. It is not always easy to distinguish between autonomous or spontaneous as against accommodating or induced capital movements or loans. But while the precise formulation of these concepts is difficult, we can console ourselves with the knowledge that as a rule it is easy to diagnose in actual practice a disequilibrium in the balance of payments, that is, the existence of a deficit or a surplus.[27]

Before describing the mechanism of adjustment of the balance of payments we shall briefly indicate how the balance of payments fits into the national income accounts. In a closed or isolated economy, national income (Y) = consumption (C) + (net) investment (I). But if a country's economy is part of the network of world trade then I must be divided into domestic investment (I_d) and foreign investment (I_f). I_d, the volume of domestic investment, corresponds to the positive or negative addition to the real capital stock: plant and equipment, buildings of all description, consumer durables inventories, etc. I_f, the volume of foreign investment, is equal to the increase or decrease in the country's total foreign investment (change in its net debtor or creditor position) through lending, borrowing and repayments, excluding changes through default or capital gains and losses.

Now, let the value of all exports (including services such as shipping, insurance, tourist expenditure, traders' commission) be X, and the value of all imports similarly defined be M; let D be the amount of income from foreign investments (interest and dividend payments, ect.); and let R be the amount of reparations, gifts,[28] etc., received. Then, $I_f = X - M + D + R$. Of course, D, R, I, and I_d, can be either positive or negative. Changes in the stock of monetary gold (excluding those resulting from home production) would be counted under I_f, for if we include them under I_d, then X and M would have to be defined as including imports or exports of monetary gold, which for most purposes is not advisable.

Our definition of national income thus becomes $Y = C + I_d + X - M + D + R$. It must be emphasized, however, that in our equation consumption (C) and domestic investment (I_d) are defined so as to include *imported* consumption and investment goods. In the theoretical literature, on the other hand, C and I_d are frequently defined as home *produced* consumption and investment goods. It is difficult, however, to implement the latter distinction statistically.

In an isolated economy, *national income, volume of production* and *total expenditures* on goods and services (or to use a cumbersome though more descriptive phrase: Sum total or money value of goods available for consumption and investment) are identical. In an open economy, however, this is not the case. For example, if a country receives income from foreign investments or reparation payments,[29] then its volume of production (P) is smaller than its national income; $P = Y - (D + R) = C + I_d + X - M$.

It is of particular importance to distinguish between national income (Y), on the one hand, and total expenditures on consumption and investment goods (V), on the other.[30] If, for example, a country increases its imports by borrowing from abroad (capital imports), either for purposes of consumption or investment, or if the country accepts foreign aid (R), its real expenditure increases; that is, more can be consumed and/or invested than before, but its national income remains constant. These relations can be written: $V = C + I_d = Y - (X - M + D + R) = P - X + M$.

It should furthermore be noted that the concept of national income is in one respect less clearcut than that of either expenditure (absorption) or volume of production, for it depends on how R is defined and this is frequently quite arbitrary. American aid to Europe, for example, was in large measure legally a gift and only partly a loan. According to our formula, each portion would have to be treated differently; for a loan is part of the national income of the country extending it, while a gift would have to be deducted. It would, of course, be possible to define the concept in such a way that gifts would be added to the income of the country making them while excluding them from the income of the recipient country. But it seems arbitrary to treat aid and reparation payments differently from interest and dividends. The latter are always treated as belonging to the income of the receiving party. Hence, if reparations are funded (as the German reparations were through the Dawes and Young loans) and reparations assume the form of interest payments, they would be treated differently in income accounting than before.

It would be easy to list further cases in which more or less arbitrary decisions and distinctions have to be made and where it is not easy to follow a clear line which does not lead to inconsistencies. But the instances mentioned should be sufficient. It cannot be emphasized strongly enough that there is nothing sacrosanct about any classification. Different classifications and definitions can be justified for different purposes.

2. Price and Income Effects in the Mechanism

We turn now to a discussion of the balance of payments mechanism. Broadly speaking three methods for reestablishing equilibrium in the balance of payments can be distinguished: (a) the gold standard method—the system of stable exchange rates; (b) fluctuating exchange rates, that is, the devaluation of the currency of a deficit country and the appreciation of the currency of the surplus country; (c) exchange control, that is, direct, quantitative regulations of trade and payments.[31]

Under the gold standard method the rate of exchange remains stable and a smooth functioning of the mechanism requires flexibility of prices and wages in the national currency. Under flexible exchange rates the national price *levels* can remain unchanged within a country while the exchange rate adjusts itself, thereby changing relative price levels as between countries. It should be noted, however, that *relative* prices in each country of different groups of commodities, such as import goods, export goods, domestic (non-traded) goods, will usually have to change in the process of adjustment, even if the general price *level*—in some meaning of the term—remains unchanged.

The advantages and disadvantages of stable versus flexible exchange rates will not be discussed in this paper. We shall deal exclusively with the pure theory of the mechanism under the assumption of flexible prices and wages and of variable rates of exchange. Moreover, we shall abstract from disturbing speculative capital movements, although the danger of such movements constitutes, rightly or wrongly, one of the main arguments against the system of flexible exchange rates. Under these assumptions, the theory developed for the case of flexible exchange rates also applies to the case of stable exchange rates.[32]

Let us assume that a sum of $100 million is to be transferred from A to B. Perhaps A has to pay reparations, or A wants to invest these funds in B, or A has to get rid of a deficit which has previously been met by outflows of gold, *ad hoc* credits, or gifts.[33] In each case A has to increase its exports and/or decrease its imports; in other words, assuming unchanged employment, A's "real expenditure" or "absorption" has to be reduced.[34] The only condition under which it would be conceivable for A to import less, export more and simultaneously increase its consumption and investment ("have its cake and eat it too") would be, if the transfer led to an increase in the level of employment from a position of severe unemployment. Under full employment no such miracle is possible.[35]

Let us assume that a decrease of expenditure in A and an increase in B is effected by raising taxes and restricting credit in the first country and by lowering taxes and easing credit in the second. Such an income or expenditure effect would improve the balance of payments of A by an amount which would depend on the *marginal propensity to import*.

The concept of the marginal propensity to import, developed out of Keynesian theory,[36] is analogous to the marginal propensity to consume and can be defined as $m = \Delta M/\Delta Y$ or $\Delta M/\Delta V$. Brief mention should be made of the distinction between marginal propensity, average propensity, and the income (as distinguished from the price) elasticity (δ) of demand for import goods. These three magnitudes are related in the following way:

$$\delta = \frac{\text{marginal propensity to import}}{\text{average propensity to import}} = \frac{\Delta M}{\Delta Y} \frac{Y}{M}.$$

Let us return to the case where $100 million have to be transferred from A to B. Assume first that the marginal propensity to import of A, $m_A = \frac{1}{3}$ and that of B, $m_B = \frac{2}{3}$, their sum being exactly equal to unity. In this case, after A's total expenditure has been reduced by $100 million and that of B increased by $100 million, A will import $33\frac{1}{3}$ million less, and B $66\frac{2}{3}$ million more. The balance of payments will improve for A by just $100 million, and thus be in equilibrium. Income effects are just sufficient to restore equilibrium.

It is generally assumed that m is so small for most countries that it is likely that $m_A + m_B < 1$. It can easily be calculated that under such conditions the direct income effects are too weak to reestablish equilibrium in the balance of payments. However, if we assume the opposite, though unlikely, case where $m_A + m_B > 1$, the direct income effects would be so strong that the disequilibrium would be overcompensated; the balance of payments would turn in favor of the paying country and show a deficit for the receiving country.

Let us go back to the more likely case where $m_A + m_B < 1$. The income effect is not strong enough to eliminate the deficit completely and price effects have to be invoked in order to bring about a full adjustment. Under the gold standard, gold would flow from A to B and prices and wages would fall in A and rise in B, both movements operating in an equilibrating manner. If wages in A should be rigid, unemployment would result. In other words, in this event *employment effects* would strengthen the income effect.[37] Although undesirable, such employment effects tend to hasten the restoration of equilibrium in the balance of payments. It would be wrong, however, or at least imply a gross exaggeration, to attribute the smoothness with which the gold standard functioned before 1914 to the fact that it operated entirely or predominantly by means of undesirable employment effects. With flexible wages and prices the gold mechanism operates, if expenditure effects are insufficient, through price effects without changes in employment. It is true, however, that with price and wage rigidity it will be easier to bring about the necessary price adjustments through a devaluation of A's currency in terms of B's.

The problem of the influence of a currency devaluation on the balance of payments and the real terms of trade has been extensively discussed during the last twenty years; this is in sharp contrast to the previous literature, which was almost devoid of such discussion. It should be observed, however, that on the level of abstraction of the present essay (disregarding rigidities as well as disturbances caused by speculation and expectations) the price effects produced by the gold standard mechanism and by changes in the exchange rate are the same; similarly the elasticity conditions discussed below apply to both institutional arrangements.

The conditions under which a *currency devaluation* would lead to an improvement in the balance of payments in the devaluing country were derived and have been discussed by Lerner, Robinson, Metzler, Meade, Stackelberg, and others. The result to be expected from an alteration in the exchange rate depends on the elasticities of demand in each country for the export goods of the other country, as well as on the elasticities of the corresponding supplies. As mentioned previously (see Section 2 above), these curves which relate the unit money price of exports and imports to the quantities demanded and supplied must be distinguished from the Marshallian reciprocal demand and supply curves which relate the total quantities where the price is the real terms of trade and not the price in terms of money.[38]

It can be shown that a currency devaluation always improves the balance of payments of the devaluing country if the sum of the elasticities of the country's demand for its imports and of the foreign demand for its exports is greater than unity. If this sum is smaller than unity, then devaluation results in a worsening of the balance of payments and we are dealing with a case of unstable equilibrium in the foreign exchange market.[39]

Let us think for a moment of the exchange market as a market in which the foreign currency, say the pound, is demanded and supplied in terms of the home currency, say dollars. A demand curve for pounds in dollars confronts a supply curve for pounds in dollars. Parenthetically, it should be remembered that the demand curve for pounds in terms of dollars must be distinguished from the American demand curve for imports from Britain. The demand for foreign currency is, however, derived from the demand for foreign goods. And the elasticity of the currency curves can be computed from the elasticities of the demand and supply curves of imports and exports.[40]

If the demand curve and supply curve of pounds have their ordinary shape, the former sloping down from left to right, the latter sloping up from left to right, the market is in stable equilibrium. If, however, the supply curve, too, slopes down from left to right (if it "bends back") and is flatter than the demand curve (that is, cuts the latter "from below") the equilibiurm is unstable. In that case, if demand exceeds supply (a deficit in the balance) and the price (the value of pound in dollars) rises, the excess demand (deficit) instead of becoming smaller as in the stable case will become even larger and the price will be driven up still higher.

Now, it can be shown that whenever the sum of the elasticities of the demand for exports and the demand for imports is greater than unity, there is stable equilibrium in the exchange market; that is to say, the supply curve of pounds cuts the demand curve of pounds from above—the supply curve is steeper than the demand curve. Instability would obtain if the sum of the elasticities of demand for exports and imports were sufficiently smaller than unity, how much smaller depending on the elasticities of supply of exports and imports.

In the older literature, until the 1930s and apart from a few hints in theoretical writings, stability in the exchange market was taken for granted. It was only in the period after World War II that a condition of unstable equilibrium was considered by many writers a common phenomenon. This "elasticity pessimism" was supported by numerous attempts at statistical measurement, which in most cases have arrived at very low estimated elasticities. However, Harberger, Machlup, and Orcutt have shown convincingly that the statistical methods (least square methods) use in these researches are biased and result in a strong and systematic underestimation of the actual elasticities. Indeed, as some of the errors have been gradually eliminated, the statistical estimates of elasticities have tended to increase steadily. Today most economists are convinced that the actual elasticities are in practice always sufficiently large to guarantee stable equilibrium in the balance of payments, except perhaps in the very short run and under very unusual circumstances, which may exist in highly specialized raw material-producing countries during depression periods. Alfred Marshall, who generally exercised great caution in such questions and never jumped to hasty conclusions, stated very emphatically: "It is practically certain that in the Ricardian example and under moden industrial conditions the total demand of each of the two countries for each other's goods is relatively elastic. And where a large and rich commercial country confronts the rest of the world, this assumption becomes absolutely certain." [41] The more diversified the economy of a country the larger will be the range of its actual and potential import and export commodities and the more rapid and smooth the adjustment. The stronger the competition of other countries, the greater the elasticities of demand for the exports of any one country and the less likely the existence of unstable equilibria.

It is, however, not difficult to understand how the appearance to the contrary may easily be created; in other words how one can get the impression that elasticities are ofteh low and the equilibrium of the balance of payments unstable. The reason is that there is often great danger that the favorable effects of a devaluation on the balance of payments will be jeopardized by incautious wage and credit policies. Pressure in this direction is strong because under full employment an improvement in the balance of payments, as shown above, is necessarily accompanied by a painful reduction in consumption or investment ("absorption" or "total expenditure"). Under modern conditions, the temptation is strong to avoid this, as well as transitional unemployment which may be necessary, by means of government spending, liberal credit policies and wage increases. This sort of policy will, of course, immediately result in a renewed worsening in the balance of payments. This can be expressed by saying that an upward, or downward, shift in an *elastic* curve creates the erroneous impression that the curve is *inelastic.*

While it thus can be taken for granted that a currency devaluation will result in an improvement of the balance of payments provided total expenditure is not allowed to expand, it is by no means equally certain that the terms of trade will be shifted in any particular direction or that they will change at all. Hinshaw, following Graham, has shown this very clearly.

It is tempting to jump to the conclusion, and as a matter of fact it is frequently assumed as self-evident, that a currency devaluation must lead to a worsening in the real terms of trade for the devaluing country, implying of course an improvement of the terms of trade for the country whose currency has appreciated. If the French franc is devalued relative to the dollar, French brandy becomes cheaper for Americans and American cotton more expensive for Frenchmen and that seems to imply that France's terms of trade have deteriorated. Such an argument, however, is based on the fallacious method of comparing cotton prices in francs with brandy prices in dollars. Obviously, export and import prices must be compared in terms of the same monetary units (it does not matter which one) in order to find the real terms of trade. In fact, both brandy and cotton prices will rise in terms of francs and both fall in terms of dollars. The real terms of trade worsen for France and improve for the United States if, in terms of francs, the cotton price rises more or, in terms of dollars, falls less than the price for brandy. Whether this will happen depends in turn on the elasticities of demand and supply. It is, *a priori*, no more probable that the real terms of trade will worsen than that they will improve for the devaluing country. It is not at all improbable that both the balance of payments and the real terms of trade would improve.

To visualize that as a consequence of a devaluation the terms of trade may improve, deteriorate or remain unchanged while the balance of payments improves, it may help if we once more reflect that a currency devaluation of, say, 30 percent is analytically equivlalent to a uniform import duty of 30 percent on all imports (including services) plus a uniform export subsidy of 30 percent on all exports.[42] Now, it is clear that a tariff alone will improve the terms of trade. A subsidy alone will make them worse. The result of their combined effect depends on the relative strength of their separate effects about which it is impossible to establish any plausible *a priori* presumption.

As to the balance of payments, the situation is different: a general tariff obviously improves it; a general export subsidy too will improve it, except where the foreign demand for the devaluing country's exports is inelastic.[43] Hence, it is very probable that their combined effect will be an improvement of the balance of payments.

The way in which a depreciation operates to improve the balance of payments can be briefly summarized as follows: In the devaluing country the prices both of export and of import goods will rise as compared with prices of domestic (not-traded) goods. This causes a shift in demand from internationally traded to domestic goods and a shift of production in the opposite direction. In the country whose currency has increased in value the prices of export and import goods will both fall relative to those for domestic goods. This will tend to bring about a substitution in consumption and production of domestic for traded commodities in the opposite direction from those in the devaluing country. The magnitude of such shifts depends on the elasticity of substitution between foreign-traded and domestic goods. As can readily be seen, these shifts will result in an increase of the stream of goods from the depreciating to the appreciating country and a decrease of this stream in the opposite direction, thus restoring the balance to equilibrium. For this mechanism to function it clearly is necessary that aggregate domestic expenditure in the depreciating country be kept constant or possibly reduced. If, *pari passu* with the depreciation and the rise in prices of export and import goods, aggregate expenditures are allowed to expand—if, in other words, depreciation is allowed to touch off an inflation of expenditure—depreciation will do no more than lead to an all-round rise in prices, leaving relative prices and the state of the balance of payments where they were before.

3. The Foreign Trade Multiplier

The above sketch deals with the pure and essentially static theory of the balance of payments mechanism.[44] Before it can be applied, the theory obviously has to be supplemented and expanded in various directions by dropping simplifying assumptions and introducing historical and institutional details, complications through rigidities, speculation and the like. Here, however, is not the place to undertake that job. We shall add only a brief account of a modest attempt to dynamize the theory of the balance of payments mechanism by means of the *foreign trade multiplier*. This theory grew out of the Keynesian system but was not developed by Keynes himself.

The dynamic version of the foreign trade multiplier is primarily the work of Machlup and Metzler. On the other hand, Harrod, to whom we are indebted for one of the first treatments of this subject, as well as Meade, developed the static version. Static theory describes and compares equilibrium conditions at different times ("comparative statics"). Dynamic theory examines the transition or movement from one equilibrium to another.

The concept of the foreign trade multiplier represents an application of the theory of the general multiplier in a closed economy to the problems of an open one. We are not dealing here with a general equilibrium theory. Multiplier theory deals only with one part of the general system and does so under greatly simplified assumptions. Its area of applicability is thus greatly restricted.

Machlup's and Metzler's dynamic models make the following assumptions: (a) All prices, including the rates of exchange and interest rates, remain unchanged; in other words, constant marginal costs are assumed and this presupposes general unemployment. This is therefore strictly depression economics and its policy implications—if one has the courage to apply such a simplified and unfinished theory—have a strong mercantilistic flavor. (b) The possibility of unlimited financing of deficits exists; that is, each country is prepared to accumulate unlimited balances in each of the other countries. (c) The marginal propensity to import, as well as the marginal propensity to consume, is constant. It would of course be possible to relax some of these rather heroic simplifications. But the further one departs from them the more complicated becomes the theory and the more uncertain the results.

In these models, the propensity to consume is defined with a time lag: Imports during the period t depend on the income (or expenditure) of the preceding period:

$$m = \frac{M_t}{Y_{t-1}}.$$

As is well known, the theory of the (investment) multiplier for a closed economy states that with a given marginal propensity to consume of smaller than unity, a stream of "primary" expenditures of 10 dollars per unit of time would finally increase national income by $10/(1 - c)$. The multiplier is $1/(1 - c)$ or $1/s$ ($s = 1 - c$, being the marginal propensity to save). The smaller is s, or the larger is c, the greater will be the multiplier.[45] This assumes that out of each additional income, a fraction (c) will be spent and the remaining fraction (s) saved. The amounts saved are considered as "leakages."

In an open economy, expenditures on imports must be added as a third kind of expenditure out of income. Thus, income or money "leak" out of circulation not only through savings but also through imports. In other words, out of each additional income a fraction (c) is spent for domestic goods, a fraction (s) is saved, and a fraction (m) is imported ($c + m + s = 1$). The multiplier therefore becomes $1/(s + m) =$

$1/(1 - c)$, while the multiplicand now contains not only investment (including government deficits or all "autonomous" expenditure) but also exports:

$$Y = I + X \frac{1}{s + m}.$$

The assumptions used can be varied in a number of ways and several refinements can be added.[46] Only one such complication, namely that concerning the indirect effects of an increase or decrease of exports, will be mentioned here as an example. Let us assume that country A launches an investment program of $10 million per month. If the marginal propensity to save is $\frac{1}{3}$, in a closed economy the multiplier would be $1/\frac{1}{3} = 3$ and A's income would ultimately increase by $30 million per month. If we assume, on the other hand, that we are dealing with an open economy and $m = \frac{1}{6}$, then the multiplier would be $1/(\frac{1}{3} + \frac{1}{6}) = 2$. Income will now increase by only $20 million since a greater part of the investment expenditures than before will "leak out." If A is a small country relative to the rest of the world, nothing further need be said as far as multiplier theory is concerned. If, however, A is important relative to the rest of the world, then it must not be forgotten that part of the amounts which have leaked abroad will flow back to A. As a rule, this will only be a fraction of the total leakage, their actual magnitude depending on the foreign c and m. The reason for such return flows is that B's economy will be stimulated by the increase of A's demand for B's products and will therefore, in turn, import more from A, thus benefiting A's export industries. Hence, what Metzler has called the *"true multiplier"* (*"complete multiplier"* might be a better term) will be greater than the foreign trade multiplier which ignores these indirect effects; but it will be smaller than the multiplier for a closed economy, because only a part of the import leakage will be restored through larger exports.

In applying multiplier theory to the reparations case ("periodic transfer of money incomes"), Metzler arrives at the following result: Money income in the transferring country will fall and it will rise in the receiving country; the balance of payments will shift in favor of the transferring country but by less than the amount transferred, regardless of the marginal propensity to import in the two countries.[47] It should also be noted here that under the assumptions of constant costs and prices underlying these models, real income and employment would parallel each other.

This result implies that the paying country indefinitely accumulates debit balances; in other words that income effects alone cannot bring about the transfer. In order to restore equilibrium in the balance of payments, price effects—a change in the exchange rate or inflation in the receiving and deflation in the paying country— must be invoked. This result seems to contradict our statement made earlier in connection with the static theory that if $m_1 + m_2 > 1$, the income effects will overadjust the balance of payments. The contradiction is, however, only apparent, not real. In the static theory we have quietly ruled out the possibility of money "leaks," or have assumed that in case of deflation (hoarding) all that happens is a fall in prices and wages leaving real income and employment unchanged. The Machlup-Metzler theory yields the same result as the static theory, if c is equal to unity in both countries; that is, if all of the income is spent and nothing is saved and hoarded.[48]

In summary we may say: Dynamic multiplier theory is superior to static and comparative static theory inasmuch as it describes the process leading to a new equilibrium while static theory confines itself to showing the end point of this process. However, on the level of refinement achieved so far in the dynamic theory the price, in the form of its sweeping simplifications, is extremely high. Not only are c and m assumed to be constant but the price effects as well as the changes in the rate of exchange are ignored. In addition, it is assumed that foreign lending adjusts itself passively to the balance of payments; this means that each country is prepared to grant and to accept loans, or to import and export gold, to an unlimited degree, and, moreover, that the volume of investment will be constant or that it is a linear function of income.

These simplifications must be considered thoroughly unrealistic. It would nevertheless be wrong to label the theory of the foreign trade multiplier as worthless. It is without question of some theoretical significance as a first step toward a general dynamic theory which would also include consideration of price effects.

Static theoretical models combining income *and* price effects, elasticities *and* propensities have been constructed by Meade, Laursen and Metzler, and Stolper. Moreover two ambitious attempts have been made by Neisser and Modigliani and by Polak to construct econometric models of this kind for an integrated world system—that is to say models based on actual statistical measures of the coefficients involved (price elasticities and income propensities) for many countries which describe in precise mathematical form the interaction of these various factors.

Nobody who has taken the trouble of familiarizing himself with this work can fail to admire the courage of these scholars, their ingenuity and the great intellectual effort involved. However, the difficulties of econometric model building for a single country (let alone for a multitude of countries or for the world as a whole) are so overwhelming and the pitfalls which beset this kind of work are so numerous and insidious[49] that, at the risk of giving the appearance of offering ungrateful and negative criticism, one cannot help having the gravest doubts concerning the concrete results of these two most impressive volumes.

4. The Purchasing Power Parity Theory of Foreign Exchanges

The theories to be discussed in the present section—different versions of the "Purchasing Power Parity" (P.P.P.) doctrine—are less elegant, hence less popular with most theorists but more down to earth, than those discussed in the preceding sections. They run in terms of necessarily somewhat vague aggregates—purchasing power, price levels, degrees of inflationary pressure and the like. As the expression "purchasing power parity" suggests, the theory states, to give a brief preliminary explanation, that the equilibrium exchange rate between any two currencies is determined by, or tends to be equal to, the ratio of the internal purchasing power of the two monies (the reciprocal of some price level) in the respective countries.

The term P.P.P. was invented by Gustav Cassel who used the theory as a rough and ready explanation of the depreciation of the German mark and other European currencies after World War I. Actually, however, essentially the same type of reasoning was employed more than a hundred years ago by members of the classical English school to explain the discount of sterling during the Bank Restriction period, 1797–1821—so called because the obligation of the Bank of England to pay cash (gold) was restricted. In fact, whenever a major currency was (or is) at a discount or under pressure (the country losing gold), we can find two types of explanation for this fact which we may call the balance of payments theory and the inflation theory respectively. The former explains the deficit in the balance or the depreciation of the currency, without (or with only minor and indirect) reference to inflation, price levels and money, by such factors as increased Government expenditures abroad for reparations or aid; loss of market of individual export industries; war losses of foreign investment, shipping; bad harvests, etc. The inflation theorist, on the other hand, speaks of general overvaluation of the currency due to inflationary pressure and of changes in the purchasing power of money; these magnitudes he defines in relative terms (compared with abroad) and he often supports his case by purchasing power parity calculations. On the policy level the balance of payments theorist usually recommends measures to influence individual items in the balance of payments while the inflation theorist urges monetary action—disinflation in the deficit country, expansion in the surplus country or a change in the exchange rate.

However, the correlation between diagnosis and explanation, on the one hand, and therapy, on the other, need by no means be perfect. Even if one stresses adverse non-monetary factors operating on individual items of the balance of payments, such as increased Government expenditure abroad, one is not precluded from recommending disinflationary policy or currency devaluation to produce the required export surplus. And those who believe that inflationary pressure is at the root of the trouble may propose restrictions on imports to correct the imbalance, at least if it is not large.

The reader will have no difficulty in recognizing these two schools of thought in contemporary discussions of the dollar shortage and dollar glut. But it may be in order to present a few samples from the writings of classical English economists during the Bank Restriction period and earlier.

Hume had already stated that international trade brings "money to a common level in all countries, just as 'all water, whenever it communicates, remains always at a level.'" He declared that "level of money" must be interpreted as "its proportional level to the commodities, labor, industry, and skill, which is in the several states. And I assert that where these advantages are double, triple, quadruple, to what they are in the neighboring states, the money infallibly will also be double, triple, quadruple."[50]

Ricardo's views are well known. He held that "the exchange accurately measures the depreciation of the currency," he attributed the discount of sterling vis-à-vis gold to the "relative redundancy of currency" and stated that "by relative redundance then I mean, relative cheapness" of money.[51]

The famous *Bullion Report* expressed the theory this way: " . . . in the event of the prices of commodities being raised in one country by an augmentation of its circulating medium, while no similar augmentation in the circulating medium of a neighbouring country has led to a similar rise of prices, the currencies of those two countries will no longer continue to bear the same relative value to each other as before. The intrinsic value of . . . the one currency being lessened, while that of the other remains unaltered, the Exchange will be . . . to the disadvantage of the former."[52]

From Henry Thornton comes this formulation: " . . . supposing an increase of paper to take place, and to augment the general price of commodities in exchange for that paper, it must also influence the state of the Exchanges, and raise the price of Bullion."[53]

All that looks to me—as it looked to others[54]—very much like modern purchasing power parity theory. To be sure, the vocabulary, style and precision of theorizing has greatly changed over a hundred years. There were no mathematical formulae in the old classical (or anti-classical) writings and no clear references to price indexes as mathematical averages of individual price changes.

The view that the modern P.P.P. theory is a reformulation or elaboration of the old classical "inflation" theory,[55] has been challenged by Viner. He says that the P.P.P. theory "differs substantially from any version of the classical theory known to me."[56] Viner's main reason is that the classical writers were either ignorant of, or rejected, the notion of a statistical average of prices or of price changes. It would be "anachronistic," he says, to impute such an idea to Hume or even to the "classical school as a whole," because Hume and many others wrote before serious attempts were made in England to measure price levels.

I cannot find this reasoning quite convincing because one can have a clear idea of a phenomenon before it has been measured and one can vaguely refer to something before anyone has given a precise definition.[57] On the other hand, I find Viner's strictures against the P.P.P. theory very convincing. But its seems to me that, in principle, the classical writers were subject to the same objections. They were shielded from such criticism only by the vagueness of their formulations. Is it not quite natural that an attempt at making a theory more precise and testable (or falsifiable) should throw into high relief all its weaknesses and shortcomings?

Let us now briefly analyze the precise meaning of the P.P.P. theory and the criticism to which it has been subjected. The theory is almost always stated in its comparative (rather than in absolute) form. That is to say, the theory asserts that the equilibrium exchange rate roughly moves parallel with the ratio of the movements in the two countries of the price levels over time (not that it is equal to the ratio of the price levels at any moment of time). Suppose that compared with a base year when the exchange rate was in equilibrium prices have doubled in country A and trebled in country B, then according to P.P.P. reasoning the equilibrium exchange rate (units of currency A exchanged pro [per] unit of currency B) will have changed in the proportion 2 : 3. If the actual exchange rate is smaller (greater) than 2/3 of its original level, currency A is overvalued (undervalued), and currency B undervalued (overvalued). The equilibrium exchange rate is that rate which keeps the balance of payments in equilibrium. The price level that is meant is usually a general price level, either at wholesale or at retail ("consumer prices").[58] General price levels in different countries are linked through the prices of internationally traded goods. Equilibrium requires that the price of each internationally traded commodity is the same in the export and import country if full allowance is made for transportation costs (comprehensively defined, including duties, taxes, special overhead costs of moving commodities, etc.).[59] It seems to follow that the level of prices of internationally traded goods will roughly move parallel in two trading countries provided we assume that changes in transportation costs of different commodities cancel each other out in their effect on the price level. This condition may not be strictly fulfilled; but let us waive this possibility.[60]

Now equality of international prices (allowing for transportation costs) is a necessary but clearly not a sufficient condition for international equilibrium. Even if there exists a large and prolonged deficit in a country's balance of payments and hence its currency is seriously overvalued, prices of internationally traded goods will not, or at least need not, show any deviation from the purchasing power par.[61] It has therefore been frequently suggested that the wholesale price index, which is heavily weighted with prices of internationally traded goods, is a poor guide for judging the existence and magnitude of a fundamental disequilibrium. For illustration, let me quote one case where the use of the wholesale price level has led policy astray. According to Keynes,[62] when Britain returned to gold in 1924–1925, Churchill's experts "miscalculated the degree of the maladjustment of money values which would result from restoring sterling to its pre-war gold parity" by comparing the British and American *wholesale* price index. The result was that sterling was seriously overvalued and the British economy remained depressed throughout the 1920s.[63]

The moral may seem to be that we should use an index of domestic prices (cost of living) or of costs (wages) which do not adjust so quickly and would show a disparity if equilibrium has not been reached. But if we do that we run into other difficulties. True, at any moment of time, given the state of international demand, quantity of money, degree of employment, and so on in each country, there must exist a definite relationship between the price and cost levels (wage levels) of the two countries, which would assure equilibrium in the balance of payments.

But a brief reflection will show that the equilibrium price or cost relationship need not be the one which is postulated by the P.P.P. theory—namely, parallel movement over time. Suppose country A exports industrial products to country B in exchange for food. Suppose further that in each country export prices are closely linked with the general price level because each country produces exports also for home consumption and factors of production can be easily shifted between the export industries and industries producing non-traded goods. Starting from an international equilibrium position, A's demand for B's exports rises for some reason which produces an improvement in B's terms of trade. In this case equilibrium clearly requires a deviation of the exchange rate from the purchasing power par: A's general price level and cost level must fall compared with B's general price and cost level because in each country the general price level is closely linked to the prices of the country's export goods and the prices of the two countries' exports have shifted one against the other (the terms of trade having changed). This change in P.P.P. can come about through an alteration in the exchange rate or with stable exchanges through a change in absolute prices in A and/or B.

Arguing along similar lines, several writers have concluded that the validity of the P.P.P. theory is confined to those cases in which the equilibrium terms of trade remain unchanged. But this need not always be the case. Suppose, for example, that in each country the general price level is closely linked with exports *and* import prices because each country has a substantial home production of the commodities which it imports. In that case, it seems that P.P.P. could be preserved even though the terms of trade have to change.[64]

It remains true, however, that there can be no assurance that the preservation of the purchasing power parity is compatible with equilibrium. Does it follow that the P.P.P. theory must be completely rejected? Many modern (and some not so modern) writers have drawn that conclusion. I am inclined, however, to agree with Metzler,[65] an author who is steeped in, or almost addicted to, the "modern" theory of foreign exchanges (to which he has contributed so much), that the criticism of the parity theory can easily go too far. It is not a precise tool of analysis, and it fits poorly into the framework of the usual simplified theoretical models which work with two or three commodities only. But, if cautiously used, along with other evidence, P.P.P. calculations have considerable diagnostic value, especially in periods of severe inflation.

Finally, let us reflect for a moment on what the P.P.P. theory implies for the shape of the demand and supply curves of one currency in terms of the other. Suppose the P.P.P. relation holds. This implies, it would seem, that demand and supply in the exchange market are highly elastic; hence demand and supply of exports and imports, too, must be highly elastic at the P.P.P. ratio. This has an important corollary. It seems that as a matter of fact under normal circumstances (i.e. when trade is not drastically controlled and regimented, and when the comparison is confined to periods that are not separated by great structural upheavals, e.g. prewar with postwar periods) the P.P.P. theory holds in an approximate fashion in the sense that it would hardly be possible to find under such circumstances a case where an equilibrium rate is, say, 15–20 percent off purchasing power par. If this is so, we have a clear indication, it seems, that international elasticities of demand and supply are in fact rather high.

6. The Theory of International Trade Policy

It is not possible here to discuss the historical, political, administrative, and strategic aspects of foreign economic policy or, for that matter, all of the economic problems involved. Nevertheless, by dealing with at least some of the purely economic aspects of foreign trade policy on an abstract theoretical level an opportunity will be afforded for further elucidation of the theories reviewed as well as of some of their limitations and weaknesses.

Every statement that this or that trade policy is "correct" or "desirable" implies a *value judgment*. The usual "economic" value or objective is maximization of the average national income per head. But shifts in the functional, personal, regional, and temporal—as between the present and the furture—distribution of income are also factors that must be taken into account. We may perhaps formulate the "economic" value judgment which more or less consciously is presupposed in policy re- commendations as follows: Any policy measure or economic change is deemed good or desirable if it leads to an increase in real national income per head, provided it does not involve a change in the distribution of income that is regarded as undesirable.[66] It is not claimed that this is the only possible or only correct criterion of valuation, but that it is the one which in most cases fits policy recommendations found in the serious literature on the subject.

Static theory tells us that under "ideal conditions"—free competition and the absence of "external economies"—free trade will maximize world income. It does not follow, however, that free trade would also necessarily be the best possible policy from the point of view of each individual country. On the contrary, it can be shown that even under these "ideal conditions" it would be in the interests of any country to restrict imports or exports to some extent (a) if the elasticity of foreign demand is not infinitely great, and (b) if no retaliatory measures need be feared. The actual level of optimium customs protection would then depend on the elasticity of foreign demand and the shape of the domestic transformation curve. In brief, the formula for optimum customs duties is that the marginal terms of trade, that is, marginal revenue or marginal receipts from exports, should be equated to the marginal rate of transformation, i.e. marginal opportunity cost in domestic produc-tion. Under free trade (free competition), on the other hand, the terms of trade, that is, the *price* of exports in terms of imports (not marginal revenue), are equated to the marginal rate of transformation, i.e. marginal costs. This rule is an application to the field of trade policy of the familiar proposition of price theory that sellers in a competitive market can improve their position by forming a monopoly and equating marginal revenue and marginal cost instead of price and marginal cost.

This tariff argument, based on the fact that protection will improve the terms of trade and therefore also called the "terms of trade argument," is not new; it was familiar to John Stuart Mill, and hinted at by Torrens, and has been accepted in principle by most of such free trade economists, for example, as Edgeworth and Pigou. In the most recent period the argument has become very popular among theorists and has been much misused for protectionist purposes. Because of the great difficulties in its practical application by any single country even in the absence of retaliation, as well as because of the danger of general application, the implications for policy of this argument are by no means as sweeping and as damaging for the free trade position as they are often made to sound in theory.[67]

Another argument for protection which is applicable even under "ideal" con-ditions, that is, under perfect competition and in the absence of external economies or diseconomies, is based on the claim that a deviation from free trade would change the income distribution in some desirable fashion. For example, if it could be shown by using the Stolper-Samuelson theorem, outlined earlier, that free trade in a particular country tends to reduce the real income of labor, many would regard this as a sufficient justification for some measure of protection, although total real income would suffer.[68] Under other circumstances (for example, those of Great Britain in the 19th century) free trade will bring about a desired redistribution of income, which provides an additional argument for its introduction.

Each departure of the actual situation from the ideal conditions[69] provides theoretical justification for some tampering with the free flow of goods and services. It depends on the concrete circumstances, however, whether such justifiable inter-ference should be an import or export duty or an import or export bounty. The literature, however, generally mentions the former although there is *a priori* no presumption one way or the other.

A particularly important deviation from the "ideal conditions" results from price and wage rigidity, and, related to this, conditions of involuntary unemployment.

General unemployment provides a theoretical justification, from the standpoint of national interest, for measures designed to improve the balance of payments via import restrictions, stimulation of exports, or some combination of these measures, such as, for example, a currency devaluation. The level of employment would improve through the multiplier; but it should be noted that this will usually result in damage abroad, except in the case when unemployment in one country is accompanied by inflationary pressures and over full employment in another. Unemployment in import competing industries could in theory justify import restrictions even if it did not result in an improvement in the balance of payments. On the other hand, if unemployment is concentrated in the export industries, it provides theoretical justification for export bounties and/or import subsidies.

It is frequently overlooked that in static terms and from the standpoint of its effects on the terms of trade (that is, ignoring possible transitional difficulties, particularly unemployment and temporary disequilibria of the balance of payments), a general export bounty has the same effects as a general import bounty of the same *ad valorem* percentage. Similarly, as Lerner and others have shown, a general import duty would be equivalent to an equally high export duty provided the customs receipts are spent in the same way and that imports and exports are of equal magnitude. On the other hand, from the point of view of the effect on the balance of payments and the level of employment, that is, in the short run, an import duty is equivalent to an export bounty in the sense that both operate in an expansionary, stimulating fashion; and an export duty is equivalent to an import bounty in the sense that both operate in an anti-inflationist depressive manner.

For our theoretical purposes, the *infant industry argument* for customs duties, which is closely related to the possibility of realizing external economies and to the problem of falling (social) marginal costs, is probably the most interesting one. The concern here is with dynamic processes of the long run and not, as for example in the theory of the multiplier, with the short run.

The free trade argument, based on the theory of comparative costs, has often been criticized for its static nature and for its neglect of the problems of long-run historical development.[70] In pure theory, economic processes are assumed to be reversible. Preference systems, production functions (technical knowledge), the stock of primary factors of production, and the forms of economic organization are all treated as constant or autonomous variables; that is, their magnitude and changes are independent of the equilibrating process itself. All of this is, of course, only approximately true and is correct at best with considerable qualification. Even a demand curve is not always reversible. Assume, for example, that the supply of tobacco temporarily rises and the price falls. When supply returns to its previous level, consumers may have acquired a habit of smoking so that the demand curve will have shifted upwards. On the supply side, where durable capital equipment, the training of workers, and so on, are involved, irreversibilities are even more frequent and important. Most theoreticians, including Edgeworth, Marshall, Pareto, and the Austrian School, have always recognized this in principle. It was particularly emphasized, of course, by the historically inclined economists (including Friedrich List).

The infant industry argument in favor of customs protection has, and always has had, a particular appeal in "young" and undeveloped countries. In the United States it was employed by Alexander Hamilton, Washington's Secretary of the Treasury, and by H. C. Carey. In Germany, Friedrich List was its most important proponent. John Stuart Mill recognized the idea in principle, but the other classical writers ignored it. Marshall was particularly impressed by Carey's reasoning. Pigou, Taussig, Viner, as well as almost all modern theorists, emphasize that it is possible, in principle, to speed the development of individual industries or of industry as a whole through such protectionist measures as import restrictions or subsidies. This will under suitable conditions result in their faster development than would be the case if all forces were permitted their free play; as a consequence, at the end of the protective period these industries may enjoy a comparative advantage and be able to meet foreign competition without benefit of protection. The condition that protection can in the end be withdrawn without endangering the existence of the industry is generally taken as a necessary though not always a sufficient, criterion for the success of a policy of infant industry protection. It is not a *sufficient* condition because against the advantage gained through successful nurturing of an industry must be set the temporary losses in national income sustained during the period of protection. It might have been more profitable if free trade had been permitted to nurture an export industry to maturity.

Neo-classical theory attempts to deal with these problems which at least partially transcend the framework of static marginal analysis, by means of Marshall's concept of *external* as distinguished from *internal economies*. By the latter are meant reductions in cost within a firm resulting from large-scale operations. It is well known that falling marginal costs due to internal economies, within the enterprise, are not reconcilable with free competition. External economies, cost reductions accruing to one or several industries from causes outside the individual enterprise, result in a downward shift of the marginal cost curve for each firm when the industry as a whole expands. Falling costs in that sense are compatible with perfect competition. Examples of such external economies are lower prices charged by such service industries as transports and communications, made possible by larger operation, improvement in the supply of labor, better technical and commercial education, cross fertilization resulting from the application of discoveries and innovations made in some industries to others, and so on.

It must not be overlooked, however, that external *diseconomies* exist too. These could be caused, for example, by traffic congestions, air pollution from smoke and pollution of rivers from industrial sewage, worsening of climatic conditions and water supply from deforestation, and so forth.

We are concerned here with very important and highly complicated sets of interrelated factors which are difficult to recognize and hard to predict. The individual producer often has no way, and frequently no interest, to foresee such conditions. Under such circumstances one cannot very well assume that the free, unregulated forces of the market, whether under competition or with all sorts of monopolistic encumbrances, will always and without exception bring about the optimum allocation of resources and the best imaginable division of labor. On the other hand, it is at least equally unjustified to expect that government officials and parliaments will usually arrive at the correct diagnoses and proper measures. One thing is clear, it is not permissible, though often done, to derive out of such considerations a presumption in favor of general customs protection.

It should also be added that it is, *a priori*, probable that in many cases not a customs duty but an export bounty would be in order inasmuch as external economies may be realizable in the export rather than in import industries. Each country's and each industry's case must be examined carefully. The fact that the infant industry argument is almost exclusively employed to recommend import restrictions and practically never to justify the opposite—import bounties—(as mentioned above, import and export bounties are equivalent from the static viewpoint) shows clearly the bias of those who employ it.

Those economists who were not satisfied with the contention of the theoretical possibility of successful and advantageous infant industry protection, but who took the pains to examine the policy as it works out in practice—for example, Taussig and Marshall, the latter making a special trip to the United States to study the practical implementation of Carey's theories—were soon disillusioned and have come to rather skeptical conclusions.

The policy of speeding a country's development through customs protection or other measures is a task of great difficulty and complexity. Recommending and evaluating such a policy, to say nothing of carrying it through, requires a good deal more than keen theoretical analysis. What is also needed is a vast factual knowledge, good judgment, and, above all, a sense for historical, political, and social development concerning the practical-political feasibility of a rational policy of protection.

In summary, the contribution which traditional, static trade theory can make to the solution of such problems is rather limited; but it should not be forgotten that static theory comprises "comparative statics," enabling the theorist to go beyond a mere "cross section" analysis and to explain the consequences of changes in the data. What is needed for a fuller treatment of economic change is a long run dynamic theory in which consumer tastes, and especially the supply of factors of production as well as conditions of production, are no longer treated as ultimate data (as they are in static theory), but as variables. Many years ago Friedrich List chided the classical school for closing their eyes to these problems. In our times, J. H. Williams has reiterated this criticism and emphasized the limitations of static cross-section analysis; and Ohlin has done more than any other theorist to show how international trade changes factor supply and moulds consumer preferences.

As far as abstract theory is concerned there exists, however, not much more than occasional hints and programmatic pronouncements concerning the necessity of dynamizing traditional theory plus a few fumbling steps in the direction of the actual construction of dynamic models. Economic history has more to offer than theoretical analysis for the solution of these problems. Those who believe that it is possible to set up model sequences of economic development should go ahead and do it, instead of merely criticizing others for not having done it. Traditional theory, contrary to the views of its critics, by no means precludes the construction of such a broader theoretical frame, although some incautious policy conclusions derived from static reasoning may have to be modified.

Notes

1. Preface to the 1961 edition. The first edition of this Survey appeared in 1955. It was an enlarged and improved version of an article written in 1952 in German which had appeared in 1954 in Volume I of the *Handwörterbuch der Sozialwissenschaften* (Gustav Fischer, Stuttgart; J.C.B. Mohr [Paul Siebeck], Tübingen; Vandenhock & Ruprecht, Göttingen). I was very grateful to the International Finance Section of the Department of Economics and Sociology of Princeton for suggesting that this article be translated and then published by them. Thanks are also due to the German publishers of the *Handwörterbuch* for generously granting permission to publish the paper in English. The new edition has been thoroughly revised and substantially enlarged.

This paper is an attempt to present in a short space an up-to-date survey of international trade theory, including a short sketch of the monetary theory of the balance-of-payments mechanism. The Survey is confined to a presentation of the theoretical skeleton, with a bare minimum of institutional details and no facts or figures. It is, furthermore, a summary in words, without the aid of mathematics.

The source citations in the body of this Survey have been kept to a minimum, but a selected bibliography has been appended. This is not intended to be exhaustive. Rather, it is designed to include only those items which seem to be of the greatest importance in the development of the particular aspects of the theory discussed here.

The bibliography is divided into sections comparable to sections of the Survey. However, many publications have dealt with several aspects of the matters considered in this Survey and so do not fit neatly into any one section. In such cases, they have been included in Section 1 of the bibliography.

In the new edition, the bibliography has been revised and brought up to date with the help of John Brandl. Section 6 has been added containing literature on the Theory of International Trade Policy. Unavoidably, there is considerable overlapping between Section 3 and Section 6.

[The bibliography of this article is not included.]

[Author's Note: The first edition was translated from German by Michael Blumenthal.]

2. In terms of the labor theory of value, however, it is necessary to make such a distinction inasmuch as the prerequisites of this theory, occupational and geographical mobility, clearly do not exist at the international level.

In the course of development of the theory, the artificial separation of international trade theory and the general theory of value and price, of the "theory of international values" and of "domestic values," has gradually disappeared and the theory of international trade has become a part of general theory as applied to international problems. Historically, in that process of assimilation of international trade theory in the body of general theory, the theory of international trade has often been the pioneer and inventor of new analytical tools which later were used for general theoretical purposes. This was especially true in the earlier phases when progress in general theory was still hampered by adherence to tenets of the labor theory of value. In the international sphere the labor theory could not be applied. This explains why the theory of comparative cost has stood up much better than other parts of the old classical theory.

3. B. Ohlin, *Interregional and International Trade*, 1935, p. 40.

4. The possible retort that his argument does not in effect imply such a value judgment (an argument which I could not accept) can be answered by pointing out that if this were true the classicists also would not be guilty of such mixing of value judgment and explanation.

5. Walter Isard, the most prominent living location theorist, has done more than anyone else to combine trade and location theory in a comprehensive general equilibrium model comprising more than two countries and commodities as well as the space factor ("distant input"). Isard's model is, however, still drastically simplified, highly abstract and formalistic and as yet hardly fit for useful application. Isard admits that traditional location theory is partial equilibrium theory. "For the most part, demand has been taken as given" and emphasis has been on the cost side. Isard is, however, mistaken when he goes on to say that trade theory "has placed greater emphasis on the [demand] blade of the scissors." He overlooks the fact that "reciprocal demand," to which he obviously refers, is just as much a matter of cost as of demand. See Isard and Peck, "Location Theory and International and Interregional Trade Theory." *Quarterly Journal of Economics*, February 1954, p. 105 and *passim*.

6. On the pre-classical literature compare the standard works, by Heckscher, Viner and Wu, for which complete citations are given in Section I of the bibliography at the end of this paper.

7. See J. Viner, *Studies in the Theory of International Trade*, 1937, pp. 442–443.

8. F. Y. Edgeworth, *Papers Relating to Political Economy*, Vol. II, 1925, p. 32.

9. It is interesting to observe that the modern theory of "linear programming" or "activity analysis" has taken up the constant cost model of Ricardo. The starting point was Graham's extension of the Ricardian theory into many-country and many-commodity models. Graham's laborious arithmetic examples have been generalized with the superior tools of linear programming. (See the papers by Whitin and McKenzie, Section III of the attached bibliography.) This strikingly illustrates the basic continuity of theoretical development.

10. Viner distinguishes (*Studies*, p. 520) between the opportunity cost approach and an "outright income approach" and says that the former has no obvious advantage over the latter. To my mind there is no such difference. The opportunity cost theory *is* an outright income approach. True, income in the first approximation is defined in terms of only two commodities. But this simplification is obviously dictated by the difficulties of handling many dimensions. It is a drastic simplification, but no more so than those of Ricardo's famous example or of any representation of such complicated relationships by means of two-dimensional graphs such as Marshall's curves.

The dispute between these various "approaches"—"real cost," "opportunity cost," "income approach"—is no longer a live, substantive issue—if it ever was one—but is in a sense a semantic snare. However, for a good recent discussion of these issues, see J. Vanek, *Review of Economic Studies*, 1959.

Most writers agree more or less on what factors are, in principle, important. But since a truly general equilibrium system, involving as it must many variables, is not easy to handle, for most economists it becomes necessary to make drastic simplifications. Differences may then well arise as to which factors should be introduced explicitly and which ones be thrown, provisionally at least, on the *ceteris paribus* dump. For example, in opportunity cost theorizing it is usually assumed that the supply of factors of production is constant and inelastic with respect to price. For labor this is clearly not true. But this assumption is obviously made for the purpose of facilitating the presentation and it can be easily dropped, though at the price of a much more cumbersome presentation. (For example, the elegant box diagram with the help of which Stolper and Samuelson derive the transformation curve from production functions presupposes constant factor supply.)

Another example is provided by the fact that the opportunity cost theory abstracts from differences in disutility ("irksomeness") of different kinds of labor—a circumstance that is treated explicitly and with emphasis by the real cost theorists. Clearly, it may be an important factor, which must not be neglected, especially when evaluating the welfare implications of international trade. Economic welfare and national income cannot be defined solely in terms of utility of output; disutility of input must not be forgotten. (But it should also be remembered that a positive value or utility may attach to labor input; the utility of leisure is not only diminishing but may be even negative from a certain point on.)

But it is only fair to add that the opportunity cost theorist regards his definition of income in terms of commodities only as a first approximation. He relegates other dimensions of welfare to verbal qualifications and *ceteris paribus* clauses.

11. In a paper in the *Quarterly Journal of Economics*, February 1956, Professor Samuelson presents what may well be a definitive clarification of the problem of "community indifference curves." He proves conclusively that it is *impossible* (except in a singular case) to derive from individual indifference maps a group indifference may which permits the derivation of offer or demand curves of the group in the same manner as an individual's offer or demand curve can be derived from his indifference map.

12. He does, it must be noted, discuss in later chapters international factor movements and the interaction between factor and commodity movements.

13. What one can perhaps hold against the first proponents of the theory is that they were not fully aware of the restrictiveness and unreality of the assumptions they had to make in order to demonstrate the equalization of factor prices under free trade.

14. In a two-commodity model that condition may not seem overly restrictive. But in a multi-commodity model, it means that each commodity is produced in all countries. In this context, the condition becomes very unrealistic indeed.

15. Ohlin thought it self-evident that the production function is everywhere the same; this, he said, followed from the fact that the same causes everywhere (and at any time) produce the same effects.

However, if the concept of the production function is to be a useful tool of analysis, it cannot be identified with, or derived from, such unverifiable metaphysical propositions as "the constancy of the laws of nature." As Samuelson has suggested, the concept of the production function should be conceived in terms of well defined, variable (although not necessarily infinitesimally divisible) inputs, leaving milieu and climate (both social and physical), factors *extra commercium*, outside the function. By hypostas[t]izing every conceivable circumstance which may affect output as a separate factor, the production function can, no doubt, be endowed with constancy, invariance, homogeneity, and what not, but at the price of emptying the theory of all empirical content and reducing it to a useless tautological system.

16. Strictly speaking, the dilemma is always there. Einstein's famous dictum about mathematics applies to all theory: "Inasmuch as mathematical propositions refer to reality they are not certain, and inasmuch as they are certain they do not apply to reality." However, the degree of uncertainty may be so slight in some cases that for practical purposes we can speak of certainty.

17. This implies, of course, that the production function in terms of the transferable factors alone is not homogeneous. Decreasing returns to scale in both industries would seem to be a reasonable assumption.

18. W. Leontief, "Domestic Production and Foreign Trade: The American Capital Position Re-examined," *Proceedings of the American Philosophical Society*, September 1953, p. 343.

19. However, recently ingenious and daring attempts have been made actually to measure, or at least to indicate the order of magnitude, of changes in the single factoral terms of trade, in terms of labor, by the method of dividing the merchandise terms of trade by an index of output per head in the production of exports. See, for example, Ely Devons, "Statistics of United Kingdom Terms of Trade" in *The Manchester School*, September 1954, pp. 258–275.

20. The result would be changed if the price of transport services were included as traded goods in the computation of the terms of trade. This would really be the correct procedure although it is rarely done, presumably because of the statistical difficulties.

21. Imlah computes all three of these measures. $Q_e P_e / P_i$ he calls the "Export Gain from Trade" index. In addition he computes what he calls "Total Gain from Trade" index which uses the quantity of total trade $(Q_e + Q_i)$ instead of the quantity of exports alone.

22. It should be observed that real national income cannot be taken as unchanged in the present *context*, because it will change as a result of a change in the terms of trade even if the volume of production (and employment) remains unchanged. The necessity of distinguishing between "volume of production" and "real national income" in an open economy will be further discussed in Section 5.

23. The reason for this assumption is that any change, however destructive it may be—a deterioration of the terms of trade, a tariff, or for that matter even an earthquake or wasteful

government expenditure—conceivably *may* (but need not) be indirectly beneficial, if it reduces unemployment and improves the balance of payments.

24. If this condition is not fulfilled, it is, e.g., possible that an improvement of the terms of trade resulting from cheaper imports might lead to widespread unemployment in the import competing industries and thus in a deterioration of the overall position. It has been said that this was the case in Great Britain during the 1930s when her terms of trade improved sharply.

25. For further remarks on the theory of "the optimum tariff" see Section 6.

26. It follows that it is correct to say that for a complete evaluation of the welfare implications of trade it is not enough to pay attention to the terms of trade; quantities must also be considered. But it does not follow that the task can be accomplished simply by putting Q_e in the formula; in other words, by substituting the income terms of trade for commodity terms of trade.

The term "income terms of trade" or "index of export gains from trade" is misleading. It is better to regard the same measure as an index of the "capacity to import" as the *Economic Commission for Latin America* does. (See their *Economic Survey of Latin America 1949*). This becomes clear if we reflect that the "income terms of trade" is the same thing as value of exports deflated by import prices; in other words, the quantity of imports bought by exports. It should not be forgotten, however, that the "capacity to import" also depends on net capital imports and interest payments.

27. Sometimes a distinction is made between the balance of payments in the *ex ante* and *ex post* sense. It is then said that in the *ex post* or "accounting" or "statistical" sense the balance must always balance. This only means that in a balance sheet, purely as a matter of double-entry bookkeeping convention, the two sides are always made equal by putting the difference, under a suitable heading, on the smaller side. It does not mean that *ex post* there can be no deficit or surplus.

Machlup in an article in the *Economic Journal*, March 1950 distinguishes three concepts, "the market balance of payments," "the programme balance of payments" and "the accounting balance of payments." For theoretical purposes the balance as defined in the text would seem to be sufficient.

28. Investment income is often included among services, that is to say, it is construed as payment for capital services. For many purposes it is, however, convenient to have the somewhat more elaborate terminology which we here propose—distinguishing services proper from investment income and unilateral transfers such as reparations and gifts. But let it be emphasized once more that there is nothing sacrosanct about any classification. It is entirely a matter of convenience depending upon the theoretical or practical problem at hand.

29. Interest and dividends are always added to the receiving country's national income and deducted from the paying country's income. In the case of reparations or foreign aid there is no generally accepted practice. They can be looked on as a part of the paying or of the receiving country's national income. But it is clear that these items belong to the paying country's volume of production and constitute additions to the resources available for consumption and investment (total expenditure) in the receiving country.

30. In the literature different terms have been used to designate what we call "total expenditure." Ohlin speaks of "buying power" and Viner (*Studies*) of "value of final purchases." Still another term has been introduced recently—"Absorption" (Alexander); the economy "absorbs" a certain amount of consumption and investment goods. There may be slight

deviations in the precise definition of these terms by the different writers, but they clearly aim at the same thing: A sort of corrected national income, national income gross of foreign lending and foreign aid. This is, of course, a different kind of "grossness" from that of Gross National Product.

31. For practical purposes a great variety of subdivisions and mixed cases would have to be distinguished, and from the practical-political point of view the difference between subdivisions belonging to the same analytical category may in some cases be greater than the difference between subdivisions belonging to different categories.

32. The distinction between (a) "the method of the adjustable peg," under which the exchange rate is rigidly pegged to a certain level which is occasionally adjusted, and (b) the system of freely floating or fluctuating exchange rates, under which the rate is allowed to fluctuate continuously in a free market, will not be discussed in the present paper although it is extremely important from a practical standpoint.

33. From a more practical standpoint than the one here adopted, where we are interested only in the theoretical skeleton, there may be a world of difference between the examples mentioned.

34. Here the previously mentioned distinction between real expenditure and real income is essential. If a country counteracts *ad hoc* borrowing or gold loss by increasing its exports, it would be incorrect to say that its income falls, although its expenditure ("absorption") (C + I_d) does go down.

35. While in monetary terms total expenditure ("absorption") has to be reduced by $100 million in order to bring about a transfer of $100 million, the change in "real" expenditure may be more or less (even if there is no employment effect), if the terms of trade are changed in the process of the transfer. If the terms of trade improve, the real burden is lightened; if they deteriorate, the real burden is increased. The change in the real burden through a change in the terms of trade, sometimes called the "secondary" burden, has received a great deal of attention in the literature.

36. Although the phrase "propensity to import" is of post-Keynesian vintage—F. W. Paish seems to have been the first to use it—the substance is by no means missing from the pre-Keynesian literature. Ohlin introduced expenditure effects in the German Reparations debate, being then more Keynesian than his antagonist—Keynes himself. As noted above, the concept "buying power" which Ohlin uses in his *Interregional and International Trade* is equivalent to real expenditure. And Viner in his *Studies* uses the term "final purchases" which, too, is equivalent to total expenditure. His table on the effects of international transfers on p. 370 implies the assumption of a constant average propensity to import. Imports are assumed to be a constant fraction of total expenditure.

37. Alternatively, we may distinguish between income changes (or better, expenditure changes) due to the transfer of reparations, foreign aid and the like, and such changes due to variations in the level of employment. A third category of income changes relevant for the balance of payments mechanism is those produced by changes in the terms of trade.

38. Some writers, notably Viner, have raised fundamental objections against the use of curves of this type and their elasticities on the ground that it involves the application of partial equilibrium analysis to a problem which is essentially of a general equilibrium nature. In other words it is illegitimate to assume that demand for imports is "independent of what happens to exports" and supply of exports is "independent of what happens to imports." (Viner)

This is a weighty issue and it cannot be settled here. Only a few remarks will be offered.

Let us start from the fact that a 20 percent depreciation of a country's currency is theoretically equivalent to a 20 percent uniform import duty plus a 20 percent uniform export subsidy.

Consider first the duty in isolation. Surely it is standard practice of economic analysis to say that the influence of the duty on the average price and the value of imports depends on the elasticity of demand and the elasticity of foreign supply—although individual import commodities may be related to one another as complements or substitutes so that the total elasticities are not simply averages of the elasticities of demand for each commodity under the assumption that nothing else (including the price of other import goods) has changed. These things are somehow supposed to have been taken care of by the method of aggregation.

The same considerations apply to the influence of an equal, uniform *ad valorem* export subsidy.

Can we simply add the result of both and say that it measures the result of the devaluation? Strictly speaking not, because there may be relationships between individual import and export goods so that their respective demands and supplies are not entirely independent. For example, imports may significantly enter exports as raw materials. Hence, when imported raw materials rise in price after a devaluation the export supply curve is shifted up.

Again such interrelations must be supposed to average out or else to be allowed for in the method of aggregation.

It is possible to adopt a skeptical and dim view of our ability to allow for such complications. Quite a few writers have taken this position and quite consistently have rejected what they call excessive aggregation—in theory at least, while in their actual practice of theoretical analysis they usually disregard their own methodological preaching and resort to aggregative reasoning. How much aggregation is permissible cannot be decided on *a priori* grounds. It would seem, however, that the degree of aggregation involved in our particular instance is not obviously greater than that which one often finds in economics, for example where we speak of demand by industry for agricultural products or of the supply of labor or saving and the like.

Apart from such connections between demand and supply of individual import and export commodities, there is the broader nexus through the monetary mechanism, through incomes and expenditures. Unless monetary expansion nullifies the effects of devaluation, real expenditure must fall (because the export volume rises and the import volume falls). These expenditure changes shift the demand and supply curves of exports and imports. But this aspect of the matter we have discussed under the heading of income or expenditure effects.

In conclusion it may be pointed out that the Marshallian reciprocal demand and supply curves are not suitable instruments for analyzing the problem of how a depreciation influences the balance of payments. Points on the Marshallian curves are possible equilibrium positions with exports equal to imports. It is true these curves can also be used to find the equilibrium position under the conditions of a *preassigned* trade gap in *real* terms. But this is not the problem in our present context.

39. To be precise: The condition that the sum of the two demand elasticities is greater than unity is a *sufficient*, but not a *necessary* condition for the balance of payments to improve, that is to say, to react "normally" rather than "perversely" to a depreciation. Even if this sum were smaller than unity, the balance of payments could still improve provided the supply elasticities are sufficiently small.

40. It goes without saying that the demand curve for pounds in terms of dollars can be translated into a supply curve of dollars in terms of pounds; and similarly the supply curve of pounds into a demand curve for dollars.

41. Alfred Marshall, *Money, Credit and Commerce*, 1923, p. 171. On page 354 of the same book, he says: "Nothing approaching to this [unstable equilibrium] has ever occurred in the real world: it is not inconceivable, but it is absolutely impossible." It is true that in the quoted passages Marshall referred to his reciprocal demand and supply curves and the "real" equilibrium. But it would seem to be permissible to transpose his statement to the monetary sphere.

42. From a practical, administrative standpoint there is of course no equivalence between the two schemes and from the point of view of economic policy the uniform tariff-cum-subsidy scheme is simply not feasible as a substitute for devaluation, although it was actually proposed by Keynes and later by Hicks. The tariff-cum-subsidy method leaves outstanding contracts unchanged, which was Keynes' motive for espousing it.

The reader will notice that there are further complications if exports are not equal to imports, because then the duties collected are not equal to the subsidies due. In that case the elasticity conditions, mentioned above, for the balance of payments to improve after a devaluation, must also be slightly modified.

43. The balance of payments will improve, if demand elasticities are large enough ($\eta_x + \eta_m > 1$). This is almost certain to be the case. It should be remembered that this is a sufficient, not a necessary condition.

The terms of trade will deteriorate (improve) if the product of the supply elasticities ($\varepsilon_x \varepsilon_m$) is greater (smaller) than the product of the two demand elasticities ($\eta_x \eta_m$). Joan Robinson, to whom we owe that formula, has tried to show that elasticities are likely to be such that devaluation will result in a deterioration of the terms of trade. Her argument is, however, not at all convincing. It would seem that the outcome depends on the concrete structure of trade of the country concerned and that no sweeping generalizations are possible.

It can be shown that in the normal, stable case, in which the balance of payments improves after devaluation, the terms of trade may improve or deteriorate. However, in the abnormal, unstable case, when the balance of payments deteriorates, the terms of trade too will deteriorate for the depreciating country.

44. This theory runs in terms of interacting price and income (or expenditure) effects; price elasticities as well as income (or expenditure) propensities play a role in the mechanism. The theory has been worked out most fully by Meade in *The Balance of Payments*.

Another approach, the so-called "income absorption approach" has been proposed by S. Alexander, in his "Effects of a Devaluation on the Trade Balance," in International Monetary Fund *Staff papers*, Vol. II, April 1952. As pointed out earlier, "absorption" is another term for expenditure. The "income absorption" approach is therefore another version of an income-expenditure analysis. Criticizing Alexander, Machlup has shown convincingly that price effects and elasticities are just as indispensable as expenditure effects and propensities to spend and "absorb," in "Relative Prices and Aggregate Spending in the Analysis of Devaluation," *American Economic Review*, June 1955.

45. If $c > 1$, the equilibrium would be unstable; any additional expenditure would draw an ever increasing stream of induced expenditures in its wake.

46. See F. Machlup, *International Trade and the National Income Multiplier*, 1943. Metzler, in his review of Machlup's book (*Review of Economics and Statistics*, February 1945) gives a succinct summary of "the principal fruits of modern long-run income analysis" in this field.

47. This applies under the assumption which is always made in models of this kind that $c < 1$ and $m < 1$. If $c > 1$, in a closed economy we would have an unstable equilibrium, since the expenditure of one additional unit of money would result in an infinite increase of incomes. In an open economy the import leakage will restore stability even when $c > 1$ if $(1 - c + m) > 0$.

48. This is not at all as improbable as it may seem at first glance if one considers that it actually does not depend on the marginal propensity to consume, but on the propensity to spend which is the propensity to consume plus the propensity to invest.

The propensity to invest, which assumes all or a part of investment expenditures as a linear function of income, should not be confused with the *acceleration principle*, according to which investment expenditures depend on the magnitude of the *change* in income.

49. Early hopes and enthusiasm have been dashed, partly by self-criticism of those involved in this kind of econometric work. For an earlier attempt at the construction of an international trade model the pitfalls have been pointed out by A. Harberger, "Pitfalls in Mathematical Model-Building," *American Economic Review*, December 1952, pp. 855–865.

50. See Essays, 1875 ed., I, 335–36 note. Quoted in Viner, *Studies*, p. 312.

51. The quotations are from Ricardo's correspondence with Malthus who was a balance of payments theorist. *See The Works and Correspondence of David Ricardo*, edited by Piero Sraffa, Vol. VI, Letters, pp. 30, 36, 39 and passim.

52. See E. Cannan, *The Paper Pound of 1797–1821, A Reprint of the Bullion Report (1810)*, 2nd ed., London, 1925, p. 17.

53. From a speech in the House of Commons, May 7, 1811, reprinted in Hayek's edition of H. Thornton's *An Enquiry into the Nature and Effects of the Paper Credit of Great Britain*, London, 1939, p. 329.

54. E.g., to J. W. Angell and C. Bresciani-Turroni.

55. It is interesting that the word "inflation" was not used in the classical literature. But I don't believe that the designation of the old theory as inflation theory will be challenged on that ground.

56. *Studies*, p. 380.

57. It is, of course, logically possible to define a concept and use it while at the same time holding that for *practical* reasons it cannot be measured. What I find difficult to swallow is the position of those who use a concept but insist that "for theoretical reasons" it is incapable of ever being measured under any circumstances.

58. Sometimes the theory is stated in terms of export prices (Bresciani-Turroni) or in terms of "cost levels" which practically become wage levels (Brisman, Hansen).

59. There are minor exceptions to this rule, some apparent, others real, e.g. in the case of discriminating monopoly.

60. Strictly speaking the P.P.P. in terms of international prices will not be preserved even in the ideal case of perfect competition and zero transportation cost. Although every single international price must then be the same in each country, the average change of these identical prices will not be the same in both countries, if a *weighted* average is used and the weights are not the same in the two countries.

I am, however, not inclined to regard this difficulty, which has been noted by several authors (e.g., by Viner, *loc.cit.*, p. 383), as one of the serious objections to the P.P.P. theory. It could be easily overcome by using equal weights in the price index.

61. According to Viner (*Studies*, p. 384), "The only necessary relationship between prices in different countries which the classical theory postulated . . . are the international uniformity of particular prices of commodities actually moving in international trade . . . after allowance for transportation costs. . . ."

For reasons stated in the text, I would say that, if the classical writers did not want to say more than that individual prices of traded commodities tend to equality in different countries (if full allowance is made for transportation cost), their theory would be true enough, but not very useful for explaining the discount of sterling or determining equilibrium exchange rates. To me it seems clear that actually they said more; they spoke of "general prices," "intrinsic value of money" and the like—terms which I find impossible to interpret without reference to some price level.

62. "The Economic Consequences of Mr. Churchill," in *Essays in Persuasion*, 1941, p. 249.

63. Another case where exactly the same mistake was made was the devaluation of the Czechoslovakian crown in the early 1930s. (For details, see League of Nations, *Monetary Review*, Vol. I, 1935–36, p. 49 et seq., Geneva, 1936.)

64. For the problem on hand as well as for others (e.g. for the related questions how the terms of trade are influenced by unilateral transfers or by currency depreciation) it matters a great deal whether one operates with a model (a) where there are only export and import goods (two-commodity model) or (b) a model with export, import and non-traded goods (four-commodity model) and how in each country export goods, import goods and non-traded goods are related to each other in production and consumption.

65. In *A Survey of Contemporary Economics* (H. S. Ellis, ed.), p. 223.

66. Needless to say, a full statement would require much more detailed specifications. Thus the term real per capita income ought to be interpreted to include not only tangible goods but also leisure, conditions of work, differences in irksomeness of different kinds of labor, and other intangibles. The use of the word "economic welfare" as against national income or output is often consciously designed to draw attention to the "imponderables" mentioned above. We have seen earlier that the "real cost" theorists (especially Viner) have laid stress on the non-physical product dimensions of economic welfare. But the opportunity cost theorist is not debarred from recognizing those factors.

67. The attitude of nineteenth century free traders on this problem, reconciling their free trade convictions with their scientific conscience, has been well and typically expressed by Edgeworth. Discussing Mr. C. F. Bickerdike's "Theory of Incipient Taxes and Customs Duties," he concludes:

"Thus the direct use of the theory is likely to be small. But it is to be feared that its abuse will be considerable. It affords to unscrupulous advocates of vulgar Protection a peculiarly specious pretext for introducing the thin edge of the fiscal wedge. Mr. Bickerdike may be compared to a scientist who, by a new analysis, has discovered that strychnine may be administered in small doses with prospect of advantage in one or two more cases than was previously known; the result of this discovery may be to render the drug more easily procurable by those whose intention ... is not medicinal. ... Let us admire the skill of the analyst, but label the subject of his investigation POISON." *Papers Relating to Political Economy*, Vol. II, pp. 365–366.

For a typical example of middle 20th century attitude towards this essentially nationalistic, beggar-my-neighbor "optimum tariff policy," see R. Kahn, "Tariffs and the Terms of Trade."

68. Actually, an argument for protection based on the Stolper-Samuelson theory would be unconvincing, because the underlying theoretical model rests on very unrealistic assumptions. It assumes two factors of production only—a homogeneous type of labor and all non-labor factors lumped together as capital. Now the factor "labor" is not homogeneous. Even excluding managerial and entrepreneurial services from the category "labor," there are tremendous differences between skilled and unskilled types of labor, white collar and blue collar labor, research and scientific personnel and manual workers, and so on and so forth. It is hard to see how a plausible ethical preference can be based on such broad aggregates composed of very heterogeneous subtotals.

69. It is often said that the "ideal conditions" implied by the free trade argument include the assumption that factors of production are freely mobile within each country. While such an assumption is implicit in the labor theory of value, it is entirely unnecessary for the logic of the free trade argument. What is required is free price competition (price flexibility) but not free factor mobility. While free mobility is obviously impossible physically, freely flexible prices are feasible. It should be noted that absence of free competition (monopoly) usually *reinforces* the case for free trade, because trade tends to reduce monopoly power.

It is true, however, that if occupational and geographical mobility of factors of production is sharply restricted a country will derive less advantage from its trading opportunities than if factors were fully mobile. Moreover, trade will then often produce sharp changes in the distribution of income as between the different immobile factors—a condition which may be undesirable in itself and is likely to lead to undesirable social reactions, to price rigidity and unemployment, thus entailing deviations from the "ideal conditions."

70. However, the free trade argument too can be given a dynamic twist: Foreign competition may and often does shock inefficient producers out of their customary lethargy or something of that sort.

5

Survey of Circumstances Affecting the Location of Production and International Trade as Analysed in the Theoretical Literature

1. Introduction

Suppose Ricardo had been asked why Portugal had a comparative advantage in wine; he surely would have answered, in effect though not in these words, because Portugal was well supplied with factors of production needed for wine growing, that is to say suitable land and plenty of sunshine. If the questioner had continued and asked whether there were not still other factors to be considered such as capital, Ricardo would have answered: Yes, certainly; in poor countries where labour is cheap capital will be invested in labour-intensive industries and in rich countries capital will be invested in industries that use comparatively little labour.

How do I know Ricardo's answers? Now, the answer to the first question is so obvious that there hardly can be any doubt. The answer to the second question I know because Ricardo said so in so many words in the *Principles* (not buried in the many volumes of letters): '...the capital of poorer nations will be naturally employed in those pursuits, wherein a great quantity of labour is supported ... In rich countries, on the contrary, where food is dear, capital will naturally flow, when trade is free, into those occupations wherein the least quantity of labour is required ...'.[1]

I say this not in order to make the point that Ricardo said everything, but merely to stress the continuity of the theoretical development from Ricardo via Mill and Marshall to Heckscher, Ohlin and Samuelson. There is an unmistakable family likeness between the modern theories, based on Ohlin's pathfinding work, and the early classical theories, just as there is between a modern jumbo jet and the Wright brothers' contraption. But I fully agree with Ohlin that Viner failed in his attempt to uphold the classical labour theory of value in the form of a real cost theory for the purpose of 'providing guidance on questions of national policy',[2] let alone as an

The International Allocation of Economic Activity, Proceedings of Nobel Symposium, Stockholm. Bertil Ohlin, Per-ore Hesselborn, and Per Magnus Wijkman, (eds.) (New York: Holmes and Meirer Publishers Inc., 1977), 1–22. Reprinted with permission.

explanation of the international division of labour. Strictly speaking the labour theory of value was already breached by the doctrine of comparative cost and the breach was widened when the assumption of geographical or occupational immobility of labour was applied to the national economy in the theory of non-competing groups. John Stuart Mill's theory of international values constitutes, in effect, an abandonment of the labour theory of value although Mill, as well as Alfred Marshall later, did not present their theories as a revolutionary new start but as elaboration and improvement of the Ricardian doctrine.

I still believe that the most fruitful way to get as much as possible out of Ricardo's theory is to reinterpret the theory of comparative advantage in terms of opportunity cost. Ohlin is surely right when he insists that this approach effectively abandons the labour theory of value, but helps 'little' unless it is 'connected with a mutual interdependence [theory of the] price system'.[3] To establish this connection was, of course, the intention of the opportunity cost interpretation right from the beginning. In the form of the 'transformation or production possibility curve' the opportunity cost approach has become one of the basic tools of the modern theory, although the word 'opportunity cost' has gradually faded away.[4] This type of analysis has been found very useful especially in the analysis of the welfare (normative) aspects, both of international trade and domestic economic problems. In fact the artificial dichotomy between international and domestic trade and value theories has disappeared.[5] The general price theory and the theory of international trade have gradually been merged and the merger has been explicitly and definitively accomplished in Ohlin's *Interregional and International trade*. The fusion process has enriched both fields and on many occasions the theory of international trade has been the source and initiator of new modes of analysis.

There has been a widespread tendency in the modern theoretical literature on international trade to exaggerate the contrast between the old classical (Ricardian) theory and what is now referred to as the Heckscher-Ohlin theory; and both theories are often interpreted rather narrowly which to my mind is unfair to both. This tendency we find both in the purely theoretical literature and among the 'empiricists' who try to test statistically (or otherwise) the hypotheses attributed to the two schools.

On the empirical side let me mention the attempts by G. D. A. MacDougall, Robert Stern and others at testing the Ricardian theory by comparing labour efficiency in some U.K. and U.S. manufacturing industries. These exercises surely have their proper uses, but as a test for the validity of the Ricardian theory of comparative advantage I find them either superfluous (if Ricardo's labour theory of value is taken literally), or inconclusive (if Ricardo's theory is interpreted more generously so as to admit factors other than labour and land.[6] Suppose the 'tests' work extremely well—even better than in fact they, surprisingly, seem to have worked—would anybody be prepared to give up modern economics and go back to the labour theory of value? Or the other way around, if the results of the 'tests' were negative, if they seemed to contradict the Ricardian theory—would anybody be prepared to give up the theory of comparative advantage?

2. Two-Factor Models: Labour and Capital

In the theoretical as well as in the empirical literature the Heckscher-Ohlin theory is often interpreted as a model that explains international division of labour solely or predominantly in terms of different endowment of different countries with *two* factors of production—labour and capital. The two-factor model lends itself to easy graphic manipulation. An elaborate, elegant analytical–geometrical theory has been developed which is displayed with great flourish and ingenuity in modern textbooks. This extension was largely the work of Samuelson and Meade. With a few additional simplifying assumptions—two commodities and two countries, constant returns to scale and identical factors and identical production functions in both countries—a highly abstract but suggestive model of world trade can be constructed. All this constitutes a permanent and most valuable addition to our analytical apparatus and an invaluable pedagogical device. But we should not forget that the extreme simplifications 'disregard', in H. G. Johnson's words, 'some of the more penetrating insights' of the original work by Heckscher and Ohlin.[7] The two-factor assumption especially deviates sharply from the original Heckscher-Ohlin theory. These theories assumed many factors right from the beginning although in illustrative examples sometimes a truncated two-factor version of the general theory was used by the two authors.

The theoretical attraction of the two-factor model is that it permits the application of the Edgworth-Bowley box diagram which has amply proved its great analytical and pedagogical worth. But it should be kept in mind that some of the best known generalisations derived from the production box diagram break down in a more-than-two-factor world—namely the Stolper-Samuelson and Rybczynski theorems, so beloved by modern textbook writers.

Also the famous theorem of factor price equalisation through free commodity trade has to be severely qualified, if there are many factors. This is in addition to several other more fundamental simplifying assumptions that have to be made, such as that factors are qualitatively the same and production functions identical in both trading countries, that production functions are homogeneous to the first degree and that there are no 'factor intensity reversals' Keeping all this in mind makes it clear that what the theory really proves is *not* that factor prices will be equalised, but on the contrary that in practice there *cannot* be a factor price equalisation.[8]

Apart from its intrinsic value and obvious ingenuity, Leontief's famous demonstration that American export industries are largely labour-intensive and import-competing industries capital-intensive had its strong impact because of the widespread misinterpreation of the Heckscher-Ohlin theory as a two-factor model. Since it was taken for granted that the United States is, compared with the rest of the world, capital-rich and labour-poor, Leontief's results came as a shock; they were widely regarded as a blow to received neoclassical theory. This conclusion is incorrect, but it had the fortunate consequence that it helped to steer empirical economists away from the two-factor models, that it forced them to distinguish different types of labour and capital, and to pay attention to dynamic, institutional and policy complications. This development marks a return not merely to the intentions but to actual observations and hints in Heckscher's article and especially in Ohlin's book.[9] Many of the modern explanations which we shall discuss presently are more or less explicitly and clearly foreshadowed in Ohlin's book.

3. 'Natural Resource Trade'

The most obvious factors that explain a good deal of international trade are 'natural resources'—land of different quality (including climatic conditions), mineral deposits, etc. No sophisticated theory is required to explain why Kuwait exports oil, Bolivia tin, Brazil coffee and Portugal wine. Because of the deceptive obviousness of many of these cases economists have spent comparatively little time on 'natural resource trade'.[10] Economic geographers have more to say no that very important subject.

While it is easy to explain why Kuwait has a 'comparative advantage' in oil, Bolivia in tin, etc., the existence of natural resources presents the economist with certain theoretical complications which should not be slurred over. Natural resources are much less homogenous and less versatile and mobile (domestically) than capital or labour. For example oil in different countries differs in chemical composition (sulphur content), geographical location (proximity to the sea), distance from the surface, etc. The same is true of other mineral deposits. In other words natural resource factors in different countries differ enormously not only in quantity but also in quality. Hence production functions can no longer be assumed to be the same in all countries or to be homogeneous to the first degree (display constant returns to scale) in terms of capital and labour. As a consequence, to speak of international factor price equalisation becomes meaningless when reference is made to *all* factors, and equalisation is quite uncertain if not practically impossible when applied to factors of comparable quality (such as capital and labour). Similarly, excluded are sweeping generalisations about the effects of trade on internal income distribution, such as the Stolper-Samuelson theorem.

If production functions in terms of capital and labour (or more generally in terms of internationally comparable factors) are different in different countries because the natural resource endowment (including climate, atmosphere) is different, the production of the same (or similar) products may be capital-intensive in one country and labour-intensive in the other. For example the production of rice in the United States is capital-intensive while in the tropics it is labour-intensive. The same is true of rubber (disregarding the quality difference between the natural and synthetic variety).[11] In the same vein several writers have suggested that the Leontief paradox can be wholly or partly explained by assuming that American capital is a better substitute for foreign natural resources than American labour.[12]

4. Determinants of Trade of Manufactured Goods

The pattern of international trade in manufactured goods is much more complex and more difficult to explain than trade in raw materials and crude foodstuffs, because the latter is largely and conspicuously dominated by the availability of 'natural resources' (including climate) and transportation costs. In recent years an enormous literature has sprung up which deals primarily with trade in manufactured goods. A bewildering array of often interrelated and overlapping explanations, refurbished old theories as well as more or less novel ones, have been presented.[13] The various strands of thought which have emerged will be discussed in greater detail and depth in the following session of this symposium. I must confine myself to giving an overview and to mentioning some forerunners of the new theories—indicating some connections between the new and the old literature. References to the older literature are almost completely missing in many recent contributions. I repeat, most of the new ideas are mentioned or foreshadowed more or less explicitly in Ohlin's *Interregional and International Trade*, but since this book is so well-known I shall refrain from making specific references.[14]

Some of the explanations stressed in the recent literature are in fact elaborations or applications of Ohlin's factor proportion theory. Thus, labour and capital are not homogeneous masses, but can and have to be subdivided in various ways.[15] This is, in effect, done in the theories that stress the 'R and D' (research and development) factor, human skills and human capital, as 'an important source of the United States' [and other industrial countries'] comparative advantage position' (Baldwin, p. 142).[16]

There are different ways to look at these problems. One is to regard them as a 'relatively abundant supply of engineers and scientists' (Baldwin). This approach continues the tradition of F. W. Taussig who explained the pre-eminence of the German chemical industry before 1914 by the abundant supply of highly trained chemists which in turn was due to cheap and easily accessible technical education.[17]

Another way of looking at essentially the same circumstances, foreshadowed by Taussig's reference to technical education, is to stress the private or social costs of providing human skills—'investment in human being', 'human capital'. Peter Kenen,[18] Harry Johnson and others have suggested that the Leontief paradox would largely disappear if labour skills were taken out of the labour supply and put into the capital coefficient where they belong.

Others have emphasised the dynamic aspects of the problem. R and D, investment in human skills, the creation of 'human capital' are, of course, essentially dynamic phenomena. R and D products are not just there for the taking but have to be continuously created, in western countries typically by private enterpreneurs.

I can do no better than to quote from the Caves-Jones treatise where the new approach is well summarised:[19]

A new product is developed or a new production process embodied in a novel kind of capital equipment. The innovating firm tests its discovery on the market—presumably first ... on its home market.[20] If the innovation proves profitable, the firm looks for wider markets abroad ... The innovation ... is likely to bestir imitators at home or abroad ... Some countries may regularly prove to be sources of innovation. Their export lists would always contain new products that have not yet been successfully imitated elsewhere. We would have to explain their trade, then, not solely by their factor endowments ... but rather in part as 'technological gap' exports. Do some countries enjoy special talents as innovators? For the United States, the answer may be yes ... The United States, as the country with the highest labour cost, seems to offer the strongest incentive to labour-saving innovations. In the nineteenth century, economic historians have argued, the scarcity and dearness of labour made the United States a fruitful source of mechanical inventions. Coupled with an abundance of labour skills (invention itself requires a high proportion of skilled labour) and congenial cultural traits, American inventive dominance has continued. Thus a significant proportion of U.S. exports probably consists of 'technological gap' trade ... The United States is of course far from being the only source of innovations. The role is also filled by countries with abundant skilled scientific labour, such as Great Britain, or ... Germany (and Japan). The empirical evidence, however, is particularly clear for the United States. Industries making the strongest research effort (measured, for instance, by research and development expenditures as a percentage of sales) account for 72 per cent of the country's exports of manufactured goods.

The process of innovation has been further analysed and 'stylised' in the theory of the 'product cycle'.[21] Typically, the innovation process runs in several distinguishable stages. Again I quote from Caves and Jones

Someone has invented and marketed the radio ... At the start its market success is uncertain. The new product does not automatically appeal to many customers. Its manufacture is small-scale. Production techniques are likely to be novel and to require large inputs of skilled labour. 'Mass production' is unsuitable because of both the small market and technological uncertainties. The good must be produced near its market, because the producer needs a quick feedback of information in order to improve its performance, reliability, and general appeal. Hence the innovator's home market will be the first served.

When the product is established at home ... the location of production may start to shift ... Standardisation and general consumer acceptance allow for mass production. This demands lesser labour skills … As the product grows standardised and its market becomes more competitive, the pull of cost advantages on the location of production grows stronger … Imitative competition is likely to arise (and to undermine the monopoly position of the original inventors of the product) …. Costs start to tell. Unless the country where the innovation first becomes established has an ultimate comparative advantage, production will spread or shift to other countries … Once again, this model helps to explain changes in production and trade in new product lines, such as electronics. The United States had been a principal innovator, but production has also spread (with a lag) to other countries … Furthermore for goods whose manufacture is spreading abroad we observe a shift from processes heavily dependent on skilled labour to automatic assembly processes using relatively more capital and unskilled labour.

'The product cycle, as an explanation of changes in production and trade, involves shifts in patterns of consumption as well as in the technology of production. As a consumer good matures, it passes from being a luxury to being a necessity. But 'necessity' is a relative term … As production standardises, a good will become cheaper relative to other goods.' (Caves and Jones op cit., p. 221).

By now any reader who is moderately versed in the recent history of economics will realise: All this is pure Schumpeter. Indeed it is essentially an elaboration, variation, verification and application to international trade of Schumpeter's classical theory of capitalist development.[22]

Another related factor which surely often is very important in shaping the pattern of manufactured goods trade is increasing returns to scale. It is one of the oldest themes in economic theory that international trade enables the participating countries to reap the advantages of large-scale production. The scale factor was analysed in depth by Ohlin and has received much attention in the recent literature along with skills, R and D and innovation.

Let me mention a few recent cases. American dominance in the market for aircaft, especially the large, long-distance jets, is surely due to the large domestic market. Heavy military demand has greatly added to the size of the market and was decisively involved in the early development of the industry. It has been demonstrated that American industries in many cases have a great advantage over Canadian industries, because the large domestic market makes long production runs possible.[23] Needless to add that protectionist policies and the ubiquitous transport costs interact with the scale factors in intricate fashion. These factors will receive further attention in other contribution to this symposium.

American industries have the same advantage over European industries. It was, indeed, one of the major economic objectives of the European economic unification to overcome this handicap. Perhaps the most important reason why this goal has been reached only to a limited extent is the enormous growth of the public sector. Without political unification it is practically impossible to coordinate sufficiently nationalised industries and public procurement policies to come near the degree of exploitation of the advantages of large-scale production that would be possible in a competitive economy.[24]

The ever present danger that new barriers of trade may be introduced or old ones increased is a great handicap for small countries; it often makes it too risky to take advantage of large-scale production by setting up factories specially for exports. Jacques Drèze has tried to show that product differentiation between national markets (not only of consumer goods but also of capital goods) is often prevalent even in the absence of tariffs, and operates like tariffs to handicap small countries with small national markets. Belgium, he says however, has partly overcome this disadvantage by exporting undifferentiated intermediate products—steel, glass, nonferrous metals, wool products.[25] Irving Kravis and Robert E. Lipsey have discovered '. . . a number of cases in which the size of the U.S. market enables U.S. producers to reach a large volume production for relatively specialised product variants for which markets are thin in any one of the smaller, competing economies. In the antifriction bearing industry, for example, the United States imports commonly used bearings which can be produced in large volume both here and abroad, but the United States has nevertheless enjoyed a net export position in bearings owing to exports of specialised kinds capable of meeting precision needs, resisting heat or rust, or bearing great weight'.[26]

These examples which could be multiplied *ad libitum* demonstrate the enormous complexity of manufactured goods trade among modern industrial countries. At first blush the facts, for example ball bearings being exported and imported at the same time, are often baffling and may give the impression of wastefulness and inefficiency. But the actors in the market, private producers and dealers, know what they are doing. While for the researching economist it requires a major effort to find out what is going on and the true answer may often elude him, the market if left alone solves even the most intricate problems with dispatch and efficiency. This is a matter of utmost importance for the development of theories and their testing as well as for trade policies. It is safe to say, nevertheless, that this fact is often not sufficiently realised in either area.

The various theories stressing labour skills, R and D innovation, technological gaps, product cycles, product differentiation, and scale economies have been subjected to numerous empirical tests—historical case and country studies and sophisticated statistical analyses. Most instructive and illuminating I find are case studies of particular industries—plastics, nylon, electronics, petrochemicals, consumer durables, etc.[27] Electronic watches is one of the most recent innovations which has started in the United States. In this case the product life cycle seems to have run its course very rapidly, judging from the fact that U.S. producers have already asked for high import duties on electronic watches to protect them from foreign competition.

Comprehensive statistical testing, using American and world trade statistics (trade matrices) have been attempted by Baldwin, Gruber and Vernon, and Hufbauer.[28] These are very ambitious studies and it would lead much too far to discuss them in detail. The authors claim that on the whole the results support their theoretical expectations. But most of the data are not very good (especially for other countries than the United States) and the vital classifications of types of product, factors (for example different skills) and processes are admittedly often rather arbitrary and haphazard. Thus it is very doubtful whether it is possible statistically to separate the effects of the skill, scale, R and D investment and innovation factors.[29] What the massive statistical operations have added to our knowledge is therefore not clear. Fortunately it is probably not very important to know the precise comparative contribution of skill, scale, R and D, product differentiation and product cycles.

5. Where Do We Stand?

Our brief sketch of post-Ohlinian theory has presented an array of overlapping models and theories which stress a variety of circumstances, factor proportions and others, that determine the 'international allocation of economic activity'. But I could consider only a part of the problem. For example, I did not address specifically the trade problem of the less developed countries (on which there exists a vast literature). These problems will occupy other sessions of this symposium. Let me make bold, however, and assert that the existing body of theories applies equally to LDCs as to countries on a higher level of development. It goes without saying, however, that the long run impact of trade on the factor supply, especially on the human factor (human capital) and the transmission of factors—including the transfer of technological and managerial knowledge—from country to country requires special attention when dealing with LDCs.

The importance of the development problem in the minds of present day economists is underscored by a remark of a participant at a recent conference on trade problems. He was moved to say the 'trade theory is foredoomed to become an extension of growth and development theory', admitting, however that 'the latter is still struggling toward its successful synthesis'.[30] This statement echoes, although in inverted from, Alfred Marshall's famous though somewhat baffling dictum that the 'the causes which determine the economic progress of nations belong to the study of international trade'.[31] No doubt, international trade and international division of labour have played an enormously important role in modern development including the first and second industrial revolution. 'It is simply not possible to imagine what sort of economic development would have taken place over the last hundred (or two hundred) years without international trade' (Ohlin op. cit., 2nd ed. p. 413).

Nor are these omissions all. Government policies, both foreign trade measures (import restrictions and export subsidies) and domestic policies such as taxes, subsidies and others, can have lasting effects on the patterns of trade. Finally I may mention monetary and business cycle phenomena. Although they have been excluded (in wise self-limitation) from the present conference, monetary and cyclical disturbances may well have permanent effects on the structure of the economy and the pattern of trade as Ohlin has pointed out. It would not be difficult to cite concrete cases of lasting effects of short-run disturbances. For example severe depressions often leave significant changes in the economic structure and comparative cost situations in their wake, largely but not wholly, via their profound impact on economic policy.

The picture which emerges is that of a mosaic of interrelated, overlapping and occasionally conflicting theories and models, each applicable to certain situations. This is a far cry from the imposing unified structure of the theory of international trade which has been developed by neoclassical writers—with appealing trasparency in graphic form for two-commodity, two-factor and two-country models and generalised by Paul Samuelson and others in mathematical terms to many countries, commodities and factors.

It could be argued that there is no use for vast general equilibrium systems covering the whole economic universe, either in disaggregated form à la Walras or in highly aggregated form as in the post-Keynesian literature. Let me quote from the celebrated *Theory of Games and Economic Behaviour* by John von Neumann and Oskar Morgenstern:

Let us be aware that there exists at present no universal system of economic theory ... Even in sciences which are far more advanced than economics, like physics, there is no universal system available at present ... It happens occasionally that a particular 'physical' theory appears to provide the basis for a universal system, but in all instances up to the present time this appearance has not lasted more than a decade at best. The everyday work of the research physicist is certainly not involved with such high aims ... The physicist works on individual problems, some of great practical importance, others of less. Unification of fields which were formerly divided and far apart may alternate with this type of work. However, such fortunate occurrences are rare and happen only after each field has been thoroughly explored.[32]

The Neumann-Morgenstern injunction against applying what they call a 'super-standard' (*loc. cit.*), in other words postulating a universal system, is surely well taken not only with respect to sweeping economic or social laws which chart the course of economic and social evolution, à la Hegel and Marx, Spengler and Toynbee, what Karl Popper[33] calls 'oracular philosophy', but also to many contemporaneous overambitious econometric models which try to describe the working of the economy as a whole and project the course of the economy of single countries or of a large part of the world with or without its cyclical ups and downs in considerable detail for longish periods in the future.

I submit, however, that the static (or comparative static) neoclassical general equilibrium theory (in the broad sense including Heckscher and Ohlin)—even the truncated two-country, two-commodity model—is an extremely useful tool of analysis. Of course the general theory does not tell us, and should not be expected to tell us, which country is going to export what, or how the international terms of trade will move, just as nobody will say that 'the ordinary single-market theory' of demand and supply 'is useless because it is not dynamic'[34] and does not tell us what the price of sugar will be and who will produce how much.

It is true, general equilibrium theory is largely competitive theory (just as a theory using demand and supply curves for a particular commodity is). Monopolistic islands in a competitive economy can be easily accommodated in the general equilibrium system. But if monopolistic markets cover large areas of the economy, it becomes difficult to incorporate them in the general equilibrium system. This is especially true of oligopolies and bilateral monopolies. But the competitive theory has two very important functions, a positive and a normative one. The positive function (in Robert Solow's words) is to give 'an idealised description of how resources are allocated and incomes distributed in a competitive capitalist economy'. However, if you try to answer not that descriptive [positive] question but the normative ... 'one of how scarce resources should be allocated by a society anxious to avoid waste', in other words a society whose aim is to maximise real national income, 'you rediscover the same theory in the guise of shadow prices or efficiency prices'.[35] The competitive equilibrium is, in a sense, an optimum. I need not here discuss in detail in what sense it is an optimum. Let me simply say in the sense of a 'Pareto optimum', which is also the sense in which Ohlin speaks of 'the gain from interregional trade'.[36]

Viner stressed the normative or 'welfare analysis orientation', as he called it, of the classical doctrine.[37] 'The classical theory of international trade', he said, 'was formulated primarily with a view to its providing guidance on questions of national policy, and although it included considerable descriptive (positive) analysis of economic process, the selection of phenomena to be scrutinised ... was almost always made with reference to current issues of public interest'.[38]

Thus the classical and neoclassical theory was and is often used to defend and propagate the policy of free trade. But it can and it has in fact been increasingly used for the opposite purpose. For example, the competitive theory can be effectively used to demonstrate the optimum tariff argument; in other words the terms-of-trade argument for import restrictions. Ohlin is surely right when he urges not 'to mix viewpoints which are tinged with normative considerations with the objective [positive] analysis'.[39] But how easy it is to slip from the objective analysis into 'normative' welfare consideration, Ohlin himself demonstrated, unwittingly I suppose, by arguing already early in his book, in the midst of the 'objective' analysis, in typical classical fashion, that interregional trade increases real national income in terms of commodities.[40] The precise meaning of such statements and the conditions under which it is true that free interregional and international trade increase and maximise real national income have been clarified in modern welfare economies. The essentials can be very effectively demonstrated diagramatically in a two-commodity model. Roughly speaking the conditions are free competition and absence of external economies and diseconomies.[41] We know that these conditions are never fully realised. Whether they are as a rule sufficiently realised to justify the free trade prescription I shall not discuss here. The purpose of this discussion is to argue that the competitive general equilibrium theory is useful or even indispensable as an ideal type which enables us better to visualise, evaluate and measure aberrations from the ideal conditions which abound in the real world.

Perhaps I have already strayed too far into welfare economics. The agenda of this conference expressly exclude the discussion of policy questions. I trust, however, that this injunction does not entirely bar the mentioning of problems of welfare economics. This would be a pity for the reason that the theories of positive and welfare economics are so closely interrelated.

Appendix A

Alfred Marshall on Technology Trade, International Transmission of Technology and the Product Life Cycle[42]

Alfred Marshall devoted great attention to the role of technology and its trans-mission in an international setting in his *Industry and Trade*.[43] He describes in detail the various methods by which technology is transmitted from one country to another, and its impact on comparative advantage. He points out the debt that British technology owes to the French in many instances, and how the British adoption of French techniques had, on occasion, reduced the volume of trade and eventually reversed the pattern comparative advantage

... the Revocation of the Edict of Nantes in 1685 was a chief incident in a sustained policy of Continental autocrats, which rid them of sturdy subjects. More than half a million of the ablest of them came to England, bringing with them that knowledge of technique, which was most needed by her just at that time. In particular the Huguenots taught her to make many light glass and metal wares, in which French genius excelled: and in a very short time such wares ... were being sent to France and sold at a good profit.

Laying particular emphasis on the British ability to standardise the inventions and new products of others, he continues

Another side of the same faculties is shown in such manufactures as those of the bicycle, motor car, submarine, and aeroplane: where French inventors have led, and a few French operative mechanics displayed a skill, a judgment and a resource which are nowhere surpassed. As these new delicate industries have reached the stage of massive production, the faculty of disciplined steadfast work becomes more important: the motor car, the submarine and the aeroplane tend to find their chief homes in other countries, as the bicycle did long ago.[44]

Another example: The German, American, and British faculty for organisation, coupled with the impossibility of French fashion designers to prevent imitation of their goods, results in the following product cycle largely foreshadowing the work of modern theorists.

This same tendency is shown even more conspicuously in those industries in which the leadership of France has been long established ... Thus new Parisian goods (dresses, etc.) are sold at very high prices to the richest customers in all countries. In the next stage copies of them, made chiefly by local hand labour, are sold at rather high prices to the richest customers in all countries. In the next stage copies of them ... are sold at rather high prices to the moderately rich. The last stage is the adoption of the new fashion for general use: and, for that purpose, people in commercial countries, endowed with a high faculty for organisation, study the imported French model, catch the keynotes of its ideas; they translate these ideas as far as possible into mechanical language and produce passable imitations for the middle and working classes.
    The meet such competition France is driven to make a little use of massive methods herself, even in industries to which they are not wholly appropriate. But the tendency of the age is to require the producer to show his goods to the purchaser. The purchaser does not, as a rule, now go to the producer unless he is in quest of goods of a very special kind: therefore, when the French goods have reached the stage of semi-mechanical imitation, the untiring push and bold energy of the travellers for German and other firms have had an advantage over their French rivals. Meanwhile, however, Paris may have made one or more new models, which can be sold at scarcity prices to those who are tired of the last model, partly because it has become somewhat vulgarised.[45]

Nor does Marshall neglect the 'public' nature of many inventions, nor the distinction between invention and innovation, nor the problem of rapid, free imitation of them abroad.

Whether he [the inventor] communicates his results to a learned society, and leaves others to earn money by them, or applies them in practice himself (with or without the protection of a patent), they become in effect the property of the world almost at once. Even if he uses them in a 'secret process', enough information about them often leaks out to set others soon on a track near to his own.[46]

In discussing the comparative advantage of Germany '... in industries, in which academic training and laboratory work can be turned to good account ...' Marshall gives the following account of German efforts to import technology by various methods

In the early stages of modern manufacture scientific training was of relatively small importance. The Germans accordingly, recognising their own weakness in practical instinct and organising faculty, took the part of pupils, whose purpose it was to outrun their teachers. They began by the direct copying of English machinery and methods: (despite the British prohibition on the exportation of machines in effect at that time) and they next set themselves to get employment in English firms; and to offer steady, intelligent services in return for a low pay in money, and a silent instruction in the inner workings of the business ... And all the while Germany has been quick to grasp the practical significance of any master discovery that is made in other countries and to turn it to account.[47]

Numerous other passages could be cited. the above should suffice to indicate the depth to which Marshall explored the role of technology, the methods of its transmission, the effects upon comparative advantage, and how

... broad ideas and knowledge, which when once acquired pass speedily into common ownership; and become part of the collective wealth, in the first instance of the countries to which the industries specially affected belong, and ultimately to the whole world.[48]

It should be mentioned that Marshall draws heavily on earlier English literature. He quotes, for example, Daniel Defoe's *A Plan of the English Commerce 1728*[49] as follows

Defoe had said, "It is a kind of proverb attending the character of Englishmen that they are better to improve than to invent, better to advance upon the designs and plans which other people had laid down, than to form schemes and designs of their own ... The wool indeed was English, but the wit was all Flemish". But he went on to show in detail how we outdid our teachers; how "we have turned the scale of trade, and send our goods to be sold in those very countries, from which we derived the knowledge and art of making them".[50]

What Defoe—and Marshall—said about the English, contemporary writers have been saying about the Japanese.

Appendix B

Some Consequences of the Expansion of the Public Sector for the International Location of Production

While the rapid technological progress in the area of transportation and communication, and the resulting reduction of the costs of transportation and communications have operated to expand international trade and international division of labour, the enormous growth of the public sector and the increasing involvement of the state in all branches of economic life have worked in the opposite direction. This is especially conspicuous in the vast area of public utilities—railways, postal services, telephone, telegraph, airlines and the governmental administration itself. But it is also true of other nationalised industries, although to a lesser extent, because these industries are usually under the discipline of competition of private firms at home and abroad.

A cursory comparison between the situation with respect to public utilities in the United States and in the European Economic Community is instructive. While in the United States public utilities, whether government operated (such as the postal service) or in private hands (such as railways, telephone, telegraph, airlines, etc.), operate freely over the whole expanse of the country and tend to select the optimum size and optimum location unobstructed by political boundaries, in Europe there exist as many such enterprises as there are sovereign States. Since the advantages of large-scale production are especially pronounced in the public utility area, the multiplicity of national enterprises involves a heavy burden of economic overhead cost and operating expenses. In other words, if Europe wanted to take full advantage of economic integration and approach the level of economic integration that has been achieved in the United States, it would be necessary to consolidate and merge many of the national railways, airlines, postal, telephone and telegraph (PTT) services. It is very doubtful whether this could be done without far-reaching political integration. If railway, telephone, telegraph and airlines were in private hands, as is the case in the United States, rational economic integration would be comparatively simple.

This does not, of course, mean that the railway, postal, telephone services inside the smaller European countries, as well as between them, are inferior to those in the United States. There exist great national differences in the quality and efficiency of these services between the different European countries and the United States. In some of the European countries these services are just as good as, or even better than, in the United States. But the point is that they could be still better, cheaper and more efficient if there were no political boundaries or if the public utilities were in private hands. In the absence of political boundaries public enterprises would presumably buy their capital equipment, instruments, materials, etc., from the cheapest sources. As it is, government-operated public utilities such as railways, telephone, and telegraph etc. produce much of their capital equipment (locomotives, freight cars, coaches, etc.,) themselves or buy them from national private firms. This is the rule even in the small countries of the European community. As the E.E.C. report on *Public Purchasing in the Common Market*, which was quoted in the text, says public procurement has remained 'unaffected by the Customs union'.

Suppose now that most of the public utilities, like the railways, telephone and telegraph, were in private hands as is the case in the United States. Then these national private concerns would merge and operate across political boundaries and their procurement policies would surely, in a customs union (i.e., under free trade and in the absence of governmental protectionist measures) ignore the political boundaries. As Jacob Viner said 'private enterprise, as such, is normally non-patriotic, while government is automatically patriotic'.[51]

It will be observed that these advantages of private enterprise over public enterprise are independent of the question whether private enterprise *as such* (that is to say given the spatial extension of the operation) is more efficient than public enterprise. I myself have no doubt that the evidence is overwhelming that private enterprise is practically always much more efficient than public enterprise, although it is true that the comparative inefficiency of public enterprise differs enormously from country to country. This inefficiency is especially pronounced in less developed countries.

Trade problems of the centrally planned countries of the East—both intra-East and East–West trade—have been excluded from consideration in this symposium. But it is clear that the rapid growth of the public sector in all Western countries make those problems increasingly relevant for the understanding of intra-Western trade.

Notes

1. Quoted from Ricardo's *Principles* by Jacob Viner in *Studies in the Theory of International Trade*, p. 504. Viner quotes other, similar passages from Ricardo, Malthus, McCulloch and other classical writers.

2. See Ohlin, 'Reflections on Contemporary International Trade Theories', Appendix II to second revised edition of *Interregional and International Trade* (Cambridge, Massachusetts, 1967), p. 307.

3. *Interregional and International Trade*, 2nd ed., p. 8.

4. In connection with intertemporal (rather than interspatial) exchange the transformation curve was already used by Irving Fisher in his book *The Rate of Interest* (New York, 1907).

5. A. Marshall's famous 1879 papers were still entitled 'The Pure Theory of Foreign Trade' and 'The Pure Theory of (Domestic) Values'. See London School of Economics *Reprint of Scarce Tracts*, No. 1 (London, 1930).

6. R. Caves' and R. Jones' view to the contrary notwithstanding. See their *World Trade and Payments. An Introduction* (Boston, 1937), p. 187.

7. Harry G. Johnson, 'The State of Theory in Relation to Empirical Analysis', in *The Technology Factor in International Trade*, conference volume edited by R. Vernon. National Bureau of Economic Research (New York, 1970), p.11.

8. This has not prevented some writers, for example, Myrdal, from criticising classical theory for teaching that free trade will equalise living standards internationally. Neither the writers in the old classical tradition, nor Heckscher nor Ohlin have taught that standards of living will be equalised. And contrary to a superficial impression the modern mathematical literature on the subject proves that factor price equalisation through free trade, although not 'inconceivable' is in reality 'absolutely impossible' (to use words which A Marshall used in another connection).

Moreover, complete equalisation of factor prices does not imply equalisation of living standards, if the latter is defined as national income per head or per unit of labour. Suppose country A is better supplied with natural resources than country B, then its national income per head (per unit of the factor labour) will be higher even if wages and other factor prices are the same in A and B.

9. It should also be observed that Leontief himself did not regard his findings in contradiction to the neoclassical tradition. (I use the world 'neoclassical' in a comprehensive sense, including Heckscher-Ohlin as well as as those who, like Marshall and Viner, emphasise the roots of modern theory in the writings of the old classical economists.) Leontief did not fully spell out the theoretical model underlying his empirical work, but it was clearly not a two-factor model; for in the verbal discussion of his results he assumed, in addition to capital and labour, the existence of other cooperating factors of production such as enterpreneurship and management in order to clear up the seeming clash between his findings and accepted principles.

10. See, however, M. A. Diab, *The United States Capital Position and the Structure of its Foreign Trade* (Amsterdam, 1956); and Jaroslav Vanek, *The Natural Resource Content of U.S. Foreign Trade 1950–1955* (Cambridge, Mass. 1963).

11. Differences in the production function should be distinguished from 'factor intensity reversals' which may occur even with identical, homogeneous production functions merely as a consequence of dissimilar endowment with qualitatively identical factors. There may exist borderline cases where it is difficult to decide whether to speak of factor intensity reversal, dissimilar production functions, factors of different quality or product differentiation. Fortunately it would probably not make much difference for most purposes.

12. See my *A Survey of International Trade Theory*, 2nd ed. (Princeton, 1961), pp. 22–23 [Chapter 4 in this volume], J. Vanek, *op. cit.*, and Robert E. Baldwin, 'Determinants of the Commodity Structure of U.S. Trade', *American Economic Review*, Vol. 61 (March, 1971), p. 142. It should be kept in mind that Leontief's statistics relate to the United States only. He does not say that *foreign* production of American imports is labour or capital or natural resource-intensive. What he does say is that *American* industries competing with imports are capital-intensive compared with *American* export industries. but some of them are also relatively natural resource-intensive compared with American export industries.

13. An attempt at classification of theories, at their statistical testing, and a comprehensive bibliography can be found in the excellent article by G. C. Hufbauer under the mouthfilling title 'The Impact of National Characteristics and Technology on the Commodity Composition of Trade in Manufactured Goods,' in *The Technology Factor in International Trade: A Conference of the Universities*, National Bureau Committee for Economic Research, edited by Raymond Vernon (New York, 1970), pp. 145–232. Robert M. Stern, 'Testing Trade Theories,' in *International Trade and Finance Frontiers for Research*, edited by Peter B. Kenen (Cambridge, 1975), pp. 3–50, presents a comprehensive account of recent theorising with an extensive bibliography.

14. Harry Johnson in his Wicksell Lectures *Comparative Cost and Commercial Policy Theory for a Developing World* (Stockholm, 1968) has put the new theories which stress the technology factor in a broader framework. He mentions that the Heckscher-Ohlin model can be 'easily adapted' to take care of differences in technology. For an early discussion of this new trend see also the excellent article by M. V. Posner, 'International Trade and Technical Change,' in Oxford Economic Papers, Vol. 13 (October, 1961), pp. 323–341.

15. It should be recalled that A. Marshall [especially in his *Industry and Trade* (1927)] and F. W. Taussig (in numerous writings) have explicitly and systematically dealt with different types of labour.

16. See especially Baldwin and Hufbauer, *op. cit.*, Donald B. Keesing, 'Labour Skills and Comparative Advantage,' *American Economic Review*, Vol. 56 (May, 1966). W. H. Gruber,

D. Mehta and R. Vernon, 'The R and D Factors in International Trade and International Investment of U.S. Industries,' *Journal of Political Economy* (February, 1967), and Gruber-Vernon, 'The Technology Factor in a World Trade Matrix,' in the *Technology Factor in International Trade* (cited above).

17. See F. W. Taussig, *International Trade* (New York, 1928). Taussig had given a similar, though less complete analysis as early as 1906 in 'Wages and Prices in Relation to International Trade,' *Quarterly Journal of Economics*, Vol. 20. For further references on Taussig, see Viner, *op. cit.*, p. 495. Irving Kravis in his well-known article '"Availability" and Other Influences on the Commodity Composition of Trade,' *Journal of Political Economy* (April, 1956) mentions Taussig and other earlier sources.

18. P. E. Kenen, 'Nature, Capital and Trade,' *Journal of Political Economy*, Vol. 73 (1965), pp. 437–460. Leontief had already pointed out that American export industries are more skill-intensive than American industries competing with imports (see W. W. Leontief, 'Factor Proportions and the Structure of American Trade: Further Theoretical and Empirical Analysis,' *Review of Economics and Statistics*, Vol. 38 (1956), pp. 386–407.

19. Caves-Jones, *op. cit.*, pp. 218–222.

20. The importance of the home market as a base for international trade was stressed by Staffan Burenstam-Linder in his well-known stimulating book *An Essay on Trade and Transformation* (New York, 1961). Furthermore he puts forward the thesis that trade in manufactured goods will be 'most intensive' between countries that are 'similar' in their basic pattern of demand which in turn is largely determined by the level of per capita income. Linder contrasts this explanation of trade in manufactured products with the factor proportion theory. He thinks that the latter applies to trade in primary products but not to that in manufactured goods. Linder's theory was statistically tested by Hufbauer (*loc. cit.*) and by Seev Hirsch and Baruch Lev ['Trade and Per Capita Income Differentials: A Test of the Burenstam-Linder Hypothesis,' in *World Development*, Vol. 1, No. 9 (September, 1973), pp. 11–19]. The results of the former test were unfavourable, those of the latter favourable for Linder's thesis.

In my opinion both tests must be judged as inadequate. For it is extremely difficult to separate the influence of differential labour skills, R and D, scale factors, transport cost, tariffs (trade barriers), product differentiation and per capita income differentials. Investigation in much greater depth would be required. But the relevance and usefulness of such an exercise must be doubted. The contrast between Linder's theory and the factor proportion theory seems to me overdrawn. It may be true that new lines of production are usually started in the home market and that international trade then first spreads between countries on the same level of development (although exceptions to this rule surely exist). But as Caves and Jones say (see text below) 'unless the country where an innovation first becomes established has an ultimate comparative advantage, production will spread or shift to other countries'. This has been confirmed in many cases by the 'product cycle' analyses (see page 114), where it is shown how the production of new product spreads to other countries. Linder says that trade in primary products is governed by factor proportions. But there is little trade in which primary products are exchanged for primary products; most trade involving primary products is an exchange of primary for manufactured products. That large chunk of trade surely is primarily determined by factor proportion.

21. See especially, Louis T. Wells, 'International Trade: The Product Life Cycle Approach,' in *The Product Life Cycle and International Trade*, pp. 3–38, edited by L. T. Wells (Boston, 1972).

22. Joseph A. Schumpeter, *The Theory of Economic Development*, Translated from the German by Redvers Opic (Cambridge, Mass., 1934; first German edition 1912). Schumpeter's theory is nowhere mentioned in the whole literature on technology trade and product cycles (nor in any of lengthy bibliographies of that subject), although these theories were largely developed in Schumpeter's own University—at the Harvard Business School where Schumpeter's work was continued in the 'enterpreneurial history' project. Schumpeter, it is true, did not put forward his theory of economic development in opposition or criticism of neoclassical economics. This may explain why he is not mentioned. Raymond Vernon, to whose initiative and drive we owe to a large extent the rapid development of this very valuable line of research, mentions J. H. Williams, Donald MacDougall and others who expressed 'discontent' with the static classical trade theory and used (rather, misused) Schumpeterian thoughts to make a case for the existence of a permanent dollar shortage—an idea which, despite its obvious weakness, was very popular in the postwar period, until the dollar shortage gave way to a dollar glut. To get a hearing for one's thoughts it is evidently better to present them as a heresy rather than as what they really are—an extension of the existing body of theory. Michael Connolly, University of Florida has drawn my attention to the fact that A. Marshall has anticipated much of the product cycle thesis. For excerpts from Marshall's *Industry and Trade* see Appendix A to this paper.

These grumbles should, however, not dampen our gratitude for the new material and insights which we owe to the recent research on technology trade, innovation and product cycles.

23. On the instructive comparison of U.S. and Canadian industries see D. J. Daly's paper 'Uses of International Price and Output Data,' in *International Comparisons of Prices and Output*, edited by D. J. Daly, Studies in Income and Wealth, Vol. 37, National Bureau of Economic Research (New York, 1972), pp. 120–121 and the literature quoted there.

24. On the situation in the European Common Market see the report on *Public Purchasing in the Common Market*, by M. Guy Charpentier and Sir Richard Clarke to the Commission of the European Communities (EC), Brussels, 1974. The authors' conclusion is that 'there exists practically no Common Market policy on public procurement and that a very large part of the European economy (bearing in mind the [large and growing] volume of the [public] purchases involved) is unaffected by the Customs Union' (see Conclusions of the Report, p. 93).

For some further reflections on the importance of the expansion of the public sector on the international division of labour see Appendix B.

25. Jacque Drèze, 'Quelques reflexions sereines sur l'adaptation de l'industrie Belge au Marché Commun,' Comptes Rendues des Travaux de la Société Royale d'Économie Politique de Belgique, No. 275 (1960). Quoted by Caves and Jones, *op. cit.*, p. 224.

26. *The Technology Factor in International Trade, loc. cit.*, p. 289. In the two authors' massive and comprehensive study, *Price Competitiveness In World Trade* (NBER, New York, 1971), can be found many examples of other 'non-price factors affecting the competitive position of the U.S.' such as technological leadership, large scale of domestic market, quality of product, speed of delivery (pp. 31–38).

27. See especially, G. C. Hufbauer, *Synthetic Materials and the Theory of International Trade* (London, 1966); Seev Hirsch, *Locations of Industry and International Competitiveness* (Oxford, 1967); and Louis T. Wells, editor, *The Product Life Cycle and International Trade* (Boston, 1972), containing eight industry and country studies by the editor and others.

28. Baldwin (*op. cit.*), Hufbauer, 'The Commodity Composition of the Trade in Manufactured Goods' (*loc. cit.*), W. H. Gruber and R. Vernon, 'The R and D Factors In A World Matrix, in *Technology Factors In International Trade*, NBER (1970).

29. On the limitations of the data and difficulties of classification of industries, labour skills, etc., see especially the lengthy explanations in small print (footnotes) in Baldwin's article where the statistical procedures are discussed at some detail. See also the critical comments on Baldwin's article by Lawrence Weiser and Keith Jay and the author's reply in *American Economic Review*, Vol. 62 (June, 1972), pp. 459–472.

30. Donald B. Keesing at Conference on *The Technology Factor in International Trade, op. cit.*, pp. 275–276.

31. Quoted from Marshall's *Principles* by Ragnar Nurkse, *Equilibrium and Growth in the World Economy. Economic Essay by Ragnar Nurkse*, edited with an Introduction by G. Haberler (Cambridge, Mass., 1961).

32. *The Theory of Games and Economic Behaviour*, 1st ed. (Princeton, N. J. 1944), p. 2.

33. Karl R. Popper, *The Open Society and Its Enemies*, revised edition, (Princeton, N.J., 1950), see especially Part II, 'The High Tide of Prophecy. The Rise of Oracular Philosophy'.

34. Ohlin, *op. cit.*, 2nd ed., p. 319.

35. Robert M. Solow, *Capital Theory and the Rate of Return*, Professor F. de Vries Lecture (Amsterdam, 1963), p. 15.

36. *op. cit.*, 1st ed., pp. 39–40, 2nd ed., pp. 27–28.

37. J. Viner, *Studies*, pp. 437 and 501 fl.

38. *Ibid.*, p. 437.

39. *Op. cit.*, 1st ed., p. 590. This passage occurs in an appendix that has been omitted in the second edition.

It should perhaps be pointed out that strictly speaking it is misleading to call welfare economics a normative science (if there is such a thing). Welfare economics is economics and not a branch of ethics. The welfare economist does not say: 'The policy-maker *should* maximise national income'. What he says is: '*if* the policy-maker wishes to maximise income, he should pursue such and such a policy'. The welfare economist does not exclude that the policy-maker may have objectives other than, or supplementary to, maximisation of income. For example, he usually has supplementary objectives with respect to the distribution of income. Of course, the welfare economist selects his hypothetical value judgements in such a way as to reflect as faithfully as possible the policy objectives that the policy-maker more or less consciously entertains or reveals by his preferences. Whether the welfare economist is, in fact, faithful in his choice, is a problem in positive science which, in principal, should be subject to empirical confirmation or refutation.

40. *Op. cit.*, 1st ed., p. 41, 2nd ed., pp. 27–28.

41. It should be observed that free competition implies flexible prices (of commodities and of factors of production including wages), not free mobility between industries of factors of production (except if immobility of factors is the consequence of monopolistic anticompetitive forces such as labour union restrictions on new entrants into a particular industry or

labour group). To say that the case for free trade maximising national income does not depend on the assumption of perfect mobility of factors does, however, not mean that increasing the domestic mobility of factors by better information, educational and training measures and the like is unimportant. Thus Staffan Linder (*op. cit.*) argues that LDCs suffer from total inability of reallocating factors of production. I think he exaggerates tremendously the alleged inability and the conclusion that it makes trade for LDCs counterproductive is quite wrong [see H. G. Johnson's review of Linder's book in *Economica*, New Series, Vol. 31, No. 121, London (February, 1964)]. But he is certainly right that comparative immobility of factors is a very important handicap for LDCs.

42. This appendix has been adapted from an unpublished PhD thesis by Michael Connolly.

43. London, Macmillan, 1919.

44. *Ibid.*, p. 118.

45. *Ibid.*, pp. 118–119.

46. *Ibid.*, p. 204.

47. *Ibid.*, pp. 132–133.

48. *Ibid.*, pp. 174–175.

49. On Daniel Defoe (1660 or 1661–1731) see *Palgrave's Dictionary of Political Economy*, edited by Henry Higgs, Vol. 1 (London, 1926).

50. *Ibid.*, p. 40.

51. Jacob Viner, 'International Relations between State-controlled National Economies,' *American Economic Review*, Vol. 34, supplement (March, 1944) reprinted in *Readings in the Theory of International Trade* (Philadelphia, 1949), pp. 437–456. See also on this whole problem G. Haberler, 'Theoretical Reflections on the Trade of Socialist Countries,' in *International Trade and Central Planning*, ed. by Alan A. Brown and Egon Neuberger (University of California Press, Berkeley and Los Angeles, California, 1968), pp. 29–46.

[The bibliography of this article is not included.]

II

International Finance

6   Transfer and Price Movements[1]

1.   The problem of unilateral transfers from country to country—whether payments of political tribute, the granting of loans or the repayment of borrowings—has for some time again been the focus of theoretical and practical attention, and it cannot be denied that the problem has to a considerable extent been clarified. The following schematic description of the relevant process has been generally agreed upon[2]: When, in the paying country, or to take the reparation payments as an example, when in Germany the requisite sums are being raised, the purchasing power of the German people is diminished, prices fall. In the recipient countries money demand strengthens, prices rise. Thus, a price differential is created, Germany exports are stimulated and imports discouraged, and quite automatically and all by itself a trade balance surplus results from which the transfer payments can be made.

There is really only *one* point on which this demonstration causes serious differences of opinion, namely the part played by *price movements* that is necessary to carry out the transfer. Two views oppose each other. The one, recently again taken by Bertil Ohlin[3], attempts to belittle the price movement; indeed, Ohlin goes as far as to maintain that in principle no movement at all of the price level is required.

The other view, in contrast, taken most pointedly by J. M. Keynes,[4] is inclined to take the price movement very seriously. It holds that, in certain circumstances, export prices of the paying country must fall severely to stimulate demand strongly enough to produce an export surplus *in money terms*. For, it should be clearly noted, the point is not to raise only the quantity[5] of exports; rather its *money value* must increase. That is, demand for German exports must be such that the quantity of exports rises more than the price declines. In other words, the elasticity of demand for German exports must not be unity or smaller.

This dispute about the part played by price movements in the transfer process is

Zeitschrift fur Nationalokonomie. Band I: 547–554 (1930); Band II: 100–102 (1931). Translated from German. Reprinted with permission.

by no means new. The *first* view, that no price level movement is necessary, goes back to Ricardo. The *second* had been very clearly developed already in 1802 by Henry Thornton in his excellent but little known work,*"An Enquiry into the Nature and Effects of the Paper Credit of Great Britain".*[6] Ricardo argued quite explicitly against Thornton, while Malthus took a very similar view. Mill (as later on Cairnes[7]) accepted Thornton's doctrine, and ever since it has been widely taken to be *the* classical doctrine, and ascribed to Ricardo. In 1917–18, there took place, in the *Quarterly Journal of Economics*, a discussion between F. W. Taussig and J. H. Hollander.[8] Taussig presented the Thornton-Mill version but was apparently of the opinion that he spoke in the vein of Ricardo. His colleague at Johns Hopkins University, however, took the orthodox Ricardian view, but believed to defend the generally recognized theory of the classics. So much on the history of the problem; now for the matter itself.

2. The Thornton-Mill theory seems to me to be clearly preferable: a price movement is almost always required to induce the necessary export surplus. Indeed, Keynes seems to me to be correct even in holding that situations can be *imagined* which make necessary price movements of such severity that serious transfer difficulties arise, or that the transfer becomes altogether impossible. On the other hand, I am convinced that Keynes greatly overestimates the difficulties in the specific case of Germany. One could say, therefore, that Keynes was right in theory but his opponents in practice.

We may think of the various possibilities as ordered along a scale. At one end there is the *limiting*, quite improbable case in which the increased money demand of the receipient country is directed at precisely those commodities which the payor country would have bought if it had not suffered the loss of the sums paid. In this improbable case, there clearly is no transfer problem. At the moment when the sums have been raised, when the budgetary problem has been solved, everything is in best order.

At the other end of the scale is the case, which is, if possible, still more improbable but which is nevertheless imaginable and which I mention only as an *illustrative limiting case* possibly approximated by actual situations. Imagine we had to deal with a country that possesses only one or a very few exportable commodities, perhaps because all other exports are prohibited. If this country had to make payments abroad, and if imports can no longer be compressed, then it clearly must force the exports of this one commodity. Then it could happen that the demand elasticity for this good is 1 or smaller, that is, that the quantity of its exports rises only by the same or even by a smaller proportion than that of the rise of its price. In these circumstances the transfer is clearly impossible. The surplus in the value of exports is simply unattainable. On the other hand, it may still be possible to raise the requisite sums in terms of domestic currency, at the ruling exchange rate, in the payor country and there to put it at the disposal of the foreign payees. One may therefore speak of an impossibility to *transfer* even when it would actually be reflected in an impossibility to balance the budget.

When therefore Keynes and Pigou speak of transfer difficulties, or rather of transfer *losses*, for the payor country, they think of a situation which approaches this extreme case where, that is, German export prices fall very sharply—be it in terms of Marks, at an unchanged rate of exchange, or in foreign currency, domestic prices remaining unchanged with the exchange rate turning against Germany. In other words, they fear that the *real terms of trade* of exports to imports turn against Germany. If that happens, German exports embody, *per unit of money*, more labor effort or "social costs" otherwise calculated, than before, which clearly may represent enormous losses.[9] Keynes expresses this, perhaps not very felicitously, by saying that German real wages would have to be cut twice over: (1) they would have to be lowered to force the export surplus, and then (2) from these already shrunk wages, the sums required for the transfer would have to be squeezed out by taxes. Perhaps the exposition becomes clearer when one reverses this order. But of course the sequence (1) to (2) must not be understood chronologically—even though Keynes' text is dangerously close to a chronological interpretation—but the two movements are parallel or even occur in reverse order. Perhaps it is altogether preferable not to speak of a "first" and "second" burden, but only of a "heavier" or "lighter" burden depending on the movement of the real terms of trade—which may, by the way, even turn *in favor* of the payor country, contrary to accepted opinion; this we shall see later on.

Concretely, the process will look as follows: First, the payor population will have to pay reparation taxes. If the thus reduced demand does not reduce prices *sufficiently* to raise exports sufficiently, that is, if the receipt for the quantitatively increased exports does not increase adequately (for which there is indeed no gurantee), then gold reserves of the central bank will fall, and the bank will be forced to restrain domestic credit.[10] This spells further pressure on prices and wages. To repeat, one may well speak, in this situation, of transfer difficulties or losses, even though these difficulties will take effect inside the payor country, e.g., in the form of severe wages disputes.[11]

That this situation *may* occur seems indisputable. We shall now have to consider how Ohlin could deny this.

3.   Ohlin accuses Keynes of having neglected the *demand* for German exports.[12] "When country B exports capital to A, this means that B puts purchasing power at the disposal of A. A's demand for goods must thus become larger, B's demand smaller, than before. Therefore, we cannot by any means reason on the basis of unchanged demand. The decisive point in the mechanism of capital transfer is precisely ... that demand has experienced a radical change ... *There is now a larger*

market in A for B's goods than before. On the other hand, the market in B for A's goods
is not so receptive as before. The local *distribution*[13] of total demand has changed ....
Before the capital movement both countries bought of all types of goods enough to
make their value equal to that of domestically produced goods.... After the capital
movement has begun, A buys more and B less of the total production of the two
countries,"[14] but both taken together—so one may continue Ohlin's argument—just
as much as before. M. Jacques Rueff speaks, in the same vein, of *"the principle of the
conservation of purchasing power"*. This "principle" says "that never in the course of
economic transformations will purchasing power be lost or created. The result is that
in all cases the loss of one is the gain of the other, and—applied to our subject—the
population of the debtor country never suffers a larger loss in purchasing power than
the size of its debt."[15]

To this one can reply only that the principle of the conservation of purchasing
power proved as little and is as empty of content, as the energy principle of
mechanics which apparently served as its model. However much the real terms of
trade turn against the payor country and however much it suffers from this, the
principle of the conservation of purchasing power—or rather, of money—remains
intact. Therefore it is totally meaningless. Neither Rueff's nor Ohlin's exposition
remove the difficulty that nobody guarantees that the recipients of the purchasing
power transferred will direct their demand to the exports of the payor country, or
that they can be induced by relatively moderate price reductions to do so.

However, there is one point on which Keynes, and all followers of the Thornton-
Mill version are wrong. Almost all authors who have immersed themselves sufficiently to be fully aware of the problem, take it as self-evident that the real terms of
international trade will turn *against* the payor country, perhaps not enough to create
difficulties but at any rate, that they will have this adverse tendency,[16] and that in the
most favorable case they will remain unchanged.

Nevertheless, this is wrong, and the reverse case, i.e. that the terms will turn *in
favor* of payor country, is perfectly conceivable. *Prima facie* one cannot even deny
that it is improbable. The justification of this becomes readily clear if one reflects on
the following situation: Assume that the demand drop in the payor country affects
principally its imports, that the demand increase in the recipient countries is directed
principally toward the exports of the payor country, then the real terms of trade will
clearly turn at once *in favor* of the payor country. Whether this favorable outcome can
be maintained in the further course of the adjustment, depends on numerous factors,
especially on the laws of return to which the affected branches of production are
subject, that is, on forces which naturally also operate when the terms have turned
against the payor country, and of which one cannot generally predict whether they
will work in one direction or the other.[17]

We have reached the end of our analytical exposition. The answer that theory gives us is, to be sure, not unambiguous. The transfer will succeed, or in the limiting case it will not; it may or may not be accompanied by price movements, and the real terms of trade may turn in favor or against the payor country. It is regrettable that theory can render only so conditional a judgment. But one should remember that suitable *empirical* assumptions may well make it possible to reduce the range of the concretely possible considerably. The circumstances that matter are clear enough. For the rest, I hold with Alfred Marshall who one said: "Every short formula for the solution of economic problems is either a misleading fragment, a fallacy or a truism." [18]

4.   My agreement with Keynes extends only to conceding to him that the result he fears *can* occur, that it is theoretically *conceivable*. In respect to his judgment of the actual economic position of Germany, and of the possibilities to transfer the German reparations, he is, I am afraid, guilty of a very large exaggeration. The thought that a country with so many actual and potential export articles as Germany could encounter a demand elasticity of 1 or smaller for a majority of them, appears altogether too improbable. The more so if one recalls that (1) Germany's exports form only a small proportion of the world market, and that (2) most German export industries are *competitive* with the corresponding industries abroad, and that the reduction of German export prices will therefore practically replace foreign by German industry. This will mean, in otherwise unchanged circumstances (especially with equal demand elasticity and equal German production capacity), that in order to achieve the same export surplus, prices would not have to fall as much as they would have to had Germany a monopoly in the commodities concerned. For these reasons, and others that cannot here be set out in detail, I do not believe that there will be severe transfer difficulties with the German reparation payments.[19] This, of course, says nothing about possible difficulties in raising the corresponding sums domestically.

Transfer and Price Movements: A Rejoinder to Bertil Ohlin

I reply in a few words to Ohlin's interesting observations on my article "Transfer and Price Movements,"[20] because I feel that we are not so far apart and that agreement, or at least a reduction of the differences to questions of fact, should easily be possible.

The principal point of the dispute is whether the shift in the distribution of purchasing power, produced by the payment of reparations, affects the balance of payments *directly* as Ohlin maintains (p. 763), or rather indirectly via a change in the relative price levels. In my essay I expressed the view that such a *direct* effect is likely because payment recipients will buy some export goods of the payor country and the payor country will reduce its demand for the exports from the payee country.

A more favorable, though highly improbable, case would obtain if the payment recipients purchased exactly the same goods which the payor country had to do without. If this does not happen, some price shifts (not necessarily a shift in the price *level*) must reconstitute the disturbed equilibrium. Opinions differ on what sort of price shifts should be expected. Keynes (and with him Pigou, Taussig and many others) believes that there will simply be a shift in relative price levels of the two countries, in the sense of a worsening of the "real terms of trade" of the payor country and thus an additional loss for it. Ohlin counters that this argumentation neglects the demand side; no shift in price levels *need* occur. For as the demand in the recipient country is strengthened, this country is enabled to purchase *more* goods from the payor country even at *unchanged* prices, and the restraint of demand in the payor country forces it to import fewer goods from the recipient country. To the objections that the demand restraints in the payor country as well as the demand expansion in the payee country may affect only domestic (non-traded) goods or goods from third countries, Ohlin retorts: "If the payor's demand restraint affects domestic goods, the output will decline and productive resources freed for export industries" (p. 764). And if the demand expansion—so we may continue his argument—in the payee countries is directed to domestic goods, their production will be expanded at the expense of export doods production and again the balance of trade will be—I do not think one could then still say, *directly*—affected. To this one can only reply that the end result will no doubt have to consist in an expansion of export industries in the payor country, for otherwise the export surplus could not be achieved. The decisive point is, however, by what price shifts this reordering of production is brought about.

However, Ohlin is right in that the dominant Thornton-Mill version—i.e., that the real terms of trade *must always* turn against the payor—is wrong. I have shown in my essay that also the *opposite* shift (i.e., one in favor of the payor) is conceivable, namely when the increased demand in the recipient country is directed predominantly to the payor's exports and at the same time the demand drop in the payor country falls on the exports of the payee.[21] This immediate price shift will of course be moderated very soon by the supply adjustments. If *constant* costs obtain over a sufficiently large range, all price shifts will disapper, and Ricardo, who generally argues under the assumption of constant costs, is only consistent when he disregards all price shifts. If we assume rising costs as the rule, the initial price shift (the "impact price", to use an apt expression of Robertson's) will be weakened though not fully reversed. Ohlin is also right, in my opinion, in that many adherents of the Thorton-Mill version neglect demand shifts. But he overlooks that I took this into account in my paper, by specifying an assumption on how the payment recipients spend the sums accruing to them, and from where the payors take the sums they pay. My attention has since been drawn, independently from three sides,[22] to the fact that

Keynes used the concept of elasticity rather carelessly.[23] Indeed, the money payments shift demand curves and these latter therefore change their shapes, so that the elasticity analysis which per force operates under *ceteris paribus* assumption, is no logner applicable. I do not object to this formulation, but must again point out that I have taken account of this circumstance through an assumption on the disposition of the amounts of the payments.

If we assume that there will be only a *parallel* shift of all, or of certain, demand curves—indeed if they suffer radical changes of shape (theoretically conceivable) then the market position will be sharply altered and we can generally say nothing at all—then the position is this: It is possible that this shift of demand curves (to the left in the payor, to the right in the payee country) suffices to produce the adjustment of the balance of trade, that is, to produce an export surplus, without price movements. If that is, however, not the case, because the "right" curves did not shift, then the equilibrium point will have to move along the supply curve (assumed unchanged), and how then prices change depends also on the elasticity of the *new* (shifted, or perhaps deformed) demand curve.

The followers of Pareto will point out that this difficulty is the consequence of the defects in the method of partial equilibrium, which analyses every single change under the assumption *ceteris paribus* and thus leads to infinite regress because the *cetera* change under the impact of the very change under consideration. This difficulty no doubt exists and, with a process of as far reaching impact as the reparations, takes on a dimension too large to neglect the resulting imprecisions. One should, however, think twice before assuming that a method of *general equilibrium* analysis exists (as it is expressed, e.g. in the system of equations of mathematical economists) that could readily be applied to the solution of specific problems. This "method" emerges, on closer inspection, as the postulate not to neglect ever the last effects of every change, however minuscule. In any concrete case there is no other approach then to analyze the various reactions step by step as they unfold in reality—up to the final equilibrium position which will certainly not be reached suddenly, and of which one cannot ever say whether it will be attained after a *finite* number of moves.[24]

Notes

1. Based on a speech to the Wiener Nationalökonomische Gesellschaft (Vienna Economic Society) on December 6, 1929.

2. See the splendid article by F. Machlup, "Wahrung und Auslandsverschuldung" ("Currency and Foreign Indebtedness"), in the *Mitteilungen des Verbandes Österreichscher Banken und Bankiers (Communications of the Austrian Bank and Bankers' Group)*, vol. 10, No. 7/8, pp. 194 ff., Vienna, 1928.

3. "The Reparations Problem," in *Index*, No. 27 and 28, March and April, 1928, issued by Svenska Handelsbanken, Stockholm, and "Transfer Difficulties, Real and Imagined," *Economic Journal*, June 1929, P. 172, and ibid., September 1929, p. 400.

4. "The German Transfer Problem," *Economic Journal*, vol. 39, p. 404, March 1929; ibid., June 1929 and September 1929, p. 179. See also [A.C.] Pigou "Disturbances of Equilibrium in International Trade," ibid., September 1929, p. 344.

5. [Melahior] Palyi, e.g., seems to have overlooked this when he says: "The only objection of importance to this (to the classical theory), it depended on the elasticity of foreign demand for the exports of the payor country. Is it, at a given point, equal to or less than one, then this means that any further price decline ... brings with it no increase, possibly even a decline *of the quantity demanded* (my emphasis), with the result that export receipts would remain unchanged or would even fall." "On the basis of this misunderstanding, Palyi can then easily say: 'Certainly, a very artificial construction'." (p. 389). *The Reparations Problem*, publications of the Fredrich List Gesellschaft, vol. I, Berlin, 1929.

6. For the history of literature, see J. Viner, *Canada's Balance of International Indebtedness*, Chapter IX, Cambridge, Mass., 1924; and, by the same author, "The Theory of Foreign Trade," in *Die Wirtschaftstheorie der Gegenwart* (*Economic Theory of the Present*), vol. 4, ed. Hans Meyer, Vienna, 1923, as well as J. W. Angell, *The Theory of International Prices*, Cambridge, Mass., 1926. In this latter work, the literature listed is almost complete.

7. [J. E. Cairnes] *Some Leading Principles of Political Economy*, 1874.

8. Taussig, "International Trade Under Depreciated Paper," vol. 31, May 1917; Hollander, "International Trade Under Depreciated Paper. A Cricitism;" Taussig, "A Rejoinder", vol. 32, August 1918. See also Knut Wicksell, "International Freights and Prices," ibid., vol. 31, February 1918, with a reply from Taussig, ibid.

9. Measured in money terms, more goods are exported than imported (an export surplus), and in addition every dollar's worth of exports contains more "real cost".

10. Whether *deliberate intervention* by economic policy is necessary to produce this additional, or if one prefers, this *increased* burden, or whether such intervention is surperfluous because currency arrangements (e.g. a *pure* gold standard) are such that it will be produced *automatically*,—all this is secondary for my purposes. The conditions at issue under which I speak of transfer loss of transfer gain consist in that the play of international demand and supply may intensify the original burden or—as we shall see below—may lighten it. In the celebrated Appendix J ("Graphical Presentation of Some Problems in International Trade") of his book, *Money, Credit and Commerce* (London, 1923), Marshall has presented the analytical apparatus for an exact study of these questions. I have not used that apparatus only because it is too little known in Germany (see also Chapters VI to VIII of the same book).
I find myself in the welcome position to say that I am in total agreement with Dr. Machlup on this matter, apart from a terminological difference about which there would be no sense to quarrel. For Machlup concedes in fact that "thus the reparation burden could become still more unbearable" (p. 559). He does, by the way, go further in his theoretical agreement with Keynes than I (at least in his original article), for he assumes, à la version Thornton-Mill, that the real terms of trade must *always* turn against the payor country (now we read that one can attribute "more probability" to this case), and that therefore there is always a transfer *loss*, while I (see below) am of the view that also the opposite can happen, i.e., that there can be a transfer *gain*.

11. Naturally, I agree with Machlup that that popular view is dilettante, which conceives of the transfer difficulty as the simple lack, one fine day, of foreign exchange. Economics has, however, other objectives than that of combatting popular mistakes, and it should not abstain from the elaboration of all details and possibilities simply to make that combat easier, and for fear that at times—and it will certainly happen—the incompetent abuse a theoretical argument that has been taken out of context.

12. See *Economic Journal*, September 1929, pp. 403–404.

13. Emphasis in original.

14. *Index*, April 1928, pp. 3–5.

15. "Mr. Keynes's View on the Transfer Problem", *Economic Journal*, September 1929, pp. 389–390. See also his pamphlet, *Une erreur economique: l'organization transferts,"* Paris 1928 and his essay "Les Idees de M. Keynes sur le probleme des transferts," *Revue d'economie politique,* 43e annee, juillet-aout 1929, pp. 1067 ff.

16. See, e.g., Taussig's excellent work, *International Trade*, New York, Macmillan, 1927. "But not only do they give up something in this way [namely, the British when they grant a loan to America, by giving without the use of the loan amount for the time being]—make a sacrifice, incur a loss, for the time being, but they incur a further loss in that the barter terms (i.e. the real terms of trade) of trade become less advantageous to them. The imports which may continue to buy are got on less fovorable terms than before" (p. 127). See also p. 131. Röpke adopts this presentation as a fully assured and recognized fact: "... we realize that the international ratio of exchange—'the real ratio of foreign exchange' ... turns against Germany, owing to the unilateral transfer of value" (p. 340 of the publication of the List Gesellschaft cited above).

17. These are strictly "short run observations", and the equilibrium of which we speak is the immediate "market equilibrium". If we focus on "long-run observations" and consider the complete or final equilibrium which will establish itself after all production adjustment processes have taken their course, we reach more or less the same result, with the following differences: the relative movements of the diverse partial price levels (export and import prices in both countries) will moderate. But they could be reversed only when many branches of production would follow the law of increasing returns or of falling costs, which in turn is possible only if—without leading to monopolistic positions—the decline in costs can be attributed to the so-called "external economies" whose extensive and regular appearance is in fact improbable. It can however not be excluded that the shifting of prices will disappear in the "long run", as Röpke thinks; that would happen if constant costs would obtain within wide ranges, such as the most modern analysis (Pigou, Knight), returning to the classics, considers likely.

18. Letter to Louis Fry, Novermber 1914, *Memorials of Alfred Marshall* (ed. Pigou), London 1925, p. 484: "My favorite dictum is 'Every statement in regards to economic affairs which is short is a misleading fragment, a fallacy or a truism'."

19. (Footnote added to the English Translation 1984.) When I wrote this in 1930, I was not aware that Alfred Marshall had made the point forcefully years ago. In his book *Money, Credit and Commerce* (London 1923), Marshall wrote: "It is practically certain that in the Ricardian example and under modern industrial conditions the total demand of each of the two countries for each other's goods is relatively elastic and when a large and rich commercial country confronts the rest of the world, the assumption becomes absolutely certain" (p. 17).

And on p. 354 he said: "Nothing approaching to this [an unstable equilibrium resulting from inelastic demand of countries for each other's product] has ever occurred in the real world. It is not inconceivable, but it is absolutely impossible."

20. This is my rejoinder to Bertil Ohlin's Reply to my paper "Transfer and Price Movements." Ohlin's Reply appeared in the *Zeitschrift für Nationalökonomie*, Vol. I, 1930, pp. 762–765. This Rejoinder appeared in Vol. II, 1931, pp. 100–102.

21. In a letter, Keynes completely agreed with me on this point and draws attention to his book [A] *Treatise on Money*, [2 Vols., London, 1930]

22. By Gerhard Mackenroth, Cambridge; Hans Neisser, Kiel; and Hans Staehle, London.

23. This debatable use of the concept of elasticity seems to originate with Marshall who applies propositions drawn from the form of individual demand curves, to the demand–supply curve of his celebrated "bales" which are insufficiently defined averages of export or import commodities.

24. On this, see P. N. Rosenstein-Rodan, "Das Zeitmoment in der mathematischen Theorie des wirtschaftlihen Gleichgewichts" (The Time Element in the Mathematical Theory of Economic Equilibrium"), *Zeitschrift fur Nationalökonomie*, Vol. I, 1930.
O. Morgenstern, *Wirtschaftsprognose* (*Economic Forecasting*), pp. 61 ff. "Ueber die Zeitqualität der Preise" ("On the Time Characteristics of Prices"), Vienna, 1928.
Umberto Ricci aptly compared Pareto's general equilibrium theory with "a splendid castle that delights the imagination but does not solve the housing problem." "Pareto e l'economia pura," *Giornali degli Economist*, 1924, p. 43.

7

The Market for Foreign Exchange and the Stability of the Balance of Payments: A Theoretical Analysis[1]

1. The Problem Stated

The present article presents a more systematic and more comprehensive treatment than can be found in the literature of a subject which has received much attention in recent years. The problem is a twofold one. First, we shall discuss how to derive demand and supply curves of one currency in terms of another, for example, of dollars in terms of francs, from the underlying demand and supply curves for exports and imports. Secondly, stability conditions in the market for foreign exchange will be stated in terms of the elasticities of those underlying curves.

These are matters of great practical importance, which arise continuously in current policy discussions. For example, whenever it is urged that the currency of a country should be depreciated, the objection is raised that the elasticities of demand for exports and imports of the country in question are such that a depreciation could not be expected to lead to an improvement of the balance of payments. The extreme position taken by many recent writers that a depreciation would actually deteriorate the balance of payments of a country (i.e., would lead to, or accelerate, an outflow of gold), is equivalent to the assertion that the market for foreign exchange (of dollars on terms of francs) is in unstable equilibrium.

In the present article, however, no attempt at application will be made. We shall present the theoretical skeleton without putting much descriptive, empirical flesh around the bare bones. Two countries or, what is the same, one country against the rest of the world will be considered, and we shall abstract from possible dynamic complications, for example, from the possibility that a change in the exchange rate may lead to anticipatory and speculative purchases or to speculative capital movements.

Kyklos, III: 193–218 (1949). Reprinted with permission.

2. Stable and Unstable Equilibria in the Market for Foreign Currency

Many writers have applied ordinary demand and supply analysis to the foreign exchange market.[2]

So long as the demand and the supply curve (of dollars in terms of francs) has its "ordinary" shape, that is to say, so long as the demand curve is negatively inclined (slopes down from left to right) and the supply curve is positively inclined (slopes up from left to right), the equilibrium is stable. The following example will make that clear. Suppose we start from an equilibrium in which demand and supply for dollars is equal; now the demand curve shifts to the right so that at the old rate demand for dollars exceeds supply. There is a balance of payments deficit and the Central Bank will lose gold. If now the price of dollars is raised, that is, if the franc depreciates, the excess demand will be eliminated and equilibrium restored.

If, however, the supply curve is negatively inclined, the equilibrium may become unstable. This will be the case, if the supply curve is less steep than the demand curve. If we are near the point where demand and supply are equal, this can be also expressed by saying equilibrium is unstable, provided the elasticity of supply is greater than the elasticity of demand.

In Figure 7.1, the point R is one of unstable equilibrium. Suppose demand for dollars increase, the demand curve shifts from D to D'. Then we get an excess of demand over supply (a deficit) of the magnitude RR'. If the Central Bank, after losing some gold, decided to raise the price of dollars in order to stop the drain on its reserve, it would find that it has made things worse: At a higher price the deficit (the horizontal difference between the S and D or D' curves) is greater, that is to say, gold will flow out at an accelerated rate. Equilibrium could, however, be restored by reducing the price of dollars to P'. An omniscient Central Bank would do just that although it would require a rather unorthodox policy, namely, an appreciation of the currency of the deficit country. But the free price mechanism could not achieve that result; it would drive the exchange rate in the wrong direction. (The reader can easily verify that the situation will be stable, if the S-curve is steeper than the D-curve. Suppose, for example, that in Figure 7.1 the S-curve is the demand schedule and the D-curve is the supply schedule. If the supply schedule shifts from D to D', there will be an excess of supply (balance of payments surplus) or RR' at the rate P. The price of dollars will fall and equilibrium restored at R".)

The question whether such a situation is at all likely to arise will be discussed later. But it may be mentioned that as a short run possibility unstable equilibria in the exchange market have been mentioned in the earlier literature.[3]

It should also be observed that in order to establish the probability that the maintenance of equilibrium in the balance of payments by means of exchange rate variations may encounter serious difficulties, it is not necessary to assume outright

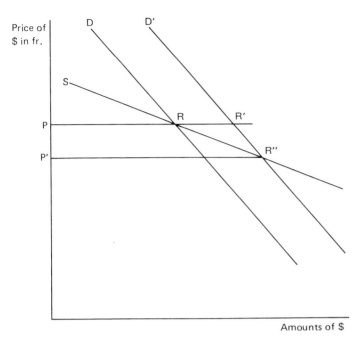

Figure 7.1
Demand and supply of foreign currency.

instability. It would be sufficient for that purpose to demonstrate that demand and supply curves are steep (inelastic). For in that case small displacements of the curves, that is to say, small deficits or surpluses would require large variations in the exchange rate. This would be decidedly inconvenient especially because it may imply large changes in the terms of trade.

It is, therefore, of great importance to have an idea of the approximate shape of the curves. Some insight will be gained, if we analyze how the shape of the demand and supply of dollars in terms of francs is determined by the shape of demand and supply curves of exports and imports.

3. Demand and Supply of Imports and Exports in Terms of Home and Foreign Currency

The shape of demand and supply curves of foreign currency is determined by the nature of the underlying transactions. Thus, the demand for foreign currency for the purpose of paying interest on fixed interest securities held abroad is of zero elasticity, if the debt is expressed in foreign currency and of unitary elasticity, if the

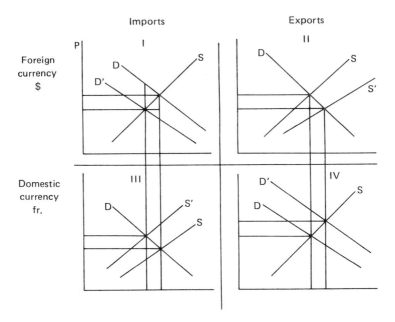

Figure 7.2
Demand and supply curves of exports and imports.

liability is expressed in domestic currency although payable abroad in foreign currency.

Let us now concentrate on demand and supply for foreign currency arising from the export and import of goods and services which is obviously related to, and derived from, the supply and demand at home and abroad of imports and exports. This derivation we shall now investigate.[4]

We are given two demand and supply diagrams, one for exports, the other for imports. There is evidently a separate diagram for each commodity exported and imported. But we assume that we have constructed a sort of average or aggregate curve; in other words, we have demand and supply curves of a "representative bale" of imports and exports. Because our curves represent averages over a variety of goods and services, it is permissible to assume that the supply curves have their normal shape, that is, are positively sloped.[5]

We have to deal with two currencies, foreign and domestic, francs and dollars. So long as no change in the exchange rate is contemplated, we can use the same curves, whether the price of exports or imports is expressed in one or the other currency. But when we wish to study the influence of a change in the exchange rate, we better draw two pairs of diagrams. Diagrams I and II in Figure 7.2 show demand and supply for exports and imports with prices expressed in terms of foreign currency (dollars); in

Diagrams III and IV prices are expressed in terms of domestic currency (francs).

The D and S curves picture the original situation before a change in the exchange rate has taken place. They are, therefore, indentical in the upper and lower part of Figure 7.2.

Now let the domestic currency depreciate in terms of the foreign currency. Throughout the present article (up to Section 8), we assume that nothing else happens, specifically that in each country the supply curve of exports and the demand curve of imports, *in terms of the respective home currencies*, remain unchanged.

This is a serious restriction. It exludes not only speculative changes resulting from anticipated further changes of the exchange rate but also shifts of the curves induced by the inflow and outflow of funds which result from the change in the exchange rate. Such shifts are, of course, an integral part of the balance-of-payments mechanism. But whether and how they come into play, depends largely on the impact-effect of the depreciation which we study in the present paper. The justification of this assumption will be further discussed in Section 8 below.

Let us now ask the question how, under these assumptions, a depreciation of the home currency (franc) in terms of the foreign currency (dollar) will influence prices, quantities and values of exports and imports. It is clear that the quantity of imports will fall and the quantity of exports will rise. But as far as prices and values are concerned, we must now carefully specify whether they are to be expressed in foreign or domestic currency, for what is true of one may not be true of the other. For example, export and import prices will rise in terms of the domestic currency but fall in terms of the foreign currency. Under certain conditions it is possible that the balance of trade will imporve in terms of one currency and deteriorate in terms of the other currency upon a depreciation.[6]

We now analyze the various changes systematically in terms of the diagrams in Figure 7.2. Let us see first what happens in terms of the foreign currency (Parts I and II of figure 7.2). The foreign supply curve of imports remains unchanged. But the domestic demand curve for imports expressed in foreign currency shifts down from D to D'. Each point of the D curve is vertically reduced in the proportion of the depreciation of the currency. In francs the D curve remains unchanged, but that means that in dollars the demand price for each quantity is less than it was before. On the export side the foreign demand curve remains unchanged whilst the domestic supply curve shifts down—for the foreigner in dollars our supply prices are lowered in proportion of the depreciation of the franc.

It follows that the price of imports and exports in terms of foreign currency falls (except if the import supply curve or the export demand curve were perfectly elastic or if the import-demand curve or export-supply curve were entirely inelastic.)[7]

The value of imports in foreign currency falls (except if the demand curve were entirely inelastic). The value exports, however, will rise, fall, or remain unchanged, depending upon the elasticity of foreign demand: If the elasticity is unity, it remains unchanged; if it is greater than unity, it will rise; if it is less than unity, it will fall.

In terms of domestic currency, the situation is different. The import demand curve remains unchanged but the supply curve shifts up, foreign goods becoming more expensive in home currency because of the appreciation of the foreign currency. The export supply curve in the exporting country's currency remains unchanged, while the foreign demand curve shifts up in terms of our currency.

It follows that import prices and export prices in domestic currency will rise (excepting again some extreme positions in which the price remains unchanged).

How the value of imports in terms of domestic currency will be affected depends upon the elasticity of demand; if this elasticity is unity, the value remains unchanged; if it is greater than one, the value of imports will fall, if it is smaller than one, the value will rise. The value of exports, on the other hand, will definitely go up (except if the foreign demand were entirely inelastic).

Let us summarize the results with respect to import and export values: In foreign currency the value of a country's imports will fall in consequence of a depreciation; but whether the value of exports rises or falls depends on the elasticity of the foreign demand for home exports. In terms of home currency, it is the other way round: The value of exports will rise, while the value of imports may rise or fall depending upon the elasticity of home demand for imports.

4. Demand and Supply of Foreign Currency as Derived from Demand and Supply of Exports and Imports

From the four diagrams in Figure 7.2 can be derived demand and supply curves of foreign currency in terms of the domestic currency or of domestic currency in terms of foreign currency. The two types of curves, (a) demand and supply curves of exports and imports in terms of domestic or of foreign currency and (b) the demand and supply curves of one currency in terms of the other, must not be confused.

Take, first, imports in terms of foreign currency which we call $ (Diagram I in Figure 7.2). The shapes of the D and S curves evidently determine the shape of the demand curve for dollars in terms of home currency which we call francs. The following relations can be easily deduced from the figure: The amount of $ demanded is represented by the rectangle under the intersection of the supply and demand curves corresponding to a given rate of $ in francs. Hence, the elasticity of demand for $ will be greater, the more rapidly this area shrinks upon a given appreciation of $ as represented by a downward shift of the D curve. It follows that given the S curve, the elasticity of the demand for $ will be the greater, the greater the elasticity of the D curve. Suppose, for example, that the elasticity of demand is infinite (the demand curve being horizontal), then the price of imports will fall by the full amount of the depreciation and the value of imports (demand for dollars) will be reduced considerably. If, on the other hand, the elasticity of demand is zero (vertical straight line), there will be no fall in the price and no reduction in the value of imports, i.e., the demand for dollars is completely inelastic.

On the other hand, given the D curve, the influence of the elasticity of the S curve on the elasticity of demand for $ is more complicated. It depends upon the elasticity of the D curve. If the elasticity of the D curve is unity, the elasticity of demand for $ is unity (i.e., the same amount of francs is spent on imports whatever the value of the $ in francs, irrespective of the elasticity of the S curve). If the elasticity of the D curve is greater than unity, the elasticity of demand for $ will be the greater, the greater the elasticity of the S curve.[8] If the elasticity of the D curve is less than unity, the elasticity of demand for $ will be the greater the smaller the elasticity of the S curve.[9]

The second diagram in Figure 7.2 yields a supply curve of $. As the $ appreciates in fr., the S curve shifts down and the rectangle under its intersection with the D curve represents the supply of $. It follows at once that the $ value of exports will increase upon a depreciation of the fr., i.e., that the supply curve of $ will be positively inclined, if the elasticity of foreign demand for our exports is greater than unity. The $ value of exports will fall upon a depreciation of the fr., i.e., the supply curve of $ will be negatively inclined, if the elasticity of foreign demand for our exports is less than unity. The numerical value of the elasticity of supply of $ (whether negative or positive) will be the greater, the greater the elasticity of the S curve (home supply of exports). If the D curve has unit elasticity, the supply curve of $ has zero elasticity, i.e., is a vertical straight line whatever the elasticity of the S curve.[10]

Similar rules can be derived for the demand and supply curves of the home currency from Diagrams III and IV of figure 7.2.[11]

5. Depreciation and the Balance of Payments

We proceed now to formulating the condition under which a change in the exchange rate will have its "normal" effect on the balance of payments, i.e., will improve the balance of payments of the depreciating country and weaken the balance of the appreciating country.

This condition is usually expressed in terms of elasticities of demand for imports and of demand for exports. It is now often referred to as the "Lerner condition", although it has been mentioned by Marshall and formulated with even greater precision later by Mrs. Robinson.[12]

The Lerner condition is that "the sum of the elasticity of [home] demand for imports *plus* the elasticity of [foreign] demand for exports" should be greater than unity. If that sum is equal to unity, a change in the exchange rate will leave the balance of payments unchanged. If that sum is smaller than unity, a depreciation will make the balance unfavorable and an appreciation will make it more favorable". The reasoning is as follows: "If the elasticity of [foreign] demand for exports is less than unity, say one third, the quantity bought [exported] will increase only one third as much as the price falls and the value of exports will fall. Suppose the price of exports falls [upon a depreciation] 3 per cent. This will result in an increase in exports of 1 per cent [one third of the fall in price] so that the value of exports will fall about 2 per cent. Now suppose the elasticity of [home] demand for imports to be two thirds (so that the sum of the two elasticities is equal to one), thus the increase of about 3 per cent of the price of imports will result in a decrease in the amount bought [imported], and in their value, of 3 per cent (two thirds of the change of the fall in price because the elasticity of demand for imports is two thirds). The values of imports and exports move together and the import balance is the same." [13] The last sentence should really read: "The values of imports and exports change in the same proportion and if exports and imports were equal to begin with, the balance would not change, that is to say, would remain zero." If exports and imports are not equal to begin with, an equal proportional change in exports and imports would change the absolute size of the balance.[14] It follows that Lerner's condition has to be modified, if exports and imports are not equal. But let us defer discussion of that aspect of the problem until later (Section 7, below).

Professor Lerner also assumes that exports and imports are supplied at constant cost, i.e., that the supply curves of imports and exports are infinitely elastic. If supply elasticities are different, a much more complicated condition obtains, because in that case a depreciation of 3 per cent would not result in a proportional change of import and export prices.

Before we go into those complications, let us consider another interpretation of the Lerner condition, which has been suggested by Dr. A. Hirschmann.[15] Instead of referring to the sum of the elasticity of demand for exports and imports (the D curves in Figure 7.2), reference may be made to the sum of elasticity of (home) demand for the foreign currency and of (foreign) demand for the home currency. The two types of demand curves, viz., for imports and exports on the one hand and for one currency in terms of the other currency, on the other hand, must be carefully distinguished. As we have seen above, only if supply elasticities are infinite (under constant cost) is the elasticity of demand for imports equal to the elasticity of (home) demand for foreign currency, and the elasticity of (foreign) demand for our exports equal to the elasticity of (foreign) demand for our currency.

If we interpret the Lerner condition in this way (as the sum of the elasticity of demand for fr. and the elasticity of demand for $), it is not necessary to assume that the elasticity of supply of exports and of imports is infinite. The supply elasticities enter into the determination of the elasticities of demand for currency and need not

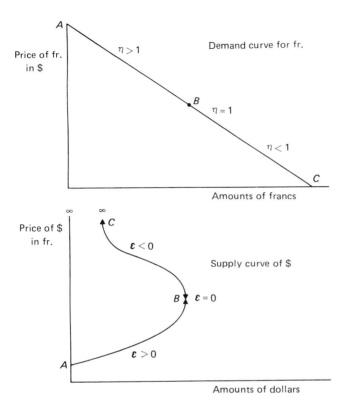

Figure 7.3
Relationship between demand for francs and supply of dollars curves.

be further considered.[16] Lerner's condition can now be written $\eta_{fr} + \eta_\$ > 1$. Now let us reflect that demand for fr. in terms of $ implies an offer or supply of $ for fr. Similarly, demand for $ implies an offer or supply of fr. In other words, from the demand curve for fr. can be derived the supply curve of $, and from the demand curve for $, the supply curve of fr.[17]

In order to convert a demand curve for fr. into a supply curve of $ we have, evidently, to plot for each point on the demand curve, the rectangle under the demand curve (that is, price times quantity which constitutes amount of $ offered at that price) against the price of $ in francs. The price of $ in fr. is the reciprocal of the price of fr. in $, which is shown on the ordinate of the demand curve for fr.

Figure 7.3 will make this relationship clear. Point A on the demand curve corresponds to Point A on the supply curve, the ordinate (price) of A on the supply curve being the reciprocal of the price at A on the demand curve. Point B, where the elasticity of demand is unity, corresponds to Point B on the supply curve, where the supply elasticity is zero. Point C on the demand curve, where the price of fr. in \$ approaches zero, corresponds to Point C on the supply curve, where the price of \$ in fr. rises to infinity. The figure shows that when $\eta = 1$, $\varepsilon = 0$, when $\eta > 1$, ε is negative and when $\eta < 1$, ε is positive.[18]

There is, thus, a simple relation between the elasticity of demand and the elasticity of the corresponding supply.[19] It is $\eta + \varepsilon = 1$. We can, therefore, rewrite the Lerner condition $\eta_{fr} + \eta_\$ > 1$, and by substituting for the $\eta_\$$ the term $1 - \varepsilon_{fr}$ we get $\eta_{fr} - \varepsilon_{fr} > 0$, or $\eta_{fr} > \varepsilon_{fr}$. It thus appears that Lerner's condition is nothing but the familiar stability condition to which we referred in Section II above: Equilibrium is stable, if the supply curve is positively inclined; or in case the supply curve is negatively inclined, if it is steeper than the demand curve, in other words, if the elasticity of demand is greater than the elasticity of supply.

The question may be asked what is the use of this reformulation of Lerner's condition? It is true, the new formula does not say more than the old. Still, it is useful inasmuch as it helps us to realize that instability in the exchange market implying perverse influence of currency depreciation, is possible even if all markets for exports and imports each are in stable equilibrium.

We get additional information if we substitute for the elasticities of demand and supply of currencies the elasticities of demand and supply of exports and imports. The result is this: A change in the exchange rate will have its normal effect on the international balance if the following expression is positive[20]:

$$\frac{\eta_m \eta_x (1 + \varepsilon_m + \varepsilon_x) + \varepsilon_m \varepsilon_x (\eta_m + \eta_x - 1)}{(\eta_m + \varepsilon_x)(\eta_m + \varepsilon_m)}$$

Following Metzler we may call this expression the "elasticity of the balance of payments" with respect to changes in the exchange rate.

From the formula it follows that if the sum of the demand elasticities for exports and imports is greater than unity ($\eta_m + \eta_x > 1$) the situation is stable. But even if $\eta_m + \eta_x$ were smaller than unity, the situation would be still stable, if the supply elasticities are sufficiently small. As Metzler points out, if one of the two supply elasticities is zero, the above expression is positive which implies that the situation is stable.[21]

6. Export Supply and Import Demand vs. Total Supply and Total Demand

From a practical point of view, it is not sufficient that the exchange market should be stable, that what Metzler aptly calls "the elasticity of the balance of payments" should be positive, but also that the elasticity should be fairly large. For if it were positive but small, large changes in the exchange rate would be required to correct small deficits, which would be decidedly inconvenient, especially because such changes may imply changes in the real terms of trade.

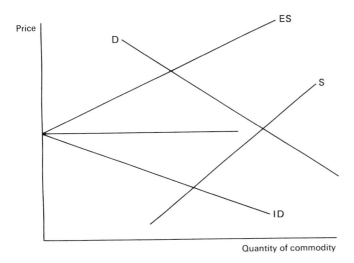

Figure 7.4
Relationship between ordinary demand and supply curves and between supply and import-demand and export-supply curves.

How large the elasticity of the balance of payments of, say, some of the large trading nations actually is, is, of course, an empirical question of great complexity. Theorists of international trade have almost always assumed that it is large. Marshall was very emphatic on that point. "All such suggestions [that there might be unstable equilibria] derive their origin from the sport of imagination rather than observable facts. For they assume the total elasticity of demand of each country to be less than unity, and on the average to be less than one half, throughout a large part of its schedule. Nothing approaching to this has ever occurred in the real world: it is not inconceivable, but it is absolutely improbable." [22]

Statistical studies, on the other hand, which have been undertaken in recent years seem to indicate that the elasticity is often not very large.

We cannot at this point enter into a thorough discussion of these empirical investigations. Only a few general considerations will be discussed which establish a strong presumption that Marshall was right and which at the same time show why the statistical findings referred to above, are probably unreliable or even outright spurious.

The first very important point is the following. It must be kept in mind that the import-demand curves and export-supply curves in Figure 7.2 are not what may be called "pure" or "primitive" demand and supply curves. In all cases where an export commodity is also consumed in the exporting country and an import commodity also produced in the importing country, the export supply as well as the import demand curve is derived from pure or primitive domestic demand and supply curves.

In Figure 7.4 , we draw ordinary demand and supply curves, D and S, for a single commodity in a particular country. In order to derive the import-demand and export-supply curves, we simply have to plot against each price the difference between home demand and home supply. The abscissa of each point on the import-demand curve, ID, is the excess of home demand over home supply. Import demand thus depends not only on domestic demand but also on domestic supply. Similarly, the abscissa of each point on the export supply curve, ES, is the excess of home supply over home demand.

It is clear from the diagram that whenever there is domestic production competing with imports, and domestic consumption competing with exports, the elasticity of import demand and export supply is much greater than the elasticity of "pure" home demand and supply.[23] The reason is that a lower price of imports stimulates imports not only by increasing consumption but also by checking domestic production. And a higher exprot price stimulates exports not only by expanding production, but also by reducing home consumption.

The fact that even on the import demand side supply changes are involved, makes the time factor so very important. Supply is likely to be comparatively inelastic in the short run, and to become much more elastic in the longer run.[24] Hence import demand and export supply curves are the more elastic the longer the reaction time which is allowed. This time factor makes statistical measurement of demand reactions very difficult and may be largely responsible for the discrepancy between statistical results and theoretical expectations.

Another closely related fact is that the list of actual import and export commodities cannot be treated as given once for all. At least in the somewhat longer run it is not a datum but a variable . The dividing line between import, export and domestic goods varies not only because of economically unexplained ("autonomous") changes in the basic data such as technology of production and transportation, consumers' tastes, etc., but also in response to price changes as an integral part of the adjustment mechanism. If foreign prices rise because of an appreciation of the currency, commodities which have not been exported so far, will enter the export list and commodities which were imported will drop out of the import list. The existence of non-traded, domestic goods which are, however, potential export and import commodities is due to the existence of transportation cost including import and export duties. Especially if all goods were traded, in a world of zero transportation cost, the shift of commodities from the export to the import side and *vice versa* would be an important factor which increases the elasticity of the balance of payments.[25] This is again a type of adjustment which takes time and is likely to cause great trouble to the statistician who wishes to measure the elasticity of international demand.

From what has been said, it follows that the danger of international demand being not sufficiently elastic is greatest in the case of highly specialized countries which have a near-monopoly in their principle export goods and are unable to substitute easily and to a large extent home produced goods for imports. Agricultural countries, especially in the tropical zone, are most likely to be in that category. Brazil is probably as good an example as any. Coffee constitutes a large percentage of its own exports and of world exports. Consumer demand for coffee is probably fairly inelastic and there is no domestic production in the consuming countries to increase the elasticity of foreign demand for Brazilian coffee. The industrial countries in their mutual dealings are in a different position, because their economies are much more diversified, most of them having also a highly developed agriculture. A. Marshall, in a famous passage, emphasized this point. "It is practically certain that the demand for each of Ricardo's two countries for the goods in general of the other would have considerable elasticity *under modern industrial conditions* even if E and G were single countries whose sole trade was with one another. And if we take E to be a large and rich commercial country, while G stands for all foreign countries, this certainly becomes absolute." [26]

7. Exports and Imports Unequal

We have seen earlier that in case exports and imports and hence demand and supply of foreign currency resulting form those exports and imports are not equal, the condition for the balance of payments to react "normally" (rather than perversely) to changes in the exchange rate must be modified. By normal reaction we mean (as before) that an appreciation of the foreign currency should improve the balance and a depreciation weaken it.

We must now carefully distinguish between the balance in terms of domestic and in terms of foreign currency. For it is clearly possible that depreciation of a currency may improve the country's balance in terms of the foreign money but make it worse in terms of the domestic currency. Suppose a country has an import surplus; in terms of foreign money, this surplus decreases by, say, 4 per cent upon a depreciation of the currency of 10 per cent. In domestic currency the new surplus will be larger than before.[27]

The way in which our stability condition has to be modified will be easily understood, if we formulate it in terms of the slopes of demand and supply curve. We have seen that the supply curve must be steeper than the demand curve. From Figure 7.5, it appears that this formulation can be applied, without change, to the case where exports and imports are unequal.

At the price P exports (supply of $) is PX and exceeds imports (demand for $) which is PM. The supply curve is steeper, therfore the export surplus increases, if the price of $ increases—the criterion of a "normal" reaction.

In terms of elasticities, however, the formula must be modified. For if demand and

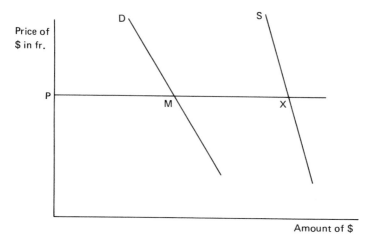

Figure 7.5
Modification of the stability condition under unequal exports and imports.

supply are not equal, the condition that the slope of the D curve be greater than the slope of the S curve, is no longer equivalent to the condition that $\eta_\$ > \varepsilon_\$$. But slopes can be easily expressed in terms of elasticities. Let D' be the slope of the demand curve and S' the slope of the supply curve. Then $D' = \eta_\$(M/P)$ and $S' = \varepsilon_\$(X/P)$.[28] Our condition $D' > S'$ becomes $\eta_\$ M > \varepsilon_\$ X$. Or if we translate the supply of $ into a demand for fr., we have $\eta_\$(M/X) + \eta_{fr} > 1$. If $X = M$, this expression reduces to Lerner's original formula.

Similarly, it can be shown that the condition for a depreciation to improve the balance in terms of the domestic currency is $\eta_\$ + \eta_{fr}(X/M) > 1$. Instead of elaborating further on the mathematics[29], let us discuss a few economic implications of these rules.

Consider the condition for the balance to improve in terms of the foreign currency. This condition is relevant for the typical balance-of-payments problem, the problem of the "dollar shortage". As Mr. Hirschmann points out,[30] it appears from the formula that the more serious the disease, i.e., the larger the unbalance as measured by an excess of imports over exports, the better the chances that a depreciation will imporve the balance. This follows from the fact that the larger M compared with X, the greater the weight attached to $\eta_\$$.[31]

One more word should perhaps be said of how to interpret "exports" and "imports". Clearly those terms must include services proper such as transportation, tourist expenditures, commissions and the like. For these items are affected by changes in the exchange rate in much the same way as exports and imports of goods.[32] Their elasticity with respect to changes in the exchange rate may be different from the elasticity of commodity exports and imports. But these individual elasticities are simply elements of the aggregate contributing to the average elasticity like that of any other individual export or import. Interest payments and receipts have to be included and, as we pointed out earlier, their elasticity with respect to changes in the exchange rate is easy to evaluate.

8. Shifts in Domestic Demand and Supply

As emphasized earlier, it has been assumed in this paper that in each country import-demand and export-supply curves in terms of the country's own currency remain unchanged. It is unlikely that this assumption will be entirely correct. As a rule, a change in the exchange rate will cause shifts in the domestic demand and supply curves, and we may distinguish two types of shifts. First there may be specific connections between individual export and import goods and their prices. For example, exports frequently contain imported raw materials or imports contain exported raw materials. This factor we can, however, eliminate by assuming that the demand and supply curves with which we operate relate to the domestic component of exports. In other words, we define exports of each commodity as *net* exports, i.e., net of the import content of those exports.[33] Another possibility is that particular imports and exports are competitive or complementary in consumption. This possibility can, however, probably be ignored when dealing with imports and exports in general.

The second reason why domestic demand and supply curves may shift in consequence of a depreciation is much more important and is monetary in nature. A depreciation of the currency is likely to result in an increase in total expenditures, in MV, implying a shift to the right of demand and supply curves; in other words, it is likely to have an inflationary or expansionary effect.

This is an important and rather complex matter which can be only lightly touched upon in the present paper, although it would deserve careful consideration.

We leave out of account at this point possible inflationary effects of a depreciation through the creation of the expectation that it is the first step in an inflationary process. Apart from that, there are two avenues through which the inflationary force of a depreciation will make itself felt: First there is the more or less automatic operation of balance-of-payments mechanism, of the "foreign trade multiplier". If the depreciation improves the balance of payments on current account, this in itself implies an increased flow in national expenditure and national income and a shift to the right of domestic demand and supply curves. If all this happens in a state of general depression and unemployment, approximately constant cost will prevail, that is supply curves will be nearly horizontal and only demand curves will shift; in that case not only money national income but also real national income and employment will rise. If it happens in a state of fairly full employment, supply and demand curves will be shifted to the right, prices and money incomes will rise, but real income and employment will be not or only little affected. Suffice it to say at this point, whether this multiplier effect comes into operation or not depends on whether the current balance is improved by the depreciation, which in turn depends, in the manner stated above, on the elasticities of demand and supply of exports and imports.

Second, this automatic expansion effect can be easily reinforced by monetary and wage policy, although it could (and on many occasions ought to) be counteracted by conscious policy.

If international demand is highly elastic and the balance of payments improves, it may be tempting to pursue a more liberal credit policy. Currency depreciation is often a means of creating a margin for more liberal credit or spending policies.

Similarly, wage policies are an extremely important factor. Suppose imports consist largely of wage goods and wage earners press through their unions immediately for higher wages when the cost of living goes up. In this case, even under conditions of depression and unemployment, will depreciation be quickly followed by price inflation.[34] But especially in a state of full or overfull employment, when the margin created by depreciations is quickly utilized, and favorable effect of a depreciation on the balance of payments may be nullified by a shift to the right of the demand for foreign currency.[35] Suppose any rise in the price of foreign currency is followed and compensated, or overcompensated, by additional inflation the impression can be easily created, that the exchange market is in neutral or even unstable equilibrium, that the sums of the two elasticities is unity or less than unity. This shows that in practice it is not easy to distinguish between movement along the curves and shifts of the curves.

To repeat what was said earlier, shifts of the monetary demand and supply curves of exports and imports resulting from income effects (multiplier effects) or from other types of repercussion are an integral part of the balance of payments mechanism. In the present paper we must adhere to the assumption that aggregate domestic demand remains unchanged.[36] It should be also observed that this is an appropriate assumption in connection with the following question of policy: Would a currency depreciation be an effective measure for improving the balance of payments? Nobody can deny that any improvement would be undone by a sufficient dose of inflation. But would there be an improvement provided inflation is avoided? This is not only a legitimate but the most relevant question in that connection.

Another limitation which the foregoing analysis shares with all that has been written on the subject must be mentioned: Competitive conditions have been assumed throughout. In the currency market that is not a serious restriction. This statement may sound paradoxical in view of the fact that there is tight exchange control in the majority of countries. In reality there is, however, nothing paradoxical about the statement for the reason that our theory is concerned with what would happen if there was no public control of the exchange market. There can be no doubt that exchange markets would be highly competitive, even if the markets of individual export or import commodities are not.[37]

It, however, often happens that the market of individual export or import goods in a country is not strictly competitive. As a consequence, the construction of a demand curve for imports in general and of a supply curve of exports in general becomes a more complicated matter. This problem, which to my knowledge has never been treated in the literature, cannot be discussed at this point. But I venture the guess that no farreaching modification of the theory would be required.

9. Summary

In this paper we were studying how the supply and demand for exports and imports determine supply and demand in the foreign exchange market. In particular, we wanted to discover the conditions under which a change in the exchange rate would have its "normal" effect on the balance of payments. In other words, we were interested in the conditions of stability in the exchange market or, in still more technical language, in the condition under which the balance of payments has its "normal" (i.e., positive) elasticity with respect to changes in the exchange rate.

By normal reaction we mean that a depreciation of a country's currency should improve the balance of payments and an appreciation should affect it adversely. If the opposite happens, we speak of abnormal or perverse behavior or of negative elasticity of the balance.

Starting with the market for foreign currency the condition for stability or normal behavior is that the supply curve of foreign currency is positively inclined, or if it is negatively inclined, that it be less steep than the demand curve. The condition can also be expressed in terms of elasticities, although it is really simpler in terms of slopes.

Since the supply curve of foreign currency can be translated into a demand curve of the home currency, the condition can be expressed in terms of elasticities of demand for foreign and for the home currency. Thus we get the well-known rule that the sum of these two demand elasticities must be greater than unity.

The demand and supply curves of foreign currency must be carefully distinguished from demand and supply curves of exports and imports.

Demand and supply curves of imports determine the demand curve for foreign currency. Demand and supply curves of exports determine the demand curve of home currency, or put differently, the supply of foreign currency. Hence the condition of normal reaction of the balance of payments with respect to changes in the exchange rate can be stated in terms of the elasticities of demand and supply of imports and exports.

This result must, however, be qualified in one important respect. It is true only, if the list of exports and imports remains unchanged. If that list changes, we have an additional factor. Concretely, if an appreciation of the foreign currency induces the exportation of goods that had not been exported so far, and eliminates goods from the import list, the demand curve for foreign currency will be turned counter-clockwise (its elasticity will increase numerically) and the supply curve will be turned clockwise (its elasticity will increase algebraically).[38] Thus the elasticity of the balance of payments with respect to rate changes will increase.

Demand and supply curves of exports and imports must not be mixed up with the underlying domestic demand and supply curves for the commodities involved. For example, the import demand curve, even for a consumer good is not a "pure", consumer demand curve, but is the excess of home demand over home supply. It is clear that whenever an imported commodity is also produced at home and an exported commodity also consumed at home, the import demand and import supply will be much more elastic than home demand and home supply, respectively.

Furthermore, it must be remembered that demand and supply of imports and exports are aggregated from demand and supply of individual import and export commodities.

We have, thus, a hierarchy of demand and supply curves, in three or four layers. First, there are what we call the "pure" or "primitive" demand and supply schedules for each commodity in each country. From these schedules export supply curves and import demand curves for each commodity are derived. Those curves are aggregated into composite demand and supply curves for exports and imports. From these aggregate curves, we derive then the demand and supply curve of foreign currency in terms of home currency (or the other way round). These various types of curves have to be carefully distinguished, if confusion is to be avoided. All these curves are in terms of money, domestic or foreign, and must not be confused with the Marshallian "reciprocal demand and supply curves" which represent a relationship of exports and imports in real terms drawn up under rigid equilibrium assumptions.

The limitations of the theory here presented must be kept in mind. It is not intended to give a complete picture of the international balance-of-payments mechanism. It is only the first step towards such a theory. In a complete theory induced shifts of the monetary curves here assumed to be fixed (in home currency) would play an integral part.

Notes

1. I wish to thank Mr. Hyman Minsky for valuable help in connection with the derivation of the formulae on pages 161–163.

2. See especially F. Machlup, "The Theory of Foreign Exchanges," Parts I and II, *Economica*, 1939 and 1940, now conveniently reprinted in *Readings in the Theory of International Trade*, ed. by H. S. Ellis and L. Metzler (Blakiston, Philadelphia, 1949). Page references are to the original.

3. See, e.g., F. Graham, "Self-Limiting and Self-Inflamatory Movements in Exchange Rates in Germany", *Quarterly Journal of Economics*, Vol. 45, p.221. Dynamic instability due to speculation and destruction of confidence in the currency or through the setting up of inflationary or deflationary spirals is probably more important than the static type of instability in which we are interested here.

4. The fullest (though by no means exhaustive) treatment in the literature can be found in Joan Robinson's essay, "The Foreign Exchanges," in *Essays in the Theory of Employment*, 2nd revised ed., Oxford, 1947, pp. 134–155, reprinted in *Readings in the Theory of International Trade*, 1949. See also Machlup, *op. cit.* Mrs. Robinson's analysis couched in words while Prof. W. A. Jöhr has, for the first time so far as I know, developed the diagramatic apparatus. See his article "Soll der Schweizer Frenken aufgewertet werden?" in *Überbeschäftigung und Frankenparität*, St. Gallen 1947.

5. A few exceptions would not be fatal so long as the average has its normal shape. For further justification of this assumption, see Section 6.

6. See Section 7. It depends on the problem on hand whether one is interested in value of exports and imports in terms of the domestic or of the foreign currency. The usual balance-of-payments problem is the task of eliminating a deficit of gold or dollars. Hence what matters is the value of exports and imports in terms of the foreign money. On the other hand, if we are interested during a depression in the stimulating effect of a depreciation on the domestic economy, export and import values in home currency are relevant. For example, Mrs. Robinson's discussion, *op. cit.*, is conducted entirely in terms of home currency, because she is interested in the domestic employment situation.

7. Remember that an inelastic (vertical) curve cannot shift downward or, expressed differently, that it shifts into itself.

8. The following consideration leads to that result: Suppose the S curve were more elastic than the one drawn in the diagram. Then it would cut the D' curve above and to the left of the point shown. If the elasticity of the D curve is greater than unity, the area under the more elastic S curve is smaller than the area under the less elastic S curve.

9. Using the usual notation of η for demand elasticities and ε for supply elasticities and denoting by subscripts x and m that the elasticities relate to demand or supply of exports and imports, respectively, and by the subscripts $ and fr. that the elasticities relate to demand and supply of dollars and francs, respectively, the precise relationship is as follows:

$$\eta_\$ = \eta_m \frac{\varepsilon_m + 1}{\eta_m + \varepsilon_m} = \frac{\varepsilon_m + 1}{\dfrac{\varepsilon_m}{\eta_m} + 1}$$

(In this formula η is taken as a positive number, as it is usually done.) From this formula the rules formulated in the text can be easily derived. It also follows that if $\varepsilon_m = \infty$, $\eta_\$ = \eta_m$. This is seen from the fact that $(\varepsilon_m + 1)/(\varepsilon_m + \eta_m)$ tends to unity as ε_m approaches infinity. (This formula is similar to that of Mrs. Robinson, *op. cit.*, p. 192. She derives it, however, for domestic currency only and her notation is a little different: She writes ε for demand, and η for supply elasticities and she uses subscripts f and h denoting whether demand or supply is foreign or domestic. Thus our η_m corresponds to her ε_h, our ε_m to her η_f, and so on.)

10. In the notation of the preceding footnote the relationship is as follows:

$$\varepsilon_\$ = \varepsilon_x \frac{\eta_x - 1}{\eta_x + \varepsilon_x} = \frac{\eta_x - 1}{\dfrac{\eta_x}{\varepsilon_x} + 1}$$

from which the rules in the text easily follow.

11. The formulae are as follows:

$$\varepsilon_{fr} = \varepsilon_m \frac{1 - \eta_m}{\eta_m + \varepsilon_m}$$

$$\eta_{fr} = \eta_x \frac{\varepsilon_x + 1}{\varepsilon_x + \eta_x}$$

From the second formula it follows that if $\varepsilon_x = \infty$, $\eta_{fr} = \eta_x$ (because the fraction becomes unity when ε_x approaches infinity). Since demand for francs constitutes supply of dollars and supply of francs constitutes demand for dollars, the corresponding elasticities are related. Concretely, as shown in the following section,

$\eta_{fr} + \varepsilon_\$ = 1$ and $\varepsilon_{fr} + \eta_\$ = 1$

This can be easily verified by inserting for $\eta_\$$ etc. the expression stated above. It should be emphasized that these are relationships by definition. The demand curve for francs in terms of dollars presents the same material as the supply curve of dollars in terms of francs, only differently arranged. On the other hand, demand for francs and supply of francs or, differently expressed, demand for dollars and demand for francs are independent of one another, although there may exist indirect causal relations between them in the sense that a change of one may influence the other.

12. A. P. Lerner, *The Economics of Control*, 1944, p. 348; A Marshall, *Money, Credit and Commerce*, p. 354; Joan Robinson, *Essays in the Theory of Employment*, 2nd ed., 1947, pp. 142–3 (first ed., 1936). See also A. C. Brown, "Trade Balance and Exchange Stability," *Oxford Economic Papers*, No. VI, 1942, pp. 57–75 (who also derived the formulae in the footnotes above), and J. J. Polak, "Exchange Depreciation and International Monetary Stability", R.E.S., Vol. 29, Aug. 1947, p. 178.

13. Lerner, *op. cit.*, p. 378.

14. That was correctly pointed out by Mrs. Robinson, *loc. cit.*

15. Albert O. Hirschmann, "Devaluation and the Trade Balance," *Review of Economics and Statistics*, February, 1949.

16. For that reason, the "condition" in terms of demand for currencies is less informative and more truistic than in terms of demand for import and export goods.

17. Professor Machlup (*op. cit.*, p. 367) says that every undergraduate ought to know how that is to be done. But experience shows that he is too optimistic in making that assumption.

18. Since we follow the usual procedure of taking η as positive (although the slope of the demand curve is conventionally called negative), we have to use the same convention for the supply elasticity. It follows that ε is positive when the supply curve is negatively inclined and negative when it is positively inclined.

19. For a demonstration, see Pigou, "Demand and Supply Equations" in A. C. Pigou and D. H. Robertson, *Economic Essays and Addresses*, London, 1931, p. 88, and J. Viner, *Studies in the Theory of International Trade*, pp. 539–540.

20. The formula was written in this form by Metzler, in "The Theory of International Trade," in *A Survey of Contemporary Economics* (1948), p. 226, but was first derived in slightly different form by Mrs. Robinson, *loc. cit.* It is derived from the formula in Footnote 2 on p. 12, as follows: Stable equilibrium requires

$$\eta_{fr} > \varepsilon_{fr}, \text{ that is: } \eta_x \frac{\varepsilon_x + 1}{\varepsilon_x + \eta_x} > \varepsilon_m \frac{\eta_m - 1}{\eta_m + \varepsilon_m} \text{ or } \eta_x \frac{\varepsilon_x + 1}{\varepsilon_x + \eta_x} - \varepsilon_m \frac{\eta_m - 1}{\eta_m + \varepsilon_m} > 0$$

After multiplication and rearrangement this expression reduces to the one in the text. The same result is obtained by using the condition $\eta_\$ > \varepsilon_\$$.

It should be observed that η_x, η_m, ε_x, and ε_m are all taken positive.

21. See Metzler, *loc. cit.*, p. 227. Thus the Lerner condition (if related to the demand for exports and imports rather than to the demand for currencies) is a sufficient but not a necessary condition. It also follows that the situation will be stable if either η_{fr} or $\eta_\$$ is greater than one. All these rules can be easily deduced from Figure 7.2.

22. *Op. cit.*, pp. 353–4. This quotation is appropriate in this connection, although Marshall's famous "reciprocal" demand-and-supply curves are in real terms and must not be confused with our curves which are in terms of money. See p. 155.

23. Only in the exceptional case that the home supply curve has a positive slope, is it possible (although by no means necessary) that the import demand curve is more elastic than home demand. But it should be observed that even if the elasticity of home supply is zero (the supply curve being a vertical straight line) the elasticity of import demand would be greater than the elasticity of home ("pure") demand. This can be seen from the fact that in this case the import demand curve is parallel to the home demand curve, but is situated to the left of it; it has the same slope but a greater elasticity than the home demand curve. See Yntema's *A Mathematical Reformulation of the General Theory of International Trade*, pp. 43–45, for a precise statement of the relation of the various elasticities.

24. Consumer demand may be also slow in reacting to price changes. But on the supply side such lags are certainly much more important, because technological changes are involved which necessarily take time.

25. F. D. Graham has stressed this factor in his article, "The Theory of International Values", *Quarterly Journal of Economics*, Aug. 1932, Vol. 46, pp. 581–616 *passim*. Strange to say, however, Graham uses this fact as an argument for the rejection of the Marshall-Edgeworth "reciprocal demand" curves. But Marshall and Edgeworth were aware of this factor and did make allowance for changes in the composition of exports and imports in the construction of their curves. Marshall's appendix H to his *Money, Credit and Commerce* makes that quite clear.

26. *Money, Credit and Commerce*, p. 176. Italics in the original.

The demand and supply curves we have been using in this paper must, however, not be confused with the Marshallian so-called "reciprocal demand and supply curves". The difference is this: Our curves relate the quantities of imports and exports to prices *in terms of money* whilst Marshall's curves relate quantities ("representative bales") of exports to quantities of imports. Marshall's curves are, therefore, in the nature of total revenue curves, whilst ours are average revenue curves. More important is, however, the following difference: Marshall's curves are drawn under strict equilibrium assumptions. They picture the final outcome of the whole process of adjustment. The curves used in the present paper, in contrast, stay at the beginning of the equilibrium process. Since each point on a Marshallian curve pictures a potential equilibrium position of equality of exports and imports, the Marshallian apparatus is entirely unsuited for the purpose of investigating changing positions of disequilibrium.

27. This cannot happen in case of an export surplus. For if the export surplus increases in terms of the foreign currency upon a depreciation, it must increase even more in domestic money. What may happen in that case is that the balance deteriorates in terms of the foreign money and improves in terms of domestic money.

28. X = exports, M = imports, both in $.

29. For a more elegant derivation of these rules, see Albert Hirschmann, "Devaluation and the Trade Balance," *Review of Economics and Statistics*, February 1949.

30. *Loc. cit.*

31. The medal has, however, another side. The larger the import surplus, the more vulnerable is the country to changes in the terms of trade or even to an equal rise in price of exports and imports.

32. Some of these items, such as commissions, banking services, and interest on certain types of short-term credit the volume of which varies with the volume of goods shipped, are likely to be closely correlated with the value of exports and imports.

33. The statistician who tries to measure the probable effect of, say, a depreciation of the currency or exports and imports will have to pay close attention to this matter. The import content of exports has been estimated for various countries. On the whole it is quite small, even for a country like Great Britain which imports a large part of its industrial raw materials.

34. It may be useful to consider an extreme case: Suppose that not only workers but all classes of a society are able to increase their money income immediately so as to offset any reduction in their living standard due to higher import prices. That would be tantamount to a refusal of society as a whole to permit an improvement in the balance on payments for any such improvement implies that fewer goods are available for domestic use.

35. The situation is essentially different (a) under full employment and (b) in a depression with much unemployment. In the latter case, an improvement in the balance of payments does not imply that fewer goods are available for domestic use. The reason is that an improvement in the balance of payments will stimulate employment (multiplier effect). Hence more goods are available for exports *and* domestic use. Under full employment an improvement in the foreign balance implies a decrease of domestic supplies. Even if a depreciation does not improve the balance, it will reduce the supply of goods at home because physical exports will increase and physical imports decrease.

It would be tempting to say that (under full employment) real national income is reduced by a depreciation irrespective of whether it improves the foreign balance or not. But I hesitate to use that expression, for the reason that "real national income" is not co-extensive with "volume of goods available for domestic use". Suppose, for example, that imports of a country rise (or exports fall) and the deficit in the balance is financed by foreign loans or sales of foreign assets. In that case (net) real income is not increased, although more goods are available for domestic use (consumption or investment). This is largely but not entirely a terminological matter. For the empirical question arises whether income effects on exports and imports attach to the one or the other magnitude.

36. It would not be appropriate to define our monetary curves so as to make allowances for some of these reactions. Professor Samuelson distinguishes "between (1) the elasticity of real exports and imports with respect to a real change in the terms of trade and (2) the elasticity of the trade balance with respect to exchange variations" ("Disparity in Post-War Exchange Rates," in *Foreign Economic Policy for the United States*, ed. S. E. Harris, 1948, p. 404). This is an important distinction, but it is insufficient, because it is not specified what kind of reactions are allowed for under (2). "Elasticity of the trade balance", as Samuelson uses the term, is not an unambiguous concept unless specific assumptions with respect to monetary conditions and policies are made.

37. Occasional exceptions may arise in cases where a large percentage of exports (or more rarely of imports) consists of a single commodity the supply of (or demand for) which is monopolistically controlled.

38. That is to say, if it is negative, it will become smaller negative or positive; if it was positive, it will become greater positive.

8

Currency Depreciation and the Terms of Trade

1

It is very often uncritically taken for granted that devaluation of a country's currency will necessarily result in a deterioration of its terms of trade, that is, in a rise of the average price of its imports in relation to the average price of its exports. It is often further assumed that this will especially be the case, if the devaluation brings about an improvement in the balance of payments, in other words, an increase in the country's export surplus or decrease of an existing import surplus, while the opposite may happen (i.e., the terms of trade may improve), if the elasticities of international demand and supply are such that the devaluation leads to a deterioration in the balance of payments.

The present writer must confess that he himself has on some occasion carelessly said or implied so much.[1] But others, notably the late Frank D. *Graham*[2] and Joan *Robinson*,[3] have correctly pointed out that this is by no means the case, that in fact the terms of trade may just as well improve as deteriorate for the devaluing country.[4]

In the present note I am trying to show by means of a simple diagrammatic analysis, that in what we may call the regular case in which the relevant elasticities are such that devaluation improves the balance of payments, the terms of trade may either become better or worse for the depreciating country, while in the exceptional or perverse case in which devaluation results in a deterioration in the balance of payments (of which the necessary but not sufficient condition is that the sum of the elasticities of demand for exports and imports is smaller than unity), the terms of trade must also deteriorate (not improve as one might be inclined to assume offhand).

The question has considerable practical importance, because the fear that an improvement in the balance of payments brought about by means of currency devaluation has to be bought at the price of worsened terms of trade is undoubtedly

Wirtschaftliche Entwiklung und Soziable Ordunung, Festschrift for Professor F. Degenfeld-Schönburg (Vienna, 1952), 149–158. Reprinted with permission of the author.

an important motive for rejecting the liberal method of currency devaluation in favor of protectionist devices for correcting an existing balance of payments disequilibrium.

It is perhaps not superfluous to remind ourselves that under full employment (more precisely constant employment) the elimination of a balance of payments deficit must be burdensome because it necessitates an increase in exports and/or a decrease in imports and thus implies that fewer goods are available for domestic consumption and investment than were available so long as there existed a deficit in the balance of payments covered by gold losses, grants, or loans. In other words, real national expenditure must be smaller.[5] This basic burden is unavoidable even if the terms of trade remain unchanged. That would, of course, be different in case of a depression when there exists a lot of unemployment. Under those conditions, through the familiar multiplier process, increased exports and reduced imports may induce an increase in domestic output and employment. In other words, it is possible under those conditions to eat one's cake and to have it too, or even to have a bigger one, at the same time! Full employment precludes such miracles.

The preoccupation with a possible worsening of the terms of trade in consequence of devaluation sometimes reflects, perhaps, a confusion between this (unavoidable) primary burden of a correction of a balance of payments deficit with a (possible) secondary burden caused by an adverse change in the terms of trade. It will be recognized that this secondary burden is strictly analogous to the so-called "transfer loss" or "transfer problem" in the case of reparations, whilst our primary burden corresponds to the budgetary problem in the case of reparations, i.e., the problem involved by the raising, with the aid of additional taxes and/or reduction of governmental expenditure, of the sums to be transferred as reparations.

It follows that if in the following pages the importance of the terms of trade argument against devaluation is discounted this does not imply a neglect of the fact that devaluation by the very fact that it brings about the desired result, namely, an improvement in the balance of payments, throws a burden on the depreciating country.

There is another disagreeable consequence which is closely connected with what we called the "basic burden," namely, the inflationary effect of devaluation: Import prices as well as export prices will tend to rise not only relatively to other prices but also absolutely in terms of the devalued currency (in terms of the appreciated currency they will tend to fall). But how far the rise in price level will go is a matter of wage policy, monetary policy, and fiscal policy. If inflation becomes serious and threatens to get out of hand, it is entirely due to wrong policies and reflects an unwillingness of society as a whole to accept the primary burden implied by the improvement in the balance of payments: If wages and salaries are on a cost of living basis and are raised as soon as the price level rises; if private investment is maintained and public expenditure not allowed to fall; in other words, if no sector of society is

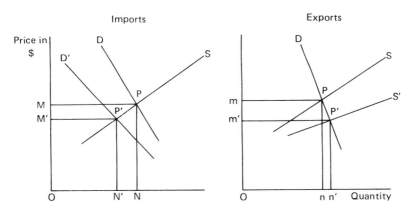

Figure 8.1
Demand and supply curves of exports and imports in terms of appreciated currency — $.

willing to accept a reduction in its real expenditures—under these circumstances depreciation cannot bring about an improvement in the balance of payments and the refusal of society to accept the unavoidable primary burden will find its expression in a seemingly irresistible inflationary pressure. After a while a rise in prices will have caused a fall in exports and rise in imports so that the *status quo ante* of the balance of payments has been restored. The deficit has reappeared or, if the reactions are quick enough, will have never disappeared or diminished. This type of reaction is often mistaken for a case of inelastic demand for exports and imports.

2

I use a diagram (see Figure 8.1) which I developed in an article "The Market for Foreign Exchange and the Stability of the Balance of Payments" in 1949.[6] In a price-quantity diagram, we draw ordinary demand and supply curves for exports and imports of, say, France with prices expressed in terms of dollars. Now suppose the franc is being depreciated. That means the French demand for imports in terms of dollars falls; each point of the demand curve for imports is vertically lowered in proportion of the devaluation, say, by 25%. Therefore, the import price will fall, but in general by less than in proportion to devaluation.
(It would fall by the full amount of the depreciation only in the limiting case where the demand curve is perfectly elastic or the supply curve entirely inelastic.[7])

In terms of francs the import price will, of course, rise, but again less than in proportion to the depreciation (except in extreme cases), i.e., American goods become more expensive to Frenchmen.

Export prices too will fall in terms of dollars, i.e., French goods become cheaper for Americans. In general the fall in export prices will be smaller than the depreciation of the franc, except, if the elasticity of supply is infinite or the elasticity of demand zero, in which case the price of French exports will fall by the full amount of the depreciation.[8] Again, in terms of the depreciated currency export prices will rise, French export goods become more expensive for Frenchmen.

We have, then, the result that export and import prices move in the same direction. Both rise in terms of the depreciated currency and both fall in terms of the appreciated currency. The effect on the terms of trade evidently depends on which falls more.[9] But irrespective of what happens to the terms of trade, the fact that prices of exports and imports (prices of internationally traded goods) fall in the appreciating country and rise in the depreciating country, is a fact of great importance. Suppose both countries follow a policy of keeping their domestic price levels approximately stable. Then in France import and export prices rise as compared with other prices. That should induce consumers to shift consumption away from international trade goods and producers to shift towards the production of international trade goods. The opposite type of inducement operates in the appreciating country. And these are precisely the types of forces which are needed to bring about an adjustment in the balance of payments.

These forces are evidently at work irrespective of what happens to the terms of trade. The terms of trade will improve for the depreciating country, if import prices in dollars fall more than export prices (or, in francs, rise less than export prices). The condition for that to happen is $\eta_m/(\eta_m + \varepsilon_m) > \varepsilon_x/(\varepsilon_x + \eta_x)$ or $\eta_m\eta_x > \varepsilon_m\varepsilon_x$. If the inequality sign is reversed, if the supply elasticities (more precisely: the product of the supply elasticities) is greater than the (product of the) demand elasticities, then the terms of trade change against the depreciating countries.[10]

For extreme cases this result can be easily checked with the help of our diagram. Suppose, for example, that either the export supply curve or the import supply curve is infinitely elastic (horizontal straight line). If import supply is infinitely elastic, import prices will remain unchanged while export prices will fall, and hence the terms of trade will deteriorate. (The only exception is that the export demand curve is infinitely elastic or the export supply curve entirely inelastic, in which case the export price too will remain unchanged and hence the terms of trade will remain unchanged). If the export supply curve is very elastic, the export price will fall by the full amount of the depreciation and, since the import price will fall less (excepting again two limiting cases), the terms of trade will again deteriorate for the depreciating country.[11]

3

Let us now ask the question whether there is any reason to expect that either demand or supply elasticities should be larger.

It is now fairly generally admitted, and the present writer is in full agreement with that view, that there is a strong presumption that for most countries elasticities of international demand and supply are such that a "normal" reaction of the balance of payments to currency depreciation can be expected. In other words, one can be confident that—in the absence of offsetting inflation in the deficit country and deflation in the surplus country—a depreciation of the currencies of deficit countries will reduce the deficit. The condition for that in terms of our elasticities is that $\eta_m \eta_x (1 + \varepsilon_m + \varepsilon_x) + \varepsilon_m \varepsilon_x (\eta_m + \eta_x - 1)$ should be positive.[12] Obviously, a sufficient (though not necessary) condition for this to be the case is that $\eta_m + \eta_x > 1$: If the sum of the two demand elasticities is greater than unity the balance of payments reacts normally and the market for foreign exchange is in stable equilibrium at the appropriate exchange rate.

It is at once clear, however, that from this it does not follow that the terms of trade must move against the depreciating deficit country, for the assumption that the sum of the demand elasticities is greater than unity (the condition for the "normal" reaction of the balance of payments) does not imply that the product of the supply elasticities is greater than the product of the demand elasticities (the condition for an unfavorable change in the terms of trade for the depreciating country). This can be easily checked graphically with the help of our diagram by drawing it with at least one of the two demand curves horizontal. It will be seen that in this case the balance of payments as well as the terms of trade improve for the depreciating country. It is, of course, also easy to imagine situations where the terms of trade deteriorate. This will happen whenever the supply curves are highly elastic and the demand curves moderately elastic (provided their sum is larger than unity).

On the other hand, it can be shown that if demand elasticities are so low that the balance of payments reacts perversely (i.e., deteriorates in consequence of devaluation) the terms of trade must deteriorate. This can be shown as follows with the aid of Figure 8.1. [Editor's Note: A redundant Figure 8.2 is not included.]

The (dollar) value of imports must fall (except in the limiting case in which the elasticity of demand is zero and the value of imports remains unchanged), from OMPN to OM'P'N'. The value of exports may rise or fall depending on whether the demand curve has an elasticity of greater or less than unity. In Figure 8.1, the demand curve for exports is inelastic and the value of exports falls from ompn to om'p'n'. The balance of payments can deteriorate only if $\eta_x < 1$. Moreover, the value of exports must fall by more than the fall of the value of imports, that is to say, only if (ompn − om'p'n') > (OMPN − OM'P'N') or, since ompn = OMPN (because the values of exports and imports are assumed to be equal before devaluation[13]), if om'p'n' < OM'P'N'. Now since after devaluation the quantity of exports is larger while the quantity of imports is smaller than before (on' > ON'), the price of exports must fall more than the price of imports (om' < OM'), i.e., the terms of trade must deteriorate, if the balance of payments deteriorates. Q.E.D.[14]

Summing up, we may say that, from the prevailing (optimistic) presumption that the balance of payments will be improved by devaluation, it cannot be concluded that there is a similar (pessimistic) presumption that the terms of trade will deteriorate. However, those who indulge in balance of payments pessimism will find additional delight in being able to point out that if the balance of payments deteriorates, the terms of trade will also worsen.

Mrs. Robinson (*loc. cit.*) has tried to establish a presumption to the effect that supply elasticities are on the whole larger than demand elasticities and that, hence, the terms of trade are likely to shift against the depreciating country. She bases this presumption on the guess that most countries are highly specialized in their exports (i.e., export a few specialities) while they import a great variety of things from many parts of the world in competition with other countries; in other words, most countries are likely to find themselves in a comparatively strong monopolistic position in their export market, i.e., as sellers, and in a comparatively weak monopsonistic position in their import markets, i.e., as buyers. But, as Mr. Hinshaw (*loc. cit.*, p. 456) has shown, this is a very unsafe generalization. It may fit some raw material producing countries, but hardly the many industrial countries. I doubt very much whether any broad generalization can be made in this matter. In that respect, the question of the terms of trade is very different from the problem of the balance of payments. For in this latter case there is a strong presumption, based on broad theoretical consideration that the balance of payments will react normally, while with respect to how the terms of trade will be influenced no such presumption exists.

How about empirical evidence? What has happened to the terms of trade in past cases of devaluation? Surprisingly little careful work has been done on this question.

It is true the deterioration in their terms of trade which Great Britain and other Western European countries suffered in the last two years has been widely attributed to the devaluation of sterling in September 1949, and it has been strongly recommended that the British pound sterling and other European currencies should be reappreciated in order to improve the terms of trade. These proposals have been convincingly criticized by Mr. Hinshaw (*loc. cit.*), who points out that United States terms of trade have deteriorated since September 1949 almost as much as the British, although the American dollar appreciated in terms of sterling, etc. On the other hand, the Australian terms of trade (as well as those of other raw material exporting countries) have improved, although the Australian currency was depreciated along with the British. This strongly suggests that the change in the terms of trade was due to other forces than the depreciation.

But the purpose of the present note is a theoretical one, and the empirical question of what happened after September 1949 will not be further pursued at this point.[15]

Notes

1. "The Choice of Exchange Rates after the War," *American Economic Review*, 1945.

2. "The Cause and Cure of 'Dollar Shortage'," Princeton, 1949, and "The Theory of International Values," Princeton, 1948.

3. *Essays in the Theory of Employment*, 2nd ed., 1947, p. 163.

4. See also the very interesting discussion by Randall Hinshaw, "Currency Appreciation as an Anti-inflationary Device," *The Quarterly Journal of Economics*, vol. 64, November 1951.

5. It is important, in this connection, to distinguish between real national income, real national product, and real national expenditure. The first two need not fall if a balance of payments deficit is eliminated. If, for example, the deficit was covered by foreign loans, the elimination of the deficit implying a cessation of borrowing abroad, does not imply a decrease in national income, because the increase in the foreign debt (or decrease in foreign assets) constitutes a minus item in the national income account. National income is equal to consumption plus investment minus (net) foreign borrowing, whilst national expenditure is defined as the sum total of consumption and investment including that part which is financed by foreign loans.

6. *Kyklos*, vol. III, 1949, fasc. 3, p. 198. [Chapter 7 in this volume.]

7. If the elasticity of the demand curve is η_m and that of the supply curve ε_m, it can be shown that PP', the drop in import prices, is equal to $[\eta_m/(\eta_m + \varepsilon_m)]k$, where k is the proportional fall in value of the franc in terms of dollars. This expression becomes equal to k when $\eta_m = \infty$ or $\varepsilon_m = 0$. It becomes equal to zero, i.e., the import price does not change, if $\eta_m = 0$ or $\varepsilon_m = \infty$.

8. If the elasticity of demand for exports is η_x and the elasticity of supply ε_x, the fall of export prices pq' is equal to $\dfrac{\varepsilon_x}{\varepsilon_x + \eta_x} \cdot k$. This becomes equal to k if either $\varepsilon_x = \infty$ or $\eta_x = 0$. It becomes zero, i.e., the export price will not change, if $\varepsilon_x = 0$ or $\eta_x = \infty$.

9. I suspect that a sort of optical illusion is frequently the cause of the careless conclusion that the terms of trade must move against the depreciating country. The argument is like this: If France depreciates her currency, French liqueurs and perfumes become cheaper for Americans (in dollars) and American cotton and coal become more expensive for Frenchmen (in terms of francs). This is, of course, true but proves nothing for the terms of trade, because export and import prices must be expressed in terms of the same currency in order to find out how the terms of trade have changed.

10. This formula has been derived in slightly different form by Joan Robinson, *op. cit.*, p. 163.

11. Incidentally, this result does perhaps indicate another reason why it is so often assumed that the terms of trade must change against the depreciating country: The reason is that it is often assumed, either as a simplifying device or because the author thinks of depression conditions, that supply elasticities are large, in other words that approximately constant costs prevail. If that assumption is made, it is indeed true that the terms of trade will shift against the depreciating country.

12. This formula is due to J. Robinson and L. Metzler. For details see my article in *Kyklos* [Chapter 7 in this volume].

13. If exports and imports are unequal, in other words, if a deficit or surplus exists before devaluation, the argument has to be slightly modified. See my *Kyklos* article for details.

14. This result can be easily proved algebraically. The balance of payments will react unfavorably, if $\eta_m\eta_x(1 + \varepsilon_x + \varepsilon_m) + \varepsilon_x\varepsilon_m(\eta_m + \eta_x - 1) < 0$. This can be also written $(\eta_m\eta_x/\varepsilon_m\varepsilon_x)(1 + \varepsilon_x + \varepsilon_m) + (\eta_m + \eta_x - 1) < 0$ or

$$\frac{\eta_m\eta_x}{\varepsilon_m\varepsilon_x} < \frac{1 - \eta_m - \eta_x}{1 + \varepsilon_m + \varepsilon_x}.$$

Now, since all elasticities are taken positive, the numerator of the expression on the left-hand side of the last inequality is smaller than unity, while the denominator is larger than unity. Hence the left-hand fraction is smaller than unity; and *a fortiori* $(\eta_m\eta_x/\varepsilon_m\varepsilon_x) < 1$. Q.E.D.

It also appears that, if the inequality sign is reversed, i.e., if the balance of payments improves, nothing follows for the change in the terms of trade; $\eta_m\eta_x/\varepsilon_m\varepsilon_x$ is then greater than a number which is smaller than unity. It can therefore be greater or smaller than unity. In other words, in the "normal" case, if the balance of payments improves, the terms of trade may either improve or deteriorate.

It may be remarked in passing that the assumptions that all four elasticities are positive is generally made in discussion of these problems. If we remember that the curves here employed are not "pure" demand and supply curves, that the "import demand" is the excess of home demand over home supply and "export supply" the excess of home supply over home demand, it appears quite reasonable to assume "normal" shapes: the demand curves have a negative slope and the supply curves a positive slope.

15. *The Quarterly Journal of Economics*, February 1952, will publish an interesting note by Mr. R. Harrod, which presents the other side of the argument together with a reply by Mr. Hinshaw. R. F. Harrod, "Currency Appreciation as an Anti-inflation Devise: Comment," Vol. LXVI, pp. 102–116; Rendall Hinshaw "Final Comment," *ibid.*, pp. 121–127.

9

A Strategy for U.S. Balance of Payments Policy

with Thomas D. Willett

1. Recent Changes in the U.S. Balance of Payments and the International Position of the Dollar

Introduction

During the last three years, remarkable, and indeed somewhat paradoxical changes have taken place in the U.S. balance of payments and the international position of the dollar. It will be recalled that in 1958–60, after several years of small deficits, the U.S. balance of payments suddenly developed a deficit which was then generally regarded to be of alarming magnitude—$3.4, $3.9, and $3.9 billion in 1958, 1959, and 1960, respectively (measured on the liquidity basis). The Eisenhower administration took drastic anti-inflationary measures which prepared the ground for a remarkable period of stable prices lasting until 1965. During these years of price stability the balance of payments improved greatly. The overall deficit (liquidity definition) fell from $3.9 billion in 1959 to $2.8 in 1964 and $1.3 in 1965. Perhaps even more important, the surplus on goods and services rose from $0.3 billion in 1959 to $8.6 billion in 1964.

The new wave of inflation starting in 1965 led to a progressive deterioration of the balance of payments which again reached alarming proportions in the fourth quarter of 1967—annual rate of $6.9 billion (liquidity definition). Huge speculation in gold, heavy pressure on the dollar, and rapid decline of the U.S. gold stock (from $13.08 billion in the third quarter of 1967 to $10.7 billion in the first quarter, 1968) prompted the Johnson administration to take drastic measures of control and to propose even more extreme steps. These proposals included an unprecedented tax on U.S. tourists abroad and generalized border taxes on imports, a program which, if carried out, would almost certainly have led to full-fledged exchange control. Fortunately, Congress refused to go along with these two measures, but severe restrictions on capital exports were imposed by executive order based on "the

With Thomas D. Willett. *Special Analysis*, no. 1. (Washington, D.C.: American Enterprise Institute, 1971). © 1971, American Enterprise Institute. Reprinted with permission.

authority vested in the President" by Congress as part of the Trading with the Enemy Act of 1917.[1]

Gold speculation continued throughout the first quarter of 1968. Then, in April 1968, the international gold pool through which the central banks of the leading industrial countries (except France which had withdrawn) had been feeding the speculators—with the U.S. contributing the major share—was abolished and the two-tier gold market established. Since then, there has existed an uncontrolled private gold market in which the price of gold is free to fluctuate under the influence of the changing pattern of demand and supply. National and international monetary authorities, on the other hand, have continued to trade gold among themselves at the official par of $35 per ounce.

Later in 1968 the situation unexpectedly improved. Huge amounts of foreign capital flowed into the U.S. For the first time in ten years, the U.S. balance of payments showed a small surplus of $0.2 billion on the liquidity basis and a much greater surplus on the "official reserve transaction" basis.[2] Foreign capital was attracted by high interest rates and the stock market boom. Moreover, the student-worker rebellion in France of May/June 1968, which almost toppled the de Gaulle regime and produced a veritable wage explosion, plus the occupation of Czechoslovakia by Russian troops, scared many investors and enhanced the comparative safety of the dollar. But while the overall balance improved, the traditional trade surplus—which had risen to almost $7 billion in 1964—all but vanished. It was clear that the improvement in the overall balance could not last. For the richest country in the world to be importing capital on a large scale was clearly an unnatural and temporary phenomenon. The expected deterioration in the balance occurred with a vengeance in 1969. In that year the deficit reached a record level of $7 billion (liquidity definition) and for 1970, according to preliminary figures, the deficit still was about $4 billion—although the trade balance substantially improved because, as a consequence of the recession in the U.S., imports into the U.S. rose less than in former years.

It is surprising, indeed paradoxical, that the large deficits of 1969 and 1970 have caused not even a ripple in foreign exchange markets for the dollar and have not disturbed the calm of U.S. policymakers, while a much smaller deficit in 1967 produced a run on the dollar and propelled the administration into frantic activity. There were several exchange crises in 1968 and 1969 affecting, for example, sterling and the French franc, which were devalued, and the German mark, which was revalued. But confidence in the dollar remained unscathed. What is the explanation?

Reasons for the Strength of the Dollar

There are several reasons for the strength of the dollar. Through the termination of the gold pool in 1968 and the surprising success of the two-tier gold market, the U.S.

dollar has been effectively shielded from private gold speculation. Also the establishment of Special Drawing Rights (SDRs), by sharply reducing the chance of a change in the gold price, has greatly discouraged gold speculation. There has been, furthermore, a sharp decline in foreign *official* dollar balances held by foreign central banks as part of their international reserve—a decline from $15.6 billion at the end of 1967 to $10 billion at the end of 1969. When foreign capital flowed into the U.S. in 1968 and the first half of 1969, private individuals obtained the dollars for investment in the U.S. from their central banks whose dollar balances thus were drawn down. This was reflected in the fact that in contrast to the great deficit in the U.S. balance of payments according to the liquidity definition, the balance on the so-called official settlement basis showed a substantial surplus in 1969 ($2.7 billion). The decline in their dollar balances mollified foreign central bankers although they must have realized all along that when the private capital flow to the U.S. receded from the high levels of 1968 and early 1969, as it would have to do, foreign official dollar holdings would go up again.

Indeed, in 1970, the official settlement balance developed a huge deficit ($11.5 billion the first quarter, $7 billion the second quarter) and official liquid dollar holdings abroad reached a record level ($17.8 billion as of September 1970). This change has been noted with uneasiness among foreign central bankers. but it has not produced an atmosphere of crisis as did the large deficits of 1967/68.

Another technical matter might be mentioned at this point. Recent rapid and pronounced changes in the balance of payments, especially the often sharply contrasting movements in the deficit as measured on the so-called "liquidity basis" and "the official reserve transactions basis," have created fresh doubts concerning the proper definition and measure of deficit and surplus. In fact, it is now fairly generally agreed that the formerly widely-accepted liquidity measure of deficit is no longer applicable (if it ever was). We shall not discuss in detail the intricate problem of the proper definition of balance-of-payments surplus and deficit for a country whose currency is used all over the world as an official international reserve medium and as a vehicle for private transactions and investment.[3] At this point it is enough to say that the liquidity definition of deficit has become obsolete and that the official reserve transactions definition, if not quite satisfactory, is certainly a much more significant measure.

Dollar Standard and De Facto Inconvertibility of the Dollar

The factors mentioned so far, important though they are, do not fully explain the surprising strength of the dollar in the face of a large deficit in the balance of payments (on either of the two official definitions). More important, we believe, are changes in the outlook and attitudes of policymakers, both in the U.S. and abroad, which have taken place in recent years. To put it bluntly, it is now fairly generally realized that in a sense the world is on the dollar standard and that the dollar is de facto inconvertible into gold, at least for large sums. That is to say, foreign central banks cannot convert large sums of dollars into gold for the purpose of changing the composition of their reserves, as France did under de Gaulle in the 1960s.

The dollar remains, of course, fully convertible into foreign exchange for private holders at home and abroad, except that the capital export restrictions can be regarded as an infringement of the principle of unlimited convertibility as far as American residents are concerned. But these restrictions do not apply to foreigners. Despite its de facto inconvertibility into gold, the dollar remains fully usable as an international reserve medium and intervention currency. Foreign central banks can use their dollars to finance a deficit vis-à-vis the U.S. They can also use their dollars to buy other currencies, because the dollar is used by most foreign central banks as international reserves along with gold and by practically all central banks as "intervention currency." In other words, foreign central banks discharge their obligation under the International Monetary Fund charter to maintain the par value of their currency (within the allowable margin of 1 percent on each side of parity) by buying and selling dollars in the market in exchange for their own currency rather than by buying and selling gold. The U.S. alone has availed itself of the option offered by the IMF charter (Article IV, Section 4(b)) to maintain the par value of the dollar by buying and selling gold rather than by buying and selling foreign currencies.[4] But this does not alter the de facto inconvertibility of the dollar into gold for large sums. No doubt, "small" amounts of gold are still available, especially for purposes other than to change a nation's reserve composition (à la de Gaulle).

What is "large" and what is "small"? Of course, no precise figure can be given. But if we look at the size of the U.S. gold stock in relation to U.S. liquid "liabilities to foreign official institutions," we find that since 1960 the gold stock has declined from $17.8 billion to $11.5 billion,[5] while liabilities have increased from $11 billion to $16.6 billion. There simply is not enough gold to permit large-scale withdrawals because, once the process is started, it could easily snowball into unmanageable proportions. Large conversion of officially held dollars into gold would, in all probability, provoke massive switches of privately held dollars into official balances. These conclusions are strengthened if we add that total liquid liabilities, to official as well as nonofficial foreign financial institutions, have grown from $21 billion in 1960 to $44 billion in October 1970.[6] Privately held dollar balances are, of course, not directly convertible into gold. But it is known that the figures for private dollar balances contain some official balances and, as recent experience has again shown, there can occur at any moment large switches from private to official holdings.

Alarming conclusions have been drawn from this apparent disproportion between the U.S. gold reserve and liquid liabilities: The gold exchange or dollar exchange standard, as the postwar international monetary system has come to be called, is inherently unstable many claim. The growing discrepancy between the U.S. gold reserve and the superstructure of foreign held dollar balances, it is said, will inevitably undermine confidence in the dollar and lead to a crisis. Economists at opposite ends of the spectrum, Jacques Rueff and Robert Triffin, agree on the instability of the present system. Their prescriptions for remedy are, of course, different. Rueff wants to go back to the gold standard (after doubling or tripling the price of gold); Triffin wants to go forward by making the IMF a real world central bank, a lender of last resort with broad money-creating power.

For some time the international monetary system appeared indeed to be moving in the direction of a crisis as foreseen by the Cassandras on the right and on the left. But since the near crisis late in 1967 and early in 1968, the system evidently has gained in stability.[7]

What is the reason? Paradoxically it has been the growing disproportion between the U.S. gold stock and liquid foreign liabilities that has strengthened the stability of the system by making it increasingly clear that the dollar is de facto inconvertible and that the world has to live with the dollar. Let us quote Dr. Edwin Stopper, president of the Swiss National Bank. In a speech in May 1970 he pointed out that "for the past months things have been astonishingly quiet in the monetary field." He listed a number of facts that contributed to the calm. The first and evidently the most important was "the progressing acceptance of a de facto dollar standard after the replacement of the Gold Pool by the Two-Tier-System and the voluntary restraint exercised by the central banks in respect of conversions into gold."[8] True, Dr. Stopper speaks of "voluntary" restraint and hints that the posture of restraint could be changed at any time, for example, if inflation in the U.S. were not brought under control.

We shall return later to the problem of "balance-of-payments discipline." But the broad fact is that the "voluntary" restraint is really imposed by the logic of the situation. Nobody wants to rock the boat and provoke a serious crisis. Since the number of large dollar holders who could jeopardize the stability of the system is small, the resulting group equilibrium can be quite stable.

In the background is the ultimate, officially unmentioned, but undoubtedly well understood sanction of the equilibrium, namely, the fact that the U.S. could at any time make the dollar formally inconvertible into gold. Such a step would not even require an act of Congress.

A few academic experts have asked that this step be taken forthwith. And some have recommended that the existing gold stock should be offered for sale at the same time, thus turning the back on gold once and for all and probably bringing about its demonetization. Others would keep the gold stock intact for any future emergency.

There would be merit in these recommendations, if the only alternatives were either a painful contraction with a lot of unemployment or the imposition of severe controls on trade and payments. We shall show, however, that these are by no means inescapable alternatives, except perhaps if the U.S. inflation gets much worse than it is. It is therefore not necessary in our opinion to take the extreme step of declaring the dollar officially inconvertible into gold. De facto inconvertibility (for large sums) and the de facto dollar standard is probably sufficient. Realization that inconvertibility could be declared at any time, and that this step probably would be taken if there were large gold conversions, should be enough to ensure "voluntary restraint."

The situation was different at an earlier stage of the evolution of the dollar exchange standard. When the gold stock covered a large proportion of liquid liabilities, it was reasonable for foreign countries to assume that they would be free at any time to change the composition of their international reserve by converting dollars into gold. The growing disproportion between liquid liabilities and the gold stock has made it clear to everyone that large conversions of dollars into gold are no longer possible. The point of no return has been definitely passed.

2. Balance-of-Payments Policies: American Options and Foreign Response

General Principles

We distinguish between (a) policies and measures designed to provide means for the *financing* of deficits and (b) policies and measures for the purpose of *eliminating* deficits and surpluses (disequilibria). The former pertain to the *liquidity* problem, the latter to the *adjustment* problem. To the former group belong, on the national and bilateral level, the holding of uncovered dollars by foreign central banks as international reserves, the swap agreements with foreign central banks, the placing of "Roosa bonds" and bilateral standby credits with foreign central banks and the like. On the international level, there is the creation of SDRs and, earlier, the GAB (General Agreement to Borrow) between the central banks of the group of ten.

It is now generally recognized that the adjustment problem is more fundamental and more intractable than the liquidity problem. The smoother and quicker the adjustment, the less international liquidity is needed. If the mechanism of adjustment were to work very slowly or not at all, the need for liquidity would become unmanageably large.

If the world were formally and irrevocably on the dollar standard, there would be no liquidity problem for the U.S. Any need for liquidity that might arise would be automatically satisfied by the accumulation of dollar balances in foreign central banks, if other countries were prepared routinely to accumulate dollar balances without limit.[9] In that case the U.S. would not have any adjustment problem either, because any deficit would be automatically financed.

Clearly there are limits to the amount of dollars that foreign central banks will be prepared to add to their reserves. The limit has, however, not been reached and is not around the corner. That is why we could say (section 1) that the world is on the dollar standard and the U.S. has no acute or imminent liquidity problem. The U.S. has considerable leeway, but a limit exists somewhere ahead. Therefore, the adjustment of the balance of payments is a matter of great concern also for the U.S.

Balance-of-payments adjustment policies can be classified in three groups: (1) internal monetary and fiscal policies, which are often called "demand management"; (2) exchange rate changes, including par value changes under IMF procedures and the various types of exchange rate flexibility, for example, "wider band" or "crawling peg," that have been proposed in recent years; and (3) the method of "controls." Controls is a portmanteau expression covering a great variety of measures or a system of measures, designed to influence particular segments or individual items in the balance of payments. Controls can be mild or severe; they can apply to capital movements or current transactions; they range from full-fledged exchange control to the imposition of more or less uniform border taxes on imports plus similar tax refunds on exports, a system which comes close to being equivalent to a change in the exchange rate. Other types of controls are tying of foreign aid, "buy American" policies for government procurement, and similar measures.

Balance-of-payments adjustment through internal financial management (expansionist or inflationary, contractive or disinflationary monetary and fiscal policies) and through exchange rate changes in one form or another can be characterized as general types of policies working with and through the price mechanism. These are the methods of adjustment that conform to, and are suitable for, our free enterprise system; they minimize interference in the price and market mechanism. Controls, on the other hand, constitute more or less serious deviations from the market system. Depending on the concrete form and degree of severity, they introduce more or less severe distortions and inefficiencies into the economy and foster the growth of an expensive bureaucracy. They, thus, reduce output and growth and are inimical to the free enterprise system. We therefore take it for granted that controls should be avoided. Their cost, degree of wastefulness, and undesirability vary, of course, greatly from type to type.

American Options

With respect to the first type of balance-of-payments adjustment policies, that is, internal financial management, the task of American policy at the present time is, of course, to curb inflation. We take it for granted and feel strongly that inflation should be brought to an end as soon as possible for purely domestic reasons, namely, to eliminate the distortions and inequities which inflation continuously inflicts on the social economy.

At the present time, clearly there exists *no* basic conflict for domestic macroeconomic policies between the directions to be followed to achieve internal and external policy objectives. Both domestic policy objectives—price stability but also long-run stability of output and growth—and the balance of payments require that inflation be brought to an end as soon as possible. But a conflict between the magnitude of policy restraint necessary to achieve external and internal equilibrium may soon arise. Concretely, a situation may develop where it could be argued that for balance-of-payments reasons the anti-inflation policy should be intensified, although such an intensification would create much more unemployment and slack than can be justified on grounds of domestic policy objectives. Many experts feel that this point has already been reached in the U.S. They argue that it is time to relax the anti-inflationary policy because it creates too much unemployment.[10] And they assume that even with the lowest rate on inflation—say 3 or 3.5 percent a year—that in their opinion could be achieved without creating too much unemployment, the balance of payments would be in large deficit. Professor Paul Samuelson and others seem to take this position when they assert that the dollar is definitely overvalued.

We doubt whether the dollar is really overvalued, at least to any substantial degree, in the sense that the deficit in the balance of payments would be uncomfortably large, even if the rate of inflation were reduced from its present level to a level that would be acceptable from the domestic standpoint. But the recent policy of more rapid re-expansion which seems to be gathering momentum may change the picture in the near future and bring about a dilemma situation in which requirements of internal and external equilibrium conflict.

Be that as it may, we feel strongly that whenever a serious dilemma or conflict between the requirements of external and internal equilibrium arises, domestic policy objectives should take precedence over balance-of-payments considerations. To be specific, in order to stop inflation, it is practically always necessary to accept a temporary rise in unemployment and a temporary slowdown of real growth. What we argue is that for balance-of-payments reasons, the U.S. should not accept more unemployment and more retardation of growth than may be necessary on domestic grounds to bring the price level under control. We are convinced that this rule, if fully thought through and correctly understood, is not only good for the U.S. but is also in the interest of other countries and of the rest of the world. There is, after all, general agreement that a serious depression or recession in the U.S. would not be in the interest of our trading partners, and the structure of the U.S. economy with a relatively low GNP percentage of imports implies that a substantial dose of internal deflation and unemployment might be required to remove even a moderate external imbalance via domestic demand management.[11]

To explain the reasons for these statements, we turn now to the *second* type of balance-of-payments adjustment policies, namely, changes of exchange rates, par value changes under the IMF rules, or some sort of exchange flexibility.

In discussing these policies, we start from the proposition now widely accepted that, because of the special position of the dollar as the world's foremost international reserve currency, the official intervention and private transactions currency and the large absolute size of U.S. exports and imports, it is extremely unlikely that the U.S. could successfully devalue the dollar vis-à-vis other currencies, by unilateral action, even if it wanted to; and, for the same reasons, it cannot unilaterally let the dollar float.[12] If the U.S. changed the par value of the dollar (in terms of gold), practically all countries of the world (with the exception of probably not more than two or three important ones) would also depreciate their currencies (in terms of gold), because only very few countries would be prepared to expose themselves to the intensified competition from American industries that would result from an appreciation of their currencies in terms of the dollar.[13] Thus the exchange value of the dollar (in terms of other currencies, as distinguished from its gold value) would remain substantially unchanged. Similarly, if the U.S. tried to let the dollar float, most other countries, again with very few exceptions, would continue to peg their currencies to the dollar.[14]

The implications of this situation are far-reaching. Whenever there exists a conflict between domestic and external policy objectives, other countries can escape the dilemma by depreciating or appreciating their currency or by letting it float up or down, whatever the situation requires. To the U.S. this option is effectively denied. This is often regarded as a severe handicap for the U.S. which may, it is said, require and justify adoption of measures in the *third* category—controls, capital export restrictions, or even import quotas.

We shall show that, in reality, the special position of the dollar and the impossibility of depreciating the dollar need not constitute any handicap and does not justify the imposition of controls, provided the U.S. does not allow balance-of-payments considerations to deflect it from the pursuit of internal macro-economic policies that are needed for the achievement of domestic policy objectives. Suppose a conflict between external and internal equilibrium arises: that is to say, suppose that restoration of equilibrium in the balance of payments requires a more energetic anti-inflation policy through monetary or fiscal measures than can be justified on domestic grounds in view of the fact that such measures would create an unacceptable volume of unemployment. How should the U.S. deal in that case with the external disequilibrium, the balance-of-payments deficit? The answer to that question is that the U.S. should leave it to the countries whose balances of payments show the surpluses corresponding to its deficit—to the surplus countries—to choose one of several options. And, as we show below, all the options they have, assuming moderately rational behavior on their part, should be acceptable to the United States.

Options of Foreign Surplus Countries

Foreign surplus countries can choose any one, or any combination, of four possible responses: (1) they can finance the American deficit by accumulating more dollars; (2) they can appreciate their currencies (or let them float as Canada did again last May); (3) they can pursue a more expansionary internal monetary policy, thereby eliminating their surpluses and the U.S. deficit; or (4) they can reduce import tariffs or other import restrictions (or export subsidies, if they have them). Let us give an example of option (4): In November 1968, instead of appreciating the DM, Germany reduced border taxes on imports and tax refunds (subsidies) on exports by four percentage points. This constituted an implicit appreciation of the DM. Later, in October 1969, when the DM was explicitly appreciated by 9.4 percent, the border tax and export subsidy were raised again by four percentage points. Thus the effective appreciation of the DM (as of October 1969) was substantially less than 9.4 percent. But compared with October 1968 (before the border tax adjustment of November 1968), the appreciation of the DM was, of course, 9.4 percent.

We assert that each of these four responses on the part of foreign surplus countries should be perfectly acceptable from the American point of view. Clearly a policy of the surplus countries which tends to reduce their surpluses and the American deficit would be very welcome, be it a reduction of trade barriers, an appreciation of the surplus country's currency (although it constitutes a depreciation of the dollar in terms of the other currency), or an internal monetary expansion (inflation) in the surplus country. From the American as well as from the world standpoint, a reduction of trade barriers would be the best response; but for obvious reasons one cannot hope that this approach will be widely adopted.

We argue that the surplus countries' first option, further accumulation of dollar balances, is also acceptable from the American standpoint, provided U.S. domestic monetary and fiscal policies are guided solely by internal policy objectives—in other words provided the U.S. tolerates no more unemployment and slack than may be needed to curb inflation. The opinion is, however, widely held that an increase in U.S. liquid liabilities to foreigners may be dangerous and damaging for two reasons.

The first is that it may endanger the U.S. liquidity position. What would happen if, for any reason, there developed a run on the dollar and dollars were thrown on the market? The answer is simple and has already been given: Private individuals cannot convert dollars into gold. They can only sell them to foreign central banks which are, under present arrangements, residual buyers for dollars. Since the dollar is de facto inconvertible into gold also for central banks, these banks could get rid of their dollars only by pursuing an expansionary monetary policy or by accepting an open or disguised appreciation of their currency. So we come back to the other three options, which clearly are acceptable for the U.S.

The second reason why an indefinite financing of a deficit by accumulation of dollar balances is said to be unacceptable can be formulated as follows: A balance-of-payments deficit implies that U.S. imports are larger and/or U.S. exports smaller than they otherwise would be. Other countries caught in such a squeeze could devalue their currency. The U.S. has to wait until the surplus countries act in any of these ways mentioned. Until they do—or if they do not—the U.S. suffers slack and unemployment. Therefore the U.S. should impose import restrictions or subsidize exports in one form or another.[15]

There would be some validity to this argument, if American domestic monetary and fiscal policy were *not* guided solely by domestic policy objectives—in other words, if the U.S. tolerated more unemployment and slack than might be needed to curb inflation, namely, the unemployment created by the shortfall of exports and increase of imports implied by the deficit. This formulation makes it clear that the argument does not hold, if internal monetary and fiscal policy (management of aggregate demand) is properly geared to domestic policy objectives.

Our analysis will perhaps be criticized on the ground that it is unreasonable to assume that monetary and fiscal policy can be so finely tuned that it irons out every dip in aggregate demand which is in excess of what must be tolerated to satisfy domestic policy objectives.

It is, of course, quite true that there are a hundred reasons—balance-of-payments changes being one of them—why there will often be slips in monetary and fiscal policies resulting in deviations of the actual level of unemployment from the target level, whatever the latter may be. But let us keep a sense of proportion. Those dips in aggregate demand that can be attributed to balance-of-payments changes are, in reality, quite small compared not only with GNP but with the annual changes in GNP, up or down, which occur as a result of the hundred other causes. Surely if there were a "gradual liquidation of American industrial potential" (to quote Professor Gottlieb) monetary and fiscal policy would cope with it.[16]

To summarize the results of our analysis in this section, surplus countries have four options: They can go on accumulating dollar balances, they can pursue an expansionary monetary policy, they can appreciate their currency or let it float, or they can reduce trade barriers. All of these options are acceptable from the American standpoint, including the first. A possible fifth option—namely, controls—is discussed in the next section of this chapter.

Reactions of Foreign Surplus Countries

Spokesmen for foreign surplus countries, both official and private, do not always take kindly to the advice that it is up to them to respond to an American deficit in any of the four ways mentioned. They often resent the suggestion that they should appreciate their currency if they do not want to accumulate more dollars or to inflate or reduce their trade barriers. A pet phrase has been that appreciation of the surplus countries' currencies instead of depreciation of the deficit country's currency (i.e., of the dollar) would be tantamount to imposing a painful cure on the healthy rather than on the sick. Why the cure should be painful is not clear. At any rate, the reaction seems to be based on the picture of a highly inflationary reserve currency country imposing inflation on the rest of the world.

If this were a true picture of the present world monetary scene, if the U.S. had much more inflation than many others and if, as a consequence, the U.S. deficit were very large and were matched by (unwanted) surpluses of a large number of other countries—in such a situation, it would indeed be possible to make a case for demanding that the dollar should be depreciated in one form or another rather than that scores of other currencies be appreciated.

Obviously, however, this is not the situation which we find today. In reality, there is only a very small number of countries that have less inflation than the U.S. and, as a consequence, have a large unwanted dollar accumulation. The great majority of countries spontaneously match or even surpass the U.S. rate of inflation.[17] To put it in other words, if the dollar were devalued (in terms of gold), the vast majority of currencies would follow the dollar and only very few, two or three important currencies in the West (and presumably the Russian ruble), would keep their par value in gold unchanged and would appreciate in terms of the dollar. From the American standpoint, it really does not matter much how the change in exchange rates that may be needed is brought about—whether by depreciation of the dollar in terms of gold or by appreciation in terms of gold of two or three currencies of surplus countries. But given the fact that the dollar is the reserve currency of the world, the foremost private transactions and investment currency, that the dollar is used all over the world (including the Communist countries) as the unit of account in innumerable private and official transactions, contracts, and financial and commodity arrangements—given this fact, from the world standpoint, it would be easier and less disruptive, economically, administratively, and psychologically, to appreciate two or three surplus currencies than to depreciate the dollar along with its vast retinue of other currencies.

There is still another reason why a devaluation of the dollar in terms of gold would be very awkward: It would imply a general rise in the price of gold. A change in the gold price by a few percent would surely give great encouragement to gold speculation, without making any contribution to the solution of the liquidity problem.[18] It will be observed that the reason why the gold value of the dollar should not be changed is that such a change would violate the interests of the world as a whole. No specific or exclusive American interests are involved.

Irrespective of what spokesmen for the surplus countries say and how unhappy they may be or pretend to be, it is difficult to see what else they could do but adopt one, or a combination of some, of the four responses mentioned above—that is, accumulate dollars, appreciate their currency, inflate, or reduce trade barriers. It is sometimes suggested that they have still another, fifth option—namely, to impose controls—and that they are likely to do just that. But if the word "controls" is used in its usual meaning of import restrictions, this reaction would make no sense, because the use of such controls would make a bad situation worse; it would increase still more the foreign countries' surpluses and the U.S. deficit. To be effective the controls would have to be negative, so to speak, restraining exports and stimulating imports. Countries usually do not like that kind of control. At any rate, that kind of control would amount to a messy, inefficient, and wasteful substitute for the appreciation[19] of the surplus countries'currencies and would constitute a violation of the letter and the spirit of the IMF charter.

A type of control that the IMF charter permits is restrictions of capital movements. For example, surplus countries could forbid or restrict U.S. direct investments in their territories. We believe that it would not be in their well-considered interest to restrict American direct investment, at any rate, not on balance-of-payments grounds. But it is obviously up to them to make that decision. It has been suggested that surplus countries could try to separate the market for "current account dollars" from the market for "investment dollars." This policy was pursued for a while by Switzerland in the years immediately following World War II. Dollars for current account purposes were kept at the official parity by pegging operations conducted by the Swiss National Bank. So-called "finance dollars" (resulting from and applicable to capital flows and certain services) were traded in an uncontrolled (or mildly controlled) market at a discount. After the war, when international trade and transactions were at an extremely low level, this system could be tolerated for a while despite its inefficiencies. At present, with the enormous volume of transactions on current and capital account and mass travel in all directions, it would require a formidable bureaucracy to administer such a system—to separate current from capital transactions, to prevent capital transactions from masquerading as current transactions. It would come very close to full-fledged exchange control, would not serve any useful purpose and would at any rate amount to a partial devaluation of the dollar and partial appreciation of the foreign currency in question.[20]

Although the inflation in the U.S. in the last few years has created uneasiness and concern about the future of the dollar among the large foreign dollar holders, confidence in the dollar is substantially unimpaired. Unless inflation goes on unchecked or accelerates, confidence in the dollar will be preserved. But it may be useful to consider briefly what would happen, if a serious confidence crisis and a "run on the dollar" should develop.

First, private dollar holders abroad could get rid of their dollar holdings only by selling dollars directly or indirectly to foreign central banks. Second, in the absence of the possibility of conversion into gold, foreign central banks could reduce their dollar balances[21] only by allowing their currency to appreciate, implying a depreciation of the dollar. This could be brought about either openly, by raising the par value of the foreign currency or by letting it float, or in a disguised form, by introducing "negative controls." None of these alternatives looks attractive from the point of view of foreign dollar holders. But there is no other way out.[22]

Summary of Conclusions

We have argued that American balance-of-payments policy should be "passive." An "active" balance-of-payments policy would use either measures of control (in the broad sense defined earlier) or changes in the exchange value of the dollar. The first of these approaches is inefficient, wasteful, and undesirable; the second is, under present institutional arrangements which make the dollar the world's reserve and intervention currency, unavailable to the U.S. We have pointed out that this policy of "passivity" with respect to the balance of payments is no handicap for U.S. general economic management, provided that American monetary, financial, and other policies are exclusively guided by internal policy objectives (high level of employment, growth, price stability, or whatever they are).

A passive attitude towards the balance of payments can be described as a "policy of benign neglect." It should be observed, however, that neglect of the balance of payments does *not* imply neglect of either the interests of the U.S. or of those of our trading partners. Nor does it imply lack of interest in the organization and functioning of the international monetary system. To be more specific, under present arrangements and policies, the U.S. cannot unilaterally change the exchange value of the dollar or let the dollar float. However, this does not mean that the U.S. is not interested in reforms of the international monetary system that would permit greater flexibility of exchange rates—directly and explicitly for currencies other than the dollar, but indirectly and implicitly for the dollar.

The subject of such reforms of the international monetary system is taken up in the following section.

3. Reform of the International Monetary System

Creation of Special Drawing Rights

For many years, international monetary reform has been a topic of endless academic discussion, numerous official and unofficial conferences, and bursts of lengthy and intense negotiations on the highest level of governments. The major recent development has been the creation and "activation," by common consent of the member countries of the IMF, of a new form of international reserves, the Special Drawing Rights (SDRs). It was an unprecedented achievement of international cooperation— in fact the first peacetime example of an international agreement to change a major feature of the international monetary system. (The Bretton Woods Charter was negotiated during the war.) We do not wish to denigrate the historic importance of that event. Nor would we argue that the creation of SDRs was in itself a harmful act. If nothing else, this action appears to have had. as already mentioned, a very useful side effect in discouraging gold speculation by greatly reducing the speculators' estimate of the probability of an increase in the official gold price.

But the scheme also has its dangers and drawbacks. Our major quarrel with SDRs concerns the opportunity cost of their creation. Years of intensive international investigation and negotiation, employing a lot of the time of scores of highpowered experts and negotiators, went into working towards the solution of the liquidity problem and so diverted attention and scarce (intellectual) resources from the search for a solution of the much more basic and difficult problem of adjustment.

Maybe the sharp and widely accepted distinction between the three problems of confidence, liquidity, and adjustment, while very useful for analyzing the working of the international monetary system, has misled policymakers into thinking that the three problems were of roughly equal importance and could be successfully solved one at a time.

The liquidity problem was chosen first, perhaps largely because the chances of reaching international agreement in that area looked most promising.[23] To be sure, the connection between liquidity and adjustment has not gone unnoticed. In fact, the amended Articles of Agreement of the IMF which contain the provisions for SDRs state the connection explicitly: "The attainment of a better balance of payments equilibrium, as well as the likelihood of a better working of the adjustment mechanism" are mentioned as conditions to be taken "into account" when the first decision is made to allocate SDRs.[24] The first decision to allocate SDRs was taken in 1969. Although things were quiet on the dollar front in that year, it is not easy to understand what evidence justified the required "collective judgment" that the adjustment mechanism was likely to "work better" in the future. Nor do the events since that year give much ground for optimism.

But be that as it may, now we have the activated SDRs. The intellectual resources which went into their creation cannot be retrieved and diverted. Why cry over spilt milk?

Unfortunately there is a danger that some of the opportunity cost of SDRs creation will continue in the future. The management of the SDRs may not become routine for some time and may continue to absorb much expert work. Furthermore, the "link" between SDRs and development assistance which is being pushed energetically by less developed countries, by international organizations and by many influential academic and official spokesmen in the industrial countries is likely to complicate things further. Under the proposed "link" scheme, a fraction of the SDRs which are allocated to the developed countries would be ceded, via some of the international lending institutions (such as the International Development Association), to less developed countries and the industrial countries would have to "buy" them back from those countries in exchange for real resources. If such a plan were adopted, there would be continuous pressure exerted by the less developed countries and the various international institutions which specialize in development assistance to increase the portion of SDRs that is channelled through the "link." Pressure from one side will inevitably induce counter pressure from the other. An inkling of what may be in store was provided by the report[25] that a movement was under way to organize the less developed countries in the International Monetary Fund for the purpose of voting against any reform of the Fund's Articles of Agreement, such as the various proposals to introduce greater flexibility of exchange rates, unless such a reform is coupled with the "link." It should be kept in mind that certain changes in the Articles of Agreement can be effectively blocked by 16 percent of the voting power in the IMF.[26]

The recently published IMF study, *The Role of Exchange Rates in the Adjustment of International Payments*,[27] is evidence that official attention has finally turned in the direction of adjustment—although belatedly and, as far as flexibility of exchange rates is concerned, grudgingly and hesitatingly.

A brief analysis of some implications of the present system, under a regime of rigidly fixed exchange rates, with or without further large SDR allocations, will show how important it is that progress is made soon in introducing some flexibility into the exchange rate structure.

Some Implications for the Present International Monetary System of Fixed Exchange Rates

A very important consequence of the present system of fixed exchanges with the dollar at its center is that the rate of inflation in all countries that peg their currency to the dollar is approximately determined by the rate of inflation in the U.S. Any country that keeps its currency fully convertible into dollars at a fixed exchange rate will, in the medium and long run, be forced to have approximately the same degree of inflation as the U.S., whatever it is—positive, negative, or zero. This proposition is not generally understood and, if expressed bluntly, will be rejected by many. It is nevertheless a fairly obvious consequence of well-known facts, requiring only few qualifications which detract little from its importance.

Let us explain carefully what it means and what it does not mean. Any country is, of course, free to inflate more than the U.S. and many make use of this license. But any country inflating much more than the U.S. will be forced to devalue its currency. There are three qualifications: First, by accumulating and "sterilizing" dollar balances, a country can slightly postpone or slow down the required price adjustment. But, like any policy that goes against the grain of economic equilibrium, it is a costly struggle and likely to be progressively hampered by speculation. The second qualification is a spurious one: Up to a point a country can use controls (import restrictions, export subsidies, et cetera) to avoid depreciation. But, as is well known, such controls are just a devaluation in disguise, and a wasteful and inefficient disguise at that. The greater the price disparity and the resulting disequilibrium, the more stringent the required controls. Experience has shown a hundred times that the wastes and inefficiencies soon become intolerable, so that open devaluation has to be subsituted for the disguise.

The third qualification is that if the degree of inflation is measured by the cost-of-living index (or some other broadly based index, such as the GNP deflator), there need not be perfect parallelism in the movement of these indices in different countries. As mentioned earlier, it sometimes happens that a country's export prices deviate significantly from its general price level, and these deviations may be in opposite direction in different countries. For example, in the U.S., export prices have often risen somewhat faster than the general price level while in Japan the opposite has been the case.[28] This has enabled Japan to have a little more inflation than the U.S. has and still enjoy a balance-of-payments surplus.

It is, however, true that large and persistent deviations in price levels are impossible with fixed exchanges and convertible currencies because, under modern conditions, there are innumerable actual and potential export and import commodities which serve to hold the discrepancies in price levels between countries to moderate proportions in the medium and long run.

Countries that wish to inflate less than the U.S. will develop a balance-of-payments surplus and will see their price levels rise unless they prefer to let their currencies appreciate. Again the three qualifications mentioned above apply, with the difference that the controls serving as a substitute for the appreciation of the currency will have to be negative, i.e., import-stimulating and export-restricting. And as we pointed out earlier, negative controls are not popular.

It will be asked why the price connection should be asymmetrical. We said inflation in the U.S. determines the pace of inflation abroad. Is there no causal force running in the opposite direction?

The answer is that the relationship is indeed asymmetrical. This follows from the special position of the dollar, from the fact that U.S. internal monetary and fiscal policies which determine the rate of inflation in the U.S. have become almost completely independent of the state of the balance of payments, and from the fact that the feedback from the deficit or surplus in the balance of payments to the U.S. economy is negligible because of the small size of U.S. exports and imports relative to the volume of GNP. As explained earlier, if there were an appreciable feedback— for example, if a balance-of-payments deficit becomes a serious drag on the economy—monetary and fiscal policy, geared as it is to domestic policy objectives, would counteract it.

Earlier we recommended that in case of a conflict in the requirements for monetary and fiscal policy between internal and external equilibrium, domestic policy objectives should take precedence over balance-of-payments requirements.In other words the U.S. should pursue a passive balance-of-payments policy, a policy of "benign neglect" of the balance of payments. (Let it be repeated that "neglect" of the balance of payments does in no way imply neglect to U.S. interests or of the interests of our trading partners.) Now we state it as a fact that such a passive policy is actually being pursued. We believe that this is a correct description of the present situation whereas it would not have described the situation ten years ago. Gradually during the 1960s, the grip of the balance of payments on monetary and fiscal policy has been loosened and by now it is practically gone. Concern with the balance of payments is still there but it expresses itself rather in terms of the policy of controls, primarily capital export controls. First controls were introduced and tightened, and now there is reluctance to loosen and abolish them although some clearly have become redundant.

Foreign Reactions

When we speak of foreign reactions we mean largely European reaction and reactions of only a very few countries. To repeat, there are only very few countries in the world that do not match or surpass U.S. inflation spontaneously—Germany, Switzerland, perhaps the Netherlands. France has, of course, been in the forefront of the complainers about the U.S. forcing inflation on others—in between her own frequent devaluations.[29]

What the European critics have been complaining of is that the U.S. is not subject to balance-of-payments discipline. That is, of course, precisely correct. (As mentioned above, it was not quite true earlier.) It is a variation of the same theme when they complain that the U.S. uses its de facto exemption from balance-of-payments constraint, or alternatively the special position of the dollar, to finance direct investments abroad ("take over European companies"), for direct investment flows are a component of the capital account of the balance of payments.

If foreign countries do not like U.S. direct investment, although it serves to close any "technological gap" (that may exist), they can restrict such investment without difficulty. In most countries foreign investment and takeovers are subject to government approval anyway. But the decision on this matter should not be made on balance-of-payments grounds. The U.S. would be well advised to leave this decision to the foreign countries. In fact, however, it has chosen to do much of the unpleasant work for them.

It is time for European as well as American policymakers to face up to the facts. Under fixed exchanges, foreign surplus countries have no choice but to share in the U.S. inflation (or to liberalize trade or impose negative controls unilaterally, both of which amount to a disguised appreciation of the currency). In the very short run they may avoid, or rather postpone, going along with U.S. inflation by accumulating dollars.

What else could they do? In the past they could signal their displeasure by converting dollars into gold. Except for small amounts this is now de facto barred.[30] Some proponents of fixed exchanges fully recognize these implications. Thus Professor Kindleberger has proposed to make them more palatable by placing European or other foreign representatives on the U.S. Federal Reserve Open Market Committee. In other words, he has proposed that U.S. monetary policy should be conducted jointly by all countries that have to share in its consequences. It is not necessary to add that this proposal is not likely to be accepted by U.S. policymakers.

Outlook for the Future

What is the outlook for the future of the dollar exchange standard, still assuming that the system of fixed exchanges is to be maintained? (Highly inflationary countries cannot, of course, maintain fixed exchanges.)

Until recently, inflation in the U.S. has been moderate compared to inflation in other industrial countries, and it surely will remain so by the standards of most less developed countries. If this is the case, the chances are that most surplus countries will grow accustomed to slightly more inflation without much fuss. (The Japanese seem to have made a more or less conscious choice to accept more inflation rather than to appreciate the yen or to sufficiently liberalize trade.) Of course, there will probably always be one or two countries which are really willing and able to have less inflation (or which, through some quirk in international demand, are able to develop a surplus while having more inflation than the U.S.). Such countries will accumulate dollars and will have to make up their minds whether they should or should not let their currency appreciate.

If inflation in the U.S. is less moderate, there will be more dissatisfied surplus countries. There will be complaint and criticism about U.S. policy but the options of the surplus countries—inflation, appreciation (open or disguised), reduction of trade barriers—remain the same. The real danger is that either the surplus countries may adopt negative controls or the U.S. positive controls (tightening of the existing ones). But once the U.S. understands that nobody can force it either to adopt controls or to create more unemployment and slack than it thinks is necessary to achieve the domestic objective of curbing inflation, it will continue its passive balance-of-payments policy and leave it to the others to choose among their options.

But, some will ask, can the dollar not be dethroned from its special position, perhaps by the creation of an attractive substitute in the form of a European or Common Market currency? Would that not be a serious matter for the U.S.? Monetary integration with the declared ultimate goal of a common currency and a unified monetary management (a Federal Reserve System for Europe) has indeed been the subject of intense official investigation and negotiations in the European Economic Community (EEC). According to present plans, it will take ten years to approach the goal. And it may take even longer, especially if Great Britain joins EEC.[31]

Let us assume, however, that a common European currency in a meaningful sense comes into being. Can it replace the dollar as an official international reserve medium or private transactions currency? It will take a long time before we come to that bridge, but let us assume the goal of monetary unification is reached. A unified Europe, by pooling its members' international reserves, could certainly manage with a smaller dollar reserve, and third countries might want to hold part of their reserve in the European currency. But even if this should happen, Europe could not get rid of its dollars without letting the European currency appreciate. For reasons mentioned earlier, the chances are that European countries would think twice before taking that step. But even if they took it, perhaps because the U.S. had too much inflation in which they did not wish to participate, such a step would stimulate U.S. exports, reduce its imports. This would indeed be a burden (transfer of real resources) and would mean an increase in inflationary pressure. Repaying debt is always a burden. Quantitatively the burden would be negligible because the U.S. deficit, even at its worst, is a tiny fraction of GNP.[32]

It is indeed mentioned as one of the advantages and purposes of a common European currency that it then would be easier to depreciate the dollar by appreciating a single European currency. This may be so, but it is also possible or perhaps probable that six governments acting in concert would be even more reluctant to change the status quo than any one of its constituents now is.[33]

But these speculations and worries are largely idle and superfluous, especially from the American standpoint. They divert attention from more pressing dangers. The greatest danger in the area of international monetary relations is that deficit countries, the U.S. as well as others, will resort to controls and will restrict trade, payments, travel, and capital flows, instead of changing their exchange rate. The corresponding danger in the case of surplus countries is less acute, because countries are reluctant to use negative (i.e., import-stimulating and export-discouraging) controls. But appreciation of one's currency is even less popular than depreciation.

It is now almost universally accepted, even by those who are against any general limited or unlimited flexibility of exchange rates, that more frequent use should be made of the possibility under the IMF charter to change exchange rates in case of fundamental disequilibrium. This proposition will be examined more carefully in the following section. Here we only note that it implicitly acknowledges the acute danger of controls. Needless to add that deflation and unemployment would be equally or more destructive. There is, however, this difference: Practically no country would accept *serious* unemployment. The propensity to control is every-where in the world much stronger than the propensity to deflate.

This brings us, finally, to the question of exchange rate flexibility.

U.S. Interest in Exchange Rate Flexibility

It is an implication of our analysis that the U.S. has less direct interest in exchange rate flexibility than other Western countries, because the U.S. cannot, under present arrangements, let the dollar float or change its exchange value, and because in the U.S., foreign trade is a much smaller fraction of GNP than that in any other Western country. The U.S. interest in flexibility is indirect and derives from the fact that greater flexibility is of great importance for our trading partners and for the international monetary system as a whole. U.S. interest in exchange flexibility is indirect and derived but real nonetheless.

This is not the place to review in detail the whole problem of fixed vs. flexible exchange rates in the abstract.[34] The practical problem is not, of course, whether the existing par value system of fixed exchange rates subject to occasional adjustments, as set up by the Bretton Woods Charter, should be replaced by a system of general flexibility under which every currency in the world would fluctuate freely in terms of every other. No such radical change is feasible, nor is it necessary to achieve a better working of the adjustment mechanism. The elements of a much more modest, although in our opinion potentially quite effective, reform may be sketched as follows: Every country that feels aggrieved because the present system, based on the dollar, imposes on it too much inflation or the opposite should be allowed to let its currency float, or to widen its band of permissible deviations of the exchange rate from the par value or to adopt a crawling peg. Persistent deficit countries should be encouraged to pursue a policy of exchange rate flexibility, rather than dissuaded from doing so. The problem of persistent surplus countries is easier to deal with. Probably no more is needed than to make it clear to them what their options are—accumulation of reserves, monetary expansion, appreciation[35] or floating of the currency, or reduction of trade barriers. There can hardly be a doubt that these are, in fact, the only practical choices and that any one of them, or any combination, should be acceptable to the U.S. and other countries.

Some people may ask—are countries not more or less free now to react in any of the ways described? Unfortunately this is not the case. They can inflate or liberalize trade but the sticking point is exchange flexibility.

It is true that as far as highly inflationary less developed countries are concerned, the IMF does not object to exchange rate flexibility. It probably encourages countries such as Brazil or Chile to make frequent changes in exchange rates. In recent years, some of them—Brazil, Chile, and others—have developed a system of flexibility which may be described as the system of "the trotting peg." Under this arrangement, the currency is depreciated at short intervals by small steps. For example, in Brazil the value of the cruzeiro is reduced by something between 1.8 percent to 1.3 percent every four or five weeks. The trotting peg has been a great improvement over the earlier system of the adjustable peg under which these countries waited six months or longer and then devalued with a bang by a large amount.[36]

The reason why the International Monetary Fund has acquiesced in those cases is, no doubt, that under rapid inflation the adjustable peg system, let alone fixed exchanges, soon leads to intolerable consequences.

In the case of the industrial countries where the disadvantages of the present system are not so pronounced, the attitude of the IMF has been much less tolerant. This was clearly revealed in the case of Canada in May 1970 when Canada returned to a floating exchange rate. The move has not hurt anybody and was a great help in Canada's internal management (fight against inflation). Nevertheless, Canada was sternly rebuked for abandoning the adjustable peg and is under constant pressure to restabilize.

The above mentioned IMF report on *The Role of Exchange Rates in the Adjustment of International Payments* evidently reflects the thinking of the fund's executive directors at the present time. The report offers a subtle, closely reasoned and well documented analysis of all aspects of exchange rate changes. It is technically of high caliber, as one would expect from a first-rate staff and a prestigious board of directors. But as policy statement which is supposed to show the way, if not to bold new ventures, then at least to new solutions of old problems which have not responded well to traditional treatment, the report has surprisingly academic flavor.

One tends to agree which the conclusion of a thoughtful and penetrating analysis[37] that the report "is on the whole a disappointing document. It suggests no real breakthrough in the direction of a genuine adjustment mechanism based on greater flexibility of exchange rates." The report is largely a defense of the existing par value system and of the adjustable peg, although it freely admits that damage is often done because countries unduly delay exchange rate adjustments beyond the time when it should be clear that a fundamental disequilibrium exists.

The report rejects outright three proposals for greater flexibility: a system of freely fluctuating exchange rates, a substantial widening of the band for permissible exchange rate fluctuations, and the various suggestions to effect parity changes frequently and automatically according to some objective indicators (the crawling peg proposals). Instead of these, it favors a slight widening of the margin of permissible fluctuations. As George Halm points out, it is somewhat surprising, in view of the rejections of any crawling peg, that the report seriously considers the seemingly more radical suggestion that "the Articles of Agreement might be amended to allow members to make changes in their parities without the concurrence of the Fund as long as such changes did not exceed say, 3 percent in any twelve month period nor a cumulation amount of say, 10 percent in any five-year period."[38]

The main thrust of the report is that the par value system may well work quite satisfactorily if countries could be persuaded to make more frequent and prompt use of the provision of the original charter to change their exchange rate in case of "fundamental disequilibrium." But the report does not give much guidance and help to the governments which are admonished to make "prompt adjustment of parities in appropriate cases." Continuing the earlier practice of the IMF, the report refuses to give a clear-cut definition of what is a fundamental disequilibrium, and substitutes for it a long and involved description of various factors and circumstances that should be taken into consideration when a determination is made whether an existing disequilibrium, presumably a balance-of-payments deficit or surplus,[39] is to be considered fundamental or not.

We submit that the greatest weakness of the report is that it does not sufficiently consider the main drawback of the adjustable peg system—that is, comparatively large parity changes at fairly long intervals induce highly disturbing capital flows. Compared with a system of truly fixed rates, as under the old gold standard on the one side, and a crawling or trotting peg on the other side, the adjustable peg system maximizes destabilizing speculation.

To be sure, recent experience with the trotting peg and also with the brief period of managed flexibility of the German mark prior to its formal appreciation in October 1969 suggests that it is not necessary to go all the way to a system of completely unmanaged, freely floating rates in order to reduce or practically eliminate speculation. This gives rise to an important problem. For anyone who rejects as the IMF report does both continuous flexibility, either of the unlimited or crawling variety, and complete rigidity, the crucial question is this: Where does the adjustable peg end and where does flexibility, sufficient to eliminate dangerous speculation, begin? Suppose we arrange alternative changes in exchange rates (depreciations and appreciations) in such an order that the size of the change becomes smaller and the interval between changes shorter. There will then be a threshold value (or threshold zone) somewhere on the scale beyond which speculation ceases to be a problem. It would be extremely important to have an idea approximately where this threshold lies. The report is silent on this central question. There is internal evidence, however, that the authors, when they speak of "prompt parity changes in appropriate circumstances" and warn of undue delays, were thinking of intervals of, let us say, substantially more than a year.

In our opinion, rather more frequent but still fairly large changes in exchange rates[40] would not offer any substantial relief from the problem of large speculative capital movements and might even exacerbate them because of the smaller likelihood of "fixity illusion" (analogous to "money illusion") which has at times been present under the adjustable peg. At just what point a more promptly adjusted adjustable peg would become in effect a discretionary crawling peg it is difficult to say. But in order to produce substantial reduction in speculative pressures resulting from the "one way option" of the adjustable peg, adjustments much more frequently than every couple of years would be needed.[41]

The point has been made many times that disregarding highly inflationary countries, over the years the structure of exchanges rates under the Bretton Woods system has become much more rigid than the founding fathers had anticipated. In our opinion this is not due to faulty or negligent management of the system, but is the consequence of the fact or suspicion, well founded in our opinion, that too frequent changes reduce the stability of the adjustable peg system.

These remarks do not pretend to give the full answer to the question posed above of where the adjustable peg ends and managed flexibility begins. But they indicate the type of problem that faces those who reject anything approaching full flexibility but recommend more frequent and "prompt adjustments in appropriate cases" than there were in the past. To repeat, the report is silent on this crucial matter.

We can be confident, however, that the report will not remain the IMF's last word on exchange flexibility. It is a milestone in a continuing process of reappraisal of the basic assumptions of the Bretton Wood system. Let us hope that in due course the crucial issue mentioned above will be faced squarely. This would force a reconsideration of some of the positions taken in the present report. A good deal of new evidence from recent experience in various parts of the world has become available and it sheds light on the question we have emphasized. No organization is in a better position to assemble and interpret the relevant facts than the IMF.

Summary and Concluding Remarks

We have argued that of the three areas of international monetary reform—confidence, liquidity, adjustment—the last mentioned is by far the most important and pressing. Problems having to do with confidence are taken care of by the close cooperation of the world's major central banks that has developed and deepened in the postwar period. The problem of liquidity has probably been brought under definite control by the creation of the SDR scheme. The task of improving the balance-of-payments adjustment mechanism remains to be accomplished.

The SDR agreement recognized the paramount importance of the adjustment problem by stipulating that, before the first decision is made to allocate SDRs, "a collective judgment" be reached to the effect that there is a good chance of "a better working of the adjustment mechanism." The first decision to allocate SDRs was made in 1969 and allocations were made on January 1, 1970 and January 1, 1971. Whether adjustment mechanism will in fact work better in the future is still very much in doubt.

The attention of the policymakers in the international monetary area has shifted to the problems of adjustment. The comprehensive IMF report, *The Role of Exchange Rates in the Adjustment of International Payments*, testifies to that shift. In our opinion, the report does not go nearly far enough in the direction of proposing new methods of adjustment through greater flexibility of exchange rates.But at least it is a beginning and it will surely not remain the IMF's last word on that important subject.

The practical problem is not to replace the par value system with a system of generalized flexibility of all currencies. Such a radical change is not only not feasible but also unnecessary to assure a better working of the adjustment mechanism. We presented the elements of a modest scheme, which in our view would be a major step forward.

We have emphasized that the American interest in greater flexibility of exchange rates is indirect, because the U.S. cannot, under present arrangements, change the value of the dollar. But nevertheless it is quite real, because the U.S. shares fully in the world interest in the smooth working of the international monetary system. The U.S. should do all it can to promote changes in the rules that will make it easier for other countries to use exchange flexibility to solve their problems—deficit countries to avoid trade restricting controls and unnecessary unemployment, surplus countries to avoid unwanted inflation and "negative" controls. By solving their own balance-of-payments problems, our trading partners also solve ours.

The special position of the dollar and the small size of U.S. foreign trade in relation to GNP makes it possible for the U.S. to continue its "passive" balance-of-payments policy, even if it takes some time and perhaps another major exchange crisis before anything decisive is done to improve the adjustment mechanism. If the U.S. is able to reduce the rate of inflation to an internally tolerable level, there will probably be very little trouble on the dollar front. But even if it is not so successful with the fight against inflation, the passive balance-of-payments policy should be continued, although in that case policymakers would have to brace themselves for continuing grumbling and criticism. But the basic strength of the dollar is such that, barring really bad inflation or any other unforeseen catastrophe, U.S. policymakers can afford to stand firm and not to change the passive stance of balance-of-payments policy in the face of foreign criticism. The U.S. should realize that nobody can force it either to impose controls or to suffer more unemployment than is needed, in its own judgment, to curb inflation.

U.S. policy should concentrate on promoting domestic economic stability, employment and growth, and should remove rather than continue to tighten barriers to international trade and capital flows. Since 1969 substantial progress has been made in the untying of foreign aid. Much less progress has been made, however, in the area of relaxing and gradually phasing out controls on capital exports. We do not wish to minimize the importance of having at least ended and even reversed a little, the trend which started early in the 1960s of ever increasing use of first voluntary and then mandatory controls and other selective measures designed to "improve" components of the U.S. balance of payments. This change in tendency is an important step forward. But residual fears concerning the U.S. balance of payments have substantially slowed the process of dismantling these measures of the 1960s. There must be considerable doubt about the continued effectiveness of capital controls in terms of improving the balance of payments. Experience has shown many times that controls, unless they become redundant, have a tendency to spring leaks as time goes on and have to be continuously tightened if their effectiveness is to be maintained. But even more important, balance-of-payments improvement via the use of controls is not an appropriate objective for a country occupying the United States' unique position in the world economy.

The removal of the remaining controls in the face of a measured U.S. deficit would be a courageous act, for it would cut against conventional wisdom that is still widespread both at home and abroad. But the benefits of final, full recognition of the United States' position in the international monetary system would be enormous.

Postscript

This paper was written late in 1970 and early 1971, eight months before the gold convertibility of the dollar was terminated (August 15, 1971), and long before floating exchange rates were reluctantly accepted by policy makers. For a brief account how floating originated, see "The International Monetary System in the

World Recession." [Chapter 11 in this volume] The 1971 paper took it as a fact that floating had no chance to be accepted and it argued that the world was practically on a dollar standard. That implied that the United States could not unilaterally depreciate the dollar or let it float because most other countries would have followed suit. On the other hand, the equilibrium was precarious, because the U.S. gold stock had declined while U.S. liabilities to foreign central banks had sharply increased, and inflation in the United States was high by the standards of the time, although quite low by present standards.

Under these circumstances the paper recommended for the United States a "passive approach" to the balance of payments problem—a "policy of benign neglect." This was defined to mean that U.S. macropolicy should be guided exclusively by domestic policy objectives—curbing inflation and preventing unemployment from going higher than was necessary to curb inflation. It should be left to other countries to bring about a change in the exchange value of the dollar or to introduce floating, by changing the dollar parity of *their* currencies, or be letting their currencies float in the market.

The policy of benign neglect received much attention and criticism in the United States and abroad; it was often misunderstood by critics and interpreted to mean that the dangers of inflation should be ignored, despite the fact that the authors emphatically stated that in their opinion U.S. inflation must be curbed.

Another criticism was that the U.S. policy of benign neglect was a selfish, nationalistic policy. This criticism overlooked the fact that our paper gives foreign countries a wide range of options. A country that developed a balance of payments surplus because its inflation rate was lower than the American rate had three options: internal expansion, appreciation of its currency, or letting its currency float. It was suggested that each of these courses should be acceptable to the United States.[42] Thus they should not lead to any serious economic conflict. This appraisal has been confirmed, we believe, by the responses to the subsequent gold convertibility of the dollar. (August 15, 1971.)

Notes

1. Section 5 (b) of the act of October 6, 1917. For details of balance-of-payments developments and policies until 1968 see *U.S. Balance of Payments Policies and International Monetary Reforms: A Critical Analysis*, by Gottfried Haberler and Thomas D. Willett (Washington: American Enterprise Institute, 1968).

2. The official balance-of-payments statistics compiled by the Department of Commerce presents two alternative measures of deficit and surplus, the "liquidity" concept and the "official transactions" or "official settlement" concept. The liquidity concept is defined as "changes in liquid liabilities to foreign official holders, other foreign holders, and changes in official reserve assets consisting of gold, Special Drawing Rights, convertible currencies, and the U.S. gold tranche position in the IMF." The official settlement concept is defined as

"changes in liquid and nonliquid liabilities to foreign official holders and changes in official reserve assets consisting of gold, Special Drawing Rights, convertible currencies, and the U.S. gold tranche position in the IMF." The official settlement definition was proposed in 1965 by a committee under the chairmanship of E. M. Bernstein. Figures for the official settlement balance are available from 1960. In earlier years, the liquidity measure was generally used.

The major difference between the two definitions is that the liquidity concept takes into account the change in U.S. liquid liabilities to all foreigners, while the official transactions or official settlement concept considers only changes in U.S. liquid liabilities to foreign official agencies.

In its recently published annual report for 1970, the Council of Economic Advisers adds two additional measures for gauging the position of the balance of payments: the "Balance on Current Accounts" and the "Balance on Current and Long-Term Capital Accounts." The latter is often called the "basic balance" and was used by the Department of Commerce until it was replaced by the liquidity definition.

3. For recent discussions, see Charles P. Kindleberger, "Measuring Equilibrium in the Balance of Payments,"*Journal of Political Economy*, November-December 1969; Raymond F. Mikesell, *The U.S. Balance of Payments and the International Role of the Dollar* (Washington: American Enterprise Institute, 1970); and Thomas D. Willett, "Measuring the U.S. Balance of Payments Position," Harvard Institute of Economic Research, Discussion Paper, 1971.

4. In recent years the U.S. too has engaged in foreign exchange transactions and holds a fraction of its international reserves in the form of "convertible currencies" ($0.8 billion compared with a gold stock of $11.5 billion as of October 1970).

5. To the gold stock could be added U.S. holdings of convertible currencies, its reserve position in the IMF and its Special Drawing Rights. As of October 1970, "total reserve assets" were $15.12 billion. Further adjustment in figures of liquid assets and liabilities could be made, but the overall position and conclusions would not be changed by such refinements.

6. All figures are taken from the *Federal Reserve Bulletin*. Stock figures relate to the end of the period mentioned.

7. For a theoretical analysis of the stability problem, see Lawrence H. Officer and Thomas D. Willett, "Reserve-Asset Preferences and the Confidence Problem." *The Quarterly Journal of Economics*, November 1969; and the same authors, "The Interaction of Adjustment and Gold Conversion Policies in a Reserve Currency System," *Western Economic Journal*, March 1970. They show that the system never was so unstable as the pessimists say.

8. "Elements of Stability and Instability in the Monetary Field," remarks made on May 18, 1970, at the Monetary Conference of the American Bankers Association, Hot Springs, Virginia (mimeographed).

9. Other countries would still have a liquidity problem unless the U.S. reciprocated and accepted foreign balances as part of its international reserve. U.S. officials have indicated they would be willing to follow such a practice, at least to some extent, in case the U.S. should run a persistent surplus.

10. It is not necessary for our purposes to discuss the controversial question of whether the adoption of an incomes policy would do any good. If it were possible by means of an incomes policy to improve the inflationary situation marginally—more than that is not expected, even by the policy's supporters—the effect on the balance of payments too would be only marginal.

11. How much unemployment constitutes a recession and how much price stability should be traded for how much unemployment, if there is such a trade-off, is a question on which views may differ, both inside the U.S. and between the U.S. and foreign countries.

12. It is not unimportant to observe that three or four years ago this situation was well understood by only a few.

13. Admittedly, many countries complain that they have to "import inflation" from the U.S. But when the chips are down, the foreign critics are extremely reluctant to accept the logical implication of their complaints, that is, to let their currency appreciate. There have been only three cases of currency appreciation in the whole postwar period (Germany in 1963 and 1969 and the Netherlands in 1963). But there were literally dozens of depreciations against the dollar.

Complaint about imported inflation combined with a refusal to appreciate amounts to wanting to have one's cake and eat it too. However, the situation would probably change if the inflation in the U.S. got out of hand, More on this later.

14. It could be argued that the outcome of a change in the gold value of the dollar would be different if it were the result of international negotiations rather than of a surprise decision by the U.S. government. In the former case, it might be said, more countries would be willing *not* to follow the American example and accept an appreciation of their currency.

This may be so, but it is extremely doubtful that an internationally agreed realignment of many exchange rates is feasible. Negotiations could not be kept entirely secret and would thus give rise to very disturbing speculation.

15. Arguments like this abound in the popular discussions, but it is not easy to find clear formulations. One of the rare, explicit and straightforward statements is contained in a letter to the *New York Times*, October 18, 1970, by Professor Manuel Gottlieb.

We quote: "Many economists ... would agree that present exchange rates significantly overvalue the dollar, especially when allowance is made for American capital outflow and governmental transfers.... The proper remedy for an overvalued exchange rate is exchange-rate adjustment ('Devaluation') and not import restrictions.... Under present institutional arrangements, our exchange rates can only be changed by decisions of our trading competitors who choose to 'revalue' ('Appreciate') their currencies or to let their currencies 'float.' I cannot watch the gradual liquidation of American industrial potential on the vain hope that foreign monetary authorities will be sensitive to our needs and capacities and will establish exchange rates that would permit competitive terms of trade at full employment. ... Rather than that, I go for the 'quota' bill with all of its imperfections."

16. Especially if it is "gradual." It goes without saying that not every fall in exports or rise in imports or change in the trade balance has something to do with the balance of payments. For example, from 1964 to 1969, the trade balance fell from $6.8 billion to $0.7 billion and unemployment did not go up but down—from 5.2 percent to 3.5 percent of the labor force.

It would be very difficult indeed to measure the amount of unemployment or slack (lost output) that is attributable to changes in the balance of payments or balance of trade. Fortunately, policymakers need no such measure to determine the thrust of monetary and fiscal policy that the situation requires.

17. If there are surplus countries that have *more* inflation than the U.S., it does not affect our argument. A country with more inflation than the U.S. may have a surplus either because it has recently devalued its currency or because its exports are low-priced (compared with its

general price level) or otherwise are in strong demand. France, after her devaluations in 1958 and 1969, illustrates the first possibility, Japan the second.

18. Those economists who recommend a rise in the gold price in order to increase international liquidity rightly speak of doubling or tripling the price of gold. A small rise of 10 percent or so would do no good.

19. It should be observed that what we call "negative" controls (export restrictions and import subsides imposed by surplus countries) are just as inefficient, wasteful, and undesirable as the ordinary controls imposed by deficit countries. Removal of existing trade barriers is, of course, a different matter. It is desirable, although it too can be regarded as a currency appreciation in disguise.

20. Surplus countries, such as Germany and Switzerland, have tried tax measures and the prohibition of interest payments on bank deposits of foreigners to reduce short-term capital inflow without much success in the longer run.

21. An objection to our argument might be that they could simply refuse to add to their dollar holdings without trying to reduce their balances. But that does not change the situation. If they refuse to buy dollars which are offered for sale, their currency will appreciate in terms of dollars (and in terms of all currencies that still are pegged to the dollar).

22. It has been suggested that the first reaction of the surplus countries would be to block further allocations of SDRs, and French officials who were reluctant to go along with the SDR creation in the first place have already voiced their opposition to further SDR allocations so long as the U.S. deficit is large. This may be a disappointment for other countries. However, for the U.S., the threat is hollow. If our assessment of the general position of the dollar is correct, it would simply mean that official dollar balances abroad would accumulate faster. It would in no way change the four options available to the surplus countries—accumulate dollars, inflate, appreciate, or reduce trade barriers.

23. The "confidence problem" (i.e., the problems that arise when confidence in a currency is lost and a run on the currency develops) would seem to be of decidedly lesser importance in the future. Any such crisis has to be dealt with on an *ad hoc* basis. But experience has shown that the close cooperation that has developed between the monetary authorities of the major countries and that has deepened in the postwar period is capable of handling confidence crises even when they involve major currencies.

24. Article XXIV, Section 1 (b).

25. The *New York Times*, September 29, 1970, and *The Economist*, September 26, 1970.

26. See Gottfried Haberler, "The Case Against the Link," *Quarterly Review*, Banca Nazionable del Lavoro, Rome, March 1971.

27. A report by the executive directors of the International Monetary Fund, Washington, D.C., 1970.

28. It is not necessary here to go into the reasons for these deviations.

29. It should be observed that the mere fact that the actual rise in the cost of living in a given country is equal to or a little higher than the rise in the U.S. does not prove by itself that the country in question spontaneously matches or surpasses the U.S. rate of inflation. It could be a case of induced inflation.

However, if prices in a country rise persistently and much faster than in the U.S., one gets the strong suspicion that it is not a case of induced inflation but one of spontaneous inflation. If a country is forced from time to time to devalue against the dollar or to maintain controls, the suspicion is confirmed beyond doubt.

30. Even if the gold policy were changed, if other countries asked for conversion into gold of large parts of their dollar holdings and the U.S. were prepared to accede to that request, it would be unrealistic to assume that internal monetary and fiscal policies in the U.S. would be changed thereby. It follows that such a change in the gold policy would not relieve other countries from the necessity to follow the U.S. inflation, so long as they maintained full convertibility of their currencies into dollars at a fixed exchange rate.

31. It is now better understood than it was a few years ago that monetary integration and the creation of a common currency presuppose far-reaching harmonization and coordination of not only monetary but also fiscal, wage, and incomes policies. The EEC countries are still far from that stage. See Gottfried Haberler. "Reflections on the Economies of International Monetary Integration" (forthcoming) [*Verstehen und Gestalten der Wirtsechaft*, J. C. B. Mohr (Paul Siebeck), Tübingen, 1971, pp. 269–278] and the literature quoted there, especially Wolfgang Kasper and Michael Stahl. "Integration Through Monetary Union—A Skeptical View," *Kieler Diskussionsbeitraege*, Nr. 7, Kiel. September 1970.

32. It should be observed, assuming as we do that monetary, fiscal, and other macro-economic policies in the U.S. are solely determined by domestic policy objectives, that the relevant comparison is with GNP. If, on the contrary, the U.S. allowed the balance-of-payments deficit to influence overall economic policies, as was the case in the early sixties, the burden could become much larger than suggested by the GNP percentage.

33. It is sometimes said that, at present, it is difficult for any single European government to appreciate its currency vis-à-vis the dollar because it would at the same time have to appreciate also vis-à-vis the other European currencies. This is, however, hardly the case—as if, say, the DM were overvalued only in respect to the dollar, and not equally or perhaps more so vis-à-vis some European currencies!

34. The authors have expressed their views in Haberler and Willett, *op. cit.* See also Gottfried Haberler, *Money in the International Economy*, 2d edition (Cambridge: Harvard University Press, May 1969).

35. In the case of appreciation of a surplus country's currency, as in the case of depreciation of a deficit country's currency, a flexible approach to the change in the exchange rate is much to be preferred to the rigid, disruptive method of the adjustable peg. Instead of waiting until a huge surplus has been built up under the accompaniment of mounting speculation and then appreciating by a large amount with a bang, it is better to let the currency float up gradually. This was dramatically demonstrated by the German appreciation in September/October 1969. Let us recall the salient events. The appreciation had become an election issue. Before the election, billions of dollars had flowed into Germany. On September 24, four days before the election, the exchange market was closed. On Monday, September 29, the day after the election, the market was reopened with the exchange rate unchanged. In a few hours, huge sums poured into Germany. The market was closed again and the decision was reached to let the mark float. The next morning, Tuesday, September 30, when the market was reopened once again, the exchange value of the mark shot up and—lo and behold—the speculation had practically vanished. It simply became too risky to speculate. Even more interesting, the speculation was not revived, at least not on a substantial scale, a little later when a more or less open debate was conducted in the press on whether the mark should be restabilized at the level of 6, 8, or 10 percent above the former parity.

It is true, in many respects, that the German appreciation was a unique case. To make the appreciation of a currency an election issue is a helluva way to change an exchange rate. But the fact that some flexibility—although it was managed (with flexibility in the direction though not the magnitude of the impending change in the rate predetermined)—was sufficient to stop speculation in its track teaches a lesson of great general importance.

36. The Brazilian system is well described and analyzed in J. B. Donges, "Neue Wege in der Wechselkurspolitik der Entwicklungslaender?—Brasiliens 'Trotting Peg'," *Kieler Diskussionsbeitraege*, Kiel. Nr. 8, Oktober 1970. An English translation of that pamphlet will be published by the American Enterprise Institute later in 1971 [*Brazil's Trotting Peg: A New Approach to Greater Exchange Rate Flexibility in Less Developed Countries*, AEI Special Analysis, No. 7].

Contrary to a widely held view, speculation has been no problem under the trotting peg, whereas it was a very disrupting feature of the earlier system of the adjustable peg. This teaches a lesson which is applicable also to the industrial countries: If speculative capital flows are no problem in the case of the trotting peg, it follows *a fortiori* that it would not be one under the more favorable conditions of the crawling peg or freely floating rates.

37. George N. Halm, *The International Monetary Fund and the Flexibility of Exchange Rates*, Princeton Essays in International Finance, 1971.

38. *Ibid.*, p. 73.

39. It is not quite clear whether the report regards an actual or anticipated balance-of-payments surplus or deficit as a necessary, though not sufficient, condition of fundamental disequilibrium. It certainly is not a sufficient condition. Maybe the report wishes to speak of fundamental disequilibrium only in dilemma cases when requirements of internal and external equilibrium conflict. If this is a correct interpretation, attention should be given to the strong possibility (a) that the diagnosis of whether a dilemma exists or not may not be easy at all and the views of the country and that of the IMF may well diverge and (b) that a dilemma case can change easily and without notice into a non-dilemma case, and vice-versa. (On these points, see Haberler, *Money in the International Economy, op. cit.*, pp. 14–18).

The balance-of-payments disequilibrium need not be "actual." Suppose a deficit is suppressed by controls or excessive unemployment. Then a policy of de-control or re-expansion would presumably bring about a deficit. Again the diagnosis and interpretation of a concrete situation is likely to be far from clear and unambiguous, especially in its quantitative aspects: How large a deficit is to be expected and how large a depreciation of the currency would be needed to take care of the deficit?

All this highlights the difficulties of operating a par value system with discrete changes in the par value in case of fundamental disequilibrium.

40. What is "large" has to be determined in reference to the possibility of forestalling speculation by high interest rates. For example, in Brazil it does not pay to speculate on an expected change in the exchange rate (precise date unknown) of 1 percent or 1.3 percent with interest rates running up to 40 percent.

41. For a detailed analysis of speculation under limited exchange rate flexibility, see Thomas D. Willett, Samuel Z. Katz, and William H. Branson, *Exchange-Rate System, Interest Rates, and Capital Flows*, Princeton Essays in International Finance, No. 78, January 1970.

42. For references to the literature, see Thomas D. Willett, *Floating Exchange Rates and Monetary Reform*, American Enterprise Institute, 1977.

The problem of the adequacy of international liquidity—or, better, of international monetary reserves—has been discussed almost as long as there has been serious discussion of the international monetary system. According to Jacob Viner, "from the late 1820s on to the end of the century a continuous succession of writers called attention to the inadequacy of gold reserves [in Great Britain], but without any visible results," and Peel himself was said to have been "aware that the metallic base of the currency was extraordinarily narrow, but did not think that either the Bank or the people would willingly bear the expense of broadening it."[1] Both before and after the Bank Act of 1844, numerous writers made proposals for a reform of the international monetary system, most of which aimed at increasing international liquidity.[2]

The Bimetallist Controversy and Commodity Reserve Currencies

The long period of falling prices from the 1870s to the 1890s, the "downswing of the Kondratieff cycle," gave rise to lively discussions in all major countries on international monetary reform; namely, the bimetallist controversy. The basic issue was the alleged inadequacy of international reserves resulting from the decline in gold production that occurred roughly during 1854–83. To my knowledge there is no satisfactory history of published works on this subject comparable to Viner's history of the English literature during the period of the bullionist controversies (in both its inflationary and deflationary phases) and during the later period of 1825–65. This is a pity, because much of the discussion was on a high level and many leading economists participated Interestingly enough, and probably surprisingly for many contemporary economists, a galaxy of famous names was ranged on the side of a double standard of gold and silver, either bimetallism or

The New International Monetary System, Robert A. Mundell and J.J. Polak, eds. (New York: Columbia University Press, 1977), 116–132 and 172–176. © 1977, Columbia University Press. Reprinted by permission.

symmetallism, against the monometallism of gold—Alfred Marshall, L. Walras, F. Y. Edgeworth, N. G. Pierson, and I. Fisher, among others.

Especially interesting is Marshall's proposal of symmetallism. The difference between bimetallism and symmetallism is, it will be recalled, that under the former, the money prices of both gold and silver are fixed by central bank pegging,[3] while under the latter the money price of a constant physical bundle, or a bar containing, say, one ounce of gold and fifteen ounces of silver, is fixed and the relative price of gold and silver in terms of money (and in terms of general purchasing power) is free to vary in the market under the influence of changes in demand and supply (cost of production).[4] The system of symmetallism is interesting because it is a forerunner of the commodity reserve-currency proposals. Marshall himself mentioned that if other commodities "suitable" for the purpose could be found, "they could be added to gold and silver to form the basis of the currency."[5] The commodity reserve-currency system has found impressive sponsor, but equally prominent critics. First proposed by W. S. Jevons in 1873, the idea was revived in the 1930s and 1940s by Benjamin Graham and Frank D. Graham and was strongly endorsed by F. A. Hayek. It has been criticized by J. M. Keynes, Milton Friedman, and Herbert Grubel, and has been supported by A. G. Hart, J. Tinbergen, and N. Kaldor.[6]

In the 1890s the bimetallist movement died down, earlier in Europe than in the United States, because in Europe the special interests (the silver producers) were too weak to maintain the pressure needed to give silver a greater role in the monetary system. Gold production picked up rapidly because of new discoveries (in the Rand district of the Transvaal in South Africa and in the Klondike–Yukon valley in Canada) and technological improvements in mining and refining. As a consequence of the increase in gold production (i.e., a more adequate supply of international liquidity) and other factors—such as the increasing use of deposit money (checks) and the early adoption of the gold exchange standard by some countries (Russia and the Austro-Hungarian monarchy)—the declining trend of prices gave way to an upward trend. Thus there could be no further question about the adequacy of international monetary reserves until after World War 1.

After the gold standard had been firmly established, a leading German bimetallist wrote, "The gentlemen of the gold standard, when they reflect on what happened must feel like 'der Reiter auf dem Bodensee'," the legendary horseman who inadvertently rode over the frozen lake and suffered a deadly shock when he suddenly realized that he just had narrowly escaped a horrible death. "Every reasonable gold standard man must admit," he continued, "that a further catastrophic price decline has been avoided only because gold production quite unexpectedly jumped from 400 million marks in 1883 to 1,600 million marks in 1906."[7] The nineteenth-century bimetallists probably had a better case than some recent prophets of disaster when they attributed the failure of their prophecy to come true, not to a defect in their argument, but to a run of undeserved good luck.

The Interwar Period

In the 1920s the problem of inadequate international reserves again became acute. The world price level in terms of dollars had about doubled since before the war, while the price of gold remained unchanged at twenty dollars an ounce. The implied a sharp drop in the value of the stock of monetary gold, the principal component of international reserves, compared with the volume of international transactions. Moreover, the lower value of gold caused a decline in the annual production of gold. To cope with the growing inadequacy of international reserves, the more general adoption of the gold exchange standard was recommended by financial experts attending the Genoa Conference in the spring of 1922.

The perils of the gold-exchange standard—which after World War II became, first *de facto* and then, with the suspenison of the gold convertibility of the dollar in 1971, explicitly, a dollar standard—have dominated the discussion of reserve adequacy until recently.

Many writers, especially Jacques Rueff and Robert Triffin in recent years, saw in the gold-exchange standard and its unavoidable collapse a major, if not the predominant, cause of the exceptional severity of the Great Depression of the 1930s; and both Rueff and Triffin have warned repeatedly that the unavoidable collapse of the dollar standard would have the same catastrophic consequences in the 1960s or 1970s as the collapse of the gold-exchange standard had in the 1930s. They were fond of quoting Santayana, "Who does not learn from the lessons of history is condemned to repeat them."

As far as the 1930s are concerned, the partial liquidation of the gold-exchange standard may have contributed a little to the severity of the world depression. But the major reasons surely were others. The gold-exchange standard was not responsible for the breakdown of the American banking system and the catastrophic deflation in the United States. One need not be an out-and-out monetarist to recognize that this was the major explanation for the severity of the U.S. depression and that, under fixed exchange rates, the U.S. depression was bound to spread to the rest of the world.[8]

There were, to be sure, other weak spots and foci of deflation in the world, for example, in central Europe and Great Britain. The central European crisis had nothing to do with the gold-exchange standard. The British weakness and difficulties, although rooted in the overvaluation of sterling since the revaluation of 1925, were possibly aggravated by the gold-exchange standard. But the American depression, which was almost entirely homemade, was the most powerful blow to the stability of the world economy, though chronologically not the first.

It is true, however, that after the depression became worldwide, there developed a severe shortage of international liquidity in the sense that international "liquidity preference" (for gold) became very strong. This was largely the consequence of the slow-motion devaluation of all currencies in terms of gold—sterling and its retinue of currencies in 1931, the dollar in 1933–34, and the "gold bloc" currencies in 1936. This was an early case of a very slowly adjustable peg, of stable but slowly adjustable exchange rates. In the end, international liquidity increased sharply through the painful process of prices declining in terms of national currencies (deflation) and national currencies being dicontinuously devalued in terms of gold. An early large injection of international liquidity, such as by doubling the price of gold, would have shortened the painful process.

The Postwar Period

In the post–World War II period the problem of international liquidity and the adequacy or inadequacy of international reserves came into its own. It has loomed very large—disproportionately large, many (including the present writer) would say—in the discussions of the reform of the international monetary system.

Following Keynes's proposal for an International Clearing Union and Robert Triffin's early seminal writings, dozens of schemes for the orderly international creation, supplementation, control, and management of global monetary reserves have been advanced, ranging from proposals for making the IMF a real world central bank or a lender of last resort for national central banks, to proposals for doubling the price of gold, for commodity reserve-currency schemes, and for multiple-currency standards.[9] In the 1950s proposals to increase international liquidity had largely been "a British-based speciality," in the words of John Williamson.[10] The "British specialty" was "transformed into a widely dispersed growth industy follow-ing Triffin's "diagnosis of a prospective liquidity shortage."[11] When the long-predicted deflation and international economic warfare *à la* 1930s failed to material-ize and it became clear that inflation, not deflation, was the menace, the diagnosis of an existing or impending shortage of international liquidity gradually shifted to one of excessive international liquidity.

The theoretical literature on the subject of international liquidity has become enormous. There have been several surveys of this literature. The latest and most extensive one by John Williamson lists about 250 items.[12] One of the highlights of this discussion was a three-day international seminar of twenty-nine experts on international reserves held by the IMF in 1970. The papers and proceedings of the seminar were published in a massive volume, together with the lengthly earlier analytical and factual–statistical papers prepared by the IMF staff in connection with the implementation of the SDR scheme.[13]

The Problem of International Reserves under Floating

While this discussion was in full swing the international monetary scene changed completely. Inflation, which had been a serious problem during most of the postwar period, accelerated to the two-digit level, even in the United States and Switzerland. As a consequence, the Bretton Woods system of stable but adjustable exchange rates broke down, giving way to generalized managed floating—which is about to be legalized through the Second Amendment of the IMF Articles of Agreement.[14]

The demise of the fixed-rate system has invalidated, or sharply reduced the relevance of, much of recent theorizing on international liquidity. For as far as I can see, almost all of the discussions of the subject (including the IMF seminar of 1970 where floating received only fleeting mention) were based on the assumption of stable, or stable but adjustable, exchange rates. The same was true four years later, after floating had become worldwide, of the deliberations of the Committee on Reform of the International Monetary System (Committee of Twenty).[15] It is true, of course, that there was a growing demand for floating, and greater exchange flexibility was often listed as one method among others for dealing with the liquidity problem.[16] But most proponents of floating took it for granted that there would be no liquidity problem under floating or that the problem would be reduced to insignificance—an assumption that many opponents of flexibility seemed to have accepted. There has been very little systematic analysis of the problem of international liquidity under floating.[17]

Admittedly, years ago Sir Roy Harrod argued that under flexible exchange rates larger official interventions in the exchange market and, therefore, larger international reserves, would be required than under fixed rates, because under fixed rates, stabilizing private capital flows that reduce the need for official financing are much more dependable than under floating.[18] But Sir Roy was very careful to add that "this, of course, assumes that there is complete confidence in the maintenance of the fixed rates." Thus, in effect, he compared flexible rates with the gold standard and not with the Bretton Woods adjustable-peg system.

Most other writers have not been so careful to distinguish sharply between credibly fixed and stable but adjustable exchange rates. Under the gold standard, when there was "complete confidence in the maintenance of the fixed rates," small interest differentials would induce large short-term capital flows. This is precisely what had enabled Britain to get along with a small gold reserve in the nineteenth century. Under the Bretton Woods system, in contrast, "complete confidence" in the existing rates was no longer possible. It has become increasingly clear and by now should be common konwledge that the method of changing rates by occasional large jumps, the adjustable peg, made it easy and almost riskless for speculators to anticipate changes in the exchange rate. Speculators could speculate against the central banks whose hands were tied rather than against each other, which is a much more hazardous proposition and which is what they have to do under floating. The consequence was a succession of currency crises with increasingly massive and disruptive capital flows. As John Williamson (and others before him) had predicted, "the adjustable peg is unlikely to be viable indefinitely. Ever increasing destabilizing speculation will result if pegs are apt to jump."[19]

Official interventions in the exchange market on an enormous, ever-increasing scale were required to hold the line. This has forced one country after another to give up pegging and to adopt floating. The only alternative would have been tight exchange control.[20] The clear implication of all of this is that the adjustable peg requires much larger international reserves than either the gold standard (credibly fixed exchange rates) or floating rates.

It does not follow, of course, that the problem of international liquidity vanishes altogether under floating. If there are official interventions in the exchange market, as there probably always will be, there is some need (or demand) for reserves. But since under floating the authorities are not restricted in their interventions by a rigid barrier, unless they restrict themselves, which would be tantamount to giving up the float, the need for reserves cannot be greater under floating than it is under the adjustable peg.

This has been denied by John Williamson, largely on the ground that during the first years of the float a number of countries used reserves in interventions to a greater extent than before the float.[21] But this is unconvincing. It does not tell us what the volume of interventions would have *been* in that same period under the same circumstances, if the world had been on the adjustable peg. The first years of widespread floating, 1973—76, was a period of high turbulence, rapid inflation, and severe recession, with sharply divergent rates of inflation and recession. This was also the period of the oil shock, which had different effects on different countries and caused different policy reactions. Can anyone doubt that under the adjustable peg there would have been enormous speculative flows of funds that could have been contained only by equally enormous interventions or by very tight controls? Given the fact (if it is a fact) that in such a disturbed period there were greater interventions, despite floating, than there were in an earlier, calmer period under the adjustable peg—should one draw the conclusion (which Williamson did not draw, although others did) that it was a mistake to give up the adjustable peg and adopt floating? I do not think so. It would be like advising sick people against going to the hospital on the ground that the death rate of hospitalized people is higher than that of the rest of the population.

While it may be an exaggeration to say that international liquidity or the volume of international monetary reserves poses no problems under floating, there can be no doubt that the problem is not pressing any more. The nature of the problem has changed in the last few years, and floating has not constituted the sole reason for the change.

To explore this subject further it will be well to follow J. Marcus Fleming and "go back to first principles," as he did in this first paper on the subject and on later occasions.[22] Fleming claimed that "practically all the important economic effects of reserve change come to pass by way of their effects on national policies; namely monetary and budget policies, policies with respect to restrictions on international trade and capital movements and policies with respect to exchange rates." Similarly, "despite the popularity of the name 'international liquidity' as a synonym for reserves, the decisive characteristic of reserve assets is not so much that they are liquid as that they are under the control of the monetary authority."[23]

Because of the essential role of policy, Fleming rejects what has been dubbed the "international quantity theory," which postulates a close parallelism between the association in each country between changes in the national money supply and changes in the national price level (or money GNP) and, on the other hand, between changes in the amount of international reserves and changes in the world price level (or volume of international transactions).[24] Jacques Polak and Egon Sohmen, too, have stressed the basic differences between national money and international monetary reserves.[25] Sohmen states his criticism of the international quantity theory this way: "Its basic fault seems to me to lie in the tendency to attribute to governments and central banks the same type of behavior with respect to monetary assets that we can expect with some confidence from private profit or utility maximizers"—that is to say, from private enterprises and households.

Fleming, Polak and Sohmen fully recognize that there are "formal similarities" between private money holdings and official reserves. But they are surely right that the essential involvement of government policies and the underlying political process introduce decisive dissimilarities, which are bound to loosen the correlation between changes in international reserves and world inflation. In Fleming's words:

> The behavior of monetary authorities with respect to international reserves is governed by considerations far more complex than those which determine the behavior of individuals with respect to money balances. Up to a point, the author-ities will react to an increase in their reserve ease as individuals would react to an increase in their monetary ease, namely by taking action intended to reduce the assets in question, reserves and money, respectively. But the authorities will be hampered in so doing by national objectives with respect to internal financial stability, exchange rate stability, etc., that have no parallel in the case of individuals.[26]

We may add that the behavior of *private individuals* with respect to their money holdings can be assumed substantially to remain the same over time (a fact that gives the velocity of monetary circulation a certain stability except in extreme situations such as hyperinflation or comprehensive rationing in wartime), whereas *public* policies bearing on the holding of international reserves are subject to frequent and larger changes over time. These changes, both cyclical and long run, often differ from country to country and are sometimes unpredictable or even internally inconsistent.[27] A particular type of change in official attitudes with respect to the desirable level of international reserves, one that has often been mentioned in the literature, is that "views held by monetary authorities on what is to be regarded as an adequate reserve seem to be subject to change without any obvious change in the underlying situation accounting for it. Once countries have enjoyed an ample reserve position for some time, they seem to get used to a comfortable cushion and to raise their sights on what is sufficient."[28] Essentially the same idea later became known as "Mrs. Machlup's wardrobe theory" of the authorities' demand for reserve.[29]

The most searching criticism of the international quantity theory has been expounded by Richard J. Sweeney and Thomas D. Willett.[30] The authors deal not only with the theory but also with the statistical measures and procedures that have been used in several recent publications to establish a close correlation between world inflation and global reserve growth. Sweeney and Willett conclude that these theories and their statistical implementation suffer from excessive aggregation. Especially with extensive floating the very concept and measures of global reserves have become highly ambiguous, if not meaningless.[31] The policy connection between international reserves and domestic money supply differs greatly from country to country and is subject to change in time. Hence, any correlation between changes in global reserves and in the world price level is apt to be spurious even if domestically the quantity theory works well. It follows that there is no presumption that stabilization of global reserves in some sense would tend to stabilize the world price level in some relevant sense. There simply are too many slips between the cup and the lip.

Recent Developments and Problems

There have been important recent cases of policy divergence between countries and of policy and institutional changes in several countries that have beclouded the very concept of international reserves and its role in the world economy. Two such developments deserve mention.

It has been charged that widespread floating since 1973 did not prevent a further inflationary expansion of international monetary reserves. It is true that global reserves as conventionally measured by the IMF grew sharply in 1973, 1974, and 1975. But the great bulk of that increase went to OPEC countries. (In 1975 and 1976 there were also substantial reserve increases resulting from intra-Eurpoean "snake" interventions—a case of stable but adjustable exchange rates.) It is now generally agreed that the largest part of the increase in OPEC reserves should go "above the line," that is to say, should be counted as "autonomous" investments and not as "accommodating" reserve changes.[32] Moreover, OPEC balances are not inflationary in the same sense as dollar balances accumulated by Japan and European countries because, unlike the latter, OPEC governments do not routinely issue national money to buy dollars (or Eurodollars) from their private exporters. Oil revenues accrue to the governments and the petrodollars are then invested abroad, partly in liquid form.

The other recent development that has blurred the dividing line between changes in monetary reserves and changes in autonomous foreign investment or disinvestment is the foreign borrowing by public and semipublic enterprises or by nominally private enterprises at the government's urging.[33] This has occurred on a huge scale in Britain and Italy. It is generally taken for granted that these operations have been undertaken, wholly or at least to a very large extent, for balance-of-payments reasons so that they are on a par with utilizing monetary reserves to finance a deficit of "autonomous" transactions. There have always existed borderline cases that made the distinction between "autonomous" transactions and "accommodating" reserve movements somewhat fuzzy. But it stands to reason that the rapidly increasing involvement of government policy in the adjustment process and the enormous growth of the public sector in many countries have made the distinction between "accommodating" reserve changes and "autonomous" investments increasingly arbitrary, if not meaningless. One consequence of this development is that it casts doubt on any attempt to define, however cautiously, an optimum level of reserves. It similarly casts in doubt the feasibility and relevance of the many proposals that detailed rules be laid down for the composition of reserves (stipulating, for example, that minimum proportions of total reserve should be kept in SDRs) and for interventions in the exchange market in order to achieve an optimum growth of global reserves or, more modestly, to prevent excessively large departures from the optimum.

Fears have been expressed that the present system as defined in the Second Amendment of the IMF charter—the "nonsystem," as it is often called by those whose blueprints have not been followed—does not eliminate the danger of global inflation (or deflation) resulting from excessive (or deficient) supply of international liquidity. The reason given, for example by John Williamson, is the "total lack of control over the international liquidity."[34] Williamson admits that this is not likely to result "from variations in the foreign-exchange component of reserves," because floating, unlike the par value system, enables countries to ward off inflationary (or deflationary) influences from abroad. But Williamson thinks that

no such reassurance exists so far as the gold component of reserves is concerned. The Jamaica Agreement gives central banks the freedom to trade gold among themselves at mutually agreeable prices. If it transpires that a willing buyer at a near-market price can always be found when a central bank wishes to sell (which is a possibility, though perhaps not a probability), the Jamaica Agreement may reverse the *de facto* demonetization of gold that occurred in August 1971. If gold is thus effectively remonetized, any new speculative bubble in the gold market would increase the value of gold reserves, and countries in general could find their reserves carried far above their optimal level. The fact that exchange rates were floating would then do nothing to prevent a competitive scramble to dispose of excess reserves; with inflationary consequences.[35]

I think we should not have sleepless nights over that danger, either. To be sure, no international agreement can prevent the world's leading economic countries from committing collectively at some time in the future the folly of remonetizing gold. But the amended IMF charter does not compel anybody to accept gold. And if the United States refuses to accept gold, other countries, even if they were in complete agreement, could not effectively remonetize gold. They could, of course, collectively go on an inflationary spending spree by buying gold from each other at an inflated price, but they could do that, if they wanted, without the help of gold.

This last thought suggests a possible inflationary danger. It is conceivable that some day in the future the holders of the huge liquid offical (or private) dollar balances abroad (largely a legacy from the prefloating period but now voluntarily held) may start to spend them. That could take the form of foreign countries engaging in inflationary policies and financing the resulting balance-of-payments deficits by drawing down their dollar balances. Not many people take this danger very seriously, for as the Bank for International Settlements states in its 1976 report[36]:

the argument, based on the global reserve statistics, that there is now a potentially inflationary overhang of liquidity in the system, the effects of which will be increasingly felt as the world economic recovery proceeds, comes rather close to saying that Germany, Switzerland, Saudi Arabia and Kuwait are about to spend the bulk of their rather large foreign assets on increased net imports of goods and services.

Since this is not a likely development, it is hardly worthwhile to discuss how the United States could protect itself against this threat.

Another scenario would be rapid inflation in the United States, which could induce other countries to try to get rid of their depreciating dollars—an attempt that would in turn intensify the U.S. inflation. This too is unlikely to happen. At any rate, it would not be the fault of the existing international monetary system of floating exchange rates and could not be prevented by controlling the volume of global reserves—unless the power of controlling global reserves were interpreted in an unconventionally broad sense to include the power of controlling the money supply in at least the major countries. Giving the IMF that power would come close to setting it up as a world government.

However, in a highly attenuated form, the possibility that the United States could be put under inflationary pressure by the operation of the present system is taken seriously by some analysts. What I have in mind is the theory that the almost universal use of the dollar as the intervention currency can lead to a depreciation of the dollar in the exchange market, even if the U.S. balance of payments is in perfect equilibrium.

Suppose, for example, that the French franc is declining and the German DM rising (or that the franc is at the "belly" and the DM at the "back" of the "snake"). If the French then sell dollars to stop or slow the slide (to keep the franc in the "snake"), the dollar will be pushed down, although there may have been no change in the U.S. balance of payments. I do not believe, however, that this is a serious threat requiring elaborate precautions such as a complicated multicurrency intervention system.

In the first place, if the dollar is the universal intervention currency, the chances are that the sales of dollars by deficit countries will at least partially be matched by purchases on the part of surplus countries. Second, if France has a deficit, the United States may be one of the surplus countries, so that the dollar will rise, and dollar sales by France will only delay the rise. Third, even if the U.S. balance is initially in equilibrium, the changes in trade flows set in motion by France's attempt to balance its accounts may change the U.S. balance. The upshot is that in our immensely complicated multilateral world trade and payment system nobody can really forsee all of the ramifications of any particular change. It is impossible to anticipate and match them by *ad hoc* tailored interventions. This task can safely be left to the market. If the dollar were the currency of a small country—say, of Switzerland— there would perhaps be cause for worry. But in the multi-hundred-billion world dollar market, including the Eurodollar market, net intervention sales even of several hundred million dollars can be absorbed without causing more than a small ripple.

Concluding Remarks: The Role of the IMF

My conclusion is that generalized floating and other developments have rendered obsolete any attempt to define an optimum level of international reserves; similarly, control of international reserves is no longer an important business for the IMF. It is the adjustment and not the liquidity problem that is of paramount importance, now more than ever before. The main task of the IMF should be "surveillance" over exchange-rate policies, prevention of "dirty floating," and of what has become known as "aggressive interventions," that is to say, "manipulating exchange rates ... in order to prevent effective balance of payments adjustment or to gain an unfair competitive advantage over other members," as the Amended Articles of Agreement put it.[37] By "dirty floating," as distinguished from merely managed or controlled floating,[38] I mean split exchange markets, multiple exchange rates, import deposit schemes, and similar devices that grossly violate one of the basic objectives of the IMF, namely, that current transactions should not be restricted.

However, to say that control of global international reserves is no longer an urgent problem does not mean that for individual countries the size of their reserves and their external borrowing potential are unimportant, nor that the use countries make of their reserves and borrowing power cannot become a matter of international concern. It is possible that in the last few years there has been much international overborrowing and excessive lending by banks to shore up shaky balance-of-payments positions. All this may, indeed, cause serious troubles in the future. But if so, it has nothing to do with a lack of international control over the volume of global reserves, and it could not have been prevented by such controls unless control over global reserves is unconventionally interpreted to include control over money supply in at least the major countries. Giving the IMF the power to control money supply in major countries would, I repeat, be almost equivalent to setting it up as a world government.

Furthermore, discounting the importance of global liquidity and its control does not mean that inflation is no problem. On the contrary, I agree with the IMF annual report for 1976 that inflation is the most pressing monetary problem.[39] But today the danger of inflation does not emanate from the working of the international monetary system. During the last years of the par value regime, the international monetary system greatly contributed to the worldwide spread of inflation, but under the present system of floating, inflation has its roots entirely in *national* monetary, fiscal, and exchange-rate policies. The primary responsibility for fighting inflation obviously falls on the leading industrial countries, especially the United States. This is so because the majority of smaller countries peg their currencies either to the currency of one of the leading industrial countries, most of them to the dollar, or to a basket of important currencies or SDRs.

One last point. To say that fighting world inflation is the task of the major industrial countries does not imply that the IMF can do nothing about inflation except preach. The IMF policies have some, though under realistic assumptions only a marginal, direct effect on world inflation. But it is easier to identify policies that would be inflationary than measures that would help to curb inflation. Steps that would add to inflationary pressures are a general increase in the IMF quotas and additional distribution of SDRs, especially if linked to foreign aid. Similarly, adding to inflation would be a further proliferation and expansion of special lending facilities—such as the Oil Facility, the Buffer Stock Facility, the Extended Fund Facility, and the Compensatory Financing of Export Fluctuations.

However, this does not mean that under no circumstances should any such measures be taken. On the contrary, emergencies must be expected to occur from time to time that would justify even large-scale credit operations by the IMF to forestall some major or minor disturbances of the world economy, including protectionist reactions. What it does mean is that the inflationary implications of such lending should not be overlooked, just as a fire bridgade when throwing water on an attic fire should not be oblivious of the damage that flooding can do to the rest of the house. The two dangers—the threatening disturbance and the inflationary side effect of the measures taken—should be weighed against each other, overreactions should be avoided, and the rescue operation should be properly dosed and pinpointed so as to minimize the danger of inflation. To illustrate the last point: Whereas an across-the-board distribution of additional SDRs would clearly be an inflationary move, the use of additional liquidity for a loan to our inflationary country as part of a comprehensive stabilization agreement that enables the country in question to get out of the inflationary rut, can be defended as an anti-inflationary move.

To pursue this highly important problem any further would burst the frame of the present study. However, one more observation may be permitted, specifically, that conditional lending by the IMF—"provision of conditional liquidity," to use official language—can be used as an inducement for countries to put their financial house in order and to pursue anti-inflationary policies. Liberal unconditional lending is likely to be counterproductive because it may well tempt countries to delay needed structural reform and antiinflationary measures and to postpone changes in exchange rates or floating that may be required.[40]

Reply to Robert Triffin

I am grateful to Robert Triffin for his thoughtful comments which give me an opportunity to clarify and amplify my paper. He questions my conclusions that "generalized floating and other developments have made obsolete any attempt to define an optimum level of international reserves" and that "control of international reserves is no longer an important task for the Fund." He does not offer a definition of an optimum level of reserves but he asks, "What are these new developments that have made the liquidity problem obsolete?"

He lists the following: "One is that expansion of reserves does not necessarily prompt ... the adoption of additional expansionary policies by governments and central banks." He here refers to my discussion of the criticism that the so-called "international quantity-theory" has received from Marcus Fleming, Jacques Polak, Egon Sohmen, Thomas Willett, and others. Triffin comments that "this certainly is not new" and does not support my position. But I did not say that this was a new phenomenon and I did not claim, nor did the writers just mentioned, that the rejection of the international quantity theory postulating as it does a fairly *precise* relationship between international reserves and world money income or world price-level changes, implies that under fixed exchanges a *sharp* increase in international reserves (an increase in gold production under the gold standard, or gold production plus foreign exchange held by central banks of nonreserve currency countries, etc.) has nothing to do with world inflation. My conclusion that control of global reserves is no longer an important task for the IMF relates to a world of floating exchange rates. Throughout his comments Triffin does not distinguish sharply enough between a floating and fixed-rate system.

Several people, including Triffin himself on several occasions, have complained that contrary to predictions of advocates of floating, floating has not stopped a further inflationary expansion of global reserves. I have tried to counter this argument by pointing out that the additions to global reserves since 1973 have largely gone to OPEC countries and the OPEC dollar reserves are not as inflationary as reserves accruing to industrial countries. Triffin's criticism of my argument is that money supply in most OPEC countries as well as OPEC imports have risen sharply and "that the reserves of Japan and most European countries ... pariculary Germany's increased enormously ... throughout all the post war years."

I am fully aware that OPEC countries have turned out to be much better spenders than was expected and that they have preferred inflation to appreciation of their currencies.[41] But what has that to do with the expansion of global reserves? Could the IMF have prevented inflation in the OPEC countries by control of global reserves? Triffin does not say nor does he ask the question whether the IMF *should* have tried. Few would answer that question in the affirmative.

It is true that Japanese and European reserves grew sharply during the postwar period. But the greatest part of the growth occurred during the par value system. According to IMF statistics, world reserves grew by about $60 billion from 1973 to October 1976. Of these more than $40 billion were OPEC accumulations. Japanese reserves were lower in October 1976 than in 1972. German reserves doubled from 1970 to 1973. Since then they rose by about 12 percent, largely as a consequence of interventions in the European common float ("snake").

Triffin agrees with me that in the last few years persistent diseqilibria have often been financed by borrowing rather than "by transfers of reserves." But he insists that "a more moderate expansion of reserves and, therefore, of high-powered reserve money would have helped to limit overborrowing and excessive lending." How the IMF could accomplish that under floating, Triffin does not explain. I discuss that problem below.

Triffin further agrees that "floating rates have made it possible for surplus countries to regain control over their money-printing press and to stem the inflationary flood of dollar balances which they had to absorb under fixed exchange rates." But, he says, under the Bretton Woods system, countries could appreciate their currencies. The trouble was that surplus countries were reluctant to do so, for the valid reason that under the par value system exchange rate changes were accompanied by disruptive captial flows, and undershooting or overshooting of the equilibrium rate of exchange was all but unavoidable. That is why floating became necessary.

Triffin is, however, mistaken when he says that "countries (e.g., Canada, Germany, and the Netherlands) continued to accumulate huge amounts of reserves well after they began floating." Canadian and Dutch reserves have fluctuated in a very narrow range since floating started (in 1970 and 1973, respectively) and, as noted, German reserves that grew explosively before 1973 have since then increased much more slowly. The main cause of further German reserve growth were interventions in the "minisnake." Thus the reserve growth was not the consequence of floating but of nonfloating.

Triffin repeats the complaint that the United States could run "enormous deficits" without being forced to adjust. According to his calculations during 1970–75, net U.S. reserve losses totaled about $70 billion and "96 percent of them were financed by piling up indebtedness to foreign monetary authorities." But most of these liabilities were incurred before floating became widespread. Liabilities to foreign central banks and governments rose from $16 billion in 1969 to $67 billion in 1973. Since then the growth of official foreign liabilities has slowed sharply, though it has not stopped. By August 1976 these liabilities had grown to $87 billion. However, such liabilities to Western Europe, whose currencies float, have remained practically unchanged since 1973.

I made it clear in my paper that by discounting the importance of control of global reserves I did not wish to minimize the dangers of inflation. On the contrary, inflation is in my opinion a major world problem. But world inflation has no longer anything to do with a lack of control over global reserves; it has its roots in *national* monetary, fiscal, and exchange rate policies primarily in the major countries. The primary responsibility for preventing world inflation thus falls on the leading industrial countries, especially on the United States. This follows from the fact that many, if not most, smaller countries peg their currencies to some key currency, most of them to the dollar, or to a basket of such currencies.

It is true that national monetary policies (inflation or deflation) in countries that peg to the dollar are profoundly influenced, if not fully determined, by the inflation, or absence of it, in the United States. If the United States lapses into inflation, dollar balances pile up in the dependent countries and inflation spreads. It follows that if the IMF could control inflation in the United States and in a few other key countries, it would substantially control world inflation. If control of global reserves is unconventionally interpreted to include control of monetary policy and, therefore, of inflation in the United States and some other major countries then, and only then, could it be said that control of global reserves is necessary to prevent world inflation. Perhaps Triffin had that in mind.

Actually the IMF can do nothing about inflation in the United States and only in exceptional cases, about inflation in other major countries. (The British borrowing may offer such an exceptional opportunity.) If the United States lapsed again into high inflation, the only effective measure to prevent the piling up of dollar balances abroad and to forestall the spread of U.S. inflation would be to stop pegging to the dollar. In other words, if there is inflation in the United States, floating is the only effective policy to prevent an excessive growth of international reserves in the form of dollar balances.

Triffin is surprised that my "only concrete suggestion ... to the Fund on how to fight inflation" is "to avoid an additional distribution of SDRs [and] the proliferation and expansion of unconditional lending facilities." He finds this odd because "88 percent of the inflationary expansion of world reserves has been derived from the accumulation of reserve currencies" and only 12 percent "of the inflationary explosion of reserves since the end of 1969" have been contributed by lending operations of the IMF. He complains that "nearly two thirds of these operations [of the IMF] have benefited the developed countries rather than the [developing countries]."

My answer is as follows. First, the subject of my paper was the importance of control of global reserves in a system of floating exchange rates. Triffin's figures relate largely to the prefloating period and hence are not relevant to my topic. Second, my remarks on the possible *direct* impact of IMF operations on world inflation were merely peripheral to my topic and were not meant to be a rounded discussion of what the IMF has done or could do to further a noninflationary expansion of the world economy. Such a discussion would have to consider what can be done indirectly in annual consultations, through prodding countries by conditional lending, and so forth. But that would go beyond the scope of my paper. Third, the question raised by Triffin whether the IMF has done enough for the developing countries I did not address at all. Triffin's answer to that question is clearly and resoundingly in the negative. My answer would be that the small percentage of total IMF lending going to developing countries throws no light at all on what benefits those nations derive from IMF activities. We should keep in mind that the industrial countries account for the great bulk of world trade; that their monetary, fiscal, and exchange-rate policies determine the stability of the world economy; that avoidance of inflationary (and deflationary) disruptions of world trade depend largely on how the major countries, the key currency countries, conduct their affairs. If by conditional lending to the developed countries, by prodding, annual consultations, and other measures the IMF is able to promote noninflationary expansion of trade, to help to avoid monetary disruptions and protectionist reactions and so to keep the channels of world trade open, then IMF activities are of immense benefit for the developing countries, even if only a small fraction of IMF lending directly goes to the developing countries.

Notes

1. Jacob Viner, *Studies in the Theory of International Trade* (New York: Harper, 1957), pp. 265 and 267. See the sections entitled 'Adequate Reserves," "Foreign Securities as a Secondary Reserve," "Silver as a Reserve," and "Cooperation between Central Banks," pp. 264–67.

2. On the English literature see Viner, *International Trade*, "Currency Reform Proposals," pp. 280–89.

3. In other words, under bimetallism the rate of exchange between gold and silver is fixed. If convertibility between the two monies is perserved and the chosen rate deviates from market equilibrium. Gresham's law comes into operation.

4. A. Marshall," Remedies for Fluctuations of General Prices," 1887, reprinted in A.C. Pigou, ed., *Memorials of Alfred Marshall* (London: Macmillan, 1925), and Marshall's evidence before the Gold and Silver Commission of 1888, reprinted in *Official Papers by Alfred Marshall* (London: Macmillan, 1926). See especially Question 9837, pp. 101–2. F. Y. Edgeworth. "Questions Connected with Bimetallism, " *The Economic Journal* (1895), reprinted in F. Y. Edgeworth, *Papers Relating to Political Economy*, vol. 1 (London: Macmillan, 1925). The term "symmetallism" seems to have been coined by Edgeworth (*Political Economy*, p. 431). It should be mentioned, however, that for Marshall (and probably also for Edgeworth), symmetallism was only a second-best solution, better than monometallism (of gold or of silver), but inferior to what Marshall called a "tabular standard," a sort of general optional indexation of debts including government securities (consols).

It is interesting to observe that according to Edgeworth, one of the advantages of symmetallism over bimetallism is that the former can be introduced independently by different countries and does *not* require international agreement on a common bundle of gold and silver. He points out that if two countries stabilized their currencies in terms of different bundles of gold and silver, the exchange rate between the two currencies would have to be allowed to fluctuate. Edgeworth does not recommend this system. He shows, however, that despite a fluctuating exchange rate the system may well ensure greater internal stability for the two currencies in terms of general purchasing power than would occur under a common monometallic standard of gold or silver, let alone in the case where one country was on the silver standard and the other on the gold standard. It should be recalled that the coexistence of the gold standard and silver standard, a situation implying that fluctuating exchange rates had lasted for a long time. China and Mexico remained on the silver standard well into the twentieth century.

5. Pigou. *Memorials of Alfred Marshall*. p. 206.

6. W. S. Jevons, *Money and the Mechanism of Exchange* (London: H. S. King, 1875); B. Graham, *Storage and Stability* (New York: McGraw-Hill, 1937) and *World Commodities and World Currency* (New York: McGraw-Hill, 1944); F. D. Graham, *Social Goals and Economic Institutions* (Princeton, N.J.: Princeton University Press, 1942); F. A. Hayek, "A Commodity Reserve Currency," *The Economic Journal* (June-September 1943), 53: 177–84, J. M. Keynes. "The Objective of International Price Stability," *The Economic Journal*, (June-September 1943), 53: 185–87; Milton Friedman. "Commodity-Reserve Currency," *Journal of Political Economy* (June 1951), 59: 203–32, reprinted in Milton Friedman. *Essays in Positive Economics* (Chicago: University of Chicago Press, 1953); Herbert Crubel, "The Case Against an International Commodity Reserve Currency." *Oxford Economic Papers* (1965), n.s., vol. 17, and the reply by A. G. Hart, "The Case For and Aganist International Reserve Currency," *ibid.* (1968), vol. 18; A. G. Hart, J. Tinbergen, and N. Kaldor, "The Case for an International Commodity Reserve Currency," paper submitted to UNCTAD, E/Conf. 46D Geneva, 1946 and reprinted in N. Kaldor, *Essays on Economic Policy*, (London: Duckworth, 1964), 2: 131–74. See also A. G. Hart, "The Case as of 1976 for International Commodity-Reserve Currency," *Weltwirtschaftliches Archiv* (1976), 112: 1–32. In the recent proposals the basic objectives of

the commodity reserve-currency proposal have changed. The objective is no longer purely monetary, that is, to provide the world with a more stable international monetary system. Equally or perhaps more important in the eyes of the recent proponents is the objective to transfer resources from the rich industrial countries to the poor raw-material-exporting countries.

7. O. Arendt, *Geld, Bank, Börse: Reden und Aufsätze* (Berlin, 1907), p. 15.

8. By out-and-out monetarists—if any exist—I mean economists who explain even minor fluctuations in business by minor fluctuations in the quantity of money and refuse to consider any other causes and cures of recessions, depressions, and the business cycle than money and monetary policy.

9. An excellent selection of these plans can be found in *World Monetary Reform, Plans and Issues*, H. Grubel, ed., Stanford University Press (Stanford: 1963) and an incisive analysis of many plans in F. Machlup, *Plans for Reform of the International Monetary System*, revised edition (Princeton, N.J.: Department of Economics, 1964).

10. John Williamson, "Survey in Applied Economics: International Liquidity," *The Economic Journal* (September 1973), 83:718 and 735. Most of these proposals misinterpreted the chronic British balance-of-payments difficulties as a worldwide shortage of liquidity. Ten years ago I wrote: "Countries with chronic blance-of-payments deficits like to blame their troubles on a lack of international liquidity. This is much more appealing than to attribute them to lack of discipline or policy mistakes. The outstanding example is Great Britain. The great majority of British experts right and left, irrespective of party affiliation, are convinced that Britain's chronic balance-of-payments difficulties are a consequence or symptom of a lack of international liquidity and more and more American experts inside and outside the government have become inclined to take the same view. ... While a real scarcity of international liquidity would almost certainly manifest itself in balance-of-payments deficits of some countries, not every balance-of-payments crisis, even of a reserve currency country, can be regarded as a symptom of an imternational scarcity of liquidity." Gottfried Haberier, "The International Payments System: Postwar Trends and Prospects," in *International Payments Problems*, a symposium sponsored by the American Enterprise Institute, Washington, D.C., 1966, pp. 9–10. R. G. Hawtrey was one of the few British dissenters. See Sir Ralph Hawtrey, "Too Little Liquidity—or Too Much?" *The Banker* (November 1962), 67:707–12.

11. Williamson, "International Liquidity."

12. Ibid., pp. 655–746. Apart from a few French items, Williamson's list covers only the literature in English, and his English list is by no means complete.

13. *International Reserves. Needs and Availability*. Papers and Proceedings of Seminar at the International Monetary Fund, June 1–3, 1970 (Washington, D.C.: IMF, 1970), pp. xiv and 552.

14. In the present paper I take it for granted that high inflation and sharply divergent inflation rates have forced the widespread adoption of floating, and not the other way round, although the opposite view that floating was responsible for the inflation still finds some support in the literature.

15. *See International Monetary Reform: Documents of the Committee of Twenty* (Washington, D.C.: IMF, 1974).

Tom de Vries, in his inside account of the reform negotiations, says: " ... Neither the Committee [of Twenty] nor the Deputies discussed the future exchange rate regime in any depth. This is quite remarkable in view of the fact that the world moved from a fixed-exchange rate system to a regime of floating rates during the very deliberations of the Committee. ... This made the work of the Committee look increasingly unreal. ... The Committee was saved from these contradictions by the quadrupling of the price of oil in ... 1973. So enormous was the uncertainty created by the disturbance ... and so evident became the fact that flexible rates were here to stay, that the Committee decided to give up its attempt at comprehensive reform." Tom de Vries, "Jamaica, or the Non-Reform of the International Monetary System," *Foreign Affairs* (April 1976), 54:585–88. Marcus Fleming once remarked in candid and rueful self-criticism, "at every stage in the discussion [of the reform of the international monetary system] reform proposals have lagged behind events and have been quickly outmoded by new events." See J. Marcus Fleming, *Reflections on the International Monetary Reform*, Princeton Essays in International Finance, No. 107, Department of Economics, Princeton University, Princeton, N.J., 1974, p. 17.

16. See, for example, F. Machlup, *Plans for Reform of the International Monetary System.*

17. Fleming's article, *"Floating Exchange Rates, Asymmetrical Interventions, and the Management of International Liquidity,"* IMF *Staff Papers* (July 1975), 22:263–83, seems to be the only attempt to squarely face the problem of international liquidity under floating. The highly involved presentation, the "meandering course" of the argument (the author's own description of his paper, on p. 281), and the author's reluctance to draw firm policy conclusions reflect the great difficulties of applying to a world of floating exchange rates the concepts and prescriptions that were developed for the par value system.

18. Roy Harrod, *Reforming the World's Money* (London: Macmillian: New York: St. Martins Press, 1965), pp. 45–47.

19. J. Williamson, *The Crawling Peg.* Princeton Essays in International Finance, No. 50, Department of Economics, Princeton University. Princeton, N.J., 1965, p. 8.

20. Experience has shown that in the long run, capital controls require current account controls, not only to prevent evasions such as illegal over- or underinvoicing of imports (or exports) for the purposes of camouflaging capital movements, but also because trade flows, for example, accumulation or decumulation of inventories of imported commodities, can serve as substitutes for international capital flows. The prevention of such perfectly legal evasions of the capital controls requires tight controls of current transactions.

21. John Williamson, "Exchange Rate Flexibility and Reserve Use," IMF Document, 1974, incorporated in "Exchange-Rate Flexibility and Reserve Use," *Scandinavian Journal of Economics* (1976), 78:327–39. Williamson also presents an ingenious theoretical model in mathematical terms that is supposed to throw light on the question whether there would be any difference in the amount of reserve use under managed floating than under a par value system. The model suffers, however, from several serious shortcomings as Stanley W. Black ("Comments on J. Williamson's 'Exchange Rate Flexibility and Reserve Use.'" pp. 340–45) has pointed out. The results of Williamson's model, as he himself summarizes them, are not very enlightening. The model hardly adds anything to the verbal argument. It seems that he, too, compares floating not with the adjustable peg system, but with more or less credibly fixed rates, that is in effect with the gold standard. See also the comments by Otmar Emminger on

Williamson's thesis in O. Emminger. *On the Way to a New International Order* (Washington, D.C.: American Enterprise Institute. 1976), pp. 16–17.

22. J. Marcus Fleming, "International Liquidity: Ends and Means," *IMF Staff Papers* (December 1961), vol. 8, reprinted as chapter 4 in J. Marcus Fleming, *Essays in International Economics* (Cambridge, Mass.: Harvard University Press, 1971). See also the chapter 5 through 7 and Fleming's powerful paper, "Reserve Creation and Real Reserves," in *International Reserves: Needs and Availability* (Washington, D.C.: International Monetary Fund, 1970), pp. 521–52. In a lengthy, closely reasoned essay, "Floating Exchange Rates, Asymmetrical Intervention, and the Management of International Liquidity," *IMF Staff Papers* (July 1975), 22:263–83, Fleming tried to assess the changes in the liquidity problem wrought by widespread floating.

23. Fleming, *Essays*, p. 97, and "Reserve Creation and Real Reserves," p. 524.

24. On the international quantity theory, see Williamson "Survey," p. 711. It should be observed that few modern quantity theorists (or monetarists, as they are usually called) have embraced the international quantity theory. Williamson mentions only Robert Mundell. Arthur Laffer also comes to mind, and Harry Johnson and Jürg Niehans came close to embracing it in their comments on Cooper's paper at the IMF seminar *International Reserves* (pp. 149 and 152). The international quantity theory seems to be coextensive with what Marina v. N. Whitman calls "global monetarism." See her paper, "Global Monetarism and the Monetary Approach to the Balance of Payments," in *Brookings Papers on Economic Activity* (Washington, D.C.: Brookings Institution, 1975), 3:531–55 and my review of J. A. Frenkel and H. G. Johnson, eds., *The Monetary Approach to the Balance of Payments*, in *Journal of Economic Literature* (December 1976), 14:1324–27.

25. See Polak's important paper, "Money: National and International," in *Essays in Honor of Thorkil Kristensen* (Paris: OECD, 1970), and reprinted in *International Reserves*, the IMF seminar volume of 1970. Sohmen's paper, "International Liquidity under Flexible Exchange Rates," is a draft for *Exchange Rate Flexibility*, proceedings of a conference held by the American Enterprise Institute and the U.S. Treasury in April 1976. *Exchange Rate Flexibility*, Edited by J. S. Dreyer, G. Haberler, and T. D. Willett (Washington D.C.: American Enterprise Institute for Public Policy Research, 1978), pp. 255–263.]

26. *International Reserves*, p. 525.

27. The international quantity theorists or global monetarists seem to be harking back to the days of the gold standard. In those days the similarity between official and private behavior with respect to cash and reserve holdings was indeed much greater than it is now, because the rules of the gold standard tended to make central banks behave like individuals: to contract the money supply, thereby inducing reductions in overall expenditures when reserves declined, and to expand the money supply when reserves increased. The growing tendency to violate the rules of the gold standard—to put *domestic* policy objectives, that is, employment, growth, and price stability in some combination (which often differs from country to country), ahead of the objective of keeping the *external* value of the currency (the exchange rate)—has progressively destroyed the similarity and has rendered the gold standard more and more unworkable.

28. Gottfried Haberler, *Money in the International Economy* (Cambridge, Mass: Harvard University Press, 1965), p. 42.

29. For references to that theory, see Williamson, "Survey," p. 694.

30. Richard J. Sweeney and Thomas D. Willett, "Eurodollars, Petrodollars, and World Liquidity and Inflation," in *Journal of Monetary Economics* (Amsterdam: North Holland, 1976). The reference list of this paper updates the bibliography in Williamson, "Survey."

31. The reasons have been spelled out in greater detail in Peter Kenen's contribution to this conference.

32. On the treatment of OPEC reserves, see especially William R. Cline, *International Monetary Reform and the Developing Countries* (Washington, D.C.: Brookings Institution, 1976), ch. 4.

33. The growing reliance on external borrowing for financing balance-of-payments deficits and propping up the exchange rate is stressed in the *IMF Annual Report, 1976* (Washington, D.C.: IMF, 1976), pp. 39–40.

34. John Williamson, "The Benefits and Costs of an International Monetary Nonsystem," in *Reflections on Jamaica*. Essays in International Finance, No. 115, Department of Economics, Princeton University, April 1976, p. 57. We can surely disregard the danger of deflation. For no country is likely to permit deflation for balance-of-payments reasons. Furthermore, the imposition of import controls for balance-of-payments reasons (rather than on protectionist grounds) has not become a very serious problem under floating, at least not yet.

Marcus Fleming stated in his last paper: "In spite of these disturbances [mainly the oil price rise, which Fleming characterized as "one of the biggest exogenuous balance-of-payments shocks of all time"] there has thus far been remarkably little resort to restrictionism by industrial or even by primary producing countries. This has been due to a combination of circumstances. Some of the credit must go to the much-abused Eurocurrency market, together with the willingness of countries to borrow where necessary from the private market. Some of it must go to the system of managed exchange rate floating which, at some cost to exchange stability in the short term, has succeeded in containing disequilibrating capital flows, and has also permitted exchange rates to adjust in the longer run to differential rates of inflation." Marcus J. Fleming, "Mercantilism and Free Trade Today," IMF Document, April 5, 1976, mimeographed [J. Marcus Fleming, *Essays on Economic Policy* (New York: Columbia Press, 1978), pp. 361–381.]

35. Williamson, "Benefits and Costs," p. 57. Similar fears that the gold provisions of the amended IMF charter may have global inflationary effects have been expressed by others.

36. Annual Report of the Bank for International Settlements, Basel, 1976, p. 109.

37. International Monetary Fund. Article IV, Section 1 (III).

38. "Merely managed or controlled floating" implies that the only measure to influence the exchange rate directly is buying and selling in the foreign exchange market. Influencing the exchange rate *indirectly* by general monetary and fiscal policy is a different matter. For example, I would not speak of a "managed float" if a decline in the exchange rate induced a country to tighten monetary policy. It is sometimes said that the monetary authorities can influence the exchange rate interventions in the money market, by buying and selling bonds, just as well as by interventions in the foreign-exchange rate. This may be true with high capital mobility if exchange rates are credibly fixed as they were under the gold standard. But when that credibility is gone, monetary policy becomes a very imperfect substitute for interventions in the exchange market.

39. To avoid a possible misunderstanding. I should like to stress that this statement does not reflect a value judgment to the effect that rising prices are a greater evil than high unemployment. On the contrary, my personal value judgment would be the reverse. What it does reflect, and what the authors of the IMF annual report probably had in mind, is that the objective of sustainable growth and full employment cannot be achieved unless inflation is curbed.

40. Some of these problems are further discussed in G. Haberler. "The International Monetary System after Jamaica and Manila," in *Contemporary Science Problems*. William Fellner, ed. (Washington, D.C.: American Enterprise Institute, 1977).

41. I discussed these problems in a previous paper: see G. Haberler, "Oil, Inflation, Recession and the International Monetary System." *The Journal of Energy and Development* (1976), 1:177–90. Available also as Reprint No. 45. American Enterprise Institute, Washington, D.C., 1976 [Chapter 14 in this volume].

11

The International Monetary System in the World Recession

1. The State of the World Economy

Scope and Causes of the World Recession

The world economy seems to be just emerging from the severest and longest recession of the postwar period. The strong rebound of the U.S. economy undoubtedly plays a major role in the global recovery. Despite the often-heard warning that the world has already started, or is just about, to slide into a deep depression, it must be stressed that the recent decline has been a recession and not a depression, if by depression we mean a decline in economic activity approaching the magnitude of the Great Depression of the 1930s or earlier depressions.[1]

Some data will show that the recent decline has been mild compared with that of the 1930s, and I shall argue that, despite certain dangers ahead, it is unlikely that a major depression will develop.

First, let us look at some global data. In the Great Depression, 1929–1933, the value of world trade in terms of gold dollars fell by about one-half and in real terms by about one-third, the difference reflecting the terrific decline in the price level, especially of internationally traded goods. In sharp contrast in the recent recession, according to the latest statistics of the General Agreement on Tariffs and Trade (GATT), in 1982 the volume of world trade fell by about 2 percent from the level of 1981, declining to about the volume prevailing in 1979. In U.S. dollars the decline of world trade from 1981 to 1982 was 6 percent.[2]

A glance at the economies of the industrial countries leads to the same conclusion, that they suffer from a recession but not a depression. In 1982–1983 U.S. unemployment reached 10.8 percent compared with 25 percent in the Great Depression.

Editor's Note: The summary that precedes this article is not included.

Essays in Contemporary Economic Problems—Disinflation, 1983–1984. William Fellner, Project Director. (Washington, D.C.: American Enterprise Institute, 1984). © 1984, American Enterprise Institute. Reprinted with permission.

Moreover, because of generous unemployment benefits, unemployment today is a lesser evil than if was in the 1930s. Today's unemployment figures contain a much larger portion of spurious, voluntary unemployment than those of the 1930s, and the hardship on the jobless is much less than it was fifty years ago. From 1929 to 1933 real GNP fell by 30 percent compared with 1.8 percent from 1973 to 1975 and −1.1 percent from July 1981 to March 1983.

The recession in Europe seems to be more severe and persistent than in the United States. Germany has the highest unemployment rate (10 percent) since the German economy rose from the ashes of the Third Reich. In France, Mitterrand's socialist government follows in the footsteps of the popular front (socialist) government of Léon Blum almost fifty years ago (1936)[3]—combining an expansionary ("Keynesian") policy with price- and wage-boosting measures and nationalization of banks and industries. The predictable result was the same—rising unemployment and inflation and huge balance of payments deficits.

Both in France and in Germany, the present difficulties are definitely a recession and not a depression. For example, unemployment in Germany at the nadir of the Great Depression, in 1932, was 43 percent, much higher than it was in the United States, and four times higher than it is in 1983.[4] In France the contrast between 1983 and the 1930s is certainly much smaller.

It would not be necessary to dwell on this if it were not for the widespread atmosphere of gloom and pessimism, not only in political circles and the media, but also among professional economists. This pessimism concerns the severity of the recession, the prospects as well as the ability, or inability, of governments to do anything about it, and the competence, or incompetence, of economists to provide an acceptable explanation or cure. Five examples of this pessimism, three from prominent noneconomists and two from well-known economists, should be sufficient.

Henry Kissinger writes in an article titled "Saving the World Economy":

John Maynard Keynes wrote that practical men who believe themselves quite exempt from intellectual influences are usually the slaves of some defunct economist. Politicians these days certainly have many economic theories to choose from, most discordant, not a few of them defunct. No previous theory seems capable of explaining the current crisis of the world economy.[5]

Ralf Dahrendorf, a political scientist, former prominent member of the German Free Democratic Party and now director of the London School of Economics, writes in an article titled "Die Arbeitsgesellschaft ist am Ende": "Whoever promises that he has a cure for unemployment, says an untruth."[6]

Somewhat pathetic is the statement of Pierre Mauroy, the socialist prime minister of France. At a meeting of seven socialist nations in Paris before the Williamsburg summit, according to news reports he said: "The world recession is the crisis of a system that is not ours—it is the crisis of the capitalist system."[7] The French situation may be serious enough to be called a crisis, but the world recession is not.

Following are two appraisals of the present state of the world economy by economists that are much too alarmist to my mind.

Peter Kenen writes:

The world is mired deeply in a macroeconomic mess, and it is getting worse. Forecasts of recovery recede before our eyes. But governments are paralyzed by myths that they [read: their economic advisers or mentors] created. It is impossible, they say, to cut taxes or to increase public spending, because budget deficits are too large. It is impossible, they say, to speed up monetary growth, because it will rekindle inflation immediately.[8]

Since Kenen wrote, the cyclical recovery, which he saw receding before his eyes, has started and gathered momentum in the United States and in other industrial countries too.

Lester Thurow comes to a similar depressing conclusion:

If one thinks of the economics profession as a navigator charged with achieving a high rate of economic growth without hitting the icebergs of inflation or unemployment, the profession has clearly failed. The world economy is sinking, yet the profession is unable to reach any consensus on what should be done. In the resulting confusion, policy makers wander at random from policy to policy, but nothing seems to work.[9]

Both authors recommend "Keynesian" policies of monetary-fiscal expansion, jointly undertaken by major industrial countries, fortified by some sort of incomes policy.[10]

Actually, the explanation of the world recession and its relative severity is easy; it was predictable and was predicted. The basic reason for the recession is that the major industrial countries were forced to bring inflation down by monetary restraint. The recession in the United States and in other industrial countries was relatively severe for two reason: inflationary expectations have become deeply entrenched by long inflationary abuse,[11] and the economy, especially wages, is becoming increasingly more rigid.

Two other factors often mentioned as being largely responsible for the recession, oil shocks and exchange rate volatility, will be considered below. But first a few observations about the basic reason.

It is simply impossible to stop an inflation without a transitional period of higher unemployment, in other words, without a recession. The size and duration of unemployment, which unavoidably accompanies the process of disinflation, depend largely on wage behavior. It stands to reason that the more rigid wages are, the more unemployment will be created by disinflation, leaving open the controversial question whether perfect wage flexibility could avoid unemployment altogether.

In recent years more and more economists have reached the conclusion that a full and sustained recovery from the present recession will require a moderate reduction of real wages, in all industrial countries (with the possible exception of Japan) to bring about a shift in the income distribution from wages and salaries to profits for the purpose of stimulating investment and growth.

I cite three examples of this trend of thought. Two years ago a group of prominent German economists, several of them monetarists, issued a statement urging a temporary wage freeze. Since there was still a significant rate of inflation at that time, a temporary freeze of money wages would have brought about the required reduction in real wages. The plea of the economists was not heeded, however; wages continued to rise, and unemployment has reached the two-digit level.

Herbert Giersch, a monetarist, has argued in several important articles that all industrial countries suffer from excessively high real wages and too low profits. He thinks it will take several years to bring about the necessary adjustment in the income distribution.[12]

The theme has been taken up by *The Economist* (London) in two excellent articles.[13] *The Economist* asks for a substantial cut in *money* wages to bring about an increase in profits for the purpose of stimulating investment, growth, and employment. Predictably, this has shocked many of *The Economist's* Keynesian readers.[14]

The main argument against cutting money wages as a recovery measure is that it reduces total spending by reducing money income of labor, and thus is a deflationary factor that would intensify the recession. This argument is, however, fallacious and rests on a misunderstanding of what wage cut is supposed to achieve. The purpose is not to reduce effective demand (nominal GNP); if such a reduction is necessary, it should be done by restrictive monetary-fiscal measures. The purpose of cutting money wages is to boost profits and stimulate investment, employment, and growth. Suppose hourly wage rates are cut by 10 percent—that does not necessarily mean that the wage bill and spending power of labor is reduced. If the elasticity of demand for labor is greater than unity (as it almost certainly is in the medium run), employment (in terms of hours) will rise by more than 10 percent, and the wage bill and spending will rise. True, if employment rises by less than 10 percent, labor income will decline; but that does not mean that total incomes and spending, too, will decline. A shift to profits will stimulate investment, employment, and growth. This tendency could be assisted by monetary expansion; the reduction of the unit labor cost would ease the inflationary danger of easier money .

What these three statements of the problem have in common is that they assume that market forces will, in due course, bring about the necessary restructuring of the economy to achieve substantially full employment, provided a moderate cut in the wage level is achieved, and macroeconomic levers are set right. The first of the two articles in *The Economist* cited above brings that assumption out very clearly. It argues that entrepreneurs would find hundreds of ways to substitute labor for capital if labor costs were reduced, just as they found ways to substitute capital for labor when wages went up.

This optimistic conclusion will be challenged by the "structuralists." In the 1930s it was widely believed that part of the unemployment problem was that labor-saving inventions had reduced the demand for labor, or that the "structure of production" had been distorted in some other way. In other words, it was argued that a large part of unemployment was "technological" and "structural," requiring large-scale reallocation of factors of production, a time-consuming, painful process. There can be no doubt that subsequent developments were entirely at variance with that structuralist theory. Experience has shown that as soon as deflation was stopped, the huge structural distortions that had been diagnosed by theorists during the depression had shriveled as quickly as they had surfaced earlier. What was called "secondary deflation" turned out to be a much more important cause of high unemployment than structural distortions that may have started the deflationary spiral. In other words, the great bulk of unemployment was "Keynesian" (or monetarist, if you like), not structural or "Hayekian."

Extreme structuralist views can be heard again today. It is said that robots and other "smart" machines have put human labor in the same position as horses were when tractors came into wide use. This is, however, a very misleading analogy. Tractors replaced not only horsepower but also manpower. But unlike horses, human labor could be shifted to producing tractors.

This is not to deny that it is possible that technological progress may require reallocation of factors of production that may cause some structural unemployment until the transfer and retraining of labor has been carried out. As we have seen, a modest decline of the share of labor in the national product is probably required now. But it is most unlikely that a large reduction of the marginal productivity of labor, an intolerable drop in the real wage, and a massive decline of the share of labor (and salaries) would occur, as the analogy with the horses suggests. As far as we can tell, the share of labor in the national product has remained remarkably stable—apart from cyclical fluctuations—despite the tremendous technological changes, including mechanization and automation, that have occurred since the industrial revolution in England.

I conclude that the present-day gloomy forecasts that disaster will befall us unless radical reforms are undertaken, involving massive redistribution of income to spread work, will turn out to be totally unfounded. These forecasts will share the fate of earlier, similar gloomy prophecies, which regularly made their appearance in periods of depression, from those underlying the Luddite movement to the most famous, Karl Marx's theory of increasing misery of the working classes—prophecies that were completely disproved and discredited by subsequent developments.

The Role of the Oil Shocks

The two oil shocks, the quadrupling of the crude oil price in 1973 and doubling in 1979–1980, have been widely held primarily responsible for the world inflation and the recession. In my opinion this is a great exaggeration. The first oil shock was preceded and accompanied by a highly inflationary commodity boom, which, in turn, was superimposed on an inflationary groundswell that encompassed the whole postwar period and went into high gear in the 1960s.[15] For the United States the additional oil import bill due to the first oil shock was about $20 billion a year. This was about 1.22 percent of the GNP at that time, or less than half of the normal annual increase in GNP. It follows that a once-for-all small decrease of about 1.22 percent in the wage level would have taken care of the problem, or, assuming that money wages were rigid downward, a once-for-all increase in the price level of about 1.22 percent would have solved the problem. An additional increase in inflation by 1.22 percentage points is a matter of minor importance in a period of two-digit inflation.

For other industrial countries the oil levy was a greater burden than for the United States, because they depend more heavily on imports. The jump in the oil import bill from 1973 to 1974 was about 4.31 percent of GNP for Japan, 3.96 percent for Italy, 3.73 percent for the United Kingdom, and 2.17 percent for Germany.[16] This is not a negligible burden, but it is not an intolerable one. For all Organization for Economic Cooperation and Development (OECD) countries as a group it was less than one year's normal growth. Hence, ideally, suspension of wage (income) growth for less than a year or a mild once-for-all rise in the price level would have taken care of the problem.

The conclusion I draw is that if one wants to assign to the oil price rise a major role in inflation and recession, it must be done by stressing *indirect* effects, for example, by assuming what J. R. Hicks has called "real wage resistance"—workers resisting not only money wage decreases but also real wage decreases, which could be brought about by widespread indexation of wages (and other incomes).

This theory has been widely applied to the second oil shock. Karl Otto Pôhl, president of the German Bundesbank, in a wide-ranging speech attributed "the present difficulties"—high inflation and unemployment—"to the delayed effect of the second oil price shock," in the sense that "all segments of society defend their acquired income levels and living standards against the dictates of OPEC." [17].

While in the first oil shock the OPEC crude oil price was quadrupled, in the second one it was "merely" doubled. For the United States the increase in the net oil import bill, the oil levy imposed by OPEC, amounted to about 0.52 percent of GNP. This can hardly be regarded as a major factor in the U.S. inflation or recession. For Germany the increase in the levy from 1979 to 1980 amounts to something like 0.86 percent of GNP. This factor can scarcely be assigned the major role in causing the

German inflation or recession—a conclusion supported by the fact that Germany did not experience any noticeable improvement when the oil price tumbled in 1982. The same is true of Britain when it became a net exporter of oil.

The general conclusion is that the two oil shocks aggravated world inflation and thereby also the subsequent recession, but they were neither the initiating nor the major cause.

The International Debt Problem

A word must be said about the international debt problem, for it is widely feared that default by some of the large debtor countries—Mexico, Brazil—would topple a number of large international banks and thus plunge the world economy into a deep depression. This would justify, it is said, a bail-out of the banks or of the defaulting countries at almost any cost to the taxpayers of the United States and of other industrial countries.

I will not discuss this danger and the likelihood of its happening but will address a narrower question: If there are a few defaults and a large number of international banks get into serious trouble, would that have the same deflationary effect on the United States and other industrial countries as the collapse of the banking system and deflation had in the 1930s?

My answer is no. This relatively optimistic conclusion is based on the assumption that it is an established fact that the exceptional severity of the Great Depression of 1929–1933 was due to a contraction of the money stock by about 30 percent. One need not be an extreme monetarist to accept that proposition. Joseph A. Schumpeter, who was definitely not a monetarist, said that the waves of bank failures in the early 1930s "turned retreat into rout"; what otherwise would have been a regular or perhaps a relatively severe cyclical recession became a catastrophic slump.

It is unthinkable today that the monetary authorities would stand idly by and let the money supply contract by 30 percent as the Federal Reserve did in the 1930s. What would be necessary to avoid a sharp contraction of the money supply is not to protect the managers or shareholders of the banks, nor to bail out the defaulting countries, but to protect the depositors.

To sum up, a default of large debtor countries would be most unfortunate. It would be much better, also for the countries concerned, if they restored their creditworthiness by putting their houses in order and by carrying out the austerity programs prescribed by the IMF. The default and its repercussions on the lending banks would put a damper on the recovery from the recession, but it would not plunge the industrial countries into a deep depression. If the major industrial countries keep their economies on an even keel, the rest of the world, too, will avoid a severe depression.

2. The International Monetary System

How Floating Originated—The Decline of the Dollar

The international monetary system, or nonsystem as some experts like to call it, is still one of widespread managed floating. All major currencies and many minor ones float, most of them with frequent interventions by central banks in the foreign exchange market.

There are, however, some areas of stable rates. Approximately 100, mostly small countries peg their currencies to the dollar, the German mark, the French franc, special drawing rights, or some other basket of currencies; and the nine members of the European Monetary System try to keep the exchange rate of their currencies in precarious stability, floating jointly against the dollar and other currencies.

It is not surprising that the recession caused exchange rate fluctuations, which in turn were and are widely regarded as excessive and as a sign of malfunctioning of floating exchange rates. As during the whole postwar period, the U.S. dollar is the center of discussion.

It will be useful to sketch very briefly the evolution of the international monetary system in the postwar period. Special reference will be made to how floating originated, because this is in danger of being forgotten.

During the early postwar period the dollar was generally accepted as "better than gold." This is underscored by the great popularity in the 1940s and 1950s of the theory of the "permanent" dollar shortage, which was especially popular in Britain, where even giants among economists such as J. R. Hicks and D. H. Robertson embraced it, though not in such a crude form as many others espoused it.[18]

The rapid recovery of Europe and Japan and the devaluation of the British pound and of many other currencies in 1949 confronted U.S. industries with increasing competition. The dollar lost some of its bloom and became "more equal." But up to the mid–1960s, the U.S. inflation was one of the lowest in the world, and the strength of the dollar remained unquestioned.

This began to change after 1965 when the Johnson administration started to finance the escalating war in Vietnam and the equally expensive Great Society programs at home through inflationary borrowing. Gradually, the emergence of a significant inflation differential between the United States and other industrial countries, primarily the three strong-currency countries, Germany, Switzerland, and later Japan, became noticeable. In 1969 the German mark and in June 1971 the Swiss franc were revalued. On August 15, 1971, the gold convertibility of the dollar was suspended, and the major currencies de facto floated. On December 18, 1971, in the Smithsonian realignment of exchange rates, the U.S. dollar was formally devalued, and most major currencies were revalued in terms of gold.

The Smithsonian Agreement did not last long. In June 1972 the British pound was set afloat, and early in 1973 the realignment became unstuck. After huge interventions in the foreign exchange markets by foreign central banks in the vain attempt to prop up the dollar, all major currencies were set afloat. Thus in 1973 the Bretton Woods regime came to an end. The adjustable peg system simply could not cope with the strains and stresses on the balance of payments caused by high global inflation.

That floating was imposed by events on reluctant policy makers is demonstrated by the fact that in 1974, a year after widespread floating had started, a prestigious Committee on Reform of the International Monetary System (Committee of Twenty) wrote in its report to the governors of the IMF, "The [reformed] exchange rate system will remain based on stable but adjustable par values."[19] According to insiders, the repeated statements by the committee that the reformed system would be one of stable but adjustable pegs "made the work of the Committee look increasingly unreal."[20]

In 1970 one dollar was worth 4.31 Swiss francs, 3.65 German marks, and 360 yen. Two years later the rates were 3.81 Swiss francs, 3.81 German marks, and 303 yen. Since then there have been fairly large fluctuations, but even after the recent surge of the dollar, its value in terms of the three strong-currency countries did not come anywhere near the 1970 level, though the average effective exchange rate vis-à-vis fifteen major countries (as measured by Morgan Guaranty Trust Company of New York) was about the same in early 1983 as in pre-June 1970.

Five years later, in 1975, the dollar had another spell of weakness, which again was the consequence of a large inflation differential between the United States and the strong-currency countries. The year 1974 was one of high global inflation. Even Switzerland had a 10 percent inflation rate. In the United States the inflation rate reached 12 percent but was brought down to a little below 5 percent by the end of 1976. It started to rise again and reached the two-digit level in 1979 when the Carter administration prematurely shifted emphasis from fighting inflation to stimulating the economy.[21]

The three strong-currency countries, in contrast, continued the anti-inflation policy. Switzerland brought its rate of inflation down to practically zero. As a consequence of this disinflation policy, the three countries had a slower recovery from the recession than the United States; they accepted a temporarily lower rate of growth of output and employment to bring inflation down, while the United States impatiently reflated the economy.

The divergent growth and price trends, the result of a divergent policy stance, produced a heavy deficit in the U.S. trade and current account balance, which was widely regarded as an alarm signal. The trade deficit was $9.3 billion in 1976, $30.9

billion in 1977, and $33.7 billion in 1978. The current account balance had a surplus of $4.6 million in 1976 and a deficit of $14 billion in 1977 and $13.5 billion in 1978. No wonder that market participants, both private and official (foreign central banks), became increasingly pessimistic about the future of the dollar and started to diversify their currency holdings. In October 1978 the foreign exchange markets became quite jittery, and on November 1, 1978, President Carter announced a sharp reversal of economic policy, the so-called (first) dollar rescue operation, consisting of a tightening of monetary policy and the mobilization of a $30 billion fund of foreign currencies for interventions in the foreign exchange market.

The response of the markets was dramatic. From October 31, 1978, to December 8, 1978, with the assistance of central bank interventions, the mark declined against the dollar by 8.2 percent, the Swiss franc by 12.9 percent, and the yen by 3.7 percent. The dollar appreciated overall by about 7.9 percent. The monetary restraint did not, however, last very long. Before the middle of 1979 the monetary aggregates resumed their rapid climb. The dollar again declined, and the markets became unsettled. At the annual meeting of the International Monetary Fund in Belgrade, according to news reports, Paul Volcker, the newly appointed chairman of the Board of Governors of the Federal Reserve System, was put on notice by some of his European colleagues that they would stop supporting the dollar if the United States did not take decisive steps against inflation. Volcker left the meeting hurriedly, and on October 6, 1979, the second dollar rescue package was announced, consisting of a sharp rise in the discount rate, higher reserve requirements for certain types of liabilities, and a shift in the operating procedures of monetary policy from emphasis on interest rate targets to emphasis on monetary aggregates.[22] Since then, the growth of monetary aggregates has slowed, and interest rates have risen sharply.

The policy shift of October 1979 was a real turning point. At last the process of disinflation had started. The response of the foreign exchange market was again favorable, though the steep ascent of the dollar got under way only a year later, after the election of Ronald Reagan.

The Rise of the Dollar since 1980 and the Recent Criticism of Floating Exchange Rates

The dramatic rise of the dollar, since 1980, as measured overall by the trade-weighted effective rate and vis-à-vis the Swiss franc, the German mark, and Japanese yen, is depicted in figure 11.1 and 11.2. The chart also shows large fluctuations. The dollar appreciated also in real terms as measured by the real exchange rate (the nominal effective rate adjusted for inflation in the countries concerned), both overall and against the three countries mentioned. This means that the recent appreciation

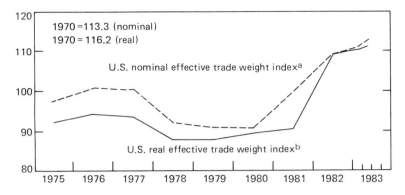

Figure 11.1
Movement in exchange rates, 1975-1983.

a. 1980 - 1982 = 100. The index measures the currency's trade-weighted value vis-a-vis
fifteen other major currencies. Annual figures are averages of months. Trade weights
based on 1980 bilateral trade in manufactures.
b. 1980 - 1982 = 100. Index of the nominal effective exchange rate adjusted for inflation
differentials, which are measured by wholesale prices of nonfood manufactures.
Source: World Financial Markets, August 1983, Morgan Guaranty Trust Company of
New York.

of the dollar, unlike its depreciation in the early 1970s, cannot, at least not fully, be
explained by inflation differentials or purchasing power parity changes.

Before taking up possible explanations, I will discuss various criticisms of floating
exchange rates that were induced, revived, and intensified by the appreciation of the
dollar.

We have seen that in official circles floating was accepted very reluctantly and
with a very costly delay.[23] In academic circles, too, much aversion to flexible
exchange rates and a deep-seated nostalgia for fixed rates quickly developed.

It is natural that advocates of the gold standard deplore floating, though it seems
that some of them are ready to settle for stable but adjustable rates à la Bretton
Woods. Now that the Gold Commission has issued its report, it is hardly necessary
to set out the reasons why a return to the gold standard and fixed rates is entirely out
of the question.

It is interesting, however, and should give satisfaction to the advocates of the
gold standard, that the basic rule of balance of payments adjustment under the gold
standard inevitably emerges again and again in present-day discussions—in modern
terminology, of course, and transposed to the inflationary conditions of our times.
This rule can be stated as follows: A deficit country that loses gold should let its
money supply decline by the full amount of the gold loss or by more. A country in

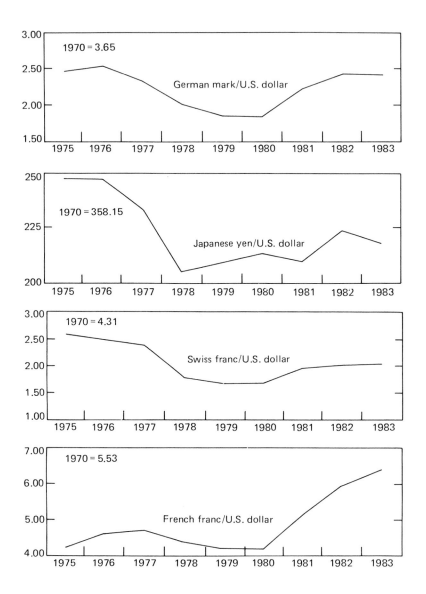

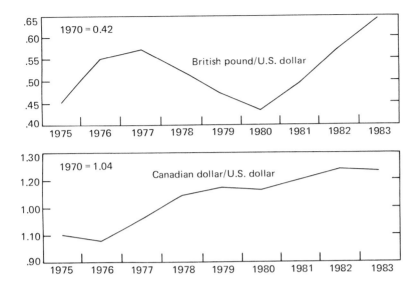

Figure 11.2
Movement in exchange rates.
Note. Data for 1983 are averages of data from the first and second quarters of 1983.
Source: Federal Reserve Board, Exchange Rate Release G-5.

surplus should let its money supply expand by the full amount of the gold gain or by more. This will bring downward pressure on money incomes and prices in the deficit country, and upward pressure in the surplus countries, and thus restore equilibrium in the balance of payments.[24]

To translate the rule into modern terminology, substitute the broader concept of "international reserves" for the gold stock and reflect that the policy of the central banks under the gold standard to buy and sell gold at the gold export and import points, respectively, to keep exchange rates stable can be described as "nonsterilized interventions." (More will be said on the distinction of "sterilized" or "pure" and "nonsterilized" interventions later in this chapter.)

To transpose the gold standard rule to the inflationary conditions of our times, substitute "changes in monetary growth targets" for "absolute changes in the money supply." Countries in deficit should lower their monetary growth targets; countries in surplus should raise their monetary growth targets.

I cite two examples of the recent reappearance, in modern dress, of the basic role of the gold standard. Ronald E. McKinnon in a widely noted paper, "Currency Substitution and Instability in the World Dollar Standard," argues that the instability of the world dollar standard stems from the fact that the United States and many other countries "define [their monetary] policy targets in terms of growth rates of purely domestic monetary aggregates."[25] He claims that "even for the United States itself, this [his] tentative measure of changes in the world money supply explains the great (dollar) price inflations of 1973–74 and 1979–80 much better than does any domestic American aggregate."[26]

What the author is really saying is best understood by turning to the last section of his paper, entitled "Policy Implications." The author says that

The solution to international currency instability is straightforward: the Federal Reserve System should discontinue its policy of passively sterilizing the domestic monetary impact of foreign official interventions. Instead, a symmetrical non-sterilization rule would ensure that each country's money supply mutually adjusts to international currency substitution in the short run without having official exchange interventions destabilize the world's money supply.[27]

He suggests that for all practical purposes "Germany, Japan, and the United States are capable of jointly bringing the world's supply of convertible money under control through a mutual non-sterilization pact and agreed-on rates of domestic credit expansion by each of the three central banks."[28]

To recognize that this is equivalent to the basic rule of balance of payments adjustment under the gold standard, only in modern dress, it should be recalled that gold sales and purchases by the central banks to keep the exchange rate stable can be described as a policy of nonsterilized intervention. This is exactly what McKinnon prescribes.

The other key concept is that of domestic credit expansion (DCE) as distinguished from an expansion of the money supply. This brings me to the second example of the resurrection of the basic rule of the gold standard where the concept of the DCE plays the key role.

William H. White of the IMF has drawn my attention to the fact that the IMF, at the suggestion of J. J. Polak, has recommended in a number of cases the use of DCE for setting the proper target for monetary policy in open economies.

In 1969 Britain accepted the advice of the Fund, and the new policy was lucidly set out by the Bank of England in its *Quarterly Bulletin*:

Put briefly, DCE may be viewed as the total arrived at after adjusting the increase in the money supply to take account of any change in money balances directly caused by an external surplus of deficit. DCE is thus approximately equal to the increase in the money supply plus those sterling funds accruing to the authorities by their provision of foreign exchange, from one source or another, for the accommodation of an external deficit or, conversely, minus the sterling finance required to accommodate an external surplus.[29]

To understand that this is equivalent to the gold standard rule, consider that in countries suffering from an external deficit, DCE indicates a larger monetary growth than does the money supply figure; it follows that restraining measures should be taken. In surplus countries, in contrast, DCE shows a *smaller* expansion than money supply figures; hence, expansionary measures should be taken.

This is, of course, part and parcel of the "monetary approach" to the balance of payments, which was independently developed by the IMF staff, J. J. Polak, Marcus J. Fleming, and their associates, and by academic economists Harry G. Johnson, Jacob A. Frenkel, and others.[30]

Two giants in the area of international monetary economics—Charles Kindleberger and Randall Hinshaw—have always been critical of floating. The latter recently gave expression to his feelings by giving the title *Global Monetary Anarchy* to the latest volume of his famous series of conference volumes.[31]

Another prominent member of the fraternity of the international monetary specialists, Fred Bergsten, who describes himself as a "traditional supporter" of the system, said that "the system of flexible exchange rates has now produced—or at least permitted—a disequilibrium situation at least as great as that which emerged during the final years of the Bretton Woods system." The dollar has become substantially overvalued, "by an average of 20–25 percent and by much more against the German mark and Japanese yen." As a consequence, "the price competitiveness of the U.S. economy has severely deteriorated" and so have the trade balance and current account balance.[32] Bergsten was thus one of the first to stress the depressive effect of the alleged overvaluation of the dollar on the U.S. economy. "Since the first quarter of this year [1982], the fall in net exports accounted for almost 80 percent of the total decline in real U.S. GNP in the second quarter, and more than explains the entire drop in the third quarter."[33]

This view has been widely accepted. The gloom cast by that theory has been lifted, however, by the U.S. economy's healthy recovery from the cyclical recession, despite the alleged overvaluation of the dollar and large trade deficits.

Except for the advocates of the gold standard, hardly anyone recommends a return to stable but adjustable, let alone fixed, exchange rates. What is widely recommended is a more vigorous policy of official interventions in the foreign exchange market to counteract what is regarded as excessive volatility of exchange rates. I will briefly discuss the views of three prominent experts, two officials and one academic.

In an important, wide-ranging speech, republished a year later in an updated version, Otmar Emminger pleads for an active exchange rate policy and judicious interventions on the foreign exchange market.[34] He distinguishes two types of cases where official interventions are justified and when judiciously executed have often been successful.

First,

foreign exchange markets, if left entirely to themselves, are notoriously volatile and erratic, at least on occasion.... They are very sensitive to psychological and political influences. Strong upward or downward movements have a tendency to feed upon themselves and become exaggerated (bandwagon-effect). Smoothing out wild, erratic fluctuations [by judicious interventions]—without trying to "stabilize"a specific rate, and without operating against basic trends—may give the market a helping hand . . . . In the past, many of these smoothing-over interventions proved to be self-reversing, and in my experience, when a currency was oversold or overbought, it needed often relatively small amounts of intervention to restore calm and reason.

He here refers to what is often called "disorderly market conditions."

The second, much more important type of malfunctioning of the foreign exchange market is this:

When a large fundamental disequilibrium in the balance of payments develops, floating exchange rates often have a tendency not only to overshoot but to overcorrect. Some overshooting, i.e., a movement beyond relative cost and price trends, may be necessary and useful in order to bring about the required adjustment of the payments balance on current-account. But sometimes exchange rate swings go clearly beyond such useful overshooting, beyond what can be justified by the underlying payments situations.

In such cases official interventions in the exchange market are justified.

Emminger makes it clear, however, that no attempt should be made to hold stable a "specific rate of exchange," and he emphasizes that the dollar presents a special case: "For the U.S. dollar there is certainly no other solution than free floating, be it with or without occasional intervention in the exchange market. There is no other currency the dollar could hang on to," and it does not seem "practical" to peg it to a "currency basket." Emminger thinks that "deliberate exchange rate policies" of countries other than the United States are "compatible with the present U.S. administration's policy not to intervene at all in the foreign exchange market except in emergency situations, provided that the administration does not object to other countries intervening as they see fit."

Clearly, Emminger is opposed to a return to a Bretton Woods system, and he gives short shrift to the idea of resurrecting the gold standard: "All the King's horses and all the King's men cannot put Humpty-Dumpty together again."

The difficulty of a policy of intervention that goes beyond the attempt at smoothing out very short-term oscillations ("disorderly market conditions") is that at any time it is impossible to be sure whether the long-run equilibrium has been undershot or overshot. True, with the benefit of hindsight, it is often possible to reach an agreement that overshooting has occurred in the sense that the market has reversed itself within a relatively short period of time. But even in retrospect problems remain. Not every reversal of the market can be regarded as a case of overshooting that should have been prevented by official interventions. It may have been due to events unforeseen by the market as well as by the authorities. Moreover, as Emminger says, some overshooting may be desirable to bring about the required adjustments in the balance of payments and, we may add, in the policies of the authorities.

The contrast between ex post facto and ex ante is neatly illustrated by Emminger's paper. Although in 1981 he was quite sure in his judgment that the dollar was undervalued in 1977 and 1978 and the yen in 1979, he said, "it *might* be that the *present* depreciation of the D mark ... will later also turn out as a case of overcorrection" (italics added). A year later his uncertainty about 1981 had disappeared. In his brilliant pamphlet, *Exchange Rate Policy Reconsidered,* he said:

American observers, official and unofficial, sometimes poked fun at the Europeans because they always seemed to complain about the dollar: in 1978 that it was far too low and in 1981 that it was far too high. But it is likely that the Europeans were right in both cases, i.e. that a rate of DM 1.70 to the dollar was just as much out of line with all fundamentals as at DM 2.50. It is indeed extremely unlikely that the fundamental factors determing the equilibrium rate between the dollar and the Deutschemark could have justified a change of 50 percent within three years.[35]

I suggest that even in restrospect the case is not at all clear. Since the under- or overvaluation of the mark is the mirror picture of the under- or overvaluation of the dollar, it will be convenient to recall why the dollar declined sharply from 1977 to 1979 and rose sharply in 1980 to 1982–1983.

Emminger explains the decline of the dollar in terms of the large current account deficits in 1977 and 1978–$14 billion each year.[36] But we have seen that these deficits as well as the decline of the dollar can be traced to inflation and growth differentials that developed between the United States and Germany, Japan, and Switzerland, when the Carter administration embarked on expansionary policies, and inflation rose to the two-digit level.

The decline of the dollar made the two dollar-rescue operations necessary. The *first* one, in 1978 under Fed Chairman G. William Miller, at first calmed the markets but then proved ineffective because the disinflation was not carried through. The *second,* in October 1979 under Fed Chairman Paul Volcker, proved to be a real turning point. It is highly doubtful that the unavoidable disinflation would have been carried through if the decline of the dollar had not scared the politicians. Call it overshooting if you like; but it was a beneficial one. Floating once again showed its disciplinary capability.

Whether the dramatic rise of the dollar since 1980 has been a pernicious overshooting that should have been prevented will be discussed presently. The intrinsic uncertainty of the judgment that overshooting has occurred is often expressed by the question, why should the judgment of the monetary authorities be better than that of the market? Alexander Lamfalussy in two important speeches rises to the challenge of this question.[37]

Lamfalussy deplores the great volatility of exchange rates in recent years and pleads for "greater stability" through "official action," including vigorous interventions in the foreign exchange market, though he makes it clear that he is not advocating a return to pegged exchanges.[38] "Floating among the dollar, the D-mark and the yen seems to be the only practical way of letting exchange rate changes play their indispensable role in the balance of payments adjustment process."

What, then, is Lamfalussy's answer to the question why should the authorities' judgment of what is the appropriate exchange rate be better than that of the market? In his words,

Why should the authorities be better than other market participants in forecasting the future? The answer is, simply, that they are "market participants" of a special kind .... The authorities know, or at least are supposed to know, what policy they are pursuing and therefore by intervening in the exchange market they signal their policy stance. In other words, intervention means that the authorities are putting their money where their mouth is.

This sounds like a plea for nonsterilized interventions. A little later Lamfalussy indeed speaks of interventions that have their "full effect on the domestic money markets." But Lamfalussy is not a monetarist. His conception of a "country's main policy thrust" comprises "interest rate policy" and "fiscal policy," not merely changes in the money supply. He illustrates his position by "the example of a sharply deteriorating currency. It clearly would be a waste of money to try to prop up [by intervention in the exchange market] their currency if the government's fiscal and monetarist policies are more expansionary than those of other countries." Interventions are useful only if "the direction in which intervention goes is compatible with the country's main policy thrust." This applies, he says, "even to 'pure' interventions, i.e. to interventions which have no effect on the domestic money supply" (sterilized intervention) and "a fortiori" to nonsterilized interventions.

As a set of principles, this sounds plausible: With optimal adjustment policies, carried out persistently, interventions would contribute to stability. Unfortunately, governments frequently lack persistence in carrying out their plans, especially in an election year. Moreover, the accuracy of their assessment of how the proposed policies will work out and how individual measures will affect demand and supply of foreign exchange and the exchange rate is not always correct, to put it mildly. It follows that there is a good chance that, contrary to what Lamfalussy says, the forecast of the markets will be more accurate than that of the authorities.

In his London speech of February 1983, Lamfalussy repeats the reason why, in his opinion, the authorities' judgment of the appropriate exchange rate may be better than that of the market, which justified vigorous intervention or, more generally, exchange rate policies. No additional comments are required on this part of his interesting speech.

He points also to recent developments that, in his opinion, signify a glaring malfunctioning of floating and of the uncontrolled foreign exchange market. Lamfalussy, correctly, points out that the depreciation of the D-mark in recent years is just the other side of the appreciation of the dollar. Both the appreciation of the dollar and the depreciation of the D-mark are in *real* terms; in other words, the exchange rate "overshot" the purchasing power parity and the inflation differential. He concludes:

To fight inflation imported through the depreciation of the real effective exchange rate, interest rates will have to serve exchange rate objectives rather than stimulating a depressed economy. This is not text-book theorizing, but a description of what happened in the Federal Republic of Germany in 1980–81; it is only more recently, since the intra-EEC exchange rate adjustments, that the problem has lost its acuteness for Germany. It is the irony of history that floating, which has been proposed as an effective way of freeing domestic policy from external constraints, has in fact, precisely in the German case, imposed such a constraint on the freedom of policy makers.

The problem will be taken up presently when I discuss the alleged overvaluation of the dollar and what can and ought to be done about it. But three comments are called for here.

First, that the inflationary effect of the rise of the dollar on Europe is not due to a malfunctioning of the market under floating becomes clear if one reflects on what would have happened under fixed exchanges (gold standard or Bretton Woods). It can be shown that under fixed rates the Europeans would have suffered much more than under floating. The reason is that high interest rates in the United States would have attracted much more capital (and gold) under fixed exchange rates than under floating. This in turn is due to the fact that under floating foreign investors in dollars have an exchange risk; they cannot be quite sure that the market has not overshot the mark and will reverse itself. Under fixed rates, this risk is absent. This is the well-known reason why fixed rates, especially stable but adjustable rates, are so vulnerable to destabilizing speculation. The upshot is that the Europeans would be put under heavy deflationary pressure and would have to raise interest rates to protect the par value of their currencies.

Thus, there is nothing ironic about the fact that floating cannot protect a country from *real* influences from abroad, such as the oil shocks or, more generally, changes in international demand and in the terms of trade; nor does it protect a country from shifts in capital flows, as the one just discussed. But fixed rates are no protection either in such cases.

It has been explained many times, however, that floating can ward off *monetary* shocks from outside. So let it be repeated once more that in the early 1970s and again in 1978–1980, floating enabled Germany, Switzerland, and Japan to enjoy a much lower inflation rate than the United States and that in the 1930s floating (or devaluation) made it possible for a number of countries to extricate themselves from world deflation long before the U.S. economy emerged from the depression. In other words, floating shielded countries from imported inflation and deflation.

Second, to speak of a "collapse" of the theory of purchasing power parity as Jacob

Frenkel does is an exaggeration. But there is probably agreement that neither purchasing power parity calulations nor inflation differentials are reliable indicators of equilibrium exchange rates in the short and medium run. Since it is based on international price comparisons the real effective exchange rate, like purchasing power parity and inflation differentials, is an uncertain guide to the equilibrium exchange rate in the short term.

Third, it is odd to say that the EMS has alleviated Germany's economic difficulties. From the economic standpoint, the EMS has been a great failure. Frequent exchange realignments, preceded and accompanied by waves of destabilizing speculation, have demonstrated once again that stable but adjustable exchange rates are not a suitable arrangement in the present world. The EMS has been an economic burden for Germany and is kept alive, at great cost, for political reasons—to forestall France's exit from the European Community. *Frankerich's Uhren Gehen Anders.*[39]

The following is an example of a prominent academic economist who has become disenchanted with floating. Peter Kenen says:

Looking back on our experience with floating rates and at the behavior of particular currencies, I have begun to wonder whether this trip was necessary. I am therefore increasingly interested in target zones and crawling pegs as second-best solutions to a difficult problem. I am likewise intrigued by Bergsten's suggestion that a temporary reinstatement of Japanese capital controls could help with the most serious exchange-rate problem facing the world right now.[40]

This is hardly convincing. Looking back at the turbulences of the 1970s, I find it difficult to disagree with what Otmar Emminger said in 1980: "No other system but floating could have coped with the enormous short-term swings in the U.S. balance on current account—from a surplus of $18 billion in 1975 to deficits of $14 billion in each of the years 1977 and 1978 . . . ," and with two oil shocks, we may add.[41] The remedies mentioned by Kenen strike me as third-best of the band-aid variety. But since the whole problem has been largely defused by the rapid recovery of the U.S. economy from the recession despite the "overvalued" dollar and larger trade deficits, it is not necessary to repeat again the arguments against the suggested measures.

The Problem of the "Overvalued" Dollar

The dramatic rise of the dollar since 1980 can be explained by two mutually supporting factors, high interest rates in the United States and the fact that the U.S. economy again offers confidence-inspiring atmosphere for foreign investors.

The high interest rates can be traced back to large current and projected budget deficits, in relation to the flow of private saving, and to lingering doubt that inflation has been definitely curbed and will not be reignited by the ongoing cyclical recovery.

The U.S. economy is a safe haven for foreign investors for several reasons, economic as well as political ones: political and economic stability, absence of controls on international transactions, and the existence of a large, efficient capital market.

Whatever the correct explanation, it is certainly true that the appreciation of the dollar and the large trade deficits have a significant depressive influence. This fact has disturbed some experts who say that it has cost the economy several percentage points of real growth.

This is, however, a very shortsighted argument. In the *first* place, it ignores the fact that despite the appreciation of the dollar and the large trade deficits, the U.S. economy has staged an unexpectedly vigorous expansion. Many experts believe that the expansion has been too fast to be sustainable. If that is accepted, by slowing down the pace of the expansion, the appreciation of the dollar and the trade deficit may well have a positive effect on real GNP growth in the longer run.

In the *second* place, and even more important, the argument overlooks the fact that the appreciation of the dollar and the trade deficits are also potent anti-inflationary factors. Some counterfactual theorizing will reveal the far-reaching implications of this fact.

Suppose the dollar had not gone up in the foreign exchange market because, say, market participants had lacked confidence in the future; in this case a powerful disinflationary factor would have been lost. It follows that, assuming we wish to bring down inflation, the Fed would have had to step harder on the monetary brake. Therefore, the recession would have been about the same as it actually was.[42] It is hardly necessary to point out that if the Fed had not stepped on the brake, the recession would have been merely postponed and would have later reappeared in an aggravated form.

Now let us change the scenario. Suppose the Fed or foreign central banks[43] had tried to prevent the dollar from rising by massive interventions in the foreign exchange market, as has been widely and even vociferously demanded, especially in weak-currency countries.[44]

There is no doubt it would have been easy for the Fed to prevent the dollar from rising, or to bring it down, by nonsterilized interventions, that is, by selling dollars and buying German marks, Japanese yen—and French francs—and by letting the money supply go up in the process at the high cost of reaccelerating inflation.

What remains in doubt is, *first*, whether such a policy would improve the competitive position of U.S. industries and thus reduce the trade deficit, and, *second*, whether interventions in the foreign exchange market, without an increase in the money supply—in other words, whether pure or sterilized interventions—would do any good. I discuss these two issues in turn.

The *first* question can be put as follows: The decline of the value of the dollar relative to other currencies, in other words, the decline of the trade weighted effective rate per se, undoubtedly stimulates exports and restrains imports and thus tends to improve the trade balance. But does not the inflation caused by the increase in the money supply operate in the opposite direction? Is there a reason to believe that the two opposite effects will offset each other, or that the one or the other will dominate the outcome?

Martin Feldstein, in a recent paper, reached the conclusion that "the essential impact of a change in the money stock [resulting from interventions] in the foreign exchange market is to alter only the *nominal* rate. Any decline in the real exchange value of the dollar would be only temporary." The result "therefore" would be "to leave the incentive to import and export unchanged."[45] This implies that the opposite effects mentioned above tend to offset each other exactly.

This conclusion is based on the assumption that inflation would accelerate quickly, in other words, that we do not live in a Keynesian world where output could be expanded without large price increases.

Many economists would probably agree that the economy is now much closer to the "classical" extreme than to the Keynesian. The elasticity of aggregate output (real GNP) with respect to an increase in aggregate nominal demand is low, despite the relatively high unemployment rate. There are two reasons for that. First, inflationary expectations have been sensitized by a long period of inflation, and, second, much of the unemployment is structural and requires time-consuming relocation of labor. The implication is to support Feldstein's conclusion: An inflationary intervention policy to bring down the value of the dollar relative to other currencies would probably improve the competitive position of the U.S. industries only slightly and temporarily.

I come to the *second* open question concerning the effectiveness or ineffectiveness of pure or sterilized interventions—a question that has received a good deal of attention recently. Under this system the Fed creates money by selling dollars in the foreign exchange market and then offsets (sterilizes) the additional dollars by selling Treasury bills in the domestic security markets (or by raising the discount rate or increasing reserve requirements of the banks). This is, however, only one half of the whole transaction. The other half relates to how the Fed disposes of the foreign currency, say D-marks, which it acquires in the foreign exchange market. If the intervention is to be fully sterilized, it must be assumed that the D-marks are invested in D-mark denominated securities, for if the Fed kept the marks the German effective demand (MV) would be reduced. This becomes clear if we consider what happens if the intervention is carried out by the Bundesbank selling dollars for marks rather than by the Fed. The final outcome must be the same. But there is this difference: If the Bundesbank sells dollars for marks, the stock of marks (M) declines; if the Fed acquires marks, the velocity of circulation of money (V) declines. In both cases effective demand (MV) declines, which makes the transaction a case of nonsterilized intervention. To sterilize the effect the mark must be invested in mark-denominated securities.

There is, I believe, general agreement that sterilized interventions are much less effective, many would say totally ineffective, compared with nonsterilized interventions in influencing the exchange rates.[46] Why this is so becomes clear when we consider that, unlike nonsterilized interventions, sterilized interventions (1) do not change the money supply and (2) tend to raise interest rates in the country whose currency is sold, compared with the country whose currency is bought. In our example, when the Fed sells Treasury bills, it tends to boost U.S. interest rates. When it buys mark-denominated securities, it tends to depress German interest rates. The incipient interest differential will attract capital from abroad. These additional capital imports constitute demand for dollars. The net effect, if any, of the whole operation on the exchange rate will depend on the comparative strength of the two forces operating in *opposite* directions: Sales of dollars in the foreign exchange market weaken the dollar; sales of Treasury bills tend to strengthen the dollar.[47] If the additional demand for dollars resulting from capital inflow exceeds the additional supply of dollars resulting from the sale of dollars, the dollar will strengthen, which means that the whole operation was counterproductive. The opposite will be true if the additional demand falls short of the additional supply: in that case the whole operation has the desired effect of weakening the dollar. If the two forces are of equal strength, the intervention has no effect on the exchange rate.

Whether sterilized interventions have an effect on exchange rates depends on whether or not the public regards securities of different currency denominations as perfect substitutes. In our example, if market participants were indifferent to whether they held mark- or dollar-denominated securities, sterilized interventions would have no effect on the exchange rate, for the slightest interest differential would lead to capital shifts from marks into dollars. Hence, an additional supply of dollars resulting from sales of dollars in the foreign exchange market would be matched by increased demand resulting from capital import.

The assumption of perfect substitutability of securities denominated in different currencies is obviously unrealistic. The reason is that there is always an exchange risk, especially under floating. This implies that sterilized interventions have some effect, as becomes clear if one considers that sterilized interventions alter the relative size of the stock of outstanding securities of different currency denominations. If the Fed intervenes, the stock of dollar-denominated securities increases. If the Bundesbank intervenes by buying mark-denominated securities to offset (sterilize) the decrease in the money supply, the stock of mark-denominated securities decreases. In either case the ratio of the stock of dollar-denominated to that of mark-denominated securities increases. To induce the market to accept the changed portfolio, an interest differential and/or a change in the actual or expected exchange rate is required. We can, then, take it for granted that sterilized interventions will have some effect.

What is still uncertain is the magnitude of the effect. It is generally assumed, rightly in my opinion, that, considering the huge volume of outstanding securities denominated in major currencies, sterilized intervention would have to be of truly massive proportions to have a significant effect—massive, that is to say, compared with the volume of interventions that have actually been made. Indirectly sterilized interventions may have an effect, for example, if they give market participants the impression that the authorities are determined to take stronger measures, if necessary, to bring about the desired change in the exchange rate—in other words, if sterilized interventions are regarded as the precursor of nonsterilized interventions.

The Recent Policy of "Coordinated Interventions" in the Foreign Exchange Market

On August 1, 1983, it was announced in Washington, with considerable fanfare, that at the urging of European countries and Japan the United States had agreed to joint "coordinated interventions" in the foreign exchange market. On the face of it, this is a sharp reversal of the present administration's policy of interventions. To describe it as a case of "correcting disorderly market conditions," as a high official put it, is rather odd. The Europeans certainly do not see it that way. They want a lower dollar. The persistent rise of the dollar may be exaggerated and undesirable, but there is nothing disorderly about it. The change in policy is better described as a gesture of good will; some would call it "appeasement." Actually, as we shall see, the U.S. concession does not amount to much.

As usual, the French were in the forefront of the critics of U.S. policy. French Minister of Finance M. Jacques Delors "sharply criticized" U.S. policy for "high interest rates and the hausse of the dollar," for "showing no concern for European interest," and for "ignoring the decisions of the Williamsburg Economic Summit." He demanded joint action and more "solidarity."[48] The minister evidently wants other countries to jump on the inflationary bandwagon to let France off the hook.

Since August 1, sizable interventions have been taken by the United States, by West Germany, and by other countries. As usual, the magnitude of interventions was not divulged, nor were the currencies involved. But according to informed sources, the total of all interventions for the first eight days or so was between $2.5 billion and $3 billion, and they have all involved sales of dollars for marks and other currencies.

Most interventions have been of the sterilized kind. When the New York Fed sells dollars, it almost simultaneously sells Treasury bills for the same amount so that the money supply is not affected. That the German interventions, too, are sterilized follows from the fact that the German minister of finance and the president of the Bundesbank have stated that interest rates will not be raised because of the fragility of the German recovery.[49] Nonsterilized interventions would do just that—raise interest rates. The Swiss National Bank, too, has intervened by selling dollars for marks; how much was not stated. The operation was officially described as "neutral with respect to Swiss monetary growth" and the president of the Swiss National Bank Fritz Leutwiler, while expressing the view that joint action of several central banks can be useful in certain situations, has emphasized the "priority of monetary policy."[50]

Fears have been expressed that the policy of internationally coordinated interventions to stop or reverse the rise of the dollar will have inflationary effects in the United States. These fears are unfounded so long as the interventions are sterilized. Sterilized interventions have no direct inflationary effect because the money supply remains unchanged. The rise of interest rates resulting from the sale of Treasury bills may even be said to be slightly anti-inflationary. Indirectly, the policy possibly may have an inflationary effect if it succeeds in reducing the external value of the dollar, for we have seen that the high dollar is an anti-inflationary factor.

But this qualification is unimportant because, as we have seen, there is fairly general agreement that sterilized interventions have little, if any, effect on the exchange rates. True, it has been shown that if market participants are not indifferent with respect to the currency composition of their assets, sterilized interventions will have some effect on the exchange rate. It should be noted that this argument involves portfolio considerations, which makes the *stock* of assets relevant. It follows that the effect on the exchange rates is likely to be minimal in view of the enormous size of outstanding assets in relation to the magnitude of interventions.

The upshot is that the effect of the whole operation is likely to be negligible. It has been argued that it may even have a negative effect. The almost daily announcements that this or that central bank will intervene, followed as they usually are by a further rise of the dollar, may fortify bullish expectations of market participants about the future course of the dollar. Since the rise of the dollar sooner or later (probably sooner than later) will come to an end or even reverse itself somewhat, not much harm will be done.

The whole operation must look very attractive to the participating central banks. When the rise of the dollar stops, they can claim that their interventions turned the tide. And it will never be quite certain whether the intervention prolonged or shortened the rise of the dollar. These conclusions are based on the assumption that the interventions continue to be fully sterilized.

Concluding Remarks on Floating: Summing Up

I will start with some general observations. Floating should be regarded as a second best. The best system would be fixed rates—provided at least three basic conditions are fulfilled. *First*, monetary policies (or more generally macroeconomic policies) in participating countries have to be closely coordinated. National inflation rates must be roughly the same. *Second*, there must be a certain amount of wage flexibility, also in the downward direction, which means that no country would have to submit to periods of general Keynesian unemployment because of its balance of payments.[51] These conditions were fulfilled in the heyday of the gold standard. Wages were much more flexible, also in the downward direction, than they are now, and the common link to gold and the rules of the gold standard game assured close coordination of monetary policy and roughly equal inflation rates in all countries. *Third*, there must be no exchange control of any kind.[52]

Unfortunately, today the conditions for fixed (or semifixed) exchange rates exist only in exceptional cases. They do not exist between the leading industrial countries—the United States, Japan, Germany, Great Britain, France, and Italy. Real exceptions are the numberous, mostly small countries that peg their currencies to the dollar, the D-mark, or some other currency or basket of currencies, provided these countries maintain their fixed exchange rates without exchange control and without intolerable unemployment or inflation. Examples are Austria, Taiwan, Venezuela, and Kuwait.

The European Monetary System is no exception. Inflation differentials between member countries are large; exchange rate realignments occur frequenctly, preceded and accompanied by very large speculative capital flights; and one country, France, was forced to introduce tight exchange control involving searches at the border, censorship of the mail, and tight rationing of foreign exchange for travel abroad—a system reminiscent of what used to be called the Schachtian system during the Nazi period in Germany—in clear violation of the spirit if not the letter of the IMF charter and the Treaty of Rome by which the EMS was set up.[53] From the economic point of view the EMS has been a costly failure. It has imposed a heavy burden, especially on Germany, and is kept alive largely for political reasons, to prevent France from isolating itself even more from the European Community. If the EMS were dissolved, some of its members—the Netherlands, Belgium, and Luxembourg, possibly also Denmark and Ireland—would peg to the D-mark as Austria does. From the economic point of view, an open-ended D-mark bloc would be a better arrangement than the EMS.

The conclusion is that floating is here to stay; a global return to fixed or semifixed exchanges is out of the question.

The principal advantage claimed for floating in our imperfect world is that it protects countries from inflationary and deflationary shocks from abroad. Thus, in the 1970s it enabled Switzerland, Germany, Japan, and some other countries to reduce their inflation rate way below the level they would have had if they had kept the link with the dollar. In the 1930s, floating (or at that time devaluations) made it possible for a number of countries to extricate themselves from the deflationary spiral long before the U.S. economy turned up.

But floating is no panacea. It has been explained many times that floating shields a country only from *monetary* shocks from abroad. Specifically, no country can be forced under floating, as it often happens under fixed exchanges, to expand or to contract the money supply more than it finds acceptable. Floating does not protect from *real* shocks from abroad. The concept of real shocks has to be defined broadly—it covers not only clearly exogenous shocks, such as the oil shock,[54] but also changes in the terms of trade that usually accompany the business cycle and can be regarded as having been caused by monetary forces. Thus in the depression of the 1930s, prices of primary products fell sharply, which implied a catastrophic deterioration in the terms of trade of less developed countries. Floating obviously does not protect a country from adverse changes in the terms of trade.

Critics of floating often assert that the insulating power claimed for floating exists only if there are no capital flows. There are, indeed, various scenarios that seem to support that assertion. One such scenario was analyzed above: We have seen, in the United States in recent years, that floating does not protect a country from the adverse effects of capital exports and depreciation of its currency caused by high interest rates abroad.[55] But it has been demonstrated that in such a case a country would be even worse off under fixed exchanges. Hence, floating can be credited with mitigating the damage.

The following is another scenario. A relatively inflationary country develops a current account deficit that is financed by capital imports of different kinds, including losses of official reserves. So long as this goes on, it reduces inflationary pressure in the deficit country and increases it in the surplus countries. The deficit country can be said to "export" its inflation to the surplus countries. Sooner or later the country will find it difficult to finance its deficit. If its currency is then set afloat, its exchange value will go down, and inflationary pressure will increase; prices of traded goods will rise, and the aggregate domestic expenditures will decline. It can then truthfully be said that floating has "caused" inflation. What has happened is better described, however, by saying that inflationary pressure has been shifted from the victims of the preexistent situation, the surplus countries, to the culprit, the inflationary deficit country.

This can also be described by saying that under floating each country has to swallow the inflation it generates because it cannot export it to others. This has increasingly been recognized by central bankers and policy makers, which in turn should be a strong inducement to resist inflation. Thus floating has a certain disciplinary effect of its own. I cannot resist quoting my observations on an earlier occasion: "The fact that floating provides an inducement for the monetary authorities to step on the brakes does not guarantee that inflation will in fact be curbed. A strong inducement to disinflate can always be overwhelmed by an even stronger propensity to inflate." [56] The same can be said about the vaunted disciplinary effect of the gold standard.

Finally, I will add a few more words about overshooting and official interventions in the foreign exchange market designed to "calm down" the market and to correct its alleged frequent overshooting. Until the recent policy shift, the present U.S. administration has pursued a strict hands-off policy. Interventions in the foreign exchange market are to be taken only "in extraordinary circumstances to counter serious market disorders." One of the few interventions occurred after President Reagan was shot on March 30, 1981, when the Federal Reserve intervened by selling a paltry sum of $76 million in foreign currencies.

The nonintervention policy has been laid down by the U.S. Treasury. It is not quite clear whether the Federal Reserve System fully supports that strict policy of nonintervention. In fact, it is no secret that the Federal Reserve Bank of New York, the operating arm of the system as far as international transactions are concerned, is in favor of a much more active policy of intervention. That attitude seems to reflect habits formed in the good old days of stable but adjustable exchange rates, when, especially in the closing years of the Bretton Woods era, almost continuous large interventions plus frequent emergency meetings of central bankers were the order of the day.

The same is true of central bankers in most other countries. They seem to be itching to act. Before I explain the reasons for doubting the wisdom of frequent interventions, let me repeat that these doubts are not meant to apply to the many countries that peg their currency to the dollar or some other currency or basket of currencies. I can see no economic objection to such a policy—provided, first, that the country keeps its currency fully and freely convertible in the market (absence of exchange controls), and, second, that it does not pay too high a price in terms of inflation or unemployment. On the second condition each country has to make its own judgment.

What, then, are the reasons for doubting the wisdom of frequent large interventions under floating? It is the great difficulty of diagnosing the existence and of estimating the extent of overshooting. Overshooting can be defined as the deviation of the spot exchange rate from the long-run equilibrium level. But what is the equilibrium exchange rate? The modern portfolio-asset market approach to the problem of exchange rate behavior under floating has highlighted the extraordinary complexity of the problem. [57]

Things were simpler, though not without problems, under the Bretton Woods regime and under the gold standard. It will be recalled that the Articles of Agreement of the IMF said that in case of a "fundamental disequilibrium" a change of the par value was in order. The concept of fundamental disequilibrium is not defined in the IMF charter, but it was usually interpreted either in terms of some purchasing power parity or loss of international reserves.

The theory of purchasing power parity appears to be going out of fashion.[58] To speak of a "collapse" seems to me exaggerated; large deviations from the purchasing power parity are still a symptom of disequilibrium, and so are large inflation differentials. But what is large? Neither purchasing power parity nor inflation differentials are suitable measures for the degree of overshooting.

Changes in official reserves obviously play a different role under floating than under fixed exchanges. If under floating the authorities use reserves to intervene in the foreign exchange market, they must have made up their minds that the market has overshot. The judgment that there is a disequilibrium must be based on other grounds than the loss of reserves.

It is true, however, that the loss of reserves may well be taken by the private market participants as a signal from the authorities or an indication of how the authorities judge the situation and how they are likely to act. This introduces expectations into the picture. Expectations play, indeed, a central role in the portfolio-asset market approach to the exchange rate problem.

Other factors that have always been regarded as influencing exchange rates and are widely watched as possible danger signals are the current account of a country and comparative monetary growth rates.[59] The asset market theory of foreign exchange rates under floating explains how these factors and events and the market participants' expectations concerning future events and government policies interact in a very complex fashion. Overshooting is not excluded, but there are no easy guides to recognizing the existence of overshooting, let alone estimating the magnitude.[60]

The upshot of this discussion is that diagnosing overshooting is a more difficult task than many policy makers and their advisers seem to realize. It follows that interventions that go beyond ironing out strictly short-run fluctuations easily can do more harm than good.

Notes

1. The sharp distinction between recession and depression is of comparatively recent origin. But in the earlier literatuare a roughly similar distinction was made between "Kitchin" and "Juglar" cycles (Joseph Schumpeter), "minor" and "major" cycles (Alvin Hansen), and "mild" and "deep" depression cycles (Milton Friedman). The National Bureau of Economic Research ranks as especially severe the cyclical downswings of 1937–1938, 1929–1933, 1920–1921, 1907–1908, 1893–1894, 1882–1885, and 1873–1879. These cyclical downswings can be

regarded as depressions. See Geoffrey H. Moore, ed., *Business Cycle Indicators*, vol. 1 (Princeton, N.J.: Princeton University Press, 1961), p. 104, table 3.6.

2. How a 6 percent decline in terms of dollars translates into a smaller (2 percent) decline in real terms in a period of inflation is a little puzzling. The reason is that, because of the recession and the appreciation of the dollar, prices of many internationally traded commodities, including oil, have sharply declined in terms of dollars, despite the ongoing inflation (rising CPI) in all industrial and developing countries.

3. Blum's policy was patterned after Roosevelt's New Deal. As a recovery policy the New Deal was unsuccessful. True, there was a long period of expansion—1933–1937, but the upswing was marred by rising prices, which led to the short but extremely vicious depression of 1937–1938. After six years of the New Deal, unemployment was still over 10 percent, and it took the war boom to restore full employment.

4. See Walter Galenson and Arnold Zellner, "International Comparisons of Unemployment Rates," in *The Measurement and Behavior of Unemployment*, a Conference of the Universities, National Bureau Committee for Economic Research (New York, 1957), pp. 455, 467.

   The figure of 43 percent mentioned in the text refers to 1932, the nadir of the cycle. In 1931 the unemployment rate was 34.3 percent, more than three times as high as now. This is important because it contradicts a widely quoted, pessimistic statement by Helmut Schmidt, the former minister of finance and chancellor of the Federal Republic of Germany. At a World Forum in Vail, Colorado, sponsored by the American Enterprise Institute on August 28, 1983 (see the *New York Times*, August 29, 1983), Schmidt said unemployment in West Germany now is as high—3 million—as it was in 1931, two years before Hitler came to power. Actually, it was over 4 million in 1931, compared with 2.2 million in June 1983. Moreover, to compare absolute numbers now with those fifty years ago is misleading because of large territorial differences and vast changes in the composition of the labor force (female labor, guest workers, etc.) Unemployment expressed as a percent of the labor force conveys a much better impression of the severity of the decline now and fifty years ago.

5. *Newsweek*, New York, January 24, 1983, p. 46.

6. *Die Zeit*, nos. 48 and 49, December 3 and 10, 1982.

7. Reported in the *New York Times*, May 20, 1983.

8. Peter Kenen, "Concluding Remarks," in *Essays in International Finance, No. 149, December 1982, From Rambouillet to Versailles: A Symposium* (Princeton, N.J.: International Finance Section, Princeton University Press, 1982).

9. Lester C. Thurow, "An International Keynesian Yank," *Challenge*, March/April 1983, p. 36.

10. I put "Keynesian" in quotation marks, because we have learned from T. W. Hutchison and Axel Leijonhufvud that the word has to be distinguished form the "economics of Keynes." Thurow admits that "Keynesian expansion" was tried by Mitterrand, but it failed, presumably because France did not have the right kind of incomes policy.

11. Kenen also wrote that "inflationary expectations have subsided." He is surely overoptimistic. Kenen, "Concluding Remarks."

12. See Herbert Giersch, "Prospects for the World Economy," *Skandinaviska Enskilda Banken Quarterly Review* (Stockholm, 1982), pp. 104–110.

13. "Work on a Pay Cut," *The Economist* (London, November 27, 1982), pp. 11–12, and "Wage Cuts," *The Economist* (London, December 18, 1982), pp. 14–15.

14. For samples of the dissenting letters, see *The Economist*, December 18, 1982. *The Economist* rightly argues that Keynes, if he were alive, would support its position and not that of its critics. It is one thing to say, as Keynes did in the 1930s, that a deflationary spiral should be stopped by expansionary measures rather than by wage reduction, and an entirely different thing to urge in a period of persistent, severe stagflation that the level of money wage rates must not be touched. One year after the publication of his *General Theory*, Keynes had urged a shift in policy to fight inflation. As I have mentioned already, we have to distinguish between Keynesian economics and the economics of Keynes.

15. See "International Financial Statistics," *Supplement on Price Statistics*, no. 2 (Washington, D.C.: International Monetary Fund, 1981).

16. Based on OECD data. See Organization for Economic Cooperation and Development, *Economic Outlook*, no. 17 (July 1973), p. 56, table 21.

17. See Karl Otto Pöhl, "Remarks on the National and International Monetary Scenario," *Deutsche Bundesbank, Auszüge aus Presseartikeln*, no. 101, November 19, 1981.

18. J. R. Hicks, "The Long-Run Dollar Problems: Inaugural Lecture," *Oxford Economic Papers*, June 1953. D. H. Robertson, *Britain in the World Economy*, London, 1954. For further references see P. T. Bauer and A. A. Walters, "The State of Economic," *Journal of Law and Economics*, vol. 18, no. 1 (April 1975), p. 5.

19. See *International Monetary Reforms: Documents of the Committee of Twenty* (Washington, D.C.: International Monetary Fund, 1974), p. 11.

20. See Thom de Vries, "Jamaica or the Non-Reform of the International Monetary System," *Foreign Affairs*, vol. 54 (April 1976), p. 587. The story is told in detail in Robert Solomon's authoritative monograph *The Internatiaonal Monetary System 1945–1981: An Updated and Expanded Edition of the International Monetary System 1945–1976* (New York: Harper & Row, 1982).

21. That this shift in policy was a grave mistake has later been frankly admitted by the administration's chief economic spokesman, former secretary of the Treasury Michael Blumenthal. See *Washington Post*, October 30, 1979.

22. For detailed analysis of the monetary policy shift, see Phillip Cagan, "The New Monetary Policy and Inflation," in *Contemporary Economic Problems 1980*, William Fellner, Project Director (Washington, D.C.: American Enterprise Institute 1980), pp. 9–38.

23. Foreign acquistions of enormous dollar balances through massive official interventions to prop up the dollar in the dying days of Bretton Woods, resulting in an inflationary increase in international liquidity, was one of the costs of resisting the float.

24. Even in the heydays of the gold standard there were frequent violations of the basic rules of the game. The introduction of the gold exchange standard constituted a major violation of the basic rule; it no longer applied to the reserve currency countries, the United States and the United Kingdom. These countries were thus liberated from the disciplinary effect of the gold standard. That was duly noted and criticized by staunch advocates of the gold standard and by others, by Jacques Rueff and Robert Triffin, to mention two names.

25. *The American Economic Review*, vol. 72, no. 3 (June 1982), pp. 320–33.

26. Ibid., p. 320. This claim has been challenged, convincingly in my opinion, by Henry Goldstein, "A Critical Appraisal of McKinnon's World Money Hypothesis" (mimeographed), Federal Reserve Bank of Chicago, 1982.

27. Ibid., pp. 331–32.

28. Ibid., p. 331.

29. Bank of England, *Quarterly Bulletin*, September 1969, pp. 363–64.

30. The most important IMF papers, which go back many years, are collected in *The Monetary Approach to the Balance of Payments: A collection of Research Papers by Members of the Staff of the IMF* (Washington, D.C.: International Monetary Fund, 1977).

31. See Randall Hinshaw, ed., *Global Monetary Anarchy* (Beverly Hills, Calif.: Sage Publications, 1981).

32. See Fred Bergsten, "Statement before the Subcommittee on International Trade, Investment and Monetary Policy, Committee on Banking, Finance and Urban Affairs, U.S. House of Representatives," November 4, 1981. See also "The Villain Is an Overvalued Dollar," interview with C. Fred Bergsten in *Challenge*, March–April 1982, pp. 25–32. He has restated his position in "From Rambouillet to Versailles: A Symposium," *Essays in International Finance*, no. 149 (Princeton, N.J.: Princeton University Press, December 1982), pp. 1–7.

33. Bergsten, "Statement before the Subcommittee on International Trade, Investment and Monetary Policy."

34. See "Exchange Rates, Interest Rates, Inflation," remarks by Otmar Emminger, September 28, 1981, Banker's Forum, Georgetown University, Washington, D.C. (mimeographed). A year later the paper appeared in an enlarged and updated version: Otmar Emminger, *Exchange Rate Policy Reconsidered*, Occasional Papers 10 (New York: Group of Thirty, 1982). The quotations come from the original version, except where indicated.

35. Emminger, *Exchange Rate Policy Reconsidered*, p. 17.

36. Ibid., p. 8.

37. See Alexander Lamfalussy, "A Plea for an International Commitment to Exchange Rate Stability" (Paper presented at the 20th Anniversary Meeting of the Atlantic Institute for International Affairs, Brussels, October 1981). A more elaborate and updated version can be found in Lamfalussy's speech "Some General Policy Conclusions for Tempering the Excesses of Floating" (Address to the Financial Times Conference on "Foreign Exchange Risk—1983," delivered in London, February 16, 1983). Excerpts reprinted in *Deutsche Bundesbank, Auszüge aus Presseartikeln*, March 13, 1983. The quotations are from the 1981 version, except where indicated. For an excellent presentation of what may be called the point of view of the Bank for International Settlements, see the interesting paper by Helmut Mayer, *The Theory of Floating Exchange Rates and the Role of Official Exchange-Market Intervention*, BIS Economic Papers, No. 5, February 1982 (Basle, Switzerland: Bank for International Settlements, Monetary and Economic Department, 1982).

38. He looks back with nostalgia at the system of stable but adjustable rates, though "a return to a new Bretton Woods" would "not be practical politics." It is "arguable," in his opinion, that "the system of pegged but adjustable exchange rates could have been saved, if the par value of

the main currencies and the price of gold had been adjusted in time and in sufficient proportion." This is difficult to accept in view of the fact that it was a basic defect of the adjustable peg (namely, "the Graham effect," which makes the system extremely vulnerable to destabilizing speculation) that brought down the Bretton Woods system and forced floating on reluctant policy makers. What Otmar Emminger said in 1980 is still true: "On the occasion of the first oil shock, Mr. Witteveen, then the managing director of the IMF, said in a major policy speech in January 1974: 'In the present situation, a large measure of floating is inavoidable and indeed desirable.' I think this is still valid today, after the second oil shock" (*The International Monetary System under Stress: What Can We Learn from the Past?* AEI Reprint No. 112 [Washington, D.C.: American Enterprise Institute, May 1980], p. 16).

39. The title of a famous book by the Swiss historian Herbert Lüthy, which means, freely translated, *France Marches to a Different Drummer.* That the second largest member of the EMS, France, has a most oppressive system of exchange control, involving searches at the border, censorship of the mail, and tight rationing of foreign currency for travel abroad further highlights the failure of the EMS to provide a well-functioning regional system of stable exchange rates.

40. Kenen, "Concluding Remarks," p. 38.

41. Emminger, *The International Monetary System under Stress*, p. 7.

42. One could perhaps argue that the effect of the recession on traded and nontraded goods would have been somewhat different. I do not think that this is an important qualification, however, because there is such a large overlap between traded and nontraded industries. To be sure, protectionists are using the high dollar and the trade deficits as an argument. But the basic cause of protectionist pressure is unemployment and the recession. And that would not be different.

43. Only those foreign central banks that hold a large reserve of dollars (or gold) or a credit line could do it.

44. For example, the French minister of finance was reported to have "accused Washington of irresponsibility toward the needs of Western Europe. He also warned that the dollar's rise could lead to more belt-tightening in France." He said: "America's partners had rallied round to help when the dollar's weakness in 1978 disturbed the world economy. With the phenomenon now reversed, Washington should do the same in return" (*Washington Post*, April 22, 1983).

45. See "Gains from Disinflation," testimony by Martin Feldstein, chairman, Council of Economic Advisers, before the Joint Econimic Committee, U.S. Congress, Washington, D.C., April 22, 1983.

46. See, for example, Michael Mussa, *The Role of Official Intervention*, Occasional Paper 6 (New York: Group of Thirty, 1981), and Martin Feldstein, "Gains from Disinflation." The *Official Report of the International Working Group on Exchange Market Intervention* comes to the same conclusion, though in somewhat veiled and guarded language, which one expects from an international body.

47. It is instructive to consider that in the case of nonsterilizing interventions, the effect of the foreign and domestic parts of the operation—that is, the sale of dollars in the foreign

exchange market and the increase in money supply—operate in the *same* direction; both tend to weaken the dollar.

48. See *Deutsche Bundesbank, Auszüge aus Presseartikeln*, no. 75, August 4, 1983, p. 2.

49. *See Deutsche Bundesbank, Auszüge aus Presseartikeln*, no. 77, August 13, 1983, p. 1.

50. See *Deutsche Bundesbank, Auszüge aus Presseartikeln*, no. 75, August 4, 1983, pp. 1–2, 4–5.

51. This statement requires a qualification with respect to *structural* unemployment. A comparison with regional adjustments makes that clear. See note 52.

52. It is instructive to reflect that these conditions are fully realized between regions in each country. For example, all Federal Reserve Banks in the United States follow the same policy. Thus inflation rates are practically the same in the east and west, north and south. Wage rigidity and wage push, if any, are also roughly the same. (Unemployment rates may, of course, differ between regions because of structural differences.) These are the main reasons why we do not hear of balance of payments adjustment problems of regions and why there are no exchange rate problems between regions.

Other factors are often mentioned that facilitate regional adjustment, such as interregional mobility of labor and capital and automatic or discretionary official income transfers from relatively prosperous to relatively depressed regions via government taxes and expenditures. But the two conditions mentioned above are basic. If they are fulfilled, the world is the "optimum currency area."

These problems have been extensively discussed in the voluminous literature on the optimum currency area. For an excellent survey, see Edward Tower and Thomas Willett, *The theory of Optimum Currency Areas and Exchange Rate Flexibility*, Special Papers on International Economics, No. 11 (Princeton, N.J.: International Finance Section, Princeton University Press, 1976).

53. The French controls apply ostensibly only to capital transactions permitted by the Articles of Agreement of the IMF. But experience has shown again and again that effective capital controls require de facto control of current transactions.

54. It is, however, a misunderstanding when some critics of floating said or implied that OPEC's "persistent" balance of payments surplus is a "disequilibrium," which in the opinion of advocates of floating should have been eliminated by floating. The *global* OPEC surplus could and should not have been eliminated by floating (or by any other means). But since *different oil* importing countries were not equally burdened by the oil shock, and since policy reactions to the oil price rise differed from country to country, floating had to play an important role in the adjustment to an oil price rise. On this point, see my chapter "The Dollar in the world Economy: Recent Developments in Perspective," in *Contemporary Economic Problems 1980*, pp. 160–65, and the literature cited there.

55. Since a change in the terms of trade is involved, it is not unreasonable to regard this and similar scenarios as involving *real* factors, and therefore not constituting exceptions from the rule that floating protects from monetary disturbances from abroad. But this is a purely semantic question, which need not detain us.

56. See my paper "The Future of the International Monetary System," *Zeitschrift für Nationalökonomie*, vol. 34 (1974), pp. 391–92. Available as Reprint No. 30 (Washington, D.C.: American Enterprise Institute, 1975). See also "The Dollar in the World Economy," pp. 151–52.

57. For an excellent, brief discussion of the "asset market approach," see Mussa, *The Role of Official Intervention*, pp. 3–12 and the literature cited there.

58. See Jacob A. Frenkel, "The collapse of Purchasing Power Parities during the 1970s," NBER Reprint No. 193, National Bureau of Economic Research, and *European Economic Review*, vol. 16, no. 1 (May 1981), pp. 145–65 (Amesterdam: North-Holland, 1981). See also the interesting comments by Roland Vaubel, "Comments 'The Collapse of Purchasing Power Parities during the 1970s by Frenkel," *European Economic Review*, vol. 16, no. 1 (May 1981), pp. 173–75.

59. Both concepts must, of course, be carefully defined. For example, a large and persistent U.S. current account deficit will cause suspicion, because the United States is generally regarded as a "natural" capital exporter, while a large current account deficit of a developing country in good financial standing may be regarded as quite appropriate. Monetary growth rates ought to be adjusted for real GNP growth to make them comparable.

60. On this point see Michael Mussa, "A Model of Exchange Rate Dynamics," *Journal of Political Economy*, vol. 90, no. 1 (1982), pp. 74–104.

12

Incomes Policies and Inflation: An Analysis of Basic Principles

1. The Essence

Incomes policy has become the hottest problem of macro-economic policy in almost all industrial countries. A rising chorus demands that monetary and fiscal measures for fighting inflation be supplemented—some would even say replaced—by incomes policies.

The call for incomes policies is based on the sharp distinction between demand inflation and cost inflation. In the United States, it is said again and again, prices were 'pulled up' by excess demand until 1970; since then excess demand has been eliminated, but now prices are being 'pushed up' by rapidly rising costs due to excessive wage demands by powerful labour unions and excessive price rises set by monopolies and oligopolies in industry.

It should be observed that the Keynesian expression 'profit inflation' would be better than 'demand inflation'. For the rise in monetary demand, contrary to what is widely claimed, has *not* been stopped. Monetary demand—whether measured in terms of money GNP or quantity of money, however defined—has grown by leaps and bounds ever since it was claimed that demand inflation had been eliminated. What has been squeezed, though of course not eliminated, is profits. Wage costs have risen faster than prices.

I do not deny that there is a wage push. On the contrary, wage push—in a sense to be defined later—is an obvious reality. The growth of militant unions and the unionisation of white-collar workers and public employees at all levels of government have made wage-push inflation in many countries a serious or even a menacing problem—jeopardising stability, growth, and employment.

These structural changes are no doubt largely the consequence of prolonged

Editor's Note: The prologue and bibliography have been replaced by the Postscript.

Inflation and the Unions (London: The Institute of Economic Affairs, 1972), 3–61. Reprinted with permission.

monetary inflation—largely, but not entirely. However, whatever their origin, they are almost certainly here to stay, even if inflation is brought to an end.

Two Basic Types of Incomes Policy

The term 'incomes policy' has come to mean different things for different people, ranging from mild policies of guiding and 'jawboning' to complete price stops and wage freezes. I distinguish two basic varieties—incomes policy one as the imposition of generalised guidelines, and incomes policy two as an assortment of specialised measures designed to eliminate monopolistic restrictions and market imperfections in different sectors of the economy and thereby to improve the performance of a flexible, competitive free-market economy. Thus incomes policy two tries to strengthen the market and to work with and through the price mechanism. Incomes policy one attempts to provide a substitute for market forces; it is beneficial in intent, but in implementation it is bound to hinder and disorganise the functioning of the market.

The almost generally accepted formula for wage guidelines—incomes policy one—is that wages on the average should rise roughly in proportion to the average rise in labour productivity (output per man-hour) in the economy as a whole. I distinguish sharply between (a) the stated target and objective of the guideline policy and (b) its implementation. The objective of the policy, to make the average wage level rise in proportion to the growth in labour productivity, is sensible and laudable; it can be shown that in a smoothly working competitive economy, if prices are kept stable by appropriate monetary management, the average wage will in practice rise approximately in proportion to the average rise in labour productivity.

The favourable judgement of the guideline formula as a policy objective must be radically reversed, however, when its implementation is considered. The plain fact is that the *average* wage is not a policy variable. It cannot be manipulated by the government without affecting—freezing and distorting—*relative* wages. Most economists agree that relative wages should be allowed to change in response to the changing pattern of demand and supply of different types of labour. Such changes are, in fact, going on ceaselessly in the economy and are essential for the efficient working of the competitive economy in general, and of the labour market in particular.

Guidelines (or generalised incomes policy) have not worked well anywhere for any length of time.[1] If enforced, either the pattern of relative wages is frozen, or else it becomes necessary to make more and more exceptions. In the latter case incomes policies degenerate into general fixing of wages—and of prices as well, because wage controls without price and profit controls are not considered politically feasible. In either case the working of the economy is progressively impaired and the growth of productivity reduced.

Price stops and wage freezes are radical versions of the guideline policy. If enforced for any length of time, for example, longer than a few months, these measures would have serious, destabilising consequences. Emergencies are conceivable during which certain short-run objectives are compellingly important. But wage push is definitely not a short-run emergency. Rather it is a more or less chronic disease which cannot be treated with short-run emergency measures.

Tax measures have been proposed as a substitute for guidelines and wage freezes. For example, an 'excess-wage tax'—that is to say, a special payroll tax on wage increases above the guideline norm—has been recommended as a way of stiffening employers' resistance to excessive wage demands. (Some have recommended that 'excess wages' should be taxed away completely. If effective, this policy would be virtually equivalent to a wage freeze.) Tax measures would certainly be preferable to the crudity of guidelines and wage freezes. But closer analysis reveals serious difficulties of implementation, and there are compelling reasons to doubt that the tax method of restraining the wage push would be more effective than tight monetary management. The latter, too, tends to stiffen employers' resistance to excessive wage demands, but it cannot prevent wage push from creating unemployment. It is not clear why tax measures would be more successful.

Re-introducing Competition into the Labour Market

What shall we conclude? Is it that nothing can and should be done to check wage push? Definitely *not*. What we should conclude is that the problem of wage push has to be attacked at its source. The excessive power of labour unions should be curbed. There simply is no synthetic substitute for restoring a larger measure of competition in the labour market and elsewhere.

Radical solutions have been proposed, such as prohibition of industry-wide bargaining and dissolution of industry-wide unions. It is, however, politically impossible and probably unnecessary to go that far. Fortunately, there are many available measures short of radical solutions which, if systematically applied, would produce a marked moderation of the wage push. Some examples are: withdrawal of the special legal or *de facto* privileges which unions enjoy and which tilt the scale in collective bargaining in favour of organised labour; modification of minimum wage laws; changes in the policy of subsidising strikes through welfare payments to strikers (and, in New York and Rhode Island, unemployment benefits also, after a strike has lasted eight weeks). Industrial monopolies or oligopolies are not much of a problem as far as inflation is concerned. (Prices in the public utility area, 'natural monopolies', are controlled, and usually over-controlled, anyway.) But any measures that strengthen competition, e.g., more vigorous anti-trust action or liberalisation of imports, have not only a direct favourable effect on prices but also serve to curb union power. For market power in the product market always strengthens the market power of labour unions.

These measures and many others (section 4) are now often recommended under the heading of the second type of incomes policy mentioned above. Any one of them, although desirable in itself, would in isolation have no appreciable effect on inflation. But collectively they would have a noticeable impact.

If little or nothing is done along these lines, we will have to resign ourselves to more inflation and eventually, since inflation cannot be allowed to continue for ever, to a permanently higher level of unemployment, lower output, and slower growth—in other words, to a sub-optimal, below-capacity performance of the economy. In practice this outcome would take the form of accentuated cyclical fluctuations, periods of excessive inflation alternating with periods of recession caused by attempts to halt inflation by monetary-fiscal measures or by ill-conceived, ineffective, and counter-productive direct controls (guidelines, wage freezes, price stops, and the like).

In the absence of effective measures for restraining cost push, nobody knows for sure how much unemployment would be required to reduce inflation to, and to keep it at, a tolerable level. The amount would depend on circumstances and must be assumed to change from time to time. The 'Phillips curve' is supposed to give a precise answer. A critical analysis of the theory of the 'Phillips curve' is presented in a Note to Section 2.

2. Demand-Pull versus Cost-Push Inflation

It has been customary for a long time to distinguish sharply between demand-pull and cost-push inflation. Sometimes the words 'buyers' inflation' and 'sellers' inflation' are used. The former, also called the 'classical' type of inflation, is said to be due to an increase in monetary demand; the latter, also called the 'new' type of inflation, is said to be caused by sellers pushing for higher prices. Sellers' inflation implies imperfect, non-competitive markets, the existence of powerful monopolies or oligopolies, of 'market power'—that is to say, the power to set or manipulate prices which is absent under competition. Cost-push or sellers' inflation becomes, in practice, largely wage-push inflation because of the strong position of powerful trade unions.

Inflation Requires Monetary Expansion

The customary formulation strongly suggests, and many fall victim to it, that demand inflation is a monetary phenomenon while cost inflation is non-monetary. This is, however, a very misleading statement. In reality, both types of inflation are monetary in nature in the important sense that they require monetary expansion.

Either M, the quantity of money, or V, its velocity of circulation, must go up. Theoretically it is possible that M may remain constant (or even decrease) and the rise in prices be entirely 'financed' by an increase in V. But it is a fact, without exception as far as I know, that there has never been a case of sustained inflation without a rise in M. It is true that V is not constant over time. It usually rises during business cycle upswings and declines during downswings. But it is only in very rare and exceptional circumstances that it moves temporarily out of a fairly narrow range. Such an exceptional case occurred during the hyper-inflation in Germany after the First World War when the velocity of circulation of money rose to fantastic heights.[2] During the Great Depression and the Second World War, V fell to an unusually low level which accounts for the sustained rise in the post-war period.[3]

Both demand-pull inflation and wage-push inflation are essentially monetary phenomena and both can be stopped or prevented by monetary restrictions. The difference is that stopping a demand inflation by monetary measures will have only a slight and temporary adverse effect on output and employment, while counteracting a cost-push inflation by monetary means will create some lasting unemployment and a corresponding loss of output. Thus the existence of powerful trade unions—labour monopolies—which force up money wages by strikes, or the threat of strikes, confronts the monetary authorities with a disagreeable dilemma: either they can create enough money to permit the rise in prices that is compatible with the rise in wages, or they can prevent inflation by refusing to expand monetary circulation, but only at the cost of 'creating' a sufficient amount of unemployment to stop wage push. It is implicit in this theory, which is very widely accepted, that under the modern organisation of the labour market (absence of competition) there exists a trade-off between inflation and unemployment. If unemployment is to be kept low, we must accept a certain amount of inflation. If we wish to avoid inflation, we must tolerate a certain volume of unemployment. This view has been formalised in the theory of the 'Phillips curve', which postulates the existence of a fairly stable relationship between the unemployment rate on the one hand and the annual rise in money wage-rates and the associated rise in the price level on the other hand.[4]

The policy conclusions to be drawn from the wage-push theory of inflation are straightforward. In order to eliminate the dilemma confronting monetary management wage push must be prevented and the rise in money wages slowed down to a rate that is compatible with stable prices. The widely-accepted formula is that money wages should rise approximately in proportion to the general rise in labour productivity (output per man-hour). To achieve this result, 'guideposts' or 'guidelines for non-inflationary wage changes' must somehow be enforced. In Europe, the same type of approach has gone for some time under the name of 'incomes policy'. Incomes policy is usually defined as the broader term, relating to other incomes as well as wages. In the 1970s the term incomes policy has become popular also in the US.

Is There a Wage-Push?

The 'guideposts' or 'incomes policy' will be further discussed (sections 3 and 4). We will first try to answer the question whether the wage-push dilemma is real and serious. Most economists believe that it is, but Milton Friedman and some others disagree.[5] They believe that the power of trade unions to raise money wages has been greatly exaggerated. If the monetary authorities stood firm and kept the money supply sufficiently tight, that is to say, if they increased the money stock by as much as is needed to keep the price level stable—say, by 4 or 5 per cent a year—then labour unions would moderate their wage demands. The transition from an inflationary to a non-inflationary price trend might be attended by some temporary unemployment; but after a while unions would realise that they could not expect the same annual increase in money wages in the absence of inflation as they could under inflation. Thus, the economy would settle down on substantially the same employment level and growth path (in real terms) at stable prices as under inflation at rising prices. Further, in the long run, real growth would be a little faster with stable prices because the periodic disturbances caused by inflation, including those brought about by futile attempts of governments to suppress inflation's symptoms, would be avoided.

On the face of it, this theory sounds too good and too comforting to be true. But let us carefully analyse it. I will first formulate a few propositions on which probably most economists could agree.

First, money wages have become almost completely rigid downward. Even before the emergence of a strong trade union movement, wages were not very flexible, but unions have certainly contributed greatly to the almost complete downward rigidity that we are confronted with today.[6] Downward rigidity of wages by itself (without any wage push) can conceivably exert some inflationary influence but is probably not a serious threat to price stability unless it is combined with an upward push.[7]

Secondly, it is generally agreed that the replacement of competition by monopoly, be it in labour or commodity markets, will push up wages and prices. This is emphasised by the critics of the cost-push theory. Thus Professor Friedman himself shows that

from 1933 to 1937, the NIRA, AAA, Wagner Labour Act and the associated growth of union strength led to *increasing* market power of both industry and labour and thereby produced upward pressure on a wide range of wages and prices.

He points out that

the concomitant rapid growth in nominal income at the average rate of 14 per cent per year from 1933 to 1937 ... reflected a rise in the quantity of money of 11 per cent per year and cannot be explained by cost push.[8] But 'cost push does explain why so large a part of the growth in nominal income was absorbed by prices' and only a correspondingly smaller part reflected by rising output and employment.

Despite unprecedented levels of unemployed resources, wholesale prices rose nearly 50 per cent from 1933 to 1937 and the cost of living by 13 per cent. Similarily, the wage cost push helps to explain why unemployment was still so high in 1937 when monetary expansion was followed by another severe contraction.[9]

This was indeed an extreme case of cost-push or sellers' inflation.

Thirdly, it follows, it seems to me, that assuming the same monopolies continue to exert their market power, they will continue to push up costs and prices. They do not need a further increase in market power. It is sufficient that they continue to do what they did from 1933 to 1937. It is true that the monetary authorities could at any time stop a further rise in the price level by making money sufficiently tight, but only at the cost of causing or perpetuating slack and unemployment.

This conclusion seems to me inescapable. If unions (and other monopolies) were able to push up wages and prices from 1933 to 1937 in the face of an 'unprecedented level of unemployment', they should a *fortiori* be able to do the same when unemployment is much lower.[10] No increase in 'market power'—for example (to give a little more precision to that vague term), more complete unionisation of labour, more aggressive union leadership, further change in legal status (extended privileges and immunities conferred by law), more lenient public policy or a more sympathetic attitude towards unions on the part of public opinion—is required.[11] The reason why unions were able to push up wages under conditions of unprecedented unemployment from 1933 to 1937 was, of course, that monopoly power was at that time created or vastly increased by the assorted New Deal policies mentioned above. But as far as the labour unions (and agriculture) are concerned, the increased market power has remained undiminished. On the other hand, the National Industrial Recovery Act (NIRA), the New Deal policy of fostering industrial monopolies, was allowed to lapse and was later replaced by more vigorous anti-trust policies. Moreover, the gradual liberalisation of trade policies (reduction of import tariffs) operated strongly to reduce monopoly or oligopoly power in many industries.

However, critics of the cost-push theory believe that the price-raising power of trade unions and other monopolies is a one-shot affair while wage-push theorists regard it as a continuing force. Thus, when the New Deal policies strengthened the market power of unions and business cartels, the newly formed or strengthened monopolies were put in a position to give a boost to prices. But it would have required a further increase in monopoly power, the critics of the cost-push theory argue, to carry forward the inflationary price-boosting.

Labour Unions and Industrial Monopolies

I am prepared to accept this argument in the case of industrial monopolies and, indeed, put it forward myself years ago.[12] But I do not believe that it applies to labour unions. The reason is that business monopolies and labour unions cannot be assumed to operate according to the same rules. This consideration is obscured by calling trade unions 'labour monopolies'. They are, of course, monopolies in the sense that they eliminate competition in the labour market and in the sense that a trade union makes workers speak with one voice. But their rules of conduct are quite different from those of industrial monopolies or oligopolies.[13]

Industrial monopolies and oligopolies try to maximise their profits making allowances, of course, for various constraints—the danger of competitors from home or abroad entering the field if prices are set too high, the risks of government intervention and of antagonising public opinion, and so on. Monopoly prices are always higher than prices would be under competition. Hence when competition is replaced by monopolies—as was the case under the early New Deal policies—prices of the monopolised commodities go up. If the monetary authorities are sufficiently firm, the overall price *level* could remain stable; prices would fall in the competitive sphere of the economy, offsetting the rise in monopoly prices.[14] If the total expenditure—nominal income as Friedman says—is allowed to go up, the price level will rise, with monopoly prices rising faster than competitive prices. Thus the introduction of numerous monopolies in the early 1930s explains, as Friedman points out, why the increase in nominal income was reflected to an abnormally large extent in rising prices and to an abnormally small extent in rising output and employment.[15] However, once monopoly prices have been established and equilibrium restored, there is no tendency for monopoly prices to go higher unless the underlying situation (on the demand or supply side) changes. Hence the substitution of monopoly for competition has a one-shot inflationary effect and is not a steady force exerting upward pressure on the price level.[16]

Labour unions behave differently. True, they too seek gains, that is higher incomes, for their members and thus they raise the price of labour. But they aim for large *annual* wage increases and not merely for a once-for-all substitution of a higher monopoly wage for the lower competitive wage. That in the absence of labour unions—i.e., in a perfectly competitive labour market—real wages rise in a progressive (growing) economy in accordance with the growing (marginal) productivity of labour, that money wages rise even if the price level is kept stable, and that money wages rise faster than prices under inflationary conditions[17]—all this makes it a perfectly natural objective for union policy to push continuously for money wage increases that are higher than is compatible with full-employment equilibrium at stable prices. There can thus be no doubt about the wage objectives of labour unions.

What can possibly be questioned is whether they are powerful enough to achieve their goal.

Moreover, in my opinion there cannot be the slightest doubt that unions very often succeed year after year (or from one contract to the other) in pushing up money wages beyond the competitive, full-employment equilibrium at stable prices. At the higher wage employment will, of course, be lower as a rule than it would be at a lower wage. But this is usually not immediately clear and is, at any rate, strenuously denied by labour leaders. In some cases, however, unions pay the price of lower employment consciously and deliberately.[18] Thus it is well known that the United Mine Workers of America, under the leadership of John L. Lewis, traded rapidly increasing wages for dwindling employment in the coal industry. It is hardly open to doubt that in public utilities and in progressive industries, where output rises rapidly and profits are high, unions are in a particularly strong bargaining position and often are able to secure wage increases way above the level to which wages in the economy at large can rise, if full employment at stable prices is to be maintained. That the same is true of steel and automobiles and many other manufacturing industries is only slightly less clear.[19]

Unions and Real Wages

What has been said about wage push and the power of labour unions to confront the monetary authorities with the disagreeable dilemma of settling for either inflation or unemployment concerns *money* wages only. Whether unions are in a position to influence *real* wages is an entirely different matter. They certainly have very little influence on the *general* level of real wages (including the wages of unionised and non-unionised labour). On balance, their long-run effect on the real income of labour as a whole is almost certain to be negative, for two reasons. First, unions are responsible for numerous misallocations of resources resulting from inefficient work rules, reduced labour mobility, excessive shortening of the work week,[20] losses caused by strikes and other work disputes, and so on. Second, they cause or intensify inflation with its associated distortion, dislocations and unemployment resulting from periodic attempts to restrain the inflation by means of inefficient direct controls or generalised financial restrictions that create at least temporary unemployment.

On the other hand, measuring the ability of unions to influence the growth of real wages for unionised labour (as compared with labour as a whole) is a much more difficult problem. There is evidence that unions create a permanent though changing wage differential in favour of unionised, as against non-unionised, labour.[21] However, since the pace of wage growth set by union wages tends to spread sooner or later to other areas and since the overall impact of unions is unfavourable for growth, it is very doubtful whether, in the long run, union wages in real terms are improved by union activities. This does not, of course, deny that well-organised unions may secure substantial and lasting gains for small groups of workers.[22]

Some Conclusions

I conclude that wage push is an undeniable fact. It is overt when wages rise under conditions of unemployment because this clearly could not happen if there were competition in the labour market. It is not so clear, but must be assumed *a fortiori* to exist, under conditions of high employment, because if unions are able to push up wages when unemployment is 'unprecedentedly high' (Friedman) or rising, they are in an even better position to do so when unemployment is low and falling. It follows that even in clear cases of demand inflation, it must be assumed that aggressive labour unions intensify and reinforce the demand pull by wage push.[23]

The critics of the wage-push inflation theory often point out that in the US only a fraction, some 25 per cent, of the labour force is unionised. This makes it impossible, they think, to attribute to labour unions the power to push up the overall wage level. No such conclusions can be drawn. Unions do have the power to push up wages. First, it is not true of other industrial countries that only a fraction of the labour force is organised in unions. Practically the whole labour force is unionised almost everywhere in Europe. Second, there has been a large increase in the union power of public employees at all levels of government (teachers, firemen, policemen, postal workers, etc.). Third, under American conditions of partial unionisation in the private sector it can be shown that wage increases forced on unionised industries by powerful labour unions tend to spread, though possibly with a lag and incompletely, to other areas. A favourable wage contract obtained by any one union under favourable conditions becomes a target and spur for others to do as well or better. Furthermore, employers often find it necessary to raise wages and salaries of non-unionised workers and employees, partly to maintain morale and wage differentials for different skills, partly to forestall unionisation of the rest of the labour force.

The point is often made[24] that in periods of high employment and rapid expalsion, wages of non-unionised workers sometimes rise faster than union wages. This is, however, merely a frictional phenomenon of strictly temporary importance. It arises because union contracts usually run for a year or two, occasionally longer. Thus it may happen that wage push is overtaken by demand pull, as it were. We can be quite sure, however, that this lag will not last long. When unions find themselves caught napping, they will quickly make up for lost time. Wage contracts will be broken by 'wildcat' strikes against the wish of union leaders or with their tacit consent. If inflation continues for long, wage-contract periods will be shortened and cost-of-living escalators will be built into wage and salary contracts.[25]

Note to 2: The Phillips Curve—A Critical Analysis

The relation between price inflation and unemployment (more particularly between the rise in money wages and the level of unemployment), the existence of a trade-off between unemployment and inflation, and the question of how much unemployment is required to stop inflation—these problems have been discussed in recent years in a rapidly growing literature. The strongest impetus came from an economic and statistical study by Professor A. W. Phillips.[26] Phillips seemed to offer a simple and elegant solution and his paper immediately acquired fully deserved general recognition and fame.[27]

Unemployment, Money Wages, and Prices

The results of Phillip's work are epitomised in the 'Phillips curve' which has become a household word in modern macro-economics. The curve depicts the relation between (a) the level of unemployment as measured by the unemployment percentage, and (b) the rate of change of money wages (in per cent per year), or at one remove, the rate of change of prices. In a diagram with the unemployment percentage plotted on the horizontal axis and the wage or price change plotted on the vertical axis, the Phillips curve slopes down from left to right: the higher the unemployment the smaller the rise in money wages and prices. At some level of unemployment, money wages would remain stable and at some (lower) level of unemployment, prices would be stabilised. At that point the Phillips curve cuts the horizontal axis; at still higher levels of unemployment money wages and prices would decline (i.e., below the horizongal axis in Fig. 12.1).

For the United Kingdom Phillips estimated that, assuming an increase in productivity of 2 per cent per year, it would take a little less than $2\frac{1}{2}$ per cent unemployment to keep product prices stable; to keep wage-rates stable would require $5\frac{1}{2}$ per cent unemployment.

The economic theory on which Phillips's empirical work is based is extremely simple and suggestive:

When the demand for a commodity or service is high relatively to the supply of it we expect the price to rise, the rate of rise being greater the greater the excess demand. Conversely when the demand is low relatively to the supply we expect the price to fall, the rate of fall being greater the greater the deficiency of demand. It seems plausible that this principle should operate as one of the factors determining the rate of change of money wage rates, which are the price of labour services. When the demand for labour is high and there are very few unemployed we should expect employers to bid wage rates up quite rapidly, each firm and each industry being continually tempted to offer a little above the prevailing rates to attract the most suitable labour from the other firms and industries. On the other hand it appears that workers are reluctant to offer their services at less than the prevailing rates when the

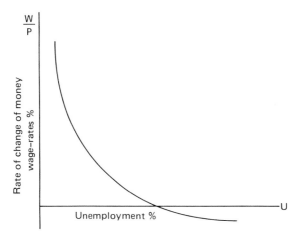

Figure 12.1
The basic Phillips curve.

demand for labour is low and unemployment is high so that wage rates fall only very slowly. The relation between unemployment and the rate of change of wage rates is therefore likely to be highly non-linear.[29]

On the left the curve is steep, reflecting the fact that in order to depress unemployment to very low levels (frictional unemployment) increasingly higher money wage and price boosts would be required. Towards the right the curve eventually flattens out because larger and larger levels of unemployment are necessary to reduce wages and prices still further.[30]

In addition to the main determinant of the change in money wages, i.e., the level of unemployment ('excess supply'), Phillips mentions two other factors: (a) 'the rate of change of demand for labour and so of unemployment' and (b) 'the rate of change of retail prices'. But he considers these two factors merely subsidiary; they do not substantially change the picture resulting from the operation of the principal factor.

Contrary to what is often assumed, Phillips's own theory of inflation is that of 'demand pull' and not of 'cost push.' He clearly regards his statistical findings as evidence in favour of the demand-pull hypothesis. The postulated relation between unemployment and the rate of change of wages and prices would seem to be perfectly compatible with attributing wage-pushing power to labour unions. Clearly, *other things being equal*, the higher the level of unemployment the weaker the position of labour unions and the weaker the wage push; and conversely, the lower the level of unemployment the stronger the position of labour unions and the stronger the wage push. Hence, even if labour is organised in well-disciplined trade unions, there will exist a level of unemployment—presumably a higher level than in a competitive labour market—at which labour unions are sufficiently weakened to assure stable prices, and a still higher level of unemployment which would stabilise the level of money wages.[31]

So much about Phillips's theory. It is only fair to add that he describes his conclusions as 'tentative'. 'There is need,' he emphasised, 'for much more detailed research into the relations between unemployment, wage rates, prices and productivity'.[32]

The call for more research has been answered in abundance. The theory has been extensively discussed and refined and innumerable Phillips curves have been constructed for many countries. For the United States, pessimistic conclusions have been reached: 6 or 8 per cent unemployment would be required to maintain price stability. Surveying this literature one cannot help getting the impression that the idea of a unique and stable Phillips curve has been gradually discussed to death. The conclusion reached in a careful study by Albert Rees and Mary T. Hamilton sums up the situation:

We have been astounded by how many very different Phillips curves can be constructed on reasonable assumptions from the same body of data. The nature of the relationship between wage changes and unemployment is highly sensitive to the exact choice of the other variables that enter the regression and to the forms of all the variables. For this reason, the authors of Phillips curves would do well to label them conspicuously: *Unstable! Apply with extreme care!*[33]

We should be quite sure, however, about what the negative verdict on the Phillips curve means and what it does not mean. It does *not* mean that the fundamental idea from which Phillips starts is wrong. It remains true that, at any point in time and over the short run, the higher the unemployment the slower the rise in (money) wages and prices. It also would seem to be plausible to assume that there always exists, at any one time or over a short period, a level of unemployment that is compatible with stable prices and another, higher level of unemployment that would stabilise money wages although it might be a socially and politically intolerable level. Furthermore, rejection of the Phillips curve does not contradict the proposition that there is a wage push in the sense explained earlier. It is one thing to say that powerful trade unions are capable of pushing up money wages, thus confronting the monetary authorities with the nasty dilemma of either allowing prices to rise or stopping inflation by creating a sufficient amount of unemployment; it is an entirely different thing to postulate, cautiously as Phillips did or incautiously as many others do, a stable, long-lasting relationship between the level of unemployment and the rate of change of wages and prices. What a negative judgement of the Phillips curve does mean is that there does not exist a *stable, long-run* relationship between unemployment and the rate of change of prices (or wages). In other words there is no long-lasting, *constant* trade-off between inflation and unemployment. The curve, if it is more or less welldefined at any moment of time, is subject to rapid shifts over time. This conclusion is based on the following considerations. Phillips derives his curve from annual British figures for the whole period 1861 to 1957. It is true he studied sub-periods separately. But his final (tentative) conclusion—that for the UK about $2\frac{1}{2}$ per cent unemployment would be required to assure price stability—is derived from the figures for the whole period of almost 100 years.

This is a highly implausible theory on the face of it. It implies that the far-reaching changes in the structure of the labour market that took place during those almost 100 years—the rise of the labour movement, the tremendous increase in the power of trade unions, the profound shifts in government policy and public attitudes to labour relations, and other structural changes—have had no influence on the power of labour unions to push up wages and on the interrelation between inflation and unemployment.[34] But even for shorter, more homogeneous periods the search for a unique, statistically meaningful and stable Phillips curve has not been successful. Let us recall the conclusion reached by Rees and Hamilton after a careful and comprehensive study: many different relations between unemployment and wage changes can be derived from the same statistical data by adopting alternative, perfectly plausible assumptions.[35]

The 'Trade-Off' versus the 'Equilibrium' View

A seemingly more radical rejection of the theory underlying the Phillips curve has come to be known as the (long-run) 'equilibrium' view. The best-known representative of the latter is Milton Friedman.[36] The 'basic defect' of the Phillips construction, according to Friedman, is 'the failure to distinguish between *nominal* wages and *real* wages'. Friedman does not deny that it is possible in the very short run to reduce unemployment by means of inflationary policies—in other words, that in the very short run there is a trade-off between inflation and unemployment. But he regards the success of such a policy as strictly temporary. For high rates of inflation this is a familiar proposition which is undoubtedly true. Suppose the Phillips curve for a particular country tells us that in order to reduce unemployment to, say, 2 per cent (of the labour force) inflation has to be stepped up to, say, 10 per cent (per year). Few would regard this as a stable situation. Inflation at that speed would soon affect expectations. Further inflation would be anticipated, in other words, 'inflationary psychology' would develop, workers would ask for higher (money) wages and lenders for higher (nominal) interest rates in compensation for the expected rise in prices. Thus a more rapid inflation, say of 15 per cent, would soon be required to maintain the real position, the existing level of output and the low unemployment percentage. This can be conceived of as an upward shift of the Phillips curve; the curve will not stay put for any length of time.[37] In other words inflation has its favourable effect on unemployment only so long as it is not generally anticipated.

Usually, prices rise faster than wages, which enables employers to hire more labour and to step up production. This implies that real wage *rates* decline or at least fall short of expectations; the worker's expectations are disappointed. Similarly, savers and money-lenders are short-changed. But you cannot fool people all the time. 'Money illusion', the belief that stable money wages and nominal interests reflect real wages and real interests over a long time to come, is bound to be eroded and sooner or later destroyed. When that happens, nominal wages and nominal interests will rise to catch up with the expected rate of inflation. Then inflation has to accelerate if the lower level of unemployment is to be maintained. To repeat, for high rates of inflation this is widely accepted and is undoubtedly true.

The 'equilibrium' theory generalises this analysis also for mild cases of inflation. It assumes that at any time there exists a 'natural' level of employment and unemployment which is compatible with stable non-inflationary equilibrium. The natural or equilibrium rate of unemployment is determined by the basic (non-monetary) facts of the economy, such as the existing structure of the labour market, the composition of the labour force, the mobility of labour, the market power of unions, the degree of competition and other institutional arrangements (including government restrictions and regulations such as minimum wages) that tend to raise the level of equilibrium unemployment. Now whenever a conscious attempt is made to increase employment above its 'natural' or 'equilibrium' level or, expressed differently, to reduce unemployment below its equilibrium level by means of inflationary policies, the train of effects described above is set in motion which tends to restore the equilibrium position.[38]

The equilibrium theorist realises, of course, that such a process takes time and that the reaction time will vary with circumstances. For example, the higher the rate of inflation, the swifter will people adjust to it. Interest rates will probably react more quickly than wage rates.[39] All this is quite true, in my view, and should dispose once and for all of the notion of a stable long-run trade-off function between inflation and unemployment.

But the equilibrium theorists sometimes give the impression that the process of adjustment can be telescoped and the long-run equilibrium point reached almost instantaneously. This is, indeed, not entirely impossible. Expectations are capable of changing and adjusting rapidly.[40] Such a state of affairs of instantaneous adjustment may be actually approached under the type of high inflation that is prevalent in many less-developed countries. When prices rise 30 per cent or more a year, as they do in some Latin American countries, then wages, interest rates and other monetary magnitudes are quickly adjusted. But it would be unfair to interpret the equilibrium theory literally as saying that under highly inflationary conditions *real* equilibrium will be closely approximated and continuously maintained. In practice the adjustment is certain to be very inaccurate because future inflation cannot be accurately foreseen. Expectation of future price rises entertained by different individuals and groups will usually not be the same, but will as a rule be different and mutually inconsistent. Moreover, since rapid inflation is bound to disturb vital economic processes, for example the rate of saving, investment and international capital flows, we must assume that the equilibrium rate of unemployment itself will be affected and cannot be closely approximated merely by adjusting money wages and interest rates to the expected rate of inflation.

However, with low rates of inflation as we usually find them in the United States and other mature countries, the equilibrium theory if strictly interpreted runs into other difficulties. It assumes that the money illusion disappears when prices rise and that the vanishing purchasing power of money is a fairly clear-cut phenomenon, unique and visible to all or most people. Actually, with prices rising at, say, 3 or 4 per cent a year on average, the money illusion seems to persist for a fairly long time. Moreover, it seems to be possible to revive it quickly, after it has been eroded, by means of comparatively short spells of uneasy price stability. In the United States it took almost 30 years of intermittent inflation and four or five years of continuously accelerating price rises (since 1965) to create the inflationary psychology (erosion of the money illusion) from which the US economy has been suffering in the late 'sixties and early seventies.' Variable, intermittent inflation is clearly much less destructive of the money illusion than continuous, uninterrupted inflation with the same average annual rise in prices. Moreover, there seems to be a 'threshold' of variable magnitude—that is, only if prices rise more than, say, $1\frac{1}{2}$ or 2 per cent a year will the money illusion be eroded. The concept and measurement of price levels and purchasing power of money is necessarily vague and means different things to different people. What matters are the expectations for the future and it would be a strange coincidence if expectations of different people did not diverge even if the historical record were clear and unambiguously the same for everybody.

Now, all these refinements can perhaps be ignored for sharp price rises, but they blur rhe picture for periods of moderate inflation.

The upshot of these critical remarks is not to reinstate a stable Phillips curve over long periods. It is, rather, to suggest that under conditions of mild or moderate inflation a slowly changing trade-off between inflation and unemployment may exist for extended periods. For the long run consists of successive short periods each with a fresh start, separated by spells of uneasy price stability which serve to restore confidence in money and revive the money illusion.

3. Wage Guideposts: Incomes Policy One

Types of Incomes Policies

In recent years the standard approach of almost all advanced Western economies to the problem of cost-push inflation has become what used to be called 'guideposts' or 'guidelines' in the US and what is known as incomes policy in Europe. Since about 1970 the term incomes policy has become popular in the US, too, and has largely supplanted the term guideposts—probably so that the new policy would not be associated with the old guidepost policy whose futility had been clearly demonstrated.

Incomes policy has indeed become a major issue in the fight against inflation. The question is whether anti-inflationary monetary and fiscal policy should, or should not, be supplemented by incomes policy. Most economists agree that a tight rein on aggregate demand through a sufficiently tight monetary and fiscal policy is a necessary condition for curbing inflation. Monetarists (Milton Friedman and his followers) believe that sufficiently tight money is not only a necessary but also a sufficient condition for stopping inflation. But an increasing number of economists, as well as officials, bankers, economic journalists, and so forth, have become convinced that monetary-fiscal policy alone cannot do the job or can do it only at an intolerable cost in terms of unemployment and slack. By 1970, they say, 'excess demand' was squeezed out of the system by tight money.[41] What remains is cost inflation which can be curbed only by incomes policy. Monetary-fiscal policy alone either could not cope with cost-push inflation at all or could stop it only by creating an intolerable amount of unemployment. But nobody knows for sure how much unemployment would be required for how long. (The Phillips curve is supposed to provide the answer: Note to Section 2.)

That incomes policy has become a popular issue has, as was to be expected, not contributed to precise thinking. Originally it meant something like generalised guideposts. Now it means different things to different people.

As already indicated I distinguish here between incomes policy one in the original sense of generalised guideposts and incomes policy two in the sense of a collection of different measures designed to improve the working of the price mechanism and bring it closer to the competitive ideal. The clearest description of the latter, the new concept of incomes policy, has been formulated by Professor Arthur Burns. Formerly, Burns was an uncompromising critic of guideline policy.[42] But when as chairman of the Federal Reserve Board he took charge of monetary policy, he soon came to the conclusion that 'the transition from an inflationary to a non-inflationary growthpath of the economy could be speeded up' and made less painful by the adoption of a variety of measures which he called 'incomes policy'. His new incomes policy includes such measures as abolishing or changing the minimum wage laws which reduce the job opportunities available to marginal workers; repealing (or suspending) the Davis-Bacon Act under which the government is frequently required to pay the highest union wages on its far-flung construction projects[43]; and compulsory arbitration of wage conflicts in certain areas (railroads, public utilities, shipping). In addition, it also includes measures that would tend to promote competition and keep down certain prices, for example, more vigorous anti-trust action and import liberalisation. This list of measures he regards as illustrative rather than exhaustive.[44]

Wage Controls and Price Controls

I shall first discuss incomes policy in the original and narrower sense and then take up some parts of the new, extended concept of incomes policy. Let me repeat, the almost universal approach to the problem of cost-push inflation in industrial countries has become the guideline policy for wages. Under such a policy, the attempt is made to hold wage increases to the rise in average productivity for the economy as a whole (output per man or man-hour).

Political considerations dictate, however, that if restraints are applied to wages they must also be applied to prices; business 'monopolies' and 'oligopolies' must be controlled as well as unions (labour monopolies). This is unfortunate for several reasons. First, industrial monopolies are not much of a problem as far as inflation is concerned. In our times industrial 'monopolies' and 'oligopolies' do not have the same power, strength and iron discipline that many unions have developed in many countries. Public opinion in most Western countries tends to be hostile to business. Therefore, 'anti-trust' policies against industrial monopoly and oligopoly are pursued with varying degrees of energy, while labour unions enjoy the protection of the law and, even though their detrimental impact on inflation and growth is now more widely recognised, are treated with kid gloves compared with the treatment meted out to alleged industrial monopolies.[45]

Second, the impact of industrial monopolies and oligopolies on inflation is, we have seen, strictly a one-shot affair, while unions exert a continuing upward pressure on costs and prices. The plain fact is that the American economy is much more competitive than most people, including many economists, realise,[46] and in smaller countries international trade effectively keeps monopolies in check.[47] Needless to say, even in the US, despite the large internal free trade area, liberalisation of trade and larger imports have had the salutary effect of counteracting monopolistic tendencies and strengthening healthy competition. The only really important exceptions are public utilities (transportation, communication, electric power).[48] But the price policies of these industries are regulated anyway, and usually over-regulated. In Europe public utilities are government-owned and are operated either by government departments or by 'public corporations'.

Price and cost policies of public utilities and their regulations have, of course, become a major problem of economic management whether they are privately owned or in the public sector. But even here the most serious aspect is the wage problem. The monopolistic nature of the industry (whether privately- or publicly-owned and -operated) confers special powers upon the unions. So the problem of public utility pricing, as far as inflation is concerned, becomes to a large extent a problem of restraining the power of labour unions and of wage guidelines.

The upshot of this discussion is that the extension of guideline policy to prices outside the area of 'natural monopolies' (public utilities) comes down to one of two things. Either it is ineffective exhortation or it degenerates quickly into general price controls with all their deleterious effects on efficiency—for example, the development of 'black' or 'grey' markets, the creation of unearned profits for some and losses for others, the gradual destruction of the allocative function of the price mechanism, the substitution of formal or informal rationing for market forces, the proliferation of red tape and bureaucracy. For these reasons, I shall confine myself mainly to a discussion of guideposts as applied to wages.

Wage Guidelines: The Target

A sharp distinction must be made between the objective or target of wage guideposts on the one hand and the practical problems of implementation and enforcement on the other. The objective is to curb union power and the target is to make the average level of money wages rise roughly in proportion to the long-run growth of average productivity (output per man-hour), say, 3 per cent a year or so for the US. The objective is laudable and, it will be argued, the target is sensible in the sense that if wage-rates—more precisely, the average wage level—could be made to behave according to the stated target, the price level would remain approximately stable. It can be shown that under competitive full employment equilibrium (in the absence of labour unions), if the price level is kept stable by appropriate monetary policy, average money wages would actually rise approximately as the guidepost target postulates. Hence the guidepost policy ideally seeks to make the economy as a whole and the labour market in particular behave as they would under perfect competitive equilibrium conditions, an objective that should command general approval. We shall see, however, that this favourable conclusion has to be changed radically when problems of implementation are considered in detail. But first a few more words about the ideal rule.

Several objections to the guidepost formula are commonly made. One is that if it were strictly applied and if wages rose in a growing economy in proportion to output per man-hour, all additional output would go to labour. This objection is not valid. If money wages grew according to the rule *and* prices remained constant, the proportion of wage income to non-wage income would remain constant; in other words, labour and non-labour incomes would share proportionately in any addition to GNP.

Another objection is that the strict application of the rule would rigidly fix the proportion of national income going to labour and non-labour income (including profits), while some flexibility in that proportion is clearly desirable. There is more to this objection than to the first. But it should not be forgotten that if wages on average rose in proportion to average productivity, the price level would remain only *approximately* stable. It is easy to show that under certain circumstances the price level *may* have to change somewhat.[49] This can be seen most easily by first considering the case of an individual industry. Suppose an industry undergoes a rapid process of mechanisation and automation; much capital equipment is installed and machines are substituted for labour. Suppose that the labour input is thereby radically reduced and a few men now operate an automated plant where formerly many men worked with simpler equipment. Output per man-hour will go up sharply. In this case, it would be absurd to attribute the whole increase in output to labour and it would not be possible to apply the rule that the wage should go up in proportion to output per man, leaving the price of the product unchanged. If this were done, there would not be enough left to cover the heavily increased capital cost. In other words, in this example the distribution of income between capital and labour has to be changed, more going to capital and less to labour. This can be brought about either by a higher product price if money wages rise in proportion to the larger physical output per man, or by money wages not rising in proportion to the rising output per man if the product price is to remain unchanged.

Something like this *could* happen in the economy as a whole. When the economy is being rapidly mechanised and automated, it may become necessary that the share of output going to labour be reduced and the share of non-labour income (including profits) be increased.[50] However, the difference is that for individual industries, the equilibrium proportion of income going to labour and capital may be subject to fairly large and rapid changes, but for the economy as a whole, as a matter of historical fact, the share of national income going to labour has remained fairly stable over time. It is not entirely constant over long periods (as some writers maintain) but it is not a magnitude that changes rapidly or exhibits *large* swings over protracted periods.[51]

This empirical fact of the relative stability of the share of wages in national income makes the guidepost formula theoretically acceptable. Prices would remain approximately constant if wages behave according to the formula. Or to put it the other way round, in an ideal competitive economy, if prices were kept constant by skilful monetary management, wages would rise *approximately* in proportion to the average increase in productivity.

If money wages rose according to the guidepost target, the small changes in labour's share of national income that might be necessary from time to time in order to maintain equilibrium would be brought about by slight variations in the price level. It can be shown that, given the relative constancy of the wage share in national income, small price changes well inside the range of social tolerance would provide sufficient flexibility.[52]

Wage Guidelines: Problems of Implementation

I turn now to the problems of applying and implementing the guidepost or incomes policy. The basic difficulty is that the average wage level is a fuzzy concept and is, at any rate, not a policy variable. The wage *level* as such, however defined, cannot be directly managed and changed by government action. It can be manipulated only indirectly by operating on wages in individual industries and locations.[53]

The government could conceivably freeze all wages and permit only uniform percentage changes. But this would be disastrous except as a short-run emergency measure and has never, as far as I know, been carried out successfully for any length of time. Most economists agree that, for the sake of efficiency, *relative* wages should remain flexible. In other words, the relations among the wages of workers of different skills and of workers in different localities, industries or even firms should be allowed to vary according to changing demand and supply, expansion and contraction of different industries and firms, and so on. Such changes are in practice going on all the time. And in our economy they are necessary to provide incentives for the gradual transfer of labour from industry to industry, or from firm to firm, and to ensure maximum employment during the process of adjustment. It is impossible through government regulation to make the average wage level behave in any particular way—for example, in accordance with the guidepost rule—without at the same time influencing and distorting relative wages by preventing or impeding adjustment to changing conditions. The government cannot simply decree the behaviour of the wage level in the aggregate. It can influence it only by influencing particular wage contracts. The attempt to manipulate the wage level (without dealing with the evil of wage push at its source by clipping the monopoly power of labour unions) necessarily remains ineffectual exhortation or becomes general wage and price control. To repeat, the wage level as such is not a policy variable.

This was implicitly recognised in the original formulation of guidepost policy in the US.[54] It was realised that a strict mechanical application to all industries of the guidepost rule—that wages everywhere should rise in proportion to the long-term growth of overall productivity—would be undesirable. Therefore, it was conceded that, for the sake of efficiency and equity, a number of exceptions must be permitted. Some of these exceptions were explicitly formulated, leaving others presumably to be spelled out from time to time. Let me quote:

The most important modifications are the following: (1) Wage-rate increases would exceed the general guide rate in an industry which would otherwise be unable to attract sufficient labour; or in which wage-rates are exceptionally low compared with the range of wages earned elsewhere by similar labour, because the bargaining position of workers has been weak in particular local labour markets. (2) Wage-rate increase would fall short of the general guide rate in an industry which could not provide jobs for its entire labour force even in times of generally full employment; or in which wage-rates are exceptionally high compared with the range of wages earned elsewhere by similar labour.[55]

These 'modifications' are sensible, as far as they go. But they do not go far enough. Economic reality is infinitely more complex than the complicated guideposts—and at least the 1962 report was aware of this. Let me again quote:

Even these complex guideposts leave out of account several important considerations. Although output per man-hour rises mainly in response to improvements in the quantity and quality of capital goods … employees are often able to improve their performance by means within their own control. It is obviously in the public interest that incentives be preserved which would reward employees for such efforts.

Also … it must be borne in mind that average hourly labour costs often change through the process of up- or down-grading shifts between wage and salaries employment, and other forces. Such changes may either add to or subtract from the increment which is available for wage increases under the over-all productivity guide.[56]

A little reflection should convince the reader that a serious attempt to apply these rules and exceptions would be bound to produce endless disputes. What are 'exceptionally low wages' compared with 'similar labour' elsewhere? Who is to decide whether alleged wage discrepancies are due to different 'bargaining positions of workers' or to other factors?[57] Who can determine convincingly whether 'special incentives' are or are not required? Any attempt at consistent application must lead to general wage control, and wage control without price and profit control is politically not feasible. Furthermore, any attempt at introducing 'guidepost[s] for non-inflationary price decisions' must lead to general price control.

Actually, until about the middle of 1965 when unemployment was fairly high, little was heard about wage guideposts being applied in specific cases.[58] When labour markets became tight and wages began to rise faster, half-hearted attempts were made at application. Success was minimal and, for all practical purposes, guidepost policy was dead by 1966 or 1967—although it was reaffirmed from time to time by the Council of Economic Advisers under the Johnson adminstration.[59]

It is not difficult to understand why the guidepost policy for wages failed. The basic reason is, to repeat, that the wage level is not susceptible to direct manipulation. It is not a policy variable and can be influenced only indirectly by influencing specific wage contracts. Wage guideposts, therefore, degenerate into either ineffectual preaching and 'jawboning' or general wage- (and price-) fixing. In the latter case they become a policy of repressed inflation, the most reprehensible and damaging kind of inflation.

The same holds, to an even higher degree, for the guidepost policy for 'non-inflationary' price behaviour. For wages, there is the fact of the great market power of tightly-organised unions which does indeed call for remedial action. However, uncontrolled monopoly or oligopoly in business is non-existent or at any rate very rare and much weaker than that of organised labour. Where industrial monopolies exist, or are supposed to exist, they are dealt with by special regulations (public utilities) and anti-trust policy. It is possible to argue that anti-trust policy should be pursued more vigorously. But general price guideposts are indistinguishable from price-fixing, which invariably leads to formal or informal rationing, black and grey markets, multiple pricing, misallocation of resources, wasteful red tape and sprawling bureaucracy.[60]

Wage guidelines, as distinguished from price guidelines, have at least the merit of calling attention to a serious problem, namely, how to curb excessive power of labour unions. This problem, of course, transcends the inflation-and-growth issue. As far as avoiding inflation is concerned, we have seen that the concrete target of wage guidepost policy, namely, to make the wage level rise in proportion to the average long-run growth of labour productivity, is sensible. But it is one thing to describe in macro-economic terms how wages and prices would behave in a competitive economy with a stable price level and to show that this is a desirable and efficient state of affairs. It is an entirely different thing to bring this desirable result about *without actually restoring a sufficient degree* of competition in the labour market.

The truth is that the evil of wage push has to be treated at its source. In other words, if wage push is to be eliminated, the excessive monopoly and coercive power of labour unions must be curbed somehow and a greater degree of competition restored to the labour market. *There is simply no good synthetic substitute for real competition.* If union power is not curbed, the only alternative is to tolerate more inflation or more unemployment than is desirable from the point of view of stability and growth.

4. Incomes Policy Two

The Problem of Restraining Union Power

How to restrain union power is a most intractable problem that has not been satisfactorily solved in any industrial country. It goes, of course, far beyond the problem of inflation, which is our only concern at this point.

It must be borne in mind that inflationary wage pressures can come only from labour unions. Non-unionised labour has no monopoly or market power and wages in that area, by far the larger part of the US labour market, can safely be left to the forces of demand and supply and do not require government regulation.[61]

A radical solution of the problem posed by powerful labour organisation would be to dissolve industry-wide unions and prohibit industry-wide collective bargaining.[62] But given present-day political and social realities, this solution is hardly practical.[63] Barring the radical solution and realising that guidelines and wage or price freezes (below, pp. 293–294) are no solution, what can be done to prevent or at least sharply reduce excessive wage pressure by powerful unions? Some well-known economists have indeed reached the defeatist conclusion that nothing can be done and that we have to resign ourselves to the unpleasant choice between perpetual inflation and high unemployment.[64]

Actually there are many other measures short of the radical solution that the government could take. They have been proposed many times and many of them have recently found their way into the proposed 'new incomes policy' (incomes policy two). They have, however, never been applied systematically and consistently and should be tried before throwing in the sponge or accepting unpalatable alternatives.

Withdrawing Union Privileges

To begin with, over the years labour unions have acquired, *de jure* or *de facto*, numerous important immunities and privileges which go far beyond anything accorded to business or other private associations and organisations.[65] It is difficult to believe that legal reforms designed to restore a more equal balance between the parties in wage bargaining by withdrawing from unions their special immunities and privileges would not have considerable effect in reducing the bargaining power of unions and relieving inflationary wage pressure. Concretely it should be possible to prevent abuses of union power and to force unions to abstain from violence and intimidation. If unions and their leaders were held financially responsible for damages caused by breach of contracts, illegal strikes, intimidation and violence, considerable moderation in wage bargains could be expected.[66]

Repeal of Minimum Wage Laws and Special Acts

We have already mentioned a series of other measures that the government could take. One is the repeal of minimum wage laws, or at least modifications such as lower minima for teenage labour. Minimum wages create unemployment among marginal workers (the unskilled, teenagers, and others). But they also strengthen union power even though the minimum is far below the level of most union wages. The reason is that the minimum wage (which has been raised many times, oblivious of any guidelines) has contributed to what Arthur Burns has called 'the overpricing of unskilled labour relative to skilled labour'.[67] This provides a strong inducement for employers to substitute skilled for unskilled labour wherever possible, either directly or indirectly through the installation of capital equipment. As a result, the bargaining position of trade unions is strengthened.

A second is the repeal or suspension of the Davis-Bacon Act and the 50 or so other federal laws that incorporate the wage-boosting provisions of Davis-Bacon. These acts require payment of prevailing wages on construction projects in which the government is involved; and frequently the 'prevailing' wages set in accordance with these requirements match the highest union rates in the area. In February 1971 the Nixon administration temporarily suspended these acts in order to slow 'sky-rocketing' wages and prices in the construction industry and to end federal encouragement of inflation.[68]

Abolition of Welfare Subsidies to Strikers
Another measure that could be taken is to withdraw government subsidies to strikers such as welfare payments and even unemployment benefits in the US and some other countries. These subsidies serve to strengthen union power and their withdrawal would make strikes much more costly and reduce union power and wage pressure.[69]

In addition, the labour supply could be increased and wage-push inflation thereby alleviated by amending social security laws to permit old-age pensioners to work and earn money without losing their benefits. It is true that such a reform would increase the money cost of social security substantially. But the advantages would be great. They would not only be economic in the form of increased output and softened inflationary pressures but also social: enforced or induced idleness is a social evil. The ideal solution would be to give those eligible for social security pensions the option to earn a larger pension in the future by continuing to work. This would probably reduce the money cost of the reform.

It was mentioned earlier that Arthur Burns includes import liberalisation and a more vigorous anti-trust policy among the measures included in his new incomes policy. Stronger competition from imports not only tends to keep down prices but also weakens labour unions. Monopoly in the labour market is always greatly strengthened by monopoly in the product market.

Price Stops, Wage Freezes, and 'Excess' Wage Taxes

In recent years many countries in desperation have decreed general price stops, usually (but not always) combined with a wage freeze. Proposals for a 'temporary' price and wage freeze have also been made in the US. (Such measures are invariably billed as temporary.) Numerous proposals to tax excessive wage or price increases have also been put forward in the US and elsewhere.

A general or partial wage or price freeze is a radical version of guidepost policy. As such it has all the deleterious effects of the latter, but in a pronounced form. It eliminates market forces, it quickly leads to distortions of the price and wage structure by making adjustment to changing conditions impossible, and it creates grey or black markets. In the case of most products, price stops can be evaded by quality deterioration; wage freezes can be circumvented by upgrading, providing more liberal fringe benefits, and any number of other manipulations. All these evasive manoeuvres impair efficiency and lead to conflicts and waste by diverting scarce and precious managerial energies and ingenuity from productive purposes to sterile activity to comply with—or to evade—government regulations. Enforcement would require detailed checking by an army of inspectors and would inevitably create a vast new bureaucracy and provide a breeding ground for corruption. Thus, price stops and wage freezes are strictly a short-run emergency measure. If maintained for longer than, say, three months it would be necessary to make more and more exceptions in order to eliminate the most glaring distortions and inequities. Thus the policy breaks down or deteriorates quickly into general wage and price control.

A policy of general or partial wage and price freezes has a strong tendency to destabilise the economy. Since the freeze cannot be maintained for long, there is great danger that when it is lifted or breaks down, prices and wages will shoot up. The policy thus leads to instability or to general price and wage control.

Emergencies are conceivable in which the achievement of certain short-run effects is the primary purpose. The outbreak of a war or revolution leading to panic buying, as well as the hoarding of goods and dishoarding of money, are examples. A decision to halt a raging wage-price spiral (a combination of demand and cost inflation) by a sharp step on the monetary brake may be another example of an acute emergency that could possibly justify a strictly temporary wage or price freeze until the monetary measures take hold. Still another emergency which cannot be excluded is the desire to win an impending election. In the eyes of the government, this may justify a temporary price stop, although hardly a wage freeze.

It should be clear, however, that the cost-push inflation and union wage pressure from which modern industrial countries suffer are definitely not acute emergency situations. On the contrary, they are a chronic disease, especially 'after excess demand has been eliminated' as the now often-repeated phrase goes.[70] These conditions cannot be dealt with by short-run emergency measures such as price stops and wage freezes which only suppress symptoms and produce instability and waste.

Numerous suggestions have been made for imposing penalties of some kind on price and wage increases. For example, Henry Wallich has called for a special tax on employers who grant wage increases in excess of a specified norm. In order to make such a policy of wage restraint acceptable to labour, Sir Roy Harrod has proposed a surcharge on dividend payments that exceed the 'normal' growth rate.[71]

The wage tax is supposed to stiffen the resistance of employers to wage demands. This approach is clearly superior to the crudity of guidelines or wage freezes, because it works through the price mechanism and does not destroy it. However, the difficulties of setting criteria for normal growth and formulating exceptions to the norm to avoid distortions and inequities would be substantially the same as the difficulties faced by guidelines. The administrative problems of carrying out such a policy would be formidable, especially if it were to be introduced, as in practice it would be, in the midst of an inflation that has had an uneven impact on different industries and firms. Thus, starting from a distorted situation it would certainly be necessary, at the outset, to make numerous exceptions for industries and firms that have lagged behind in the inflation race. If no exceptions were made, the 'excess-wage tax' would have the same type of increasingly distorting effects as guidelines, although presumably to a somewhat lesser extent.

Furthermore, it is not at all clear why a complicated system of excess-wage and excess-profit taxes would induce more resistance on the part of employers to excessive wage demands than would be induced, without any additional difficulties and administrative complications, by keeping a suitably tight rein on aggregate demand through appropriate monetary and fiscal policies. The trouble with the monetary-fiscal approach in the case of a cost inflation is, as we have seen, that powerful labour unions force wage increases on employers which the latter cannot absorb. If money is sufficiently tight to prevent employers from passing on the higher wage costs in the form of higher prices, a curtailment of production and a rise in unemployment will result. There is no reason to believe that an excess-wage or excess-profit tax would change the dilemma in any way. If the employer cannot absorb the tax, he has to pass it on (together with the wage increase) in the form of higher prices or else he will be forced to curtail output and employment. Similarly, there is no reason to assume that unions would be more moderate in their wage demands if employer resistance to higher wages stemmed from an excess wage or profit tax than they would be if it resulted from tight aggregate demand.[72]

5. The British Scene

This essay was finished just when President Nixon announced his New Economic Policy on 15 August 1971. The text was not changed, but the American edition had a Prologue on the price and wage freeze of 90 days which was the integral part of the new policy.

In the meantime, the freeze has been followed by 'phase two', to be administered by a 'Price Commission' in charge of price control and a 'Pay Board' for wage control. There is, furthermore, a high-level Cost-of-Living Council and a Committee on Interest and Dividends whose task is continuous 'surveillance' of interest and dividend levels on a 'voluntary' basis. These bodies are supposed to develop comprehensive rules and standards. There is no point in republishing the Prologue to the American edition and I shall not speculate what the standards and rules of control will be. But it is pretty clear that the US is going down the road of full-fledged incomes policy, resembling more what I call incomes policy one—generalised guideposts—rather than incomes policy two—specialised measures to promote competition and restrain monopolies in the labour market and elsewhere. One can only hope that there will be enough of the latter to mitigate the damage done by the former.

Recent Proposals Examined

In this section I shall make further comments and raise questions, partly concerning the British situation, inspired by the two studies from Professors Frank Paish and James Meade published in 1971 by the IEA which came to my notice only after I had finished my original essay.[73]

On fundamental issues the two eminent British economists reach the same conclusions as I do. Both authors make it quite clear that the real problem lies in the labour market, in the monopoly power of labour unions. 'Wage restraint is the basic problem', as Professor Meade puts it. He further emphasises, and Professor Paish presumably agrees, that a method of wage restraint must be found which leaves relative wages free to vary. Meade develops an ingenious and rigorous scheme to restrain wage push without endangering the flexibility of relative wages. Whether it has a chance of being adopted, and if applied in some form is likely to achieve its goal, I cannot judge. But it faces up to the real problem and should be required reading for all those in charge of incomes policy.

Meade also is emphatic that wage and price controls are entirely unsuited for redistributing income either between workers, for example from the skilled and well-paid to the unskilled and poorly-paid, or between labour and non-labour income. And he argues convincingly that controlling 'producers' monopolies' (what I call business monopolies) requires entirely different measures from restraining labour monopolies (unions). The most effective anti-monopoly policy is free imports.

Until 1970 Paish was not an advocate of incomes policy (which in practice he identifies with wage policy, i.e., a policy to restrain labour unions).[74] The reason for his rejection of incomes policy was not so much scepticism concerning its feasibility, but rather his conviction that until 1969 or so Britain suffered from demand rather than cost (wage) inflation and therefore no incomes policy was needed. But he now thinks that 'cost push has come at last'. (This is reminiscent of the claim of the American money managers that by 1970 'excess demand' had been eliminated and the inflation had become purely cost-push.) Since 1969 a most dramatic change in the labour market has taken place. On the basis of careful statistical analyses Paish concludes that, whereas from the 1952 to 1966 experience one would have expected the unemployment existing between the middle of 1969 and the middle of 1970, about 2.5 per cent, to have been associated with an increase of 3.8 per cent in incomes from employment, the actual increase in money earnings was 13.7 per cent. (This phenomenon could be described as a sudden shift or jump of the Phillips curve; but neither Meade nor Paish uses that expression.)

Meade accepts Paish's finding that since 1969 'a most dramatic and marked change' in the relation between unemployment and wage increase has taken place. To express it differently, the phenomenon of 'stagflation'—co-existence of high unemployment and sharp wage and price rises—has raised its ugly head. (Similarly in the US the 'trauma of rising prices at a time of substantial unemployment' [75] in the late 1950s and early 1960s made a profound impression on economists and policy-makers.)

Intensified Use of Trade Union Power?

How do Meade and Paish explain this dramatic change? They attribute it to a more energetic and aggressive exercise of existing monopoly or market power by labour unions. But labour unions have been there for a long time and there has been no conspicuous increase in their market or monopoly power recently. By contrast, a dramatic change in the power structure, greatly enhancing union monopoly power, occurred in the US in the middle 1930s when Roosevelt's extensive New Deal legislative reforms fostered the growth of labour unions and industrial monopolies. This spectacular increase in market power all-round explains why, from 1932 to 1937 when unemployment and excess capacity were still at very high levels, money wages and prices rose sharply.[76] No such dramatic increases in monopoly power of unions have taken place in Britain in recent years. But Paish offers reasons for the unions' more *vigorous* use of *existing* monopoly power. Meade amplifies, and adds to, Paish's analysis in a most illuminating way.

Meade is frankly baffled by the 'very dramatic increase in wage inflation':

No one can at present give a confident explanation. There are many possible factors at work and very probably it is a combination of many different influences which has caused so large a change.[77]

He enumerates four possible influences.

Four Causes of Intensified Wage-Push

He dismisses, for lack of empirical foundation, the view that an increase in *structural* unemployment may account for the changed wage-unemployment relationship.

The important factors contributing to the intensified wage-push mentioned by Paish and Meade are

1. more liberal unemployment benefits;

2. diversion of productive resources from consumption to exports following the devaluation of sterling in 1967;

3. intensified awareness on the part of workers and unions that it is *real* and not *money* wages they are interested in;

4. better realisation by workers and union leaders of their large accumulated monopoly power.

1.   The introduction of redundancy payments and higher unemployment benefits in 1965 and 1966 'reduced the terrors of temporary unemployment' (Meade) and made it easier for unions to engage in long strikes. The same phenomenon can be observed in the USA (above, pp. 290–291).

2.   The necessity to balance the international accounts after the 1967 devaluation forced the Government to reduce private consumption by fiscal measures and to direct resources to export industries. This policy has been successful, as seen in the improvement in the balance of payments. But it implied a temporary reduction in the standard of living. It is natural that wage-earners and their unions after a lag attempted 'to restore the situation through more urgent demands for increased money wages' (Meade). In the US, because of the small share of exports in GNP, such balance-of-payments effects are negligible.

3.   Meade says that 'higher prices of imports and higher direct and indirect taxes', which resulted from the necessity to balance the international accounts, 'may have made wage-earners more conscious of the rise in the cost of living'. There are really two factors here: (a) the erosion of 'money illusion' through prolonged inflation, and (b) the basic interest of the workers in 'take-home pay', i.e., income after taxes, social security contributions and other deductions from their gross wage. If these deductions are enlarged, unions take steps to restore their disposable income (take-home pay); they do not regard the larger social benefits they may get for larger deductions as part of the income for which they bargain in wage negotiations; they accept them as windfalls like sunshine or manna from heaven.

This surely is a very important matter, on which the Editor of Paish's *Paper* rightly lays emphasis in his Preface to the Second Edition.

4.   These recent developments 'may have given individual trade unions an unexpected glimpse into the very large monopolistic powers which they possess for pushing money wage-rates up and which they have not fully exploited in the past. The consequence may have been a basic [permanent] change in their attitudes' (Meade).

Monetary Policy Crucial to Successful Attack on Inflation

All this is extremely interesting and important. The factors mentioned above have certainly played a large role in the changed labour market picture and the increased aggressiveness of trade unions. I would like, however, to add a few comments.

First, there is another factor which neither Meade nor Paish mentions, perhaps because it is so obvious. 'Money illusion' has been eroded and everybody has become more conscious of the difference between money and real income *because of the prolonged inflation*. Monetarist economists are inclined to say that this is all there is to it. In their opinion, the increased militancy of unions is nothing but a hangover from a long spell of inflation and would disappear if inflation were stopped.

This explanation is too simple and too optimistic. Even if it were true that it was largely inflation that first brought about this change, I am inclined to agree with Meade that the change in union attitudes is basic and permanent.

The range of compressible types of income has become much smaller than it used to be. The once 'fixed' incomes of the proverbial widows and orphans, of teachers, government officials, social security beneficiaries, etc., are now more or less automatically adjusted for changes in the purchasing power of money. As a consequence inflation, no matter for whose benefit it is intended, spreads more rapidly throughout the economy.

The monetarist is surely right when he emphasises the importance of inflation for the enchanced aggressiveness of trade unions (p. 272 above). But I believe that Meade is also right to speak of a 'basic', meaning a permanent, change in attitudes. It is much too optimistic to assume, as monetarists do who deny the reality of a wage-push, that unions would promptly shed their aggressiveness if inflation were stopped by monetary restraint and that therefore no policy of market-directed wage restraint (incomes policy two as I call it) is necessary. To invalidate the monetarists' precept it is sufficient to make the weaker assumption that unions would eventually adjust to a change in the rate of inflation, but only after a considerable lag. In that event, it is true, full employment equilibrium would eventually be restored after inflation was ended by monetary restraint, but only after a prolonged period of transitional unemployment, which modern society just will not tolerate.

Professor Friedrich Hayek and the late Albert L. Hahn drew attention years ago to the dangers threatening the free enterprise system when the money illusion is eroded and labour monopolies bargain for real rather than money wages.[78]

In some countries union aggressiveness obviously has also a political root, for example in Italy and in Latin American countries. But even in countries where labour unions are socially and politically conservative, as in the US, they have been strengthened by the general rise of lawlessness and emergence of radical-anarchist leftist movements in the universities and elsewhere. True, the unions have spurned the advances of radical students. But these radical movements have given the unions an aura of respectability, responsibility, and conservatism. They deserve that reputation, but it enhances their political power and makes it easier for them to pursue their wage-pushing activity with little interference from government.

Meade and Paish are surely right that heavier taxation, including larger social security contributions (and union dues), intensify the wage-push because unions try to protect their members' take-home pay. In his Preface to Paish's *Paper* the Editor asks:

Has increasing taxation lost its power to restrain consumption? May it *intensify* inflation by reducing "take-home" pay and inciting wage demands when "social wages" are not valued as part of income?

The second question can be definitely answered in the affirmative: heavier taxation has a tendency to intensify inflation. But whether this effect is so strong that taxation has completely 'lost its power to restrain consumption' is doubtful. However, one thing is certain, I believe: if there were no monopolistic unions, in other words if there was competition in the labour market, the situation would be entirely different. In that event heavier taxation would not necessarily have inflationary consequences, or if it had (indirectly, e.g., by discouraging saving investment and risk-taking or by reducing the effort on the part of employers/entrepreneurs and workers), the inflationary effect could be offset by monetary restraints *without creating additional unemployment*.

Conclusions

The upshot of this whole discussion is that wage-push by powerful labour unions is an undeniable reality. For various reasons wage-push has become much stronger everywhere in recent years. This put the monetary authorities into the nasty dilemma, either to permit or create inflation, very likely at an accelerating rate if the emergence of unemployment is to be prevented, or to counteract inflation by tight money and thereby 'create' unemployment.

If nothing is done to remove the evil at its *source* by curbing the monopoly power of unions we have to accept more inflation and more unemployment, probably much more of both than there would be present in a competitive market.

Finally, let me reiterate a conclusion which is repeated again and again in the text above: *inflation is a monetary phenomenon*. With a loose monetary and fiscal policy all other measures for fighting inflation, such as wage restraints and anti-monopoly policies in general, must be in vain.

Postscript—1985

Rereading my 1971 paper, as well as my earlier paper *Causes and Cures of Inflation*,[79] which covers much of the same ground, was an interesting experience. During the last 14 or almost 20 years, the terminology of macroeconomics has changed greatly, theories have become much more sophisticated, and expert opinion has shifted on several important issues, but I confess that I find few new substantive insights.

I begin with what I regard as merely terminological or semantic changes. Nobody would say today, as many did 20 years ago, that there are two kinds of inflation: "demand pull" and "cost push." With every inflation prices are "pulled up" by rising demand (an increase in M and/or in V), but it is also true that there is such a thing as "cost push," "wage push," and monopolistic price rises in certain areas, e.g., the two oil shocks. All this greatly complicates anti-inflation policy.

The word "stagflation" is, I believe, of a more recent vintage, but the phenomenon of "inflationary recession" was not entirely unknown, although it has become more pronounced and received increasing attention in the 1970s and 1980s.

Expert opinion has sharply shifted away from the Phillips curve concept. It is now fairly generally realized that there is no permanent or long-run trade-off between inflation and unemployment. The extreme opposite of the Phillips curve is the theory of rational expectations, which came into vogue after my 1971 paper was written, although its "invention" is usually attributed to J. F. Muth's paper on security and commodity markets ("Rational Expectations and the Theory of Price Movements").[80] In its most radical form, which is found in the writings of Robert Barro and Robert E. Lucas, it sounds the death knell of macroeconomics. It is said that monetary and fiscal policy cannot affect the real economy, output, and employment, only prices, money GNP, and nominal interest rates, because rational individuals will realize what the government is up to and will take immediate defensive action.

In this extreme version the theory is surely a gross exaggeration. It ignores the plain fact that wages are rigid and that, therefore, a policy of disinflation (reduction of the rate of inflation), let alone a real contraction of the money stock, produces unemployment from which it follows that a policy of expansion reduces unemployment and increases output.

However, the basic idea that rational market participants try to figure out what the consequences of monetary expansion and contraction will be and that they do not simply extrapolate the current state of affairs but are guided by their expectations of future events is surely correct. But in that sense the theory is not new. In my 1966 and 1971 papers I argued that inflationary policies will after a while lose their stimulating power and will require ever increasing rates of inflation to maintain, let alone increase, employment.

In my paper I distinguish what I call Incomes Policy I from Incomes Policy II.

Incomes Policy I comprises more or less comprehensive wage and price controls, wage and price freezes, wage guidelines, and the so-called Tax-oriented Incomes Policy (TIP). These types of incomes policy are rejected; they have never worked and are a bureaucratic nightmare.

Incomes Policy II is described as a bundle of measures designed to make the economy more competitive, flexible, and efficient. In Europe this type of incomes policy is called supply-oriented policy. Examples are deregulation of industry and the scaling down of excessive welfare measures, overly generous unemployment benefits, higher minimum wages, and severance payments. These measures raise wage costs, impede labor mobility, cause unemployment, and reduce the rate of growth. Free trade is vitally important. Few private monopolies, oligopolies, and cartels would survive in a free-trade world.

Supply-oriented policy should be distinguished from supply side economics, which flourishes in the United States. The latter, to my mind, is a dangerously overoptimistic and unrealistic notion: Reduce taxes and the economy will respond by more savings, investments, and more work effort so that tax revenues will not decline. Too simple to be true. The valid core of the theory, that high marginal tax rates are counterproductive because they reduce saving, investment, and work effort, is of course recognized by the proponents of a supply-oriented policy. Elimination of that impediment to rapid growth would be one way to increase supply.

Finally, supply-oriented policy should not be contrasted with demand-oriented policy, i.e., monetary fiscal policy designed to keep aggregate demand (nominal GNP) on an even keel. The two are not mutually exclusive alternatives but complements.

Notes

1. Incomes policies have recently been reviewed by Eric Schiff in *Incomes Policies Abroad* (Washington: American Enterprise Institute, Vol. I, 1971, Vol. II, 1972), and Lloyd Ulman and Robert J. Flanagan, *Wage Restraints: A Study of Incomes Policies in Western Europe* (Berkeley: University of California Press, 1971). Both works come to the conclusion that incomes policy has not worked well anywhere.

2. People got rid of their money as fast as they could. For a while wages and salaries were paid twice or even three times a day, and people rushed to the shops to buy what they could before prices were again marked up. Thus velocity of circulation rose to many times its usual level. As a corollary, the 'nominal' quantity of money (in terms of depreciating marks), although it multiplied fast, rose much less sharply than prices and the 'real' quantity of money (nominal quantity corrected for the loss of purchasing power of money) fell sharply. It is amusing to report that some well-known German economists argued at the time that the increase in the (nominal) quantity of money had nothing to do with the rise in prices, because the *real* quantity of money (money stock expressed in constant purchasing power or gold) declined! It can be laid down as a general proposition that an increase in the *nominal* quantity of money at a rate which causes inflation (a rise in prices) will lead to a decrease in the stock of *real money*.

The reason is that people will economise in the use of money if its purchasing power is expected to decline.

3. However, the drop during the Great Depression was of an entirely different order of magnitude than the rise during hyper-inflation. There is a striking asymmetry between inflation and deflation. It has often happened that prices have risen to many times their former level. But even in the worst deflation the price level falls, perhaps by 50 per cent—and that happens very rarely. A 20 per cent general price decline due to monetary contraction is a calamity. This asymmetry has its roots in the downward rigidity of prices, especially of wages, and in the existence of fixed money contracts and debts.

4. The theory of the Phillips curve is briefly discussed in a Note to this section (pp. 277–282).

5. For example, M. Friedman, 'What Price Guideposts?', in *Guidelines, Informal Controls and the Market Place*, eds. G. P. Shultz and R. Z. Aliber (Chicago, 1966), reprinted in M. Friedman, *Dollars and Deficits*, 1968; Allan Meltzer, 'Is Secular Inflation likely in the U.S.?', in *Monetary Problems of the Early 1960s* (Atlanta, Ga.: Georgia State College, 1967). Frank W. Paish has taken a position similar to Friedman and Meltzer in his *Rise and Fall of Incomes Policy*, Hobart Paper 47, IEA, London, 1969. But in the Second Edition which appeared in 1971 he says that the situation has changed in Great Britain since about 1969. He believes that wage push has become a reality. He therefore now favours a policy of wage restraint (see section 5).

6. What is rigid is money wages. 'Efficiency wages' are not quite so rigid. The reason is that labour efficiency declines when the labour market is tight and employment is full or overfull and increases when the labour market is slack and unemployment high. That means that even when money wages remain constant, efficiency wages fall somewhat in depressions and rise faster than money wages when unemployment declines.

Real wages, too, are less rigid than money wages, because as a rule money wages are not promptly corrected for changes in the cost of living. But it is true that cost-of-living clauses in wage contracts tend to make real wages rigid and money wages more flexible upwards. (Such 'escalator clauses' usually work only in an upward direction.)

7. Suppose aggregate demand rises in proportion to the gradual growth of output. There is, thus, no inflationary demand pull. Now assume that there are, from time to time, shifts of demand from one group of commodities to others. Then wages will rise where demand increases, but will not fall where demand declines. Thus in the long run it is possible that through this ratchet mechanism the price level will be jacked up. A theory of inflation along these lines was put forward by Charles L. Schultze in his study, *Recent Inflation in the U.S.*, Study Paper No. 1, Joint Economic Committee, 86th Congress, 1st Session, September 1958; see also my criticism in *Inflation: Its Causes and Cures*, 1966 edition, p. 86.

8. Indirectly the cost push has probably greatly contributed to the rapid expansion of nominal income. For it is very likely that the authorities would not have let the quantity of money increase so fast if unemployment had fallen rapidly and output had approached the full-employment level more quickly. It remains true, however, that the cost push and monopolistic price increases were largely due to the ill-advised policies of the New Deal. They were responsible for the fact (to use Alvin Hansen's words) that 'the monetary expansion was to such a large extent dissipated in price rises'.

9. M. Friedman, 'What Price Guideposts?', *op. cit.*, p. 22.

10. For example, during the recession from July 1957 to April 1958 wages continued to go up in the face of substantial unemployment. This clearly suggests union pressure and since unemployment, though large, was much smaller than in 1933–37, less 'market power' was required than in the earlier period.

It would, furthermore, not be difficult to find cases where unions were able to secure wage increases through strikes in particular industries (e.g., the steel industry) despite the high level of unemployment in that industry at that time. Another glaring case is the construction industry. For years wages of construction workers have risen sharply despite much unemployment and slack in the industry. If unions are able to push up wages in slack periods and in depressed industries, they are a fortiori able to do it in boom periods and in industries that operate at or near full capacity. That is to say, wage push reinforces demand pull.

11. It could be argued that a decrease in unemployment by itself constitutes an increase in market or monopoly power on the ground that under fuller employment the demand curve for union labour is less elastic. But this would give away the case against the theory of the wage push and would come close to accepting the Phillips curve.

12. See my 'Wage Policy and Inflation', in P. D. Bradley (ed.), The Public Stake in Union Power, Charlottesville, 1958, p. 75, and Inflation: Its Causes and Cures, op. cit., pp. 71–73.

13. The basic difference between industrial monopolies and labour unions is often overlooked or ignored. When talking about cost-push inflation, many economists feel the urge to demonstrate their social impartiality by blaming industrial monopolists and oligopolists along with labour unions. That there is a difference between the two has, however, been clearly recognised by a group of leading economists representing a cross-section of experts from left, right and centre who wrote the remarkable report, The Problem of Rising Prices (Organisation for European Economic Co-operation, Paris, 1961). They unanimously reached the conclusion that in the United States in the late 1950s wage push played a major role: 'With demand pressure [in the United States] less intense than in Europe, round after round of wage increases have weakened the competitive position of American industry' (p. 62). They also agreed unanimously that there is no counterpart to continuous wage push on the business side. 'We believe that the danger of aggressive pricing to raise profit margins is a limited one. It can add fuel to the fire in an inflationary situation. But it is not likely to be the starting cause, nor can it be a cause of continuously rising prices. In this respect, an increase in profit margins differs from an increase in wages; there can be a wage-price spiral but there cannot be a profit-price spiral' (p. 70). The committee thus rejected the theory, popular at that time in the US, that large corporations in oligopolistic industries continuously 'push up' prices in the same way as unions push up wages.

It is not surprising that the group split on policy recommendations. The majority, including Bent Hansen and Richard Kahn, recommended incomes policies while William Fellner and Friedrich Lutz were in favour of treating the evil at its root by curbing the power of industry-wide labour unions.

14. Except if wage or price rigidities prevent the price decline.

15. The price rise was abnormal in view of the large amount of unemployed resources then existing. From 1933 to 1935 over 20 per cent of the labour force was unemployed. In 1936 it was still 16.9 per cent, in 1937 14.3 per cent and in 1938 again 19 per cent. This analysis is fully acceptable, in principle at least, for Keynesians. Thus Alvin Hansen in his A Guide to Keynes (New York, 1953) points out that 'to the extent that this occurs [viz., that money wage-

rates rise before full employment is reached] the increase in aggregate demand is unnecessarily dissipated in higher prices with correspondingly less effect on output and employment' (p. 193). It is true, however, that few other Keynesians have emphasised this point as much as Hansen has.

16. Naturally, this does not exclude the consideration that it may take some time before a newly-created or strengthened monopoly has tested the market, evaluated the various constraints mentioned earlier and found the price that suits it best. Thus, during a transitional period prices may rise after a monopoly has been created or strengthened.

17. It is true that inflation strengthens the hand of trade unions because it offers them an opportunity to secure large increases in money wages which bolsters their prestige and reinforces their hold on the workers, even though a part of these increases is not real. It also stands to reason, as was pointed out earlier, that the transition to a non-inflationary situation is made difficult because, when inflation is stopped, labour unions have to get used to the fact that the money wage increases cannot be so generous in a non-inflationary situation as they were under inflation. But this does not alter the fact that, apart from any transitional intransigence, unions naturally wish to achieve large wage increases than are compatible with stable prices and full employment.

18. The close connection between wages and employment often becomes clear in export industries. This is especially true in small countries, for example, the Netherlands or Switzerland, where exports constitute a large proportion of output and a small fraction of the world market so that the elasticity of demand for the product is high. In such situations, workers know that exports would fall and they would lose their jobs if wage costs were to rise more than elsewhere. That is probably the main reason why wage discipline is better maintained in these countries than elsewhere.

19. It is generally agreed among economists and is implicit in the 'guidepost' policy that, in a growing economy, prices of the products of progressive industries, where rapid technological improvements take place and cost of production declines more quickly than elsewhere, have to decline if the price level is to remain stable. If this decline is prevented by strong unions that are able to capture, as it were, the fruits of technological progress for themselves instead of letting them be passed on to the consumer, the chances are that the price level will eventually be pushed up. The required price differential between fast and slowly progressing industries is restored in the end, at least to some extent—but in the form of prices of progressive industries rising less fast than other prices, not in the form of such prices actually falling. This process requires, of course, that the wage increases obtained in the progressive industries spread, at least to some extent, to the less progressive industries. How this happens is explained below.

20. It is natural that, with rising affluence, the work week becomes shorter because people wish to consume part of their larger income in the form of more leisure. But it is also clear that in most countries the work week has been shortened, by government regulation and union pressure, much below the level of people's preference for leisure. This policy has become a device to push up money wages by exacting high payment for overtime. It has thus added to the wage push and inflation and also leads to inefficient 'moonlighting' and similar practices.

21. See the thorough theoretical and statistical study by H. G. Lewis, *Unionism and Relative Wages in the United States, An Empirical Inquiry*, Chicago, 1963.

22. This is especially true of unions of specialised, skilled workers (craft unions). But it is by no means confined to such unions, as is clearly shown by the success of the United Mine Workers in raising the real wages of their members.

23. For a minor qualification of this statement see two paragraphs below.

24. For example, by A. Meltzer, *op. cit.*

25. It has often been pointed out that union leaders as well as union members have become sophisticated and price-conscious and that nowadays they tend to bargain for *real* income rather than for *money* wages. Keynes has come in for criticism because in his *General Theory* he assumes that workers are under a strong 'money illusion'. The alleged fact that workers accept reductions in their real wage when it comes in the form of rising prices, while strenuously resisting any cuts in money wage-rates, is indeed a cornerstone of Keynes's theory and essential for many of his policy conclusions. This aspect of Keynes's theory has been criticised by F. A. Hayek ('Unions, Inflation and Profits', in *The Public Stake in Union Power, op. cit.*, reprinted in F. A. Hayek, *Studies in Philosophy, Politics and Economics*, London and Chicago, 1967) and A. L. Hahn (*The Common Sense of Economics*, New York, 1956). Also James Tobin, a good Keynesian, has pointed out (in *The New Economics*, ed. S. E. Harris, New York, 1947) that Keynes assumes contradictory behaviour of the same individuals in their capacity of savers (in which they are supposed to be swayed entirely by real income) and in their capacity as bargainers for wages (in which they are supposed to be concerned with money wages only). It is true that prolonged inflation has the effect of making more and more people price-conscious and of bringing about more frequent and quicker adjustment of incomes, even of 'fixed' incomes, to changes in the price level. This clearly makes the economy more vulnerable to inflationary stimuli. If money illusion were fully destroyed and almost all incomes were automatically adjusted to changes in the purchasing power of income, the consequences would be serious indeed. But this stage has not yet been reached; it is indeed surprising that it takes so long to erode the money illusion altogether and that it seems to be still possible to revive the faith in money fairly rapidly by comparatively short periods of stable prices.

26. 'The Relation Between Unemployment and Rate of Change of Money Wage Rates in the United Kingdom, 1861–1957', *Economica*, November 1958, pp. 283–99. There have been, of course, many earlier attempts to connect inflation with the level of unemployment. But Phillips's work was couched in econometric terms. This fact probably accounts for its strong appeal to contemporary economists.

27. There exist several good reviews with lengthy bibliographies of the literature that took its starting point from Phillips's work. Monographs are: R. G. Bodkin, *The Wage-Price Productivity Nexus* (Philadelphia, 1966) and G. L. Perry, *Aggregate Wage Determination and the Problems of Inflation* (Cambridge, Mass., 1967). Elaborate discussions and fairly complete bibliographies can be found in the articles by Edwin Kuh, 'A Productivity Theory of Wage Levels—An Alternative to the Phillips Curve' (*The Review of Economic Studies*, October 1967, pp. 333–60) and Edmund S. Phelps, 'Money Wage Dynamics and Labor-Market Equilibrium' (*Journal of Political Economy*, July–August 1968, pp. 678–711).

28. In a progressive economy, where output per man-hour (labour productivity) increases steadily, price stability is compatible with rising money wages and, of course, with rising real wages as well. Hence it takes less unemployment to keep prices stable than it would take to keep money wages stable.

29. *Economica, op. cit.,* p. 283.

30. If there exists an irresistible wage push which imposes a minimum wage increase of, say, 2 per cent, the curve would become horizontal at that rate. This situation would still be compatible with *price* stability if the annual wage increase imposed by the wage push is lower than the annual rise in labour productivity.

31. If money wages (more precisely, the wage *level*) remained stable, prices would fall roughly in proportion to the increase in labour productivity so that *real* wages would rise just as much as with rising money wages.

32. *Economica, op. cit.,* p. 299.

33. 'The Wage-Price-Productivity Perplex,' *The Journal of Political Economy,* Vol. 75, February 1967, p. 70.

34. Phillips's assumption of a stable trade-off over this long period thus reflects an extreme version of the demand-pull theory of inflation because it implies that the market power of labour has no influence on wages and unemployment. This goes far beyond the position of the modern critics of the wage-push theory of inflation which we discussed earlier. These critics do not deny that the large increase in market or monopoly power of labour unions that has taken place during the period studied by Phillips has had a profound influence on the level of unemployment and presumably also on the *short-run* trade-off between inflation and unemployment.

35. *Op. cit.*

36. See especially his masterful presidential address, 'The Role of Monetary Policy', *American Economic Review,* March 1968, pp. 8–11, and his contribution to *Guidelines, Informal Controls and the Market Place (op. cit.),* pp. 55–61. The 'trade-off' and 'equilibrium' views have been well analysed and compared by R. W. Spencer, 'The Relation Between Prices and Employment: Two Views', *Review,* Federal Reserve Bank of St. Louis, March 1969. This article contains numerous references to the literature.

37. As explained earlier, this does not mean that inflation must inexorably accelerate. Restrictive monetary policy can always prevent acceleration, in principle at least, notwithstanding certain technical difficulties to keep it exactly at a particular level. But what monetary policy cannot prevent is adjustment of nominal wages and interest rates to the (constant) rate of inflation. When these adjustments are made, unemployment will rise again; in other words, the Phillips curve will shift upwards. With the same rate of inflation more and more unemployment will be associated.

38. This does not, of course, mean that government policy cannot reduce the equilibrium level of employment and unemployment. Improvements in the structure of the labour market, better information for workers about job opportunities, training and retraining programmes, elimination of minimum wages and similar regulations, restraints on the monopoly power of labour unions through the withdrawal of the far-reaching legal and *de facto* privileges which they presently enjoy—these and similar measures would serve to reduce the equilibrium level of unemployment and bring about a lasting increase in output and employment.

39. Friedman offers some cautious observations and guesses about the time these various reactions may take in his presidential address, *op. cit.,* p. 11.

40. Henry Wallich in his remarkable paper, 'The American Council of Economic Advisers and the German Sachverstaendigenrat: A Study in the Economics of Advice,' *Quarterly Journal of Economics*, August 1968, has some interesting observations: 'The Phillips curve retains its familiar shape only so long as there is money illusion.... Without money illusion, i.e., if inflation is fully and instantaneously discounted, the Phillips curve becomes a vertical line over the point of "equilibrium unemployment". This is the rate of unemployment where wage increases equal productivity gains plus changes in income shares. The unemployment-price stability trade-off is gone'. (pp. 356–57)

The Phillips curve becomes a vertical straight line, because if inflation were fully foreseen and instantaneously anticipated the equilibrium rate of unemployment would persist whatever the price rise. Needless to add that perfect foresight and full anticipation are extreme assumptions describing an 'ideal type' which may be approached but will never be fully realised in the real world.

41. As mentioned earlier, the Keynesian expression 'profit-in-flation' would be more descriptive than demand inflation. For aggregate demand in the sense of money GNP (MV, aggregate expenditure) has *not* been stopped from rising. Only its rate of increase has been slowed. Thus from the second quarter 1968 to the third quarter 1969 'total spending' (GNP in current dollars) rose at an annual rate of 7.8 per cent. From the third quarter 1969 to the fourth quarter 1970 it rose by 4 per cent while 'real' GNP (in 1958 dollars) declined slightly by $1\frac{1}{2}$ per cent. What has been squeezed is profits. Increases in monetary demands have not been 'eliminated'.

42. 'Wages and Prices by Formula,' *Harvard Business Review*, March–April 1965, reprinted in A. F. Burns, *The Business Cycle in a Changing World*, New York, 1969, pp. 232–53. He has spelled out his ideas on the new incomes policy in numerous speeches and testimonies before congressional committees, especially in his speech, 'The Basis for Lasting Prosperity', Pepperdine College, Los Angeles, December 1970 (mimeographed).

43. The Davis-Bacon Act was suspended temporarily in 1971 (below, pp. 290–291).

44. Other measures are 'expansion of Federal training programmes to increase the supply of skilled workers', the 'establishment of national building codes to break down barriers to the adoption of modern production techniques', and 'liberalisation of depreciation allowances to stimulate plant modernisation'. General wage guidelines, wage or price freezes are not part of Burns's incomes policy. He has, however, edged towards at least a partial acceptance of guidelines by suggesting that a wage and price review board be set up which would be expected to evolve principles of wage and price setting in certain areas. Similar proposals have been made by the Committee for Economic Development (in *Further Weapons Against Inflation—Measures to Supplement General Fiscal and Monetary Policies*, Committee for Economic Development, New York, 1971).

45. See the authoritative study by Roscoe Pound, *Legal Immunities of Labor Unions*, American Enterprise Institute, Washington, D.C., 1957.

46. This does not mean that perfect or pure competition in the strict theoretical sense is the rule. Far from it. I have discussed elsewhere why I think that 'monopolistic competition' is largely competition rather than monopoly. ('Wage Policy and Inflation', in *The Public Stake in Union Power*, 1958; also my paper, 'Theoretical Reflections on the Trade of Socialist Countries', in A. A. Brown and E. Neuberger (eds.), *International Trade and Central Planning*, University of California Press, Berkeley, 1968.)

47. The other side of this coin is that monopolies are created if imports are restricted by tariffs or quotas. The smaller the country, the more serious the problem. The highly protectionist countries in the less-developed world suffer grievously from government-created and protected monopolies.

48. Even here monopoly power should not be exaggerated. In many cases it has substantially declined because of technological progress. Electricity has come to compete with natural gas and the railways have been subjected to the powerful competition of road and air transport.

49. This has been pointed out many times. I commented on it in *Inflation: Its Causes and Cures, op. cit.*, pp. 14, 65, 116–17.

50. The opposite shift, an increase in the share of GNP going to labour, is also possible. This may happen because of technological change and improvements, despite the fact that historically the capital-labour ratio has gone up more or less continuously. It should be observed that we speak here of the capital-labour ratio, not the capital-output ratio. Also as a consequence of technological change and improvements, the latter (capital-output ratio) historically does not display a continuous increase.

51. It changes, of course, in the short run, i.e, during the business cycle. Profits rise more rapidly during cyclical expansions and fall more rapidly during contractions than labour income.

52. On this point, see R. M. Solow, 'The Case Against the Case Against the Guideposts', *Guidelines, Informal Controls and the Market Place, op. cit.*, pp. 48–49. It should be observed that this argument applies to *money* wages only. It assumes that *real* wages are not entirely rigid. If the rate of growth of real wages were set at the level of the rate of growth of labour productivity (for example, by adjusting the money-wage growth continuously or at short intervals to the rise in the cost of living), unemployment would result whenever the situation required a decline in labour's share of national income, irrespective of whether, and at what speed, prices were allowed to rise.

53. This is certainly true for the US. In some foreign (non-communist) countries that have all-embracing labour unions, for example, the Netherlands, it has sometimes been possible to negotiate uniform wage changes over a large part of the economy. Thus incomes policy was thought to have been relatively successful in the Netherlands for several years. But after a while it broke down, partly because many Dutch workers could take jobs at much higher wages across the border in Germany. Holland thus experienced a veritable wage explosion.

54. *Report of the Council of Economic Advisers*, January 1962, p. 189.

55. *Ibid.* The rules—or 'guides' as the report says—for 'non-inflationary price behaviour and the corresponding modifications' are even more complicated than those for wages. They largely turn on comparative productivity trends in different industries.

56. *Ibid.*, p. 190. CEA reports for later years have added nothing to the analysis of the problem. On the contrary, the formulations have become cruder and more dogmatic and the 'modifications' have been de-emphasised for the simple but unconfessed reason that they are in practice totally unworkable without quickly degenerating into general wage-and price-fixing, which even the Kennedy and Johnson Councils of Economic Advisers always rejected.

57. Indeed, years before the guideline approach to wage setting was first proposed by the Council of Economic Advisers, some of the problems and dilemmas were clearly foreseen and

analysed by no less than the late Professor Sir Dennis Robertson in the *First Report* of the Council on Prices, Productivity and Incomes (HMSO, 1958). (The first report of the so-called 'Cohen Council', named after its chairman, Lord Cohen, was largely Sir Dennis's handiwork, especially its analytical parts.) Concerning 'the suggestion that from time to time a percentage figure should be announced by which average money wages could increase without damage to the national interest', the report has this to say:

We are conscious of the attractiveness of this proposal offering as it does the hope of establishing a link between the rate of wage increases and the growth in overall productivity. There are, however, serious practical objections to it. There would always be industries in which there were good reasons for the advance in wages to exceed the average; others in which much less good reasons for it to do so could be thought up; very few in which the case for lagging behind the average would be readily conceded. There would thus be a real danger that the prescribed average would always become a minimum, and the process of wage inflation therefore built into the system.

58. *The Report of the Council of Economic Advisers*, January 1966, said that 'during recent years of still excessive unemployment and idle capacity, strong competition for jobs and markets reinforced a growing sense of responsibility on the part of labour and management'. The 'growing sense of responsibility' is vaguely attributed to the operation of the guidepost policy. This sounds like a witch rainmaker saying, when the rains came, that favourable atmospheric conditions reinforced his efforts!

59. The experience of seeing guidepost policy fall into disuse and disrepute under the weight of its own ineffectiveness has not prevented the economists who unsuccessfully tried to make it work from chiding their successors for not using it.

60. It should not be forgotten that there is a basic difference between regulating a monopoly price and fixing a competitive price. If by government decree or by imports from abroad a monopoly price is reduced below the level which an uncontrolled monopolist would charge, the monopolist will produce even more (assuming the prescribed price is not set below the competitive level). Attempts at fixing a competitive price below the equilibrium level have all the deleterious consequences mentioned in the text. Competition need not and must not in this connection be interpreted in the strict theoretical sense of infinitely elastic demand. 'Workable' or 'monopolistic' competition is sufficient.

61. This does not mean, of course, that the labour market would necessarily be perfect in the absence of unions and that nothing can be done to remove imperfections.

62. This has been often proposed and seems to be the proposal of the two members of the above-mentioned OEEC group of experts who did not go along with the majority in recommending general incomes policy: 'Reservations by Professors Fellner and Lutz', *The Problem of Rising Prices, op. cit.*, pp. 63–65.

63. The only major country where industry-wide collective bargaining still seems to be the exception rather than the rule is Japan. Partly for that reason, Japanese wages have retained considerable flexibility downwards. This fact surely is largely responsible for Japan's remarkable ability to cope with inflationary bouts and balance-of-payments difficulties by means of orthodox monetary measures (credit restriction) without creating more than very mild and short recessions.

64. The late Sumner H. Slichter argued that, given the strength of labour unions in what he called 'our labouristic society', we would have to accept perpetual inflation of something like 3

per cent a year. The only alternative would be to permit intolerable unemployment. At the same time, he was confident that the monetary authorities, by standing firm, could and would prevent inflation from accelerating to, say, 5 per cent or more per year.

This theory is, however, quite unconvincing. It implies unions will never realise that gains in money wages are lost through rising prices or, alternatively, that it is possible, even in the long run, to squeeze so-called 'fixed' incomes sufficiently to provide labour permanently with a real growth above the equilibrium level.

Neither assumption is tenable. Unions fully realise the implications of rising prices. Interest rates go up when borrowers and lenders expect rising prices and, increasingly, even many of the so-called fixed incomes—particularly salaries of teachers, firemen, policemen, government employees in general—tend to be adjusted more or less automatically when the cost of living rises for protracted periods. Unionisation of these government employees has sharply reduced the size of the so-called fixed-income group. Also, social security and other welfare payments and pensions are now being raised to keep abreast of rising prices.

It is interesting to recall that, as already mentioned, Keynes too, in *The General Theory*, made the untenable assumption that workers are under such a strong 'money illusion' that they do not realise the difference between money and real wages. Keynes compounded his mistake by assuming that other members of the social economy are entirely free of the money illusion. He assumed, in fact, that wage earners 'are under the spell of money illusion only in their capacity as suppliers of labour'—not, for example, in their capacity as savers. (James Tobin, 'Money Wage Rates and Employment' in S. E. Harris (ed.), *The New Economics*, New York, 1947, pp. 572–90.)

65. See the authoritative study by Roscoe Pound, 'Legal Immunities of Labor Unions', in *Labor Unions and Public Policy*, American Enterprise Institute, Washington, 1958. The same volume contains an excellent analysis, 'Economic Analysis of Labor Union Power', by E. H. Chamberlin.

66. In Britain where union power has been more abused than in the US, the Conservative Government under Mr. Edward Heath has undertaken a major reform of the rules of collective bargaining.

67. Arthur F. Burns, *The Management of Prosperity*, New York, 1966, p. 46.

68. The suspension was later rescinded and replaced by a complicated 'largely self-regulating system of wage constraints' and 'monitoring' of construction prices. Many states have their own 'little Davis-Bacon acts' which have contributed to the 'skyrocketing' wage and price increases in the construction industry. All these wage-boosting measures are the legacy of the Great Depression.

69. The reform of collective bargaining proposed by the British Government tries to end or at least sharply reduce public financing of strikes. In the US, the unemployment compensation laws of 48 states specifically exclude striking workers from unemployment benefits. New York and Rhode Island, however, permit payments to strikers after a strike has lasted for eight weeks. It is not difficult in many states for strikers to meet eligibility requirements for welfare payments.

70. As pointed out earlier, the Keynesian term 'profit inflation' would be more appropriate. For the rise in monetary demand, measured either by money GNP (MV) or by the supply of money (M), has *not* been eliminated. It has at best been slowed down. Profits have been sharply reduced in the process.

71. See also Sidney Weintraub, 'An Incomes Policy to Stop Inflation', *Lloyds Bank Review*, London, January 1971; F. W. Paish, *Rise and Fall of Incomes Policy*, Hobart Paper 47, IEA, 2nd Ed., 1971; James Meade, *Wages and Prices in a Mixed Economy*, Occasional Paper 35, IEA, 1971. (Section 5 comments on the Paish and Meade proposals.)

72. *The Economist* ('A Real Incomes Policy', 24 April 1971) has proposed that increases in wage incomes exceeding the growth in labour productivity—say, 3 per cent per annum—should be taxed away 100 per cent. That would indeed remove any incentive to ask—or strike—for larger wage increases. But an 'incomes policy' as stiff as that would be equivalent to a wage freeze. In an acute crisis, such a measure might become necessary. But it could not be maintained for any length of time without causing most serious distortions and wastes.

73. F. W. Paish, *Rise and Fall of Incomes Policy*, Hobart Paper 47, IEA, Second Edition, 1971, and J. E. Meade, *Wages and Prices in a Mixed Economy*, Second Annual Wincott Lecture published for the Wincott Foundation by the IEA as Occasional Paper 35, 1971.

74. *Rise and Fall of Incomes Policy*, First Edition, 1969 (and *Policy for Incomes?*, Hobart Paper 29, IEA, 1964, Fourth Edition, 1968). The Second Edition adds a Postscript under the title 'Cost-Push At Last'. Another prominent British economist who finds that inflation has changed its character recently is Lord Robbins: 'Inflation: The Position Now', *Financial Times*, London, 23 June 1971. Lord Robbins used to stress demand-pull. Now he believes that wage-push has become the villain.

75. This apt expression comes from a paper by Thomas Moore, *US Incomes Policy, Its Rationale and Development*, American Enterprise Institute, Washington, D.C., December 1971.

76. Above Section 2, sub-section 'Is there a wage-push?', pp. 272–273.

77. Meade, *op. cit.*

78. E.G., Hayek, 'Unions, Inflation and Profits', in *Studies in Philosophy, Politics and Economics*, London and Chicago, 1967.

79. Second edition, American Enterprise Institute, Washington, D.C., 1966.

80. *Econometrica*, July 1961. Thomas M. Humphrey traces 'the idea of an inflation unemployment trade-off' back to David Hume (1752) and Henry Thornton (1802). See his paper 'The Evolution and Policy Implications of Phillips Curve Analysis' (*Economic Review*, vol. 71/1, March/April 1985).

13   International Aspects of U.S. Inflation

Introduction

The adoption of a New Economic Policy on August 15, 1971 was prompted to a large extent by the sharp deterioration in the U.S. international payments position in early 1971 and by the ensuing speculation which, on May 9, had forced the floating of the German mark and the Dutch guilder and the appreciation of the Swiss franc and Austrian schilling. The previous year, 1970, had brought a slight improvement in the U.S. balance of payments. The surplus in the widely watched trade balance had risen from $0.6 billion for 1969 to $2.2 billion. Later in 1970 this surplus declined and in the second quarter of 1971 a large deficit of $3.6 billion (annual rate) suddenly developed.

The Smithsonian Agreement of December 18, 1971 brought a far-reaching realignment of parities. It provided for a depreciation of the dollar in terms of gold and SDRs of almost 8 percent, producing a devaluation in terms of the major currencies of about $7\frac{1}{2}$ percent on a trade-weighted basis.

It was generally realized that devaluation would not improve the U.S. balance of payments quickly, but further deterioration in the trade balance in 1972—to a record deficit of $6.8 billion for the whole year—came as a shocking surprise. Thus on February 12, 1973, fourteen months after the Smithsonian conference, the dollar was again depreciated by 10 percent in terms of gold and SDRs, resulting in a trade-weighted devaluation of 6.5 percent in terms of fourteen major currencies.[1]

Before describing and analyzing these events in greater detail, it will be useful to put the recent developments into somewhat broader perspectives.

Editor's note: The summary that precedes this article is not included.

A New Look at Inflation, Economic Policy in the Early 1970s, AEI Domestic Affairs Study (Washington, D.C.: American Enterprise Institute, May 1973), 79–105. © 1973, American Enterprise Institute. Reprinted with permission.

Historical Perspectives

During the first fifteen years after World War II the dollar ruled supreme in the world economy. The economies of Western Europe and Japan were shattered by the war and American industry had an unchallenged quasi-monopoly position. But with lavish American help, Europe and Japan recovered much more quickly than was generally thought possible. Germany's recovery started in 1948 when Ludwig Erhard put the German economy on the path of sustained rapid growth and prosperity by discarding wartime controls and by radically slashing the monetary overhang inherited from the war, thus giving Germany a sound monetary system.

The German example, which Japan surpassed by using essentially the same type of policies, had a tremendous impact. It showed that the "classical medicine," [2] sound money and free enterprise, could still work if given a chance.

During the 1950s Europe and Japan managed to accumulate a substantial international reserve consisting of gold and dollars. While many well-known and influential economists, especially in Great Britain, spoke of a perpetual "dollar shortage," the U.S. had a small deficit of about $1 billion in each year from 1950 to 1956. In 1957, the year of the Suez crisis, the U.S. had its last small surplus. Then in 1958, 1959, and 1960, a series of large deficits appeared—$3.4 billion, $3.9 billion, and $3.7 billion, respectively.[3]

These deficits caused great concern. They greatly contributed to the decision of the Eisenhower administration to take energetic anti-inflationary measures on the fiscal and monetary front. The anti-inflation policy produced a mild recession from May 1960 to February 1961 and laid the foundation for the remarkable stability of prices that lasted until 1965. The trade balance improved from a surplus of $1.1 billion in 1959 to one of $5.6 billion in 1964 and the surplus in the balance of goods and services rose from $0.3 billion to $8.6 billion.

In 1965 inflation started again when the Johnson administration began to finance the escalating war in Vietnam and rising Great Society expenditures by borrowing and inflating rather than by higher taxes. Actually, in 1964, taxes had been reduced and the rate of increase in the money supply had quickly accelerated.[4] The export surplus fell to a low level in the fourth quarter of 1968. In that quarter and the first half of 1969 the trade balance was slightly in the red. It improved somewhat in the second half of 1969 and 1970 but, as mentioned earlier, it then fell deeply into the red in the first half of 1971 and has not yet recovered. The balance of goods and services and the current balance tell pretty much the same story.

Of course, we cannot gauge a country's balance-of-payments position by the trade or the current balance alone. But on the plausible assumption that the United States, in view of its great wealth, is a "natural" net capital exporter, a current account deficit implies a disequilibrium in the balance of payments.[5]

We do not know precisely the magnitude of U.S. net "natural" capital exports, but it must be quite substantial. Direct investment clearly falls into that category. But the concept surely is not coextensive with long-term capital exports. These are often swelled by purely speculative movements and by capital flows induced by contra-cyclical movements in this country and abroad.[6]

In the last quarter of 1967 the dollar came under strong speculative pressure. Sterling was devalued in November, which cast doubts on the dollar. The trade and current account balances were not negative, but the surplus was small and clearly insufficient to cover normal capital exports. The deficit in the so-called basic balance shot up to $7.3 billion (annual rate), the net liquidity deficit was at the same level, the official settlement deficit was $4.2 billion, and the gold stock fell by $1 billion in one quarter.

This was an alarming deterioration. It prompted President Johnson to announce, in a dramatic New Year's Day speech (January 1, 1968), a sweeping new "program of action to eliminate the external deficit." These proposals, had they been accepted by the Congress, would have amounted to almost full-fledged exchange control. They included a heavy tax on "nonessential" foreign travel outside the Western Hemis-phere (15 percent on tourist expenditures between $8 and $15 a day and 30 percent on expenditures exceeding $15 a day!), plus a border tax on imports and a tax refund on exports to offset the burden of domestic indirect taxes.[7] These two proposals were rejected by Congress. But mandatory restrictions on direct investment abroad and mandatory repatriation of foreign earnings, as well as a tightening of "voluntary" restraints on foreign lending by American banks and of a number of petty restric-tions, were immediately put into effect by presidential executive order.[8]

Speculation, largely in the form of gold hoarding abroad, continued. This led in March 1968 to the closing of the "gold pool," a cooperative arrangement by which the major central banks, with the U.S. carrying more than half of the burden, sold gold in the London market to keep the gold price from rising. But in the first quarter of 1968, before the "two-tier" gold price system was established, the United States had lost $2 billion in gold. Later in 1968 and in 1969 there occurred an unexpected improvement: capital flows turned around sharply, the official settlement balance improved, and liquid liabilities to foreign official agencies declined despite the fact that the trade and current account balances were very weak. What happened was that capital was attracted to the United States by high interest rates and a booming stock market. At the same time the European sense of security was being shaken by the student-worker revolt in France—which caused a wage explosion, eventually led to the departure of de Gaulle, turned the French franc from one of the strongest currencies into a weak one, and forced its devaluation in August 1969. The invasion of Czechoslovakia in summer of 1968 heightened the feeling of insecurity in Europe and, by contrast, revived confidence in the dollar. But it was clearly an unnatural and unsustainable phenomenon for the richest country in the world to import capital on a large scale.

In 1970 capital flows reversed themselves once more and there was again a large deficit in the official settlement balance—although the trade balance showed a small improvement, due probably to the mild American recession that had started in November 1969 and lasted for one year. As mentioned earlier, the trade balance deteriorated sharply in the second quarter of 1971 and the deficit in the official settlements balance jumped from $9.8 billion in 1970 to $29.8 billion in 1971, reflecting a large increase in U.S. liquid liabilities to foreign central banks which had to buy dollars to keep their currencies from rising above parity. On May 9, 1971, the German mark was allowed to float up and, following the mark, the Swiss franc and the Austrian schilling were appreciated by 7 percent and 5 percent, respectively. Austria and Switzerland had learned from their experiences in 1969 and 1970 that they exposed themselves to strong inflationary impulses ("imported inflation") from Germany, their most important trading partner, if they did not follow the mark.

Recent Developments: August 15, 1971 to June 1973

The New Economic Policy brought two important changes in the international area, suspension of gold convertibility of the dollar and a general surcharge of 10 percent on dutiable imports (equivalent to 4.8 percent surcharge on all imports).

De facto, the dollar had been inconvertible into gold for some time, in the sense that large foreign dollar holders such as the German and Japanese central banks knew that the gold window would be closed if they tried to convert some of their dollars into gold. Earlier in 1971, however, there had been some small gold conversions of dollars held by smaller countries. Since August 15, 1971, the dollar has not been convertible for anybody. This meant that, until general floating started in March 1973, the world was formally on the dollar standard rather than on the dollar-gold exchange standard.

However, two facts should be kept in mind. First the declaration of inconvertibility only legalized an existing situation. Dr. Edwin Stopper, president of the Swiss National Bank, put it this way: "According to a widely held view on 15 August 1971 the dollar-gold exchange standard was put to rest. Actually it was not the existing monetary system that broke down, but the notion that it was based on the dollar-gold exchange standard. In reality it functioned, practically from the beginning, as a dollar standard." [9]

Second, while the dollar has been inconvertible into gold for a long time (with the small exception noted above), it has remained fully convertible in the market all along. In other words, holders of dollars, foreigners as well as Americans, can use their dollars as they please to buy or invest or disinvest in the United States and can exchange their dollars in the market for other currencies either at a fixed rate if the foreign currency is pegged to the dollar or at the prevailing market rate if the foreign currency floats. (For Americans the market convertibility of the dollar is somewhat restricted by the various capital export restrictions.)

It stands to reason that market convertibility of the most important currency, the dollar, is of the utmost importance to world trade. The fact that world trade has continued to grow by leaps and bounds despite frequent currency crises is to a large extent due to the fact that the dollar, and most other major currencies as well, have remained convertible in the market.[10] This is in sharp contrast to what happened during the 1930s.

The import surcharge of 10 percent was a temporary measure designed to bring pressure on surplus countries to appreciate their currencies. In that it was successful and it was promptly removed after it had served its purpose. The surcharge helped to induce the Japanese to let the yen rise. It also helped to bring about the Smithsonian agreement, which was reached on December 18, 1971, after intensive negotiations and numerous conferences at the highest level. This agreement brought a drastic realignment of exchange rates, including a depreciation of the dollar in terms of gold of 7.6 percent, a sharp appreciation of the mark, yen and Swiss franc, and a smaller one for several other currencies including sterling and the French franc.

The turmoil in the exchange market subsided, but the calm did not last long. The British balance of payments deteriorated again and, on June 23, 1972, the government was forced to let sterling float—the first post-Smithsonian crisis. The appreciation of sterling vis-à-vis the dollar in the Smithsonian Agreement thus proved to have been a mistake which probably had been made for political reasons.

The devaluation of sterling stimulated speculation against the dollar. Between July 1 and September 1, the Federal Reserve intervened in the market to support the dollar by selling a few million German marks and Belgian francs, a trifling sum of $31.5 million. This move was played up in official statements and in the press as a historic change in policy. It was merely a gesture of goodwill, one that was well received abroad and that may have eased the situation momentarily as was widely claimed by making foreign central banks more willing to buy dollars. But it could not restore confidence of the market because the American trade deficit remained throughout the year at the record level of over $6 billion (annual rate) that it had reached in the first quarter.

The second post-Smithsonian currency crisis was touched off by European developments. The Italian lira had been weak for some time, because of unsettled internal political and economic conditions that have produced continuous uncontrollable flight of capital. On January 22, 1973, the authorities decided to follow the French example and to split the exchange market into a pegged one for current transactions and an unpegged one for capital transactions. The Italian crisis was an alarm signal. The flow of speculative funds—dollars—into Switzerland and Germany rose immediately. But the Swiss had learned their lesson. When they saw the avalanche coming, they let the franc float up (January 23, 1973) and the flood of dollars poured into Germany and Japan. Both countries at first categorically refused to either appreciate or float. So in one week (February 1 to 9) the Bundesbank had to buy over $6 billion to prevent the mark from going through the roof. Then the exchange markets were closed and the United States had to take things in hand. By offering a 10 percent devaluation of the dollar in terms of gold and SDRs, it took Germany and Japan off the hook. Japan agreed to float the yen (February 14),[11] and Germany accepted the 11.1 percent appreciation of the mark vis-à-vis the dollar (and many other currencies) that the depreciation of the dollar implied. Germany's common market partners—minus Italy and Great Britain, who continued their independent floats—went along with the mark, and a number of other countries appreciated their currencies vis-à-vis the dollar by varying smaller amounts.

But when the markets were reopened on February 14, it soon became clear that the new pattern of exchange rates had not restored confidence. Speculation continued and on March 1 the Bundesbank had to buy $2.7 billion—the largest daily flow of hot money ever recorded—to prevent the mark from rising above the new intervention point.

On March 2 the exchange markets were again closed and they remained closed officially until March 19. However, unlike the earlier cases, "closing of the markets" this time merely meant that there was no official pegging. The central banks stayed out of the market, but private trading was allowed to continue and exchange rates were quoted. Speculation practically stopped as soon as the central banks stopped offering the speculators a one-way option by pegging, and exchange rates changed only slightly.

During the breathing spell of the float, the members of the Common Market—minus Great Britain and Italy whose currencies continue to float independently—agreed on a common float of their currencies against the dollar, after Germany had agreed to appreciate the mark by 3 percent vis-à-vis its Common Market partners and also de facto vis-à-vis the dollar and other currencies (although it has not declared a legal par value).

Since March 19 when the markets were officially reopened, the situation has been this: Yen, lira, sterling, Swiss francs and Canadian dollars float independently. The currencies of the Common Market countries—France, Germany, the Benelux countries and Denmark—plus Norway and Sweden have a "common float" against the outside. In other words, these countries link their currencies together by intervention with a $2\frac{1}{2}$ percent band (maximum spread between the strongest and the weakest currency), the so-called "snake," but refrain from fixing the rate of the dollar. Thus, no attempt is made to keep the "snake" inside a "tunnel."

Actually the snake remained inside the old tunnel until early May. At that time speculation once more turned against the dollar and drove the gold price to record highs. Under the old system this would have produced a first-rate crisis and foreign central banks would have had to buy billions of dollars to keep their currencies from rising. Under the floating system some of the strong currencies, such as the mark and the Swiss franc, rose by roughly 8 percent vis-à-vis the dollar and many other currencies. Instead of ministers of finance and governors of central banks rushing around from one emergency meeting to the other, the market took care of the problem with comparatively mild fluctuations.

It is beyond the scope of this paper to describe the working of this system in detail. I confine myself to two remarks: First the various floats are by no means entirely "unmanaged." Undoubtedly the interventions have been, and still are, numerous, although it is impossible for an outsider to estimate their frequency and size.[12] Second, for almost two months after March 19 a remarkable tranquillity reigned in the exchange markets.[13] When speculation against the dollar started again in May—probably largely because of the unsettled political situation and resurgence of inflation in the United States, but also because Germany took strong anti-inflationary measures that made an appreciation of the mark a distinct possibility[14]—the market took care of the problem with mild fluctuation of exchange rates.

How long the calm will last depends primarily on how long the authorities will leave exchange markets alone and refrain from pegging. An uncertain question is how long it will be possible to keep the Common Market currencies together in a common float. That will depend on whether the members of the block will be able to coordinate their monetary, fiscal, and wage policies sufficiently. If past experience in the Common Market and elsewhere is a guide, the chances are dim that the common float will last very long.[15]

The Nature of the Recent Crisis

The currency crisis of February–March 1973 is usually called a crisis of the dollar—and so it undoubtedly was. But it was also a mark and a yen crisis. I would speak of a pure dollar crisis if the dollar were overvalued with respect to all or most currencies so that a devaluation of the dollar was all that were needed to restore equilibrium. A pure mark and yen crisis would exist if these two currencies were undervalued with respect to all or most currencies so that their up-valuation was all that were needed to restore equilibrium. The recent crisis clearly was a mixture. The dollar was devalued with respect to many but by no means all currencies, and the mark and yen were up-valued with respect to many currencies but not all.

It should be observed, however, that even in a pure mark and yen crisis, the dollar would be prominently involved. Whenever one or two important currencies get out of line and seem ripe for up-valuation, dollars from all over the world, not only from the United States, will flow into these currencies. This flow will give the impression of a dollar crisis, even if the dollar is not out of line vis-à-vis any currency other than the two or even if the U.S. balance of payments is in equilibrium. This is the consequence of the fact that the dollar still is the world's foremost reserve, official intervention and private transactions currency.

It is useful to carry this thought one step further. Suppose SDRs or gold replaced the dollar as the international reserve and official intervention currency. Suppose further that one or two important currencies became undervalued. The consequences would be much the same as now—gold, SDRs and dollars would rush into the under-valued currencies. I say "and dollars" because, even if the dollar were shorn of its official reserve and intervention functions, it would still be an important private transactions currency and the American economy would still be the leading economy in the world.

This confirms the now widely accepted view that the basic defect of the present monetary system is the malfunctioning of the balance-of-payments adjustment mechanism, the "adjustable peg" system. What is needed most is greater flexibility of adjustment. It is possible that sufficient flexibility has already been achieved by widespread floating, however "dirty" or intensively managed it may be.[16] I doubt that a grand revision of the International Monetary Fund charter is at all feasible or desirable. But this problem will not be further pursued in the present paper.

To say that smoother adjustment is the most pressing problem does not mean that the managment of the dollar and the American inflation are unimportant for the functioning of the international monetary system. Far from it. I now turn to an analysis of the weakened position of the dollar with special emphasis on the American inflation.

The Weakness of the Dollar and the American Inflation

The American balance of payments and the dollar have been chronically weak since the late 1950s. Is this entirely a consequence of the American inflation? Our inflation surely has had much to do with it. When there was little or no inflation from 1958 to 1964, the balance of payments greatly improved: the surplus on goods and services rose from practically zero in 1959 to $8.6 billon in 1964. There can be little doubt that the U.S. balance would again improve if inflation were brought under control, even if this were done without causing a recession.[17]

However, American inflation is emphatically not the only cause of the weak U.S. balance of payments. A factor of major importance is the rapid recovery of industrial Europe and Japan and other countries, causing American industries to lose the semimonopolistic position they enjoyed during the first years after the war.[18] Another important factor is the numerous devaluations of most currencies against the dollar that occurred during the first twenty-five years after the war: the wholesale devaluation of currencies against the dollar in 1949, four devaluations of the French franc between 1948 and 1958 (when de Gaulle put the franc on a firm basis) and one more after de Gaulle's departure in 1969, and many others.

All this, of course, does not mean that the dollar is lost or that the American inflation is irrelevant. It means, however, that in view of the weakened competitive position of American industry, equilibrium at stable exchange rates requires a much lower inflation rate, possibly a zero or negative rate, than we have actually had.

The reference to zero or negative inflation needs careful explanation. The degree of inflation is usually measured in terms of the consumer price index (CPI). Using that definition, it is definitely not true as a general proposition that all countries with less inflation than the average will enjoy surpluses and all those with more inflation will develop deficits. As a conspicuous and very important example, take the case of Japan. Starting from 1953 as 100, the Japanese CPI almost doubled by the first quarter of 1970 (rising to 197.3) whereas the U.S. consumer price index rose by less than 50 percent (to 141.4). But Japan's wholesale price index (WPI) rose by only 14 percent (to 114.1) and its export price index (EPI) even declined by 5.2 percent (to 94.8). For the United States the figures were 125.3 for the WPI and 129.6 for the EPI.

Japan's case is extreme, but it is not the only case. It has been found that the higher a country's productivity growth (output per man-hour), the greater is the gap between the CPI and WPI. Thus, the rapidly growing economies of Germany, Italy and Japan have displayed a significantly higher CPI/WPI ratio than the slowly growing economies of Canada, the United States and the United Kingdom.[19] The well-known reason is that the CPI is heavily weighted with services, including distribution services at each stage on a product's way to the final consumer. These services are on the whole labor-intensive and have a slower productivity growth than manufacturing industries and agriculture. With respect to the CPI/EPI ratio, the contrast between the high and low productivity countries is even greater. The explanation is partly the same as in the case of the CPI/WPI ratio. In addition, the good performance with respect to export prices of the three high-productivity countries mentioned above, Germany, Italy and Japan, surely is connected with the rapid recovery of those countries after the war. The principal rapidly growing exports of the three countries are manufactured commodities, especially durable ones. These are the industries with the most rapid recovery and productivity growth.[20]

But whatever the complete explanation, the difference between the United States and some other important countries with respect to the divergence between consumer prices on the one hand and wholesale and export prices on the other has

far-reaching economic consequences. Suppose the United States succeeds in stopping inflation in the sense that consumer prices remain stable. Since the prices and
price levels of internationally traded goods in different countries are closely linked
and move together, the larger gap in Germany and Japan between the WPI and EPI
on the one hand and the CPI on the other implies that their CPIs would have to rise
substantially vis-à-vis that of the United States if equilibrium in the balance of
payments is to be maintained at fixed exchange rates. In other words, there is a sort
of inflation-transmission multiplier at work. Inflation in the United States whether
zero or positive, is transmitted in a significantly amplified manner to some other
countries in terms of the CPI.

This has important implications for the furture of the international monetary
system, especially for one that is based on the dollar. It has often been said that as
long as the world is on the dollar standard—that is to say, as long as most countries
peg their currencies to the dollar and keep them convertible—the U.S. sets the pace
for world inflation. It is true that in principle the price relationship is reciprocal: U.S.
inflation induces inflation in all countries that maintain fixed exchange rates and
inflation abroad induces inflation in the United States. But, as an empirical proposition, the relationship is asymmetrical. This follows from the fact, or what I take as a
fact, that American inflation is almost entirely determined by domestic policies—
domestic policy objectives and constraints—and is only marginally influenced by
forces from abroad.[21] Twenty years ago monetary and fiscal policies which
determined the pace of inflation in the United States were still influenced by balance-
of-payments considerations. This is no longer the case and most economists agree
that it should not be the case. It is the principal postulate of the policy of benign
neglect that macroeconomic policies should be determined by domestic policy
objectives and not by the balance of payments. Even officials who reject the policy of
benign neglect accept its basic postulate. Thus, Arthur Burns's famous Ten Com-
mandments for international monetary reform state that the "international monetary
system will have to respect the need for substantial autonomy of domestic monetary
policies.... No country ... should have to accept sizable increases in unemployment
to reduce its deficit. Nor should a surplus country have ... [to accept] high rates of
inflation [to reduce its surplus]."[22]

The cyclical situation and the rate of inflation in the United States are, of course,
subject to some influences from abroad via the balance of payments and more
directly through exchange rate changes. For example,the large trade deficit of $6.8
billion in 1972 must have helped a little to dampen inflation, and the 1973
devaluation of the dollar somewhat exacerbated the inflationary trend through the
rise in import prices even before it began to have a favorable effect on the balance of
payments.

But for the United States these repercussions and feedbacks are normally minor and can be offset, and are likely to be offset, by domestic policy changes. For all other Western countries, however, they are of major importance.[23] Because of this quantitative asymmetry, we can say that the United States sets the pace for world inflation, that is, it sets the pace for inflation in the many countries that peg their currencies to the dollar and keep them convertible.

So long as exchange rates are fixed and currencies remain convertible, this is a fact of life that would not be changed even if the dollar were replaced by SDRs. Only by changing parities or by floating can other countries stay out of the backwash of the American inflation.

To say, as I do bluntly, that the United States sets the pace of world inflation, does not mean that the United States is responsible for every inflation in the world. Many countries have managed to generate, autonomously and voluntarily, more inflation than we have. This is clearly true of the many countries that have been forced at one time or another to devalue vis-à-vis the dollar. It is also true of some that have kept their currencies stable in terms of dollars, although in that case the fact is a little more difficult to establish. If a country has trouble keeping its external balance in equilibrium (symptoms: use of controls, loss of reserves) and is forced from time to time to depreciate, we can conclude that it is generating its inflation autonomously, although this often does not inhibit such a country from loudly complaining that the U.S. is exporting inflation.

On the other hand, if a country has more inflation measured by the CPI than the United States, it may nevertheless be argued that it has been subject to unwanted inflationary pressure from the U.S., for its more rapidly rising CPI may be due to the working of what I have called the inflation-transmission multiplier.

Some writers have tried to demonstrate that most countries that have been complaining about being forced to "import inflation" from the United States have in reality made their inflations all by themselves. The demonstration takes the form of showing that, in the crucial years, the central banks of those countries have increased their domestic assets just as much or more than their foreign assets. The idea is that we can speak of imported inflation only if the increase in the money supply is substantially equal to, and is due to, an increase in the international reserve, reflecting a favorable balance of payments, irrespective of whether the reserve flow stems from current transactions (trade surplus) or capital movements (including speculative funds).

This seems to me an unduly narrow interpretation of the matter. True, both an imported inflation (rise in prices) and a homemade one have to be supported by an increase in the quantity of money. But whether this increase comes entirely from central bank purchases of *foreign* assets (increases in their international reserves) or partly or predominately from purchases of *domestic* assets (open market operations or loans) is a matter of secondary importance. If the latter is the case, that is, if the acquisition of domestic assets is partly or largely responsible for the increase in the money supply, it may reflect a deliberate policy designed to forestall an undue accumulation of dollars or it may be the consequence of a boom touched off by heavy orders from abroad. In neither case does it preclude a perfectly honest statement to the effect that the inflation was imported, in the sense that it would not have occurred if the balance of payments had not gone into surplus. The basic fact is that prices and price levels in countries engaged in intensive trade with one another are closely connected through the medium of tradable-goods prices which, allowing for transportation costs, are the same at home and abroad. Therefore such price levels react promptly to inflationary impulses from abroad and to changes in exchange rates.[24] Whether a given country follows the U.S. inflation reluctantly, is seriously inconvenienced and hence can be said to be subjected to unwanted imported inflation, or whether it generates enough inflation at home to get into balance-of-payments troubles even if there were no U.S. inflation—the answer to this hypothetical question cannot be deduced solely from the ratio of foreign to domestic assets in the central bank of the country concerned. Additional evidence is required to decide this question, such as a loss of reserves, resort to controls and occasional devaluations.

This analysis should not be interpreted, however, as a denial or disregard of the fact that no country need submit to imported inflation. On the contrary, I believe that any country can, in principle, shield itself from foreign inflation by appreciating or floating.[25] In fact, appreciation and floating are the only really effective defenses against imported inflation. Large countries with a small foreign trade sector may be able to resist inflationary pressures from abroad by using open market operations to offset the monetary expansion caused by the influx of reserves and to reduce the prices of nontraded goods as a counter to the price increases of traded goods. But there obviously are economic, political, psychological, and institutional limits to this increasingly costly policy. Small countries will reach these limits quickly. The longer a country resists, the more the inflationary pressure will be intensified by speculation. Small countries are likely to be overwhelmed in a short time.

But let me repeat, the compulsion to submit to imported inflation arises only under a regime of fixed exchanges and convertibility.[26]

Some Implications for the Future of the International Monetary System

The fact that the U.S. inflation rate, whether positive or zero, is amplified as it is transmitted to some other countries makes the operations of the fixed-rate system more difficult. For this means that even if the United States managed to keep its rate of inflation at an internally tolerable and sustainable level of not more than, say, a 2 percent annual rise in the CPI, it may involve what may be an unacceptable rise of, say, 4 percent in some other countries such as Germany and Japan. In other words, because of this multiplication factor, the United States is capable of "exporting inflation" even if it has none internally.[27] This clearly strengthens the case for flexible exchange rates. The problem is, of course, greatly aggravated when the United States has rates of inflation of 4 or 5 percent because then many currencies, not just a few, become undervalued vis-à-vis the dollar.

The problem would not go away if the dollar were replaced as an international reserve and official intervention currency by SDRs, for it will always be a difficult job to devalue the world's most important private transactions currency. The reluctance of surplus countries to appreciate their currencies vis-à-vis the dollar has, one gets the impression, little to do with the reserve and official interventions function of the dollar. Rather it seems primarily motivated by the fear of losing a trade surplus, a mercantilistic attitude to be sure, and the superstition that changing an exchange rate as such is a burden.[28] There is furthermore the understandable apprehension in surplus countries about the danger of overadjustment (overshooting the equilibrium rate). After all, the equilibrium rate is not known and nobody wants to see a surplus position turned into one of deficit. For this reason, there is an entirely rational tendency under the adjustable peg system to appreciate too little rather than too much. If this appraisal is approximately correct, putting SDRs in the place of the dollar would achieve very little.[29]

The upshot is that, in the future, we have to expect the emergence from time to time of disequilibria which require parity changes. The dollar will probably be involved even if the United States manages to curb inflation. But with a U.S. inflation, the problem becomes much more serious.

Under the adjustable peg, parity changes are bound to be preceded and accompanied by currency crises triggered by increasingly massive flows of speculative funds. Controls on speculative capital flows is not the answer. The longer they last and the more often they are applied, the less effective they become unless they are progressively tightened. They hit "legitimate" or "virtuous" capital along with "speculative" or "bad" capital and sooner or later require current account controls as well. This cannot be further discussed here. I confine myself to drawing attention to a neglected aspect that has become very important in the last crisis: When speculative capital flows are increasingly subjected to controls, speculation turns more and more to commodities. When it becomes difficult and expensive to speculate in marks and yens, the next best thing is to get out of currencies expected to depreciate by making speculative purchases of international traded commodities.[30] This seems to have happened on a very large scale during the last crisis and to have greatly contributed to the sharp rise in raw material prices.[31] This development is a natural extension of the familiar phenomenon of "leads and lags." Gold speculation is another manifestation of the same phenomenon. But, fortunately, the price of gold does not enter the cost-of-living index or the wholesale price index. Given the current huge volume of world trade, leads and lags, forward buying, and commodity speculation can move many billions of dollars from country to country in a short time. To restrict this sort of speculative flow would require tight controls going far beyond the financial area.

The conclusion is that floating is the only way to effect parity changes without setting in motion increasingly massive and disruptive capital flows. This is now being widely recognized in official circles.[32] How much floating is required remains to be seen. Rapidly accumulating experience suggests that even extensively managed floating creates enough uncertainty about the future movements of exchange rates to discourage most speculators. The German periods of floating (1969, 1971 and 1973), the Canadian case and the Brazilian "trotting peg" all point in that direction.[33]

Let me end with a cautionary note. If the American inflation is not stopped and if the dollar becomes overvalued from time to time vis-à-vis numerous currencies, there will be plenty of trouble in the international field. This trouble can be greatly reduced by floating of the currencies concerned, but it cannot be completely eliminated. Repeated devaluations of the dollar are bound to make more acute attempts on the part of official dollar holders to diversify their reserves by shifting some of their dollars into other currencies. This dangerous development, which seems to have started already, cannot be dealt with by floating.[34] But this is not an argument for the adjustable peg. On the contrary, because it breeds more and more crises, the adjustable peg system is apt to heighten the danger of instability by causing shifts of the ballast of official reserves in the hold of the international monetary ship.

It would go beyond the scope of an essay devoted to analyzing the internatioal implications of the American inflation to discuss the proposals that have been made to cope with the danger of official reserve shifts.[35] If inflation were curbed in America, the danger of shifts of dollar reserves would be dramatically reduced if not entirely eliminated.

Ceterum censeo inflationem esse delendam.[36]

Postscript: Developments since Completion of This Paper[37]

Since this paper was completed (late May 1973) exchange markets have remained troubled and confidence in the dollar has not been restored. The exchange value of the dollar against some major currencies has sharply dropped—especially the German mark and the Swiss franc. On June 29 the mark had to be appreciated again vis-à-vis the other currencies in the common float, this time by 5.5 percent, to prevent it from piercing the back of the "snake" and so demolishing the common float. The Swiss franc continued its independent float, but substantially followed the course of the mark. On July 2 the Austrian schilling was appreciated by 4.8 percent to neutralize the inflationary backwash of the German appreciation. The pound, the lira and the Canadian dollar continued their floats but stayed more or less with the dollar. From June 4 to July 6 the mark rose vis-à-vis the dollar by 15.41 percent, the Swiss franc by 12.62 percent, and the French franc by 10.28 percent.[38]

It should be noted that these figures, which have been widely publicized, give a greatly exaggerated impression of the depreciation of the dollar since the beginning of the float or since May. Actually the value of the dollar has not much changed since March vis-à-vis the great majority of currencies. It has not declined in recent months against the currencies of countries with which the United States does about three-quarters of its trade. Among these currencies are not only sterling, the lira, the Canadian dollar and many others of lesser importance, but also the yen.[39] Until July 13 the overall trade-weighted depreciation of the dollar against twenty-one OECD countries has been 3.7 percent from March 30 and 4 percent from May 4, 1973. What has happened since May is best described as a sharp appreciation, vis-à-vis the dollar and most other currencies, of the mark, the Swiss franc and the Austrian schilling to a lesser extent of the other currencies in the common float.

The lack of confidence in the dollar is not difficult to explain in general terms.[40] After two formal devaluations, the dollar's stability is no longer taken for granted. This has induced many foreign dollar holders, private ones as well as some official institutions, to diversify their currency holdings by shifting part of their dollars into other currencies, especially the mark. It also has alerted many people to the need to watch for symptoms of weakness in the dollar. The resurgence of inflation in the United States and the debilitating effect of the Watergate affair on the administration's ability to pursue a consistently vigorous anti-inflation policy and to resist spending pressures from Congress and special interests surely were two of the major factors sparking the new wave of speculation. Others were Germany's very energetic anti-inflation measures and the strong showing of its balance of payments, which made the mark an obvious candidate for appreciation. Because of the common float arrangement the mark pulls up other currencies.[41] As explained above, any such speculation is bound to focus particulary on the dollar.

It is true that, measured in terms of the consumer price index, the American inflation has been substantially less than the inflations in Germany, Switzerland, Japan and elsewhere. But the German export boom has not yet faltered and the market has learned that differential rates of inflation are not always, at least not in the short and medium run, a good guide for exchange rate developments. (The reasons are analyzed above, page 319).

Sophisticated observers and speculators are perturbed by the failure of U.S. monetary authorities to control the money supply. In 1972 the rate of monetary growth was at its highest level since the Korean War, 8.9 percent. True, it was down

2.2 percent during the first quarter of 1973, but it shot up to 10.3 percent during the second (annual rates). The attempt to substitute suppression of symptoms of inflation for resolute elimination of inflation's causes, to freeze and control prices instead of putting a firm rein on monetary growth and raising taxes, does not inspire confidence. The unanimous support of the Democratic caucus in the Senate for a "90-day freeze on prices, profits, rents, wages and salaries, and consumer interest rates"—many even asked for a rollback of prices—and the inability of an embattled administration to stand up to such irrational and hysterical demands has made a deplorable impression.[42] So has the haphazard imposition of restrictions on the export of important commodities.

It will be recalled that in 1971 one of the main justifications for controls was that "excess demand had been eliminated from the system"—presumably by monetary restraints. The remaining inflation, it was said, was due to cost-push pressures and inflationary psychology, for which wage and price controls were the only cure. It was difficult to attach a precise meaning to the phrase "excess demand has been eliminated," for neither the quantity of money (M) nor total expenditure (nominal income, MV) had stopped growing.[43] But whatever the advocates of controls originally had in mind, there seems to be general agreement that wage-push has not been the moving force in 1973. The new inflation is a demand inflation. Therefore the original justification for controls is no longer applicable.[44] The new price freeze was imposed at a most inopportune time and it caused most serious wastes and distortions almost immediately.

It almost looks as if the administration had wanted to demonstrate the absurdity of a price freeze. In that it may have succeeded. The majority of the senators who had demanded a general freeze voted a few weeks later, when beef became scarce, to abolish the freeze on beef prices. Moreover there is some evidence that the debacle of the American price freeze and control of 1973 served as a warning example to some foreign countries such as Germany which have not yet tried it themselves. (The 1971 freeze and Phase II may have had the opposite effect, because it was oversold as a great success, although in retrospect few would continue to make the exaggerated claims that were made earlier.)

The disillusionment with controls is a very healthy development. But there is danger that it may go too far in one respect: Wage pressure by labor unions will again become the most serious stumbling block to regaining price stability. Much praise has been heaped on unions for their moderation. But workers' earnings are rising at an annual rate of 7 percent. This may be moderate under present inflation. But will unions accept a slower wage growth of, say, 3 to 4 percent—which is probably the maximum compatible with price stability? I doubt it. I am afraid that we shall soon be confronted again with the problem of wage push by monopolistic unions. Monopolies require controls. The tragedy was that price controls were applied indiscriminately to a largely competitive economy. The debacle of this policy should not be allowed to compromise monopoly control. And labor unions are the most powerful monopolists.

The 1973 surge in prices has made the international character of inflation more conspicuous than it was formerly. Monetary authorities in most countries have seized the opportunity to plead innocence and to blame inflation on other countries and on anonymous international markets. Small and medium sized countries are indeed, as we have seen, powerless to avoid world price trends unless they are ready to float. (And even floating does not ensure immediate success.) But for very large countries such as the United States, the scope for blaming others is very limited. Without the excessive monetary expansion and large government deficit in 1972, the domestic component of the U.S. inflation would have been at least much smaller than it was, and the imported component would also have been smaller because it is partly the result of inflation previously exported from the United States.

As mentioned earlier a shift of foreign official dollar holdings into German marks and possibly other currencies has been underway. The German Bundesbank stated in its last annual report that the mark has become the second largest reserve currency (but did not divulge the names of the countries involved). This type of portfolio readjustment by official dollar holders may put pressure on the dollar for a considerable period, unless U.S. inflation is credibly curbed or an international agreement on official reserve holdings is reached. Readjustment of private currency holdings on the other hand can be assumed to run its course quickly.

Given these adverse factors, the present system of widespread floating surely has worked much better than the former system of the adjustable peg would have. It is not hard to visualize what would have happened under the earlier arrangements: huge flows of dollars into Germany, Switzerland, Japan, and so forth; ministers of finance and presidents of central banks rushing around from one emergency meeting to another; a rash of controls on the international movement of funds and eventually devaluations, upvaluations—and floats.

This is not to say, however, that the present situation is satisfactory. In particular there is almost general agreement—this time shared not only by officials, who have to profess optimism, but also by the great majority of independent experts—that the dollar is now undervalued in the sense that, at current exchange rates, the United States is likely to develop after some delay a large exports surplus. In other words, it is widely believed that speculation against the dollar has gone too far and that the current pessimism about the dollar's future is excessive.

It is argued in the body of this paper that occasional judicious management of a float by intervention in the exchange market need not deprive the float of its beneficial effect or signify a return to the crisis-prone system of the adjustable peg, so long as such management stops short of rigid pegging at a specific rate. I have argued elsewhere at greater length that situations may arise, especially when noneconomic, political factors are involved, where the speculators and the markets are wrong.[45] In such cases government intervention in the market—that is, counter-speculation—is in order.

There is reason to believe that we have such a situation today, in which case the dollar should be supported by official intervention in the market. From a technical standpoint it does not matter who intervenes, the United States selling gold and foreign exchange for dollars, or foreign central banks buying dollars. But since psychology and politics are heavily involved it is very imporant that intervention, if it takes place, be done with international agreement. These highly important tactical problems can be discussed here only briefly.

As far as the U.S. is concerned, it should use its gold stock which is quite large at the current free market price, to bring down the price of gold and support the dollar.[46] The alternative—or supplement—to gold sales would be to borrow marks and other currencies from the International Monetary Fund (IMF) or from foreign central banks. This course has been strongly urged by the Europeans. From the standpoint of impact on the exchange market, it comes to the same whether Germany buys dollars with marks or the United States borrows the marks to buy dollars. Moreover, both alternatives would cause the German money supply to expand, a consequence that would tend to counteract the anti-inflation policy of the Bundesbank. The economic difference, however, is that by borrowing foreign currencies abroad the United States in effect would give an exchange guarantee to the foreign central bank.[47] But if we are sure that the dollar is undervalued and is likely to rise after the wave of adverse speculation has been broken or reversed, the exchange risk should be no serious deterrent.

One last word: it should be clear that even massive interventions would do no good in the absence of a firm anti-inflation policy that does not tinker with symptoms by imposing haphazard controls on prices and exports but goes to the root of the trouble by putting a tight rein on money supply and doing something decisive about the budget by reducing expenditures or raising taxes.

After the last meeting of the Committee of Twenty of the International Monetary Fund, the ministers of finance expressed great optimism that agreement on reforming the international monetary system could be reached early next year and the reform be put into effect a year later. Details have not yet been divulged but several ministers have stated that the new system will again be based on semi-fixed parities; exchange rates will be "stable but adjustable," as the disingenuous phrase goes.

Before abandoning floating, the ministers would be well advised to do their homework and curb inflation. The reason behind this advice is that fixed or semi-fixed exchange rates require close coordination of monetary, fiscal and wage policies—or, expressed differently, mutually consistent rates of inflation. (In other words, not "equal" rates but "consistent" rates, meaning a little more inflation for some countries, a little less for others, according to circumstances.) It is conceivable, although by no means easy or certain, that the major countries may achieve such a mutually consistent pattern, if the rates of inflation are very low everywhere. For in that case no country would find itself saddled with a very high rate of inflation. But it is practically inconceivable that there can be found such a mutually acceptable and consistent pattern, except perhaps among small groups of countries, if inflation rates cluster as they do now around an 8 percent price rise or more per annum.

Notes

1. This figure is taken from *World Financial Markets* (New York: Morgan Guaranty Trust Company, February 23, 1973). The depreciation from the Smithsonian Agreement central rates was 6.05 percent. From the pre-June 1970 parities the trade-weighted depreciation against fourteen major currencies was 16.64 percent. (By the end of May the figure was about 18 percent.)

2. These words are Keynes' in his famous posthumously published paper "Tha Balance of Payments of the United States," in which he castigated his radical followers, calling their writings "modernist stuff gone wrong and turned silly and sour." (*The Economic Journal*, June 1946, p. 186).

3. These figures relate to the so-called "liquidity" definition then in general use as the measure of imbalance. Under that concept, a deficit is defined as the loss of monetary gold plus an increase in U.S. liquid liabilities to foreigners. This is in contrast to what is now called the "net liquidity balance," which includes, in addition, changes in U.S. liquid *assets* abroad. The old liquidity balance is now called "gross liquidity."

4. A budget deficit without supporting monetary expansion would not be inflationary.

5. A trade deficit does not imply a current account deficit. It could be offset by a surplus on services. For the United States, the largest positive service item is investment income, which has been rising steadily and reached the level of $8 billion net in 1971. But since other services (including tourist expenditures) are negative and since there are remittances and military expenditures abroad to be covered, investment income though large cannot turn a sizable trade deficit into a current account surplus. No quarter showing a trade deficit has registered a current account surplus. It is therefore legitimate to regard a trade deficit for the U.S. as a sign of disequilibrium. This could change in the future if investment income continues to grow. However, this growth has been stopped by interest payments on the huge liquid liabilities (dollar balances held by foreign central banks) that have piled up in recent years.

6. Balance-of-payments analyses often identify long-term capital flow with normal or natural movements and changes in short-term flows with speculation and cyclical fluctuations. The correspondence is, however, far from perfect. What is now called the "basic" balance, that is, current account plus long-term capital, is often not basic in any real sense but also reflects speculation and other short-term fluctuations. One example is the sudden rise in the basic deficit in late 1967 mentioned in the text below. It would be easy to cite other examples.

7. Details and a critical analysis of this amazing program can be found in Gottfried Haberler and Thomas D. Willett, U.S. *Balance of Payments Policies and Internal Monetary Reform: A Critical Analysis* (Washington, D.C.: American Enterprise Institute for Public Policy Research, 1968), p. 19, et seq.

8. This was done "by virtue of the authority vested in the President by the act of October 6, 1917 as amended (12 U.S.C. 95a)."

9. Address to the annual general meeting of the Swiss National Bank on 28 April 1972 (mimeographed).

10. However very few currencies are as completely convertible in the market as the dollar.

11. From that day on, the Italian lira, too, was allowed to float. But Italy kept its dual exchange rate—so it had a double float, one for current transactions, the other for financial transactions.

12. Even the Canadian float has been a managed one since 1970, judging from the fact that the Canadian international reserve has grown substantially during that period. This is in contrast to Canada's earlier period of floating (1950–1962) when the authorities claimed that their interventions were confined to ironing out short-run fluctuations.

13. At that time several people suggested that the quiet in the exchange market should be attributed not to floating but rather to the restrictions on capital inflows that had recently been put in place, especially in Germany.

This explanation is unconvincing. Twice, once in 1969 and once in 1971, Germany had gone through the exercise of first resisting appreciation and then retreating into a temporary float. In both cases, speculation ceased immediately after the authorities stopped giving the speculators a one-way option by pegging, despite the absence of elaborate capital import restrictions. On all three occasions the Bundesbank lost billions of marks by buying billions of dollars in the vain attempt to keep the mark down (not counting, as unavoidable, the loss on previously accumulated dollars).

One more example: The Swiss had elaborate capital import controls in place in 1973, but still had to resort to floating to stop speculation.

14. Some highly respected German economic research institutions expressed doubts that the anti-inflationary policy could succeed without "protection from imported inflation" ("Aussenwirtschaftliche Absicherung" is the German expression) through a rise of the mark in the exchange market. Actually in May the mark was still at the bottom of the snake.

15. In June Germany was, in fact, forced to appreciate the mark once more by 5.5 percent. See Postscript: Developments Since Completion of This Paper, below.

16. I personally would distinguish between "dirty" floating and "managed" floating. If management is confined to buying and selling of foreign exchange in a free market for the purpose of ironing out short-run fluctuations, it does not deserve to be called "dirty." I would go further and say that even if the purpose of buying and selling is somewhat more ambitious, namely, to restrain a rapid rise or decline of the exchange rate that seems to be unjustified—in other words, if the purpose of management is to moderate an emerging trend without trying to suppress it altogether—this policy will not upset the smooth working of the system in the same way as rigid pegging does. Floating becomes "dirty" when markets are split, when special rates for different types of transactions are established in either an open or disguised

form and other controls are used to influence the rates. The borderline between merely managed and "dirty" floating is fluid, but experience seems to show that the system can stand a good deal of management without developing the defects of the adjustable peg.

17. It is not, however, absolutely certain because it is conceivable that some countries would want to secure a surplus by devaluation, either in order to increase their international reserve or to stimulate their economy. But in view of the high propensity to inflate everywhere, I would not expect this to happen on a large scale. Moreover, the United States should not be alarmed if it happened. At any rate, foreign complaints about the excessive accumulation of dollar balances would be less insistent if the purchasing power of the dollar remained intact.

18. To show that this is not just hindsight, let me quote what I said in my pamphlet, *Inflation: Its Causes and Cures* (Washington, D.C.: American Enterprise Institute, 1959), revised and enlarged, 1961 and 1966. "The rapid deterioration in the U.S. trade and payments position since 1957 has to be attributed mainly to the rapid recovery of industrial Europe and Japan from war destruction and dislocation ..." (p. 68, 1961 edition).

19. See Ronald McKinnon, *Monetary Theory and Controlled Flexibility in the Foreign Exchanges*, Essays in International Finance, No. 84 (Princeton, N. J.: Princeton University Press, 1971). See also Bela Balassa's important paper, "The Purchasing Power Parity Doctrine: A Reappraisal," *Journal of Political Economy*, vol. 72 (1964). A careful statistical analysis has been made by Hirotaka Kato, "Statistical Analysis of the Gap between Consumer Price and Wholesale Price Movements in Japan, 1960–1964," in *Shokei Ronso* (Kanagawa University, Japan), vol. II, no. 4 (March 1967).

20. It should be kept in mind that in the United States, and presumably elsewhere too, the EPI is statistically a much poorer and less reliable index than the CPI and WPI. In the case of Japan one could also think of lower "dumping" prices as an explanatory factor. But in view of the American sensitivity to dumping, flagrant cases of dumping are unlikely to escape detection and are subject to countervailing and anti-dumping measures.

21. William D. Nordhaus, "The Worldwide Wage Explosion," *Brookings Papers on Economic Activity*, 2: 1972 (Washington, D.C.: The Brookings Institution, 1972), reaches a fair conclusion. "How does the U.S. exert such a powerful influence on prices abroad? Paradoxically, the answer is because the U.S. is the only country that does not (or can afford not to) care seriously about the effect of its price level on its external position." (p. 459.) Actually there is nothing paradoxical about that.

22. Arthur F. Burns, "Some Essentials of International Monetary Reform," Federal Reserve Bank of New York *Monthly Review*, June 1972, p. 132 (address to the 1972 International Banking Conference, Montreal, Canada, 12 May 1972).

23. If the U.S. trade balance shifted from the current deficit of almost $7 billion to a larger surplus of $13 billion, which sometimes is mentioned as a target, it would be a highly inflationary factor.

24. By appreciating its currency a country exerts inflationary pressure on its neighbors who refuse to go along. For example the German appreciation in 1969 had a strong inflationary impact on Austria and Switzerland. These countries learned their lesson and followed Germany immediately in its next appreciation in 1971. In 1973 Switzerland floated before Germany moved.

By parity of reason, it follows that by depreciating its currency a country exerts *anti-inflationary* pressure on its neighbors who refuse to go along. This is, of course, true only if currencies are convertible in the market.

25. It should not be overlooked, however, that monetary influences from abroad—inflationary and especially deflationary influences—often have an admixture of *real* shifts in international demand. These real shifts cannot be obviated by monetary measures such as parity changes.

26. It is well known that inconvertibility, that is, propping up a nominally fixed exchange rate by a battery of controls, is analytically (not merely definitionally) equivalent to disguised devaluation or upvaluation with multiple exchange rates.

27. In the early 1960s when there were complaints abroad that the United States "exported inflation" through its deficit, American officials replied indignantly that America had no inflation and therefore could not export it. This was little comfort to other countries which had to submit to inflationary pressures from the American deficit. But the Americans were right in the sense that it would not be reasonable in the modern world to ask for more than price stability. To avoid exporting inflation—in other words to enable some other countries to enjoy a stable CPI at fixed parities—the United States would have had to let its CPI go down. But if the United States had a slightly declining price level—which, it will be remembered, many economists used to regard as the optimal policy—it surely would be accused by some of "exporting deflation" because quite a few countries would not be able to maintain parity with a dollar that gained steadily in purchasing power.

28. Economists have nurtured this superstition by emphasizing, for want of economic arguments, the alleged "political" and "psychological" burdens of changing parities. In France, where the mercantilistic tradition is especially strong, official spokesmen have made it abundantly clear that their reluctance to see the franc appreciate vis-à-vis the dollar is motivated by the wish to protect French industries from what they regard as excessive American competition.

29. To replace the dollar as a "pivot" or "numéraire" in which parities are expressed has already been achieved to some extent because numerous new par values or central rates including that of the dollar have been officially declared in terms of SDRs. It is, however, a change of negligible importance except on the question-begging assumption that it will make parity changes, including that of the dollar, easier.

30. "Speculation" should be interpreted in a broad sense. It means not only speculation in commodities by people who are not engaged in production or in exporting and importing of the commodities concerned—"pure speculators" we may call them—but also, and primarily, speculative purchases and orders by producing firms (national and multinational corporations) and by professional exporters and importers.

31. See an illuminating article in *The Economist* (April 14–20, 1973).

32. The German Bundesbank in its annual report for 1972, after a careful examination of what capital controls can and cannot do, reaches this conclusion: "The main lesson of past experience is that in case of confidence crises involving the dollar, in view of the large dollar balances which can be shifted around, the only effective defense against unwanted inflows is temporary setting free of the dollar exchange rate"—that is, temporary floating.

33. On the Brazilian experience, see Juergen B. Donges, *Brazil's Trotting Peg: A New Approach to Greater Exchange Rate Flexibility in Less Developed Countries*, with an introduction by Gottfried Haberler which discusses the lessons of the Brazilian experiment for the industrial countries (Washington, D.C.: American Enterprise Institute, 1971). On the Canadian case, see Paul Wonnacott *The Floating Canadian Dollar: Exchange Flexibility and Monetary Independence* (Washington, D.C.: American Enterprise Institute, 1972).

34. It can, of course, be argued that the adoption of a general system of freely floating parities would not require large official reserves and would therefore automatically eliminate the danger in question. But such a radical reform surely is most unlikely to materialize and, even if it did, the problems of official reserves would remain during a long period of transition.

35. Let me mention, however, a proposal by Professor William Fellner that would be helpful in this connection. He recommended that the U.S. consider offering to official holders of dollar balances abroad "low interest securities carrying a purchasing-power guarantee." (William Fellner, "The Dollar's Place in the International System," *The Journal of Economic Literature*, American Economic Association, vol. X, no. 3 (September 1972); available also from American Enterprise Institute, Washington, D.C., AEI Reprint No. 8.)

36. "For the rest, I hold that inflation ought to be destroyed." Paraphrased from Marcus Porcius Cato, The Censor.

37. Written July 15, 1973.

38. The figures represent averages of buying and selling rates at noon in New York.

39. There has been a sharp contrast between the yen and the mark. While the mark has sharply appreciated, the yen-dollar rate has changed little since March. Space does not permit an analysis of this remarkable development. But it may be mentioned that the Bank of Japan has been able to reduce its dollar holdings by about $4 billion. Without these interventions the yen would have depreciated somewhat and the dollar would be correspondingly higher. The Japanese current account surplus has for the time being disappeared. Japan seems to have been importing raw materials on a grand scale.

40. This is true only ex post. I do not claim that I have foreseen the recent appreciation of the mark and other currencies or any of the specific crises mentioned earlier in this paper. I could easily give documentary evidence for this statement, but I could also prove that the same is true of the vast majority of economists, official as well as academic, working in the field of international finance. It is one thing to demonstrate that the system of the adjustable peg is crisis-prone, and an entirely different thing to forecast with any accuracy the timing and intensity of particular crises or waves of speculation.

41. Thus once again the disruptive power of fixed exchange rates in the absence of a sufficient coordination of policies has been strikingly demonstrated. Before appreciating the mark on June 29 the Bundesbank had to buy DM 4 billions' worth of the other currencies in the common float in a futile attempt to keep the mark in the snake. True to form the German minister of finance vehemently denied any intention to appreciate only a few hours before the decision to do so was announced. He went out of his way to attack the "irresponsible professors" at the Institute in Kiel. Their transgression had been to warn that the German anti-inflation policy could not succeed and would lose its credibility without protection against inflationary influences from abroad.

42. An overwhelming majority of the Democratic senators also voted for a large increase in the minimum wage—which is, in effect, a vote for more inflation and more unemployment, especially of underprivileged workers (such as teenagers and blacks).

43. What had been squeezed, though of course not eliminated, was profits. It would have made more sense to use the Keynesian phrase that inflation was no longer a "profit inflation," but an "income inflation" (cost inflation).

44. It is sometimes said that we still have a case of cost-inflation because the sharp rise in raw material prices has raised production costs. But this makes little sense, since most raw materials, feedstuffs and foodstuffs are traded in highly competitive international markets. If the worldwide surge in demand for raw materials is not a case of demand inflation, it is difficult to see what would be one.

45. See "The Case Against Capital Controls for Balance of Payments Reasons," a paper prepared for the Geneva Conference on *Capital Movements and Their Control*, June 15–16, 1973 (in *Capital Movements and Their Control*, A. K. Swoboda, ed. (The Netherlands: A. W. Sijthoff, 1976); AEI Reprint 62). It is argued there that these are exceptional cases and that it is much easier to think of cases where the speculators' judgment about the strength or weakness of a currency was right and that of the authorities wrong than of cases where the opposite was true. But we cannot exclude the possibility of waves of excessive optimism or pessimism concerning the true value of a currency.

46. It has been suggested that the U.S. should sell large amounts of its gold in the free market even if no international agreement on such sales could be reached. This would, however, not be advisable for, as Professor Fellner has pointed out to me, this policy would run the risk that some foreign central banks might seize the opportunity to get rid of some of their dollars. In that case selling gold would mean throwing gold into a bottomless pit.

47. In case of borrowing from the IMF even a gold guarantee would be involved according to the Articles of Agreement. This is another instance where recent events have made the Articles of Agreement obsolete.

14

Oil, Inflation, Recession and
the International Monetary
System

In this paper I discuss the impact of the enormous rise of the price of crude oil on
inflation and recession in the importing countries and on the international monetary
system. I first deal with the *domestic* impact in the importing countries of the levy
imposed on them by the Organization of the Petroleum Exporting Countries
(OPEC). What was the contribution of the oil price rise to the world-wide inflationary explosion in 1973 and to the subsequent recession? The indirect effects through
the parallel price rise of domestic energy supplies as well as sectoral price rises in
other areas will also be considered. In the second section I discuss the international
monetary aspects of the oil price rise, its bearing on the issue of fixed versus flexible
exchange rates, and the accumulation by OPEC countries of foreign investments,
liquid assets ("petrodollars") as well as portfolio and direct investment.

1. The Domestic Impact

It will be useful first to consider the impact of the fourfold or fivefold increase in the
oil price on a representative importing country, say, the United States, under
simplifying assumptions. How would a perfectly competitive, well-managed market
economy deal with, or react to, an annual levy of $20 or $22 billion imposed by
OPEC? Since in a competitive economy wages and prices are flexible, there would be
no serious problems of maintaining price level stability and full employment at the
same time by monetary policy.[1] If the price of imported oil has gone up, and the
price level is to be kept stable by monetary measures, other prices than those of oil
(and oil-related products) have to go down. That requires, if full employment is to be
maintained, a reduction of money wages (or more generally of money incomes),
reflecting the fact that the oil levy (deterioration in the terms of trade) involves some

Editor's note: The biographical reference to the author is not included.
Journal of Energy and Development, 1 (2): 177–190 (Spring 1976). Reprint 45. Reprinted with
permission of the International Research Center for Energy and Economic Development.

belt tightening (reduction in *real* income) which cannot be avoided by any monetary manipulation although it can be postponed by borrowing abroad (see below).

Now suppose that money wages are rigid downward as in fact they are almost without exception. In that case keeping the price level stable by pushing other prices down would create unemployment. If full employment is to be maintained, the price level must be allowed to rise and the unavoidable reduction in real wages be effected by inflation.

Let us consider the magnitude of the problem for the United States. The annual extra cost of imported oil since the quadrupling of its price is estimated at about $20 billion.[2] This is a large sum, but it is not more than about 1.4 percent of GNP in our trillion and a half dollar economy. It happens to be a little smaller than the average annual increase in what our government spends on goods and services (excluding transfer payments).[3] It follows that the real burden of the OPEC price rise for the United States is small. It is less than half of the normal annual increase in GNP. This means that in our ideal, competitive economy only a small, once-for-all, reduction in money and real wages (incomes) would be required. Cessation of the normal wage increase for half a year would take care of the problem. After six months the normal wage growth could be resumed.

From the same type of reasoning it follows that in the alternative case when money wages are rigid and the unavoidable reduction of real wages is brought about by inflation, a comparatively small, once-for-all rise in the price level would take care of the problem. If the price level rose by, say, 1.4 percent, the real purchasing power of money incomes would be reduced by what is needed to pay the oil levy imposed by OPEC.

For other industrial countries the oil levy is a greater burden than for the United States, because they depend more heavily on imports. The jump in the oil import bill from 1973 to 1974 was 4.31 percent of GNP for Japan, 3.96 percent for Italy, 3.73 percent for the United Kingdom, and 2.17 percent for Germany.[4] This is not a negligible burden, but it is not an intolerable one; for all OECD countries it is less than one year's normal growth, except for the United Kingdom it may be a little more than that. Hence, ideally suspension of wage (income) growth for less than a year or a mild once-for-all rise in the price level would take care of the problem.[5]

On this reckoning the contribution of the oil price rise to the United States inflation is minimal. How can that conclusion be reconciled with the widely held belief that the oil price rise was a major factor in our and in the world wide inflation? And how can it be squared with the view, also widely held, that the oil price rise was the cause of, or greatly contributed to the recession?

Let me give a straight answer to these questions and then try to justify it. The oil price rise was not a major factor in bringing on inflation and recession. It was no more the cause of inflation and recession than the proverbial last straw that broke the camel's back. In fact, it was not the heaviest straw, nor was it the first or last one. If one wants to assign an important role to the oil price rise, it could be done only by stressing *indirect* effects through the reactions of the economy and of government policies. But the economy and the government reacted to several things which happened more or less simultaneously. At any rate, what is of primary importance, and what could and should be changed, is the policy reactions. This holds for the United States as well as for other countries, but let me explain what I have in mind with reference to the United States by putting the problem in proper historical perspective.

The whole postwar period was one of slowly accelerating inflation, interrupted only by spells of precarious price stability in recessions. The spectacular acceleration of inflation to the two-digit level started late in 1972, long before the October 1973 Middle East war, the oil embargo, and the sharp rise in oil prices. The inflation record of other industrial countries, let alone the less-developed ones, was if anything worse than that of the United States, with the exception of Germany in recent years, but not excepting Canada which has no oil problem (or one in reverse because it is an oil-exporting country).

Monetarists will say that inflation is the consequence of the fact that the money supply has been allowed to grow too fast and that is all there is to it. I agree with the monetarists that any *substantial* inflation, however brought about, is a monetary phenomenon in the sense that it requires an increase in the money supply and that no inflation can be stopped without reducing monetary growth and keeping it at an appropriately low level.[6] The 1973–1975 inflation, whatever the role of the oil price rise, is no exception. But I insist that this is emphatically not all that there is to it. Monetary restraint is a necessary but not a sufficient condition for an economically efficient and politically feasible anti-inflation policy.

Arthur Burns was quite right when he told a Congressional committee that the Federal Reserve could have kept the price *level* constant, despite higher oil prices, but only by driving down other prices. However, this course of policy would have caused an intolerable amount of unemployment. Another way of expressing the same thought is that, since a part of consumer spending is absorbed by the higher cost of oil, less is left for other purchases. Under rigid money wages, this drop in demand for other things would create unemployment unless the deficiency in monetary demand is offset by expansionary monetary or fiscal measures. There is truth in this argument, but it should not be forgotten that *real* wages (incomes) have to decline a little to pay for the higher cost of imported oil. Under rigid money wages, the reduction of real wages must be effected by higher prices (inflation). The loss of purchasing power through the oil price rise and inflation cannot be offset by monetary measures.

We have seen, however, that quantitatively speaking, only a small fraction of the two-digit inflation in 1973 and 1974 can be explained—and "justified"—in this manner. To this the Federal Reserve can reply that there were other "special" factors at work than the OPEC price rise. Domestic energy prices rose along with the price rise of imported oil and, for reasons we need not go into here, there was in 1973 also a sharp rise of prices of basic foodstuffs and other raw materials vis-à-vis the prices of manufactured goods.

It should be kept in mind that the oil price rise came at a time when an unsustainable cyclical boom was in progress in all industrial countries. In a boom, prices of primary products always rise faster than prices of finished goods. However, prices of other primary products rose less than prices of basic foodstuffs, petroleum, and energy-related products (such as fertilizer). Those other prices have come down rather sharply since the peak of the boom in 1974.

The consequence of these developments was an *internal* income transfer from manufacturing and service industries to farmers and domestic energy producers. The internal income transfer, unlike the external one to the OPEC countries, does not require an *overall* reduction in real wages, but indirectly it, too, can have inflationary effects. If farm and energy prices rise, monetary policy can keep the price level stable only by driving down prices of manufactured goods and services. With money wages rigid, this policy necessarily creates unemployment. The monetary authorities, thus, have the unpleasant choice between "creating" inflation or recessions.[7]

But wage rigidity alone, in conjunction with the "special" factors—the oil price rise imposed by OPEC, and a crop shortfall (plus the Russian wheat sale)—could explain and "justify" only a fraction of the two-digit inflation that has occurred.[8] The dilemma of the monetary authorities either to permit inflation or to stand firm and "create" unemployment has been greatly intensified by labor unions pushing for higher wages. As Hayek and others have pointed out, unions think increasingly in real terms because money illusion has been eroded by chronic inflation. It is, however, not only labor unions but many other pressure groups which, by political means, compel the government to force up prices and incomes. Organized farmers who force government to adopt enormously expensive farm price support policies is the most glaring example. Naturally the problem becomes acute when external circumstances ("special factors"), such as the oil price rise, temporarily reduce real national income or interrupt its normal growth. There develops what John Hicks calls a "real wage resistance,"[9] that is, unions and other pressure groups refuse to accept a reduction in real wages, even in the form of higher prices. In other words, they press for higher money wages (incomes) to maintain the real wage.

The upshot of this discussion is that the oil price rise would not have aroused so much passion and concern, and it would and could not have been regarded as a major cause of inflation and recession, if it had not come so suddenly and if it had not impinged on a highly inflationary, unsustainable boom which, in turn, was superimposed on an inflationary groundswell. Furthermore, if the present inflation were merely a monetary demand inflation in a highly competitive economy, it could be stopped by monetary–fiscal restraints without causing more than a mild short recession despite the oil price rise. The situation has become so untractable because labor unions, other pressure groups, and government regulations have dangerously reduced the area of effective competition. This development was clearly seen more than thirty years ago by the great Chicago economist, Frank H. Knight, one of the founders of the Chicago School. Speaking of business cycles he said:

In a free market these differential changes [in the prices of different types of goods] would be temporary but even then they might be serious; and with important markets as unfree as they actually are—and prices as sticky and labor and capital as immobile—the results take on the proportion of a social disaster.[10]

Since 1941 when Knight wrote those lines, the situation has become much worse. There are many more powerful labor unions—just think of the unions of public employees that have grown up including teachers, firemen, policemen who do not hesitate to use the strike weapon to push up their salaries—and there are many more powerful pressure groups and government regulations which raise costs and curtail competition and have multiplied by leaps and bounds. The public sector of the economy has grown enormously and enormous government deficits have piled up.[11] All that puts terrific pressure on the monetary authorities to expand the money supply. If nothing is done to relieve the pressure by reducing the power of the pressure groups, restoring competition, and checking the cancerous growth of the public sector, we have to expect more inflation and more unemployment, intermittent recessions, more stop-and-go around a steepening price trend. Sooner or later the political reaction will probably be more and more controls with dismal prospects for the free enterprise system and for democracy itself. The oil price rise imposed by the cartel of the oil producers is only a minor facet in that depressing picture.

2. International Aspects

So far we have ignored the international aspects. We have analyzed the impact of the oil price rise on the domestic economy on the assumption that the higher prices have been collected, and the proceeds of the sales have been transferred to the exporting countries.

This is a realistic assumption, for it is a fact that the swollen proceeds from oil sales have been and are being continually transferred to the OPEC countries. World trade has been going on as before. It has somewhat declined in the recession as was to be expected, but we have seen that the recession had little to do except indirectly with the oil price rise. So far, the international monetary system of widespread managed floating has taken the oil price rise in its stride. A large amount of recycling of surpluses[12] of the OPEC countries ("petrodollars") has been effected by the international money markets, especially the Euro-dollar market.

All this is in sharp contrast to the widespread apprehension, shared by many experts, when the oil crisis erupted in 1973 and the magnitude of the sums involved became understood. It was widely predicted that the existing international monetary system could not cope with the huge flow of funds involved, that floating exchange rates were of absolutely no use in dealing with a sudden change of that magnitude, that OPEC surplus funds would be sloshing around the world, disrupting international trade and payments, and that large parts of American industry were in danger of being taken over by Arab sheikhs.

I shall try to show that these fears and apprehensions are unfounded, that the present international monetary system can cope with the oil transfer problem, and that floating of many though not all exchange rates is indispensible to bring about the required balance-of-payments adjustments.

This relatively optimistic appraisal is not a result of hindsight; it is not merely an extrapolation of the successful and fairly smooth adjustments that have been effected in the last two years. On the contrary, it is based on a theoretical analysis using the relevant tools of theory, the theory of international transfers which is part and parcel of the general theory of balance-of-payments adjustment.[13]

The transfer of huge sums to OPEC countries is often compared with the German reparations in the 1920s. This is an appropriate comparison, but it is apt to be misleading, especially for noneconomists, because of the widely held view that the German reparations were difficult if not impossible to transfer and were an important cause of the depression of the 1930s. Since I have explained elsewhere why I think that this pessimistic appraisal of the German reparations problem is quite wrong.[14] I shall not go into that problem here. But I will try to show that it is also incorrect to assert, as it is often done, that the oil transfer is a more difficult problem than the transfer of the German reparations was.

When analyzing the problem it is crucially important to make clear whether one treats oil-importing and exporting countries each as a unit, or whether one considers the differential impact on different oil-importing and exporting countries.

Let me start with the simpler case, treating as it is often done, each group as a unit. In this case it can be shown that the transfer, in other words, the balance-of-payments adjustment between the two units, present practically no problem and that there would be little point in recommending changes in exchange rates, concretely that the oil-importing country's currency, say, the dollar, should be depreciated in terms of the exporting country's currency, say, the Saudi Arabian rial or Kuwaiti dinar. The reason is that the oil-exporting countries, unlike the recipients of the German reparations in the 1920s, are either wide-open economies which import almost everything save oil or less-developed countries which, too, have a very high propensity to import. The oil bonanza flows into the governments' coffers, and as a group the OPEC governments have no other choice but to use their swollen revenues to import from, or invest in one form or another, in the importing countries.

It is common knowledge that the oil countries spend only a comparatively small part of their increased revenues on additional imports. Thus their current account surplus rose from $6 billion in 1973 to $70 billion in 1974 and is estimated to be $50 billion in 1975.[15] The rest of the world has a corresponding "deficit," that is to say it "imports capital from," and runs into debt with, the oil countries. Thus the industrial countries had a current account surplus of $6 billion in 1973 and a deficit of $12 billion in 1974—a swing of $22 billion in one year.[16] This change undoubtedly reflects the increase in the oil price and thus represented capital investments, both liquid (monetary reserves) and illiquid (portfolio and direct investment), of OPEC money. It should be observed, however, that it is not easy, nay impossible to make a precise statistical separation of oil and nonoil deficits. This is important to remember, because it casts doubt on the many plans that have been put forward for dealing separately with the oil and nonoil deficits. Fortunately, there is no good reason why oil deficits should be handled differently from other deficits, as we shall see presently.

To the extent that the OPEC countries invest in the oil-importing countries (rather than increase their imports from them), the burden of the oil price rise for the importing countries is temporarily reduced. There could be even a permanent reduction of the burden expressed as a percentage of GNP, if the capital imports from the oil exporters result in a *net* increase in real investment in the importing countries. The reason is that the additional investments would result in a larger GNP. Whether this actually happens or not depends on the policies of the importing countries themselves. For fairly obvious reasons which need not detain us here, it is very unlikely that this will in fact happen on a large scale.

It is widely feared that the cumulative OPEC investments abroad, liquid, portfolio, and direct investment, will lead to all sorts of trouble. The early estimates which ran as high as $400–600 billion in five years or so have been drastically scaled down to $150–200 billion. The recession and energy conservation have reduced consumption of oil. Even more important, oil countries have proved to be much better spenders than many Western observers, highly respected oil experts among them, had assumed. Exports to the oil countries have increased sharply and some major oil exporters, Iran and Venezuela among them, have been reported to be ready to enter the Euro-dollar market as borrowers for their development plans. Others have started rather fancy "investment" projects at home. In the old days, teachers of international trade told their students that it would be possible to grow grapes in Scotland in hot houses, but that it was more economical to import them from Portugal in exchange for cloth (Ricardo's famous illustration of the principle of comparative cost). Now we are treated to the spectacle of grapes and apples being grown in cold houses in the Arabian desert.[17]

True, when the recovery in the industrial countries picks up speed or if the oil price is raised again, the accumulation of funds by OPEC countries may quicken. But compared with the multitrillion size of outstanding United States and European securities, one or two hundred billion more OPEC investment spread over several years simply do not matter much.

Our conclusion then is that in global terms, taking oil-importing and exporting countries each as a unit, there is no transfer or balance-of-payments problem, nor should the accumulation of OPEC investments abroad cause serious trouble. Furthermore, from the global standpoint there would be no point in changing exchange rates.

Needless to add that the absence of balance-of-payments and exhange rate problems does not change the fact that the oil price rise is a burden on the importing countries, although not an intolerable one for the industrial countries. Nor does it exclude that particular industries in the importing countries may come to grief.[18]

Some of the conclusions, especially those with respect to the superfluousness of changing exchange rates, have to be altered radically, when we consider the differential impact on individual countries. Take first the case of the oil-exporting countries. For some of them an appreciation of their currencies might be beneficial because it would reduce inflation and let their people, as distinguished from their governments, more fully participate through cheaper imports in the oil riches. But if countries like Iran, Venezuela, or Saudi Arabia prefer inflation to appreciation of their currencies, it is their bussiness.

I now come to the more important case of the differential impact of the oil price rise on different oil-importing countries. The frequently made assertion that exchange rate changes or floating may be necessary to deal with "nonoil" deficits but are of no use whatsoever for the adjustment fo "oil" deficits makes sense only when importing countries are considered as a unit.

Obviously different importing countries are very differently affected by the oil price rise in three different ways. First, the basic burden is very different because of the unequal dependence on imported oil. Second, different countries are very differently placed with respect to the possibility of stepping up their exports to OPEC. Third, OPEC surplus funds, "petrodollars," are very unequally distributed among importing countries—not in proportion to their oil-created balance-of-payments gap (additional cost of imported oil minus additional exports to OPEC countries), nor in proportion to the basic burden, let alone in proportion to the per capita GNP level of the importing countries. In view of this diversity and considering the fact that the policy reactions of different countries to the impact of the oil price rise on their economy will be very different—some being financially disciplined, others not, etc.—in view of all this, exchange rate changes and floating will be necessary in many cases.

As far as the basic burden is concerned, there is nothing that can be done about it. But for none of the industrial countries is it intolerable, although it is lighter for the United States than for others. As far as some very poor less-developed countries that are really hard hit are concerned, the problem is one of international charity and foreign aid. It is all right to plead with the oil countries not to exploit their monopoly power ruthlessly and to contribute more to aid and charity. But from the economic point of view it makes no sense to treat oil differently from any other commodity.

Floating does not prevent a country from stretching out and thereby softening by foreign borrowing the sudden blow suffered through the precipitous rise of the oil price. Some countries have, in fact, made lavish if not reckless use of this opportunity. The outstanding example is Britain. It has borrowed abroad on an enormous scale to obviate or rather postpone the belt tightening that will be necessary in the end—unless North Sea oil will flow much more abundantly than now seems likely. Since the borrowing has been done largely by the government and nationalized industries, the British policy is better described as "dirty fixing" of the exchange rates than as "dirty floating.¹⁹

The unequal distribution of petrodollars has received much attention and numerous schemes have been proposed to "recycle," that is to redistribute petrodollars through official lending from the countries that receive the petrodollars to those that fail to attract them. All these proposals for international planning suffer from two fatal weaknesses. First, they fail to appreciate the complexities and uncertainties of the situation. Even *ex post* it is extremely difficult to ascertain where the petrodollars went. The statistics that have been collected are fragmentary and unreliable. Oil-related deficits and nonoil deficits, petrodollars, and other dollars are hopelessly intermingled. Second, even if they could be separated statistically there is no good reason why they should be treated differently.

The market, especially the Euro-dollar market, has done an excellent job of recycling, especially as far as the industrial countries are concerned. Ironically, many proposals for offical recycling were designed expressly for the industrial countries which need it least. What holds for industrial countries also holds for the wealthier, semi-industrialized less-developed countries—Brazil, Mexico, Argentina, and others. If it is felt that some very poor countries need special help, it should be called what it is—international aid or charity. There is no objection to speak of a "special oil facility on concessional terms," if it helps to get funds from OPEC. But there is no rational economic or "ethical" reason why such aid or charity should be tied to the oil price rise. A country that has been hit by the rise of the oil price is not more deserving than another one that received a blow from high food prices, a string of crop failures, or some other calamity.

The rational solution of the balance-of-payments problems caused by the oil price rise—as distinguished from international aid and charity—is this: Let each country grapple with its overall balance of payments (whatever the precise definition), using exchange rate changes, managed or unmanaged floating,[20] borrowing from the IMF, or internal monetary-fiscal measures as it sees fit or as determined in consultation with the IMF. Then oil and nonoil disequilibria in the balance of payments will be adjusted or financed in one wash and it will not be necessary to distinguish between oil and nonoil deficits.

Notes

1. It would be easy to relax the assumption of perfect competition by assuming lags in the adjustment of wages and prices and search periods for workers who have lost their jobs. Under these assumptions there would be some transitional, frictional unemployment even in a highly competitive economy. But for our purpose, it is not necessary to complicate the analysis. Let us, therefore, stick for a moment to the ideal picture of instantaneous adjustment and continuous full employment.

2. The OECD estimates the increase from 1973 to 1974 at $17.25 billion which is 1.33 percent of 1973 GNP; see Organization for Economic Co-operation and Development, *Economic Outlook*, no. 17, July 1973, p. 56. Table 21. For an excellent quantitative analysis of the oil price rise in global terms for different groups of countries (including less-developed areas), see Hollis B. Chenery, "Restructuring the World Economy," *Foreign Affairs*, January 1975.

3. The difference is that government expenditures go up and up relentlessly, while the oil price rise was a one-shot affair in the sense that after the price had been raised fourfold, it has remained on the higher level since the end of 1973. This could, of course, change in the future. But the recent price rise of 10 percent (or in practice a little less than 10 percent) imposed by OPEC in September 1975 can be regarded as an adjustment for inflation and does not change the real picture.

4. Based on OECD data. *loc cit.*

5. The Europeans and Japan have reacted more rationally to the oil price rise than the United States. Since they depend almost entirely on imports, they had no choice but to take the price rise on the chin and could not follow the foolish American policy of holding down the price for "old" oil by direct controls administered by a huge, wasteful, inefficient and self-perpetuating bureaucracy—a policy which plays right into the hands of the OPEC cartel by holding down domestic production, discouraging conservation, and keeping up oil consumption.
    The folly of the American oil policy was compounded by The Energy Policy and Conservation Act of December 1975. The price of "old oil" was (slightly) rolled back in an election year. That the price is to be decontrolled in the future—slowly after the election!—is not much of a consolation, because there will be plenty of time to reconsider. This policy merely serves to perpctuate a huge bureaucracy and is bound to strengthen the oil cartel by increasing the American dependence on imported oil. The irony of calling the act a "conservation" measure was lost on the Congressional committees responsible for the legislation.

6. What the appropriate level is I need not discuss here. Due to fluctuations in the velocity of circulation of money, there occur short-run and long-run deviations between monetary

growth and the movement in the price level. But there has never been a case, as far as I know, where a substantial inflation was not preceeded or accompanied by a substantial increase in the money supply. Our present inflation is no exception.

7. This is an application of the theorem formulated by F. A. von Hayek and Charles Schultze to the effect that wage rigidity alone (without an actual wage push) creates unemployment or inflation as a consequence of *shifts* in demand. Wages and prices rise where demand has increased, but fail to decline where demand has decreased. See F. A. von Hayek, "Inflation From Downward Inflexibility of Wages," in *Problems of U.S. Economic Development,* edited by the Committee for Economic Development (CED), (New York, 1958), vol. 1, pp. 147–152; reprinted in F. A. von Hayek, *Studies in Philosophy Politics and Economics* (Chicago, 1967), and Charles L. Schultze, *Recent Inflation in the United States,* Study Paper No. 1. Joint Economic Committee, 86th Congress, 1st session (Washington, D.C.: Government Printing Office, September 1959).

8. That has been acknowledged by the Arthur Burns. In a recent speech (at the University of Georgia, September 19, 1975) he said:

The truth is that, for many years now, the economies of the United States and many other countries have developed a serious underlying bias toward inflation. This tendency has simply been magnified by the special influences that occasionally arise ... such as a crop shortfall that results in higher farm prices, or the action of a foreign cartel that raises oil prices.

9. Sir John Hicks, "What is Wrong With Monetarism?" *Lloyds Bank Review* (London), October 1975. Consideration of an extreme example will help to clarify the nature of the problem. Suppose the economy is "fully indexed," that is to say, *all* types of income—wages, salaries, rents, interest, ect.—are continuously adjusted for changes in the price level. Now assume something happens that requires a reduction in real incomes, for example, a deterioration of the terms of trade due to the rise in the oil price. The result will be an impasse. With rigid wages (money incomes) the assumed deterioration will trigger either an explosive inflation or a recession, depending on the reaction of the monetary authorities. Now, fortunately our economy is not fully indexed, but with money illusion having been badly eroded by inflation, it has come dangerously close to full indexation.

Two further remarks are in order. First, proponents of indexation are aware that not all incomes can be indexed. For example, nobody has suggested that profits should be indexed. (In fact, profits are not fixed in monetary terms. They act as a shock absorber or cushion. But the cushion has become thin and cannot absorb heavy blows.) Second, pointing out the dangers of full or close-to-full indexation does not preclude advocacy of indexation in certain areas. For example, William Fellner, who rejects general indexation, strongly favors indexation of taxes. See William Fellner. "The Controversial Issue of Comprehensive Indexation," in *Essays on Inflation and Indexation* (Washington, D.C.: American Enterprise Institute, 1974), and William Fellner, Kenneth W. Clarkson, and John Moore, *Correcting Taxes for Inflation* (Washington, D.C.: American Enterprise Institute, 1975).

10. Frank H. Knight, "The Business Cycle, Interest and Money," reprinted from *Review of Economic Statistics,* May 1941, in F. H. Knight, *On the History and Methods of Economics. Selected Essays* (Chicago, 1956), p. 224.

11. The growth of the public sector at the expense of the productive private sector has been especially pronounced in Britain. According to *The Economist* (London). November 15, 1975, p. 18, two Oxford economists (Robert Bacon and Walter Eltis) have demonstrated that

Britain's (economic) disaster in the past decade . . . has been that . . . in 1961–1973 the numbers of men employed in industry fell by 14%. . . . The great emigration has been into the public sector employment, where the marginal producitivity of labour is often tiny or nil, with a . . . 53% increase in local government employment . . . and a 14% increase in central government employment.

Britain has been leading the way, but the United States is moving in the same direction: see Warren Nutter, "Where Are We Headed?" speech given before the Southern Economic Association (Reprint No. 34, American Enterprise Institute, Washington, D.C., 1975).

12. I use the word "surplus" here in a loose balance-of-payments sense. For our purpose, it is not necessary to distinguish between what goes "below the line" (international reserves) and "above the line" (foreign investment). For most of the OPEC countries this distinction would be quite arbitrary anyway. Nor need I go into the important question whether in a deeper sense the word "surplus" is not inappropriate, for the reason that these surpluses merely reflect the depletion of an exhustible resource—of oil in the ground—and do not represent an addition to real wealth.

13. To show that it is not merely hindsight, I may be allowed to mention that I have sketched the analysis as early as January 1975 in a postscript on "The Impact of The Energy Crisis" to *Two Essays on the Future of the International Monetary Order* (Washington, D.C.: American Enterprise Institute, 1974). An excellent, much more elaborate analysis along similar theoretical lines has been offered by Dr. Jan Tumlir, "Oil Payments and Old Debts in the World Economy," *Lloyds Bank Review* (London), July 1974.

14. See my *Theory of Internation Trade* (London and New York, 1936) and my essay *The World Economy. Money and the Great Depression. 1919–1939* [Chapter 16 in this volume] which was written for the German Bundesbank and has appeared in German in a volume published by the German Bundesbank in 1976 on the occasion of the hundredth anniversary of the foundation of the German Reichsbank in 1876. An English version has been published by the American Enterprise Institute in January 1976. The principal transfer pessimist with respect to reparations was J. M. Keynes: his chief critic was Bertil Ohlin. There is fairly general agreement among experts now that Ohlin was right. But the transfer pessimism found a reincarnation in the theory of the permanent dollar shortage which was widely held, even among economists, in the postwar period. Some writer, e.g., Lord Balogh, managed to be optimistic with respect to reparations, while at the same time, to believe in the permanent dollar shortage without noticing the contradiction.

15. Internation Monetary Fund, *Annual Report 1975*, p. 16.

16. *Ibid.*

17. See the story in *The Wall Street Journal*, October 18, 1975, "Easy Come, Easy Go. Oil Nations Discover Ways to Spend Money." But apples in the desert is not quite the obverse of grapes in Scotlan, because know-how, machinery, equipment and their replacements must be imported from abroad. Import demand is not likely to be reduced much by these extravaganzas.

18. The automobile industry immediately comes to mind. I do believe, however, that a setback to automobile production was bound to come anyway. But it surely was magnified by the oil price rise.

19. In Britain an ominous development strongly reminiscent of the 1930s is the call for general import restrictions—not only by the labor unions, but also by well-known economists. See, for example the new *Economic Policy Review* (University of Cambridge, Department of Applied Economics), no. 1, February 1975. This organ of the so-called "New Cambridge School," one branch of the split Keynesian community, has come out flatly for general import restrictions. A devastating criticism of that view has come from Oxford; *Import Controls versus Devaluation and Britain's Economic Prospects*, by W. M. Corden, I. M. D. Little, and M. F. G. Scott (Trade Policy Research Center, Guest Paper No. 2, London, 1975). The authors show convincingly that import restrictions cannot do anything that cannot be done more efficiently and more cheaply by devaluation.

20. It is important to distingusih between "managed" and "dirty" floating. Examples of dirty floating are split exhange markets, multiple exhange rates for different types of transactions (capital versus current transactions, necessary versus luxury imports, and the like). Managed floating means that the exchange rate is influenced by official interventions, buying and selling of foreign exchange in the market, maintaining the uniformity of the (fluctuating) exchange rate. Dirty floating shades off into the system of comprehensive exchange control.

15

The Problem of Stagflation

Introduction

About a year ago, in March or April 1975, the American economy passed the trough of the sixth postwar recession (not counting the mini-recession of 1966, nor the February–October recession of 1945, the latter being clearly not a cyclical recession but a period of physical changeover from war to peace). The last recession was the longest and most economists would say the severest of the six.[1] The contrast between the last and the earlier recessions was much greater in Europe and Japan than in the United States. This was, in fact, the first truly worldwide recession in the postwar period. But it was a recession and not a depression, if by depression we mean a slump of the order of magnitude of the Great Depressions of the 1930s (1929–1933 and 1937–1938) and the (so-called first post-World War I) depression of 1920–1921. However, the 1974–1975 recession had a feature that made it perplexing and disturbing from the theoretical as well as from the policy point of view: it was a highly inflationary recession, a pronounced case of stagflation.

Stagflation and inflationary recession are usually used as interchangeable terms. But it is better to make a distinction. Stagflation can be defined as the coexistence of significant inflation and substantial general unemployment and slack over a considerable period. Inflationary recession is a cyclical recession characterized by rising unemployment and declining output combined with significant inflation. The *rate* of inflation may go up as was the case in the last recession until about the end of 1974, or it may decline as was the case in the last three or four months of the recession in 1975. Stagflation is the wider concept; it covers inflationary recessions as well as those cyclical upswings (or phases of cyclical upswings), like the present one, that are characterized by substantial general unemployment and inflation. The rationale of this definition is, as we shall see presently, that the coexistence of high general

Contemporary Economic Problems, William Fellner, ed. (Washington, D.C.: American Enterprise Institute, 1976), 225–272. © 1976, American Enterprise Institute. Reprinted with permission.

unemployment and inflation poses the same problems for economic theory and economic policy in recessions as well as in recoveries.

Stagflation of the present scale and duration is a new phenomenon. It has not happened before that a long and severe recession was accompanied by rapid and for some time even accelerating inflation on a two-digit level; and no earlier cyclical recovery has started with 6 to 8 percent inflation with which the present one started. It is true that faint symptoms of the new disease had been noticed in some of the earlier postwar recessions when prices failed to decline or even continued to rise although at a much lower rate than in the last recession. Moreover, it is significant that the cyclical recoveries in the postwar period have shown a tendency to start from successively higher inflation rates. (See Table 2 in Geoffrey Moore's contribution.)[2]

An earlier episode resembling the current stagflation was the price rise that occurred after the great contraction of 1929–1933 and before the short but very sharp depression of 1937–1938. The price rise was deliberately brought about by the various New Deal measures—NRA, AAA, the Wagner Act and dollar devaluation. But after a while it caused great alarm although, compared with our recent inflation rates, the price rise was modest. It was a case of cost-push inflation and stagflation. Although the expansion from 1933–1937 was fairly rapid and long (fifty months), unemployment was still very high (14.3 percent at the upper turning point of the cycle in 1937). In the following depression unemployment rose again to 20 percent and there was a mild decline in the price level in 1938 and 1939.

Theoretical and Policy Problems Posed by Stagflation

The coexistence of substantial unemployment and rising price and wage levels is a puzzling phenomenon for the economic theorist and it confronts economic policy, and more precisely macroeconomic ("Keynesian") policies of demand management, with a nasty dilemma.

The theoretical puzzle is well expressed by the repeated rueful complaints by Arthur Burns that the economy does not seem to behave as it used to. How is it possible that in the face of substantial unemployment and excess capacity—in other words, that despite excess supply in labor and commodity markets—wages and prices continue to rise sharply? The answer is that in an ideal fully competitive economy stagflation would be impossible and that in moderately competitive economies as we had them in the not too distant past stagflation would be mild and confined to short periods.

The policy dilemma of stagflation is this: If macroeconomic monetary and fiscal policies try to counteract inflation, they increase unemployment; if they try to reduce unemployment they intensify inflation. In the "classical" recessions (depressions) and booms of the past the dilemma did not exist or existed only to a small extent and in an ideal competitive economy there would be no such dilemma. The policy conclusion is obvious: To eliminate the dilemma or to reduce it to more tolerable proportions, the economy must be made more competitive by removing at least the most serious restraints and restrictions on free competitive markets.

The crucial importance of the fact that the economy has increasingly deviated from the competitive ideal can perhaps be most clearly demonstrated if we analyze the impact of the so-called "special factors" on inflation, recession, and stagflation under alternative assumptions about the competitive structure of the economy.

Let us take as an example the enormous rise in the oil price decreed by OPEC. First, let us ask how an ideal fully competitive economy would react to a levy (deterioration in the terms of trade) imposed by the foreign oil cartel. If the price of oil (and of oil-related products) were forced up and the price level were to remain stable other prices would have to decline. If full employment were to be preserved, this would require that money wages (more generally, money incomes) go down. In an ideal competitive economy where wages were flexible downward (as well as upward) a suitably tight monetary policy would bring about the necessary wage and price adjustments without creating more than temporary, frictional unemployment.[3] The resulting decline in *real* wages would reflect the unavoidable decline in real national income.

Second, let us assume money wages to be entirely rigid downward—a quite realistic assumption indeed. In that case, keeping the price level stable by monetary policy would cause unemployment (a recession). That is what Arthur Burns told Congress; the Federal Reserve System, he said, could have prevented inflation, despite the oil price rise, but only by forcing down other prices and thereby creating an intolerable amount of unemployment. It was therefore necessary to allow prices to rise in order to bring about the unavoidable reduction in *real* wages by inflation. The argument is unexceptionable.[4] But it should be observed that with wages rigid downward (without any wage-push upward) the rise in the price of imported oil, representing a burden of about $20 to $22 billion for the $1.5 trillion U.S. economy, would merely cause a once-for-all price rise of about 1.4 percent. In other words, only a small fraction of the inflation that actually occurred from 1973 to 1975 could be explained—and justified—in this manner. To say that only a small degree of inflation can be "justified" merely means that with rigid money wages the oil price rise would create some unemployment if the price level were kept stable. It is not intended to prejudge the question whether the inflationary reaction to the oil price rise would reduce the *real* burden of the oil price rise—something which depends on the reaction of OPEC. If the nominal price of oil (in dollar terms) remained unchanged, the *real* burden of the oil price rise would be reduced by inflation in the importing countries, because the terms of trade would be better than they would be if the importing countries kept the price level stable. But it is probably realistic to assume that OPEC would react by raising the nominal price of oil so as to keep the real price at some preassigned level.

It is true, there were other "special factors" at work (there always are): the rise in domestic energy prices, the Russian wheat sale, a moderate crop shortfall not to mention the temporary disappearance of the anchovies from the Peruvian coast, a disappearance that caused a sharp rise in soybean prices. The result of all these changes was *an internal* income transfer from the urban sector to energy producers and farmers. This, in turn, had an inflationary impact through the Hayek-Schultze effect. But all special factors combined in conjunction with money wage rigidity can explain only a fraction (perhaps a fourth) of the two-digit inflation. The comparative unimportance of the special factors in the inflation picture has been acknowledged by Arthur Burns. In a recent speech he said: "The truth is that, for many years now, the economies of the United States and many other countries have developed a serious underlying bias toward inflation. This tendency has simply been magnified by the special influences that occasionally arise—such as a crop shortfall that results in higher farm prices, or the action of a foreign cartel that raises oil prices." [5]

Third, downward rigidity of money wages is unfortunately not the only nor the most important present deviation from the competitive ideal. As William Fellner, Friedrich Hayek, and others have pointed out, labor unions, like everyone else, have become "inflation conscious"—in other words, money illusion has largely disappeared and "real wage resistance" (in the phrase of Sir John Hicks) has developed. The same is true of other pressure groups that manage by political means to force the government to raise the price of their products and the incomes of their members. Organized agriculture is the best and most important example. The resistance to real-income reductions finds its expression in aggressive wage contract bargaining and widespread indexation. Furthermore, labor unions and other pressure groups are in general not satisfied with preserving their real incomes but wish to increase them. The recent wage contract won by the teamsters' union under pressure of a nation-wide strike in an election year is a perfect example. It provides for a substantial (10 percent) annual increase in money wages for the next three years plus full indexation. The precise magnitude of the real wage increase is not quite clear. But there can be no doubt that the terms of the contract must, therefore, be judged to be highly inflationary. If, under these circumstances, an attempt is made to hold the lid on inflation by monetary restraint, unemployment develops. This is stagflation.

Enough has been said to make clear that in an ideal, fully competitive market economy stagflation would be impossible. The spectacle of wages rising rapidly in the face of heavy unemployment, both overall and in particular industry, could not be seen in a free-market economy.

But why has stagflation suddenly reached such a high level in 1974–1975? There has been no sudden burst but rather a gradual (though since the 1930s rapidly accelerating) rise in restrictions on the competitive market economy. The answer is to be found in the inflationary history of the postwar period. Prolonged inflation, whatever its origin, was bound to erode money illusion and to generate inflationary expectations. If most people expect an inflation of (say) 15 percent and the actual rate is then reduced to 7 or 8 percent, losses, retrenchment and some unemployment must be expected even in a much more competitive economy than the one we actually have. But it is still true that the resulting stagflation, unemployment, and slack would never have become so serious and intractable if so many restrictions, rigidities, and deviations from the competitive ideal had not piled up over the years, (especially since the 1930s).

How about the monetary factor? The monetarists are, of course, right that stagflation, like any other kind of inflation, is a monetary phenomenon in the sense that it would be impossible without monetary growth. But we must keep in mind that what monetarists have established is a close relationship between monetary growth and the growth of *money* GNP. The relationship between monetary growth and *real* GNP is a different matter. In the words of a prominent monetarist "we still know very little about the division of short-run changes in nominal GNP between changes in output, on the one hand, and changes in prices, on the other. This is a deficiency of both the Keynesian and the monetarist analyses."[6] It is true that macroeconomic theories of the monetarist or Keynesian type cannot tell us how a change in money GNP will be divided between price change and quantity change. To solve that problem microeconomic considerations are needed. But Meiselman underestimates what we know about that problem. In particular he is much too pessimistic when he says that we do not know why the recovery after 1933 was so slow and why the "revival was aborted in 1937."[7] I find Milton Friedman's microeconomic explanation of "why [in 1933 to 1937] so large a part of the growth in nominal national income was absorbed by prices" entirely convincing. It was "the cost push" he said, from the "NIRA, AAA, Wagner Labor Act and the associated growth of union strength" that was responsible.[8] In 1937 the alarming price rise induced the Federal Reserve System to raise reserve requirements in order to remove excess reserves. This, in turn, led the banks to contract credit and brought on the depression. This explanation should be acceptable for Keynesians as well as for monetarists. Alvin Hansen, for example, was fully aware of the danger that an "increase in aggregate demand [may be] unnecessarily dissipated on higher prices with corresponding less effect on output and employment."[9] And Keynes himself did mention the importance of downward flexibility of *relative* wages, of prices, and of exchange rates for the smooth functioning of the economy and the effectiveness of macro-policies.[10]

There exists a substantial modern literature on the "Microeconomic Foundations of Employment and Inflation Theory."[11] This theory is essentially one of frictional or structural unemployment, inasmuch as it describes and analyzes in detail the search for suitable jobs on the part of employees who have lost their previous job and the search for suitable candidates for job openings on the part of employers. Stress is laid on the cost (both money and opportunity cost) of gathering information about jobs, including the income foregone by not accepting second- or third-best options that may present themselves. One aim of most contributors to this literature is to explain unemployment without reference to labor unions and money illusion. It is unquestionably true that the picture of a perfectly competitive labor market in which wages immediately adjust to the market-clearing level does not correspond to reality. Even if there were no unions and no money illusion, workers who have lost their jobs would not immediately accept wage cuts in their old employment (if that were an option) or inferior job offers elsewhere. They would take their time and invest time and money to search for acceptable openings. What is true of labor markets is also true of many commodity markets, especially of the market in durable manufactured goods where seller–buyer and manufacturer–customer relationships are important. In these markets prices are sticky and respond sluggishly to changes in demand, even in the absence of monopolies and oligopolies. This stickiness implies that in the short run quantity adjustments resulting in ups and downs of employment and of capacity utilization play a great role. All that is well described in Okun's paper.[12]

This analysis of frictional or structural unemployment is an extremely useful exercise. It has greatly enriched our knowledge of the way the economy works. The perfectly competitive economy in which all prices and wages immediately adjust to any change in the data and in which markets are cleared continuously at the full-employment level is an ideal never fully realized—even in the absence of monopolies or oligopolies in commodity and labor markets.

What I find unfortunate and unacceptable is the tendency in that literature to obliterate the distinction between general depression or recession unemployment (often called Keynesian unemployment) on the one hand and frictional or structural unemployment on the other hand, to play down the importance of labor unions, to ignore the fact that unions have made money wages almost completely rigid downward, to neglect the inflationary implications of the fact that the unions often push up wages even in the face of heavy unemployment.

I find equally unconvincing the reinterpretation of Keynes's theory of involuntary unemployment. It runs as follows: Unemployment is the "consequence of a decline in demand when traders do not have perfect information on what the new market-clearing price will be. No other assumption . . . needs to be relinquished . . . in order to get from the Classical to Keynes' Theory of Markets."[13] If, as Keynes says, workers do not accept a reduction of their *real* wage when it comes in the form of a reduction of their money wage, while they do accept it in the form of a rise in prices, it is not because unions rule out money wage reductions or because of money illusion. The real reason is said to be different: A rise in the price level "conveys" the information that "money wages everywhere have fallen relative to prices." Workers reject an equal cut in their real wage in the form of a money wage reduction because "a cut in one's own money wage does not imply that options elsewhere have fallen." [14] Tobin offers the same interpretation of Keynes's theory of involuntary unemployment. "Rigidities ... of money wages can be explained by workers' preoccupation with relative wages and the absence of any central economy-wide mechanism for altering all money wages together." [15]

This interpretation is in my opinion unconvincing. Keynes was confronted with the mass unemployment and misery of the 1930s; he surely did not want to say that workers were unemployed (more or less voluntarily) because they were shopping around for better opportunities or that they were "preoccupied" not so much with their own plight as with the possibility that if they accepted a lower money wage other groups might get away with a better bargain. Keynes was, of course, opposed to *general* wage reduction as a recovery measure. But even at that time few economists favored that policy. [16]

The upshot of this discussion is that the literature on the microfoundations of inflation and employment theory is of little help for explaining the stagflation dilemma, because it abstracts from the most important factors—wage rigidity, wage push, real wage resistance from labor unions, similar activities of other pressure groups, and the effects of the widespread government regulation of industries. I find Frank H. Knight's explanation much more convincing. With the Great Depression in mind Knight wrote in 1941: "In a free market these changes [in demand and prices of different types of goods] would be temporary, but even then they might be serious; and with important markets as unfree as they actually are ... the results take on the proportion of a social disaster." [17] Since 1941 the economy has moved much farther away from the competitive ideal. There are many more powerful unions—for example, public employees (including not only bus drivers, subway personnel, garbage men but also teachers, civil servants, firemen, policemen) are now unionized and do not hesitate to use the strike weapon to push up their wages. Many other pressure groups have organized themselves, and government regulation of more and more industries has made more prices rigid downward while they remain elastic upward. In addition the public sector has grown enormously—which is bound to slow GNP growth. [18] Slower growth of aggregate supply collides with ever increasing claims on the available national product. This puts heavy pressure on the monetary authorities to make a choice between giving way and financing an inflation or standing firm and bringing on a recession. Monetarists are right when they say that stagflation like any other type of inflation cannot be stopped without an appropriate monetary policy. Monetary restraint is a necessary condition for stopping an inflation but it is not a sufficient condition for an economically efficient and politically feasible anti-stagflation policy. I agree with William Fellner, Herbert

Giersch, Friedrich Hayek, Hendrik S. Houthakker[19] and others that a tight monetary and fiscal policy must be supplemented by measures designed to make the economy more competitive. If we rely on monetary and fiscal restraints alone, we will create so much unemployment that the fight against inflation will be broken off prematurely. This premature breaking off has in fact taken place in country after country. The result will be more inflation and more unemployment, a stop-and-go cycle around a steepening price trend. The great danger is that the cry for comprehensive wage and price controls will become irresistible despite the dismal failure of controls whenever and wherever they have been tried. Since the people will remember from the last time how to anticipate and evade the controls, the next time around the system of controls will run its course rapidly: that is, it will break down, merely disrupting the economy, or (perhaps more likely) will be quickly followed by consumer rationing and allocation, leading straight into a fully planned and regimented economy.

**Structural Reform or How to Make the Economy
More Flexible and Competitive**

In recent years government policies and regulations that restrain competition, protect (or even created) private monoplies, restrict production, and raise or fix prices have come under closer scrutiny. Economists have unearthed and described dozens of such cases.[20] Phasing out these restrictions and changing these policies would go a long way toward making the economy more competitive and flexible than it is now, thus making macroeconomic recovery and anti-inflation policies more effective. Here only a few examples can be mentioned.

In the field of agriculture, although output restrictions on some basic foodstuffs were belatedly lifted after food prices had exploded in 1973 and 1974, such restrictions still exist on several important products. Furthermore, interregional trade in many agricultural commodities (especially dairy products, fruits, and vegetables) is severely restricted by federal and state marketing orders or by producers privately organized—organizations in restraint of trade that are government-sponsored, government-licensed, government-enforced, and of course, exempt from antitrust laws. Imports of many agricultural products from abroad, especially of meats and fruits, are sharply restricted. Such policies freeze and distort prices and reduce output because they prevent a rational interregional and international division of labor. There exist, furthermore, many import restrictions on industrial products, apart from tariffs, including the so-called "voluntary restrictions" imposed on foreign exporters, ranging from exporters of steel to exporters of textiles. These "voluntary" restrictions are especially damaging and costly because they force foreign producers to organize themselves in export monopolies at the expense of the American consumers. There is, furthermore, the Buy American Act which prevents foreign competition and costs the U.S. taxpayer many hundreds of millions of dollars. The field of transportation and energy is full of government-imposed restrictions on competition.[21]

Most difficult to deal with, but crucially important, are restrictions in the labor market imposed by labor unions. The importance of unions has been often questioned on the ground that in the United States only 20–25 percent of the labor force is unionized. But it has been demonstrated many times that, for various reasons that need not be repeated here, nonunion wages tend to follow union wages although at a distance and usually with a lag.[22] Leaving aside far-reaching structural reforms of the present methods of wage determination by industry-wide collective bargaining under the constant threat of crippling strikes, there exist a number of policy changes that could reduce wage pressure, increase competition, and expand output and employment. Houthakker mentions the following: "Unions should be prevented from restricting membership by apprenticeship requirements, nomination procedures, or excessive entrance fees; nor should they be allowed to operate hiring halls. The Davis-Bacon Act and similar laws requiring excessive wages to be paid under government contracts have interfered seriously with the performance of the construction market [and cost the taxpayer hundreds of millions of dollars]; they should be phased out not only at the federal but also at the state level."[23] Today, moreover, the government finances strikes by generous unemployment benefits and welfare payments. In some states such benefits go even to the strikers themselves, and in that connection a proposal of Arthur Burns should be mentioned. In an important speech he has recommended that "public employment" be offered "to anyone who is willing to work at a rate of pay somewhat below the Federal minimum wage." Burns stressed that a low rate of pay in such public service employment is essential to prevent "such a program from becoming a vehicle for expanding public jobs at the expense of private industry."[24] Public service employment would largely take the place of the present system of unemployment benefits which have become so generous that they "blunt incentives to work."[25] It has been found that in many cases unemployment benefits and various welfare grants (all of which are tax-free) exceed the income after taxes that a person could earn if he accepted a job for which he was qualified.

Minimum wage laws cause considerable unemployment among teenagers and other underprivileged groups, especially blacks and high-school dropouts. The minimum wage laws deprive thousands of young people of their first crucial on-the-job training and may seriously damage their whole future working career. These laws are a social and economic crime and should be phased out.[26] Unions strenuously object to the phasing out of minimum wage legislation. They even reject a reduction of the minimum wage for teenagers on the grounds that such a change would give employment to some teenagers at the expense of adult workers; "sons would displace their fathers on the jobs." This argument completely misses the purpose of policies designed to make the economy more competitive and flexible. Such structural reform is not a zero-sum game: The purpose is not a redistribution of a given pie but the enlargement of the pie. Overall employment and output would increase, and so would real wages, partly because more expansionary and more effective monetary and fiscal policies would be possible if the threat of rekindling inflation were eliminated (or at least sharply reduced) by measures that would make the economy more competitive and flexible.

What about incomes policy? A policy along the lines indicated above, designed to make the economy more competitive, is sometimes called an "incomes policy." Arthur Burns has used that terminology. In earlier publications I have called it "incomes policy II" as distinguished from incomes policy I in the usual sense of wage and price guidelines, price stops, wage freezes, and similar measures. Because of these connotations of the term incomes policy, it is perhaps better not to use it for the policy here recommended.

Keynesians and monetarists alike should be able to agree on the desirability of structural reform for the purpose of making the economy more competitive and more flexible. The Keynesian (or, more precisely, the Phillips-curve advocate) would say that such a reform would improve the terms of the trade-off between unemployment and inflation, while the monetarist would assert that the reform would reduce the level of "natural" unemployment.[27]

Concluding Remarks

I am painfully aware that structural reform along the lines sketched here will be at best a very slow process. Vested interests fiercely resist any attempt at deregulation and liberalization and the beneficiaries of present policies hold on, tooth and nail, to their privileges and monopoly positions. What, then, are the policy options if quick relief through structural reform is beyond our grasp?

There is, I believe, no other choice but to continue the present policy of letting the economic expansion proceed slowly in the hope that inflation will not accelerate too rapidly. In my opinion it would be a great mistake to speed up the expansion in order to reduce unemployment quickly, whatever the political appeal of such a policy may be in an election year. Quick expansion surely would speed up the ongoing inflation. The consequence would be either that the monetary brake would be applied and the expansion give way to a new inflationary recession or (perhaps more likely) that the call for wage and price controls would become so strong that the system of controls would be tried once more despite the dismal failure of earlier attempts. The controls would either soon become ineffective, merely further disrupting the economy and burdening it with a new bureaucracy without preventing a recession, or worse (but perhaps more likely) lead to consumer rationing, compulsory allocation of factors of production, and full regimentation of the economy in the guise of economic planning.

The many Keynesians who argue that large unemployment and slack in the economy make a quick expansion safe at present forget that the experiment has been made: much unemployment and slack have *not* prevented the rapid inflation of the last three years. (The operation of "special" inflationary factors can, as we have seen, "explain" only a fraction of the price rise that has occurred.) To say as some do that a more rapid monetary expansion would reduce the rate of inflation because it would stimulate production and so increase aggregate supply is like saying that one can make a drunk sober by forcing whiskey down his throat to pep him up. True, if the poison is withdrawn from him too rapidly a situation may arise where one must increase the dose of the stimulant temporarily to forestall an imminemt collapse. But I do not believe that the economy faces that danger now. The economic recovery that started a year ago has gathered momentum and is likely to continue for a considerable period without any additional monetary or fiscal stimulation.

Notes

1. Geoffrey Moore doubts, however, that it was the severest recession. G. H. Moore, "Employment, Unemployment and the Inflation–Recession Dilemma," in *Contemporary Economic Problems*, edited by William Fellner (Washington D.C.: American Enterprise Institute for Public Policy Research, 1976), pp. 163–182.

2. *Ibid.*, p. 167.

3. For our purposes it is not necessary to discuss how the money supply would have to be managed to keep the price level stable.

4. It is in effect an application of the theorem formulated by F. A. Hayek and Charles Schultze that says downward wage rigidity (even without any wage push upward) is inflationary as a consequence of *shifts* in demand. Wages and cost of production rise where demand has increased, but fail to decline where demand has decreased. See F. A. Hayek, "Inflation from Downward Inflexibility of Wages," in *Problems of U.S. Economic Development*, ed. by Committee for Economic Development (CED), (New York: The Committee, 1958), vol. 1, pp. 147–52. Reprinted in F. A. Hayek, *Studies in Philosophy, Politics and Economics* (Chicago: University of Chicago Press, 1967), and Charles L. Schultze, *Recent Inflation in the United States* (Study Paper No. 1, Joint Economic Committee, 86th Congress, 1st session, Washington, September 1959).

5. Speech at the University of Georgia, Athens, Georgia, September 19, 1975 (reproduced from typescript).

6. David I. Meiselman in *Answers to Inflation and Recession: Economic Policies for a Modern Society* (New York: National Industrial Conference Board, 1975), p. 23. Friedman, too, notes

that the highly aggregated macro-models of the monetarist and Keynesian type have nothing "to say about the factors that determine the proportions in which a change in nominal income will, in the short run, be divided between price change and output change." See Robert J. Gordon, ed., *Milton Friedman's Monetary Framework: A Debate with His Critics* (Chicago: University of Chicago Press, 1974), pp. 49–50 and 135.

7. Meiselman, *Answers to Inflation and Recession*, p. 23.

8. Milton Friedman, "What Price Guideposts?" in George P. Shultz and Robert Z. Aliber, eds., *Guidelines, Informal Controls and the Market Place* (Chicago: University of Chicago Press, 1966), p. 22.

9. Alvin H. Hansen, *A Guide to Keynes* (New York: McGraw-Hill, 1953), p. 193.

10. J. M. Keynes, *The General Theory of Employment, Interest and Money* (New York: Harcourt, Brace & Co., 1936), p. 270.

11. See especially a volume of essays under that title edited by Edward S. Phelps (New York: W. W. Norton, 1970). See also the interesting article by Arthur Okun, "Inflation: Its Mechanics and Welfare Costs," in *Brookings Papers on Economic Activity*, 1975 (2), pp. 351–90.

12. Okun, "Inflation: Its Mechanics and Welfare Costs." Sir John Hicks, too, has stressed the difference between what he calls the "fixprice" and "flexprice" sectors of the economy. See his booklet *The Crisis of Keynesian Economics* (Oxford: Clarendon Press, 1974), passim.

13. Axel Leijonhufvud, *On Keynesian Economics and the Economics of Keynes* (London and New York: Oxford University Press, 1968), p. 38.

14. Armen A. Alchian, "Information Costs, Pricing and Resource Unemployment," in *Microeconomic Foundations of Employment and Inflation Theory*, ed. E. Phelps, p. 44.

15. James Tobin, "Inflation and Unemployment," *American Economic Review*, March 1972, p. 5.

16. It is true, there can be found passages in *The General Theory* which suggest that Keynes held the theory criticized here. On p. 264, for example, he wrote: "since there is, as a rule, no means of securing a simultaleous and equal reduction of money wages in all industries, it is in the interest of all workers to resist a reduction in their own particular case." This could be interpreted to mean that workers were primarily interested in relative wages. True, no one wants to be discriminated against, and the invisible hand of free competition would bring about equal pay for equal work and eliminate any discrimination. But the process of competition requires that the price be bid down when there is excess supply. To say that despite the heavy unemployment, wage reductions are refused because workers are primarily concerned with relative wages—in other words, because they are unwilling to work at a lower wage than that of workers in some other industries—implies that the individual workers who become unemployed (as distinguished from their unions) prefer a zero-wage to a positive wage. That is not a plausible behavior assumption and it is difficult to believe that Keynes meant to make it. The situation is, however, quite different if we drop the assumption of competition and instead assume collective bargaining through a union. For a union it is perfectly rational to accept a certain amount of unemployment, provided the total wage (of those employed and those unemployed) is greater than under full employment. Obviously, generous unemployment benefits will make it much easier for the unions to solve the difficult problem of sharing the burden of unemployment among their members and thus will induce the unions to accept a larger amount of unemployment than they would otherwise accept.

In the next sentence after the one quoted above, Keynes makes it clear that he was thinking of general wage cutting: "In fact, a movement by employers to revise money-wage bargains downward will be much more strongly resisted, than a gradual and automatic lowering of real wages as a result of rising prices." There can hardly be a quarrel with that proposition up to the point where money illusion has been fully eroded by prolonged inflation and real wage resistance and real wage push have developed. That point marks *The Crisis of Keynesian Economics* of which Hicks speaks (see note 12 above). As was noted earlier, Keynes favored changes in relative "wages of particular industries so as to expedite transfers from those which are relatively declining to those which are relatively expanding." (*The General Theory*, p. 270)

17. F. H. Knight, "The Business Cycle, Interest and Money," reprinted from *Review of Economics and Statistics*, vol. 23, no. 2 (May 1941), in F. H. Knight, *On the History and Methods of Economics* (Chicago: University of Chicago Press, 1956), p. 335.

18. This ominous development has gone farthest in Great Britain. *The Economist* of London recently (November 15, 1975, p. 18) reported about a study by two Oxford economists (Robert Bacon and Walter Eltis) which reaches the conclusion that, "Britain's [economic] disaster in the past decade ... has been that ... in 1961–1973 the numbers of men employed in industry fell by 14%. ... The emigration has been into the public sector employment, where the marginal productivity of labor is often tiny or nil, with a ... 53% increase in local government employment ... and a 14% increase in central government employment." The study by Bacon and Eltis was summarized in three articles in the *Sunday Times* (London), November 2, 9, and 16, 1975, and will be published in full by Macmillan (London) later this year.

The same alarming development threatens Italy. Guido Carli, the former governor of the Italian National Bank, has warned that the government deficits in Italy have now grown beyond the capacity of the economy to absorb them, crushing the economy and cutting living standards. These deficits result from the growth of the bureaucracy, generous social security and health insurance payments, liberal unemployment benefits, and the massive cost of what Carli calls "concealed unemployment"—that is, in many industries workers produce goods, at public expense, for which there is no demand. (*See New York Times*, December 9, 1975.) The United States is rapidly moving in the same direction. See Warren Nutter, *Where Are We Headed?*, AEI Reprint No. 34 (Washington, D.C.: American Enterprise Institute, 1976).

19. William Fellner, "Lessons from the Failure of Demand-Management Policies: A Look at the Theoretical Foundations," *Journal of Economic Literature*, vol. 14, no. 1 (March 1976). pp. 34–53; Herbert Giersch, "Some Neglected Aspects of Inflation in the World Economy," *Public Finance* (The Hague, 1973), esp. pp. 104–08; F. A. Hayek, "Unions, Inflation and Profits," in *Studies in Philosophy, Politics and Economics* (Chicago: University of Chicago Press, 1967), and "Inflation, the Path to Unemployment," in *Inflation: Causes, Consequences, and Cures* (London: Institute of Economic Affairs, 1974), "Zwölf Thesen zur Inflationsbekämpfung," in *Frankfurter Allgemeine Zeitung*, August 19, 1974; Hendrik S. Houthakker, "Incomes Policies as a Supplementary Tool," in *Answers to inflation and Recession: Economic Policies for a Modern Society* (New York: The Conference Board, 1975). The title of Houthakker's speech is misleading. He argues that price and wage controls and incomes policies (in the conventional sense) can make only an "extremely modest contribution." His thesis is that macroeconomic policies must be supplemented by "structural reform."

20. See, for example, Hendrik S. Houthakker, "Specific Reform Measures for the United States," in *Answers to Inflation*, pp. 83–85; Murray L. Weidenbaum, *Government-Mandated*

Price Increases: A Neglected Aspect of Inflation (Washington, D.C.: American Enterprise Institute, 1975), and numerous other AEI publications; and *Annual Report of the Council of Economic Advisers, 1975*, Chapter 5, "Government Regulations."

21. See especially the CEA report for 1975, Chapter 5, and numerous AEI publications.

22. See, for example, Gottfried Haberler, *Economic Growth and Stability* (Los Angeles: Nash, 1974), p. 107.

23. Houthakker, "Specific Reform Measures for the United State." pp. 83–85.

24. Speech at the University of Georgia, Athens, Georgia, September 19, 1975 (reproduced from typescript). Britain's economic disaster in the past decade, which was mentioned in note 18 to this paper, should serve as a warning not to expand employment without proper safeguards.

25. Ibid.

26. Actually there is a strong movement in Congress to raise the minimum wage from $2.30 to $3.00 an hour and henceforth to adjust it automatically for any rise in the consumer price index (indexation). This measure would sharply reduce job opportunities for teenagers and other underprivileged persons, it would magnify and perpetuate, even in boom times, unemployment among such groups and would accentuate the inflation.

27. Such an agreement would not compel the two groups to forego the pleasure of continuing their quarrels, the monetarist insisting that the trade off cannot be permanent and the Keynesian objecting that the "natural" level of unemployment will never be reached.

16

The World Economy, Money, and the Great Depression 1919–1939[1]

Introduction

This essay describes the restoration of the gold standard in the 1920s, its collapse under the impact of the Great Depression, and major international economic and monetary developments in the 1930s—especially those under the "Tripartite Agreement" between the United States, Great Britain, and France in 1936—up to the outbreak of the Second World War in 1939. During this interwar period, the world economy and the international monetary system were, of course, decisively influenced by economic developments in the leading countries—in the United States and, at some distance, in Great Britain, Germany, France, and Japan. Therefore attention is paid here to the internal problems and policies of these countries, especially of the United States.

Section 1 gives a chronicle of events with a minimum of attention to why things happened as they did. Section 2 discusses various explanations—advanced at the time and later—as to why the gold standard broke down and why the depression in the world at large and in the United States in particular was so severe and lasted so long. This discussion offers opportunities for some reflections (summarized in the Concluding Remarks) on what can be learned for the future from considering the events—failures and successes—of the past, keeping in mind that economic, social and political institutions and policies as well as our economic knowledge and the whole intellectual climate have undergone profound changes since the interwar period.

"Die Weltwirtschaft und das international Währungssystem in der Zeit zwischen den beiden Weltkriegen," in Deutsche Bundesbank, *Währung und Wirtschaft in Deutschland 1876–1975*, (Frankfurt [main]: Fritz Knapp Verlag, 1976). English version in American Enterprise Institute Foreign Affairs Study 30 (Washington, D.C.: American Enterprise Institute, January 1976). © 1976, American Enterprise Institute. Reprinted with permission.

1. A Chronicle of Events

From the Stabilization of the Mark to the Outbreak of the Great Depression: 1923–1929

When the mark was stabilized in 1923–1924, Europe's recovery from the ravages of the war had already made good progress and the international gold standard had been restored in large parts of the world. The reparation of physical damage, the rebuilding of worn out or destroyed capital equipment and buildings, the replenishment of inventories, and the reopening of disrupted transport and trade channels between the warring countries were achieved much more quickly than most people, including many economists, had thought possible. But the speed of the reconstruction would not have surprised the classical economists. John Stuart Mill wrote: "The possibility of a rapid repair of disasters mainly depends on whether a country has been depopulated. If its effective population has not been extirpated at the time and not starved afterwards, then with the same skill and knowledge which they had before, with their land and its improvements undestroyed . . . they have nearly all the requisites of their former amount of production." Similarly Alfred Marshall declared: "Ideas, whether those of art and science or those embodied in practical appliances are the most 'real' of the gifts that each generation receives from its predecessors. The world's material wealth would quickly be replaced, if it were destroyed but the ideas by which it was made were retained." [2]

These statements have been put to an even more severe test—and their truth has been again confirmed—by the much greater destructions and dislocations caused by the Second World War.

In the monetary and financial area the return to normal was slower and the road much rougher than it had been in the rebuilding of physical capital. The continental European belligerents—Austria, Belgium, France, Germany, and Italy—had their severe postwar inflations, indeed it was hyperinflation in Austria and Germany, and the United States had a severe depression from January 1920 to September 1921, the so-called first postwar depression. (The second postwar depression was the Great Depression of 1929–1933. Between these two there were two mild recessions in 1923–1924 and 1926–1927.)

The stabilization of the mark in 1924 was preceded by the stabilization of the Austrian currency; the crown was replaced by the schilling in 1922 and pegged to the gold dollar. After the stabilization of the mark many other European currencies were stabilized in rapid succession. The Swiss franc and Swedish crown were slightly depreciated vis-à-vis the dollar and reached their prewar parities late in 1924. Poland, Hungary, and Finland introduced new currencies which soon were pegged to the gold dollar. On April 28, 1925, Winston Churchill, then chancellor of the exchequer, announced in his budget speech the immediate return of Great Britain to the gold standard at the prewar parity. Holland restored the gold standard at the same time.

In France in August 1926 the government of the *Cartel des Gauches* was overthrown in the Chamber of Deputies, and Raymond Poincaré assumed office. He proceeded immediately with the task of eliminating the budget deficit. By early 1927 the French franc was stabilized de facto and, on June 25, 1928, the stabilization was legalized and gold convertibility restored. In 1926 Belgium stabilized the franc and returned to the gold standard. In 1927 the Italian lira was stabilized on gold. In 1928 Bulgaria, Luxembourg, and Norway went back on gold, in 1929 Portugal, and in January 1930 Japan stabilized at the prewar parity.[3]

The upshot is that by 1928 the world was back on the gold standard. This event was almost universally acclaimed by central and commercial bankers and monetary experts. The following statement by O. M. W. Sprague, trusted financial counsellor of the U.S. government and for several years American adviser to the Bank of England, is typical:

The gold standard has emerged triumphantly from the welter of disordered currencies of the World War period and gold has now become more universally than ever before the foundation of the structure of credit throughout the world. This return to the haven of familiar monetary practice is significant of the widespread conviction that the gold standard is an essential factor in the maintenance of a reasonable measure of international stability, for which there is no promising or practical substitute.[4]

The gold standard of the 1920s was, however, very different from the gold standard before 1914, let alone from the ideal textbook variety. Circulation of gold coins and internal gold convertibility of paper money had disappeared; the new gold standard was a gold bullion rather than a gold specie or coin standard. More important, it became largely a gold exchange standard. Many countries held their international reserves not in the form of gold but as sterling or dollar balances. This practice went back to the late nineteenth century. The Russian example of the 1890s had been followed by several countries in Europe (especially by the Austro-Hungarian National Bank) and in other parts of the world. After the war the gold exchange standard was officially recommended for general adoption by the Genoa Conference of financial experts which met in spring 1922 to make proposals for monetary reconstruction. The reason for the recommendation was that there clearly seemed to exist a shortage of gold: As a consequence of war inflation world prices in terms of dollars and gold had about doubled since 1914. This implied a sharp rise in the cost of producing gold, which caused a substantial decline in gold production.[5]

Later, in the 1930s and after World War II, the wide adoption in many countries of the gold exchange standard in the 1920s was widely criticized as a great mistake which, it is held, greatly contributed to the exceptional severity and length of the Great Depression. I shall return to this issue later.

The working of the new gold standard was bedevilled from the start by the misalignment of important parities. The British pound was overvalued and the French franc undervalued. Immediately after the war the pound had fallen to a discount of about 20 percent vis-à-vis gold and the dollar. By deflationary measures the prewar parity was gradually restored. As a consequence the British economy was mildly depressed throughout the 1920s while the rest of the world enjoyed a high level of prosperity.[6]

France could not make the same mistake because the franc's purchasing power was impaired to such an extent and its discount vis-à-vis the dollar was so large— the franc stood at or below one-fifth of its prewar parity—that a return to the prewar parity was out of the question, although it was nevertheless demanded by many Frenchmen. It soon became clear that the new parity undervalued the franc. As a consequence France developed a strong balance of payments through capital inflows and repatriation of French capital on a large scale and a favorable current account. The Banque de France accumulated a very large international reserve in the form of gold and balances in London and New York, which put France in a strong bargaining position. Later actual or threatened conversions of sterling and dollar balances into gold put strong deflationary pressure on Great Britain and the United States. (History repeated itself after 1958 when de Gaulle stabilized the franc.)

Another factor that hampered the smooth operation of the gold standard in the 1920s was the problem of reparations and war debts. Many economists believed then and many still believe that the obligation of Germany to pay reparations and of France and Great Britain to pay war debts to the United States was one of the main causes of the breakdown of the gold standard. For some time American capital exports to Europe, especially to Germany, kept the system going. But when in 1928 the capital flow sharply declined and later stopped or was reversed, the gold standard broke down. Later on I shall return to the problem of reparations and war debts.

One very important development that made the operation of the gold standard (and of any system of permanently fixed exchange rates) more and more difficult was the growing downward rigidity of money wages—a change that was especially pronounced in Great Britain. During the first postwar depression money wage rates in Great Britain declined sharply. That was the last time this happened. From 1929 to 1931 union wage rates fell only marginally.[7] The increased downward rigidity of money wages had made deflation a much more painful and costly operation than it had been before 1914.[8]

An equally important and lasting handicap of the restored gold standard was that it had to operate in a changed and increasingly unfavorable intellectual and policy environment—a changed environment that to a large extent was the consequence of the growing wage rigidity which made deflation extremely painful. Economists, policy makers, business leaders and the public at large had become business-cycle conscious and public policy became increasingly ready to counteract cyclical swings by monetary measures. Internal policy objectives—primarily price stability in the 1920s, full employment in the 1930s, and growth thereafter—were more and more emphasized even if their realization conflicted with the requirements of external equilibrium. As a consequence the rules of the gold standard game were increasingly violated; surplus countries tried to "sterilize" inflowing gold by offsetting monetary measures in order to prevent prices from rising and deficit countries became reluctant to let gold losses affect the price level. Inviolably fixed exchange rates under the gold standard (and the absence of exchange controls) made violation of the rules of the gold standard much easier and more attractive for surplus than for deficit countries. Thus, in the 1920s both France (after the stabilization of the franc) and the United States pursued conscious policies of sterilizing the influx of gold and other reserves. This could be justified on the ground of internal price stability, but it was a violation of the rules of the gold standard. Thus the burden of adjustment was shifted to the deficit countries, a shift that was very painful for Great Britain.[9]

The tendency to flout the rules of the gold standard became even stronger later in the depression. To be sure, the gold standard was never quite so automatic and mechanical as the idealized textbook picture suggests; but in the postwar period it became much more energetically managed than it had been before 1914, and this development gave rise to policy conflicts between countries and to stubborn balance-of-payments disequilibria and was largely responsible for the final break-down of the gold standard.

However, if we look back over the whole period from 1922 to 1928, it is difficult to disagree with the judgment of the great majority of contemporary observers that it was a period of high prosperity and progress. World production and world trade grew steadily. In the United States there were some areas of speculative excesses—the Florida land boom (1924) and the stock exchange boom (1928–1929)—but unlike what had happened in earlier business cycle upswings, the *overall* price level remained remarkably stable from 1922 to 1929. This gave great satisfaction to policy makers and misled most experts to assume that the business cycle had been conquered and a "new era" of permanent stability through skillful monetary management had dawned. The next few years brought a rude awakening.

The Great Depression

In an analysis of the Great Depression, American developments must take first place.

United States

The U.S. economy stood in the center of the storm; the depression in the United States was deeper and lasted longer than the depressions in most other industrial countries, and it was almost entirely homemade. It is true there were phases in the course of the U.S. depression when it was intensified by influences from abroad. In 1931, for example, the devaluation of the pound and of many other currencies affected the U.S. trade balance adversely and induced speculative pressure on the dollar. But these adverse foreign influences were largely the feedback from earlier phases of the American depression. Moreover, given the large size of the American economy, the feedback was comparatively small and could have been offset and neutralized by a more skillful and vigorous monetary policy than the one actually pursued.

Given the dominant position of the U.S. economy and of the dollar in the world economy, and the monetary arrangements and policy maxims of the time—fixed exchanges under the new gold standard—the depression that came about in the United States was bound to spread to the four corners of the world. This does not mean that there were no other focal points of depression elsewhere in the world, for example in Central Europe; but the American infection clearly was the most virulent and the United States was in the strongest position to stop the slide. It failed to do so and in 1930 it struck a heavy blow at the world economy by imposing skyscraper duties on imports through the Smoot-Hawley tariff. To these problems we shall return presently. But first we may draw a brief sketch of the course of the depression in the United States.

The term Great Depression either refers to the catastrophic cyclical downswing from 1929 to 1933 or to the whole depressed period from 1929 to 1939—or to 1941.[10] The long cyclical contraction of 1929–1933[11] was followed by a long cyclical expansion which was, however, interrupted far short of full employment by a brief but precipitous depression lasting from May 1937 to June 1938.[12] In 1937 unemployment was still over 14 percent of the labor force, and at the outbreak of the war in Europe in 1939 it was over 17 percent. The slump from 1929 to 1933 was worldwide, but a number of countries, notably Nazi Germany, managed to stay out of the sharp relapse of 1937–1938.

The onset of the depression is usually associated with the crash on the New York Stock Exchange in October–November 1929. Actually the decline in output and employment had started earlier; the "official" date of the peak of the cycle (the beginning of the downswing) is August 1929.

Apart from the stock market crash the depression at first did not look unusually serious—the decline of output and employment was much more precipitous in 1937–1938 than in 1929–1930. Early in 1930 there were even faint signs of a revival. But in October 1930 the financial situation deteriorated drastically. Confidence in the banking system waned, and there were runs on the banks by depositors who wanted cash. In several waves of panic (October 1930, March 1931, September 1931, March 1933) thousands of banks suspended operations—over 9,000 out of 24,700 banks in existence at the beginning of 1930 had failed by the end of 1933! The final banking crisis came early in 1933. It culminated in the complete shutdown of all banks for all transactions, the "banking holiday" that was declared by President Roosevelt on March 6, 1933. The banks resumed operations on March 13 and within a month things were back to normal.

The bank failures enormously intensified the deflation, directly through the destruction of deposit money and reduced lending and indirectly by shattering confidence and spreading gloom. From the peak of the cycle to its trough (August 1929 to March 1933) the stock of money was allowed to decline by 33 percent, moeny GNP and industrial production fell by about 50 percent, real GNP (in terms of 1958 prices) fell by 28 percent, unemployment rose to over 25 percent of the labor force and the value of imports of goods and services fell to almost a third of its previous level.

The following cyclical recovery, the longest peacetime expansion in the annals of American business cycles, lasted fifty months (March 1933 to May 1937), but stopped far short of full employment and was marred by rapidly rising wages and prices. The unusual phenomenon of sharply rising wages and prices in the midst of still heavy unemployment[13] was largely the result of two sets of government policies: First, there was the policy of President Roosevelt's New Deal of promoting business and labor monopolies. (The active promotion of business monopolies was later declared unconstitutional and was discontinued; but the enormous strengthening of labor unions was a permanent change.) Second, in 1933–1934 the dollar was devalued vis-à-vis gold and the gold price pushed up by gold purchases in the market for the explicit purpose of raising the general price level. In 1934 the dollar was restabilized at $35 per ounce of gold compared with the earlier par of $20.67 per ounce—a devaluation by about 40 percent. The devaluation of the dollar put heavy deflationary pressure on the gold bloc countries—France, Switzerland, Belgium, the Netherlands, and Poland. (In addition, to help American silver producers in six western states, the price of silver was sharply raised by purchases in the market, thereby spreading depression to China and Mexico, the two countries still on the silver standard.)

The alarming rise in prices induced the American authorities to step hard on the monetary brake. The consequence was a short but precipitous depression: starting from a still depressed position, money GNP fell by 12 percent, industrial production by 32 percent, and unemployment rose from 11 percent to 20 percent in the short span of thirteen months (May 1937 to June 1938). The upswing that followed lasted through the war, but full employment was not reached until after the United States entered the war in 1941.

Great Britain

The British economy, already depressed in the 1920s as a consequence of the overvaluation of the pound and undervaluation of the French franc, was hard hit by the American depression. After the crash of the Austrian Kredit-Anstalt in May 1931 and the German banking crisis a month later, the pressure on the pound became unbearable. The historic departure of the pound from gold occurred on September 21, 1931. Along with Great Britain, or soon after, many other countries broke the link with gold, specifically members of the British Commonwealth of Nations (excluding Canada whose currency took a middle course between the U.S. dollar and the pound) and British dependencies, as well as Egypt, the Scandinavian countries, and Portugal. These countries formed the nucleus of the sterling area, a changing group of countries that stabilized their currencies in terms of sterling. In addition, there were several other countries, including Japan and Argentina, which for many years kept their official exchange rate fixed in sterling, without being formal members of the sterling bloc.

If a death certificate for the gold standard is required, September 21, 1931 would be a reasonable date to put on it. Actually a number of countries had abandoned the gold standard before September 1931, either by depreciation (Australia,[14] Argentina, Brazil, Chile, New Zealand among them), or by imposing tight exchange controls, which is analytically equivalent to a disguised, wasteful, and disorderly depreciation (Austria and Germany among others), or by floating alone.

In addition to letting the pound float down, in 1932 Great Britain reversed completely and definitively its traditional free trade policy and imposed a high tariff. The devaluation of the pound put heavy deflationary pressure on Germany, France, the United States and other countries and the policy of high protection greatly contributed to the disintegration of the world economy. But the two measures served their purpose of stimulating the British economy, although at least as far as the tariff was concerned the stimulation came in a beggar-thy-neighbor fashion. Thus, in Great Britain the trough of the depression occurred in 1932, a year earlier than in the United States. The ensuing cyclical upswing merged into the rearmament and war boom, but the U.S. depression of 1937–1938 caused a short relapse, although much milder than the relapse in the United States.

Germany

The depression in Germany was very severe, of at least the same order of magnitude as that in the United States.[15] It started and ended earlier than in the United States (April 1929 to August 1932).

Unlike the American depression, the German depression was dominated by international developments, especially by reparations and capital flows. As mentioned earlier, many experts have argued that reparations and the closely related problem of the Allied war debts due the United States played a major role in bringing about the world depression. I doubt that these were a major factor in the *world economy*. (To this question I shall return later.) But that the reparations and the sharp fluctuations in international capital flows had a strong impact on the business cycle *in Germany* cannot be doubted. The sharp decline in American capital exports to Germany after 1928—and later the reversal of the capital flows through withdrawals of foreign credit, especially by France,[16] and capital flight from Germany—were unquestionably very powerful depressing factors. Whether the *early onset* of the depression in 1929 can be attributed to the decline in American capital exports and whether the latter was due to the American stock market boom's pulling capital away from other uses (as some economists have asserted) are questionable. But whatever the first trigger of the German depression, it cannot be doubted that it was tremendously intensified later by the outflow of capital, the devaluation of the pound, and the Smoot-Hawley tariff.

The lower turning point came in August 1932 and the ensuing upswing carried without interruption into the armament and war boom. The mark was not formally devalued, but increasingly tight exchange control, a complicated system of import restrictions, export subsidies, bilateral clearing arrangements, and so on, insulated the German economy from outside shocks. Thus the German expansion, unlike the British, French, and others was *not* interrupted by the American depression of 1937–1938. Exchange control, which became notorious as the Schachtian system, was equivalent to a disguised, discriminatory, and exploitative devaluation of the mark. It was a messy and inefficient system, but it served its purpose of permitting rapid expansion while keeping the facade of an unchanged international value of the mark. That this line of policy was, so to speak, in the air and in the spirit of the times is shown by the fact that in 1931 Keynes had proposed an essentially similar system of import duties and export subsidies as an alternative to the devaluation of the pound.[17]

It is interesting to compare the American recovery after 1933 with the German. Roosevelt and Hitler came to power at about the same time and both found a sadly depressed economy.[18] The American expansion after 1933, although long and pronounced, was marred as we have seen by unusual price rises in the midst of still high unemployment. These price rises, by inducing a policy of monetary restraint, led to the sharp interruption of the upswing by the severe depressions of 1937–1938; moreover, the U.S. economy failed to reach full employment before the American involvement in the war. The German recovery, on the other hand, proceeded without interruption and reached substantially full employment within two or three years. Even more important, the price level in Germany, unlike that in the United States, remained remarkably stable for several years.

It would be tempting to attribute the rapid German recovery to massive expenditures on armament. Heavy public spending there was indeed, but massive rearmament came only later. Possibly German public spending was comparatively larger than the American, but this would not explain the different price performances. The main difference between the American and German recovery policies lies elsewhere: The New Deal combined spending with deliberate price and wage boosting. As a consequence, an exceptionally large part of the rising nominal GNP in the United States took the form of higher prices rather than larger output and employment. In Germany, in contrast, money wage rates remained fairly stable, although the average annual earnings of labor rose rapidly in monetary and real terms along with the rising output and employment, because unemployment disappeared and the workweek lengthened.[19]

Japan

As mentioned above, in Japan the gold standard was restored at the prewar parity as late as January 1930. Although wages and prices were much more flexible in Japan than in the United States or Great Britain, the overvaluation of the yen, accentuated by the rapidly worsening world slump, could not be absorbed without a depression. Less than two years later, in December 1931, the yen was again cut loose from gold and was allowed to depreciate by 40 percent vis-à-vis the depreciated pound. In 1933 the yen was pegged to the pound and Japan became for some time a de facto member of the sterling bloc. The Japanese economy responded quickly to the double stimulus of devaluation and sharply increased expenditures for the conquest of Manchuria and the war in China. Thus the country was launched upon a highly inflationary, imperialistic war boom.[20]

France

The French economy, like the German but unlike the American, was dominated by international developments. Thanks to the undervaluation of the franc, prosperity lasted longer in France than in the United States, Germany and most of the other countries. But in the second quarter of 1930 depressive forces from abroad took hold. As in many other countries there was a revival in 1932 but the upswing was not vigorous and lasted only a year. The advantage of the undervalued franc was whittled away by the depreciation of the pound and of the many currencies that followed the pound. During the World Economic Conference in London early in 1933, the so-called gold bloc constituted itself under the leadership of France; the other original members were Switzerland, Belgium, Italy and the Netherlands. Poland, too, clung to the gold standard but its association with the gold bloc was informal and intermittent. These countries tenaciously held the gold parity of their currencies and defended it by deflation and increasingly severe import restrictions, largely in the form of import quotas. But Italy, in preparation for the Ethiopian conquest (1935), drifted away in the direction of the German system of full-fledged exchange control.[21]

The devaluation of the dollar in 1933–1934 put France under strong deflationary pressure and plunged it again into depression (July 1933 to April 1935). The French franc and the other gold bloc currencies became badly overvalued.

In March 1935 Belgium gave up the struggle and devalued the belga by about 28 percent. This devaluation was a great success. The high rate of 28 percent was deliberately chosen to leave a margin for expansion. The Belgian economy responded quickly, expanding so fast that the first twelve months after the devaluation witnessed a sharp rise in the import surplus because of the increased demand for foreign raw materials.[22] But the Belgian devaluation put pressure on the currencies of the remaining members of the gold bloc.

Despite the precarious state of its balance of payments France managed through internal expansionary measures to engineer a cyclical revival in 1935. However, the "reflation on gold" required ever tighter import restrictions.

In May 1936 a Popular Front government under the premiership of Léon Blum came to power. It instituted social and economic reforms modeled after the U.S. New Deal (the forty-hour week, collective bargaining, public works, price support for agricultural products, nationalization of the armament industry, and so on). These measures did not inspire confidence. The government tried to stem the ensuing capital flight by control measures, but having been elected on an anti-devaluation platform, resisted the rising calls for devaluation coming from different sides, including conservative economists and politicians (for example, Charles Rist and Paul Reynaud). The Banque de France lost gold at an alarming rate.

One reason why the Blum government refused for so long to bow to the inevitable was that the United States and Great Britain were negotiating secretly to work out a common position. In fact the French wanted to restore the international gold standard as part of the currency realignment. This was impossible, but the so-called Tripartite Monetary Agreement, revealed on September 25, 1936, in simultaneous statements from Washington, Paris and London was a substitute face-saver for the Blum government to announce its intention to devalue the franc. The three-power agreement was hailed by Secretary of the Treasury Henry Morgenthau as "a new kind of gold standard." It became quite famous and is even now often referred to as a forerunner of later, more comprehensive schemes of monetary cooperation. Actually it was a rather vague declaration of good intentions of the governments to "continue the policy which they have pursued in the course of recent years, one constant object of which is to maintain the greatest possible equilibrium in the system of international exchange, and to avoid to the utmost extent the creation of any disturbance of that system by British monetary action" and so on, and so on.[23] The agreement did not fix exchange rates or pledge mutual pegging. Actually there was some mutual support, although subject to a famous "24-hours" clause. Britain and the United States accepted the French devaluation. Exchange rate fluctuations did not stop, but they became milder. I shall return to this development below.

The French franc was devalued on October 1, 1936, with its limits being set at 25.2 percent and 34.4 percent below the former parity. However, unlike what happened after the Poincaré stabilization in 1926–1928 (and after the de Gaulle devaluation in 1958), confidence in the Blum franc was not restored and the franc depreciated further until it was virtually pegged to sterling in May 1938.

The French devaluation was quickly followed by the devaluation of the other two remaining gold bloc currencies, the Swiss franc, and the Dutch guilder. Despite an earlier pledge by Mussolini to defend the lira at all costs (he had ordered his words to be graven in stone) the lira was depreciated by 40 percent on October 5, 1936— "not devaluation but equalization" was the official phrase used.[24] Among other currencies whose parities were adjusted were the Polish, Greek, Turkish, and Latvian—the last three joining the sterling bloc by pegging to the pound.

To finish the French story, it may be noted that prices rose very rapidly after the devaluation, partly because of the rising cost of imports as a result of the devaluation, but also because of increasing internal costs from the increased labor costs, which in turn were caused by social reform measures introduced by the French New Deal.[25]

Partly as a reaction to the sharp price rises and partly as a consequence of the American depression of 1937–1938, the French economy again moved into recession in June 1937. However, a change in the tenor of French economic policy (still under the Blum administration) in favor of business and the rapidly rising outlays on armament brought the recession to an end in August 1938.

The International Monetary Order

In the light of what has been said about developments in some important countries—what were the effects of the Great Depression on the international monetary order as a whole? They were profound and lasting. The departure from gold of the oldest and most prestigious gold currency—sterling—was a mortal blow from which the gold standard has never recovered. Gold still plays a role, but the monetary mystique of gold is largely gone and there is no chance that a real gold standard will be restored. Another lasting effect of the historic British decision of September 21, 1931, was the creation of a separate currency bloc. Over the years the sterling area has changed its composition, its scope, and its operating rules. But the idea of a group of countries forming a monetary bloc with fixed exchange rates among the members but a floating (or at any rate potentially changeable) exchange rate against the outside world is still alive.[26]

The sanctity of fixed exchange rates was a casualty of the Great Depression. It is true that there had been many exchange-rate changes in the nineteenth century and earlier. But the devaluation of the leading currencies of the world—the pound, the dollar, the Swiss franc and the Dutch guilder—made the operation "salonfähig," that it, fit for gentlemen. The basic reasons for frequent parity changes have been (a) that economists, policy makers, and the public at large have become cycle-conscious and have come to expect the authorities to intervene to counteract cyclical swings, especially to cure or prevent depressions and (b) that wages have become very rigid, which rules out deflation (reduction in the price level) or at any rate makes it an extremely costly operation.[27] The Great Depression brought this home to everybody. Everywhere, when a conflict arises, internal policy objective—full employment, growth, and price stability in some combination—take precedence over the external policy objectives—balance-of-payments equilibrium at fixed parities.[28] In a world of independent sovereign states, conflicts between internal and external policy objectives of different countries are bound to arise. These conflicts are incompatible with permanently fixed exchange rates.

I shall return to this problem in the next section. Here I wish to show how the concrete manner in which exchange-rate changes were effected during the fateful years of the Great Depression compromised the idea of flexible exchange rates for some time to come.

The method used was essentially what now is called in official language the "par value" system and colloquially called the method of "the adjustable peg," that is, large discrete changes of one or a few currencies at a time combined with pegged rates in between. The depreciation of the pound came in 1931, of the dollar in 1933–1934, of the gold bloc currencies in 1936, to mention the most important cases. In between the big changes, there was some movement of exchange rates, but very little free floating. Most of the devaluations were forced by acute balance-of-payments pressures intensified by massive speculation and could be justified as necessary conditions for domestic expansion and relaxation of import restrictions.[29] But each of these devaluations put deflationary pressure on all the other countries that maintained their gold parities, pushing them deeper into depression, import restrictions, and exchange control. This vicious sequence became known as "competitive depreciation" or "exchange dumping." As we shall see in the following section, it was, and often still is, attributed to floating, but in reality it was the consequence of overly rigid exchange rates—in other words, of the refusal to make adjustments until the situation became critical.

When, after the devaluation of the gold bloc currencies and the conclusion of the Tripartite Agreement, exchange rates settled down in a sort of semi-permanent pattern, the relationships between the principal free currencies were not greatly different from what they had been in 1930. To give only a few examples, the exchange value of the pound was $4.86 until September 21, 1931. After suspension of gold convertibility it fell to $3.21 (December 1932), after the devaluation of the dollar it rose to $5.06 (July 1934), and by December 1936 it was back at $4.90. The value of the Swiss franc was about $0.19 from 1913 until March 1933. The devaluation of the dollar pushed it to $0.32 (1934 and 1935). After the devaluation of the gold bloc currencies it was again close to its original parity ($0.22). The French franc was $0.039 from the time of its stabilization in 1926 until the dollar devaluation. It rose to $0.066 when the dollar was devalued in 1933–1934. In December 1936 it was down to $0.046 and drifted lower to about $0.026 when it was effectively pegged to the pound in 1938. Naturally, tightly controlled currencies, such as the German mark, nominally kept their original gold parity. The value of the mark was about $0.237 until 1933 (the same as it had been in 1913) and rose to $0.402 after the devaluation of the dollar in 1933–1934, where it remained until the outbreak of the war.[30]

What had been achieved by the long series of devaluations? The relative changes in exchange rates were not very large, at least so far as the major currencies were concerned. Moreover, there was no assurance that the new pattern of rates was in any sense closer to a hypothetical equilibrium situation. The outstanding "achievement"—if it deserves that appellation—was the great increase in international liquidity. The ratio of reserves to the value of world trade had risen dramatically as a consequence of four factors—first, the depreciation of all national currencies in terms of gold[31]; second, the sharp decline of prices in terms of national currencies (deflation), implying an even sharper decrease of prices in terms of gold; third, the sharp rise in gold production[32]; and fourth, the catastrophic contraction in the volume of world trade (in constant prices) and even more so in the value of world trade (in current prices).[34]

The increase in liquidity did not go unnoticed.[34] In the middle 1930s there was much concern that the plethora of gold, due to the greatly enhanced purchasing power of the existing stock and the sharply increased production (induced by the high price of gold), had gone too far and would lead to inflation. There were rumors that the U.S. Treasury was planning to reduce the gold price. This produced a wave of dishoarding of privately held gold.[35] The American depression of 1937–1938, the armament boom and the rumblings of the rapidly approaching war diverted attention from the gold problem.

In summary, the method that was used to remedy the alleged deficiency of gold reserves and to bring about a comparatively small parity realignment was perverse in the extreme. If I may use an analogy I have used before, it was like cutting the tail of a dog piece by piece instead of all at once. "All at once" would have meant doubling or tripling the price of gold, as might have been done if the International Monetary Fund had been in existence.[36] But there simply was no mechanism available to perform that operation.[37]

Given the American depression and given the impossibility of an across-the board change in gold parities, the best method of currency realignment would have been extensive floating. If in September 1931 Germany and the gold bloc countries, following the British example, had depreciated their currencies against the dollar and started expansionary policies, they all could have cut short the deflationary spiral in their countries, just as the devaluation of the pound cut short the deflationary spiral for the sterling bloc. This would, of course, have intensified the U.S. depression, but it might have induced the United States to take expansionary measures.[38] However, the discussion of what might have been—"counter-factual" arguments, as the economic historians say—implies explanations on the basis of a theory. It therefore belongs to the following section.

2. Some Explanations

In this section, with the benefit of hindsight, I venture upon a somewhat more systematic discussion of the various explanations of the Great Depression and the breakdown of the gold standard put forward at the time and later. "Explaining" a world-shaking event such as a world depression raises, of course, many portentous and intricate questions, not only of an economic but also of a social, methodological and philosophical nature. However in a short paper such as this I have to confine myself to the technical-economic aspects of the question, except for some remarks on the broader issues at the end.

Maladjustments and the Depression

It was a view widely held in the 1930s and voiced occasionally later, that deep-seated maladjustments and distortions, caused either by the war or by faulty policies or of earlier origin, together with the increasing rigidity and lessened adjustability of the economic system, were largely responsible for the exceptional severity and length of the depression.

The war had caused great changes in the economic structure inside each country as well as in international trade flows. Two well-balanced economic units, the Austro-Hungarian monarchy and Czarist Russia, had been broken up and replaced by several independent countries. New sources of supply had been developed and numerous industries, such as shipbuilding and munitions, had been expanded far beyond normal requirements. No wonder that the resulting economic structure did not fit the peacetime requirements and that there were overdeveloped industries and depressed areas. These dislocations and strains were for several years papered over by inflation and capital exports from the United States. The growing rigidity of the economy prevented speedy adjustment and the maladjustments piled up until the bubble burst in the Great Depression.

Although this short summary of what they believed does not do full justice to all of those who held such views, it was essentially the explanation given, for example, in the majority report of the Gold Delegation of the Financial Committee of the League of Nations, a group of highly respected financial and economic experts who labored from the summer of 1929 until 1932 to study the working of the international monetary system.[39] There was, however, a Memorandum of Dissent by a minority, of which Gustav Cassel was perhaps the most prominent member. The minority rejected "the view that the sharp fall in the level of commodity prices and the consequent breakdown of the international gold standard are primarily due to the various economic maladjustmens enumerated by our colleagues."[40]

The minority's explanation stressed monetary factors and reparations and war debts (to which I shall come presently). It pointed out that up to 1929 the world enjoyed a remarkable progress, despite maladjustments. The supply of monetary gold was sufficient until about 1928. Then a "maldistribution of gold" developed— that is to say, there was a high concentration of gold in France and later in the United States. This was the consequence of the undervaluation of the French franc, the overvaluation of the pound, the cessation of U.S. capital exports, and the U.S. depression—all monetary phenomena. Gustav Cassel's remarks in the Memorandum of Dissent are especially striking: "What we have to explain is essentially a monetary phenomenon and the explanation must therefore essentially be of a monetary character. An enumeration of a series of economic disturbances and maladjustments which existed before 1929 is no explanation of the breakdown of the gold standard."[41]

The allegedly crucial importance of "maladjustments" was the theme of two very influential studies. In 1944 the Royal Institute of International Affairs in London published a report of a study group on postwar economic problems. The report, which reviewed the economic lessons of the 1930s, was drafted by H. W. Arndt. It reached the conclusion that

> the root cause of the failure and final breakdown of the gold standard system was the combination of two factors, the large maladjustments in the balances of payments and productive structure of most countries and the world economy as a whole which the war had left behind, and rigidities in the economic systems of all countries which made the correction of these maladjustments by market forces alone impossible ... [Of the enumerated maladjustments] only the German reparations problem can be entirely attributed to the war. .... The others were the result of accumulated failures of adjustment to long-term economic changes. The war merely hastened these changes and for five years and more prevented the forces from working which might otherwise have made for adjustment.[42]

In 1954, the United Nations published a massive volume by Ingvar Svennilson entitled *Growth and Stagnation in the European Economy*.[43] Eric Lundberg summarized Svennilson's results as follows:

The interwar stagnation tendencies in European countries have been persuasively related to the economic disorganization, dislocation, and postponed adaptation to fundamental changes caused by the First World War and the consequent peace settlements. Although Svennilson admits that an insufficient level of aggregate demand may be part of the reason for the slow recovery after the First World War, he puts the weight of his argument on the faulty and sticky distribution of resources in relation to the changed distribution of actual and potential demand at home and abroad, which resulted in overcapacity problems in a number of traditional European key industries, in particular, coal mining, steel, shipbuilding, and cotton textiles.[44]

Post World War II experience is completely at variance with the maladjustment explanation of the Great Depression. Surely, destructions, maladjustments, and dislocations were much greater after the Second than after the First World War. But they did not cause a severe depression—only mild recessions and inflation. True, there were no reparations after World War II of a comparable magnitude and duration to those after World War I, and there was the Marshall Plan. However, American aid hardly provided full compensation for the enormous destruction caused by the Second World War.

Another type of maladjustment explanation of the Great Depression must be briefly mentioned, namely, the so-called neo-Austrian theory of the business cycle and depression as developed primarily by F.A. von Hayek and adopted, among others, by Lionel Robbins.[45]

According to Hayek and Robbins, every depression is the inevitable consequence of the maladjustments in the "vertical" structure of production created by the preceding inflationary boom. Inflation distorts the interest rate, depressing it below the equilibrium level. This leads to excessive investment—that is, to an overexpansion of "the higher stages of production" and to "forced saving," involving an unsustainable shift of original factors of production (labor) to the capital goods industries. The boom can be prolonged by larger and larger inflationary injections, but the longer it lasts, the greater the maladjustment and more painful the unavoidable correction.[46]

A major difficulty in the application of this theory to the Great Depression is that in the United States wholesale and consumer prices remained virtually stable from 1921 to 1929. Hayek and Robbins faced this problem squarely. Robbins puts it as follows:

A stationary price-level shows an absence of inflation only when production is stationary. When productivity is increasing, then, in the absence of inflation, we should expect prices to fall. Now the period we are examining was a period of rapidly increasing productivity. The comparative stability of prices, therefore, so far from being a proof of the absence of inflation, is a proof of its presence.[47]

Expressed differently the theory asserts that absence of inflation ought to be defined not as a period of constant prices, but as a period of constant money income.[48] The implication is that equilibrium would have been preserved and that there would have been no business cycle and no depression if there had been no inflation in that sense, that is, if money national income had remained constant and prices had been allowed to decline.

It is difficult, however, to believe that with stable prices from 1921 to 1929, very large real maladjustments could have developed which would have necessitated a massive reshuffling of real resources between capital goods and consumer goods industries ("higher and lower stages of production") that would be capable of explaining the extraordinary depth and length of the depression.[49]

Why is it that the transition from a war to a peace economy after the First and after the Second World War could be achieved without a major depression, despite the fact that both wars, especially the Second, had left behind very large real maladjustments which required a large reshuffling of real resources (labor and equipment)? This question has never been squarely faced, let alone answered by the proponents of the maladjustment explanation.[50]

Robbins later abandoned the maladjustment theory of the depression. He did not exclude that "inappropriate investments fostered by wrong expectations" and by the stock exchange boom may have triggered the downturn. But these real maladjustments, whatever their nature, "were completely swamped by vast deflationary forces."[51] What he evidently had in mind were the destruction of money and the wave of hoarding (sharp increase in liquidity preference, implying a sharp reduction in the velocity of money) on the national and international level, caused by runs on the banks, the collapse of the banking systems in the United States and in central Europe, competitive depreciation, and the termination of the gold exchange standard. These monetary developments were not essential features of the business cycle but must be attributed to institutional weaknesses and policy mistakes of commission and omission—primarily mistakes that were committed after the depression had started.

I have already mentioned that Albert Hahn and Wilhelm Röpke had stressed maladjustments caused by inflationary booms as the reason why a smooth transition to a noninflationary equilibrium position—"growth path" we would call it today— is impossible. But as the depression deepened, they came to distinguish sharply between what Röpke called the "primary depression," resulting from the maladjustments, and what they called "the secondary deflation." By "secondary deflation" they meant the above-mentioned monetary complications and repercussions which Robbins had in mind when he spoke of the "vast deflationary forces" which "completely swamped" the real maladjustments that may have caused the downturn.[52]

Still another explanation of the Great Depression is the *secular stagnation* hypothesis. Few would defend it now in the light of postwar developments, but it should be mentioned, because it was very popular in Keynesian circles in the 1930s and 1940s and because it strongly influenced the planning and execution of postwar economic policies. Alvin Hansen was the most prominent representative of the school.

According to this theory modern capitalism has a chronic tendency toward oversaving and deflation, because investment opportunities tend to become inadequate to absorb the forthcoming savings. This inadequacy is, in turn, basically due to slower population growth and the alleged fact that for various reasons there are fewer and fewer capital-absorbing inventions and discoveries, such as the railroads in the nineteenth century and the automobile in the twentieth. The theory can be and has been elaborated in many different ways. Suffice it to say that post-World War II developments have been in total conflict with the predictions of the stagnation theory. The postwar period was one of inflation and not deflation, of heavy investment and capital scarcity and not capital glut, of prosperity and not stagnation. If in 1975 we were heading for a serious depression, as many said we were, the scenario would have been quite different from what the stagnation theory would postulate. But this is outside the scope of the present paper.

Reparations and War Debts

Before taking up the monetary factors. I now discuss the problem of reparations and the closely related problem of war debts. Reparations profoundly influenced German policies and dominated German discussions of the depression.

There is no doubt that from the political viewpoint the decision of the European victors of World War I to collect huge reparations from Germany was a first-class disaster. It led to sharp conflicts between Germany and France, poisoned the political atmosphere throughout the whole period, and greatly contributed to the rise of Nazism. The conflict over reparations which culminated in the occupation of the Ruhr by France and Belgium in January 1923 enormously intensified the ongoing inflation. The political consequences of the German hyperinflation were grave and prolonged, although the economic dislocations were surprisingly short-lived.[53] The early demands for reparations were fantastically high and open-ended. Even in the Dawes plan(1924), the number of annuities was not limited. Not until the Young plan(1930) were the reparations claims finally reduced to a definite number of annuities of tolerable magnitude. But by that time the depression was in full swing. This changed the picture completely. With fixed exchange rates and increasingly protectionist policies in the recipient countries and elsewhere, the transfer of reparations would have become very painful if not virtually impossible. At any rate, under such circumstances, when productive resources were allowed to go to waste in idleness and countries everywhere were restricting imports to protect jobs, it made no economic sense whatsoever to insist on the transfer of real resources from abroad as reparations.

There was even a direct connection between the German policy of deflation and the unemployment which it created, on the one hand, and reparations, on the other. Chancellor Heinrich Bruening thought that his deflationary policy would "offer the chance ... to pay the reparations ... by means of an export surplus and thereby to tear apart ('auseinanderzubrechen') the structure of the whole world market." He "estimated that in twelve to fourteen months his policy would call forth a cry in the world for cancellation of the reparations."[54] The memoirs of Hans Luther, then president of the Reichsbank (Central Bank), tell a similar story.[55] He reports that in 1931 when the pound was allowed to float, not only "prominent scholars" but also the Bank for International Settlements (BIS) in Basel "strongly urged" that the mark should be attached to the pound. He admits that this would have enabled Germany to reduce unemployment by implementing the "Lautenbach plan" of deficit spending and credit expansion. He is fully aware that the British devaluation had a most unfavorable effect on the German economy and its balance of payments. But he insists that all this does not "dispose of Brüning's argument [against devaluation] based on the necessity to get rid of reparations."[56]

We can say, then, that given the severe depression in the United States and in the world at large, the protectionist consequences of that depression, and Germany's unwillingness or political inability to depreciate the mark, the reparations greatly intensified the German depression. This was fully recognized by many economic experts in the West and found its expression in the minority report of the Gold Delegation.[57] But Gustav Cassel in his Memorandum of Dissent surely (and probably intentionally) exaggerated when he said: "The fundamental cause [of the final breakdown of the gold standard after 1928] was the claim of reparations and war debts, combined with the unwillingness of the receiving countries to receive payment in the natural form of goods and services."[58]

However, from what has been said about the deflationary consequences of reparations for Germany, it does not follow that the reparations had much influence on the depression in America or in the world at large. The German depression surely had a strong, unfavorable impact on the surrounding European countries, but the U.S. depression was substantially homemade and in the world economy Germany was not a dominating factor.

What is true of reparations is even more true of the war debts of the European allies to the United States. There is no question that they caused much passion and political friction, partly because they were linked with the reparations. But their magnitude was quite small compared with the volume of trade or GNP of the debtor countries and, needless to say, the annual war debt claims were a small fraction of the U.S. federal budget, let alone of GNP. The great psychological and political impact of the war debts was out of all proportion to their economic weight.

Whether the reparation payments as finally laid down in the Young plan would have been a serious *economic* problem, if the world depression and the consequent protectionist explosion had been avoided, is another question. The magnitude of reparations compared with Germany's GNP and volume of trade was much greater than that of the interallied war debt. The average annual annuity under the Young plan was about 2 percent of the pre-depression German GNP. This was not an intolerable burden, as can be seen by comparing reparations with armament expenditures: by 1935 the latter had already risen to a level more than twice as high as the reparations.[59]

What about the transfer problem? The average annual reparations payments under the Young plan amounted to a little over 10 percent of German exports (or imports) of goods and services in 1929.[60] That means that a rise in exports of, say, 6 percent plus a decline in imports of 6 percent spread over a few years would have taken ample care of the transfer. In the absence of a depression and the resulting wave of protection, this would not have been difficult to accomplish.

It is a fact, however, that a large part of the enormous literature of the 1920s and 1930s on the subject was very pessimistic about the feasibility of the transfer.[61] The theory of the perpetual dollar shortage and "elasticity pessimism" of the 1940s and 1950s—of which Thomas Balogh, Geoffrey Crowther, Charles P. Kindleberger, and Donald MacDougall were the most prominent protagonists—was the direct descendant of the transfer pessimism of the interwar period. It is fair to say that this theory has been completely disproved and discredited by events and theoretical analyses. In the light of these developments there can be hardly a doubt that the transfer of the reparations as fixed by the Young plan would have been possible—in the absence, to repeat, of a serious depression and depression-induced protectionism. But let me emphasize that this optimistic economic appraisal does not change the judgment that, from the political standpoint, reparations were an unmitigated disaster and certainly would have been so, even if the world depression had not changed the picture completely.[62]

The Monetary Factor

One need not be an extreme monetarist to recognize the enormous importance of monetary disturbances and shocks—the weakness and collapse of monetary institutions and the mistakes of commission and omission in monetary policy on the national and international level—in making the depression so long, deep and destructive as it was.

Take first the case of the United States. There may have been some real maladjustments, and the unavoidable crash of the stock market surely had serious repercussions, so that a recession more serious than those of 1923–1924 and

1926–1927 was to be expected. But there can be no doubt that the collapse of the banking system, the bankruptcy of many thousand banks, and the inept and overly timid monetary policy which permitted the money stock to shrink by about one-third was to a large extent responsible for the disaster. The depression would not have been nearly so severe, if there had existed then, as there exists now effective insurance of bank deposits to prevent runs on the banks,[63] or if the United States had not had the archaic unit-banking system but an efficient branch-banking system like the Canadian and British (on July 29, 1929 there were over 25,000 independent banks, a number that fell to 15,000 four years later), or if the Federal Reserve Board at an early stage had taken vigorous action by large open-market operations to stop the deflation and to prevent the collapse of the banking system.[64]

Surely a catastrophic contraction of the money supply and a breakdown of the banking system were not the unavoidable consequence of real maladjustments or of insufficient investment opportunities or of oversaving or of the interaction of multiplier and accelerator.[65] These events were not an essential part of the ordinary business cycle, but rather the consequence of institutional defects and horrendous policy mistakes. They had nothing to do with basic weaknesses and contradictions of the modern capitalist, free enterprise economy. In country after country, whenever the monetary deflation was stopped, whether by orthodox or unorthodox measures, the alleged real structural contradictions and maladjustments, lack of investment opportunities, chronic oversaving, and so on, disappeared as fast as they seemed to have appeared a few years earlier.

But I am running ahead of the story. We must now turn to money in the international economy. Given the great weight of the United States in the world economy, under a regime of fixed exchange rates the American depression was bound to spread to the four corners of the world. We have mentioned already that other American policies in the international area—the Smoot-Hawley skyscraper tariff in 1930, the gold and silver purchases in 1933–1934—intensified the international impact of the depression.

To repeat, there existed other focal points of deflation and depression in the world. The overvaluation of the pound and the undervaluation of the French franc kept the British economy in a semi-depressed position. Some influential economists, among them, Jacques Rueff, Robert Triffin and their followers, have put much of the blame for the depression on the gold exchange standard. No doubt the liquidation of the gold exchange standard—that is to say, the withdrawal of gold from London and New York by official holders of sterling and dollar balances, mainly by France—added to the deflationary pressure. But there can be no doubt about the overwhelming importance of the American depression which was, to repeat, almost entirely homegrown. The liquidation of the gold exchange standard was quantitatively altogether much less important than the repercussions of the U.S. depression.

The overwhelming importance of the monetary factor is underlined by the fact that countries that applied expansionary measures under the cover of open or disguised devaluation or of floating managed to extricate themselves from the maelstrom of deflation one or two years ahead of the United States. Britain and the sterling bloc including the Scandinavian countries and Japan belonged to that group, as did Germany, where expansion started in 1932 under the cover of tight controls ("aussenwirtschaftliche Absicherung" as the modern phrase goes, although it is today used with reference to floating rather than to exchange control and import restriction). Countries that later restabilized their exchange rate de facto or de jure in terms of gold, such as Great Britain, were forced to share the U.S. depression of 1937–1938. It should be observed that expansion ahead of the United States was possible despite the continued existence of the Smoot-Hawley tariff in the United States,[66] which further underscores the paramount importance of the monetary factor.

There has been general agreement that competitive depreciation of currencies greatly contributed to the world depression. This agreement found its expression in the Articles of Agreement of the International Monetary Fund (IMF). Article I lists as one of the fund's main purposes "to avoid competitive exchange depreciation." But the IMF charter does not define the term. It is indeed an imprecise term and there has been much confusion about its meaning and its causes. Competitive depreciation has been and often still is attributed to floating. Thus in recent years when floating became widespread, fears were voiced that it might again lead to competitive depreciation as in the 1930s. Some regard the mere existence of exchange-rate changes in the 1930s as evidence of competitive depreciation. This completely confuses the problem. Not every devaluation was of the competitive kind. A devaluation which merely restores equilibrium or "clean," unmanaged floating (as distinguished from "dirty," mismanaged floating) has nothing to do with competitive devaluation. Given the U.S. depression, fixed exchange rates were not only impossible but most undesirable. Fixed rates would have meant that no country could have extricated itself from the deflationary spiral before the United States did; all countries would have had to wait until, at long last, the American slump came to an end.

A reasonable definition of competitive depreciation—also called exchange dumping, a species of beggar-thy-neighbor policies—would be this: a deliberate undervaluation of a currency (either actively pushing it down, or keeping it down if it has temporarily been pushed down by capital flight or speculation),[67] in order to develop an export surplus and/or to promote a capital inflow, and thereby to stimulate the economy at the expense of other countries that would have to accept a deterioration of their foreign balance and its depressive consequences.[68]

At the time when currencies were depreciated or stabilized it was often not possible to know whether the change would usher in a period of "unneighborly exchange dumping" or restore equilibrium. *Ex post* it was clear that the French franc after 1926 was undervalued. But it is difficult to criticize the French policy of accepting the rate existing in the market at the time of stabilization. This point illustrates the dilemma in the method of the adjustable peg—a dilemma which was only imperfectly realized in the 1930s: nobody can be quite sure beforehand what the equilibrium rate will be. Hence in a decision to stabilize or to depreciate it is sensible to choose a rate that is likely to be too low rather than too high, because in the latter case one runs the risk of being forced to repeat the painful operation in the near future.

A good example of that mistake was the depreciation of the Czechoslovak crown in March 1935. The rate of devaluation (16 percent) was chosen on the basis of purchasing power parity calculations in terms of wholesale prices. It soon proved to be too low and the crown had to be devalued again in October 1936.[69]

A counterexample of a successful devaluation was that of the Belgian currency in 1935. As was mentioned earlier this devaluation was deliberately large (28 percent) to allow for a domestic expansion. But despite its large size, the depreciation did not produce an export surplus, because the ensuing expansion was so rapid that imports of raw materials rose rapidly. As far as the outside world as a whole was concerned, it was therefore not a beggar-thy-neighbor policy. But it put deflationary pressure on France and the other remaining members of the gold bloc by inducing speculative capital outflows from these countries and also by inducing sharper competition for their manufactured goods exports.[70]

The depreciation of the pound in September 1931 was a very different case. Great pressure on the balance of payments had built up before September. Thus the pound was driven down sharply after convertibility was suspended and was, as Nurkse said, "undoubtedly undervalued" for some time.[71] Unavoidably there was deflationary pressure on Germany, the gold bloc countries, and the United States, pressure which was intensified by the imposition of a high tariff in 1932. This was clearly a case of competitive devaluation.[72] However, as Nurkse points out, strong expansionary monetary measures, a bank rate reduction, and open market operations were taken almost immediately after the devaluation. The economy responded by expanding and the pressure on other countries gradually diminished.

The depreciation of the dollar in 1933–1934, which was not forced by an adverse balance of payments, comes close to the textbook case of competitive devaluation. The right policy would have been to concentrate on domestic expansion and, if balance-of-payments difficulties had developed (which in retrospect seems unlikely), to let the dollar find its own level.

As was mentioned earlier, in December 1931 the Japanese yen was depreciated by 40 percent vis-à-vis the depreciated pound. This surely was excessive and thus constituted competitive depreciation.

Given the fact of the depression, the basic trouble with the international monetary system was the complete lack of coordination of national policies of expansion. Nurkse puts it this way in his authoritative *International Currency Experience*: "What made the long succession of devaluations inevitable was the fact that monetary expansion was completely uncoordinated in time as well as in degree."[73] He was, however, much too optimistic when he continued: "If the leading industrial nations had initiated ... a simultaneous policy of monetary expansion in, say, the spring of 1931, they would probably have had little difficulty in keeping their mutual exchange rates stable." Post-World War II experience has shown again and again that in the modern environment, which is characterized by rigid wages and by the fact that domestic policy objectives of full employment, growth, and price stability (in different combinations in different countries) take precedence over stable exchange rates, the conditions needed for there to be sufficient policy coordination to obviate exchange rate changes are very exacting—so exacting indeed that they are unlikely to be generally fulfilled between sovereign countries. Coordination of monetary policy alone is not enough. Other phases of economic policy would have to be coordinated as well, and this is rarely possible without political unification.

Furthermore, what was not realized—even after the necessity of occasional exchange-rate changes had been generally accepted, as they were by Nurkse[74] and the framers of the Bretton Woods Charter—was that the method of the adjustable peg—or "jumping parities," meaning occasional large changes of parities—is bound to lead increasingly to disruptive speculation and anticipatory capital flows across national borders. The reason is that the adjustable peg loads the dice in favor of the speculators. A currency under pressure can only go down; it cannot go up. If the speculator against a weak currency is right and the currency is in fact devalued, the parity change is likely to be large (for the reason just explained) so that the speculator makes a large profit. If he was wrong and no depreciation occurs, he cannot lose much because a weak currency cannot go up. The case is different under floating. A floating currency can go up or down, which makes speculation much more hazardous.

Moreover, if the parity changes are made at shorter intervals—every two years or every year on the average instead of every five years or more—the destabilizing speculative flows are likely to become larger rather than smaller because people in general become more and more alert to the likelihood of further changes.

To eliminate the danger of destabilizing speculation it is necessary either to float or at least to make parity changes at very short intervals, as is done in the well-known case of the Brazilian "trotting peg."[75]

Competitive depreciation was not the consequence of freely fluctuating exchanges, but of excessive rigidity in rates and of the adjustable peg. In fact, as Nurkse pointed out,[76] there was very little free floating in the 1930s. In that respect the situation was very different from what it is now. It was very different in another respect as well: With the problem in the 1930s being deflation rather than inflation and with high unemployment, the temptation to engage in competitive depreciation was very strong. In view of this, it is indeed surprising that there was not more outright competitive depreciation in the 1930s. Today, under chronic inflation, the temptation to depreciate is much less because it is generally realized that depreciation increases inflationary pressures. In 1974–1975, rising unemployment may change the picture again, although the simultaneous threat of more inflation is still very real. But our present troubles are not the subject of this paper.

3. Concluding Remarks

The Great Depression was truly a world-shaking event. Its political repercussions were enormous. Without the misery of mass unemployment, Hitler probably would not have come to power; or if he had, early economic successes would have been denied him, for he could not have provided butter and guns at the same time. Soviet Russia's apparent immunity to the depression greatly raised its standing and reputation in Western eyes and enhanced its economic weight: it was only during the depression years when domestic markets in the West were contracting that trade with the Soviet Union amounted to a sizeable proportion for some Western countries and industries. For example, from 1929 to 1931 German exports to Russia rose from 2.6 percent to 7.9 percent of total German exports.[77] In 1931, 55 percent of U.S. exports of machine tools went to Russia and in 1932, 81 percent of British and 74 percent of German exports of machine tools found a market in Russia.[78]

Economic policy was profoundly influenced by the trauma of the depression and that trauma imparted an inflationary bias to economic policies for years to come. The depression of the 1930s was widely misinterpreted as a normal cyclical downswing with dismal implications for the viability and stability of the capitalist system. Quite naturally, Marxists saw it as confirmation of the master's theory that, under capitalism, depressions would become increasingly severe until the system would collapse in a final big bang.[79] Many Keynesians, too, were led to believe, or confirmed in their view, that depressions are bound to become chronic and more serious unless counteracted by permanent deficit spending and measures to reduce the "excessive" propensity to save. This view greatly contributed to the inflationary bias of postwar economic policies.

In retrospect it should be clear that the Great Depression was not an ordinary cyclical downswing. Its extraordinary severity and length (using the word depression in the broad sense of the whole period from 1929 to 1939) was clearly due to what Schumpeter called "adventitious circumstances."[80] These adventitious circumstances were essentially of a monetary nature—the combination of weak monetary institutions and horrendous policy mistakes. That these flaws in monetary policies and institutions are not inherent in the modern free enterprise system has been confirmed by the fact that they were avoided after World War II. (I do not believe that our present difficulties—worldwide inflation and recession—are of the same order of magnitude. At any rate they are of a different nature.)

Let me repeat, one need not be an extreme monetarist to recognize the enormous importance of monetary factors. But this recognition does not imply that non-monetary factors should be ignored or minimized. First, it is possible to argue that in 1929 there may have existed some real maladjustments which would have caused a recession more serious than the earlier ones in the 1920s, even if the monetary mistakes ("secondary deflation") had been avoided. In other words, one should perhaps put a little more weight than the monetarists do on what Röpke called the "primary depression," although for reasons given earlier, I would find it entirely unrealistic to put equal weights on monetary and non-monetary factors.

Second, in my opinion, one should recognize the importance of the growing downward rigidity of wages. This rigidity is one reason why monetary deflation is a much greater threat to real stability in modern times than it was before 1914 when wages still had a certain downward flexibility.[81]

Third, deflation and depression had non-monetary consequences which greatly intensified the depression—such consequences as the protectionist explosion and social unrest.

Fourth and most important, emphasizing monetary policies and institutions does not preclude examining the non-monetary or even non-economic reasons why makers of monetary policy acted as they did and why monetary institutions were so vulnerable to collapse. All this offers virtually unlimited opportunities of putting forward more or less plausible non-monetary or even non-economic "explanations" of the Great Depression which are perfectly compatible with recognizing the crucial importance of monetary factors.[82]

Fifth, emphasizing the central importance of monetary factors in starting and propagating a depression is perfectly compatible with the view that once a depression has acquired momentum, monetary measures—that is, easy money—may not be sufficient to pull the economy out of the tailspin, or at any rate may be intolerably slow. Fiscal measures—that is, deficit spending—may be required, at least for quick recovery. For a depression is a cumulative, self-reinforcing process. As Friedman says: "there are such things as chain reactions and cumulative forces ... [An] economic collapse often has the characteristics of a cumulative process. Let it go beyond a certain point, and it will tend for a time to gain strength from its own development."[83] Or as a prominent British monetarist (of a somewhat different color), Ralph G. Hawtrey,[84] put it, in a serious depression a "credit deadlock" may well develop, a situation of deep pessimism and gloom, when even ultra-cheap money fails to revive economic activity except after a long delay. In such a situation a direct injection of money into the income stream through fiscal measures is indicated. This is not the place to go into details—for example, into the question whether the proper fiscal measures are tax cuts or expenditure increases. All I am trying to do here is to put the real meaning and implications of a monetary explanation of the depression into proper perspective.

Finally I return to the international monetary system. The lessons of the interwar period have been exhaustively studied and evaluated by private and government experts. The "official" conclusions were drawn at the conference in Bretton Woods, New Hampshire, and laid down in the Articles of Agreement of the International Monetary Fund.

The IMF has come in for a good deal of criticism in recent years. No doubt, the charter needs revision in some of its basic assumptions. The principal lesson that was learned from the Great Depression and that is enshrined in the Articles of Agreement is that exchange rates have to be changed from time to time, in an orderly fashion and by international agreement. The major misinterpretation of the lessons was blaming the competitive depreciations of the 1930s on flexible exchange rates rather than on excessive rigidity of those rates and on the defects of the method of the adjustable peg. As a consequence floating was ruled out. Actually, in many cases, the practice of the IMF was much more flexible than the principles of its charter. A problem that was largely ignored in the charter is the systematic provision of international reserves to keep pace with the growing needs of world trade. In practice the problem was "solved"—faultily and disastrously many would say—by the evolution of the system into a dollar standard.

But these problems go beyond the scope of the present paper. Suffice it to say that, for reasons that cannot be discussed here, the gaps and defects of the charter did not become clearly visible and disturbing immediately but only much later. However, there can be no doubt in my opinion that the agreement at Bretton Woods was a great achievement. To bring the world's leading experts, gathered in New Hampshire, to agree on a workable plan on many controversial subjects on which most of them had taken a by-no-means identical stand, was a feat unique in the history of international collaboration.

There can be no doubt, furthermore, that the influence of the International Monetary Fund has been highly beneficial. The IMF has greatly contributed to the phenomenal growth of world trade during the postwar period. True, the most important reason why trade has grown much faster in the postwar period than it did between the wars and earlier, and why the growth has not been interrupted by any of the numerous currency crises, was that all the major countries, including the United States, have managed to maintain substantially full employment and avoid severe depression.

Some credit for the satisfactory development of world trade since the war is due also to the General Agreement on Tariff and Trade (GATT) and the numerous trade agreements (the "Kennedy round," and so on) negotiated under the auspices of GATT by which tariff walls were substantially reduced. In the first postwar years, the IMF greatly contributed to freer trade by prodding countries gradually to eliminate exchange controls and import quotas on balance-of-payments grounds, thus restoring convertibility of currencies. This was not easy, for the depression- and war-induced restrictions were deeply entrenched. Many influential experts, especially in Great Britain (in and outside the bureaucracy), attached as they were to the idea of the permanent dollar shortage, resisted every move away from wartime regimentation of trade.[85] The most decisive step toward liberalization of trade and convertibility of currencies was the currency reform in Germany in 1948 and the simultaneous abolishment of all wage and price controls by Ludwig Erhard. The astounding and sustained success of this bold move made a tremendous and lasting impression everywhere. It demonstrated that "the classical medicine still worked" (to use Keynes's words).[86]

At the time of the writing (1975) many countries have again reached a crisis point in their economic policy. The combination of inflation and recession—stagflation— seems to defy the accepted rules of economic policy. But the present crisis is quantitatively and qualitatively vastly different from that of the 1930s: Quantitatively, it is much less serious, for the contraction of economic activity is much milder than in the Great Depression (although greater than in earlier postwar recessions) and the misery of *mass* unemployment has not reappeared.[87] Qualitatively, the present crisis is different from and more difficult to deal with than that of the 1930s, for macroeconomic anti-inflation policies tend to intensify the recession and macroeconomic anti-recession measures accentuate inflation. The easy "Keynesian prescriptions"[88] which have become the "classical" medicine of today, and which were so beneficial in the 1930s whenever they were applied, do not work well any more. However, the real "classical" medicine, in a broader sense than what Keynes had in mind, has not lost its potency.

But this, too, is not the subject of the present essay.

Notes

1. This paper was prepared for a volume of essays to be published by the German Bundesbank in 1976 under the title *Währung und Wirtschaft in Deutschland 1876–1975*. (Fritz Knapp Verlag Frankfurt [Main]) The occasion is the hundredth anniversary of the founding of the German Reichsbank in 1876. The volume contains sixteen contributions by German authors dealing in considerable detail with the monetary, banking and fiscal developments and policies in Germany during the period from 1876 to 1975. The present paper, written in English and translated into German, provides the international background for four chapters dealing with

the period from the stabilization of the German mark in 1924 to the outbreak of the Second World War in 1939.

2. John Stuart Mill, *Principles of Political Economy*, Book 1, Chapter 5, Section 7; Alfred Marshall, *Principles of Economics*, 5th ed., p. 780.

3. During the war Japan experienced a great boom which pushed wholesale prices much higher than in United States. After the war the prewar gold (and dollar) parity was maintained despite the deterioration of the balance of payments. The disastrous earthquake of 1923 forced the depreciation of the yen by about 20 percent. After a severe financial crisis in 1927 the yen was brought back to parity by deflationary measures and the prewar gold parity was restored in January 1930, at the worst possible time. In December 1931 the yen was again cut loose from gold and was allowed to depreciate by about 40 per cent vis-à-vis the depreciated pound (see below).

For details, see W. Arthur Lewis, *Economic Survey, 1919–1939* (London, 1949), pp. 115– 123, and Hugh T. Patrick, "The Economic Muddle of the 1920s," in *Dilemmas of Growth in Prewar Japan*, ed. James William Morley (Princeton, N.J., 1971), pp. 211–266.

4. Speech given in 1930, reprinted in *Selected Documents Submitted to the Gold Delegation of the Financial Committee* (Geneva: League of Nations, 1930), p. 53.

5. World output of gold (including the U.S.S.R.) in millions of dollars of old parity ($20.67 per fine ounce) was estimated at 448 in 1914, 472 in 1915, 330 in 1921 and 320 in 1922. During the depression, the value of gold in general purchasing power rose sharply as a consequence of the devaluations of all currencies in terms of gold and falling commodity prices in terms of national currencies (deflation). As a consequence, world output of gold rose from 390 in 1928 to 780 in 1938 (in millions of dollars of old parity). See Ragnar Nurkse, *International Currency Experience* (Geneva: League of Nations, 1944), p. 233.

6. Keynes had correctly predicted this outcome in his famous pamphlet, *The Economic Consequences of Mr. Churchill* (London, 1925) reprinted in J. M. Keynes, *Essays in Persuasion*, several editions. Keynes objected not to restoration of the gold standard as such, but to the timing and to the rate of $4.86. The full story of the British return to gold in 1925 has been told only recently after hitherto secret official papers have become available. See D. E. Moggridge, *British Monetary Policy, 1924–1931: The Norman Conquest of $4.86* (Cambridge, 1972). The subtitle is an allusion to Montague Norman, the powerful governor of the Bank of England, who was to a large extent responsible for the return to gold at the prewar parity of $4.86. The new material tends to exonerate Churchill. In a remarkable "most secret" memorandum addressed to his advisers before the decision to return to gold at the old parity was made, Churchill had asked all the relevant questions. But he received wrong or misleading answers from his advisers.

7. See Moggridge, *British Monetary Policy, 1924–1931*. "Between their peak in January 1920 and their nadir in December 1922 average weekly money wage rates fell by 38 percent— while the cost of living fell by over 50 percent. ... A large proportion of these [wage] reductions were accomplished under sliding scale agreements through which money wages were related to the cost of living" (p. 110). The author points out that the experience of 1921–1922 made indexations of wages "unpopular" with unions. Further reductions of money wages could be effected only after crippling strikes and much unemployment. "The General Strike [1926] removed the possibility of widespread reductions in money wages and

costs, if only because attempts at reductions were too expensive socially and economically" (p. 235). On the failure of union wages to fall from 1929–1931, see the excellent article by Otmar Emminger "Die englischen Währungsexperimente der Nachkriegszeit," *Weltwirtschaftliches Archiv*, Band 40, Heft 2 (September 1934), table on page 21.

8. *Relative* wages are much less rigid than nominal wages, but their changes are effected by differential money wage *increases* and only in exceptional cases by *decreases* in money wages.

9. The British policy of restoring the gold standard at the prewar parity was *inter alia* based on the expectation that prices in America would rise. See Moggridge, *British Monetary Policy, 1924–1931*, p. 111. Otmar Emminger pointed out that the British authorities would not have made this mistake if they had read "carefully" the Annual Report of the Federal Reserve Board for 1923: "There, for the first time gold movements and gold stock were abandoned as regulator of credit policy and stability of production was made the lodestar of monetary policy. Internal stability versus external equilibrium! Is it not the leitmotiv of all monetary policy in postwar period?" See Emminger, "Die englischen Währungsexperimente," p. 29.

10. Milton Friedman and Anna J. Schwartz call the downswing of 1929–1933 "The Great Contraction," which is the title of Chapter 7 of their great book, *The Monetary History of the United States, 1867–1960* (New York: National Bureau of Economic Research, 1963); this fascinating chapter is also available in a paperback edition. Lester V. Chandler's impressive monograph is entitled *America's Greatest Depression, 1929–1941* (New York, 1970) and Charles P. Kindleberger's lively volume has the title, *The World in Depression, 1929–1939* (London–New York, 1973).

11. In the third quarter of 1932 there were clear signs of revival of economic activity but the improvement was cut short by the outflow of gold and a new flurry of bank failures.

12. Monthly dates for cyclical changes in the United States, France, Great Britain, and Germany have been compiled with meticulous care by the National Bureau of Economic Research. See Arthur F. Burns and Wesley C. Mitchell, *Measuring Business Cycles* (New York, 1946), pp. 78–79. The American monthly dates for cyclical peaks and troughs have been slightly revised in a few instances by Geoffrey Moore. The U.S. cyclical calendar is republished from time to time in *Business Conditions Digest* (*B.C.D.*, formerly *Business Cycle Developments*), a monthly publication of the U.S. Department of Commerce, Washington, D.C.

13. What were in the 1930s generally regarded as alarming price rises may appear moderate in the mid-1970s.

14. Australia devalued in January 1931. After Britain left gold, Australia pegged to the pound as a member of the sterling bloc. See Douglas Copland, *Australia in the World Crisis, 1929–1933* (New York, 1934).

15. According to the official figures, the drop from 1929 to 1932 in real national income, overall and per capita, was about the same in the United States as in Germany. But in 1932 unemployment in Germany was much higher, 43.8 percent. [For national income figures, see Ingvar Svennilson, *Growth and Stagnation in the European Economy* (Geneva: United Nations, 1954), p. 233.] The unemployment figure comes from Walter Galenson and Arnold Zeller, "International Comparisons of Unemployment Rates," in *The Measurement and Behavior of Unemployment*, a Conference of the Universities National Bureau Committee for Economic Research (New York, 1957), pp. 455 and 467.

16. The credit withdrawals of France from Austria and Germany in 1931 were assumed to have been made largely for political reasons—a reaction to the proposed Austro-German customs union. They were said to have triggered the collapse of the Austrian Kredit-Anstalt and of the German banking system.

17. See the memorandum that Keynes together with six other members submitted to the Macmillan Committee (Committee on Finance and Industry, *Report*, Addendum 1, London: His Majesty's Stationery Office, 1931, esp. pp. 190–209). Keynes at first had recommended a uniform ad valorem duty on all imports and an equal ad valorem bounty on all exports. This would have been roughly the same as a devaluation. But he later dropped the uniformity principle and recommended different taxes and subsidies for different commodities. "A plan of this kind would be immeasurably preferable to devaluation" because it "would avoid the injury to the national credit and to our receipts from foreign loans fixed in terms of sterling which would ensue on devaluation." (Ibid., pp. 199–200.) The scheme was, thus, essentially nationalistic and exploitative, for it would have sharply increased the burden of foreign debtors, largely less developed countries—a burden which had already been enormously increased by the sharp decline in commodity prices.

This was Keynes's nationalistic and protectionist period. In the early 1930s Keynes, like many other liberals, despaired of the prospects that liberal policies would work. See also his article "National Self-Sufficiency," in *Yale Review* (Summer 1933, pp. 755–769) where he "sympathize[d] with those who would minimize . . . economic entanglement among nations" and exclaimed "let goods be homespun wherever it is reasonably and conveniently possible." (Ibid., p. 758.) On Keynes's nationalistic period, see Lord Robbins, *Autobiography of an Economist* (London, 1971)—"Even Keynes succumbed to the current insanity. . . . A sad aberration of a noble mind"—for the judgment of one of Keynes's great admirers (p. 156).

The Schachtian system, in different variations and guises, was admired and advocated for adoption elsewhere by Keynes's radical disciples. Keynes himself, when he later worked on plans for postwar reconstruction, returned to advocating liberal trading methods. In his famous posthumously published article, "The Balance of Payments of the United States" (*Economic Journal*, June 1946, pp. 172–187) he expressed optimism that "the classical medicine would work" and castigated the views of his erstwhile radical followers (who in the meantime had become his critics) as "modernist stuff gone wrong and turned sour and silly." (Ibid., p. 186.)

18. It is true the German economy had a head start, for it had turned the corner in August 1932, six months before Hitler came to power. But that does not seriously vitiate the comparison because in the first six or seven months the German expansion was slow and the date of the trough of the U.S. depression, 1933, is not quite clear-cut; the depression has been described as "double bottomed," the first bottom occurring in 1932.

19. See Gerhard Bry (assisted by Charlotte Boschan), *Wages in Germany, 1871–1945* (Princeton: National Bureau of Economic Research, Princeton University Press, 1960).

There was, of course, strict wage and price control right from the beginning of the Nazi dictatorship. Later, when full employment was approached and rearmament went into high gear, scarcities, unavailabilities, and deteriorations of quality of certain products gradually began to appear, making the official cost-of-living index increasingly unreliable. Gerhard Bry tried to make adjustments. His figures show that from 1937 on, the official index understates the real rise in the cost of living. For example, from 1932 to 1939 the rise was 4.6 percent according to the official index, while Bry's adjusted index shows an increase of 9.5 percent.

(Ibid., p. 264.) These corrections do not invalidate the statements in the text which are concerned with the earlier period when the index was not yet seriously distorted.

20. See Lewis, *Economic Survey, 1919–1939* and Patrick "The Economic Muddle of the 1920s."

21. See H. V. Hodson, *Slump and Recovery, 1929–1937: A Survey of World Economic Affairs* (London, 1938).

22. See Nurkse, *International Currency Experience*, p. 128.

23. Quotation from the text of the British declaration. Similar statements, *mutatis mutandis*, were issued by the American and French governments. See Hodson, *Slump and Recovery, 1929–1937*, p. 414.

24. Ibid., p. 421.

25. In France as in the United States the New Deal caused a cost-push inflation. I might mention that the concept of a "wage- or cost-push inflation" is still controversial. But the idea that a sudden great strengthening of the monopoly power of labor unions and business organizations, as was produced by the American and French New Deal, caused a *once-for-all* increase in the price level is recognized even by those who reject the idea of a *continuing* wage push.

26. It has been said that the gold bloc can be traced back to the old Latin Monetary Union between France, Belgium, Switzerland, and Italy (1865), to which Greece acceded later. But the Latin Union was a very different animal. It established monetary units of equal value (one Swiss franc = one French franc = one lira, et cetera). This ruled out changes in the exchange rate, but under the rule of the gold standard with permanently fixed parities, the equal value of the monetary unit was not an important matter.

27. Since 1938 there have been several mild recessions and much inflation but no case of real deflation in the sense of either falling prices, declining money, national income (MV), or declining quantity of money (M).

28. O. Emminger diagnosed this change as early as 1934. See Emminger, "Die englischen Währungsexperimente."

29. The devaluation of the dollar in 1933–1934 was an exception inasmuch as it was not preceded by substantial gold losses in the early 1930s. The fact that there was a very large gold inflow in every year from 1934 to the American entry into the war suggests that the expansion would not have been hampered by reserve losses if the dollar had not been devalued. At any rate, the aggressive depreciation of the dollar was a flagrant case of beggar-thy-neighbor policy.

In his remarkable article, "Währungsentwertung und Krisenüberwindung in England," *Weltwirtschaftliches Archiv* Band 40, Heft 3 (November 1934), p. 61, Otmar Emminger puts it this way: "In all the years since 1929 there was nothing [that is, no balance-of-payments constraint] that would have prevented the United States from stopping its credit deflation. . . . The difference between England and America in the crisis can be summarized by saying that America was an active center of deflation, while England was forced from abroad [that is, by a weak balance of payments] to deflate."

30. All figures come from *Banking and Monetary Statistics* (Board of Governors of the Federal Reserve System, Washington, D.C. 1943).

31. According to R. Nurkse (*International Currency Experience*, p. 18), the increase in the price of gold in terms of national currencies was about 70 percent on the average.

32. World output rose from $U.S. 390 millions (of gold parity $20.67 per fine ounce) in 1928 to 780 millions in 1938. (Ibid., p. 233.)

33. From 1929 to 1932 the quantum of world trade fell by about 25 percent and its value (in terms of dollars and gold) by about two-thirds reflecting the sharp drop in prices. Because of the devaluation of the pound in 1931, the value decline of world trade in terms of sterling was less (about 46 percent). See *Review of World Trade, 1937* (Geneva: League of Nations, 1938), p. 10.

34. From 1928 to 1937 the ratio of reserves (of all countries excluding the Communist bloc) to world imports rose from 42 to 117. See *International Reserves and Liquidity*, A Study of the Staff of the International Monetary Fund (Washington, 1958), p. 18.

35. See Nurkse, *International Currency Experience*, p. 133.

36. The Articles of Agreement of the International Monetary Fund provide for the possibility of "a uniform proportionate change in the par values of the currencies of all members." (Article 4, section 7.)

37. This was pointed out as early as 1934 by Otmar Emminger in "Währungsentwertung," p. 67. See also Nurkse, *International Currency Experience*, p. 133.

38. This would, of course, have influenced the pound rate vis-à-vis the dollar. It might be objected that the British recovery which resulted from the devaluation of the pound would have been jeopardized, if the gold bloc currencies and the mark had followed the pound promptly. This objection is, however, not valid as Otmar Emminger convincingly demonstrated. (See his "Währungsentwertung," *passim*, especially pp. 68–69 and 100–105.)

39. See *Final Report* (Geneva, June 1932). In the spirit of the times the question that the committee was asked to investigate was phrased in terms of gold and price stability: "To examine into and report upon the causes of fluctuations in the purchasing power of gold and their effect upon the economic life of the nations." (Ibid., p. 5.) Naturally, the committee interpreted its task broadly and the result was a report on the international monetary system and the depression.

40. Ibid., p. 64.

41. Ibid., pp. 74–75.

42. *The Economic Lessons of the Nineteen-Thirties*, Report drafted by H. W. Arndt (London: Oxford University Press, 1944), pp. 287 and 288. In the spirit of the times this report is imbued with despair about the viability of modern capitalism (Späkapitalismus, although the word is not mentioned) and reflects the "stagnation" theory (see below).

43. United Nations, Economic Commission for Europe (Geneva, 1954) *passim*.

44. Eric Lundberg, *Instability and Economic Growth* (New Haven, Conn., 1968), pp. 32–33. It should be stressed however that, although Svennilson's main conclusion is unconvincing, the book contains a wealth of most interesting and valuable statistical materials and economic analyses.

45. See F. A. von Hayek, *Prices and Production,* 1st edition, London, 1931; 2nd ed., 1935. Lionel Robbins, *The Great Depression* (London, 1934). Robbins later changed his mind (see below). Gustav Cassel, too, developed a theory of the business cycle and depression which is similar to Hayek's and Robbins's, but he did not make the mistake of regarding the Great Depression as an ordinary cyclical depression. Two prominent German economists, Albert Hahn and Wilhelm Röpke, put forward a theory, similar to that of Hayek and Robbins, on how an inflationary business cycle upswing breeds maladjustments which bring about the downswing. But they soon realized that the Great Depression had quickly degenerated into something much more serious than an ordinary business cycle recession (see below).

46. According to Hayek and Robbins, precisely this mistake was made by the Federal Reserve Board in 1927. Partly to ease pressure on the pound and partly to counteract the mild recession of October 1926 to November 1927, the Federal Reserve Board engaged in what in retrospect must be described as mild expansionary policy. Robbins comments as follows: "The policy succeeded. The impending recession was averted. [Actually it was cut short, not averted.] The London position was cased.... But from that date ... the situation got completely out of hand." See Robbins, *The Great Depression,* p. 53. What he had in mind was that the stock exchange boom was rekindled. Few would doubt that the eventual unavoidable collapse of the stock exchange boom was a highly disturbing factor of a monetary-financial kind capable of distorting money flows and creating some real maladjustments. What is difficult to believe is that it should have caused in a short time massive shifts of real factors of production (a great distortion in the real structure of production) which would have made a deep depression inevitable, as the theory postulates.

47. Ibid., pp. 48–49.

48. In technical terms, constant money national income equals quantity of money (M) times velocity of circulation (V). An alternative definition which Hayek seems to prefer would be a constant M. For our purposes it is, however, not necessary and it would lead us too far afield to discuss this issue—which was extensively discussed at the time under the heading of "neutral money."

49. However, this statement does not deny that good reasons can be adduced for the proposition that a mild secular decline in the price level, reflecting the growth of productivity (rising output per man-hour), would be desirable on grounds of equity and efficiency. See, for example, Milton Friedman, *The Optimum Quantity of Money* (Chicago, 1969). This theme can be found in the monetary literature going back to the eighteenth century.

50. After World War I there was the sharp depression of 1920–1921. But this was a financial-monetary aftermath of the war and had nothing to do with physical difficulties of the transition from war to peace, as is demonstrated by the fact that there was no such depression after World War II. For the United States the National Bureau of Economic Research has registered short recessions from August 1918 to March 1919 and from February 1945 to October 1945. It is generally recognized that these two "recessions" reflected unavoidable difficulties and frictions in the relocation of factors of production involved in the transition from a war to a peace economy and that they lacked many of the features of a regular business cycle recession. These were the depressions one would expect to result from "maladjustments": they were short, mild and inconsequential.

51. See Lord Robbins, *Autobiography of an Economist* (London, 1971). There he gives a most interesting, frank, and moving account of why he accepted the theory in the first place and

how he later convinced himself that the theory and the policy conclusion—opposition to deficit spending as an anti-deflation measure—were quite wrong (pp. 153 et seq.).

52. See L. Albert Hahn, *Fünfzig Jahre Zwischen Inflation und Deflation* (Tübingen, 1963), especially pp. 73–106, and Wilhelm Röpke, *Crisis and Cycles* (London, 1963), especially p. 120. Friedrich von Hayek has recently said that he always was of the opinion that the prevention of "an actual shrinkage of the total demand" is justified—in other words, that the "secondary deflation" should be counteracted. But his emphasis is still on the real maladjustments. See his *Inflation: Causes, Consequences, Cures* (London: The Institute of Economic Affairs, 1974), pp. 116–117. He has spelled out his views in greater detail in *Full Employment at Any Price?* (London: The Institute of Economic Affairs, 1975) and in *A Discussion with Friedrich von Hayek* (Washington, D.C.: American Enterprise Institute, 1975).

53. Economically the open hyperinflation suffered after World War I was much less damaging than the repressed inflation suffered after World War II until the currency reform in 1948. The inflation in the early 1920s even had one economic advantage: it shielded Germany from the United States and from the world depression of 1920–1921. See Frank D. Graham, *Exchange, Prices and Production in Hyperinflation: Germany 1920–1923* (Princeton, N.J.: Princeton University Press, 1931), pp. 287–288.

54. See Heinrich Bruening, *Memoiren 1918–1934* (Munich: Deutscher Taschenbush Verlag, 1972), Band I, p. 204. The story had a bizarre sequel. Bruening called Hitler in and explained to him his strategy to get rid of the reparations. He asked Hitler for his understanding, but Hitler remained noncommittal. Three weeks later an American journalist informed Bruening on behalf of the American ambassador that Hitler had sent his press chief to the American ambassador to inform him that Bruening had tried to get Hitler's support for a policy whose purpose was "to confront the United States with the sudden elimination of reparations and to push it [the United States] thereby into a severe economic crisis." When Bruening asked what the ambassador's reaction was, he was told that the ambassador just laughed. (Ibid., pp. 207–208.) The irony is that on this occasion Hitler did not stray far from the truth.

55. See Hans Luther, *Vor dem Abgrund, 1930–1933. Reichsbank präsident in Krisenzeiten* (Berlin, 1964), especially pp. 155–157.

56. "Aber das schien mir Brünings reparationspolitisches Argument nicht zu erschüttern." (Ibid., p. 155). Luther also cites legal obstacles to devaluation. "The Young plan explicitly demanded maintenance of the gold parity of the mark." (p. 156.) He evidently did not try to overcome this hurdle, something which should have been possible with the help of the BIS. Luther mentions Edgar Salin as one who "strongly urged" that "Germany should follow the British example, abandon the gold standard, depreciate the mark or ... peg it to the pound." At that time and later many economists in Germany recommended depreciation or even floating (although the word "floating" was not used). This is, for example, the clear implication of Dr. Emminger's two articles, "Die englischen Währungsexperimente" and "Währungsentwertung." Another example is an excellent article by Dr. Hans Richter-Altschäffer (now of Washington, D.C., then of Berlin), "Organische Anpassung" (in *Wirtschaftsdienst* Heft 17, April 27, 1934, Hamburg). He recommended expansionary measures to get out of the depression but argued that this could be done efficiently only by letting the mark float. ("Durch Freigabe des Aussenwertes der Währung, sich dasjenige Niveau zu suchen und darauf einzuspielen, das der Unterschiedlichkeit in den wirtschaftlichen Bedingungen und

Verhältnissen Deutschlands einerseits und der übrigen Volkswirtschaften anderseits ontspricht.")

These papers and many others (especially those by Wilhelm Lautenbach in the German economics ministry, whom Luther mentions) demonstrate that what in the Anglo-Saxon literature later became known as "Keynesian" policy prescriptions, were fully anticipated in the German literature. The same is true of the Scandinavian literature, especially the Swedish. But Keynes had a strong influence on the German literature through his earlier writings, especially *Treatise on Money* (1930) and as co-author of the Macmillan Report (1931). The German literature is extensively reviewed in Wilhelm Grottkopp, *Die Grosse Kirse. Lehren aus der Überwindung der Wirtschaftskrise 1929–32* (Düsseldorf, 1954).

57. The minority report listed among "the most important conditions" for the restoration of the gold standard: "First, some reasonable settlement of the reparations and war-debts questions must be effected, and the settlement must be of such a character as to make quite clear that (a) reparations and war debts can be paid and the payments received, and (b) how this can be accomplished without serious interference with the gold standard." (*Final Report,* p. 70.)

58. Ibid., p. 74. Cassel subscribed to the minority report and added a separate Memorandum of Dissent.

59. See figures in Dietmar Keese, "Die volkswirtschaftlichen Gesamtgrössen für das Deutsche Reich in den Jahren 1925–1936," in *Die Staats- und Wirtschaftskrise des Deutschen Reichs 1929/33,* edited by Werner Conze and Hans Raupach (Stuttgart, 1967).

60. Ibid.

61. The pessimistic school was led by Keynes. His chief theoretical antagonist, Bertil Ohlin, was optimistic. This controversy is well known and need not be reviewed here. Suffice it to say that the modern theory of the balance-of-payments adjustment mechanism clearly shows that Ohlin had the better of the argument.

62. Fortunately the world has learned that lesson. There were no long-lasting reparations or war debt problems after the Second World War. It is a matter of regret, however, that the right lesson has, to a large extent, been learned for the wrong reason—namely, for the reason that the transfer was inherently impossible or prohibitively expensive, even if reasonable full employment had been maintained and the channels of trade kept open.

63. I leave the question open whether a sharp reduction of the number of banks would not have been necessary, even with extensive deposit insurance.

64. The tragic mistakes of monetary policy, not only of omission—that is, failing to counteract the deflation—but on several occasions also of commission—that is, actually contracting the money supply, are convincingly demonstrated by Milton Friedman and Anna Schwartz, in "The Great Contraction," in *The Monetary History of the United States, 1867–1960.* That their overall judgment is correct cannot be doubted even though some will not accept every detail of their analysis. Lester Chandler reached substantially the same conclusions in *America's Greatest Depression, 1929–1941.* On the weakness of the American banking system, Jacob Viner had this to say: "The depression ... was more severe in the United States than in most other countries ... the weakness of the banks must be held largely responsible for this.... What are the causes of this peculiar weakness of the American banking system? The

explanation, I am convinced, lies in the fact that of all the modern national banking systems it alone has adhered predominantly to the eighteenth-century model of individual small-scale units, as distinguished from large-scale banking institutions with many branches." See Jacob Viner, "Recent Legislation and the Banking Situation," *American Economic Review*, Supplement, vol. 26, March 1936, pp. 106–107.

65. The editors of *The Economist* of London retrospectively rely heavily on this Keynesian or rather post-Keynesian multiplier-acceleration mechanism for an explanation of the economic catastrophe of the 1930s, without even mentioning the monetary complications ("secondary deflation"). They think "it is entirely possible for such a spiralling to happen" again (see issue of November 30, 1974, p. 85).

66. In 1934 Cordell Hull, U.S. secretary of state, started the Reciprocal Trade Agreement policy which eventually brought the American tariff sharply down. But the policy had a slow start, and it took many years to reduce the tariff to the predepression and pre-Smoot-Hawley level. During the depression the tariff wall was raised not only by the Smoot-Hawley act but also by the operation of deflation: the incidence of specific duties (in contrast to *ad valorem* duties) is automatically raised when the price level declines. During and after World War II inflation operated in the opposite direction scaling down the tariff wall.

67. This covers the French stabilization of 1926–1928.

68. It should be observed that situations are conceivable in which a country's policy of stimulating its economy by developing an export surplus through depreciation would also benefit the outside world. Suppose country A is in depression while country B suffers from inflation and overfull employment. If country A devalues its currency and develops an export surplus, it alleviates its own depression and at the same time dampens inflation in country B. Such situations are conceivable and have occurred. In this possibility, see my *Money in the International Economy*, 2nd edition (London, 1969). But this was, of course, not the situation in the 1930s when the whole world was depressed and nobody had an inflation to dampen.

69. According to Keynes, Churchill's advisers made the same mistake of comparing the movement of wholesale prices in the United Kingdom and the United States to estimate the degree of undervaluation of the pound. Wholesale prices adjust quickly and therefore are apt to convey a spurious picture of equilibrium. See Keynes, *The Economic Consequences of Mr. Churchill* (London, 1925), reprinted in *Essays in Persuasion* (London, 1931 and later editions).

70. The Czechoslovakian and Belgian cases are compared in Nurkse, *International Currency Experience*, p. 128, and analyzed at greater length in *Monetary Review, Money and Banking, 1935–36*, vol. 1 (Geneva: League of Nations, 1936), pp. 49 ff.

71. See Nurkse, *International Currency Expansion*, p. 127.

72. Continued free floating would have corrected the imbalance after a short while. But the rebound was prevented by intensive interventions. It was, however, understandable that the authorities wanted to replenish their international reserve which had been badly depleted. This illustrates, once again, the intrinsic defect of the method of the adjustable peg for changing exchange rates. Competitive depreciation is the almost inevitable consequence of that system, for, as has been explained many times, under that system it is a matter of elementary prudence to depreciate too much rather than too little.

73. Nurkse, *International Currency Experience*, p. 130.

74. Ibid., p. 211.

75. See Juergen B. Donges, *Brazil's Trotting Peg: A New Approach to Greater Exchange Rate Flexibility*, with a foreword by Gottfried Haberler (Washington, D.C.: American Enterprise Institute for Public Policy Research, 1971).

76. Nurkse, *International Currency Experience*, p. 211.

77. See *Statistisches Handbuch der Weltwirtschaft*, Bearbeitet Im Statistischen Reichsamt (Berlin, 1936). In absolute terms German trade with the U.S.S.R. was in the same order of magnitude as that of Sweden or Switzerland, but German exports to Switzerland fell from 4.9 percent in 1929 to 4.4 percent in 1931. (In the severe recession of 1974–1975 Soviet Russia has again become a more attractive market for some Western countries and the economic prestige of Soviet Russia has been enhanced by the fact that it does not suffer from recession. Since the present recession is much milder than the Great Depression of the 1930s, the contrast between the Western and Eastern economic developments is less pronounced.)

78. See Alexander Gerschenkron, *Economic Relations with the U.S.S.R.* (New York, 1945), p. 20.

79. On the Soviet interpretation, see Laszlo M. Tikos, "Waiting for the World Revolution: Soviet Reactions to the Great Depression," in *The Great Depression Revisited: Essays on the Economics of the Thirties*, edited by Herman van der Wee (The Hague, 1972), pp. 76–85.

Communist hopes for a collapse of the capitalist system in the post-World War II period practically vanished when one after the other of the postwar recessions turned out to be exceedingly mild. They have, however, been revived by the severe recession of 1974–1975.

80. Schumpeter, it is true, played with the idea that the severity of the depression of the 1930s could be explained by the coincidence of a "Kondratieff," "Juglar" and "Kitchin" downswing. But he did not take this idea very seriously. His considered view was "(a) that the darkest hues of cyclical depressions ... are not essential to business cycles per se but due to adventitious circumstances and (b) that these adventitious circumstances might be eliminated and those darkest hues banished without interfering with the cyclical mechanism itself." (See "Historical Approach to the Analysis of Business Cycles," in *Conference on Business Cycles*, held under the auspices of the Universities-National Bureau Committee for Economic Research, New York, 1951, p. 150.)

81. The importance of the growing stickiness of wages and prices has been stressed by Frank H. Knight. In 1941 he wrote: "In a free market these differential changes [in the prices of different types of goods] would be temporary, but even then they might be serious; and with important markets as unfree as they actually are—and prices as sticky and labor and capital as immobile—the results take on the proportion of a social disaster." (Frank H. Knight, "The Business Cycle, Interest and Money," reprinted from *Review of Economics and Statistics*, vol. 23, no. 2, May 1941, in F. H. Knight, *On the History and Methods of Economics—Selected Essays* (Chicago, 1956), p. 224.) Since Knight wrote those lines, the situation has become much worse. There are now many more powerful labor unions (especially among public employees—teachers, firemen, policemen, et cetera) and many other pressure groups which make prices and wages rigid in the downward direction and push them up even in the presence of unemployment and slack. This development goes a long way to explain the perplexing phenomenon of "inflationary recessions" or "stagflation."

82. It is therefore unwarranted and superficial to construe, as is sometimes done, a basic contradiction between (a) theories that regard the Great Depression as the result of a series of historical accidents and (b) theories that explain it as the consequence of monetary factors. Thus, Milton Friedman, the chief monetarist, discusses at length "the climate of intellectual opinion" which, in his opinion, "helps to explain ... the behavior of the Federal Reserve System from 1929 to 1933." He and another prominent monetarist, Lester Chandler, attribute crucial importance to the "historical accident" of the sickness and untimely death in 1928 of Benjamin Strong, the governor of the New York Federal Reserve Bank whose inspired leadership had dominated Federal Reserve policy throughout the 1920s. See Milton Friedman and Anna J. Schwartz, "Why Was Monetary Policy So Inept?" last section of Chapter 7 on "The Great Contraction," and the last chapter "Summing Up," in *The Monetary History of the United States, 1867–1960*, and Lester V. Chandler, *Benjamin Strong, Central Banker* (Washington, D.C.: The Brookings Institution, 1958), p. 465.

83. Friedman and Schwartz, *The Monetary History of the United States, 1867–1960*, last paragraph of Chapter 7. Surely every recession or depression (and every boom for that matter) acquires "the characteristics of a cumulative process" long before it degenerates into an "economic collapse."

84. Of his many books, see, for example, *Trade Depression and the Way Out* (London, 1933), pp. 146–147, 159–160.

85. The miscarriage of the premature introduction of sterling convertibility of the Anglo-American loan agreement of 1946 had discredited the principle of convertibility and nondiscrimination and made British statesmen and experts allergic to these principles for years to come. The failure of convertibility came about because inflation was still rampant and the pound grossly overvalued. The situation changed quickly after the pound was drastically devalued in 1949.

86. Keynes, "The Balance of Payments of the United States," p. 186. However, Keynes had not—not yet—completely freed himself of the depression mentality. For he makes it clear that he did "not suppose that the classical medicine will work by itself." In his view, the classical medicine has to be supported not only by what we now call "demand management" and "exchange variations," but also by "overall import control." (Ibid.)

87. To indicate the difference it should be recalled that from the cyclical peak in August 1929 to the trough in March 1933 in the United States industrial production fell by 53.4 percent and unemployment reached 25.4 percent of the labor force. In the current recession which in the United States probably passed its trough in May or June 1975, industrial production declined approximately 14 percent and unemployment reached about 9.4 percent. Moreover, owing to generous unemployment relief and welfare payments, human suffering and the social implications of unemployment today are much less serious than they were in the 1930s. Moreover, since these measures blunt the incentive to look for jobs, the figure of 9.4 percent probably overstates the magnitude of the problem.

However, the long period of prosperity and rapid growth the West enjoyed after World War II until 1974, interrupted only by very short and mild recessions, has raised our sights. More optimistic expectations and the changed intellectual climate have made public opinion impatient and increasingly sensitive to even comparatively mild setbacks.

88. To call these prescriptions "Keynesian" is actually a misnomer. For these same prescriptions—easy money and deficit spending to counteract deflation and depression—could have been derived and have in fact been derived by "classical" economists from "classical" economic theory. Who doubts that should consult T. W. Hutchison, *Economics and Economic Policy in Britain 1946–1966* (London, 1968), especially the appendix, "Pigou and Keynes on Employment Policy," pp. 277–301; and J. Ronnie Davis, *The New Economics and the Old Economists* (Ames, Iowa, 1971).

17

The Great Depression of
the 1930s—Can It Happen
Again?

1. Introduction

The fiftieth anniversary of the outbreak of the Great Depression and the crash on the New York Stock Exchange in October 1929 coincided with high inflation, an impending recession in the United States, decline of the dollar and a fantastic rise of the price of gold, a veritable gold mania. No wonder that the question is asked with increasing urgency and anxiety—will it happen again?

Let me recall that it is not the first time that a repetition of the dismal experience of the 1930s has been widely expected. During World War II and the first years after the war many economists, especially the Keynesians—not so much Keynes himself as his followers—expected that deflation and stagnation were the dangers the world would face in the post-war period, and in the early post-war recessions many saw the beginning of a deep depression. When the depression again and again failed to materialize the general mood changed. The 1950s and 1960s were the heydays of Keynesianism. It was widely assumed that the business cycle had been finally tamed, if not eradicated, by clever fine-tuning of the economy. It did not turn out this way; the business cycle which had been declared dead on earlier occasions (for example in the 1920s) is still with us. In the 1970s the rising inflation and the worldwide recession of 1973–75 produced again a change; the euphoria of the 1950s and 1960s gave way to pessimism and gloom.[1]

Actually, the first quarter century after the war, or even the 35 years since 1945, including the recent years of the world recession of 1973–75 and high inflation 1976–80, has been a period of almost unprecedented prosperity and growth for the United States and the rest of the Western World, including the less developed countries. It is true, however, that rising affluence has been marred increasingly by

96th Congress, 2nd Session, *The Business Cycle and Public Policy 1928–1980*, A compendium of papers submitted to the Joint Economic Committee, Congress of the United States 1–19 (Nov. 28, 1980).

inflation, and in the last few years the rate of growth has decreased in all industrial countries. Still, the contrast of the post-War War II period and the twenty years after World War I is tremendous. The interwar period saw two severe depressions, the so-called first post-war depression of 1920–21 and the Great Depression of the 1930s. Since 1945 there were six mild recessions in the United States, but no depression, if by depression we mean a decline in economic activity of the same order of magnitude as the two depressions of the interwar period and earlier ones.[2] It should be stressed that even the recession of 1973–75, although longer and more severe than the earlier ones, was definitely a mild recession compared with the Great Depression of the 1930s and earlier ones.

2. The Great Depression

The Great Depression of the 1930s was a world-shaking event. For the world economy and economic policy it was a watershed. It gave rise to the Keynesian revolution and shook the confidence in the free market-capitalist economy. It led to far-reaching government interventions in the economy and made central planning popular in the West. It gave a tremendous boost to the communist system of the East which seemed to be impervious to the economic disaster that had engulfed the Western World.

The economic depression had enormous political repercussions. It helped Hitler come to power and gave him the opportunity for great economic successes which he effectively used to prepare for World War II which he unleashed in 1939, it made the Soviet system and Stalin's dictatorship respectable in the West, and it strengthened the militarist regime in Japan. The depression-inspired U.S. policy of boosting the price of silver ruined the Chinese monetary system that was still based on silver and so contributed decisively to the defeat of the Chiang Kai-shek regime ("The Nationalists") and to the rise to power of Mao Tse-tung in China.

The principal center of the depression was the United States which had emerged from World War I as the world's dominant economic power. Let me briefly recall the salient facts. The U.S. depression was almost entirely homemade. Comparatively minor adverse influences from abroad (which were largely feedbacks of the previous foreign impact of the U.S. depression) will be mentioned later. The depression started slowly in the summer of 1929, several months before the stock exchange crash in October. It lasted 43 months (August 1929–March 1933), the longest and deepest depression in the twentieth century. Money GNP declined by 50 percent, real GNP by 33 percent, industrial production by 53 percent, and unemployment rose to 25 percent of the labor force. The depression was followed by an expansion which lasted 50 months (March 1933–May 1937). But the expansion came to an end long before full employment was reached. For 1937 as a whole unemployment was still over 14 percent. The long expansion was followed by a short but extremely precipitous slump (May 1937–June 1938). Money GNP fell by 16 percent, real GNP by 13 percent, industrial production by 32 percent and unemployment shot up from 11 percent in March 1937 to 20 percent in June 1938—all in the short span of 13 months. At the outbreak of the war in Europe (1939) U.S. unemployment was still sbout 17 percent. Full employment was not reached before the United States entered the war in 1941. Thus the whole decade 1929–1939 was a severely depressed period.

The depression was worldwide almost from the start and there were some epicenters, for example, in Germany and central Europe. It is controversial to what extent the depression in Europe was due to autonomous forces or was caused by the U.S. depression or, as some say, by the sudden cessation of U.S. capital exports in 1928 (which in turn has been attributed to the boom on the New York stock exchange that preceded the depression). But we need not go into that question; for whatever the answer, under the then-existing system of fixed exchanges (gold standard), the depression in the dominant U.S. economy was bound to spread swiftly to the rest of the world.

World trade, as measured by exports, fell in nominal terms (gold dollars) to about one-third, from $33 billion in 1928 to $13 billion in 1932. In real terms it shrank by about 25 percent, the difference reflecting the enormous deflation—the sharp decline of prices of internationally traded goods; or in other words, the enormous rise in the value of gold (gold's purchasing power in terms of real goods).

In passing it may be mentioned that the rise in the real value of gold operated sharply to increase world liquidity by encouraging gold production and boosting the real value of the existing gold reserves. Thus the ratio of the Western World's international reserves to world imports rose from 42 percent in 1928 to 117 percent in 1937.[3] This is the classical way by which the economy under the gold standard works its way out of a depression—a slow and painful process.

During the 35 years since the end of World War II, in sharp contrast to the interwar period, international trade has grown by leaps and bounds. In nominal terms (U.S. dollars) world exports and imports have sharply increased without interruption throughout the period.[4] In real terms there was a slight contraction in one year: in the recession year 1975 the quantum of world exports declined by 2 percent.[5]

3. Why Was the Depression So Severe and Why Did It Last So Long?

A. Non-Monetary Explanations

I think that with the benefit of hindsight a straightforward answer can be given to the question why the depression of the 1930s was so severe and why it has not happened after World War II—at least not so far. However, when it happened in the

1930s few economists were aware of what was going on and even now controversies about the origin and cause of the Great Depression are still going on.

I will first mention some explanations that were popular in the 1930s and 1940s,
some of which have been echoed in recent years.

Marxist economists and communist propaganda took the disaster of the 1930s
simply as a confirmation of Marx's theory that under capitalism depressions would
become more and more severe until in a final big crash the capitalist system would
collapse. In the 1950s and 1960s this view had lost its power of conviction even
among faithful Marxists; but their hope has been revived in recent years.

Those who lacked the prophet's guidance had a harder time to explain the slump.
The Keynesians fashioned the theory of secular stagnation, chronic oversaving and
of vanishing investment opportunities due to the drying up of technological
progress and slower population growth. Keynes himself never fully embraced this
pessimistic theory, although he came very close to accepting it in the General
Theory. There was, however, a convergence of Keynesian and Marxian thought.
Among Keynes' followers we may distinguish a right wing and a left wing. Keynes,
especially in his later years, belonged to the right or conservative wing of his school.
Keynes' radical followers, led by Joan Robinson—the Marxo-Keynesians as Joseph
A. Schumpeter used to call them—accepted the Marxian thesis that capitalism was
beyond repair. The right wing, among them Roy Harrod and most American
Keynesians (whom Joan Robinson calls "bastard Keynesians"),[6] have not accepted
the secular stagnation theory or have abandoned it. In the light of later developments the secular stagnation explanation of the Great Depression makes little sense
indeed. Excessive saving, lack of investment opportunities and slow technological
progress can hardly be said to be characteristic of the post-war period or even the
last five years.[7]

There is another related explanation of the Great Depression that was very
popular in the 1930s and later, namely the theory that the depression's exceptional
severity and length was due to deep-seated real maladjustments and distortions,
both on the national and international level, "in the productive structure of most
countries and the world economy as a whole which the war had left behind, and
rigidities in the economic systems of all countries which made the correction of these
maladjustments by market forces alone impossible."[8] These maladjustments were
for several years papered over by inflation and capital exports from the United
States until the bubble burst in the Great Depression.

The maladjustment explanations are refuted by the fact that in country after
country the alleged giant maladjustments disappeared as myteriously as they had
suddenly made their appearance earlier, as soon as deflation was stopped. Furthermore, the maladjustment theory of the Great Depression is at variance with the
post-World War II experience. Surely destruction, maladjustments and dislocations

wrought by World War II were much greater than those caused by World War I. Yet there has been no depression after World War II—mild recessions yes, but no severe depression. Why? Because there has been no case of monetary deflation since the end of the war.

The same criticism applies to another type of maladjustment explanation of the Great Depression, namely that based on the so-called Austrian theory of the business cycle as developed primarily by Friedrich A. Hayek and Lionel Robbins—a theory that has important monetary elements.[9]

According to this theory every depression is the inevitable consequence of maladjustments in the "vertical" structure of production created by the preceding inflationary boom. Inflation depresses the interest rate below its equilibrium level, which leads to overinvestment, an overexpansion of the "higher stages of production" involving an unsustainable shift of original factors of production to the capital goods industries. The boom can be prolonged by larger and larger monetary injections, but the longer it lasts, the greater the maladjustments and the more painful the unavoidable correction.

It would lead too far to discuss this theory in greater detail.[10] Suffice it to say that Robbins later changed his mind and abandoned the maladjustment theory of the depression. He did not exclude the possibility that "inappropriate investments fostered by wrong expectations" and perhaps by the stock exchange boom may have triggered the downtrend. But these real maladjustments, whatever their magnitude and nature, "were completely swamped by vast deflationary forces."[11]

B. Monetary Explanations

There can be no doubt in my opinion that the most important cause of the exceptional length and severity of the Great Depression was massive deflation in the United States. Through acts of commission (deflationary measures) and omission (failure to take sufficiently strong anti-deflationary, expansionary measures) the Federal Reserve system caused or permitted the quantity of money to contract by about 30 percent from 1929 to 1933.

This explanation is now firmly associated with the work of Milton Friedman who in his and Anna J. Schwartz' "truly great book", *A Monetary History of the United States 1867–1960*,[12] has given the most convincing and best documented monetary explanation. It is not necessary, however, to be an extreme monetarist to realize that a destruction of a third of the money stock was bound to produce a catastrophic depression. And there can be no doubt that it was in the power of the Federal Reserve to stop the monetary contraction in its track and to prevent the collapse of the American banking system.[13] This is convincingly demonstrated in "the masterly"—Sir Roy Harrod's words—Chapter 7 of the *Monetary History* on "The

Great Contraction 1929–1933". There it is shown in great detail that the Federal Reserve not only failed to counteract the ongoing deflation, but took highly deflationary steps on several occasions.

The failure to prevent the collapse of the banking system through massive open market operations or other means can be described as a failure of the Federal Reserve to perform the function of a lender of last resort. It will be recalled that Charles P. Kindleberger in numerous writings has stressed the absence of a lender of last resort as the main cause of the great debacle of the 1930s. It follows that Kindleberger's explanation is very close to that of Milton Friedman, although he argues vigorously against the monetarist explanation.[14]

It will be observed that my formulation of the monetary explanation does not exclude the possibility that the depression may have been triggered by some "real" factors, by "real maladjustment" as Lord Robbins said. Nor does it deny that there occurred powerful aggravating real shocks later in the course of the depression. The authors of The Monetary History are fully aware of this. Good examples of aggravating real shocks are protectionist moves such as the introduction of a skyscraper tariff (Smoot-Hawley Tariff) under the Hoover administration in 1930, the abandonment of free trade and imposition of a high import tariff by Britain in 1932 and protectionist reactions elsewhere. In their global effect these protectionist measures greatly aggravated the world depression, although such measures, regarded in isolation and in the short run, did stimulate the economy of the country in question. However, the preponderant importance of monetary factors and reflation of aggregate demand is demonstrated by the fact that the Smoot-Hawley Tariff did not prevent numerous countries from extricating themselves long before the United States from the world depression by cutting their currencies loose from gold and the dollar and taking expansionary monetary and fiscal measures. (See below.)

Another important point that must not be overlooked is that every deflation (just as every inflation) tends to become cumulative and to feed on itself. The authors of The Monetary History mentioned this, although a little bit as an afterthought, in the last paragraph of Chapter 7: "... small events at times have large consequences ... there are such things as chain reactions and cumulative forces. It happens that a liquidity crisis in a unit fractional reserve banking system is precisely the kind of event that can trigger—and often has triggered—a chain reaction. And economic collapse often has the character of a cumulative process. Let it go beyond a certain point, and it will tend for a time to gain strength from its own development as its effects spread and return to intensify the process of collapse. Because no great strength would be required to hold back the rock that starts a landslide, it does not follow that the landslide will not be of major proportions." (p. 419)

In this passage the authors refer specifically to the "liquidity crisis", the run of frightened depositors on the banks. But what they say about chain reaction and cumulative forces applies also to the depression as a whole. The Great Depression became a major landslide. Prompt monetary measures of moderate strength may have "held back the rock that started the landslide". But it is not unreasonable to argue that after a depression has gathered momentum stronger measures than open market operations and lower discount rates are indicated to stop the slide. These stronger measures are direct injections of money into the expenditure stream through government deficit spending. Eventually expansionary monetary measures will turn the tide, but it will take a long time. Relying on monetary policy alone courts the danger that a large pool of liquidity will be created which later, after the economy has turned the corner, will lead to an unhealthy inflationary boom.[15] Thus, as far as combating an ongoing cumulative deflation is concerned, monetarists and Keynesians should be able to agree on a common strategy.[16]

The Keynesian revolution pushed money and monetary policy into the background, but the so-called monetarist counterrevolution had started long before the advent of modern monetarism. Many earlier writers emphasized the monetary causes of the Great Depression. For example, as mentioned above, Lauchlin Currie (The Supply and Control of Money in the United States, 1934) and William Fellner (Monetary Policies and Full Employment, 1946) had given inept monetary policy its full due for causing the exceptional severity of the Great Depression. And Friedman himself has pointed out that emphasis on money was in the Chicago tradition of Frank H. Knight, Henry Simons, Jacob Viner and others.[17]

Many writers have pointed out that under the gold standard (fixed exchanges) great wars breed deep post-war depressions, because countries often deflate to restore the prewar gold parity of their currency. Edward M. Bernstein put it this way: "War [inflation] exhausts the money creating power of gold standard countries. Consequently, after a war the monetary authorities were unable to provide the economy with the expanding money supply required to maintain economic growth in an environment of price stability. [Thus] in virtually all countries a severely restrictive monetary policy was begun in 1920" which led to the first post-war depression.[18]

This theory had many adherents in the 1920s (and later) among economists and there was much apprehension in financial circles that a scarcity of gold, due to the rise in prices (reduced real purchasing power of gold), would cause serious deflationary pressure on the world economy. Thus, a conference of financial experts in Genoa in 1922 recommended the adoption by many countries of gold exchange standard and other measures to reduce the demand for gold to forestall the emergence of deflationary pressures.[19] The well-known French economist and financial expert Charles Rist made the same point in numerous writings. J. R. Hicks in his *Contribution to the Theory of the Trade Cycle*,[20] put forward a "real" theory of the business cycle in terms of interaction of multiplier and accelerator; but he realized that for the slump after 1929 the multiplier-accelerator explanation was wholly inadequate: "The monetary system of the world had never adjusted itself at all fully to the change in the level of money incomes which took place during and after the war of 1914—18; it was trying to manage with a gold supply which was in terms of wage-units extremely inadequate. Difficulties in the postwar adjustment of exchange rates (combined with the vast changes which the war had produced in the creditor-debtor position of important countries) had caused the consequential weakness to be particularly concentrated in certain places; particular central banks, as for instance the Bank of England and the Reichsbank, were therefore particularly incapable of performing their usual function as "lenders of last resort." [21]

The best-known recent example where the Rist-Bernstein explanation applies is the British revaluation of sterling in the 1920s. It will be recalled that during World War I the British pound was pegged to the dollar. When the peg was removed after the war the pound depreciated in the foreign exchange market by about 20 percent. It was then decided to restore the prewar parity, and in order to achieve that purpose the Bank of England applied deflationary measures. As a consequence Britain found herself throughout the 1920s in a depressed position with unemployment of about 10 percent while the rest of the world enjoyed a high rate of growth. [22] Keynes criticized the policy in his famous essay "The Economic Consequences of Mr. Churchill" who as Chancellor of the Exchequer was responsible for the policy. [23]

Keynes' warning was based on orthodox classical principles. A hundred years earlier, after the Napoleonic wars, the same mistake of restoring the prewar gold parity was made with the same consequences. In 1821 David Ricardo wrote to John Wheatley: "I never should advise a government to restore a currency which was depreciated 30 percent to par; I should recommend ... that the currency should be fixed at the depreciated level." [24] Under twentieth century conditions of wage rigidity we would say even 10 or 5 percent overvaluation is too much to be dealt with by deflation rather than by devaluation of the currency.

It is interesting that another great depression in the United States, that of the 1870s, offers striking parallels with the British depression in the 1920s. Large budget surpluses followed the deficits during the Civil War and the premium on gold was gradually reduced from 57 percent in 1865 to zero in 1879, the terminal year of the depression. [25] True, the general economic background in nineteenth century America was quite different from that of twentieth century Britain. But the difference in the surrounding conditions makes the similarity of the consequences of the same kind of policy all the more remarkable and supports the view that monetary factors were decisive.

Summarizing, we may say that the three episodes mentioned—the developments after the Napoleonic war in Britain, after the Civil War in the United States and after

World War I in Britain—as well as the so-called first postwar depression of 1920–21 mentioned by Bernstein, support the hypothesis that during the era of the gold standard, due to monetary mismanagement, big wars were apt to be followed by deep depressions.

But the theory does not explain the Great Depression of the 1930s.[26] The United States was not forced to take deflationary measures by gold losses, a weak balance of payments, a weak dollar or the wish to restore the prewar parity of the dollar. The U.S. depression was homemade; it was due to inept monetary policies as the authors of the *Monetary History of the United States* have made abundantly clear. The United States had emerged from the war as the dominant economic power. Under fixed exchanges (gold standard) a severe depression in the dominant economy was bound to spread swiftly to the rest of the world. Let me repeat that there were other weak spots in the world economy. The British economy was semi-depressed as we have seen. When Britain was hit by the Great Depression, unemployment rose from about 10 percent to 20 percent. Germany and Central Europe were in bad shape. But these and other trouble spots had only a negligible impact on the dominant U.S. economy and could not have dragged the whole world into depression if the United States had not sunk into deep depression or had experienced merely a mild recession like the ones in 1924 and 1927.

Before examining the role of the international system, a look at the depression in Germany is instructive. The depression hit the German economy, the second or third largest in the western world, even harder than the American economy. As in the United States monetary deflation was the dominant force, but unlike the United States international developments had a strong impact—reparations, international capital flows, the U.S. depression, the Smoot-Hawley tariff, and the devaluation of the British pound all had a powerful depressive impact. In Germany the depression started earlier and ended earlier than in the United States (April 1929 to August 1932). Whether the early onset of the depression was due to the cessation of U.S. capital exports and whether the latter was caused by the New York stock exchange boom pulling capital away from other uses (as some economists have argued) is debatable. But it cannot be doubted that later capital flight from Germany, because of the rapidly deteriorating economic and political situation, had a strong depressing effect. Reparations that the victorious powers, especially France, imposed on Germany, had a most unsettling effect largely by poisoning the political atmosphere throughout the interwar period until they were formally abolished, along with the allied war debts to the United States, by the Hoover moratorium in 1934. In January 1923 France and Belgium occupied the Ruhr to collect reparations. This greatly intensified the hyperinflation in Germany, whose political consequence—contributing to the rise of Nazism—was grave and prolonged.

Later on there was a direct link between reparations and deflation. The German

Chancellor Heinrich Bruening thought that his deflationary policy would enable him to get rid of the reparations. This would be accomplished by large German exports disrupting world markets. He "estimated that in twelve to fourteen months his policy would call forth a cry in the world for cancellation of the reparations".[27] The British devaluation in 1931 had a strong depressive effect on the German economy. Germany did not follow the British example of devaluing the currency as had been recommended by many experts, partly because this would have interfered with Bruening's policy of bringing about the end of reparations by forcing disruptive German exports on foreign markets.

The depression reached its lowest point in the summer of 1932. The recovery was slow at first, but picked up speed after Hitler came to power early in 1933. It is interesting to compare the American and German recovery. Roosevelt and Hitler came to power at approximately the same time and both found a deeply depressed economy. The American recovery, although long and pronounced, was marred by unusual price rises in the midst of still heavy unemployment—an early case of stagflation. These price rises induced the Federal Reserve to step on the monetary brakes which led to the sharp slump of 1937–38. As we have seen, full employment was not reached before the American entry into the war in 1941.

The German recovery, in contrast, proceeded without interruption and reached substantially full employment within two or three years. The price level, unlike that in the United States, remained remarkably stable.

It would be tempting to attribute the rapid recovery to large spending on armaments. Heavy government spending there was, but massive rearmament came later. Possibly German public spending was comparatively larger than in the United States, but this would not explain the different price performance. The main difference between the American and German recovery policy lies elsewhere. In the United States the New Deal combined deficit spending with deliberate wage and price boosting, through NRA, AAA, the Wagner Act and other measures. Thus, an exceptionally large part of the rising nominal GNP took the form of higher prices rather than larger output and employment.[28] In Germany, by contrast, money wage rates remained fairly constant, although the average annual earnings of labor rose rapidly in monetary and real terms, because unemployment disappeared and the workweek lengthened.[29]

True, under the Hitler dictatorship there were wage and price controls which later, after full employment was reached and massive preparation for war came into full swing, became very oppressive. Scarcities, unavailabilities and quality deterioration of numerous commodities combined with rationing made the stable price index increasingly unreal. But this does not alter the fact that the recovery from the depression was handled very effectively. Hitler was able quickly to liquidate the miseries of the depression and to provide guns and butter at the same time. The great economic successes strengthened his hold on the German people enormously. The gold parity of the mark was formally not altered. There was no devaluation, but an increasingly tight web of exchange control, import restrictions and export subsidies amounted to a disguised, messy, discriminatory and exploitative devaluation of the currency— the Schachtian System.[30] Hitler's economic success made a deep impression on many economists, on Keynes himself, who however soon changed his mind,[31] and on Keynes' radical followers who were strengthened in their conviction that only comprehensive controls and central planning can assure full employment and rapid growth without inflation. Fortunately, another German economic miracle, the sustained economic recovery and growth after World War II, conclusively demonstrates that liberal trade policy and sound finance, the "classical medicine" as Keynes called it, works even better than the Schachtian system of comprehensive controls. Equally important, the German economic success also shows that a liberal policy can successfully be carried out in a democracy.[32]

4. The International Monetary System During the Interwar Period

It is misleading to speak of an international explanation of the Great Depression in contrast to explanations in terms of mistakes of U.S. monetary policy, or other domestic circumstances in the United States or elsewhere.[33] There can be no doubt, however, that the world depression had been intensified—greatly in smaller countries and slightly, primarily through feedback-effects, in the United States—by the malfunctioning and mismanagement of the international monetary system then in operation. Contrary to a widely held view, the trouble was not excessive volatility of floating exchanges rates, but rather excessive rigidity of exchange rates under the gold standard.[34]

To bring out the perversity of the operation of the system, consider how it should have operated and would have operated if it had been properly managed. After the depression gathered momentum, the ideal policy would have been an internationally agreed policy of joint monetary-fiscal expansion—the dominant economic power, the United States taking the lead. Since the United States did not take the lead but let its economy sink deeper into depression, the second-best policy would have been for other countries to go ahead with expansionary measures and promptly let their currencies depreciate as many countries did in the end. This, however, was against the spirit of the times. What actually happened was that most countries took deflationary measures to protect the parity of their currency. As a consequence, protectionist propensities became very strong. As mentioned above, the United States gave a bad example by imposing in 1930 the highly protectionist Smoot-Hawley tariff. In Britain Keynes recommended first a "revenue tariff", then a uniform import tariff plus an equal export bounty (which would have been roughly equivalent to a depreciation of the currency), and still later a system of differentiated import tariffs and export bounties (which would have been equivalent to what later became known as the Schachtian (Nazi) system).[35] On September 21, 1931 Britain took the historic step of cutting the link to gold and let the pound float. On top of that, she introduced in February 1932 a stiff import tariff.[36] The combination of devaluation and protection served its purpose; it stimulated the British economy but exerted strong deflationary pressures on other countries including the United States where the Federal Reserve reacted by deflationary measures.[37]

In 1933–34 the gold value of the dollar was gradually reduced from $20.67 per ounce of gold to $35 for the purpose of raising the price level and so stimulating the economy—a flagrant case of beggar thy neighbor policy which resulted in heavy deflationary pressure on the countries whose currencies were still linked to gold— France, The Netherlands and Switzerland among them. They reacted by further deflating and imposing import restrictions. In 1936 the "gold bloc" countries devalued. In the meantime other countries—Australia and the Scandiavian countries among them—had cut the link to gold and the dollar, launched expansionary measures, and so extricated themselves from the deflationary spiral.[38]

The upshot is that, although each devaluation can be detended as unavoidable and serving its purpose of relieving deflationary pressure in the country concerned, the time pattern of the process, the slow-motion adjustment of exchange rates, stamps the whole approach as a sadistic policy, calculated to maximize the pains of adjustment. If I may use a simile that I have used before, it was like cutting off the tail of a dog piece by piece instead of all at once as it might have been done (if there had existed an International Monetary Fund) by raising the gold price all around, thus enabling simultaneous expansion in all countries.

5. Fifty Years Later: Can It Happen Again?

Can it happen again? The short answer is: It is thinkable but very unlikely. Why? A plausible but not entirely satisfactory answer, that only a few years ago would have been given by many economists, mainly Keynesians,[39] is this: The Great Depression and earlier ones were due to deflation (a sharp decline of the money stock and aggregate expenditures) and this is not likely to happen again. True enough, but avoidance of monetary deflation may not be enough to prevent recessions and depressions. In recent years it has become general knowledge (what previously was known only to a few economists) that inflation is not incompatible with unemployment. The recession of 1973–75 was a highly inflationary one. Is an inflationary depression with unemployment as high as in the 1930s (25 percent) not possible?[40]

The probability of this happening is, I believe, greater (probably much greater) than the probability of a monetary deflation (sharp decline in money GNP). The reason is that it is much easier to stop a monetary contraction than an inflationary recession or depression. A decline in money and money GNP can always be stopped by monetary-fiscal measures. But that may not be enough to stop an inflationary depression. Keeping the growth of money and money GNP at the level that corresponds to the growth of full employment real GNP ("growth potential" as it is often called) is a necessary but not a sufficient condition for preventing an inflationary recession or depression. Even if the monetary stability condition is fulfilled, that is to say, even if monetary growth is equal to the full employment real GNP growth, inflation accompanied by unemployment (an inflationary recession) is thinkable, namely if organized pressure groups push wages and other costs, such as energy, above the full employment level. This could also be described as a case of cost-push inflation and stagflation.

The crucial question thus is what one assumes about the power and behavior of such pressure groups. The answer to this question has important implications. Monetarists assume that, provided the monetary authorities stand firm, labor unions and other pressure groups would not want to, or would not be strong enough to, push up the cost level significantly so as to produce a recession or depression, although some transitional unemployment may have to be accepted to eliminate inflation after it has been allowed to gather momentum. This assumption implies that by and large the economy still operates according to the competitive rules.

I, myself, believe that this diagnosis is too optimistic. Wage push is a real threat. After all, there have been inflationary recessions. The question is: Can the wage push become strong enough to produce a real inflationary depression of an order of magnitude of the Great Depression? In my judgment the answer to this generation is: no; an inflationary depression is not likely to occur. This judgment is based on the assumption that at an unemployment level of, say, 12–15 percent or more unions would moderate their wage demands substantially.

However, this conclusion does not justify great optimism for the future. For one thing, our society's tolerance for unemployment is much lower today than it was 50 years ago. As a consequence, governments react strongly even to low levels of general unemployment and to patches of unemployment in limited areas, by all sorts of measures, massive deficit spending, ill-conceived regulations, large subsidies to, or nationalization of, inefficient and uncompetitive industries or firms, restriction of imports, and so on. The result is an enormous growth of the public sector, a stifling tax burden, lower productivity, sluggish growth and more inflation. In some western countries there are strong reactions to these collectivist tendencies. But it remains to be seen whether there will be a real reversal of the trend.

For another thing, paradoxical though it may sound, an old-fashioned, classical depression with falling prices, even a depression of as catastrophic dimension as the Great Depression of the 1930s, is easier to stop than the mild inflationary recessions of our times. Easy money and crude deficit spending is the straightforward cure for old-fashioned depressions, while an inflationary recession—stagflation—poses a nasty policy dilemma: If fiscal-monetary expansion is used to combat unemployment, inflationary pressures increase; if tight fiscal-monetary measures are applied to curb inflation, unemployment goes up.

Space does not permit a thorough discussion of the dilemmas and perils of stagflation. I must confine myself to a few remarks.

First, inflation must be stopped by tight monetary-fiscal policies, because the cost of long-lasting inflation is much greater than is commonly realized.[41] Second, most economists, including Keynesians and Monetarists, should be able to agree that the transitional (or long-lasting) unemployment caused by disinflation will be less and thus the chances of a disinflationary policy to be adopted and successfully carried out will be greatly improved, if the economy is brought closer to the competitive ideal by removing impediments to competition, vigorous anti-monopoly policy (keeping in mind that free trade is the most effective and administratively easiest anti-monopoly policy), deregulation of industry and similar measures. However, since such reform measures take a long time to be adopted and to become effective, curbing inflation by monetary-fiscal policies cannot wait until institutional reforms have been carried out. Third, recent theoretical developments (monetarism, rational expectations theory, William Fellner's credibility approach) as well as practical experience have demonstrated the crucial importance of inflationary expectations. If market participants (including labor unions and other pressure groups) are convinced that inflation will continue, they raise their wage and price demands and inflation accelerates. As William Fellner[42] has stressed, the government can help to induce market participants to change their expectations by making it clear that it will stick to its anti-inflation policy. If a credible anti-inflation policy persuades market participants that the government will pursue its anti-inflation policy consistently and will not change course as soon as unemployment goes up a little bit, unions will moderate their wage demands in order not to price themselves out of the market. The difficulty is how to make the policy credible after many years of stop and go.

The international monetary system of the post-war period was a great improvement over the gold standard of the interwar period. The Bretton Woods system served the world well for 25 years. It provided a forum for continuous consultations so that necessary exchange rate changes could be made more promptly than under the gold standard and convertibility of currencies could be restored. Tariffs were reduced and world trade was liberalized under the aegis of GATT.

Although protectionist pressures have increased in recent years, a protectionist explosion has been avoided because, unlike what happened in the 1930s, balance of payments adjustment is being effected by exchange rate changes and floating rather than by exchange control and import quotas.[43]

In the later 1960s, however, the Bretton Woods system came increasingly under stress and in the early 1970s it broke down because its method of changing exchange rates, the "adjustable" or "jumping" peg, was too slow to cope with the strains and stresses caused by rising inflation and increasing international mobility of capital. Bretton Woods was followed by widespread managed floating of all major and many minor currencies although a large number of smaller countries continue to peg their currencies to the dollar, the German mark, the Japanese yen, to SDRs or some other baskets of currencies.

Despite much criticism and disenchantment, it can be said that the present system of managed floating—or non-system as some prefer to call it—has served the world quite well, certainly much better than the adjustable peg would have. Floating has enabled the world economy to adjust to a series of nasty shocks—a major inflationary commodity boom followed by the oil shock, the severe recession of 1973—75 and the large inflation differentials between major countries that have developed in recent years.[44]

The dollar is still the world's most important reserve and transactions currency. The dramatic decline of the dollar, mainly vis-à-vis the German mark, Swiss fanc, Japanese yen and currencies linked to the mark, is due to the fact that the strong currency countries have managed to reduce the rate of inflation to a much lower level than the United States. True, the United States inflation declined from 12 percent in 1974 to below 5 percent at the end of 1976; but it got stuck at that level and rose again to the two-digit level after the new administration in 1977 prematurely switched emphasis from fighting inflation to more rapid expansion while strong currency countries continued to wind down inflation. This divergent policy stance created a (temporary) growth differential as well as an inflation differential between the United States and the strong currency countries. No wonder that the dollar slumped! The greatest, nay indispensable, contribution to a smooth working of the international monetary system and further growth of the world economy that the United States could make is to bring down its rate of inflation to the German level.

But floating is here to stay. It has served the world well. Despite turmoil in the foreign exchange markets and protectionist pressures, world trade has continued to expand rapidly. Only in one year, the recession year of 1975, was there a small decline in the volume of world trade.

5. Concluding Remarks

The Great Depression of the 1930s was not a regular cyclical down-swing; its catastrophic severity and length did not signify a basic instability of the capitalist free enterprise system, as Marxists and Keynes' radical followers, Marxo-Keynesians (as Schumpeter used to call them) believe. It was due to horrendous monetary-financial policy mistakes of commission and omission on the national and international level. The international monetary system then in operation, which provided for fixed exchanges under the gold standard, was responsible for the rapid worldwide sweep of the slump and greatly added to its severity.

These basically monetary mistakes were not repeated in the post-war period and are most unlikely to be committed in the future. The international monetary arrangements of the post-war period, first the Bretton Woods regime then the present system of managed flexibility of exchange rates, have been a great improvement over the regime of fixed exchange rates in the 1930s. It follows that another depression of the same kind and severity as the Great Depression, a *deflationary* depression, is almost inconceivable.

This conclusion is, however, no reason for complacency. There are different ways of getting into serious difficulties. Chronic inflation has become a grave calamity and we have learned that in the longer run inflation, far from being a remedy, becomes the cause of stubborn unemployment. There are good reasons to believe that an inflationary *depression* approaching the severity of the Great Depression of the 1930s, although not unthinkable, will be avoided. But we have already had several *inflationary recessions;* the last one of 1974–75 was serious and worldwide. The tolerance of our society for unemployment is much lower today than it was 50 years ago. The consequence is that governments overreact even to comparatively low levels of unemployment and associated inflation—by excessive monetary-fiscal expansion, thus accelerating and perpetuating inflation; by ill-conceived regulations, by price and wage controls, and by import restrictions and subsidies in different forms to noncompetitive firms and industries. This leads to an enormous growth of government bureaucracy and stifling taxation—a potent discouragement of saving and investment—and to economic inefficiencies. Thus, the growth of productivity slows down and comes to a halt which makes it still harder to stop inflation. This vicious circle undermines the foundation of the capitalist, free market economy, and endangers the future of democracy itself.

Notes

1. See my paper "The Present Economic Malaise," in *Contemporary Economic Problems 1979,* American Enterprise Institute, Washington, D.C., 1979, pp. 261–292.

2. The terminology "recession-depression" is of recent origin. Earlier writers made a roughly similar distinction between "Kitchin" and "Juglar" cycles (Schumpeter), major and minor cycles (Hansen), mild and severe depression cycles (M. Friedman). The distinction is one of degree, but it is clear-cut in most cases.

3. See *International Reserves and Liquidity,* A study of the Staff of the International Monetary Fund, Washington, D.C. 1958, p. 18. The increase in international liquidity did not go unnoticed. There was concern in the middle 1930s that the plethora of gold could produce

inflatory dangers. See references to the literature in my essay *The World Economy, Money and the Great Depression 1929–1939*, American Enterprise Institute, Washington, D.C., 1976, p. 20. [Chapter 16 in this volume]

4. See *International Financial Statistics*, International Monetary Fund.

5. See *International Trade 1978–79*, General Agreement on Tariffs and Trade (GATT), Geneva 1979, Table 1, "Growth of World Exports and Production 1963–1978," p. 2.

6. This does not mean that there are no radical economists in the United States. There are quite a few but they have broken allegiance to Keynes and have organized themselves in the Union of Radical Political Economists (URPE).

7. The theory that slower population growth and its impact on construction was at the root of the Great Depression was recently revived. See Clarence L. Barber, "On the Origin of the Great Depression," *Southern Economic Journal*, vol. 44, No. 3, January 1978, pp. 432–455. This factor could conceivably have helped to trigger a recession. But the recession could not have snowballed into a catastrophic depression without massive mistakes of commission and omission on the part of the monetary authorities.

8. The quotation comes from the report of a study group on post-war economic problems organized by the Royal Institute of International Affairs. London. *The Economic Lessons of the Nineteen-Thirties*, report drafted by H. W. Arndt, London Oxford University Press, 1944, pp. 287–288. The role of real maladjustments in the depression was the central theme of two other very influential studies. One is the majority report of the so-called Gold Delegation of the Financial Committee of the League of Nations, a group of highly respected financial and economic experts, with the task to study the working of the international monetary system. See *Final Report*, Geneva, 1932. (There was, however, a minority report signed by Gustav Cassel, the famous Swedish economist, among others, which rejected the view that the trouble was due "to the various economic maladjustments enumerated by our colleagues" (ibid., p. 64) and put forward an essentially monetary explanation.) The other study stressing real maladjustments is a large volume by Ingvar Svennilson, *Growth and Stagnation in the European Economy*, United Nations, Economic Commission for Europe, Geneva, 1954.

9. See Friedrich A. Hayek, *Prices and Production*, 1st edition 1931, 2d edition, London 1935. Lionel Robbins, *The Great Depression*, London, 1934. In my book *Prosperity and Depression*, I discussed this theory in greater detail under the title "Monetary Over-Investment Theories."

10. See my *The World Economy, Money and the Great Depression, 1929–1939*, ibid., pp. 24–25. There it is pointed out that a major difficulty of the application of the Hayek-Robbins theory to the Great Depression was that in the United States the price level was virtually stable from 1921 to 1929. Thus, there seems to have been no period of inflation preceding the Great Depression. Hayek and Robbins tried to overcome this difficulty by arguing that there was a *hidden* inflation. The 1920s was "a period of rapidly rising productivity. The comparative stability of prices, therefore, so far from being a proof of the absence of inflation, is a proof of its presence." (Robbins, ibid., pp. 48–49) It would lead too far and is hardly necessary any more to show why this is not a satisfactory answer.

11. See Lord Robbins, *Autobiography of an Economist*, London, 1971, pp. 153 et seq. The present writer fully agrees with Lord Robbins. He, too, had accepted Hayek's theory at one point, but has long since given it up. (See Gottfried Haberler, "Money and the Business Cycle," in *Gold and Monetary Stabilization*, Harris Foundation Lectures, Quincy Wright, editor,

University of Chicage Press, 1932; reprinted in *The Austrian Theory of the Trade Cycle and Other Essays*, Center of Libertarian Studies, Occasional Paper No. 8. New York, 1978.)

Two prominent German economists, Albert Hahn and Wilhelm Röpke, both of conservative and anti-Keynesian persuasion, had stressed real maladjustments caused by inflationary booms that made a smooth transition to a non-inflationary equilibrium impossible. But when the depression deepened, they distinguished between the "primary depression" (caused by the real maladjustments) and the "secondary deflation" due to monetary policy mistakes of commission or omission. Like Robbins they realized that the "secondary deflation" completely swamped the so-called "primary depression." See Wilhelm Röpke, *Crises and Cycles*, London, 1963, p. 120.

12. National Bureau of Economic Research, Princeton University Press, 1963. The words "truly great" come from Sir Roy Harrod's review of the book in *The University of Chicago Law Review*, Vol. 32, No. 1, Autumn 1964. pp. 188–196. This is high praise coming from an avowed Keynesian, but is by no means inconsistent with the author's Keynesian beliefs. Harrod emphatically rejects the view adopted by many Keynesians "that the events of 1929 to 1933 proved the impotence of monetary policy" and emphasizes that "monetary policy was not attempted in the United States in 1929 to 1933" (Ibid., p. 196). The same conclusion had been reached earlier by Lauchlin Currie, *The Supply and Control of Money in the United States*. Harvard University Press, Cambridge, Mass. 1934 passim, William Fellner, *Monetary Policies and Full Employment*, California University Press, Berkeley, Calif., second edition 1947, pp. 212–213, and Walter S. Salant, *Some Comments on the Effectiveness of Credit Policy in Combatting a Recession*, Memo presented to a Staff Committee of the Council of Economic Advisers, May 21, 1948 (mimeographed).

13. This categoric statement has been challenged on two grounds: First, it has been said that psychologically, ideologically and politically it was not possible for the Federal Reserve to engage in sufficiently massive open market operations. Second, it has been questioned whether a prevention of monetary contraction would have had a strong effect on the real economy. The first doubt is inconsistent with the fact that the New York Federal Reserve Bank, surely not a hotbed of monetary radicalism, was in favor of strong monetary antideflationary measures. Friedman and Schwartz have shown that the power in the system shifted from the New York bank to the Federal Reserve Board after the untimely death in 1928 of Governor Benjamin Strong who had dominated the system. The point is that if the Board instead of overruling the New York bank had joined forces with it, the System need not have been afraid of ideological or political obstacles.

The answer to the second question is this: What is asserted is that prevention of the breakdown of thousands of banks and of the tremendous contraction of money and credit would have drastically reduced the catastrophic fall in output and employment. This can hardly be doubted but leaves open two more questions: First, would monetary measures also have prevented a recession, perhaps a somewhat more severe one than the two mild recessions of 1924 and 1927? Second, can it not be argued that, after the depression had gathered momentum, stronger measures than easy money were required to stop the slide quickly? (For an affirmative answer to the second question see below.)

14. This was pointed out in the review of Kindleberger's latest book *Manias, Panics and Crashes. A History of Financial Crises*, New York, 1978, by Patrick Minford in *The Economic Journal* (Vol. 89, December 1979, p. 948). "... it is not clear how one distinguishes between a failure of the Federal Reserve Board to maintain the money supply (as Friedman says) and such

a credit contraction (as Kindleberger puts it); for credit is simply the other side of the bank's balance sheet. Kindleberger's views are much closer to Friedman's than he recognizes, if not identical."

15. A mechanism of this kind has been used by several economists (e.g., by Ralph G. Hawtrey, the great British monetarist) to explain the business cycle.

16. This thought has been developed in my paper "Austria's Economic Development After the Two World Wars: A Mirror Picture of the World Economy," in *Empirische Wirtschafts-forschung und Monetäre Ökonomik*, Berlin 1979, pp. 177–197. See also my paper "Notes on Rational and Irrational Expectations," in a Festschrift for Odolf Jöhr, Tübingen 1980. [Chapter 27 in this volume] Both papers are available as American Enterprise Institute reprints.

17. The older members of the Chicago School have emphasized a development that greatly intensifies the disastrous impact of monetary deflation, namely the increasing rigidity of wages and prices—a factor that the next generation of monetarists tends to neglect or to minimize. Thus, in 1941 Frank Knight wrote with the Great Depression in mind: "In a free market these changes (in aggregate demand and prices of different goods) would be temporary, but even then they might be serious; and with important markets as unfree as they actually are ... the results take on the proportion of a social disaster." (F. H. Knight, "The Business Cycle, Interest and Money", reprinted from *Review of Economics and Statistics*, Vol. 23. May 1941, in F. H. Knight. *On the History and Methods of Economics*, Chicago, 1956, p. 335.) A. C. Pigou in his classic book *Industrial Fluctuations*, second edition, London, 1927, assigns equal weight in explaining the business cycle to monetary and banking arrangements and to wage rigidity. Recent research has demonstrated the decreasing responsiveness of inflation to declining aggregate demand due to increasing rigidity of wages. (See Jeffrey Sachs. *The Changing Cyclical Behavior of Wages and Prices 1890–1976*. National Bureau of Economic Research Working Paper No. 304. New York, 1978, mimeographed.)

18. Edward M. Bernstein. *The Nature and Causes of Deep Depression*, EMB Ltd., Washington, D.C., 1962 (mimeographed). See also his article "International Monetary Organization," in *International Encyclopedia of the Social Sciences*, Vol. 8, New York, 1968, p. 19.

19. On the origin of the gold exchange standard, its growth and the deflationary consequences of its breakdown in the depression see Ragnar Nurkse, *International Currency Experience Lessons of the Inter-War Period*, League of Nations, 1944, pp. 27–46.

Several writers, especially Jacques Rueff, have argued that the gold exchange standard had been an inflationary factor and then through its inevitable breakdown and liquidation was largely responsible for the extraordinary severity of the depression. The liquidation of the gold exchange standard surely was a deflationary factor. But compared with the massive internal deflation in the United States, which was almost entirely due to domestic causes (institutional weaknesses and monetary mismanagement), it must be judged a factor of minor importance.

20. London, 1950.

J. A. Schumpeter, whose theory of the business cycle is usually not classified as a monetary one (although it has monetary elements), flirted with the idea that the severity of the depression was due to the confluence of the depression phase of several superimposed types of concurrent fluctuations. But his considered view was that "the darkest hues of cyclical depression ... are due to adventitious circumstances". (J. A. Schmpeter, "The Historical

Approach to the Analysis of Business Cycles," in *Conference on Business Cycles*, National Bureau of Economic Research, New York 1951, p. 150.) By "adventitious circumstances" he meant deflationary shocks due to collapse of the banking system, and other complications which are not regular features of the business cycle.

21. Op. cit. p. 163.

22. In most countries on the European continent inflation had reached a much higher level than in Britain. Therefore, a return of their currencies to the pre-war parity was out of the question. For example, the French franc was stabilized at a low level which enabled France to accumulate a large gold reserve which put additional deflationary pressure on Britain.

23. London, 1925. Reprinted in *Essays in Persuasion*, various editions. The whole episode is analyzed in depth in D. E. Moggridge, *British Monetary Policy, 1924–1931: The Norman Conquest of $4.86*, Cambridge 1972. The subtitle is an allusion to Montague Norman, the powerful governor of the Bank of England who was to a large extent responsible for the return to gold at the prewar parity of $4.86. The new material tends to exonerate Churchill. In a remarkable "most secret" memorandum addressed to his advisers before the decision to return to gold at the old parity was made, Churchill had asked all the relevant questions. But he received wrong or misleading answers from his advisers.

24. *The Works and Correspondence of David Ricardo*, edited by Piero Sraffa, Vol. IX, Cambridge, 1952, p. 71.

25. See Rendig Fels. "American Business Cycles 1865–79." *American Economic Review*, June 1951, pp. 335–349, and his book *American Business Cycles 1865–1897*, Chapel Hill, N.C., 1959.

26. This was pointed out with reference to J. R. Hicks in my paper "The Quest for Stability: The Monetary Factor," in *Stability and Progress in the World Economy. The First Congress of the International Economic Association*, edited by Douglas Hague, Macmillan, London, 1958, p. 165. An abridged and slightly altered version appeared under the title "Monetary and Real Factors Affecting Economic Stability. A Critique of Certain Tendencies in Modern Economic Theory," in the *Banca Nazionale del Lavoro Quarterly Review*, No. 38, September 1956, Rome p. 25.

27. See the memoirs of Heinrich Bruening, *Memoiren 1918–1934*. Münich, Deutscher Taschenbuch Verlag, 1972. Vol. 1. p. 204. For further details see my *The World Economy, Money and the Great Depression 1919–1939*, American Enterprise Institute, Washington, D.C. 1976, pp. 413–415 [Chapter 16 in this volume.]

28. Keynes sympathized with Roosevelt's reform measures but felt that "undue haste in the reform program" would prejudice recovery; and recovery should have priority over reform. For Keynes' criticism of the New Deal, see R. F. Harrod, *The Lift of John Maynard Keynes*, London-New York, 1951, p. 447.

29. See Gerhard Bry. *Wages in Germany 1871–1945*, National Bureau of Economic Research, Princeton University Press. 1960.

30. So named after Hjalmar Schacht, Hitler's economic wizard.

31. Richard (Lord) Kann in his paper "Historical Origins of the International Monetary Fund" (in *Keynes and International Monetary Relations*. The Second Keynes Seminar held at the

University of Kent at Canterbury, 1974, edited by A. P. Thirlwall, St. Martin's Press, New York, 1974) quotes a memorandum that Keynes distributed in the Treasury in September 1941 entitled *Post-War Currency Policy*. In this memorandum Keynes said "It was only in the last years, almost in the last months, before the crash, that ... Dr. Schacht stumbled in desperation on something new which had in it the germs of a good technical idea.... Dr. Schacht's idea was to introduce 'what amounted to barter'.... In this way he was able to return to the essential character and original purpose of trade whilst discussing the apparatus which ... had been supposed to facilitate, but was in fact strangling it. This innovation worked well, indeed brilliantly." Two years later (October 1943) Keynes wrote in the same vein to a U.K. Treasury official: "I believe that the future lies with (I) state trading for commodities; (II) international cartels for necessary manufacturers; and (III) quantitative import restrictions for non-essential manufactures. Yet all these instrumentalities for orderly economic life in the future you (and the U.S. State Department) seek to outlaw" (quoted in R. F. Harrod. *The Life of John Maynard Keynes*, London-New York, 1951, p. 568). Harrod remarked: "In the preceding ten years he (Keynes) had gone far in reconciling himself to a policy of planned trade: these ideas had sunk deeply in. Even for him, with ... his power of quick adaptation, it was difficult to unlearn so much." (loc. est.) But unlearn he did, and very fast indeed. In May 1944 in a letter to The Times defending the Bretton Woods agreement against criticism by Thomas Balogh. Keynes wrote: "Since we are not (so far as I am aware), except perhaps Dr. Balogh, disciples of Dr. Schacht, it is greatly to our interest that others should agree to refrain from such disastrous (Schachtian) practices." (*The Times*, May 20, 1944, reprinted in Thomas Balogh's *Unequal Partners*, Vol. II, Oxford, 1963, p. 118.) Keynes, reconversion to liberalism (which was probably due largely to listening to James Meade, Redvers Opie, and Lionel Robbins) is described in detail in Harrod's book (see especially p. 609). In his famous posthumously published article, "The Balance of Payments of the United States" (*The Economic Journal*, June 1946) Keynes urged that "the classical medicine" should be allowed to work and concluded "that the chances of the dollar becoming dangerously scarce ... are not very high," thus rejecting the theory of the permanent dollar shortage which was propounded by his radical disciples as the basis of their violent objections to the policy of non-discrimination. Keynes criticized these theories "as modernist stuff, gone wrong and turned sour and silly." (See ibid. pp. 185–186.) In a letter to Lord Halifax he expressed himself even more strongly (see *The Collected Writings of John Maynard Keynes*. Vol. 24, *Activities 1944–1946, The Transition to Peace*, edited by Donald Moggridge, Cambridge, 1979, p. 626).

32. It is not surprising that the German economic "miracle" which started with the currency reform of 1948 and the simultaneous abolition of all controls by Ludwig Erhard, was completely unforeseen and misjudged, even after its early success had become apparent, by British admirers of Schacht. On this see T. W. Hutchison "Notes on the Effects of Economic Ideas on Policy: The Example of the German Social Market Economy," in *Zeitschrift für die Gesamte Staatswissenschaft. Currency and Economic Reform, West Germany after World War II, A Symposium*, Vol. 135. Tübingen, September 1979, pp. 436–441. I cite only one example: Thomas (Lord) Balogh predicted that the policies of Erhard could not be sustained. "The currency was reformed according to a wicked formula." It "helped to weaken the Trade Unions.... Their weakness may even inhibit increases in productivity, since large scale investment at high interest does not pay at the present low relative level of wages. In the long run the income pattern will become intolerable and the productive pattern unsafe." Balogh said that Dr. Erhard and his "satellite economists" are trying to discredit "enlightened Keynesian economic policies" and "to apply to real life an abstract obsolescent and internally

inconsistent economic theory and certainly did not succeed." Balogh predicted alarming political consequences and pointed in "a final warning to the gains which the Soviet Zone of Germany has been able to record." Balogh was however right in pointing out the extreme contrast between the economic ideas and policies prevailing in the Federal Republic of Germany and those in Britain. However, the results were the opposite of what Balogh and the other critics had predicted: German real GNP per capita has grown to almost twice that of Britain. (See T. W. Hutchison, op. cit. pp. 435–439 and Thomas Balogh "Germany: an Experiment in 'Planning' by the 'Free' Price Mechanism," *Banca Nazionale Del Lavoro Quarterly Review* 3, Rome 1950, pp. 71–102.) Hutchison also shows that German economic policies were similarly misjudged by American representatives of the "New Economics", Walter Heller among them.

I offer a supplement to Hutchison's list of misjudgments by advocates of central planning and comprehensive controls of the German revival of laissez faire liberalism: In 1948, criticizing the view "that if, somehow, the German economy could be freed from material and manpower regulations, price controls and other bureaucratic paraphernalia, then recovery could be expedited", John K. Galbraith concluded: "... There never has been the slightest possibility of getting German recovery by this wholesale repeal [of controls and regulations]". (J. K. Galbraith, "The German Economy," in *Foreign Economic Policy for the United States*, edited by Seymour E. Harris, Harvard University Press. Cambridge, Mass. 1948, p. 95). Galbraith's paper abounds with predictions of dire political and economic consequences of Erhard's dash for economic freedom. To quote Keynes again: Rarely has "modernist stuff gone wrong and turned sour and silly" so fast!

33. Charles P. Kindleberger "takes exception to the findings of those" who stress monetary policy in the United States and other major countries, slower population growth or autonomous changes in the propensity to spend, and "insists that the origins of the Great Depression were international." Charles P. Kindleberger "The International Causes and Consequences of the Great Crash," *The Journal of Portfolio Management*, Fall 1979, p. 11. This paper summarizes Kindleberger's full-dress analysis, *The World in Depression 1929–1939*, London-New York 1973.

34. However, criticism of the gold standard in its dying phase does not mean that it was a bad system under more propitious circumstances in the liberal era before 1914.

35. This was Keynes' nationalistic-protectionist period. One of Keynes' great admirers commented: "Even Keynes succumbed to the current insanity ... A sad aberration of a noble mind." Lord Robbins' *Autobiography of an Economist*, London 1971. p. 156. Keynes later changed his mind, but some of his followers have continued the "insanity" to this day.

36. Keynes opposed the devaluation and pleaded for his import-tariff, export-bounty scheme. After the devaluation had occurred he argued that protectionist measures were no longer necessary. But it was too late, "Die ich rief, die Geister, die werd ich nun nicht los." (Goethe, "The Sorcerer's Apprentice".)

37. See Friedman-Schwartz, *Monetary History*, p. 317.

38. For details, see my, "The World Economy Money and the Great Depression 1929–39" and the literature mentioned there. [Chapter 16 in this volume]

39. Keynesians rather than Keynes himself. Already in 1937, one year after the appearance of the General Theory. Keynes had become very worried about inflation and called for a shift in

policy, although inflation was low by present day standards (less than 10 percent) and unemployment was rather high (about 11 percent). See T. W. Hutchison, *Keynes versus the "Keynesians,"* Institute of Economic Affairs, London, 1977.

40. It could be argued that 25 percent unemployment today is not equivalent to 25 percent in the 1930s, because generous unemployment benefits and welfare payments have not only reduced the cost of unemployment in terms of human suffering, but also means that an unknown but surely significant fraction of the registered number of the unemployed represents voluntary unemployment. It follows that 25 percent unemployment in the 1930s would be equivalent, to, say, 35 percent now.

41. See Martin Feldstein, "The Welfare Cost of Permanent Inflation and Optimal Short Run Economic Policy," *Journal of Political Economy,* vol. 87, No. 4, August 1979, pp. 749–768.

42. William Fellner, *Towards a Reconstruction of Macroeconomics, Problems of Theory and Policy,* American Enterprise Institute, Washington, D.C., 1976, and "The Valid Core of Rationality Hypotheses in the Theory of Expectations," paper prepared for a Conference on Rational Expectations held at the American Enterprise Institute, Washington. D.C., Feb. 1, 1980. The proceedings are published in the *Journal of Money, Credit and Banking.* Volume 12. No. 4, Part 2, November 1980, Columbus, Ohio.

43. On the trade front there has been some backsliding. Import restrictions have been imposed in a number of cases, usually not by higher tariffs but by "non-tariff" measures including the so-called "voluntary" export restrictions forced on foreign exporters. But these restrictions are protectionist in nature designed to protect particular industries; they are not across the board to "protect" the balance of payments as they were in the 1930s.

44. See Otmar Emminger, *The International Monetary System Under Stress. What Can We Learn from the Past?,* Reprint No. 112. American Enterprise Institute, Washington, DC 1980 and Gottfried Haberler. "The Dollar in the World Economy: Recent Developments in Perspective". *Contemporary Economic Problems,* 1980, William Fellner, Project Director, American Enterprise Institute. Washington, D.C. 1980.

18

The World Economy,
Macroeconomic Theory and
Policy—Sixty Years of
Profound Change[1]

1. Overview

In the last sixty years the economies of the world have undergone great changes; the same is true of macroeconomic theory and of economic policy. In the present paper I shall try to sketch these changes and to analyze the interactions of economic change, changing macroeconomics theories and policies.

The First World War and the Interwar Period

The fratricidal European war of 1914—1918, the first global conflict since the Napoleonic wars a hundred years earlier, was a watershed. It marked the end, or the beginning of the end, of an epoch—the epoch of liberalism, of free trade and the gold standard, of free migration and free travel, *without a passport*, between most countries (excepting Russia but including the United States). True, in the 1920s most countries recovered faster from the ravages of the war than had been expected, trade was resumed and the gold standard restored. But tariffs were much higher than before; free migration and free travel without a passport were gone forever; the United States and most other countries had a severe depression in 1920—21; the continental European countries went through a period of high or hyper-inflation; communism was firmly established in Russia, and the recovery lasted barely eight years, 1921—1929.

The Great Depression of the 1930s

The great Depression was a world-shaking disaster. The United States, emerged as the dominant economic power from the war, was in the center of storm. From

Paper prepared for the occasion of the award of the Antonio Feltrinelli Prize by the Academia Nazionale dei Licèi (Italian Academy of Science) (Rome, Italy: 1982). Also published by the American Enterprise Institute as an Occasional Reprint. Reprinted with permission of Academia Nazionale dei Licèi.

August 1929 to March 1933 money GNP fell by about 50 percent, real GNP by about 33 percent, industrial production by 53 percent and unemployment reached 25 percent of the labor force. The slump was followed by a long recovery (April 1933–April 1937) but it was interrupted "long before full employment had been reached" by a short, but extremely vicious slump. In the short period of thirteen months real GNP slumped by over 16 percent, industrial production by 32 percent and unemployment again shot up to 20 percent. Full employment was reached only in 1942, after the United States had entered the war.

The depression was worldwide although only a few countries were hit as hard as the United States and several countries managed to extricate themselves from the depression long before the United States. The third world, the less developed countries, experienced a devastating deterioration of their terms of trade. The money value of world trade (in gold dollars) shrank to about a third of its predepression level and the real volume to about half—the difference indicating the enormous decline in the price level.

The economic and political repercussions of the depression were tremendous. If Germany had not been hit so hard by depression, Hitler might not have come to power and the Second World War might have been avoided. The power and prestige of Soviet Russia received a great boost because the communist economy seemed to be immune to the depression. The depression gave rise to the "Keynesian revolution" (see below) and Marxist thoughts became very popular. Confidence in the capitalist, free market systems was badly shaken and government policies everywhere and in every sphere veered sharply to the left, in the direction of more government interventions, tighter control and central planning. These tendencies were accentuated by the Second World War. Stalinist Russia, the true victor, was enlarged by a string of satellites and its prestige and power greatly enhanced. Thus, the prospects for the postwar period were rather grim.

The Post-World War II Period—A Great Surprise

Despite the seemingly poor prospects and contrary to the pessimistic forecasts especially by Keynesian economists—not so much Keynes himself—that the dismal developments of the interwar period would repeat themselves, the first thirty-five years since the end of the war have been a period of almost unprecedented growth and prosperity. Few would doubt the truth of this statement for the first quarter century since the war as far the industrial countries are concerned. Let me mention a few facts. The U.S. economy enjoyed a high rate of growth except for the last few years; it experienced several mild recessions, but not a single depression, if by depression we mean a decline in economic activity of the same order of magnitude as the depression of the 1930s, or 1920–21, or earlier depressions. Even the recession of November 1973–May 1975, the longest and severest of the postwar period, was a mild setback compared with the depressions of the interwar period.

Everyone knows of the German and Japanese economic miracles. But there was also an Italian economic miracle and a French and an Austrian one. I shall come back to the question of what accounts for the contrast between the economic performance in the interwar and postwar periods. But let me mention right here that the various economic miracles had one thing in common: All of them were the result of the application of what Keynes called "the classical medicine" and Schumpeter the "capitalist methods", that is, the principles of sound finance. In Italy it was Luigi Einaudi the great economist and statesman who, as Governor of the Central Bank and later as President of the Republic, was the architect of the economic miracle. The excessive growth in the money supply was stopped and the government budget brought under control.

The various economic miracles were made possible by generous American aid through the Marshall Plan. Trade was liberalized under the aegis of GATT and world trade grew throughout the postwar period as never before. Only in one year, the recession year of 1975, was there a small decline in the volume of world trade. The contrast between the postwar years and interwar period could not have been sharper.

The question will be asked how this cheerful picture of the postwar period can be reconciled with the widespread economic malaise that has gripped the world in the last few years? There certainly has been a marked change. The prevailing mood in the 1950s and 1960s was one of optimism, skillful demand management along Keynesian lines, it was widely thought, had eliminated the business cycle and assured lasting stability, high level employment and steady growth.

It did not work out that way. Rising inflation and especially the vicious modern form of inflation, stagflation (the combination of inflation and high or even rising unemployment), two oil shocks, declining productivity and slow or zero growth— all that has turned the euphoria of the 1950s into pessimism and gloom.

I do not want to minimize the dangers of inflation nor belittle the consequences of slow growth or the evils of unemployment. I shall come back to the present situation and the dangers for the future. But whatever the prospects for the years to come, it is a fact that even the troubled years of the 1970s were a period of high prosperity compared with the depressed years of the 1930s.

I now come to the changes that have taken place during the last sixty years in macroeconomic theory and policy.

2. Changes in Macroeconomic Theory and Policy—The "Keynesian Revolution" and the "Monetarist Counterrevolution"

The "Keynesian Revolution"

A revolution it was in the sense that ever since the appearance of Keynes' *The General Theory of Employment, Money and Interest* (1936) his ideas have been in the center of the vast literature on macroeconomic theory as well as in policy discussion; the great changes in policy that have taken place have been strongly influenced by Keynes' ideas. No one less than Sir John Hicks has suggested that historians may well call the third quarter of the twentieth century "the age of Keynes." [2] It is not easy, however, to identify the novel features in Keynes' thinking that justify its characterization as a scientific revolution for two reasons. The first is that Keynes changed his views frequently. He adapted his conclusion to take account of changing conditions; a striking example will be mentioned presently. Moreover, his most famous book, *The General Theory*, is as Hicks points out "by no means wholly self-consistent" (*ibid.*, p. 5), but suggests alternative answers to the same question. Secondly, as a consequence of these rapid changes and inconsistencies many different views are "claiming a place under Keynes' umbrella" (Hicks, *ibid.*).

Time does not permit an extended analysis of the Keynesian theory; that has been done many times and I myself have tried it on two occasions. [3] Instead, I turn immediately to Keynes' principal policy recommendation—government deficit spending; and since this recommendation was clearly prompted by the traumatic experience of mass unemployment in the 1930s, I will discuss the Keynesian explanation of the exceptional severity of the Great Depression.

The Keynesian explanation was provided by the theory of secular stagnation due to vanishing investment opportunities, drying up of the flow of technological innovations and initiatives and chronic oversaving. This development was thought to impart a deflationary bias upon the later stages of capitalism. The obvious remedy was government deficit spending to offset the chronic deflationary expenditures gap in the private sector of the economy.

Later developments—a veritable burst of technological progress (new products, new methods of production) requiring enormous investments—have completely discredited the thesis of vanishing investment opportunities and drying up of the stream of technological progress. But the theory was widely accepted in the 1930s and Keynes clearly embraced it in *The General Theory*. However, a year later Keynes shifted his position. In 1937 in three remarkable articles in *The Times* he warned about the dangers of inflation and called for a change in policy, although unemployment was still high (about 11 percent down from over 20 percent in 1931, 1932 and 1933) and the price rise was not very high (a little over 10 percent) by present-day standards.[4] He did, of course, not recommend outright deflation, but did say "we are in more need of rightly distributed demand than of a greater aggregate demand" and if demand is stimulated in some lines "the Treasury would be entitled to economize elsewhere" (ibid., p. 66)—a veiled call for the end of deficit spending. As on many other occasions, Keynes' shift in position came too fast for most of his followers. Most of the numerous influential Keynesian economists remained unconcerned about the dangers of inflation throughout the postwar period.

I return to the question of government deficit spending in a depression. It has been widely accepted that the existence of mass unemployment justifies the use of deficit spending, irrespective of what caused the depression. Contrary to what his followers often say,[5] this was not a discovery of Keynes. Advocacy of deficit spending and public works to combat unemployment in a depression has a long history and the proponents of such policies were not only idealistic social reformers but also hard-headed professional economists of conservative persuasion. Thus when Keynes proposed public works in the early thirties he was joined by many British economists, D. H. Robertson and A. C. Pigou among them.[6] In the United States, too, deficit spending and public works were recommended during the depression by many economists, including conservative economists such as Jacob Viner and Henry Simons in the University of Chicago, the cradle of modern monetarism.[7]

But it is time now to discuss the role of money and monetary policy in the Keynesian system and the monetarist counterrevolution.

The Monetarist Counterrevolution

Money is not absent from Keynes' theoretical system. But in practice money was pushed into the background and had to be "rediscovered" in the postwar period.[8] Specifically, according to the Keynesians, money had little or nothing to do with the Great Depression, monetary developments were not the cause of the depression nor was monetary policy an effective remedy. "For many of his [Keynes'] followers, there is nothing important that can be done with monetary policy . . . Keynesianism, in practice, has become fiscalism."[9]

We now know that money had a lot to do with the Great Depression. The depression in the United States would never have become so severe and lasted so long if the monetary authorities had not allowed the stock of money to contract by about 30 percent from 1929–1933. Through mistakes of commission (deflationary measures applied on several occasions during the depression) and, even more important, mistakes of omission (failure to counteract with sufficient vigor the contraction of the money supply due to several waves of bank failures), the Federal Reserve System must take a large share of the responsibility for the disaster.[10]

The U.S. depression was almost entirely homemade. Deflationary influences from abroad were relatively minor and were largely feedback effects of the U.S. depression. Under fixed exchanges (gold standard)[11] a severe depression in the dominant U.S. economy was bound to spread swiftly around the world. Thus the United States was in the center of the storm. But there existed some epicenters, for example, in Germany and Britain—countries that experienced severe deflation, inflicted on them largely by their own actions.[12]

Thus the exceptional severity and length of the Great Depression was due to horrendous mistakes of monetary policy in the United States and in other major countries. In addition, the international monetary system was very badly managed which greatly intensified the depression, especially for smaller countries.

Stubborn defense of the gold parities of overvalued currencies by deflation, import restrictions and exchange control and uncoordinated, unduly delayed, discontinuous changes of exchange rates—devaluation of the British pound in 1931, of the dollar in 1933–34, the currencies of the so-called gold bloc (France, Switzerland, etc.)—all this maximized the pains of adjustment. The result was a catastrophic contraction of world trade.[13]

Before trying to apply the lessons of the 1930s to the period after World War II, the role of fiscal policy (deficit spending) in a deep depression must be defined. Even if it is accepted that monetary factors made the depression as long and severe as it was and that timely antideflationary monetary measures would have averted the disaster, it does *not* follow that after deflation and depression had taken hold and deflationary expectations had become entrenched there was no place for expansionary fiscal policy. Every depression (and recession for that matter) tends, if it lasts long enough, to become cumulative, to feed upon itself and to gather momentum. Once that happened, a strong case can be made for the proposition that the deflationary spiral should be stopped by direct injection of money into the income stream through government deficit spending. True, monetary expansion (open market operations and changes in reserve requirements) would eventually succeed in reviving the economy by inducing people to spend on consumption and investment. But in a deflationary environment monetary expansion is bound to work very slowly, and in the meantime a large pool of liquidity would be created which would become the source of inflation after the economy has turned the corner.[14] Keynesians and monetarists should be able to agree on this.

3. The Present Economic Malaise and Prospects for the Future

We have seen that the first quarter century after World War II was a period of almost unprecedented prosperity for the whole world, and that compared with the interwar period even the whole postwar period of 35 years, including the recent years of rising inflation and slowing growth, was very successful.

Two questions arise. *First*, what accounts for the success of the post-World War II period as compared with the failure of the interwar period? *Second*, will the vaunted prosperity last? Have we not paid too high a price in terms of high inflation?

The first question is the easier. We have seen that the exceptional severity and length of the Great Depression was due to horrendous policy mistakes on the national level (deflationary policies in the United States, Britain, Germany and elsewhere) and on the international level (delayed adjustment of exchange rates causing a protectionist explosion and exchange control). These mistakes have been avoided in the postwar period. There was no case of serious deflation anywhere, and under Bretton Woods and later under a system of managed floating, exchange rates were adjusted more or less smoothly. Furthermore, under GATT trade was liberalized. Thus, private enterprise and comparatively free markets were given a chance to show their mettle on the national and international level. This, basically, explains the success of the postwar period.

Keynesians claim full credit for the success. There is some justification, for Keynes and his followers certainly pressed the fight against deflation. This is why Hicks calls the third quarter of the century "the age of Keynes." But the good showing can just as well be called a triumph of monetarism, for monetarists, too, have been strongly opposed to deflation. And the Keynesians, not so much Keynes himself, must take much blame for the rising tide of inflation that threatens to cut short the era of prosperity. For they, the Keynesians, have pushed expansionary measures far beyond the point where they cease to yield significant additions to output and result mainly in rising prices. Their relaxed unconcern about the dangers of inflation has greatly contributed to make our time "the age of inflation." [15]

This brings us to the second question. Will the prosperity last? Will it not turn out that we have paid too high a price in terms of inflation?

We have learned that inflation is not a permanent cure for unemployment. There is no permanent trade-off between inflation and unemployment. The longer inflation goes on, the less stimulus it provides for output and employment and the harder it becomes to stop it. Inflation reduces the rate of productivity growth and after a certain point its net effect on output becomes negative. It is futile to try to "stabilize" a significant inflation rate. Only a zero or near-zero rate of inflation can be regarded as a stable condition.[16]

Two basic questions arise. First, what will happen if inflation continues unchecked and, second, how can it be stopped? I shall discuss these two questions in turn and concentrate on American conditions for two reasons: First, because I am more familiar with the American situation and, second, because the American inflation is specially disturbing.

Since the dollar is still the world's foremost private and official transaction, reserve and intervention currency, inflation in the United States is bound to have profoundly disturbing effects on the international monetary system. But I shall not discuss in the present paper the international aspects of the problem. That has been done elsewhere.[17]

Now to the *first* question. If inflation is not brought under control soon but allowed to continue, the outlook is very bleak indeed.[18] I rule out two extreme scenarios that are often said to be the probable outcome of unchecked inflation, a repetition of the Great Depression or hyper-inflation. A deflationary depression as in the 1930s is almost unthinkable; no country will deflate itself into depression. Hyper-inflation as happened in Germany and some other countries after World War I leading to complete destruction of money in existence and forcing a fresh start with new money is perhaps not quite so unlikely. But I am confident that as far as the United States and other industrial countries are concerned, inflation will be stopped one way or the other long before it approaches the state of hyper-inflation.

What cannot be so confidently excluded is an *inflationary* depression. To explain let me recall that we had in recent years the unusual and unpleasant phenomenon of *inflationary* recessions. Unlike in all previous "classical" business cycle recessions or depressions that were accompanied by declining prices, "deflationary recessions or depressions," the recent recessions were accompanied by rising prices, "inflationary recessions." Is it not possible that the next one will become so severe, output falling so much and unemployment rising so high, that it will qualify to be called an inflationary *depression?*[19]

That certainly is a possibility. There are reasons, however, to expect that things will not get quite so bad. It should be realized that the combination of inflation and high or rising unemployment, "stagflation," would not be possible, at least not on a large scale, in a highly competitive economy, especially not in a competitive labor market. It requires strong labor unions—and similar pressure groups—to drive up wages and prices in the face of high unemployment and slack. Is it not plausible to assume that unions would scale down their wage demands if unemployment reached depression proportions of, say, 15 percent or more?

Be that as it may, what is likely to happen, if inflation is not checked, is that governments will step in with comprehensive wage and price controls. This is very tempting because stagflation poses a disagreeable dilemma: If monetary and fiscal policies are used to combat inflation, unemployment will go up; and if tight financial policies are used to reduce unemployment, inflation will accelerate. This policy dilemma makes it very tempting to try to cut the knot by controls, alias incomes policy.

This is not a pleasant outlook. Comprehensive controls would deal a heavy blow to the market economy and they would reduce productivity growth—not an acceptable option.

This brings us to the second question posed above. How to stop *inflation without controls?* I take it for granted that to bring down inflation, monetary growth has to be restrained; for there has never been a significant inflation without an increase in the stock of money. Conversely, the growth of the money supply has to be reduced to roughly the normal rate growth of real national income.

There remains however, a number of technical questions which cannot be discussed here, e.g., how to define precisely the stock of money and whether monetary growth should be reduced gradually or abruptly. The question of gradualism versus shock treatment has been much debated recently. I confine myself to saying that, unless inflation has advanced very far, bordering on hyper-inflation, a gradual reduction of monetary growth is to be preferred—at least from the economic point of view.[20]

Leaving aside all that, I now discuss what we may call *the limits of monetarism.*

Restraint on monetary growth is certainly a necessary condition for a successful anti-inflation policy. But is it also a sufficient condition as monetarist economists often seem to imply?

Monetarists themselves usually make one exception: they often say that a tight monetary policy has to be accompanied by a tight fiscal policy; in other words, that the government budget deficit must be reduced or eliminated.[21] This concession of the monetarists has important implications. There can be no question that sufficiently tight money can bring down the rate of inflation, irrespective of the size of the budget deficit. If monetary policy can do the job, why insist on the help of fiscal policy? The answer is simple: the adverse, hopefully merely transitional, side effects of anti-inflationary monetary measures on output and employment will be much more serious, if there is a large budget deficit; for tight money combined with a large budget deficit will drive up interest rates, "crowd out" productive private investment, and thus in the short run will start or intensify a recession, and in the long run reduce productivity growth. This, surely, is an excellent reason for insisting that monetary policy should be supplemented by a tight fiscal policy.

If this is accepted the question arises: are there no other factors that, too, aggravate the adverse side effects of an anti-inflationary monetary policy? There surely are such factors which are in a sense even more basic and important than the budgetary problem. This brings me to a point of crucial importance which has been sorely neglected and downplayed in most of the modern monetarist literature. Inflation has become so intractable and the fight against inflation so difficult because the economy has become so inflexible and so far removed from the competitive ideal. In particular, labor unions have made industrial money wages almost entirely inflexible downward and in many countries, through widespread indexation, real wages, too, have become very rigid. Labor unions are, of course, not the only culprits. There are other pressure groups which do the same for their constituents as unions do for workers. Organized agriculture is the most conspicuous and important example.

Harry G. Johnson, the great monetarist, gave eloquent expression to his concern about that deplorable development. In one of his last papers he wrote: "In some countries, there now appears to be a commitment not only for every man [woman and child, we may add] to be employed, but for him [or her] to be employed in the occupation of his [or her] choice, in the location of his [or her] choice, and, it would sometimes seem, at the income of his [or her] choice." [22]

That development finds its clearest expression in protectionist pressures and governments' readiness to yield to these pressures. Instead of adjusting to changing conditions by letting uncompetitive firms go out of business and uncompetitive industries contract, governments protect such firms and industries not only by import restrictions in the form of tariffes, quotas, so-called "voluntary" agreements forced on foreign exporters to reduce their sales ("orderly market agreements"), and other devices, but also increasingly by subsidies to, or takeover by the government of, lame-duck firms and industries that should be allowed to contract or be liquidated. [23]

I have argued earlier that stagflation, the coexistence of inflation and high or even rising unemployment, would be impossible in a truly competitive economy. Since this is often misunderstood, let us consider how a competitive labor market economy operates.

Inflation is, of course, perfectly compatible with competitive markets but unemployment combined with rising prices is not. What counts is real involuntary unemployment which means that the supply of labor exceeds demand. [24] It is one of the basic principles of economic theory that under competition the price declines when supply exceeds demand. Applied to our case under competition, wages would decline if there is unemployment, i.e., if supply of labor exceeds demand. But in an inflationary situation this does *not* mean that there must be an absolute decline in money wages. Since under inflation wages rise, it only means that under competition money wages will rise less fast than they would in the absence of unemployment. Whether real wages rise, remain constant or decline depends on whether there is productivity growth, that is to say, whether output per man-hour rises, remains constant or declines. This follows from the generally accepted proposition that the rise of real wages is determined by the growth of productivity. [25]

Contrary to what is often assumed, the rise of inflationary expectations does not invalidate the proposition that stagflation would be impossible in a truly competitive economy. This is not to deny that inflationary expectations, in other words the erosion of money illusion, is a matter of capital importance; it progressively drains all pleasure from inflationary policies, and we have seen that neglect of the importance of inflationary expectations has been a serious weakness of Keynesian policy discussions. Entrenched inflationary expectations make labor unions and other pressure groups more aggressive and tempt them to jump the gun, that is to say push for wage increase in anticipation of future higher inflation. This deprives anti-inflationary polices of their stimulating power. Workers in competitive labor markets, too, become aware of what is going on and expect higher wages in the future. But refusing to accept in an inflationary situation a slower rate of growth of money wages and withholding their services, in other words to accept the hardships of unemployment in expectation of a higher wage in the future, would be irrational— and if some workers behaved like that, perhaps because they can afford such behavior in view of high unemployment benefits, the unemployment would be voluntary.

In summary, the conclusion that in competitive markets there would be no stagflation, at least not on a large scale, still stands.[26]

4. Summary: Some Policy Conclusions and Prospects for the Future

It is widely if not generally accepted that chronic inflation in its vicious modern form of stagflation has become the most serious economic problem confronting the Western industrial countries. For chronic inflation and its underlying causes are responsible for the poor growth performance and the widespread economic malaise that has developed in recent years.[27]

This is particularly true of inflation in the United States. For the U.S. economy is by far the largest in the world and the dollar, despite its recent decline, is still the world's foremost private and official transactions, reserve and intervention currency. Without a stable dollar the international monetary system cannot function smoothly and efficiently; and there can be no stable dollar if the U.S. inflation is not stopped. Inflation cannot be stopped without restraint on monetary growth and we have seen that tight monetary policy must be supported by a tight fiscal policy; that is to say, the deficit in the government budget must be sharply reduced to a manageable level. Theoretically, a sufficiently tight monetary policy could bring down inflation despite a large government budget deficit, but the adverse side effects on private investment and growth would be unacceptable. Moreover, in the United States and other Western countries, apart from the budget deficit, the size of the government budget has become a crushing burden on the economy and the tax system in most countries reduces saving and investment. It follows that in order to stimulate investment and accelerate growth the budget deficit should be reduced as far as possible by reducing government expenditures rather than by increasing taxes, and the structure of the tax system which has been greatly distorted by inflation should be changed. But this theme cannot be further pursued in this paper.

To summarize, restraint on monetary growth, supported by a tight fiscal policy, is a necessary condition to stop inflation and eventually re-accelerate growth and revitalize the economy.

Unfortunately, the adoption of an anti-inflationary austerity program of monetary and fiscal restraint, before it produces its beneficial effects, is bound to have temporarily adverse effects on output and employment. Some transitional unemployment is well-nigh unavoidable. In a truly competitive economy the transitional difficulties would be shortlived and mild. But in an economy as far removed from the competitive ideal as it has become in recent years, an economy overregulated and overtaxed, and shot through with monopolies and pressure groups largely due to government actions—in such an environment the transitional unemployment caused by an anti-inflationary policy is apt to be large and protracted.

It is therefore imperative to support the anti-inflationary monetary-fiscal policy by measures of "structural reform" designed to make the economy more flexible and bring it closer to the competitive ideal. From a long list of measures that should be taken only a few examples can be mentioned: Deregulation of industry, elimination of excessive price supports for agriculture, and elimination of minimum wage laws. The toughest problem in most countries, in the United States and the United Kingdom in particular, will be to curb the monopoly power of labor unions. Excessively large unemployment benefits (in some American states even striking workers are eligible for unemployment benefits) should be reduced. As far as business monopolies are concerned, the best antimonopoly policy is freer trade.[28] If nothing is done along these lines, the transitional unemployment caused by an anti-inflationary monetary-fiscal policy will be large and protracted. In that case the chances are that the pattern of the last fifteen years, the pattern of stop-and-go, will continue; the rate of inflation will be reduced temporarily in recessions, but "to get the economy moving again" before the next election the anti-inflationary policy will be reversed before inflation has been eradicated.

This is a dismal pattern. For successive recoveries from recessions will start from a higher inflation rate, inflation expectations will become more firmly entrenched, and it will become more and more difficult to break out of the vicious spiral.

I realize that structural reform along the lines indicated is bound to be a slow process. It will take time to design and put in place the measures that will make the economy more competitive and flexible. And after the reform measures have been adopted it will take more time for such measures to yield their beneficial effects. But I submit that the mere adoption of a firm policy along these lines, if it can be made credible, if people can be persuaded that the policy will be firmly pursued, will have an important announcement effect by shaking entrenched inflationary expectations. The same is true of a tighter monetary and fiscal policy. The adoption of such a policy will have an announcement effect on inflationary expectations if the public can be persuaded that this time the authorities mean business and will not, as so often in the past, give up the tighter policy as soon as unemployment rises a little bit.

In conclusion I sketch once more very briefly the two policy approaches—scenarios—that have emerged and indicate some political consequences.

The first senario: If the policy of stop-and-go is continued with half-hearted attempts at curbing inflation, the outlook is grim. Inflation will accelerate, though temporarily slowed from time to time in recessions. Labor unions and other pressure groups will assume that the government will bail them out through inflation and other measures, and thus ratify even outrageous wage and price boosts. The clamor for direct wage and price controls[29] will become irresistible and sooner or later even a conservative government will give in as the Nixon Administration did in 1971.

Direct controls have never worked[30]; they merely suppress sympions of inflation—repressed inflation, the most reprehensible kind of inflation. After a while either the controls will break down, leaving behind a bitter harvest of distortions and a lower growth rate, or they will lead to a permanently regimented, socialist economy. Whether such a system is compatible with democracy is more than doubtful. As the great Austrian economist, J. A. Schumpeter, a not unsympathetic student and critic of socialism said: "Socialism is likely to present fascist features."[31]

The second scenario: Suppose a firm policy of tight money and tight government budget is instituted, supported by measures designed to stimulate saving and investment and to make the economy more competitive and flexible along the lines indicated above. Furthermore, suppose the government makes it quite clear that it will stick to the policy, even if unemployment initially increases, until inflation is eradicated within a reasonable period, say, two years. The chances then are, that inflationary expectations will evaporate and labor unions and other pressure groups will scale down their wage and price demands in order not to price themselves out of the market.

The big problem, of course, is how to make the policy credible. An initial increase in unemployment and some bankruptcies will have to be accepted. This is not a policy of deflation, that is to say, an attempt to bring down the price level through monetary contraction. It is a policy of eliminating excessive growth of the money stock and of money GNP, although an initial slack, or stabilization crisis may occur and has to be accepted.[37] If such a program is carried out successfully, it can be expected that the rate of growth in the industrial countries will recover from the present abnormally low level, to the enormous benefit not only of the industrial countries themselves but to that of the whole Western world including the less developed countries.

Notes

1. This paper was prepared in 1980 for the occasion of the award of the Antonio Feltrinelli Prize by the Academia Nazionale dei Licèi [Italian Academy of Science], Rome, Italy. A discussion of subsequent events can be found in my paper "Inflation and Incomes Policy," in *Economic Notes by Monte dei Paschi di Siena*, No. 2, 1982, Italy.

2. John Hicks, *The Crisis of Keynesian Economics,* Oxford 1974, p. 1. The second quarter, Sir John says, historians call "the age of Hitler"—a dubious suggestion in view of the fact that Keynes and Hitler were prominent in rather different spheres of human affairs. The implication that Keynes' impact on world events was of the same order of magnitude as that of Hitler greatly exaggerates Keynes' impact on world history.

3. See my *Prosperity and Depression,* second and later editions, Chapter VIII, and my contribution to *Keynes' General Theory. Report of Three Decades,* edited by R. Leckachman, New York, 1962, pp. 269—288 [chapter 26 in this volume].

4. These articles are reprinted in T. W. Hutchison, *Keynes Versus the Keynesians? An Essay on the Thinking of J. M. Keynes and the Accuracy of Its Intepretation by His Followers,* Institute of Economic Affairs, London, 1977.

5. Two typical examples: "He [Keynes] preached what has become commonplace since he wrote: Government should spend more and tax less in depression and spend less and tax more in boom. These simple truths were discoveries of Keynes which had to be repeated a hundred times before they made the required impression". Seymour E. Harris, *John Maynard Keynes: Economist and Policy Maker,* New York, 1964, p. 263. Robert Skidelsky in an otherwise excellent article "Keynes and the Reconstruction of Liberalism" makes the amazing statement: "Keynes was at first the *only* professional economist in Britain and the United States who grasped the point that unemployment could be seen as a technical problem in economic analysis to be solved by economic means". (*Encounter,* London, April 1971, p. 29. Italic in the original).

6. For details, see T. W. Hutchison, *On Revolution and Progress in Economic Knowledge,* Cambridge 1978, Chapter 6, "Demythologizing the Keynesian Revolution" (pp. 175—199). In a letter to *The Times* (July 28, 1933) Keynes went out of his way to emphasize his agreement with Pigou on policy. (See T. W. Hutchison, *op. cit.,* p. 187)

7. Herbert Stein's celebrated monograph, *The Fiscal Revolution in America* (Chicago, 526 pages) presents an exhaustive and detailed picture of the development of American thinking and its relation to the Keynesian revolution. J. Ronnie Davis, *The New Economics and the Old Economists* (Ames, Iowa, 1971, 170 pages) tells the same story in shorter space.

8. The "rediscovery of money" was broadly based but is usually associated with Milton Friedman's and Anna J. Schwartz's famous book, *A Monetary History of the United States 1867—1960* (National Bureau of Economic Research, New York, 1963, XXIV and 860 pages). Other economists who have stressed the importance of the monetary factor are mentioned in Gottfried Haberler's "The Great Depression of the 1930s—Can It Happen Again?" in *The Business Cycle and Public Policy, 1929—79, A Compendium of Papers Submitted to the Joint Economic Committee,* Congress of the United States, U.S. Government Printing Office, Washington, D.C., 1980, pp. 1—19. Also available as an American Enterprise Institute Reprint, Washington, D.C. 1981 [chapter 17 in this volume].

9. John Hicks, *op. cit.,* pp. 31—32. As in many other respects a distinction ought to be made between Keynes himself and many of his followers. The master was not so uncompromising as his disciples in denying money any explanatory or curative role as far as the Great Depression is concerned.

10. That the contraction of the stock of money was exogenous and not endogenous to the economic system has been convincingly established by Milton Friedman and Anna J.

Schwartz (*op. cit.*) and Phillip Cagan, *Determinants and Effects of Changes in the Stock of Money, 1875–1960* (Studies in Business Cycles, No. 13, National Bureau of Economic Research, New York, 1965). See especially Chapter 6 in Phillip Cagan's book.

Friedman's diagnosis has been endorsed by no one less than the great Keynesian economist (and biographer of Keynes) Sir Roy Harrod. In his review of *A Monetary History of the United States* (*The University of Chicago Law Review*, Vol. 32, No. 1, Autumn 1964, pp. 188–196) Harrod rejects emphatically the view held by many Keynesians "that the events 1929–1933 proved the impotence of monetary policy" and states categorically that "monetary policy was not attempted in the United States in 1929–1933" (*ibid.*, p. 196).

The opposite position was taken by another Keynesian, Nicholas (Lord) Kaldor. In "The New Monetarism" (*Lloyds Bank Review*, No. 97, July 1970), he argued that, since in July 1932 the monetary base (what Friedman calls high-powered money) was 10 percent higher than it was in July 1929, the monetary explanation of the extraordinary severity of the depression is invalid. He evidently thinks that the monetary authorities had done their duty by keeping the monetary base barely stable in the face of a massive decline of the money supply as a consequence of the stock exchange crash and several waves of bank failures. Kaldor does not mention that the monetary base declined a little from November 1929 to November 1931 and that it was only in April 1932 that large scale open market operations were undertaken. Harrod's statement that "monetary policy was not attempted" surely is the appropriate description of the performance of the Federal Reserve System.

Kaldor evidently believes in the existence of the liquidity trap as a more or less permanent condition. For he says again and again that velocity of circulation of money goes down whenever the quantity of money increases, and increases when the quantity of money goes down. At the bottom of a deep depression, when deflationary expectations (in other words Pigou's and Keynes' excessive pessimism) have become firmly entrenched, a liquidity trap— what Hawtrey called a "credit deadlock"—may develop as a temporary situation. If people expect demand to shrink and prices to decline even a zero rate of interest will not quickly stimulate investment. But this is not a stable equilibrium position. It is true, however, that in such a situation a strong case can be made for injecting money directly into the expenditure stream by government deficit financing instead of relying entirely on monetary policies, such as open market operations and changing reserve requirements. That should be acceptable also to monetarists. (See text which follows note 10.)

What was said above about the likelihood of excessive pessimism (deflationary expectations) becoming entrenched in a severe depression leading to a sharp decline in the velocity of circulation of money, disposes also of another argument of Kaldor in favor of the existence of a permanent liquidity trap—to wit, that Canadian developments support his theory. Friedman shows in his *Monetary History of the United States* (p. 352 quoted by Kaldor), that Canada had no bank failures because it had an efficient branch banking system (rather than the archaic U.S. unit banking system). Therefore, during the depression (1929–1933) in Canada the quantity of money declined by only 13 percent compared with 33 percent in the United States. On the other hand, velocity declined by 41 percent compared with 29 percent in the United States. This proves according to Kaldor that velocity adjusts automatically to changes in the quantity of money.

What Kaldor does not mention is that the Canadian economy was rigidly linked to the U.S. economy by a fixed exchange rate and therefore shared fully in the U.S. depression; net national product fell by 49 percent compared with 53 percent in the United States. No wonder that pessimism (deflationary expectations) became entrenched as in the United States and velocity declined sharply. Friedman points out (*ibid.*) that, because there were no bank failures in Canada the public's confidence in the banks was not shaken and the demand for the bank-deposit portion of the money stock declined not nearly as much as in the United States; hence, velocity declined more sharply.

The upshot is that this strictly cyclical development in a severe depression does not support Kaldor's theory of a permanent liquidity trap.

11. That the gold standard contributed to the spread of the Great Depression does not mean that it was a bad system as such. No regime of fixed exchanges could have performed better in a period of world deflation.

12. The British economy was depressed throughout the 1920s because the monetary authorities applied deflationary measures to restore the gold parity of the pound after World War I. (This policy was duly noted and criticized by Keynes at the time). Germany was put under heavy deflationary pressure by capital flight and Chancellor Bruening took strong deflationary measures deliberately to get rid of reparations. For details see Gottfried Haberler, *The World Economy, Money and the Great Depression, 1919–1939*, American Enterprise Institute, Washington, D.C. 1976. [chpater 16 in this volume.]

13. The *value* of world trade (in terms of gold dollars) shrank to about a third of its 1929 level; the *volume* fell to about one-half of its 1929 level, the difference reflecting the enormous decline in the price level.

The gold standard was a casualty of the depression. It might perhaps have been saved if the gold price (in terms of national currencies) had been raised in an early stage of the depression; in other words, if the dollar and all other currencies had been depreciated simultaneously in terms of gold in order to increase international liquidity. That perhaps might have been accomplished if the International Monetary Fund had existed at the time. For the Articles of Agreement of the IMF had a provision that empowered "the Fund [to] make uniform proportionate changes in the par values of the currencies of all members". (Article IV, Section 7). As it was, international liquidity was increased through the exceedingly painful process of price deflation plus a long drawn-out, uncoordinated sequence of parity changes which in the end encompassed all currencies of the world.

14. In fact, a mechanism of this kind relying on the lagged effect of monetary expansion has been used by some economists as an explanation of the business cycle, for example, by the great British monetarist, R. G. Hawtrey.

15. Neglect of the role of inflationary expectations on the part of the public is probably the greatest weakness of Keynesian policy discussions. This is strange because expectations play a great role in Keynes' *The General Theory*. I cite one example from no one less than the great Keynesian James Tobin. As late as 1973, in his truly brilliant presidential address, Tobin extolled the virtures of inflation. "Inflation lets this struggle [for mutually inconsistent claims on the social product] proceed and blindly, impartially, impersonally and nonpolitically scales down all its outcomes." (James Tobin, "Inflation and Unemployment", *American Economic Review*, Vol. 62, March 1973, p. 13). Tobin was right, however, when he added "There are worse methods of resolving group rivalries and social conflict". By worse methods he meant direct wage and price controls.

Tobin later graciously admitted that he had "been overoptimistic about the trade-off [between unemployment and inflation] and too skeptical of accelerationist warnings". (James

Tobin, "Comment of an Academic Scribbler", *Journal of Monetary Economics*, Vol. 4, 1978, p. 622). The "accelerationists" are the economists who had argued that any significant inflation has a tendency to accelerate, and to lose its stimulating power.

16. In technical terms this means that the Phillips curve which was so popular in Keynesian circles ten years ago is not a stable relationship but at best a short-run phenomenon. As inflation goes on, the short-run curve shifts up and becomes steeper.

17. See my papers "The International Monetary System after Jamaica and Manila", *Contemporary Economic Problems 1977*, "Reflections on the U.S. Trade Deficit and the Floating Dollar", *Contemporary Economic Problems 1978*, and "The Dollar in the World Economy: Recent Developments in Perspective", *Contemporary Economic Problems 1980*, American Enterprise Institute, Washington, D.C.

18. This holds for continuous as well as intermittent inflation; in other words, irrespective of whether the picture of the upward sweep of the price level is a smooth curve with a rising slope or an upward sloping staircase, the rate of inflation declining in cyclical recessions, but the successive business cycle upswing starting with higher and higher rates of inflation. The U.S. price level since 1965 has presented the latter shape. Thus, the last business cycle upswing which is now underway has started with an inflation rate of 11 to 12 percent.

19. The distinction between recession and depression is one of degree. But historically, most cyclical declines in economic activities can be unambiguously classified as a recession or a depression.

20. From the political standpoint shock treatment may be preferable. For example, a newly elected government simply may not have the time, before the next election, to adopt an economically optimal gradualist policy. Technical questions which cannot be discussed here refer to the degree of gradualness and the precise methods of reducing monetary growth, open market operations, changes in reserve requirements, etc.

21. Again, I cannot go into finer but very important points. In order to reduce the deficit, should taxes be raised or government expenditures reduced? Which taxes? Which expenditures? Nor can I discuss a rather comforting theory that has become popular in the United States under the name of "supply side economics": Reduce taxes, the theory says, and the economy will quickly be stimulated to such an extent that tax revenue will not decline or may even increase so that the budget deficit is likely to shrink. I confine myself to a short remark. A strong case can be made for the proposition that in many countries, partly because of the distorting effects of inflation (people being pushed into higher and higher tax brackets), the tax system has come to seriously reduce incentives to work, to save, and to invest. It follows that a tax reduction and a reform of the tax structure will have a beneficial effect on output and employment. But those beneficial effects will be slow in coming. In the short and medium run a tax reduction will almost always reduce tax revenues and increase the deficit. It does not follow that tax reduction and tax reform should not be sttempted. What follows is that the tax relief should be accompanied by cuts in government expenditures to forestall an increase in the budget deficit.

22. Harry G. Johnson, "Foreword" to *Trade Effects of Public Subsidies to Private Enterprise*, by Geoffrey Denton, Seamus O'Cleireacain and Sally Ash, London, 1975, p. XIII.
   The older generation of the Chicago economists (Frank H. Knight, Henry Simons, Jacob

Viner and others), unlike the modern monetarists, did not ignore or minimize the great importance of the growing rigidity of wages and prices for the working of the monetary system and for monetary policy. Frank H. Knight wrote: "In a free market these differential changes [in aggregate demand and prices of different goods] would be temporary, but even then might be serious; and with important markets [especially the labor market] as unfree as they actually are, the results take on the proportion of a disaster" (Frank H. Knight, "The Business Cycle, Interest and Money", reprinted from *Review of Economics and Statistics*, Vol. 23, May 1941, in Frank H. Knight, *On The History and Methods of Economics*, Chicago, 1956, p. 224). Knight wrote with the deflation of the 1930s in mind. But what he said about the implications of wage and price rigidity applies in principle also to the case of disinflation (anti-inflationary monetary measures). And the rigidification of the economy has made much progress since Knight wrote forty years ago. For statistical evidence of the growing rigidity of wages and prices, see Jeffrey Sachs, "The Changing Cyclical Behavior of Wages and Prices, 1890–1976", *Working Paper No. 304, National Bureau of Economic Research*, New York, 1978.

23. The unwillingness to adjust is the main theme of two remarkable studies by Richard Blackhurst, Nicolas Marian, and Jan Tumlir, *Trade Liberalization, Protectionism and Interdependence*, General Agreement on Tariffs and Trade (GATT) Studies in International Trade, no. 5 (Geneva, 1977), and by the same authors, *Adjustment, Trade and Growth in Developed and Developing Countries*, GATT Studies in International Trade, no. 6 (Geneva, 1979). See also the trenchant analysis by Melvyn B. Krauss, *The New Protectionism: The Welfare State and International Trade* (New York, New York University Press, 1978).

24. The essential distinction between "involuntary" and "voluntary" unemployment has been made popular by Keynes' *General Theory*, but has been well known in the earlier literature on the subject. (See, for example, the masterly discussion in A. C. Pigou's *The Theory of Unemployment*, London, 1933, chapter 1, "Definition of Unemployment"). In fact Keynes' definition of involuntary unemployment is unnecessarily complicated. The entirely satisfactory common sense definition is: A worker is involuntarily unemployed if he cannot find a job although he is willing and able to work at the wage ruling for the type of work for which he is qualified. Voluntary unemployment can be defined as consisting of those who do not work because they find the ruling wage for the type of work for which they are qualified too low or who prefer leisure to work. A borderline case may be people who find the difference between unemployment benefits and the ruling wage too small to make it worth their while seriously to seek work. These concepts, as most others in the social sciences, are fuzzy on the edges and the statistical separation of voluntary and involuntary unemployment is never quite sharp. No doubt, published unemployment figures always have an admixture of spurious, voluntary unemployment. But for clear thinking the distinction obviously is necessary.

Keynes criticized what he called the classical school, for recognizing only voluntary unemployment. This is clearly unjustified. As mentioned above, the arch-classical economist Pigou dealt with involuntary unemployment although he used different words (*loc. cit.*). But Keynes' criticism seems to apply to the modern rational expectations school.

I give one typical example. Karl Brunner, Alex Cukierman and Allan H. Meltzerin "Stagflation, Persistent Unemployment and the Permanence of Economic Shocks" (*Journal of Monetary Economics*, Vol. 6, No. 4, October 1980, North Holland Publishing Co., Amsterdam, pp. 467–492) try to show that stagflation—"rising prices and unemployment"—"can occur in a neo-classical framework" (p. 483) "in which all expectations are rational and all markets clear instantaneously" (p. 490). This implies perfect competition. The authors speak repeatedly of "persistent" unemployment, although in a footnote (footnote 12, p. 470) they say that "since the focus of this paper is on cyclical unemployment, we do not discuss types of unemployment that arise for other reasons". It would be interesting to know whether they regard the mass unemployment of the 1930s as "cyclical".

For the problem on hand the gist of the theory is in the supply function of labor. To determine the amount of labor they are willing to supply, "workers compare the currently prevailing wage to the wage they currently perceive as permanent" (p. 470).

Let us start from a full employment equilibrium where the prevailing wage is equal to the perceived permanent wage. Now suppose the economy is subject to a "shock"—the authors usually speak of a change "in productivity". If productivity goes up, the actual real wage is raised "on impact". But the workers cannot know immediately whether the change is permanent. Therefore, "the currently perceived permanent wage" will for sometime be below the ruling wage. This will induce workers to supply more labor, in other words, "to substitute future for current leisure", resulting in "negative unemployment" (p. 470), what usually is known as overfull employment.

If the shock is unfavorable ("negative"), if productivity declines, the real current wage will be reduced "on impact". But again the workers cannot be sure what the permanent wage will be. Therefore, the actual wage falls below "the currently perceived permanent wage". This will induce "part of the labor force which looks for work [to] abstain for accepting current employment. This group is counted as unemployed in the official statistics" (p. 470). Unemployment will persist until the growing perception of the changed situation has reduced the perceived permanent wage to the level of the current wage.

If overfull employment means the substitution of "future for current leisure", unemployment means "substitution of present for future leisure". To describe unemployment as "leisure" is very odd indeed. It suggests that unemployment does not involve much hardship. The statement that "current leisure is subsituted for future leisure" implies that the current loss of employment and output is offset by more work and output in the future. This, too, makes little sense.

At any rate, what the authors are talking about is voluntary unemployment, "part of the labor force" being on the margin of indifference between work and leisure.

If unions create unemployment by pushing up wages or preventing them from falling, one can perhaps argue that the unemployment is voluntary from the point of view of the union, for it is possible that the union wishes to maximize total labor income which requires that part of the labor force "abstain from work". But this union policy inflicts hardship on their unemployed members. From the point of view of individual workers, the unemployment is involuntary.

25. Two qualifications are in order. *First*, it is now widely realized that in the long run inflation has an adverse effect on the productivity trend which makes adjustments to changing circumstances more difficult.

Second, strictly speaking it is not true that in a competitive market the growth of real wages is determined by the growth of *average* productivity of labor; the determining factor is *marginal* productivity. A simple mental experiment will clarify the problem. Suppose an industry undergoes rapid mechanization; much labor being replaced by machinery and computers, and output per worker goes up sharply. Clearly, wages cannot go up parallel with average productivity. That would not leave enough money for the reward of indirect labor and capital. The implication is that the share of labor in the revenue of that particular industry must decline. The same *may* happen for the economy as a whole. Depending on the elasticity of substitution of capital for labor, the share of labor in the national product may go down, go up or remain constant. It follows that the real wage trend may have to deviate somewhat from the productivity trend to maintain equilibrium with full employment.

However, it is a fact that historically for the economy as a whole in the *long run* the share of labor income in national income does not change much. This makes it possible to uphold, *as a rule of thumb*, the widely accepted proposition that real wage growth is determined by the growth of productivity.

26. The qualification "on a large scale" is intended to take care of friction, minor deviations from the competitive ideal. In the real world only few markets are perfectly competitive; in other words, clear instantaneously. For example, workers who have lost their jobs usually take their time and invest money to find suitable employment. The concept "competitive market", must be interpreted to allow for this sort of thing.

Another qualification: It can be argued that unorganized workers sometimes behave almost as if they were organized. Thus, in the depressions of the nineteenth century (or in the Great Depression of the 1930s) when unions were nonexistent or weak, workers resisted wage cuts. Moreover, declining demand for labor in a depression is a strong inducement for workers to organize themselves in order to strengthen their bargaining power. For this and other reasons employers, on their part, are reluctant to push hard for wage cuts. The upshot is that wages were sticky downward even in the absence of well organized unions. This is what F. H. Knight had in mind when he wrote that even then, when the economy was more free than at the time he wrote, monetary deflation was a serious matter. (F. H. Knight, *loc. cit.*).

There surely is something in this argument, but it must not be pushed too far. After all, in the Great Depression of the 1930s and earlier depressions wages did decline sharply despite the workers' resistance. Today's almost total downward rigidity of money wages, both in the aggregate and in particular industries, combined with real wage push upward often in the face of heavy unemployment, would be inconceivable without the existence of strong unions created, fostered and abetted by government policies. The power and aggressiveness of other pressure groups, too, has increased enormously. This accounts for stagflation on the present scale.

27. The statement that inflation is the major problem facing the industrial countries will perhaps be questioned by those who have become greatly alarmed about what is now often called the North-South dialogue or even confrontation allegedly resulting from the growing income gap between the developed industrial countries, the "North" and the less developed countries, the "South". This problem has recently been dramatized by the report of a prestigious "independent commission on development issues" under the chairmanship of Willy Brandt of Germany. The title of the report is: *North-South. A Program for Survival.* (MIT Press, Cambridge, Mass. 1980) The subtitle indicates the alarmist, not to say hysterical tone of the report. No one would deny that the existence of stark poverty in some less developed countries presents serious problems. But to say, as the Brandt Commission does, that poverty in less developed countries and the great inequality between the "North" and the "South" is responsible for wars, violence and tensions in the present day world cannot be taken seriously. None of the recent wars had anything whatsoever to do with the North-South income gap— not the two world wars nor any of the many local post-war conflicts (the wars in Korea and Vietnam, the Israel-Arab wars, the Persian Gulf war between Iran and Iraq, the conflicts between Greece and Turkey, Ethiopia and Somalia, etc., etc.). The East-West tensions and

confrontations are a real global threat compared with which the North-South skirmishs are of minor importance. On recent U.S. and other Western policy statements (especially but not only before the invasion of Afganistan) that take the opposite view see the article by the great historiam and Soviet expert Adam B. Ulam, "How to Restrain the Soviets" (*Commentary*, Vol. 70, No. 6, New York, December 1980, p. 99).

The so-called "South", or Third World, is a very heterogenous group. It comprises many countries and areas (Argentina, Brazil, Taiwan, etc.) that are well on the way to joining the industrial "North". The really poor countries, sometimes called the Fourth World, are but a fraction of the "South".

I repeat, I don't want to minimize the problem of the poor counrties. But here is not the place to discuss the commonly proposed policies to deal with that problem ("resource transfer" from the rich to the poor countries, foreign aid and international charity, commodity price stabilization, etc., etc.). I confine myself to saying that the industrial countries, if they put their economic houses in order, curb inflation, resume normal growth and liberalize trade, they will make a great contribution to the development of the less developed countries, including the very poor, by providing markets for the Third World exports. World Bank statistics show that the less developed countries, as a group, have made excellent progress during the prosperous period after World War II. (The largely dubious policy proposals of the Brandt Commission have been critically analyzed by P. T. Bauer and B. S. Yamey in "East-West/North-South. Peace and Prosperity?", *Commentary*, New York, September 1980, and P. D. Henderson in "Survival, Development and the Report of the Brandt Commission", *The World Economy. A Quarterly Journal on International Economic Affairs*, Vol. 3, No. 1, June 1980. For a thorough discussion of the so-called New International Economic Order (NIEO), see *Challenges to a Liberal International Economic Order*, edited by Ryan C. Amacher, Gottfried Haberler and Thomas D. Willett, American Enterprise Institute, Washington, D.C., 1970).

28. The elements of such a policy of liberalization are well known. In my book *Economic Growth and Stability. An Analysis of Economic Change and Policies* (Los Angeles 1974), I discuss this policy and refer to it as "Incomes Policy II" which must be distinguished from "Incomes Policy I", that is incomes policy in the usual sense which implies direct price and wage control of some sort.

29. In view of the strength of labor unions in many countries wage control, in the form of a temporary wage freeze, is especially tempting. But wage control without price control is politically impossible.

30. Comprehensive wage and price controls are incompatible with the present, comparatively liberal international economic order, symbolized by the International Monetary Fund and GATT (General Agreement of Tariffs and Trade). The impossiblity, in the absence of a fully regimented economy, of controlling import and export prices became an increasingly intractable problem in the United States after 1971 and greatly contributed to the breakdown of the controls, although in the U.S. economy international trade is a comparatively small fraction of the GNP.

31. See his famous prophetic book *Socialism, Capitalism and Democracy*, first edition, New York 1942, second edition, New York 1947, third edition, New York 1950, p. 375 in the second and third editions.

32. After World War I in the 1920s a number of countries (Germany, Austria, Poland, Hungary) experienced hyper-inflation. In those cases it was possible to stop inflation abruptly

and restore price stability seemingly without a stabilization crisis. But it is very doubtful whether the experience under hyper-inflation is applicable to the present cases of peacetime, chronic though much milder inflation.

Drawing on German experience, I mention three typical developments in hyper-inflation that made abrupt stabilization possible. First, hyper-inflation wiped out the mark-dominated private and public debts; there were no mark-dominated debt contracts outstanding. Second, at the peak of inflation wages and salaries were paid twice or three times a day to enable people to buy before prices were again marked up. Thus, the velocity of circulation of money rose to fantastic heights and the real money stock fell to a small fraction of its normal level. Third, the trauma of the collapse of the currency (and of the recent war) made drastic stabilization measures acceptable. People were ready for a fresh start and accepted the new money with relief and confidence. Payment habits returned to normal and the velocity of circulation of money declined rapidly; in other words, the demand for money rose sharply.

This enabled the monetary authorities and the banks to expand the money supply without endangering price stability. The money was put into circulation partly by extending credit to private businesses and the public sector, partly by buying gold and foreign money that emerged from hoards. The increase in the international reserve, in turn, strengthened the confidence in the soundness of the new money.

In these crucial respects the situation is very different today. This explains why, paradoxically though it may sound, a hyper-inflation is much easier to stop than the present much milder but chronic inflation.

IV

Economic Development

19   Terms of Trade and Economic Development

1. Introduction

The present essay tries to elucidate various connections between the terms of trade and economic development. It utilizes existing statistical and other factual material, but it does not present any new empirical facts nor does it contain new computations. The paper is, to a large extent, critical and polemical. That is to say, it tries to disprove certain widely held notions, historical generalizations, as well as policy conclusions which have been derived from such generalizations. No originality is claimed for these critical analyses, but no apologies are offered either. It is hoped that a systematic stocktaking of existing facts and arguments may clear the air and lead to useful results. In the first section, I discuss some general propositions of international trade theory concerning the terms of trade in their relation to economic welfare. In the succeeding sections, some applications of these propositions to the problems of economic development are made.

2. The Terms of Trade and Economic Welfare: A Theoretical Discussion

Under-developed countries are rightly much concerned with their international trade position, because for all of them international trade is vitally important as a source of supply of the technological know-how, skill, capital, machinery, implements, etc., which are essential for their economic development. Many of them, for example, all Latin-American countries, are very closely knit into the world economy in the sense that an exceptionally large percentage of their output is exported and an equally large part of their total expenditures on capital as well as consumption goods is made on imports. In view of these circumstances, it is altogether natural that much attention is paid to the terms of trade as one of the factors affecting the supply of badly needed imports.

Economic Development for Latin America, Howard Ellis and H. C. Wallich, eds., (New York: St. Martin's Press, 1961), 275–297. Reprinted with permission.

Later on I shall have occasion to distinguish different types of terms of trade, but throughout the paper, when not otherwise stated, I shall always refer to the ordinary commodity terms of trade, that is to say, to the ratio of the export and import price indices, Px/Pm.

Any improvement in the terms of trade, that is to say, any rise in export prices relatively to import prices is generally regarded as a factor favourably affecting economic welfare as measured by real national income per head. (Unless otherwise stated, I shall in this paper disregard possible divergences between economic welfare and real national income.) This proposition as well as many others of this paper applies to developed countries as well as to underdeveloped ones, except that for many of the latter group, owing to the importance of trade, the terms of trade are a matter of greater quantitative concern than for most members of the first group.

The statement that a deterioration in the terms of trade can usually be regarded as an unfavourable factor does, of course, not mean that if the terms of trade of a country have deteriorated over a certain period the country in question is worse off at the later date. It does not even mean that the chain of events which brought about the deterioration in the terms of trade has unfavourably affected economic welfare. If, for example, productivity in transport or in the production of export goods has gone up by, say, 10 per cent, so that the same factor input yields a 10 per cent larger output (or the same output can be produced by a 10 per cent smaller factor input), and if the prices of exports in terms of imports have fallen by less than 10 per cent, the country is still better off than before. The substitution of the single factoral terms of trade for the commodity terms of trade is designed to take care of such a situation. In the case envisaged we would have to say that the single factoral terms of trade have improved, that is to say, the average price of factors exported (embodied in the exported commodities) in terms of imported commodities has gone up despite the fact that the commodity terms of trade have deteriorated. Hence, in this case, the single factoral terms of trade are a better index for changes in economic welfare than the commodity terms of trade.

It is true that factoral terms of trade is a concept much more difficult to define and to measure statistically than the commodity terms of trade, because the problems involved in defining factors of production and an index of factor prices are much more complicated than the index number problem in the commodity field. (This is so at least as soon as we get away from the oversimplified notion that labour is the only factor of production.) In fact, as far as I know, only very few and purely exploratory attempts at statistical measurements of factoral terms of trade, single or double, have been made so far. But that in no way reduces the importance of forming a judgment on whether a given deterioration in the commodity terms of trade reflects only an increase in the productivity of the export industries, or goes beyond such an increase, or is due to altogether different causes.

But even if a given deterioration of the commodity terms of trade is fully or more than fully accounted for by an increase in the productivity of the export industries (that is to say, if the single factoral terms of trade have not worsened), it is still true that the country would be better off if the foreign demand for its exports had been infinitely elastic so that the commodity terms of trade had remained unchanged. In this case, the more elastic the foreign demand and hence the better the terms of trade, the better for the country. Similarly, the less elastic the foreign demand, hence the worse the terms of trade, the worse for the country. But if we use this language, we must not forget that the implied comparison is not between the present situation and a previous one (before the increase in productivity has occurred), but between the present situation and a hypothetical one (one in which the elasticity of foreign demand is assumed to be different from what it actually is).

An improvement in a country's terms of trade which results from a change abroad (a shift, for any reason, of the foreign reciprocal demand and supply curve) is always favourable for a country, unless it leads to widespread unemployment in the country's export industries, as was the case in the United Kingdom in the 1930s. But given the level of employment (or unemployment), an improvement in the commodity terms of trade resulting from an intensification of foreign demand is always favourable. Similarly, a deterioration is always unfavourable.

On the other hand, a change in the terms of trade resulting from a shift in the country's own offer curve cannot be unambiguously said to be good or bad according to the direction of the change, even if full employment is maintained continuously.[1] It is generally recognized that a country or group of countries, if it is large enough to influence prices in the markets in which it sells or from which it buys (in the world market, or in sheltered regional or bilateral markets), can improve its terms of trade by restricting the volume of trade (assuming, of course, that the improvement is not cancelled by retaliatory measures by foreign countries). But it is equally well known that, from a certain point on, further improvement in welfare resulting from further rise in export prices in terms of import prices is offset by a fall in the volume of trade. Just as the optimum price of a monopolist, the price which maximizes monopoly profits, is not the highest price which the monopolist would be able to charge, the optimum terms of trade which maximize welfare is not the highest price of exports in terms of imports which a country could possibly obtain. The optimum tariff theory has tried to define the optimum tariff and optimum terms of trade. The location of the optimum point depends on the elasticities of foreign demand and supplies. The larger these elasticities, that is to say, the larger the percentage reaction of foreign demand and supply to a given percentage change of the prices charged, the sooner this point is reached, and the lower is the optimum tariff.

Suffice it to say at this point that once the optimum has been reached, a further improvement in the terms of trade, brought about by a further contraction of the volume of trade, will reduce economic welfare instead of increasing it. We may also express this by saying that the terms of trade should be optimized, but there is no sense in trying to maximize them.

It has been suggested that for this reason a better indicator than the commodity terms of trade can be found for the welfare change associated with a given trade change. Specifically, volume changes of trade have to be brought into the picture in addition to price changes. This is done by multiplying the index of the commodity terms of trade (Px/Pm) by an index of the volume of exports Qx. The resulting index has been called the income terms of trade or an index of the export gains from trade or of the total gains from trade.

While it is correct that in order to evaluate a welfare change it is necessary to consider volume changes in addition to price changes, it can be easily shown that the income terms of trade $(Qx \, Px/Pm)$ is not a satisfactory indicator of the direction (let alone the magnitude) of the welfare change associated with a trade change. Suppose Px/Pm has risen by 10 per cent and Qx fallen by 10 per cent—other things, viz., total output, employment, and the balance of payments remaining unchanged. In that case, the country is better off because it exports less and receives the same volume of imports, but the income terms of trade have remained unchanged. Similarly if Px/Pm is down by 10 per cent and Qx is up by 10 per cent, the country is worse off, but the income terms of trade are unchanged. In both cases the commodity terms of trade correctly indicate the direction of the change in welfare.

This does not mean, however, that an index of the income terms of trade is of no use at all. For example, the Economic Commission for Latin America in their *Economic Survey of Latin America*, 1949, uses the same measure as an index of Latin America's capacity to import. That seems to me a much more appropriate description and application than to regard it as a measure of the gain from trade or an indicator of welfare change.[2]

The upshot of these discussions is that the relations between the terms of trade and economic welfare are intricate. Therefore, great care must be exercised in the interpretation of given changes in the terms of trade and in the formulation of policy objectives with respect to the terms of trade. The mere knowledge that the terms of trade for a country or group of countries have changed in a certain way over a certain period of time is of precious little importance unless it is combined with other types of information. Did the change originate primarily at home or abroad? In other words, has the foreign or the domestic offer curve shifted? If it was the domestic offer curve which has changed, what was the main reason for that shift? Has the supply of export goods become more plentiful—for example, because of technological improvements—or has the demand for imports changed and for what reason?[3] What changes in the volume of exports and imports have been associated with the given change in the terms of trade?

Some of these questions are not at all easy to answer, especially when long run comparisons are involved. Comparisons between distant years are, of course, also marred by the fact that changes in the statistical measures of the terms of trade themselves (quite apart from the difficulty of ascertaining and interpreting attending circumstance and causes) become increasingly dubious to the point of being completely meaningless for the reason that the composition of trade changes fairly rapidly over time as a consequence of the appearance of new commodities, of quality changes of old ones, and of shifts of others between the categories of traded or non-traded, or even between the categories of export and import, commodities.

Looking through the trade statistics of any country, or at the shop windows in any city, one is struck by the large number of commodities which did not exist at all ten, twenty, forty years ago, or which have changed their quality profoundly. Examples are machinery of all description, household appliances, vehicles, aeroplanes, chemicals, pharmaceuticals, and synthetic fibres. At great effort and expense it should be possible to make allowance for some of these changes by introducing new commodities, as they appear, in a chain index number. Existing terms of trade indices are grossly deficient and it stands to reason that neglect of new commodities and of quality changes affects primarily the export indices of the developed industrial countries.

In the light of these general theoretical considerations, I shall now discuss some specific issues relating to under-developed countries.

3. Alleged Secular Tendencies in the Terms of Trade and Their Consequences

I will first discuss the well-known theory that the terms of trade have a secular tendency to deteriorate for the exporters of primary goods and to improve for the exporters of manufactured products. We may divide the argument into five phases: first, the alleged fact that the said deterioration did in fact occur from the 1870s to the eve of the Second World War[4]; second, the proposed explanation of this alleged tendency; third, the extrapolation based on this alleged tendency; fourth, the welfare interpretation—what does the alleged tendency imply for the economic welfare of the underdeveloped countries and the contribution thereto made by international trade? fifth, policy recommendations derived from the foregoing.

Several writers have questioned whether as a matter of historical fact the terms of trade have deteriorated for primary producers or for underdeveloped countries over the period from the 1870s to the 1940s. It is indeed on the face of it highly improbable that such a broad generalization should hold—that the terms of trade for all, or for the majority, of underdeveloped countries should have the same trend. Where do we draw the line between developed and underdeveloped countries? It should be borne in mind that while all underdeveloped countries are, on balance, exporters of primary products, there are developed countries, such as Australia and Denmark, that also are net exporters of primary products.

However we draw the line, it is clear that the economic structure, or at any rate the composition of exports, of different underdeveloped countries is very dissimilar. Considering for the moment Latin American countries only, it would be a very strange coincidence indeed if, in the long run, the commodity terms of trade, let alone the factoral terms of trade, moved parallel for coffee countries, mining countries, petroleum exporters, and exporters of wheat, wool, and fats. The same holds for the other side of the fence. The dissimilarity of the trade structure of developed countries is hardly less pronounced than that of underdeveloped countries.

It is well known that the hypothesis under consideration is based entirely on the annual index of the United Kingdom's commodity terms of trade. This is much too narrow a statistical base for the generalization that historically the terms of trade for underdeveloped countries have deteriorated by 40 per cent or so from the 1870s to the late 1930s.

There are at least three basic objections. First, this index does not allow for quality changes and makes very insufficient allowance for new products. This introduces a bias because, as has been repeatedly pointed out, industrial products have tremendously improved in quality, and literally every year a host of new products are introduced, while the quality and range of most primary products have remained very much unchanged. Copper remains copper, cotton remains cotton, and wheat remains wheat, while an automobile, a rubber tyre, a radio, an antibiotic, either did not exist at all or was an entirely different, less durable, and infinitely less serviceable commodity in earlier periods.

Second, as is also well known, the terms of trade index leave out services. In the above-mentioned index of the British terms of trade, import prices are taken c.i.f. at British ports of entry and export prices f.o.b. at British ports of exit. In case of a change in transportation cost, this makes it impossible even in a two country model to regard the terms of trade of one partner as an accurate index of the terms of trade of the other. As has often been pointed out, it is possible that, in a period of falling transportation costs, the terms of trade improve for both countries. That this has often happened has been shown by C. M. Wright in a remarkable article.[5] Wright cites many cases where in depressions prices of primary products fell sharply in the United Kingdom but rose in the distant ports of shipment. For example, from 1900 to 1904, wool prices fell in London 8 per cent, while prices in Argentine gold pesos rose 12 per cent.[6]

Professor Ellsworth, using more aggregative methods, reaches the conclusion that for the period from 1876 to 1905 a 'large proportion, and perhaps all, of the decline in the British prices of primary products can be attributed to the great decline in inward freight rates. Since the price of British manufactured exports fell in this period by 15 per cent, the terms of trade of primary countries, [if] f.o.b. prices [were] used for their exports as well as for their imports, may well have moved in their favor.'[7] Professor Kindleberger in his monumental study on the terms of trade of Europe has constructed a rough index of 'Current-Account Terms of Trade' (including services) which seems to confirm Ellsworth's findings.[8]

Third, the British terms of trade cannot without verification be taken as representative of the terms of trade of other industrial countries. Professor Kindleberger has computed indices for other European countries and has concluded that they do not support the generalization which is based on the United Kingdom terms of trade alone. In fact, he fails to detect 'much uniformity in the terms of trade between manufactures and primary products'.

We can say, then, that the proponents of the secular deterioration of the terms of trade for primary products have not been able to prove that such a change has actually taken place. It is true, however, that Professor Kindleberger thinks that he found some support for a somewhat different proposition. He states that the question of the terms of trade between developed and underdeveloped countries should not be identified with that between manufactures and primary products because developed countries also export primary products and relatively underdeveloped countries often export manufactures.

He believes that in intra-European trade the terms of trade have, on the whole, been favourable for the relatively highly developed (progressive is perhaps a better term) countries and unfavourable for France and Italy whom he regards as relatively less developed. 'Moreover, if the terms of trade of Industrial Europe with other areas are computed, and inverted, to get an impression of the terms of trade of the rest of the world with Industrial Europe, it . . . will be found that the underdeveloped world has fared' less well than, for example, the United States.

Special attention should be drawn to the fact that Professor Kindleberger's unit value index of machinery is computed by dividing values of machinery by their physical weight. Hence, if machines become more efficient but lighter in weight (a very common form of progress), even if the price per machine remains unchanged, the unit value will indicate a rise in price, while the efficiency price has fallen. Machinery, of course, plays a very important, in fact an increasingly important, role in the export of the industrial countries to underdeveloped areas.[9]

The support which these findings provide for the thesis under consideration is, however, very weak. For the underlying indices suffer from all the defects mentioned above. They do not allow for quality changes and allow insufficiently for new commodities, and the inversion of the European terms of trade is of questionable validity for the reasons given earlier. We may conclude that it has not been established that the terms of trade have deteriorated for underdeveloped countries over the stated period.

I now come to the second phase of the argument, the proposed explanations for the alleged tendency. Two main reasons are given: first, monopolistic manipulations in the industrial countries, and, second, the operation of Engel's Law.

On the first point, it is said that in the industrial countries the fruits of technological progress are not passed on to the consumer in the form of lower prices, but are retained by the producers in the form of higher wages.

It is true that for most periods and countries, monetary policy and wage policies have been such that economic progress has taken the form of rising money wages and stable or rising prices rather than the form of stable money income and falling prices. Many economists in the developed countries have felt (and a few still do feel) that from the point of view of cyclical stability and social justice stable wages and falling prices would be a better system than the one we have. But there is no evidence that it has hurt the producers of primary products (except perhaps if it really produced serious instability, which few economists would accept today). The victims are not the farmers and other primary producers who know very well how to protect their interests, but fixed-income receivers in the developed countries. In other words, the explanation under review confuses movements in the absolute price level with shifts in the relative prices of manufactures and primary products.

In the early nineteenth century, especially before the rise of economic liberalism and free trade, many attempts were made at preventing the export of machinery and technological know how in order to slow down the spread of industry and protect the monopoly of the old countries. However, these attempts were never very successful and even after the demise of the free trade era they were not revived except in isolated cases. There is much more competition between manufacturers and producers of capital goods now than there used to be one hundred years ago, because there are now many countries that supply capital goods, machinery, industrial know how, while there was only one, England, a hundred years ago.

On the second point, it is said that Engel's Law operates in such a way as to reduce secularly world demand for primary products. Engel's Law states that the percentage of expenditure on food is a decreasing function of income.

Now Engel's Law is well established as a description of household behaviour in homogeneous populations, but it is a long way from there to an explanation of an alleged trend in the ratio of world expenditures on primary products to expenditures on manufactures over extended periods.

Engel's Law applies to food but not to raw materials. Moreover, relative prices depend not only on demand but also on supply conditions which are likely to change profoundly over long periods. The importance of this last fact is dramatically revealed by the reflection that the hypothesis of the secular deterioration of the terms of trade for primary products, due to the operation of Engel's Law, is the exact opposite of another hypothesis which has been and still is very popular among an influential group of economists. I am thinking of the theory going back to Torrens,

Ricardo, and Malthus to the effect that, owing to the law of diminishing returns in primary production, prices of primary products are bound to rise relatively to prices of manufactures. This pessimistic theory—pessimistic from the point of view of the industrial countries—has held a strange fascination for English economists from Ricardo and Malthus, via Marshall and Keynes (in his controversy with Beveridge in the *Economic Journal*, 1912) to Professor Austin Robinson.[10] This theory was also popular in Germany around the turn of the century among a group of economists who looked with apprehension at the rapid industrialization and urbanization which was then in progress in Germany. There were, of course, also other considerations in their minds such as the alleged military and social disadvantages of industrialization and urbanization, but the expected unfavourable tendency of the terms of trade for industrial products was one reason why economists such as Richard Pohle,[11] Adolf Wagner,[12] and others asked for increased protection of German agriculture against imports from overseas.

Needless to say, the dire predictions of that school have proved just as unfounded as the *ex post* interpretation of the opposite school of thought which we have been considering. Both schools are wrong, because there has been no clear-cut trend one way or the other, but rather irregular, or at best, cyclical fluctuations.[13]

The reason why those predictions went wrong and why it is impossible to forecast future movements of the terms of trade—this brings us to the third phase of the argument, extrapolation—is the complexity and unpredictability of long-run technological and population changes. Methods of production and transportation, world production and world trade, world population and standards of living have undergone tremendous changes since 1870 and are still changing before our eyes. Nobody could foresee these changes then or gauge their impact on various countries or on the terms of trade, and nobody can perform such a miracle now. Surely Engel's Law and the Law of Diminishing Returns alone or in combination are totally inadequate to predict or interpret, or even to throw much light on such structural upheavals.

In addition to references to Engel's Law one finds frequently direct appeal to the fact that the import coefficients of the industrial countries, particularly of the United States, have declined. By import coefficient is meant the ratio of national income or GNP to imports, the average propensity to consume or simply the percentage of national income spent on imports.

The fact seems to be fairly well established for recent decades.[14] German economists (especially Werner Sombart) generalized the meagre evidence they had and then elevated the generalization to the dignity of a historical law—the law of the falling importance of international trade.[15]

To the extent that the fall in import-income ratio is due to protectionist policies in the industrial countries or to any other factor which shifts the industrial countries' offer curve inward, it tends to make the terms of trade for the underdeveloped countries less favourable. To the extent that it is due to protectionist policies in the underdeveloped countries themselves, or any other factor which tends to shift the underdeveloped countries' offer curve inward, it tends to improve the terms of trade for the underdeveloped countries. It would not be easy to answer the question which one of these various forces have been most powerful and I do not know of any attempt to answer it. In fact, I do not even know of any attempt at a clear formulation of the issues involved. So long as that is not done, the mere reference to the simple fact of the falling import-income ratio does not contribute anything to the solution of the problem on hand.

I now come to the fourth phase of the argument, the welfare implications of the alleged secular deterioration of the terms of trade for underdeveloped countries. As we have seen in section 2, a deterioration of the commodity terms of trade even if it is not wholly spurious (due to neglect of changes in transportation cost, of quality changes, and of new products) does not imply a decrease in economic welfare. When the United Kingdom's terms of trade improved in the last quarter of the nineteenth century as a consequence of the opening up of new sources of supply of agricultural products from the United States, Canada, and Argentina—that did not mean that this was an unfavourable change for the producers in those then underdeveloped areas, although they would have been still better off if the British market could have absorbed the additional supplies at unchanged prices. We can express this by saying that the single factoral terms of trade of those areas improved although their commodity terms of trade deteriorated.[16] The improvement in the British and other European terms of trade hurt British and European competitors of cheap imports, that is, British and European agriculture, but not the underdeveloped countries whence the cheap imports came.[17]

I now come to the fifth phase of the argument—the policy conclusions drawn from the alleged secular tendency of the terms of trade to deteriorate for the underdeveloped countries. Tacitly or explicitly it is usually concluded that those countries should protect themselves from, and anticipate, the threatening deterioration in their terms of trade by protectionist measures. It is interesting that the opposite school in the industrial countries often draws the same protectionist conclusion from their contrasting forecast of the future development of the terms of trade. This is, of course, not true of the old classical writers, but it is true of the German group of economists mentioned above, and this line of argument can also be found in Professor Robinson's paper.

We have, then, the intriguing situation that two schools recommend reduction in the trade between developed and underdeveloped countries starting from contradictory forecasts, but on the basis of a common theoretical proposition, namely, that it is better to anticipate an expected unfavourable development of the terms of trade than to wait until the deterioration actually occurs and induces a shift in production.

A few comments on this theoretical proposition seem to be in order. First, it would seem to be clear that what matters is an *expected* deterioration. The mere historical proposition that the terms of trade have deteriorated in a certain way does not prove anything, unless it can be proved that the economy for one reason or the other has failed to adapt itself fully to the changed conditions. If the latter is claimed, then it has to be shown in which way or for what reasons the adaptation has failed to occur. According to the answer given to that question the argument then becomes a species of one of the familiar *genera*: the infant industry argument for protection; the unemployment (including disguised unemployment) argument; or the lower productivity in agriculture than in industry argument.

Second, since future events are involved, the policy recommendations suffer from all the uncertainties to which forecasts are subject. Nobody really knows what changes in the terms of trade the future will bring. It is presumptuous and very incautious, in view of the poor record of economic forecasts, for economists to base policy recommendations on such uncertain foundations.

Third, even if we were sure that certain future changes are inevitable, as long as we are uncertain about the date, it surely would be better not to cross the bridge before it is reached. And if, as is likely, the change comes gradually, if it comes at all, the adaptation too can be gradual and can be left to the forces of the market.

Summing up, we may conclude that this case for protection rests on exceedingly weak foundations. It is therefore not surprising that members of both schools frequently try to strengthen their case with extraneous considerations. Thus the argument for protection based on the alleged historical tendency of the terms of trade to deteriorate for one or the other group of countries is frequently linked with the well-known static terms of trade argument for protection (optimum tariff theory). The latter is entirely independent of the former. The optimum tariff case depends on the elasticities of international demand and supply *at any moment of time* and in no way on the alleged historical development of the terms of trade over time.

In the German discussion mentioned above (of which one finds echoes in Professor Robinson's article), much is made of the argument that the inevitable industrialization of the now underdeveloped countries will rob the industrial countries both of the supply of raw materials and foodstuffs and of markets for their manufactures. And while it is comparatively easy to industrialize and to draw people from the country into the cities, the reverse process is infinitely more difficult. Even if the terms of trade become unfavourable for agriculture it will be difficult or impossible to get people from the factories in the cities back to the farms on the land.

Leaving aside considerations of military strategy and preparedness for war, the above reasoning overlooks two important and related facts. First, even if the whole world becomes industrialized in the sense that a larger and larger percentage of the working force is engaged in secondary and tertiary production, many countries will retain a comparative advantage in agriculture and hence remain exporters of agricultural products. The United States, Australia, Denmark, and Holland are conspicuous examples.

Secondly, advances in technology affecting agriculture have been so rapid that the surpluses of agricultural products available for export in the industrial countries with comparative advantage in agriculture have remained large. In other words, the terms of trade have not turned permanently or catastrophically against industry. And the same technological advance—we may call it the industrial revolution of agriculture—makes it possible for industrial countries to step up agricultural output even at fairly short notice (*vide*, war experience), although, of course, at higher relative prices than those at which they can import those materials. It may be impossible to reverse the process of urbanization, but it is possible to industrialize agriculture. The greatly increased application on the farms of machinery, fertilizer, scientific know how, and other products of industry means that a larger and larger percentage of food and other agricultural products is virtually produced in cities, or at any rate in factories.

4. Cyclical Instability of the Terms of Trade of Underdeveloped Countries

While there is no uniformity or common pattern in the long run movement of the terms of trade of underdeveloped or primary producing countries, the chances of finding such a pattern in the cyclical fluctuations of their terms of trade would seem to be better. But in this area too the degree of uniformity over time and space is by no means as great as is often assumed. A really comprehensive study is still lacking, although the cyclical and other short run instability of prices of primary products has received a great deal of attention.

It is a well-known feature of the business cycle that prices of agricultural products and primary commodities in general fluctuate more widely than prices of manufactured products and finished goods in general. From that it would seem to follow that the terms of trade of countries whose exports consist largely of primary products and whose imports consist largely of manufactures will tend to deteriorate during business cycle downswings and improve during business cycle upswings. One would expect to find the opposite pattern in the terms of trade of industrial export countries. Thus, while the industrial countries get some relief from their depression pains through an improvement in their terms of trade, the underdeveloped countries (and other net exporters of primary products) find their depression woes intensified by adverse changes in the terms of trade.

As far as industrial Europe, and especially the United Kingdom, is concerned,

these expectations were subjected to some statistical testing by Professor Kindleberger. For the inter-war period he found much support in the facts, although even
in this period there are a number of exceptions. For the period before 1914 he found,
as others found before him, that the cyclical pattern of the British terms of trade was
different. They improved as a rule in booms and deteriorated in depressions. The
same was true in some instances of the terms of trade of France and Germany. The
reason for the cyclical behaviour of the British terms of trade before 1914 was that
coal, iron, and steel prices fell sharply in depressions. After 1914, these items no
longer loomed so large in British exports and so the cyclical pattern changed.

But even in the short run of the business cycle, we must not assume, without
proof, that the British terms of trade are always indicative of the direction of change,
much less of the amplitude of movements in the terms of trade of exporters of
primary products. It is true that quality changes and the appearance of new
commodities can hardly make much difference in the short span of a cycle. (I am not
discussing now the long Kondratieff waves.) But the cyclical pattern of other
industrial countries is not always the same as the British. And cyclical changes in
ocean freight rates have been often very pronounced. C. M. Wright, in an article
already cited,[18] has shown that, especially before 1914, in almost all depressions, due
to drastic falls in freight rates (especially in the direction towards the industrial
centres), lower prices c.i.f. in Britain meant higher prices f.o.b. at distant ports of
shipping.

The Wright effect was perhaps not so regular, pronounced, and pervasive as its
discoverer thinks. He believes that it worked in every depression prior to 1931 when
the pattern changed because of the disruption of triangular trade and convertibility.
Professor Kindleberger did not find it always confirmed by his more comprehensive
data. But there can be no doubt that on many occasions the impact of depressions in
the industrial centres on the overseas primary producers has been greatly lessened
by the cyclical play of transportation costs. This is confirmed also by Professor
Kindleberger's finding that the inclusion of services in the terms of trade index (the
substitution of what he calls the current account index for the merchandise index of
the terms of trade) dampens the cyclical amplitude, even if it does not reverse the
cyclical pattern of the terms of trade of the industrial countries.

The converse of Wright's theory, that the cyclical play of transportation costs
reduces the improvements in the terms of trade of primary producers during
business cycle upswings, has not been explored in detail so far as I know. But it
stands to reason that, if the impact of depressions is reduced, the relative improvement of prosperity is also lessened.

The purpose of these remarks is not to deny that there are cyclical fluctuations in
the terms of trade of primary producers or to suggest that they are always
negligible. It is rather that we should not exaggerate the magnitude of the problem

and the degree of regularity of the cyclical pattern over time and space. Especially we should not allow the consequences of a unique catastrophe such as that of the Great Depression in the 1930s to dominate our thinking.

By and large the terms of trade of underdeveloped countries usually do deteriorate in depressions. With the same export volume and the same interest and capital balance (in real terms), the fall in the terms of trade obviously reduces the import capacity or foreign buying power of those countries. The cyclical fluctuations in the terms of trade add to the instability of export proceeds. It seems, however, that fluctuations in the physical volume of exports usually contribute more to the instability of export proceeds than do price changes. In other words, the percentage increases in cyclical upswings and decreases in downswings of export volumes of primary products are greater than those of prices (unit values).[19] In the post-World War II period of 1948–52 this pattern changed. In this period fluctuations in the value of the foreign trade of underdeveloped countries were primarily due to price changes and only to a much lesser extent to quantity changes.[20]

If the cyclical fluctuations in the terms of trade disappeared or became milder, volume changes remaining what they are, it would be better for the underdeveloped countries. Similarly, if the cyclical patterns were reversed, terms of trade improving during downswings when quantities decline and deteriorating during upswings when quantities rise, it would be nice, provided this cyclical pattern was of the right amplitude, and not so violent as to create again instability in the export proceeds.

But there is not much use in wishful thinking. Let us rather think in terms of concrete measures and policies, keeping well in mind that such measures and policies will never operate on the terms of trade alone, but also on other relevant magnitudes such as trade volumes.

I suppose it will be generally accepted that the task of eliminating or drastically mitigating world-wide cyclical swings falls squarely on the industrial centres, predominantly on the United States. Without engaging in undue wishful thinking, we may perhaps assume that very violent depressions, anything approaching the Great Depression of the 1930s, will in the future be prevented by fiscal and monetary measures. This will automatically eliminate radical shifts in the terms of trade of the underdeveloped countries and at the same time stabilize export volumes.

The price which the industrial countries seem to have to pay for that comparative stability in output and employment is a slowly but steadily rising price level—creeping inflation in other words. I am not here going to speculate on how long the developed countries will be willing to accept that condition, what can be done about it, or what the final consequences will be. As far as the underdeveloped countries are concerned, it seems to me that mild inflation in the industrial centres serves them well so long as full employment and import demand are maintained. Since most underdeveloped countries, especially those in Latin America, have a strong propensity to inflate, their balance of payments position is somewhat eased if inflation, though in milder form, is going on in the industrial countries too. In addition, the burden of their external debt is lightened by steadily rising prices.

The driving force in the process of creeping inflation is the relentless pressure of monopolistic trade unions for higher wages which, in view of the generally accepted full employment postulate, necessitates continuous monetary expansion. The policy of driving up wages parallel with, and in excess of, the gradual rise in productivity, far from hurting the interests of the importers of industrial products (as the theories previously criticized assert), turns out to be in their interest.

It would be wishful thinking to assume that even mild depressions can be avoided. Depressions of the order of magnitude of the recessions which the American economy experienced in 1946–49 and 1953–54, and probably somewhat more severe slumps than those two will again occur. Also, inflationary booms like the one started by the Korean war together with their aftermaths cannot be excluded. Such occurrences will inevitably have their effects on the price ratios between primary products and manufactured commodities.

If it is impossible to eliminate this type of fluctuation at the source, can they be offset or counteracted by special measures? The special measures which at once come to mind are international commodity agreements and buffer stock schemes. When the fluctuations under consideration can be assumed to be produced primarily by inventory fluctuations, international commodity agreements and buffer stock arrangements can best be regarded as attempts by the authorities in charge of these schemes to offset those inventory fluctuations by means of counter-cyclical accumulation and depletion of government-held stocks.

Innumerable schemes of this sort have been proposed. Few, if any, cases of successful counter-cyclical buffer stock schemes are on record. I cannot hope to give a thorough discussion of the issues involved, much less to make any novel contributions to this much studied and reviewed area, but will confine myself to asserting somewhat dogmatically that national and international experience does not justify optimism that anything decisive can be done along these lines. *Ex post* it looks simple to institute counter-cyclical accumulation and decumulation of commodity stocks. But *ex ante* the difficulties of diagnosing and anticipating cyclical changes are formidable. The dissensions and conflicts of interests are enormous and the pressure by special interests to influence the action of the buffer stock authorities must be terrific. If the difficulties into which the American policy of parity price regulation of agricultural products has run offers any guidance, the obstacles to the satisfactory operation of a similar scheme on an international level must be well-nigh insurmountable.

Rather than try to promote administratively and politically if not economically unworkable commodity price stabilization and buffer schemes, the underdeveloped countries would be better advised to learn to live with a certain degree of cyclical instability in their terms of trade and balance of payments. It has been claimed that this instability makes for inflation in good years as well as in bad years[21]—in good years because the high export proceeds are all spent, in bad years because the deficit is offset by domestic credit expansion, the government taking up some of the non-exportable surpluses.

This surely is not an inescapable consequence, but the result of faulty financial policies.[22] There is no reason why the central bank should not accumulate foreign exchange in good years, sterilizing at least partly the proceeds, and then maintain imports for development and other purposes by dipping into the accumulated reserves. There are, in addition, the International Monetary Fund and other international or foreign national agencies from which credit may be obtained in depressions. Furthermore, if a country maintains a sound financial position it may be able to get private credits. This is what I mean by learning to live with a certain amount of cyclical instability in terms of trade and export proceeds.

Changes in the terms of trade and export prices are, of course, not the only factors making for instability in export proceeds and the capacity to import, and, as we have seen, often not the most important factor. Export quantities of underdeveloped countries have been frequently affected unfavourably in depressions by increased protectionism in the developed countries. Underdeveloped countries surely have a right to protest against such unneighbourly policies on the part of the developed countries. They should raise their voices in GATT and the United Nations in protest, but would be in a much better position to do so effectively if they themselves did not engage, as many of them unfortunately do, in hyperprotectionist policies, and did not claim a special right to such policies based on their being underdeveloped or in the process of development. Who is not developing nowadays, one might ask? Saner, more liberal commerical policies would greatly contribute to minimizing cyclical instability of the terms of trade and its consequences.

Another aggravating factor which in many depressions has increased the pressure on the balance of payments of underdeveloped countries (and of debtor and capital importing countries in general) has been the interruption or even reversal, through credit withdrawals and capital flight, of the capital stream. This is highly disturbing and tends to affect unfavourably the terms of trade of the countries concerned.

This aggravation too is not an entirely inescapable, god-sent concomitant of every depression, but is at least partially preventable or curable. Prevention is usually better than cure. Sounder financial management, less inflation, larger international monetary reserves would go some way to counteract the incentive to withdraw capital and the reluctance to invest new capital, at least in mild depressions. I would argue that up to a certain point such a policy would not really cost anything because the loss involved by the holding of a larger liquid reserve (in the form of gold or short term dollar balances) would be offset by the elimination of the high social cost of continued inflation. Moreover, it surely would be worth some expense to make the financial structure capable of withstanding the high winds of financial crises even if we could not possibly make it fully resistant to the hurricane of a really severe depression. To attempt the latter would be tantamount to living permanently in a storm cellar.

5. Summary and Conclusions

International trade is vitally important for all underdeveloped countries—at least for all those that have a strong urge to push their economic development as quickly as possible. Hence the terms of trade as one of the factors determining the gains from trade in general and the capacity to import in particular are matters of legitimate concern.

It seems to me, however, that the concern with the terms of trade has been greatly overdone. Sinister secular tendencies which simply do not exist have been conjured up. Past developments have been given an unwarranted pessimistic interpretation. Reasons have been advanced for the alleged trend which are either fallacious or are entirely inadequate to explain what they are supposed to explain.

The same criticism applies to the opposite theory, popular among certain economists in developed countries, notably Britain, which states that because of the operation of the law of diminishing returns, the terms of trade must inexorably become unfavourable for the industrial countries.

Nobody can be quite sure about what the future will bring. If synthetic coffee were invented, it would be a catastrophe for the coffee exporters. If all underdeveloped countries could, in a few years, raise themselves to the level of the developed countries, the latter standing still in the meantime, the developed industrial countries would indeed find themselves in a very precarious position.

But these things are not likely to happen, and at any rate economists are not in the possession of any law which would enable them to predict a price trend for or against primary producers, or for or against underdeveloped countries, however we define that ambiguous term.

With regard to short-run, especially cyclical, variability, there would seem to exist some possibility of broad generalization. Prices of primary products fluctuate more violently over the course of the business cycle than prices of finished goods. Hence the terms of trade of underdeveloped countries tend to deteriorate in depressions and to improve in prosperity periods. One would expect the opposite cyclical pattern in the terms of trade of industrial countries.

But the degree of regularity and the magnitude of these cyclical fluctuations have been greatly exaggerated. Theorizing in this field has been unduly dominated by the experience of the catastrophic slump of the 1930s and other recent war-induced changes which are, after all, unique occurrences which we may hope will not continuously repeat themselves.

The amplitude of cyclical fluctuations of different primary products is very different (agricultural products versus minerals, petroleum versus mining products, foods versus fibres, etc.). Many developed countries have sizable exports of primary products, some being net exporters of primary products. Some underdeveloped countries have begun to export finished goods. For these reasons, the uniformity in the cyclical pattern of the terms of trade as between different developed and underdeveloped countries is limited with respect to amplitude and subject to exceptions with respect to direction.

Furthermore, the comparative stability or rigidity of finished goods prices is by no means an unmixed blessing for the industrial countries. The other side of the medal is great fluctuations in output and employment.

The excessive stress on terms of trade has deflected attention from more strategic points. It has led to preoccupation with symptoms or with factors which cannot be controlled or eliminated, or which can be controlled only at a heavy price in terms of lost opportunities for profitable trade, bureaucratic regimentation of the economy, and great administrative expense. Instead of learning to live with a certain amount of instability, making the economy flexible, and evolving methods to offset some of the consequences of the fluctuations in international demand and export proceeds, administratively and politically, if not economically, hopelessly unworkable schemes of price stabilization are being proposed and discussed.

The prevention of severe world-wide slumps is, of course, a task which falls squarely on the shoulders of the leading industrial countries, primarily on the shoulders of the dominant economy, the United States. In view of the fact that the prevention of severe depressions is also in the interest of the developed countries and that we undoubtedly know much better now how to control them, it seems to me not unreasonable that severe depressions will in fact be prevented in the future.

The milder ups and downs in business which are likely to persist, and the fluctuations in the terms of trade which they engender, should not be a major handicap and it should be possible for the underdeveloped countries, acting on their own and in cooperation with the developed industrial countries and international agencies, greatly to soften their impact. What is needed for that purpose is a strengthening of the financial structure of the underdeveloped countries and a counter-cyclical manipulation of gold and dollar reserves—less inflation, larger reserves, accumulation of reserves, and partial sterilization of export proceeds in boom times. This would enable these countries to maintain their imports in depression years by dipping into the accumulated reserves and would counteract the tendency to capital flight and withdrawal of foreign credits in depression years.

In the commercial policy field, attempts should be made to prevent protectionist reactions which in the past have so often intensified the contraction of trade in depressions. Cooperation in the existing international organizations, especially in the International Monetary Fund and GATT, will further the attainment of those objectives.

Notes

1. I must apologize for having slipped on this point in my *Survey of International Trade Theory*, International Finance Section, Princeton University (Princeton, N.J., 1955). [Chapter 4 in this volume.]

2. The authors of that report are, of course, fully aware of the fact that the capacity to import also depends on funds made available through capital imports, the necessity of repaying loans and interest payments.

3. Why the foreign offer curve has changed need not concern us except for the reason that this knowledge may give a clue about its likely future behaviour.

4. The statistical basis is to be found in United Nations, *Relative prices of Exports and Imports of Underdeveloped Countries* (New York, 1949).

5. C. M. Wright, 'Convertibility and Triangular Trade as Safeguards against Depression', *Economic Journal*, September 1955, pp. 425−426.

6. Many other examples are cited in Wright, *op. cit:* p. 726.

7. Paul T. Ellsworth, 'The Terms of Trade between Primary Producing and Industrial Countries', *Interamerican Economic Affairs*, vol. x, Summer 1956, pp. 55−56.

8. C. P. Kindleberger, *The Terms of Trade, a European Case Study* (New York, 1956), ch. 11, 'Primary Products and Manufactures'.

9. It is only fair to add that Professor Kindleberger is aware of the weakness of his machinery index; but he is unable to do anything about it.

10. E. A. G. Robinson, 'The Changing Structure of the British Economy', *Economic Journal*, September 1954.

11. Richard Pohle, *Deutschland am Scheidewege* (Jena, 1902).

12. Adolf Wagner, *Agrar und Industriestaat* (Jena, 1902).

13. Colin Clark has put forward the theory that there are long-run swings in the terms of trade and has freely extrapolated them into the future.

14. It cannot have been true for earlier periods. The British import-income ratio rose steadily throughout the nineteenth century but seems to have declined somewhat since the 1880s. See Robinson, *op. cit.* p. 458.

15. See, for example, Sombart, 'Das Gesetz der fallenden Export Quota', in *Die Deutsche Volkswirtschaft im 19. Fahrhundert*, 3rd ed. (Berlin, 1913), p. 371.

16. In many cases not even the commodity terms of trade deteriorated, for when we convert the British terms of trade into their partner's terms of trade, and make proper allowance for changes in freight rates, it may turn out that the latter improved too.

17. Professor Kindleberger, it will be remembered, thinks he found some support for the thesis that the commodity terms of trade of underdeveloped countries have behaved unfavourably. He remarks that this would be even more true of the double factoral terms of trade. His reason is that productivity in the developed (progressive) countries rises faster than in the underdeveloped (less progressive) countries. Hence a representative bale of the developed countries' exports contains, as time goes on, less and less labour (or factors of production in general) than a representative bale of the underdeveloped countries' exports.

This may be so, but it should be remembered that what matters for the economic welfare of a country is the single factoral terms of trade, and not the double factoral terms of trade. (If a country receives more or better goods per unit of its exported labour, it is better off irrespective of whether these goods contain more or less foreign labour than before.) And the single factoral terms of trade are not a symmetrical concept in the sense that an improvement in the single factoral terms of trade of one partner implies a deterioration of the single factoral terms of trade for the other partner. They may improve for both trade partners at the same time. Concretely, in the 1880s the United States, Canada, and Argentina received more in terms of import goods per unit of labour contained in the wheat or meat which they exported, while at the same time the United Kingdom received more in terms of goods for a British labour unit contained in the machinery and railway equipment which they sent abroad.

18. 'Convertibility and Triangular Trade', *Economic Journal, September 1955.*

19. That at least is the conclusion of the United Nations' report, *Instability of Export Markets of Underdeveloped Countries* (New York, 1952), p. 3 and *passim.*

This report states that it makes very little difference whether export prices (unit values) of primary products are taken in United States dollars (United States import unit values which are computed on an f.o.b. basis at the point of exit from underdeveloped countries exclusive of subsequent transport charges) or in real terms (that is to say, deflated by a price index of U.K. manufactured exports). This is rather strange, because it means that the import prices of underdeveloped countries remain virtually unchanged during the cycle. The fact that the deflator does not make allowance for changes in transportation cost may provide part of the solution.

20. United Nations, *Repercussions of Changes in Terms of Trade on the Economies of Countries in Process of Development*, U.N.E/2459, June 1953 (Mimeographed).

21. See, for example, United Nations, *Instability in Export Markets of Underdeveloped Countries* (New York, 1952), p. 1.

22. This is also the opinion of W. A. Lewis. See his celebrated volume *The Theory of Economic Growth* (London, 1955), p. 291. Similarly, Norman S. Buchanan and Howard S. Ellis, *Approaches to Economic Development* (New York, 1955), pp. 383–385.

20

Integration and Growth of
the World Economy in
Historical Perspective[1]

We live in the age of integration. Every conceivable—or inconceivable—combination of countries has been proposed, more or less seriously, as a candidate for integration—other planets and outer space being almost the only areas that do not yet figure in any of the many plans and proposals. With the formation of the European Economic Community, the European Common Market as a going concern, integration has passed from the talking stage, where it had remained for many years, into the stage of concrete realization. The example of the Common Market, beside spawning a rival European combination (EFTA), has induced the creation of similar schemes in other parts of the world—in South and Central America—and still others are on the drawing board. I do not intend to offer yet another comparative analysis of any of those schemes. What I should like to do is to put the modern integration movement into broader historical perspective of the growing world economy.

Without wishing to engage in a lengthy discussion of the proper or useful definition of terms, I think I should first indicate very briefly what we mean by integration—I say "we" and not "I" because I hope for fairly general agreement. We mean by integration closer economic relations between the areas concerned. This is clearly a concept capable of continuous gradation. One first stage is characterized by free commodity trade, greater division of labor, tending toward equalization of commodity prices. We have a higher stage of integration when factors of production can move freely with a consequent tendency for factor price equalization. (Allow me to skip the famous controversy whether complete factor price equalization would result from free commodity trade alone, with the remark that such equalization could indeed result, but only under such unrealistic assumptions that for practical purposes we can say that it would *not*. I hope that speaking of "unrealistic assumptions" will not embroil me in another famous and as yet unresolved controversy—namely, whether it is possible to reach reasonable conclusions from absurd premises.) We

American Economic Review, LIV (2), Part 1; 1–22. (March 1964). Reprinted with permission.

have a still higher stage of integration if all or the most important phases of economic policy are coordinated, and positive steps are taken to equalize commodity and factor prices.

I shall refrain from arbitrarily designating, as some have done, any one stage as that of "true integration" and shall not go into the substantive question whether the achievement of a lower stage of integration by itself may have undesirable results which would involve probing the mysterious depth of the theory of the "second best."

1. Waves of Integration

The recent movements toward integration are often regarded as an entirely new development which has been envisioned and proposed by many but has never before made headway on a significant scale. I submit that this is true only in a formal and narrow sense.

Looking over the evolution of the world economy during the last two hundred years or so, we can clearly discern three big waves of integration—preceding and dwarfing the regional integration movements of the last ten years. The secular trend toward integration and growth of the world economy was interrupted by one period of sharp decline and disintegration.

Let me first briefly identify these partly overlapping waves and then discuss them in turn.

The first wave was the internal integration of the economies of the nation states which we find today on the map of the world. The economy of Great Britain was the first to be unified and integrated, the French and American followed soon after. Later came other Continental European and overseas countries.

The second wave overlapping or, if you prefer, superimposed upon the first was the free trade movement that reached its high point at the end of the 1870's. The movement towards freer trade was reversed in 1878, but despite the fact that in most countries tariffs became higher and higher, world trade continued to grow rapidly up to World War I. For the underlying forces of rapid technological progress in transport and mass production, as well as massive migration of labor and capital toward the regions of "recent settlement" in the Western Hemisphere, Oceania, and South Africa, still dominated over increasingly protectionist commercial policies in many parts of the world. The more drastic modern methods of trade restriction, quotas and exchange control, had not yet made their appearance, and the movement toward collectivism, interventionism, and national economic planning, which later became a formidable obstacle for world-wide integration, had not yet made much headway.

The first serious disintegration of the world economy, foreshadowed by the rising protectionism and economic nationalism from 1880 on, became a fact during and immediately after the World War of 1914–18. After a brief interlude of freer trade in the 1920's, real disintegration and rapid decline of world trade set in with the Great Depression. After an incomplete and hesitant recovery, disintegration reached its nadir in World War II.

The third wave of world-wide integration and growth started soon after the end of World War II, gathered momentum after 1948, and is still in progress. It has been centered on and propelled by the spectacular recovery and rapid growth of all industrial countries, including the United States and United Kingdom, notwithstanding their recent troubles and their lower growth rates compared with the Continent of Europe and Japan. Contrary to what is often said, the prosperity of the "industrial centers" of the world economy did spread, though not as rapidly and fully as one would wish, to the "periphery" of the less developed countries, to use Raul Prebisch's picturesque designation of the two areas. This wave of world-wide integration has had more powerful and beneficial effects than the much more advertised and talked-about series of regional integrations.

2. National Economic Integration

Let me now add some observations on each of these phases of the growing world economy. Later I shall analyze recent developments in somewhat greater detail in the light of the historical perspective gained.

The internal integration of the British and French economies was vigorously pursued during the mercantilistic era. The economy of Great Britain emerged as a fully integrated unit in the eighteenth century and the economic integration of France was completed when the French Revolution swept away all still existing internal barriers to trade and migration. In both countries, as well as in almost all others, political and administrative unification and centralization preceded and promoted economic integration. Early attempts at close Anglo-French economic co-operation, sponsored by the physiocratic advisers of Louis XVI and by Adam Smith's influence on the younger Pitt, culminated in the Eden Treaty of 1786 which brought drastic tariff reductions. But the movement toward freer trade was premature and was soon interrupted by the French Revolution and the following wars. Not before 1860 was the time ripe to accomplish what had been tried 75 years earlier.

The American economy had the good fortune of having been integrated at a very early stage. When the War of Independence came to an end, the economic relations between the states resembled those of the German states after the Congress of Vienna. Under the Articles of Confederation each of the 13 states of the Union pursued its own tariff policy. But through the Constitution a huge free trade area for the unimpeded movement of goods and services, of labor and capital was created, which was surely a major factor in U.S. economic development.

On the Continent of Europe the major steps toward integrated national economies were the economic unification of Germany through the German *Zollverein* (1834) and the emergence of a unified Italian state in 1861.

Alfred Marshall called the *Zollverein* "the most important movement toward free trade that the world had ever seen, except the contemporary reform of the British fiscal system" [12, p. 399]. I think Marshall was right, for from the political and historical standpoint, if not from the economic one, national economic unification was an indispensable prerequisite not only for the economic development of the various countries concerned, but also for the growth of the world economy. This remains true even though we now know that the hopes and expectations so widely held in the mid-nineteenth century, that national free trade and integration would lead in straight and unbroken succession to world-wide free or near-free trade, were not fulfilled. To question Marshall's judgment concerning the *Zollverein* on the ground of the next hundred years of German history would imply extreme and untenable historical determinism.

There is no doubt that the Italian unification did for the development of the Italian economy as a whole what the German unification did for the German economy. This would be true even if the widely held theory were correct that the economic integration and internal free trade caused a retardation of the economic development of the Italian South as a region in an absolute sense, not merely relatively to the more progressive North.

The German and Italian national economic integration was preceded and followed by similar movements in many other European and overseas countries.

3. World-Wide Integration through Freer Trade

While this was going on, the second wave of world-wide integration as I called it, started—namely, the free trade movement of the mid-nineteenth century. It was spearheaded by Great Britain, but spread widely (especially after 1860) to the Continent of Europe. Let me briefly recall a few landmarks—abolition of the Corn Laws in 1846, the Cobden-Chevalier Treaty of 1860 between Great Britain and France, which brought a radical reversal from high protection to something near free trade in France, and following the Franco-British accord a number of commercial treaties which substantially reduced tariffs all over Western and Central Europe. The impact of the free trade movement was not confined to commercial policy and tariffs. Shipping policy, which was extremely restrictive everywhere in the early nineteenth century, was radically liberalized, first in Great Britain as early as the 1830's and later in other countries. Furthermore, the introduction of the "open door" policy in the British crown colonies and in others was a major step towards the liberalization of world trade.

As far as tariff policy is concerned, the movement towards freer trade came to an end in the last years of the 1870's. The two major factors that caused the reversal of liberal commercial policy, first in Germany (1878) and a little later in France and elsewhere, were the accelerated influx of agricultural products from overseas countries—United States, Canada, Argentina, Australia—and the impact of the severe depressions of the 1870's and 1890's. But although import tariffs in many countries showed a definite tendency to go higher during the last quarter of the nineteenth century and the first decade of the twentieth century, the volume of world trade rose rapidly throughout the whole period up to World War I. From about 1895 the rate of growth was indeed substantially higher than during the preceding two, and possibly three, decades.

A number of factors account for the growth of trade in the face of rising tariffs. The technological revolution in production and transportation continued, of course, without let-up. However this factor alone might not have been sufficient to support the growth of world trade as is shown by the development during the next period, namely the interwar years during which world trade did not show much growth, although one could hardly say that technological progress had slowed down.

The flow of capital and especially of labor from Europe to the Western Hemisphere and a few other areas continued at a rapid and increasing rate until 1914, after which it slowed down sharply. Moreover, while tariffs went higher after 1878, they were on the whole still moderate compared with those prevailing after World War I and, what is equally important, much more stable. Furthermore, the international payments mechanism improved with the adoption of the gold standard by many countries in the last quarter of the nineteenth century. International clearing of balances aided by the easy flow of short-term credit through London and other financial centers in Western Europe and elsewhere promoted multilateral trade around the globe. Payment restrictions were, of course, almost totally absent, and so were other quantitative trade restrictions such as quotas and export or import monopolies.

We are thus justified, it seems to me, to speak of a long period of world-wide integration during which most countries were knit together ever more closely in a network of multilateral trade and payments. It is true that many writers—most of them later with the benefit of hindsight, though one can also find a few contemporary prophets of doom—thought that they could detect tendencies of incipient disequilibrium and disintegration. As far as the economics of the matter is concerned, these are merely *ex post* rationalizations and explanations of what happened later. It is only in the field of ideologies, it seems to me, that a case can be made for the theory that later events were the likely and natural (though not the unavoidable) consequence of earlier tendencies. Concretely, it can perhaps be argued that the rising tide of economic and political nationalism and antiliberal thinking and policies in general led to World War I and its aftermath. But there surely was no inevitable economic nexus in the sense that a deep-seated real maladjustment had arisen in the world economy, something analogous to what is supposed by many business cycle theorists to develop in major if not all business cycle upswings—a real disequilibrium which makes a painful and long drawn out readjustment all but inevitable.

The statement that there was nothing basically wrong with the pre-1914 world economy will probably not encounter strenuous objections from the present generation of economists, although it is contradictary to Marxian-type theories, especially the neo-Marxian theory of imperialism, and to the Keynesian secular stagnation doctrine.

But the justification of what I have said must to a large extent rest on the plausibility of an alternative explanation of the events of the next thirty years.

4. Disintegration of the World Economy, 1914–45

The period from 1914 to 1945, bordered by two world wars and bisected by a catastrophic depression, can surely be described as one of distintegration of the world economy and declining world trade, under any reasonable definition of these terms.

The disintegrating forces were so strong that it is surprising that world trade did expand at all. Let me briefly recall the major developments.

World War I was followed by acute financial disorders, rapid inflation in many countries and hyperinflations in some. In the United States, the period of inflation ended in the severe depression of 1920–21 which had repercussions in many countries around the world, while in Europe inflation was stopped abruptly in a series of successful stabilization efforts between 1922 and 1925 without any immediate depressive effects.

By the middle of the 1920's the world was back on what looked like a normal course with most currencies again convertible. It is true, tariffs were higher and less stable than before and had a tendency to go higher; moreover, the integrated area of the Austro-Hungarian monarchy was fragmented into several pieces. But despite these unfavorable developments, world trade expanded fairly rapidly to something like 30 per cent above the prewar level. The effective exclusion of Russia from the world economy, although an event of tremendous political consequence, had a very limited economic impact on the world economy during the interwar period.[2]

Then came the Great Depression and the picture changed completely. The few remaining free trade countries, Great Britain[3] first, switched abruptly to high protection. Tariffs everywhere were raised rapidly and almost all countries introduced quotas, exchange control, import prohibitions, bilateral clearings—methods of international trading which in peacetime had literally not been known for centuries. By 1932 the dollar value of world exports had tumbled to about a third of its 1929 level and its quantum was where it had been in 1913.

The quantum of trade in manufactured articles declined much faster than that of trade in primary products, but the value of the latter fell more, which reflects the extremely sharp deterioration of the terms of trade for the exporters of primary products.

In 1938 the quantum of trade of primary products was again 16 per cent above the 1913 level. While the world index of manufacturing activity in 1936–38 was 85 per cent above the 1913 level, the quantum of trade of manufactured articles was some 8 per cent below 1913 [3] [25, Ch. 2].[4] This contrast can be regarded as a rough indication of the degree of disintegration of the world economy that had taken place.

For the purposes of this paper as indicated above, I have to venture to express my views on the basic causes of the exceptional severity and length of the Great Depression. At the time when it happened most economists did not know what had hit them. Marxian economists, of course, took the economic catastrophe simply as a confirmation of Marx's theory that depressions would become more and more severe until the capitalist system would come down in a final big crash. (In the 1960's this view has lost conviction, even among the faithful.) Others who lacked the prophet's guidance through the maze of world history had a harder time to explain the slump. Some spoke vaguely of big real maladjustments in the structure of production that had accumulated during the 1920's and others of the coincidence, accidental or otherwise, of the contraction phase of several superimposed types of concurrent economic fluctuations.[5] The Keynesians later fashioned their theory of secular stagnation.

From the present vantage point, the explanation of the exceptional virulence of the Great Depression seems much simpler. It was mainly due to the wholesale destruction of money, which in turn was largely the consequence of institutional weaknesses and incredibly poor policies, on the national and international level. Let me mention only a few of these. The collapse of the American banking system, the bankruptcy of thousands of banks, and the overly timid[6] monetary policy which failed to counteract energetically and to stop the raging deflation explain, I venture to say, the "darkest hues" (Schumpeter) of the depression in the United States. Money supply contracted by something like 30 per cent from 1929 to 1933. The deflation could not have been nearly as severe if there had existed then, as there exists now, effective deposit insurance, or if the United States, instead of the archaic unit banking system, had had an efficient branch banking system like Great Britain,[7] not to mention "100 per cent banking."

The mistakes of the early New Deal of pressing hastily for often poorly conceived reforms, of fostering monopolies of business (N.R.A.) and labor and thus raising costs and frightening investors, instead of concentrating at first all energies on expansionary measures to bring about quick recovery (as Keynes among others recommended), explain why in 1939 unemployment was still over 17 per cent. Policy mistakes of a similar kind and magnitude were made in several other important countries, for example in pre-Nazi Germany and under the popular front government in France. Just as Roosevelt ignored Keynes' suggestion that he postpone reforms until recovery had made good progress, so did Léon Blum the advice of his Scandinavian and British socialist friends who recommended that expansion take precedence over reform.[8]

On the international level the slow-motion, beggar-my-neighbor devaluation of all currencies of the world at intervals of a few years—sterling in 1931, the dollar in 1933–34, the gold bloc currencies in 1936 and so on—inflicted upon different groups of countries protracted periods of overvalued currencies, causing deficits and losses, further trade restrictions, and more depression. Although each of these devaluations in isolation can be defended as unavoidable, their time pattern stamped the whole approach as a sadistic policy, calculated to maximize pain and destruction. It was like cutting off the tail of a dog piece by piece instead of all at once, the way it surely would have been done had there existed the *International Monetary Fund*.

These institutional defects and horrendous policy mistakes have noting to do with basic weaknesses or contradictions of the capitalist, free enterprise economy, or with a tendency toward secular stagnation, lack of investment opportunities and a chronic tendency toward oversaving, or gigantic real maladjustments. At any rate, wherever the monetary deflation was stopped by orthodox or unorthodox measures without at the same time sharply raising costs, the alleged real, structural contradictions, weaknesses, and maladjustments disappeared as fast as they had appeared a few years earlier.

It is true the methods used to stop deflation were very unorthodox in many countries (not in all), and there remained almost everywhere a legacy of high tariffs, tight quotas and many other restrictions on international trade and payments. But the point is that this was not necessary; deflation could have been stopped and the economy "reflated"[9] in a more orderly, less unorthodox fashion with less structural change and without damage to the international division of labor. Even as it was, if in the meantime the threat of war had not arisen and the war had not come, surely a good part of the new trade barriers would have been removed and trading methods would have returned to a more normal state of affairs. Actually, the outbreak of World War II delayed the return to something resembling the pre-1929 conditions until the 1950's.

Before going on to those recent developments, let us look back once more at the interwar period. As it recedes into the past and we gain perspective, it becomes increasingly clear, it seems to me, that the interwar or two-war period in general and the Great Depression in particular were in many important respects a singular historical phenomenon.

Let me become more concrete. I have already mentioned that the exceptional severity and length of the Great Depression were due to special circumstances, institutional weaknesses, and incredibly inept and timid policies on the national and international level. This has been misunderstood by the Marxians and Keynesians. The doctrine of secular stagnation, the widely held expectation that World War II would soon be followed by a deep depression—an expectation which was still entertained by many when the second and even when the third postwar recession came around—all these misjudgments as well as the theory of the stubborn dollar shortage and the low elasticity of international demand stem largely, if not wholly, from the misinterpretations of the depressed 1930's as a more or less regular business cycle downswing. A period of singular catastrophes plays havoc with trend extrapolations, and many an analysis has come to grief. Examples in the domestic field are the numerous estimates of saving propensities and investment opportunities for the postwar years on the basis of interwar experience and figures. Formidable difficulties arise for another type of analysis—namely, that which assumes the existence of some sort of supercycle, be it Kondratieff or the now much more popular Kuznets cycle. It is difficult to see how an endogenous mechanism producing such swings or cycles could fail to be completely disrupted by the elemental forces of a world war or the Great Depression.[10] In the international field, the famous conjecture that the terms of trade have a secular tendency to deteriorate either for the less developed countries or for primary producers is to a large extent the consequence of not recognizing the interwar period with its two very sharp price declines—in 1920–21 and 1929–33—as a singular event. In the light of later developments, this conjecture has lost its statistical support entirely.[11] We shall encounter other cases of analyses that have gone astray for the same reason.

5. The Growth of World Trade since the War: The Case of the Industrial Countries

I now come to the third wave of world-wide integration or reintegration during the postwar period.

Since the end of the war, especially since 1948, world trade has grown very rapidly. World exports rose from some $54 billion in 1948 to over$140 billion in mid-1963, and for the decade 1950–60 the compound rate of growth of the volume of world exports was about 6 per cent a year.[12] It seems that for the first time in almost a hundred years world trade has grown faster than world production for a period of more than ten years. I mention this fact for two reasons, first, to convey an idea of the rapidity of the growth and, second, because so much has been made of the alleged fact that since the late nineteenth century international trade has in most countries grown less fast than national income. You will remember that years ago Werner Sombart tried to establish a "historical law" of the "declining importance of international trade."[13] This alleged tendency has held a strange fascination for many economists.[14] But I myself cannot see much importance in this particular criterion. Whether trade has grown somewhat more or less fast than GNP is hardly very significant unless the divergence is very pronounced as it was in the 1930's. Here again the contours of the trend have been blurred by the singular events of the Great Depression.[15]

The rapid rise in world trade is the consequence of, but has also powerfully contributed to, the rapid growth of world production. The performance with respect to growth and stability of the majority of national economies of the world has, on the whole, been satisfactory—not in an absolute sense of perfection, but satisfactory compared first with earlier periods (not only the definitely unsatisfactory interwar period), compared secondly with what was expected by many economists 20 years ago, and compared thirdly, I dare say, with what one would gather from current statements of many experts, not to mention politicians, statesmen, and other laymen.

Let me first discuss the case of the highly developed industrial countries. As far as Continental Europe, Japan, and Australia are concerned, my optimistic statement will probably not be questioned. These countries can indeed look back to a decade and a half of almost unprecedented and unbroken growth and prosperity, which has definitely gone beyond the stage that could be reasonably regarded merely as recovery from the low levels reached at the end of the war. But I go on to say that an objective evaluation shows that, contrary to what is often said or implied, the overall performance of the American economy, too, has been quite satisfactory in the sense defined above. This holds for the whole postwar period including the last five or six years of slightly slower growth and somewhat higher unemployment of which we have heard so much in recent years. True, the U.S. rate of growth has been much lower than that of Europe and Japan, but it has been somewhat higher, over all and per capita, than it was, not only during the whole interwar period, but for any period of similar length (leaving out the Great Depression) since 1909 when reliable deflated GNP figures begin. In the nineteenth century, aggregate GNP grew faster, but as far as we can tell per head or per man-hour growth was slower than during the postwar period.

The great improvement of the postwar years over earlier periods is, of course, the complete absence of deep depressions. This is common knowledge and it is, I think, fairly generally agreed now that there are excellent reasons for assuming that deep depressions are a thing of the past. I share this conviction and shall not repeat the well-known argument. But let us recall that this consensus, which now seems to extend even to Marxist economists, did not exist or was at least much less widespread only ten years ago.

But how about the last five years of somewhat slower growth and higher unemployment? The critics of our economic system call it semi-depression, just about the best one can expect under a capitalist free enterprise regime. Many others agree with the diagnosis of an intolerable stagnation, but think that it could be cured by bold expansionary measures. Some think that monetary and fiscal expansion alone would not be enough, that drastic structural reforms (retraining of workers on a massive scale, redistribution of income, and others) would be required to get the economy back to a high level of employment and to keep it there.[16]

To me any comparison with the 1930's, quantitative or qualitative, seems to be entirely unwarranted, and structural factors explain only a small fraction of the problem. The explanation of the slack is really quite simple: It is the consequence, directly and indirectly via somewhat tighter monetary and fiscal policies than otherwise would be necessary, of the deficit in the balance of payments.[17]

To put the matter in the simplest terms, suppose the deficit in the balance of payments disappeared all by itself—as it well may through continued inflation abroad—can anyone doubt that our economy would expand substantially, partly from rising exports and import substitution, partly in response to easier money and fiscal policies which then would become possible?

It is really as simple as that although, looking at the size of the deficit compared with GNP itself or with its annual increases, it may sound astonishing that such a tiny tail should wag such a huge dog. But let me get back to my main theme by brushing aside a mountain of real and imaginary difficulties and controversies with the remark that it cannot be beyond the wit of men—that is, us economists—to get this tiny tail removed, with or without the surgery of a change in exchange rates, and without in the process restricting trade in goods and services or reducing growth itself below the otherwise attainable level.[18]

An indispensable condition for the rapid recovery and growth of the industrial countries and the expansion of world trade was the removal of the jungle of internal and external direct controls that had grown up in many countries during the depression and the war. Price controls, consumer rationing, allocation of raw materials, etc. were removed quickly in some countries such as Germany and more gradually elsewhere. By the middle 1950's the process was substantially finished almost everywhere and the price mechanism had again taken the place of the wartime system of direct controls. The liberation of the economies of the industrial countries in Europe and elsewhere from the shackles of direct control released great energies which led to the spectacular rise in output and consumer satisfaction. I add "consumer's satisfaction" because improvements in quality of products and a great increase in the variety of products (including services such as increased opportunity to travel) surely are factors adding greatly to economic welfare while finding inadequate expression in output figures.

In the international sphere the replacement of direct controls by the price mechanism was much slower and in some countries less complete than in the domestic area. But by 1959 the currencies of all industrial countries were again more or less convertible; in other words, exchange control was dismantled although restrictions on capital movements still exist in many countries. Moreover, import quotas were gradually removed, first in intra-European trade, but then largely also on dollar imports and later, although still incompletely, on imports from Japan.

This freeing of trade constitutes a movement towards world-wide integration that has preceded and overlapped the regional reduction of trade barriers and regional integration in the European Common Market and other similar schemes of which we hear so much. There can be hardly a doubt that, up to now, the quantitative effects on trade of the world-wide integration and liberalization have been much greater than those of the much more discussed and advertised regional schemes.

6. The Growth of World Trade and the Less Developed Countries

Now to the controversial and extremely important question of the participation of the less developed countries in the over-all expansion of world trade. From a careful study of postwar facts and figures, the conclusion emerges, I believe, that the less developed countries have greatly benefited from the expansion of world trade and that the prosperity in "the industrial centers" has spread to "the less developed periphery."

This result is not surprising; both classical and Keynesian theory, speaking with complete harmony on this matter, lead to the strong presumption, though not the absolute certainty, that the rapid growth of the industrial countries will benefit the less developed countries by increasing the demand for their exports, by making a more liberal supply of capital and aid funds possible and, taking a broader and longer view, by developing numerous new technologies and products, many of which are extremely useful for the less developed countries. It is nevertheless necessary to dwell on the matter and carefully to establish the meaning, validity, and implications of the above statement because it runs counter to widely held pessimistic views. The extreme form of these heretical doctrines—heretical to the classical as well as the Keynesian theory—is represented by the transference to the international sphere of the Marxian theory of "increasing misery" (*Verelendungstheorie*). Since it really makes no sense any more to say that the American, European, or Japanese workers are getting poorer all the time, modern Marxists have given up this theory for the developed countries. But it has survived in the international sphere. Thus Paul

Sweezy admits that in the developed countries workers have a "tolerable if degraded life"; but the advanced countries "increasingly impose the burdens on the people of the colonies and the raw-material-producing countries" [21, p. 221]. A somewhat less extreme theory has been put forward by non-Marxist writers. Thus Gunnar Myrdal holds that "trade operates (as a rule) with a fundamental bias in favor of the richer and progressive regions (and countries) and in disfavor of the less developed countries." His thesis is not only that the poor countries derive less benefits from trade than the rich, but that, in the absence of strong protective policies, the poor become poorer if and because the rich get richer.[19]

Baldly stated like that, these extreme views are not widely accepted, but their influence in coloring the general thinking on these problems, especially in the less developed countries, should not be underrated. However, since they have been adequately criticized in the literature, I shall not discuss them further [13] [2].

The moderate version of the pessimistic view concerning the international position of the underdeveloped countries asserts that these countries have had no, or only a very inadequate, share in the expansion of world trade and that their international position has deteriorated continuously for the last ten years as evidenced by the lagging volume of exports and unfavorable terms of trade.

Looking at the broad facts, we find indeed that while the volume of exports and imports of the developed countries has grown at an annual rate of about 7 per cent from 1950 to 1960, the volume of exports of the "developing countries" (the official U.N. designation of less developed countries) has grown by 3.6 per cent and that of their imports by 4.6 per cent during the same period.[20] During the same period, the terms of trade of the developing countries in the aggregate have deteriorated by about 9 per cent as a consequence of a rise of about 10 per cent in unit value of the imports of the developing countries and a slight rise of unit value of their exports.[21]

To speak of developing countries in the aggregate—or, what comes to much the same thing, of a "typical" or "representative" underdeveloped country—is, of course, a bold abstraction from which purists will recoil in horror. The less developed countries are a much more heterogeneous group than the industrial countries. Among them there are semideveloped and wholly undeveloped countries; tropical and temperate zone agricultural countries; petroleum, mining, and agricultural product exporters; many pursue inflationary policies of varying degrees of severity, others are more disciplined; a few have convertible currencies but the majority suffer from overvalued currencies and their trade is restricted and distorted by controls and multiple currency practices of varying impenetrability.

In view of this great diversity of basic structures and policies, it is not surprising that the trade and growth performance of the less developed countries is very widely scattered. To search for systematic connections between the latter—performance—and the former—basic structures and policies—would be a challenging task but cannot be undertaken in one lecture. It would seem possible, however, to draw some useful conclusions from the over-all picture.

The most important fact is that the volume of trade of the less developed countries has grown and is growing at a substantial rate. The more rapid growth of the volume of imports than that of exports reflects the fact that these countries have been able to attract capital and have received substantial aid from the industrial countries.

This on the whole favorable picture is not changed by the fact that trade of, and between, the industrial countries has grown faster. The more rapid growth of the trade of industrial countries is not a new phenomenon. Even before 1914 it has often been observed, especially by free trade economists with obvious satisfaction, that "the industrial countries are their own best customers." But during the Great Depression trade in manufactured products (which can be taken as a rough index of trade of developed countries) contracted more sharply than the volume of trade primary products.

There are, however, good reasons to believe, as Professor Samuelson recently reminded us [17, p. 48], that lower total volume of trade between the developed and underdeveloped countries may bring more material benefits and consumer satisfaction to both partners than the larger volume of trade between the developed countries. The reason is that the intramarginal cost differences underlying the trade of manufactures between industrial countries are probably much smaller than those on which the trade between industrial countries and the exporters of primary products is based.[22]

There is another factor involved. One of the reasons for the lower rate of growth of the trade of the less developed countries is surely that practically all of them pursue highly protectionist policies. In my opinion, they are going in their protectionism far beyond what can possibly be justified on infant-industry, terms-of-trade, or any other rational grounds. But whether one accepts this judgment or not, high protection reduces the volume of trade[23] and by the same token increases the *marginal* benefit from trade.

As for the terms of trade, the deterioration from the early 1950's is, of course, regrettable in the sense that the less developed countries would be better off if in 1960 their terms of trade were the same as in 1950. But we must keep a sense of proportion. The deterioration was not catastrophic and cannot be compared with what happened in the 1930's. The comparative order of magnitude is indicated by the fact that while, according to the U.N., from 1950 to 1960 the deterioration was 9 per cent, Kindleberger found that in 1938 the terms of trade of industrial Europe with a large part of the underdeveloped world stood at 149, with 1928 = 100 [22] [6].[24] To convey an idea of the absolute magnitude of the "burden" or "loss" involved, let me mention that the U.N. report computes that "had the terms of trade of the less developed countries been stabilized at their 1950 level the aggregate purchasing power of their exports in terms of imports in 1960 would have been greater to the extent of $2.3 billion." This is not a negligible sum, but compared with the national income of the less developed areas of the world or its annual increase it is quite small.[25] The incidence of the 9 per cent over-all deterioration of the terms of trade on different areas was, of course, very uneven. Latin America, for example, suffered a deterioration almost double the average, the Middle East none at all, and the rest of Asia (excluding Japan) one much smaller than the average. But even in the area hardest hit—Latin America—the "importing power of exports" (volume of exports multiplied by terms of trade, also called "capacity to import") has substantially increased throughout the period of 1950 to 1960 [4, p. 61]. As has frequently happened in the past, the impact of the change in the terms of trade on the primary exporters was partly offset by a sharp decline in freight rates which were very high in the early 1950's.[26] Since the middle of 1962, the international trade situation of the less developed countries has improved greatly, prices of many primary products have risen substantially, the terms of trade did not show any further deterioration, and export earnings have registered sizable increases.

Nobody can be sure how long that improvement will continue and how far it will go. But assuming that the industrial countries avoid serious depressions and maintain a good rate of growth, barring further revolutionary technological changes (such as the invention of cheap synthetic coffee) and highly protectionist policies on the part of the industrial countries—under these not unreasonable assumptions the less developed countries can look forward to a continuously expanding market for their exports, and a sharp deterioration of their terms of trade comparable to what happened in the 1930's is virtually excluded.

I should add that this fairly optimistic appraisal relates only to the international trade position of the less developed countries.[27] Far be it from me to belittle the severe handicaps from which many less developed countries suffer, such as poor natural resources and bad climate, population pressure, political and social instability, and, I am afraid one has to add, exceedingly bad economic policies. All I have said was that a shrinking or stagnant world market has not been among the handicaps since the war.

7. Outlook for the Future

Instead of summarizing what I have said, let me try to peer a little into the future. Since economists are not endowed with the gift of prophecy, I shall not try to predict what will happen to world trade in the future but do the next best thing and suggest what would be the course of events if certain conditions are fulfilled.

I see no reason why the the growth of world trade and the ever closer integration of the major areas of the world should not continue if two conditions are met. The first, basic requirement is maintenance of a high level of employment and growth in the industrial countries. On this nothing more need be added, except to say that to me the chances look good that this condition will be fulfilled. But it is a necessary, not a sufficient, condition. At least in the larger countries economic activity could grow quite satisfactorily (although not at the highest attainable speed) without a corresponding growth of trade.

The second presupposition is further liberalization of trade or, as a minimum, avoidance of increases in trade barriers for balance-of-payments or protectionist reasons. I am afraid we cannot be so sure about this condition being met as about the first. Balance-of-payments troubles among industrial countries could easily become a serious roadblock to freer trade, as is already the case to some extent in the United States through the tying of loans, buy-American policies, and similar protectionist devices. Paradoxically, attempts at regional integration in various parts of the world constitute an imminent danger to world-wide integration and further growth of multilateral trade.[28]

As to the balance of payments, I must confine myself to a few remarks. The current American difficulties will somehow be resolved, but will hardly remain the last case of serious disequilibrium among the industrial countries. With the rate of growth slowing down and inflation going on in some countries, with anti-inflationary and growth-promoting measures being taken in different countries with different degrees of vigor and success, it would be very surprising indeed if strains in the international payments system did not develop from time to time in different places.

The extreme reluctance to change any exchange rate and the stubborn rejection of floating rates not only for reserve currencies, which is understandable, but also for nonreserve currencies throw a very heavy burden on internal price and wage adjustments. The successful operation of the present system requires, if world-wide inflation is to be avoided, a degree of financial and wage discipline which few countries have so far been able to muster.[29] But the problem is not insoluble and, since the imposition of financial and wage discipline is, after all, the most important advantage that can be claimed for the system of stable exchange rates, we can only hope that sufficient discipline will in fact be forthcoming to bring about the necessary adjustments smoothly and speedily without causing severe restrictions of trade or serious unemployment in the process.

I suppose I have to mention international liquidity. I can only say that it does not strike me as a problem of major importance or difficulty. The policy-makers have a great number of plans to choose from—Bernstein, Posthuma, Roosa, Triffin, Zolotas, to mention only a few luminaries. Even the more modest ones would banish the danger of a general lack of liquidity, at least for many years. I wish, therefore, that a large part of the professional ingenuity that is now being spent so lavishly on that issue were diverted to the basic and mush more difficult problems of internal price and wage restraints and adjustments.

The regional integration schemes that are now in the process of realization have developed strongly protectionist features which go far beyond their unavoidable discriminatory effects. This is true of the European Common Market and even more so of its Latin American counterpart. In fact, as far as the latter is concerned, it is an understatement to say that protectionist tendencies have appeared. The Latin American Free Trade Area (LAFTA) has been conceived openly and frankly as a protectionist device from its beginning.[30] On the other hand, many of the managers and supporters of EEC inside and outside the six members sincerely regard the Common Market as a step towards freer trade. But good intentions even on the part of the managers are not enough. An international enterprise of that magnitude, once it has been launched with a tremendous effort and enthusiasm and has been institutionalized through the creation of a heavy politico-bureaucratic machinery, tends to develop its own logic and movement. After it has gathered momentum, it becomes very difficult to steer it in another direction. This has been discovered, to their sorrow, by the vocal and vigorous forces which, working from within and from without EEC, have been trying to persuade the Community to adopt an "outward looking attitude," as the phrase goes. A crucial test as to whether or not it can be made to move in the direction of freer trade will come next year when the negotiations begin in earnest on the so-called Kennedy-round of tariff reductions in Geneva.

Let us hope that this noble experiment will succeed, that tariffs between the industrial countries and on imports from the less developed countries will be drastically reduced. Then the future economic historian will be able to say of the European Economic Community what Marshall said of the German *Zollverein*—it was a big step toward freer multilateral trade.

Notes

1. Presidential address delivered at the Seventy-Sixth Annual Meeting of the American Economic Association, Boston, December 27, 1963.

2. It is interesting that only at the lowest point of the depression in 1931–32 did trade with Russia temporarily assume a somewhat greater importance for some European countries.

3. It is true that during and immediately after World War I Great Britain applied a stiff dose of tariff protection (the so-called "MacKenna" and "Key Industry" duties). But they applied only to a short list of industrial articles, and some were temporarily removed by Philip Snowden, Chancellor of the Exchequer in the first MacDonald ministry in 1924.

4. The concept "world manufacturing activity" is, of course, somewhat nebulous and its measure arbitrary and imprecise. But the statements in the text could be restated in terms of GNP, industrial production, and trade of the major countries, concepts that are less objectionable than "world production," etc.

5. Schumpeter himself did not really take seriously his suggestion that the coincidence of a Kondratieff, Juglar and Kitchin depression accounted for the severity of the 1930 depression. On the contrary, he said that "the darkest hues of cyclical depressions ... are due to adventitious circumstances." See [19, p. 150].

6. The timidity of monetary policy should be judged by the magnitude of the problem (the intensity of the deflation which was to be offset) and not by historical standards.

7. If anybody doubts this statement, let him read Jacob Viner's brilliant, convincing, and blunt but well-balanced analysis in [24]. Also see [1].

8. On Keynes' criticism of the New Deal policies compare R. F. Harrod, *The Life of John Maynard Keynes*, New York, 1951, p. 447. Keynes was critical not of the reforms as such, but of the timing of their introduction and of the methods of putting them through, which, by frightening the businessman, unnecessarily delayed full recovery.
    The information concerning Léon Blum I owe to Gunnar Myrdal.

9. This does not mean that the price level would have to go back to the 1929 level.

10. It is possible by means of population or investment echos or some financial mechanism to make a plausible case for the proposition that a tendency for long swings is started by those powerful disturbances. But the attempt to carry the chronology of the long swings right through the disturbed period of 1914–45 and thereby to suggest that the mechanism, whatever it is, which produces the long swings should function more or less undamaged right through that period, punctured though it was by tremendously powerful exogenous shocks, seems to me entirely unconvincing and to compromise the long-swing hypothesis.

11. The latest extremely careful evaluation is contained in Robert E. Lipsey's important book [11].

12. In average of 1955–60 prices. See [4] [22].

13. "*Die These von der abnehmenden Bedeutung der internationalen Handelsbeziehungen*" or "*der fallenden Exportquote*," Werner Sombart in [20, pp. 368–71].

14. See [16] for a good, brief discussion and references to the recent literature.

15. Lipsey [11, p. 44] found that as far as the United States is concerned "over the whole period [1879–1960] the only suggestion of a downward trend in the ratio of the quantity of trade to output was the low interwar export and postwar import ratios. Both now appear to have been temporary." Lipsey reached his results by using constant dollar rather than current value trade figures. The difference between current and deflated dollar value ratios of trade and output stems from the fact that both export and import prices have fallen in the long run compared with domestic prices. Hence a different deflator has to be used for the two items of the ratio. If "invisible" exports and imports could be added to merchandise trade, the statistical support for the theory of the declining trade-GNP ratio would be further weakened.

16. The most extreme position has been taken by Gunnar Myrdal in [14].

17. William McC. Martin, Jr., Chairman of the Board of Governors of the Federal Reserve System, has acknowledged the role of the balance of payments. "I am convinced that our failure to solve the problem [of the balance of payments] up to now has not only been damaging to our international relations but has also impeded the achievement of even high levels of output and resource utilization" (statement before the House Committee on Banking and Currency, July 22, 1963, *Fed. Reserve Bull.*, Aug. 1963, p. 1062).

Since the slack is small, it cannot be far off the mark to say that the external deficit has been the major cause of the slowdown.

18. I do not wish to say, of course, that in the absence of a balance-of-payments deficit there will never again be a recession or a period of slack. For example, if at a higher level of employment wage-push became stronger and prices started to creep up again, the monetary and financial brakes would sooner or later be applied as they were in the late 1950's with the same general result. But demand inflation, wage-push, Phillips curves, income policy, and all that are not the subject of this talk.

19. See [15]. Myrdal's policy conclusions are, of course, not the same as the Marxists'.

20. See [22, p. 1]. Developed countries are North America, Western Europe, Australia, Japan, New Zealand, and South Africa. Developing countries are the rest of the world, excluding the "centrally planned economies" (Communist countries) in Europe and Asia.

21. Measured from the peak in 1951 caused by the Korean War boom and massive U.S. stockpiling, the deterioration in the terms of trade would be substantially greater—14 or 16 per cent. The fact that the deterioration reflects a rise in import prices rather than a fall in export prices is significant because unit values of manufactured goods have a notorious upward bias, due to the fact that the gradual improvements in quality and the continuous appearance of new manufactured products are not, or very insufficiently, taken into account. In other words, a rise in import prices (of manufactured goods) is much less "real" than a fall of export prices (of primary products) would be.

22. Alfred Marshall has alluded to that; Richard Schueller in [18] has commented on this fact. See also D. H. Robertson [16]. It should be observed, however, that freer trade between the industrial countries, although it may be less valuable than trade between industrial and tropical countries on comparative cost grounds, can be beneficial through stimulating competition and counteracting monopolistic tendencies. This effect of free trade has been stressed by J. S. Mill and reiterated by modern theorists of integration, e.g., by Tibor Scitovsky and Harry Johnson.

23. In underdeveloped countries the theory has been widely accepted that in less developed countries import restrictions do not reduce the volume of imports or exports; they merely cause a shift of imports from, say, luxury goods to capital goods. In the developed industrial countries, it is said, the classical rule still applies that import restrictions reduce the volume of trade in both directions. This is the official doctrine of the U.N. Economic Commission for Latin America (ECLA). See, e.g., [23, esp. p. 61]. The reason usually given is that these countries spend all their export proceeds anyway. This, of course, overlooks that protection draws factors of production into the protected industries from the export sector. Only under extreme and entirely unrealistic assumptions concerning the existence of large masses of disguised unemployment (including that of skilled workers), of surplus capacity, and very elastic capital supply could the conclusion be overthrown that export supply will contract as a consequence of massive import substitution brought about by heavy protection.

24. Kindleberger's figures are not quite comparable with the U.N. figures because his area breakdown is a different one. The figure quoted in the text refers to industrial Europe's terms of trade with "all other areas," i.e., the world excluding the rest of Europe, the United States, and the "countries of recent settlement." With the last-mentioned area the index of industrial Europe's terms of trade stood at 138 in 1938 (1928 = 100).

25. Some may question the relevance of a comparison with national income. In my opinion, it is relevant with certain qualifications: A large and sudden change in the terms of trade might cause serious transitional difficulties. Or, if a country by extreme protectionism has reduced its imports to a bare minimum and has neglected its export industries, a decline in the terms of trade may necessitate a further reduction of imports which have already been stripped to essentials. In that case the impact on GNP would be out of proportion to the money cost of the deterioration quoted in the text because the "marginal benefit" of imports would be much higher than the marginal benefit of domestic production. If my income falls by 5 per cent and I were forced to skimp on food rather than spread the shortfall over the whole range of expenditures, the result would be disastrous. But I doubt whether any country really finds itself in such a predicament, although extreme protectionism could conceivably put it there.

26. Charles Kindleberger has pointed out to me that a veritable revolution has taken place in ocean transportation. Thus, while the world wholesale price index in dollars has about doubled since before the war, oil tanker rates are just about where they were, and dry cargo rates have gone up on a very rough average by 50 per cent. This great cheapening of transport cost constitutes a powerful integrating force in the world economy and has bestowed great benefits, especially on many less developed countries, by improving their f.o.b. terms of trade.

The drastic reduction in transport cost, made possible by technological advances, applies primarily to the very competitive international routes. Many countries rob themselves of those very large benefits by highly protectionist shipping policies. This is especially true of coastal shipping, including sometimes shipping between neighboring countries. For example, freight rates between Rio de Janeiro and Buenos Aires are often as high as between Buenos Aires and New York, because of nationalistic policies. See [8, p. 297].

The jet aircraft promises to produce another revolutionary advance in transport technology..

27. W. Arthur Lewis has reached similar conclusions in two important papers [9] [10]. Speaking of Latin America, he said: "Puzzling are those cries which seem to be founded on the belief that it is particularly difficult to expand exports because the world is buying fewer and fewer exports. The opposite is true. World trade has never grown faster. Between 1950 and 1960 the quantum of world trade in primary products increased at an average rate of 6 per cent per annum, and the quantum of world trade in manufacturers by more than 7 per cent per annum. The terms of trade for primary products could not retain the heights to which they were raised by the speculative fever of the Korean War and the heavy American stockpiling in the early fifties; nevertheless the average terms of trade for the decade of the 1950's were better than for any previous decade in all the preceding hundred years. I do not know whether it is in fact true that in the 1950's, Latin America had difficulty in keeping her exports growing at the same rate as national income but if this was so, it cannot possibly have been due to failure of world demand to grow adequately, since the quantum of world trade was growing by about 7 per cent per annum throughout the 1950's. Taking the continent as a whole, rather than individual countries, failure on this score can only have been a failure of effort" [10, pp. 10–11].

28. Another acute danger, which cannot be discussed here, is regimentation, contraction, and distortion of trade through the numerous international price-support schemes of important commodities now under active consideration.

29. I would agree that a floating rate system, too, requires price and wage discipline for successful operation. But I would argue that the fixed rate system calls for much sterner discipline.

30. This does not necessarily mean that it is undesirable. There are valid arguments for protection which theoretically can be applied to customs unions or free trade areas. In the case of LAFTA, the protectionist effects are, however, so strong that it would be very difficult to make a rational case for it on, say, infant-industry grounds. It could conceivably be defended with the help of a theory of the third or fourth best. Let me briefly indicate what I have in mind. By means of a policy of partly repressed inflation, tight exchange control, etc. a country can maneuver itself into a position where trade is so sharply contracted and distorted that even bilateral trade is better than no trade. Similarly, a regional trade expansion may be better than no expansion at all, although a relaxation of controls and general expansion of trade would be infinitely better.

References

1. Milton Friedman and Anna Schwartz, *Monetary History of the United States.* New York, 1963.

2. Gottfried Haberler, "International Trade and Economic Development," National Bank of Egypt, *Fiftieth Anniversary Commemoration Lectures.* Cairo, 1956. [Chapter 21 in this volume.]

3. Folke Hilgerdt, *Industrialization and Foreign Trade.* League of Nations, 1945.

4. International Monetary Fund, *Annual Report*, 1963.

5. ———, *International Financial Statistics*, recent issues.

6. C. P. Kindleberger, *Foreign Trade and the National Income.* New Haven, 1962.

7. ———, *The Terms of Trade.* New York, 1956.

8. Guillermo W. Klein, "Die Lateinamerikanische Integration und die Weltwirtschaft," in A. Hunold, ed., *Lateinamerika: Land der Sorge und der Zunkunft.* Zurich, 1962.

9. W. Arthur Lewis, "Economic Development and World Trade," submitted to the International Congress on Economic Development organized by The International Economic Association. Vienna, 1962. (Mimeo.)

10. ———, "Closing Remarks," Conference on *Inflation and Economic Development.* Rio de Janeiro, January 1963. (Mimeo.)

11. R. E. Lipsey, *Price and Quantity Trends in the Foreign Trade of the United States.* Nat. Bur. of Econ. Research. Princeton, 1963.

12. Alfred Marshall, *Official Papers.* London, 1926.

13. Gerald M. Meier, "International Trade and International Inequality," *Oxford Econ. Papers*, Oct. 1958, N.S. 10, 277–89.

14. Gunnar Myrdal, *Challenge to Affluence.* New York, 1963.

15. ———, "Development and Underdevelopment," National Bank of Egypt, *Fiftieth Anniversary Commemoration Lectures.* Cairo, 1956. Revised version, *Economic Theory and Underdeveloped Regions.* London, 1957.

16. D. H. Robertson, "The Future of International Trade," *Econ. Jour.,* March 1938, 48, 1–14.

17. Paul Samuelson, *Stability and Growth in the American Economy. Wicksell Lectures 1962.* Stockholm, 1963.

18. Richard Schueller, *Schutzzoll und Freihandel.* 1905.

19. Joseph Schumpeter, "Historical Approach to the Analysis of Business Cycles," in *Conference on Business Cycles,* Universities-National Bureau Committee for Economic Research. New York, 1951.

20. W. Sombart, *Die deutsche Volkswirtschaft im 19. Jahrhundert,* 3, Auflage. Volksausgabe, Berlin, 1913.

21. Paul Sweezy, "Marxism: A Talk to Students," *Monthly Rev.,* Oct. 1936.

22. United Nations, *World Economic Survey 1962.* Part I: *The Developing Countries in World Trade.* New York, 1963.

23. ———, *International Co-operation in a Latin American Development Policy.* New York, 1954.

24. Jacob Viner, "Recent Legislation and the Banking Situation," *Am. Econ. Rev.,* March 1936, Supplement, 26, 106–19.

25. W. S. and E. S. Woytinsky, *World Commerce and World Government.* New York, 1955.

21

International Trade and
Economic Development

First Lecture

I regard it as a signal honor that you have invited me to give three lectures in this series which has been made famous among economists all over the world by the contributions of earlier speakers—such as F. A. v. Hayek, Per Jacobsson, Arthur Lewis, G. Myrdal, Ragnar Nurkse, to mention only a few. I am all too conscious of the fact that my illustrious forerunners in this series as well as the high position of the institution, the National Bank of Egypt, and its officers, under whose auspices these lectures are being given, have put me under a very heavy obligation. However hard I try, I am afraid, I shall not be able fully to discharge this heavy debt.

1

As a topic for my lectures I have chosen *Economic Development and International Trade.* I shall discuss the contribution, positive or negative, favorable or unfavorable, which foreign trade can make to the economic development of underdeveloped countries. I shall make a special effort to bring the tools of economic theory, i.e., the theory of international trade, to bear upon the problem on hand and shall also draw some policy conclusions from my analysis.

What I have to say will, to some extent, be critical and polemical. But since widespread misconceptions have greatly and in my opinion perniciously influenced policy, I regard criticism of these views as a highly constructive task.

For the purposes of our discussion I shall conform to the general usage and define development as the growth of per capita real income. A factor or institution or policy—international trade or a change of trade or trade policy, free trade or

National Bank of Egypt, Fiftieth Anniversary Commemoration Lectures, Cairo, 1959. Reprinted in *Expansion of World Trade and the Growth of National Economics*, Richard S. Werkstein, ed. (New York: Harper Torchbooks, 1968), 97–136. Reprinted with permission of the author.

protection—are said to be conducive to economic development, if it can be shown that they speed up the rate of growth of per capita real income as compared with the rate that would obtain in the absence of the factor or policy or institution in question.

I should like to say, however, in passing that the level of per capital real income is not always a sufficient criterion to decide whether a country should be said to belong to the "developed" or "underdeveloped" part of the world. In fact it is not easy at all to give a precise and acceptable definition. If we were satisfied with a mere enumeration of the developed and underdeveloped countries, there would be little disagreement. The economically underdeveloped part of the world consists of the Western Hemisphere south of the Rio Grande, Central and South America (with one or two exceptions), most of Asia and Africa, excepting Japan, the Union of South Africa, and one or two other countries. But when it comes to framing a formal definition and to giving precise criteria of development and underdevelopment, we run into difficulties and controversies.

Let me pursue the matter a little further, although it would be, in my opinion, a mistake to worry much about the lack of a precise definition. The following statement by one of the great mathematicians and philosophers of our time may comfort you, as it did me. Hermann Weyl, in his celebrated book *Philosophy of Mathematics and Natural Science*,[1] speaking of the natural sciences, in the context in question especially of the biological sciences, says that it often happens in scientific pursuits that "the typical may be elusive in terms of well-defined concepts and yet we handle it with intuitive certitude, e.g., in recognizing persons." Surely, what is good enough for the natural sciences should also satisfy the social scientist.

Per capita real national income as criterion for the comparative *level* of development of different countries is often grossly misleading because of the difficulties and ambiguities of international income comparisons; it would be easy to cite examples of naive, misleading or even fraudulent comparisons of national income figures for different countries. But even waiving statistical difficulties of measurement and assuming that we have developed meaningful and comparable measures of real per capita income of different countries, the level of economic development of a country in a basic sense cannot always be accurately gauged by its results in terms of output. Suppose Country A is highly developed in the sense that its population is highly educated, well trained, reliable, efficient in the use of modern means and methods of production—this is what I call real, genuine development—and suppose, furthermore, that Country B is not highly developed in that sense, but is better endowed than A with natural resources, mineral deposits, good soil and climate and so on per head of its its population; then it is quite possible that the less developed country will enjoy a higher per capita income than the more developed country.

It is true that a well trained, hard working and frugal people can make up to an astonishing degree for lack of natural resources as the example of Switzerland shows. Nonetheless, it would be a mistake to expect a perfect correlation between the real level of development and output per head. It would be an even greater mistake to identify the level of development with the degree of industrialization, especially in the sense of having a large percentage of the working force employed in the manufacturing ("secondary") industries. Urbanization and having a large percentage of the working population employed in "tertiary" industries, i.e., in service industries such as education, entertainment, research, scientific and artistic pursuits, is probably a much better indicator of economic development than industrialization proper.[2]

It is true there may not yet exist an underdeveloped country that is highly industrialized. But some underdeveloped countries seem to be on the way to that status, and the results are not happy. Argentina, e.g., has managed to hurt its thriving agriculture badly and has steadily been going down, financially and economically, during the regime of Colonel Peron. On the other hand, there may be no developed country in existence at the present time that is not industrialized in the sense that a large percentage of the labor force or population (the two measures are not quite the same because of the larger families one finds often in the country) is in industry, mining and especially services. But some countries were highly developed before they ceased to be predominantly agricultural. New Zealand, Denmark and Australia are examples and there is nothing backward and underdeveloped about Nebraska and Iowa, American states that are predominantly agricultural. It is an extremely important fact that there exists no highly developed country that has not also a highly developed agriculture in the sense of a high degree of literacy, efficient application of modern methods of production, high input of machinery, fertilizer, etc. and high value of output per head.[3] Moreover, and this too is a very important fact, many highly industrialized countries (in the sense that a large percentage of the labor force is engaged in non-agricultural pursuits), have remained large net exporters of food and agricultural raw materials. The U.S., Canada, Australia, and Denmark are conspicuous examples.

These facts have important policy implications which are often ignored. The fact that in developed countries not only industry, but also agriculture, is more highly developed than in underdeveloped countries lends further weight to the warning that development policies should not concentrate exclusively on industry. And the fact that highly industrialized countries can remain efficient producers and cheap exporters of food and agricultural raw materials should help to dispel the fear that it would be dangerous for industrial countries to fill a large share of their food and agricultural raw material requirements from foreign sources (possibly from underdeveloped countries) and to give up a correspondingly large part of their own high cost agriculture, on the ground that if they did that, later when industrialization has proceeded farther in many parts of the world, they may not be able to buy food and agricultural raw materials except at exorbitant prices.[4] Such fears were widespread among German economists around the turn of the century when Germany was making rapid strides towards industrialization. But one finds them also occasionally today. They are, e.g., implicit in certain versions of the Marxian theory (espoused also by non-Marxist writers such as G. Myrdal) that the underdeveloped countries of today are handicapped as compared with the now developed countries in the corresponding stage of their development because the underdeveloped countries today, when they push their development (identified by those writers with industrialization) are not surrounded by an underdeveloped world, as the now developed countries were in the early stages of their development—an underdeveloped world which provided industrializing countries with cheap supplies of raw material and food and a market for their industrial products. If my strictures draw the reply that it was the colonial status of the *then* underdeveloped countries which gave the now developed countries their comparative advantage over the underdeveloped countries *now*, my answer would be this: I am not going to discuss to what extent colonial rule has exploited the colonies and retarded their development. To some extent and in some cases it has undoubtedly done that. Not being an expert in that area, I shall not try to make any generalization. And fortunately I need not form a judgment on that matter because for the problem in hand another question is crucial, namely, the question to what extent the development of the colonial powers themselves was speeded by their possession of colonies. With respect to this question, I feel much more confident. My answer is that the possession of colonies was not a decisive or even very important factor in the development of the colonial powers. If it had been, it would be difficult to explain why colonial powers have done quite well after having lost their colonies (e.g., the Netherlands) and why other countries such as Germany,[5] Sweden, Switzerland, not to mention the USA, which never possessed colonies (or whose colonies were economically unimportant) developed just as well, or better, than others that had colonies.

But let me return to my main topic—the contribution of international trade to economic development. In this context growth of real income or output per head can be used with greater confidence as criterion, than in connection with the question as to which countries should be regarded as developed or underdeveloped, for in this case no intra-country comparisons are involved.[6]

2

I shall now positively and systematically state what I think the contribution of international trade to economic development was in the past and what it can be in the future. My overall conclusion is that international trade has made a tremendous contribution to the development of less developed countries in the nineteenth and twentieth centuries and can be expected to make an equally big contribution in the future, if it is allowed to proceed freely. It does not necessarily follow that a 100% free trade policy is always most conducive to most rapid development. Marginal interferences with the free flow of trade, if properly selected, may speed up development. But I do not want to leave any doubt that my conclusion is that substantially free trade with marginal, insubstantial corrections and deviations, is the best policy from the point of view of economic development. Drastic deviations from free trade can be justified, on development grounds—and this is very nearly the same thing as to say on economic grounds—only if and when they are needed to compensate for the adverse influence of other policies inimical to economic development, for example, the consequences of persistent inflation or of certain tax and domestic price support policies. Let me guard against a possible misunderstanding. If I say that drastic interferences with the market mechanism are not needed for rapid development, I refer to trade policy and I do not deny that drastic measures in other areas, let me say, land reform, education, forced investment (if the projects are well chosen) etc. may speed up growth. But I shall in these lectures not further elaborate on those matters.[7]

I shall make use of the so-called classical theory of international trade in its neoclassical form associated with the names of Jacob Viner, James Meade, and Bertil Ohlin, to mention only a few. I shall not try to modernize the theory more than, say, Ohlin and Meade have done, although I shall make an attempt to spell out in some detail the implications of classical trade theory for economic development, an aspect which has perhaps been somewhat neglected. On the other hand, I shall, of course, avoid using the caricature of the theory which is often presented as a portrait by its critics.

Later I shall then take up in detail objections to the orthodox conclusions and shall consider alternative or rival theories put forward by the critics of the orthodox theory.

Let us then start with first things first. International division of labor and international trade, which enable every country to specialize and to export those things that it can produce cheaper in exchange for what others can provide at a lower cost, have been and still are one of the basic factors promoting economic well-being and increasing national income of every participating country. Moreover, what is good for the national income and the standard of living is, at least potentially, also good for economic development; for the greater the volume of output the greater can be the rate of growth—provided the people individually or collectively have the urge to save and to invest and economically to develop. The higher the level of output, the easier it is to escape the "vicious circle of poverty" and to "take off into selfsustained growth" to use the jargon of modern development theory. Hence, if trade raises the level of income, it also promotes economic development.

All this holds for highly developed countries as well as for less developed ones. Let us not forget that countries in the former category, too, develop and grow, some of them—not all—even faster than some—not all—in the second category.

In most underdeveloped countries international trade plays quantitatively an especially important role, that is, a larger percentage of their income is spent on imports, and a larger percentage of their output is being exported, than in the case of developed countries of comparable economic size. (Other things being equal, it is natural that the "larger", economically speaking, a country, the smaller its trade percentages.) Many underdeveloped countries are highly specialized also in the sense that a very large percentage of their exports consists of one or two staple commodities. I am sure that here in Egypt, which depends on cotton for more than 60% of its exports, I need not cite further examples for that.

This high concentration of exports is not without danger. One would normally not want to put so many of one's eggs into one basket. But the price of diversification is in most cases extremely high. I shall touch on that topic once more. At this point, let me simply say that a high level of concentrated trade will, in most cases, be much better than a low level of diversified trade. How much poorer would Brazil be without coffee, Venezuela, Iran and Iraq without oil, Bolivia without tin, Malaya without rubber and tin, Ghana without cocoa, and, I dare say, Egypt without cotton. The really great danger of concentration arises in case of deep and protracted slumps in the industrial countries—slumps of the order of magnitude of the Great Depression in the 1930's. In my opinion, and here I am sure the overwhelming majority of economists in the Western World agrees, the chance that this will happen again is practically nil.

The tremendous importance of trade for the underdeveloped countries (as well as for most developed ones, with the exception of the US and USSR, which could, if need be, give it up without suffering a catastrophic reduction in their living standard) follows from the classical theory of comparative cost in conjunction with the fact the comparative differences in cost of production of industrial products and food and raw materials between developed countries and underdeveloped countries are obviously very great, in many cases, in fact, infinite in the sense that countries of either group just could not produce what they buy from the other.[8]

The classical theory has been often criticized on the ground that it is static, that it presents only a timeless "cross-section" view of comparative costs and fails to take into account dynamic elements that is, the facts of organic growth and development. Of modern writers, it was especially Professor J. H. Williams of Harvard and recently Gunnar Myrdal[9] who have voiced this criticism of the classical doctrine and have demanded its replacement by a dynamic theory. This type of criticism is, in fact, about as old as the classical theory itself. Williams mentions many earlier critics and especially the German writer Friedrich List who more than anyone else in the nineteenth century has attacked the classical theory on exactly the same grounds, that is, for being "unhistorical and static,"[10] with the same vehemence and the same strange tone of bitterness and irritation as the modern writers.

Now it is true that the theory of comparative cost is static; it is also true that the economies of most countries are changing and developing and that the theory should take account of that fact. But it is not true that a static theory, because it is static, is debarred from saying anything useful about a changing and developing economic world. There is such a thing as "comparative statics," that is, a method for dealing with a changing situation by means of a static theory. How much can be done by means of comparative statics (as distinguished from a truly dynamic theory) depends on the type of problem on hand. I contend that the problems of international division of labor and long-run development are such that the method of comparative statics can go a long way towards a satisfactory solution.[11] That does not mean, however, that a dynamic theory would not be very useful. Unfortunately, not much of a truly dynamic theory is available at present. What the critics of the static nature of traditional theory have given us over and above their criticism and methodological pronouncements is very little indeed and thoroughly unsatisfactory. But a well known Burmese economist, H. Myint, has recently reminded us that the classical economists, especially Adam Smith and J. S. Mill, were by no means oblivious of the indirect, dynamic benefits which less developed countries in particular can derive from international trade. Going beyond the purely static theory of comparative cost, they have analyzed the "indirect effects" of trade (as J. S. Mill calls them) and thereby presented us with at least the rudiments of a dynamic theory, which Myint aptly calls the "productivity" theory of international trade.[12] Let us then enquire how we can deal by means of the theoretical tools on hand with the problems of change and development. The tools on hand are the static theory of comparative cost and the semi-dynamic "productivity" theory.

For our purposes I will distinguish among the changes which constitute economic development two types—those that take place independently of international trade and those that are induced by trade or trade policy.

As far as the first group—let me call them autonomous changes—is concerned, I can see no difficulty resulting from them for the applicability of the classical theory of comparative cost. Such changes are the gradual improvement in skill, education and training of workers, farmers, engineers, entrepreneurs; improvements resulting from inventions and discoveries and from the accumulation of capital—changes which in the Western World stem for the most part from the initiative of individuals and private associations, but possibly also from conscious Government policies.[13]

These changes come gradually or in waves and result in gradually increasing output of commodities that had been produced before or in the setting up of the production of goods that had not been produced earlier. Analytically, such development has to be pictured as an outward movement of the production possibility curve (often called substitution or transformation curve). Depending on the concrete turn that autonomous development (including improvements in transportation technology) takes, the comparative cost situation and hence volume and composition of trade will be more or less profoundly affected. But since these changes only come slowly and gradually and usually cannot be foreseen (either by private business or Government planners) in sufficient detail to make anticipatory action possible, there is no presumption that the allocative mechanism as described in the theory of comparative cost will not automatically and efficiently bring about the changes and adjustment in the volume and structure of trade called for by autonomous development.

I turn now to the second type of changes in the productive capabilities of a country which are more important for the purposes of my lectures, namely, those induced by trade and changes in trade including changes in trade brought about by trade policy. Favorable as well as unfavorable trade-induced changes are possible and have to be considered. Alleged unfavorable trade-induced changes have received so much attention from protectionist writers from List to Myrdal (which has induced free trade economists, too, to discuss them at great length), that there is danger that the tremendously important favorable influences be unduly neglected. Let me, therefore, discuss the latter first.

If we were to estimate the contribution of international trade to economic development, especially of the underdeveloped countries, solely by the static gains from trade in any given year on the usual assumption of given[14] production capabilities (analytically under the assumption of given production functions or given or autonomously shifting production possibility curves) we would indeed grossly underrate the importance of trade. For over and above the direct static gains dwelt upon by the traditional theory of comparative cost, trade bestows very important indirect benefits, which also can be described as dynamic benefits, upon the participating countries. Let me emphasize once more that the older classical writers did stress these "indirect benefits" (Mill's own words).[15] Analytically we have to describe these "indirect", "dynamic" benefits from trade as an outward shift (in the northeast direction) of the production possibility curve brought about by a trade-induced movement along the curve.

First, trade provides material means (capital goods, machinery and raw and semifinished materials) indispensable for economic development. Secondly, even more important, trade is the means and vehicle for the dissemination of technological knowledge, the transmission of ideas, for the importation of know-how, skills, managerial talents and entrepreneurship. Thirdly, trade is also the vehicle for the international movement of capital especially from the developed to the underdeveloped countries. Fourthly, free international trade is the best antimonopoly policy and the best guarantee for the maintenance of a healthy degree of free competition.

Let me now make a few explanatory remarks on each of these four points before I try to show how they fit into, and complement, the static theory of comparative advantage.

The first point is so obvious that it does not require much elaboration. Let us recall and remember, however, the tremendous benefits which the underdeveloped countries draw from technological progress in the developed countries through the importation of machinery, transport equipment, vehicles, power generation equipment, road building machinery, medicines, chemicals, and so on. The advantage is, of course, not all on one side. I stress the advantage derived by underdeveloped countries (rather than the equally important benefits for the developed countries), because I am concerned in these lectures primarily with the development of the less developed countries.

The composition of the export trade of the developed industrial countries has been changing, as we all know, in the direction of the types of capital goods which I have mentioned away from textiles and other light consumer goods. This shift has been going on for a long time; it is not a recent phenomenon. But it has proceeded rapidly in recent years, and there is no reason to doubt that it will continue.

Secondly, probably even more important than the importation of material goods is the importation of technical know-how, skills, managerial talents, entrepreneurship. This is, of course, especially important for the underdeveloped countries. But the developed countries too benefit greatly from cross-fertilization aided by trade among themselves and the less advanced industrial countries can profit from the superior technical and managerial know-how, etc. of the more advanced ones.

The late-comers and successors in the process of development and industrialization have always had the great advantage that they could learn from the experiences, from the successes as well as from the failures and mistakes of the pioneers and forerunners. In the nineteenth century the continental European countries and the U.S. profited greatly from the technological innovation and achievements of the industrial revolution in Great Britain. Later the Japanese proved to be very adept learners and Soviet Russia has shown herself capable of speeding up her own development by "borrowing" (interest free) immense amounts of technological know-how from the West, developing it further and adapting it for her own purposes. This "trade" has been entirely onesided. I know of not a single industrial idea or invention which the West has obtained from the East.[16] Today the underdeveloped countries have a tremendous, constantly growing, store of technological know-how to draw from. True, simple adoption of methods developed for the conditions of the developed countries is often not possible. But adaptation is surely much easier than first creation.

Trade is the most important vehicle for the transmission of technological know-how. True, it is not the only one. In fact this function of trade is probably somewhat less important now than it was a hundred years ago, because ideas, skills, know-how, travel easier and quicker and cheaper today than in the nineteenth century. The market where engineering and management experts can be hired is much better organized than formerly. There is much more competition in this field as well as in the area of material capital equipment. In the early nineteenth century Great Britain was the only center from which industrial equipment and know-how could be obtained, and there were all sorts of restrictions on the exportation of both. Today there are a dozen industrial centers in Europe, the US, Canada, and Japan, and even Russia and Czechoslovakia all ready to sell machinery as well as engineering advice and know-how.

However, trade is still the most important transmission belt. What J. S. Mill said 100 years ago is still substantially true: "It is hardly possible to overrate the value in the present low state of human improvement, of placing human beings in contact with persons dissimilar to themselves, and with modes of thought and action unlike those with which they are familiar.... Such communication has always been, peculiarly in the present age, one of the primary souces of progress."[17]

The third indirect benefit of trade which I mentioned was that it also serves as transmission belt for capital. It is true that the amount of capital that an underdeveloped country can obtain from abroad depends in the first place on the ability and willingness of developed countries to lend, which is of course decisively influenced by the internal policies in the borrowing countries. But it stands to reason—and this is the only point I wanted to make at this juncture—that, other things being equal, the larger the volume of trade, the greater will be the volume of foreign capital that can be expected to become available under realistic assumptions. The reason is that with a large volume of trade the transfer of interest and repayments on principle is more easily effected than with a small volume of trade; and it would be clearly unrealistic to expect large capital movements if the chance for transfer of interests and repayments is not good. There is, furthermore, the related fact that it is much easier to get foreign capital for export industries with their built-in solution of the retransfer problem than for other types of investments which do not directly and automatically improve the balance of payments. This preference of foreign capital for export industries is regrettable because other types of investment (such as investment in public utilities, railroads, manufacturing industries) may often (not always) be more productive and may make a greater indirect contribution, dollar per dollar, to economic development by providing training to native personnel and in various other ways than export industries which sometimes (by no means always) constitute foreign enclaves in native soil. If the direct and indirect contribution of non-export industries to national income and economic development are in fact greater than those of the export industry, they should be preferred, because their indirect contribution to the balance of payments position will then also be such as to guarantee the possibility of smooth retransfer of principle and interest—*provided* inflationary monetary policies do not upset equilibrium entailing exchange control that then gets in the way of the transfer. But with inflationary monetary policies and exchange control practices as they are in most underdeveloped countries, the preference of foreign capital for export industries is readily understandable and must be reckoned with and foreign capital in export is better than no foreign capital at all.

The fourth way in which trade benefits a country indirectly is by fostering healthy competition and keeping in check inefficient monopolies. The reason why the American economy is more competitive—and more efficient—than most others is probably to be sought more in the great internal free trade area which the US enjoys rather than in the antimonopoly policy which was always much more popular in the US than in Europe or anywhere else. The importance of this factor is confirmed by the fact that many experts believe that the main economic advantages of the European Common Market, towards the realization of which the first steps have just been taken, will flow from freer competition rather than merely from the larger size and larger scale production which it entails.

Increased competition is important also for underdeveloped countries, especially inasmuch as the size of their market is usually small (even if the geographic area is large). A reservation has nevertheless to be made. The first introduction of new industries on infant industry grounds may justify the creation of monopolistic positions, depending on the size of the country and the type of industry. But the problem will always remain how to prevent the permanent establishment of inefficient exploitative monopolies even after an industry has taken root and has become able to hold its ground without the crutches of imports restriction.

The general conclusion, then, is that international trade, in addition to the static gains resulting from the division of labor with given (or autonomously changing) production functions, powerfully contributes, in the four ways indicated, to the development of the productive capabilities of the less developed countries. Analytically we have to express that, in the framework of modern trade theory, by saying that trade gradually transforms existing production functions; in other words, that a movement along the production possibility curves in accordance with the pre-existing comparative cost situation, will tend to push up and out the production possibility curve.

I have stated my conclusions rather boldly and uncompromisingly. Some qualifications and reservations are obviously called for, because trade may have also unfavourable indirect (or direct) effects. But I shall discuss these exceptions and qualifications after I have discussed and considered opposing views.

Second Lecture

In my first lecture I presented the case for a maximum of international trade in the interest of economic development. I started with the static theory of comparative cost but pointed out that the classical economists especially Adam Smith and John Stuart Mill were not oblivious of indirect dynamic influences of international trade. International trade not only increases national income within given production functions, thereby enabling a country to save and invest more, but trade also increases productive capabilities, analytically speaking, pushes out production functions and production possibility curves. I distinguished four different ways in which trade operates to bring that about. (1) It enables a country to import capital goods of all description which are needed for economic development. (2) Trade serves as transmission belt for the dissemination of ideas, technological know-how, skills, managerial and entrepreneurial services. (3) Trade is the vehicle for international capital movements. (4) Free trade is the most effective anti-monopoly policy; in other words, trade makes for healthy competition.

My conclusion was that free trade is extremely desirable from the point of view of economic development especially of the underdeveloped countries.

3

I am aware that my conclusions are not shared by everybody. In fact, influential experts, both academic and official, as well as certain branches of the United Nations, have been contending almost the exact opposite of what I have been trying to say. I shall now consider these opposing views and while by and large, after careful weighing of evidence and arguments, I shall stick to my conclusions, certain not negligible qualifications and reservations will have to be made.

While I have sung the praise of international trade as a factor spurring the rate of economic development, especially in the less developed countries, I must voice a warning against certain exaggerations. There are certain things trade cannot do. No amount of trade can be expected to bring about a complete or even a nearly complete equalization of real wages or more generally of real per capita income as between different countries and areas. It is not even certain that trade will in all cases result in a lessening of the existing degree of international inequality (assuming that an unambiguous measure of degrees of inequality as between different countries can be agreed upon).

Contrary to what is sometimes said, even by experts,[18] classical or neo-classical theory does not teach that free trade will result in international equalization of real income. What the theory does teach is that everybody will be better off with trade than without trade and that every country will be best served by free trade. Needless to add that the latter conclusion, the free trade conclusion, is subject to important exceptions and qualifications. There hardly exists a single free trade economist who does not recognize certain exceptions to the rule that free trade is the best commercial policy and it is widely accepted that in less developed countries the exceptions are more numerous and important than in the advanced industrial countries.

It is true that in recent years a highly abstract discussion has been carried on in the learned journals in the course of which some participants thought they were able to prove that under certain assumptions free commodity trade would be a perfect substitute for free international migration of labor and free movement of factors of production in general and would thus lead to complete equalization of factor prices as between the trading countries. But the assumptions necessary for that happy result proved to be much more restrictive and unrealistic than was at first thought. So that theoretical flurry really wound up with the opposite conclusion of the one that was at first announced: it has shown that an equalization of factor prices is in reality almost inconceivable. I shall not go into that highly esoteric disputation. It can be credited with having clarified certain theoretical puzzles, but "the factor price equalization theorem" should not be pronounced as one of the conclusions of classical trade theory. To repeat—what classical theory really teaches is that trade will benefit every country, rich and poor, but not that mere trade will necessarily remove or even reduce international inequality.

It is true that in my first lecture I have advanced reasons to the effect that underdeveloped countries are likely to derive special advantages from trade. If we lived in a static world it would follow that trade has an equalizing tendency (although not necessarily that it would lead to a *complete* equalization of incomes). In the dynamic, developing world of ours, which is subject to many other influences than those connected with international trade, there is no guarantee, even with a lot of unrestricted trade, that historically international inequalities will become smaller. In such a world it does not even follow from what has been said about the special importance of trade for the less developed countries, that international inequality will be less with trade (or with much trade) than without trade (or with little trade).

Let me mention two reasons why international inequality *may* increase (I do not say, of course, *must* increase) despite the special advantages of trade to the poorer countries. First, population pressure is stronger in many less developed countries than in most advanced countries and may even become stronger if trade leads initially to higher living standard, better health, to improved sanitation and lower mortality. It is then possible that the relatively greater advantages from trade accruing to the less developed countries may be insufficient to completely outweigh this handicap.

Secondly, the developed countries do not stand still, they too develop, and some of them even grow faster than some underdeveloped countries. Thus the greater advantage of trade for the latter countries may not completely offset for some of them the head start (not only with respect to the *level* but also with respect to the *rate of growth* of income) of some of the former.[19]

4

The exact opposite of the classical theory that all participating countries profit from international trade is the neo-Marxian theory to the effect that trade, capitalistic, unregulated trade of course, far from benefitting the poor countries, actually operates in such a way as to make the poor countries in the world poorer and the rich richer; according to this theory, a version of which has been adopted (or independently invented) by non-Marxist writers, the poor as a rule get poorer because the rich get richer.

I said *neo*-Marxist—advisedly—because Marx himself, although as you know not an ardent supporter of the capitalist system, gave the devil its due, which cannot be said of all his followers. He had a very high opinion indeed of the power of capitalism to raise productivity. In truly dithyrambic language he described in the famous *Communist Manifesto* how capitalism industrializes backward countries and increases their productive capacities.[20] Needless to add that Marx did not teach that capitalism increased the productivity of backward countries for the purpose of raising the welfare of the masses of their population. And, like the English writers of the classical school whose disciple he was, Marx was not in favor of colonialism. But an appreciation of the power of international trade and international capital movements, especially of the indirect, dynamic aspects which I discussed earlier, is implicit in Marx's position. The exploitative aspects of the theory, the theory that is to say that the gains from trade are so unequally distributed as to make trade operate to the detriment of the poorer countries, the less developed countries, the primary producing or "peripheral" countries (all these terms are now used more or less synonymously)—this part of the theory has been carried over by neo-Marxists and some non-Marxists into the post-colonial period.

You will remember that Marx taught that under capitalism in each country the working class, the proletariat, was getting poorer all the time. This "theory of increasing misery" ("Verelendungstheorie") has more or less grudgingly and reluctantly (more often silently rather than explicitly) been given up, even by orthodox Marxists; for it simply makes no sense to say that American or European workers are getting poorer all the time. But the theory of increasing misery survives in the international sphere; here it has even been adopted, or independently invented, by non-Marxist writers.[21] I shall examine, however, only the non-Marxist version of the theory that "trade operates (as a rule) with a fundamental bias in favor of the richer and progressive regions (and countries) and in disfavor of other regions" (i.e., underdeveloped regions and countries)[22] that "by itself freer trade would even tend to perpetuate stagnation in the underdeveloped regions" (and countries).[23]

The theory rests on several pillars which have been widely accepted as very strong several years ago, but have been badly shaken in recent years by critical examination and by new empirical evidence that has been turned up by later experience and research. Let me briefly discuss the following three pillars of the modern theory of the pernicious effect of international trade on less developed countries.

The first is the alleged tendency of unregulated trade to turn the terms of trade in the long run against the primary producers and to impart to them an excessive cyclical instability. Secondly, there is the assertion that trade creates or at least perpetuates, or at any rate is unable to eradicate, and takes advantage of, disguised unemployment. Thirdly, there are alleged "backetting" (i.e., unfavorable) effects that are said to emanate from the developing industrial countries and impinge upon the underdeveloped countries. These effects are largely taken from alleged interregional developments; they are blown up beyond recognition and uncritically transferred to the international scene.

The theory of the secular tendency of the terms of trade to deteriorate for primary producers, i.e., for prices of primary, especially agricultural, products to fall relatively to the prices of finished goods is a big topic and raises many intricate questions. I can nevertheless be brief, because recent researches, both theoretical and statistical[24] have made it abundantly clear that the theory under review is based on grossly insufficient empirical evidence, that it has misinterpreted the facts on which it is based, that the attempted explanation of the alleged facts is fallacious and that there is no presumption at all that the alleged unfavorable tendency of the terms of trade will continue in the future.

The theory under review is generally known as the Singer-Prebisch thesis.[25] Its empirical basis is the fact that the ratio of British import prices to British export prices fell from 163 for 1876–80 to 100 in 1938. For the following reason, however, the improvement of the British terms of trade does not support the conclusion that the terms of trade of all exporters of primary products have suffered a corresponding deterioration.

First, as Kindleberger has shown, the British terms of trade cannot be taken as indicative of the terms of trade of all other industrial countries. Kindleberger's extensive calculations reveal large divergences between the movement of the British terms of trade and those of other industrial countries. Secondly, the British terms of trade cannot without question be taken as the reciprocal of the terms of trade of the raw material exporting countries with which Britain was trading because British import prices are taken c.i.f. and British export prices f.o.b. In other words, imports are valued including transport costs to British ports of entry and export prices excluding transport costs from British ports of exit to the foreign destination. In order to evaluate the true terms of trade of the exporters of primary products both export and import prices must be measured at the ports of entry of those countries. As Viner, Baldwin and others have pointed out, in periods in which freight rates change, such a shift of the geographical base makes a great difference for the terms of trade. Professor Ellsworth, who has investigated that problem, statistically concludes, e.g., that "a large proportion, and perhaps all, of the decline in the British prices of primary products in the period between 1876 and 1905 can be attributed to the great decline in inward freight rates.... Since the prices of British manufactured exports fell in this period by 15 per cent, the terms of trade of primary countries, were f.o.b. prices used for their exports as well as for their imports, may well have moved in their favor." (loc. cit., p. 55–57.) Mr. Carl Major Wright of the U.N. in a remarkable paper[26] cites numerous examples when in a period of falling import prices in Great Britain the prices of the same goods rose in the distant ports of lading, the difference having been absorbed by falling freight rates. This was often true even of cyclical price drops. I might add that during the recent recession price declines in raw materials have been greatly softened as far as the exporters are concerned by the sharp drop in freight rates.

Thirdly, over long periods all terms of trade figures have a strong bias, because they cannot make proper allowance for changes in quality of old products and for the appearance on the market of hosts of new commodities. Since it is primarily industrial products which improve in quality while primary products remain qualitatively more or less the same and since literally hundreds of new products are added over the years to the list of finished industrial goods, this bias operates in such a way as to make the movement in the terms of trade of the primary exporters (finished goods importers) appear much less favorable than it actually was. To present but one example, let me mention that Professor Kindleberger, who computes an index of machinery prices, is forced to define the price of machines in dollars per physical weight! Hence when a machine becomes lighter and more efficient—a typical form of development—and the dollar price per machine remains unchanged, the index will indicate a price rise instead of a price fall as it should.

It follows from these considerations that it is very doubtful whether actually, over the stated period, the alleged deterioration in the terms of trade has taken place.[27] Moreover, suppose for argument's sake, the commodity terms of trade of primary producers, or of a certain group of such countries, has really deteriorated. The implications for the welfare of the country or countries concerned depend on the causes that are at the root of the change. If export prices have fallen because the cost of production has been reduced, the "deterioration" in the terms of trade has no sinister implications. For example, in the late nineteenth century when the United

States, Canada and Argentina gradually came into the European market with their agricultural products, the basic reason for the relative price fall of primary products was that the costs of production of the newly opened areas (including the cost of transport on land and across the ocean) had been sharply reduced (or were much lower in the first place than the cost of the European competitors). Hence one cannot say that the price fall hurt the overseas suppliers although it did injure European agriculture. Economists express that by saying that what matters from the welfare standpoint is not the commodity terms of trade, but the single-factoral terms of trade. The criticized theory simply takes no notice of all this.

In the attempted explanation of the alleged facts, the theory is just as careless as in the ascertainment of what really happened. Two reasons are usually given for the alleged change in the terms of trade against primary producers: (a) monopolistic manipulations in the industrial countries and (b) the operation of "Engel's law."

(a) Employers and labor unions in industry in the industrial countries are said to conspire to keep prices up in the face of declining real cost. Thus they fail to pass on to the consumers in the form of lower prices, the fruits of technological progress, but keep them for themselves by raising wages and profits.

It is, of course, true that monetary policy in the industrial countries has been most of the time (especially in the recent period) such as to let money wages (and money incomes in general) go up with stable or even rising prices instead of keeping money wages (incomes) constant and letting prices fall. Union policies have surely contributed to that result. But there is not the slightest indication that this policy has led to a shift in *relative* prices of primary products and finished goods. The criticized theory thus rests on a confusion of the absolute price level and relative prices. In passing, it might be pointed out that if the advanced countries followed the policy of keeping money wages constant and letting prices fall (a policy which is often recommended by conservative economists in the industrial countries) it would be definitely injurious to the less developed countries on two grounds: First, the real burden of debt would rise and second, the difference in the degree of inflationary pressure as between the two groups of countries would become even greater than it actually is—thus adding to the balance of payments woes of the less developed countries.

As far as monopolistic pricing of finished goods, either consumer or capital goods, is concerned, there is very little of it, surely less in international trade than within some of the industrial countries, and much less than there was 50 or 100 years ago. The reason for that I have mentioned before: There are now many industrial centers competing with one another in the world market. The rise of the U.S. as an industrial power has greatly contributed to making world markets more competitive because the U.S. economy has always been more competitive and U.S. industry less secretive than their European counterparts.

(b) Engel's law states that the percentage of consumer income spent on food is a decreasing function of income. When income rises people spend smaller fractions of their income on food. Inasmuch as services ("tertiary industries") become more and more important as people get richer, one can probably also say that the percentage of national income spent on raw materials (including those from mining) tends to fall.

But from this bare fact it does by no means follow that prices of primary products must fall as compared with prices of finished goods. The reason is that there are numerous counteracting and conflicting forces and tendencies at work, for example, technological changes, industrialization in the developed as well as in the underdeveloped countries, population growth and the law of diminishing returns in primary production.

It is very interesting to observe that there exists a school of thought, which teaches that the terms of trade must inexorably turn *against* the *industrial* countries because of the operation of the law of diminishing returns in agriculture and extractive industries. This theory, which has had a remarkable hold on British economic thinking, goes back to Ricardo. A. Marshall greatly worried about the terms of trade and Keynes at one time (1912) got alarmed by a deterioration of the British terms of trade.[28] In our time Professor Austin Robinson ("The Changing Structure of the British Economy," *Economic Journal,* Sept. 1954) has again taken up this theme.

This pessimistic theory—pessimistic from the point of view of the industrial countries—is the exact opposite of the Singer-Prebisch-Myrdal thesis. One of the strange things in this strange economic world of ours is that no one in either group seems to be aware of the fact that those in the other group say exactly the opposite and hence no one takes issue with the arguments of the opponents.

If you ask me which of the two schools is right, my answer is that both are wrong. It might be objected that this is impossible—the terms of trade cannot go in opposite directions at the same time. This, of course, is true. But let us not forget that the terms of trade may not change at all or may for some time go one way and then move in the opposite direction. That is what they seem actually to have done.[29]

At any rate, it is rash to make forecasts on the basis of such flimsy foundations and it is irresponsible to recommend policies on the strength of such uncertain extrapolations. These irresponsibilities are committed by each of the two opposing schools. One recommends protection for agriculture in the advanced countries because the terms of trade will turn against the industrial countries. The other group recommends protection of industry in the less developed countries because the terms of trade will move the other way. So protectionists everywhere unite, unknowingly, on the basis of contradictory forecasts, to bring about the same result—a reduction in the volume of trade to the disadvantage of both groups of countries.

The complaint about the short run instability, especially cyclical variability of the terms of trade of raw material producers, has more substance than their alleged secular tendency to deteriorate. But the cyclical fluctuations are by no means so regular, big and pervasive as they have been pictured. Different types of raw materials and foodstuffs have different cyclical patterns and different amplitudes. The cyclical swings are greatest in the case of metals and are greater in raw materials than in food. Even in the short run substantial relief is often afforded by a drop in freight rates during depressions.

The really serious adverse changes in the terms of trade of primary producers happen in severe depressions. But such catastrophies hit the advanced countries probably just as hard as the less developed countries, although in the form of unemployment rather than in the form of lower prices. It would be idle, however, to speculate who has fared worse on these occasions. For, let me emphasize once more, deep depressions are a thing of the past. I don't want to exaggerate. Mild recessions like the three recessions through which the American economy has passed during the post-war period will certainly recur. However deep, prolonged depressions are definitely out. There can be no doubt that the problem of creeping inflation is much more acute than that of serious depressions. I personally do not take the dangers of creeping inflation as lightly as many of my fellow economists do in the West, precisely because creeping inflation can easily lead to mild recessions and to a lower level of employment on the average over the cycle than otherwise would be the case. But severe depressions are not being tolerated any more—not even in the most capitalist countries. The problems posed by mild recessions for the exports of the less developed countries can be solved with the help of existing machinery—*ad hoc* credit arrangements through I.M.F. and other international and national institutions and possibly some commodity stabilization schemes. The remaining instability surely is not nearly large enough to put a serious handicap on the development in the raw material exporting countries or to call in question the immense advantages for them of unhampered international trade.

Third Lecture

In my second lecture I pointed out that, opposing the classical theory according to which free trade is beneficial to all, rich and poor, because there is a basic harmony of interests, there exists a Neo Marxian theory espoused (or independently invented) also by non-Marxist writers which postulates a basic disharmony between rich and poor, developed and underdeveloped countries. Free trade, according to this view, is inimical to the poor and an instrument of exploitation (even apart from colonialism) by the rich. The non-Marxist version of that theory rests on several pillars. The first one, the theory that the terms of trade have a tendency in the long-run to move against the primary producers I have criticized the last time. It is I think the weakest of the three.

The other two pillars I shall criticize in the current lecture and then state reservations to my own free trade position which I have promised.

5

The second pillar of the theory under consideration—the assertion that there are available in underdeveloped countries, mainly in agriculture, large masses of unused but more or less easily usable labor, "disguised unemployment"—has not fared much better than the theory of the long-run deterioration of the terms of trade. Under the criticism of economic experts in underdeveloped as well as in developed countries, this pillar has all but collapsed. Among the early critics of the theory of disguised unemployment were men like Dr. N. Köstner, Eugenio Gudin, Professor Jacob Viner, Professor Theodore Schultz.[30] It is now admitted even by former enthusiasts that "the early easy optimism about transferring the disguised unemployed from agriculture to industry has disappeared. It is recognized that in many underdeveloped countries *static* disguised unemployment in agriculture is at a very low level.... Substantial numbers could not be released from agriculture without a drop in agricultural production, unless the average size of holdings is increased and some degree of mechanization introduced." This statement by Professor Benjamin Higgins[31] is typical of the disillusionment that has taken place.

Professor Schultz, one of the world's foremost agricultural experts who has had wide experience in underdeveloped countries in different parts of the world, has declared flatly that he knows of no evidence for any poor country anywhere that would suggest that a transfer of even a small fraction, say, 5 per cent, of the labor force from agriculture to industry could be made, with other things equal, without reducing output.[32] Later he added that development "programs based on disguised unemployment have not performed as expected: instead of labor resources responding to an increase in the money supply or to new industries in the way that one would have expected if there were considerable underemployment, workers act as if the marginal productivities of laborers in agriculture and in other fields are about the same."[33]

The term "unemployment" in connection with underdeveloped, poor countries was most unfortunate indeed because it suggested that the situation is approximately the same as depression unemployment in developed countries which can be easily cured (at least up to a certain irreducible minimum) by strengthening effective demand.[34] What the proponents of the concept should have said is that in underdeveloped countries productivity of labor is very low, which is about the same as saying that those countries are desperately poor and backward; this, of course, nobody would have denied. They might have added that productivity is lower in some branches of the economy than in others. But it is surely not true to regard agriculture as the only sector of the economy where marginal productivity of labor is especially low. Dr. Köstner has pointed out to me the fact that productivity is also low (occasionally even zero or negative) in certain non-agricultural urban pursuits, as a short stroll through the streets of any city in a poor country—and in some not so poor countries—will convince even a casual observer.

Far be it from me to deny or minimize these deplorable conditions or to suggest that nothing can or should be done to improve them. But the description of the situation as disguised unemployment suggests that there is unlimited, if not efficient, then at least usable, manpower available to start new industries without reducing output anywhere else. This simply is not so. Such oversimplifications encourage easy solutions which must come to grief and result in disappointment and in waste of scarce resources, which poor countries can ill afford.

Let me cite one erroneous policy conclusion which has been drawn from the facile, but entirely unrealistic, assumption that there are large masses of unused resources free for the asking and ready to be put to work. This erroneous conclusion occurs again and again in ECLA publications and abounds in Myrdal's writings, and its pernicious influence on policy of many underdeveloped countries must have been strong.

It is said that in underdeveloped countries the restriction of imports by high tariffs, quotas and other measures will not lead to a reduction of the volume of trade, but only to a shift in the composition of imports—from consumer goods (possibly of luxury type) to capital goods. This is in contrast to the developed countries where the classical rule still holds that a restriction of imports leads to a fall in exports and an all round reduction in the volume of trade.

The argument which is often put forward in support of this theory to the effect that poor countries spend all their foreign exchange earnings anyway, and that any dollars they do not spend on those things that are kept out by import restrictions will be spent on something else, is obviously fallacious. It overlooks the fact that the amount of foreign exchange available will be less if resources are drawn into the protected industries away from the export industries. This could be different only if it were true that the protected industries can be staffed wholly or at least to a large extent by workers drawn from the pool of unused resources, i.e, of disguised unemployed rather than by drawing away resources from other industries, including the export industries. This pool of unused resources unfortunately does not exist. The underdeveloped countries are not exempt from the general law of scarcity— they least of all, unfortunately. The theory of disguised unemployment is simply four-dimensional, *deus ex machina* economics—better described as wishful thinking.

Let me emphasize once more that my discounting the idea of disguised unemployment and reducing it to the less exciting and less paradoxical if not trivial and humdrum notion of low, though not uniformly low, productivity in underdeveloped countries, is not meant to add up to a counsel of despair. I do not want to say that nothing can or should be done to raise output and productivity. You will not expect me in three lectures on international trade to give an outline of development policies. There would not be time, and I am not competent for that job. I must confine myself to a few remarks.

I am convinced that the main job has to be done inside each country and that protectionist trade policies can make only a marginal contribution. What needs to be done is to raise gradually the quality of labor by better education, health measures, and the like; to increase mobility, improve the "infra structure" by investment in public utilities of all description. Probably as much can be done by *removing* social and policy impediments to growth, mobility, private initiative and enterprise as by positive measures involving large investments.

6

The third pillar of the theory that free trade always, or at least normally, hinders rather than helps the development of underdeveloped countries, is the assertion that the very fact that the rich countries themselves develop and grow and increase their output and income has as a rule "backsetting", i.e., unfavourable effects rather than favourable ones on the poorer countries.

This is indeed a novel view, which flies in the face of classical trade theory. Let me first discuss how the old-fashioned classical economist would argue on this matter. If the industrial countries develop, that is to say, if output and incomes rise, their import demand for raw material, food, tourist services and goods in general will rise. This, the old-fashioned economist would say, is a clear gain for the less developed countries which sell all those things. (With this conclusion the modern and ultra-modern Keynesian economist would heartily agree—for one of his tenets is that the propensity to import is positive, barring the most unlikely case that the majority of imports consist of inferior goods.) The old-fashioned economist will then go on to say that as incomes rise in the developed countries their rate of saving will increase and that there is a good chance that some of the additional capital will become available for investment in less developed countries. This conclusion again will be heartily approved by Keynesians, especially by those who believe in secular stagnation (admittedly a little outmoded now) due to chronic oversaving and lack of investment opportunities in rich countries. Broadly speaking, the conclusion that with increasing wealth in the rich countries more capital becomes available for the poor countries would seem to be borne out by past developments. But it is of course not true that investment opportunities have become less and less in the advanced countries and it is possible that development in the industrial countries may temporarily take such a turn as to absorb a larger proportion of the savings that become available and leave less for export.

By developing and increasing their output, the old industrial countries often deplete their exhaustible resources which gives other countries a chance to export. Britain has practically exhausted her mineral deposits and had to rely more and more on imports from abroad. The U.S., better supplied than the Old World, has been forced to import iron ore from Canada and Venezuela, oil from Venezuela, copper, lead and zinc from Chile, Peru and Africa. Despite occasional setbacks, produced by temporary depressions, protectionist policies and occasionally by discoveries of new mineral deposits or new processes, this development has been proceeding and will undoubtedly continue.

The old-fashioned economist would, of course, readily admit that technological progress in the industrial countries (or for that matter in underdeveloped countries) often is such as to injure particular underdeveloped countries (or particular developed countries). The introduction of synthetic nitrate reduced demand for Chilean natural nitrate, the invention of rayon and nylon was a heavy blow for Japanese silk and to a lesser extent for cotton. The invention of synthetic coffee would be a terrible blow for Brazil and the other coffee countries. But in the meantime Indian textile exports have hurt Lancashire, and Japan's industrial development has stepped on dozens of toes in the older industrial centers.

Admitting all that, or rather stressing it in the first place, the old-fashioned economist, taking a broader view over the last hundred or hundred and fifty years, would nevertheless conclude that the expansion and development of the now comparatively rich countries has been a great boon for the less developed countries, leaving aside the unanswerable question who has gained most. (He would, of course, deny the frequently heard contention that the underdeveloped countries have made no progress at all, being at the same time fully aware of the fact that in some of them a rapid increase in population has swallowed up a larger or smaller part of the rise in aggregate output.) Where would the underdevelopment countries be, and what would their chances of further development be, if they had not at their disposal all the technological and medical improvements, not to mention the purely scientific and the "cultural" advances made in the advanced countries? Where would Brazil sell its coffee, Malaya its tin and rubber, Iraq, Venezuela, etc. their oil—if the developed countries had not sufficiently developed to have effective demand for these things? Where would India sell her textiles and how could other semi-industrialized countries hope to export certain finished goods or export materials more and more in refined rather than raw form, if the highly developed countries did not rapidly develop and pass on from the production and export of the more simple kinds of goods to the production and export of more refined and complicated products, from

cotton goods to rayon and nylon, from textiles to machinery, vehicles, pharmaceuticals, and instruments, from simple models to more and more highly fabricated
commodities requiring more and more skill, scientific know-how and so on? The old-
fashioned economist might go on and ask, as Professor Albert Hirschman has done
in his highly challenging and original book *The Strategy of Economic Development*,[35]
how could there be any progress at all, for anybody, unless some countries (and
individuals) forged ahead of others? Or should we assume that if the advanced
countries (or individuals) had not developed as they did, the others would have done
it all by themselves? Maybe they would, but how many centuries would have been
lost?

These considerations seem to me to establish an overwhelming presumption that
the further development of the rise of developed industrial country will benefit the
poorer underdeveloped countries. But let us now consider, against this background,
the so-called "backsetting" or "backwashing" effects which the development in the
advanced countries is supposed to have on the less advanced, underdeveloped
countries.

First it should be recorded that Myrdal does not altogether neglect the favorable
effects—the "spread effects" as he calls them. But he pictures them as uncertain and
unimportant compared with the "backwash", the unfavourable effects. He makes a
molehill out of a mountain and views the problem of how development spreads from
the growing points to the surrounding area from an exceedingly narrow and overly
static and myopic point of view.

What are, then, the "backsetting", unfavorable effects? It is very difficult to come
to grips and find out precisely what these effects are. There is much talk of
"interlocking and cumulative causation", of "vicious spirals", and the like. "Suppose
that in a community an accidental change" causes "a large part of the population" to
lose their jobs. Then the tax rate will go up, "the community will be less tempting for
outside business ... the process gathers momentum ... " and a "vicious circle" of
contraction is set up.[36]

This kind of reasoning is well known from business cycle theory, but the
cumulation of an adverse shock into a vicious spiral is essentially a short-
run phenomenon and does not upset equilibrium analysis although the new equilibrium, after a disturbance, is usually approached gradually and not established
immediately.[37]

Much is also made of the familiar fact (well known to the classical writers as
indeed to anyone who has a modicum of historical perspective) that for fairly
obvious reasons, the first steps towards economic progress from low levels of
development are especially hard.[38]

This may explain why some regions or countries increase for some time their lead
over others once they have gotten over the threshold at which growth becomes

faster, but it does not explain why that should make it harder for others to do the same, provided the objective (social or physical) conditions there are not less favorable. The few concrete examples of backsetting effects which I have been able to discover are the following[39]: The developing region may attract key personnel from the stagnant region. In other words, a selective migration may start from the poor to the rich country—young, skilled and enterprising people leaving the stagnant area. This cannot be altogether excluded *a priori*, but it is more likely to happen inside a country than between countries. The case of Italy where the North is progressive and the South backward is the standard example. East and West Germany at present is another example—but the political causes are obvious in that case: West Germany enjoys the blessing of a progressive free enterprise system and of liberal democracy, while the economy of the East labors in the stifling atmosphere of an inefficient collectivist system imposed on the country by a dictatorship which is hated and despised by the overwhelming majority of the people. It is at any rate clear that this movement of skilled labor plays at present no important role in the international relationship between the developed and underdeveloped parts of the world wherever we draw—arbitrarily—the line between the two.[40]

The progressive part of a country may also draw capital away from the stagnant part. This again is more likely to happen interregionally than internationally and cannot be an important factor in the relation between the developed and underdeveloped parts of the world.[41] True, there have occasionally occurred capital movements out of underdeveloped countries towards industrial countries (e.g., from Latin America to the U.S. or Europe), but these are instances of capital fleeing from inflation or political dangers as is clearly indicated by the fact that these movements go upstream, as it were, from areas of high to areas of low interest rates. These more or less pathological aberrations do not alter the fact that the *net* capital flows have been on the whole in the right direction, i.e., from the rich to the poor countries.

There remains the vague notion that the developing centers aided by increasing returns due to external economies, will have a "competitive advantage" over the relatively stagnant "peripheral" areas extending over the whole range of industry, leaving to them only primary production where no external economies can be expected.[42]

But these are very extreme assumptions. There exists probably not a single case which fully corresponds to that pattern. The comparative advantage of the developing industrial countries will hardly extend over the *whole* range of industry. Development does not consist exclusively in the reduction of cost of production of existing industries and old products, but largely in the introduction of new commodities and new industries. This is then certain to create gaps in the chain of comparative cost which gives an advantage in certain industrial products to the backward countries. Moreover, external economies often attach to the export sector of the economy even if the exports consist of agricultural products. For example, in the U.S. and Canada the export of agricultural products helped to stimulate the construction of railroads and the opening up of the western part of the North American continent—external economies of gigantic dimensions. Hence less developed countries may benefit from external economies by concentrating on the production of those things where they have a comparative advantage.

I conclude that the argument under consideration can at best justify a certain amount of infant industry protection, but can never invalidate the strong presumption that the rapid growth and development of the rich countries will benefit the poor.

7

But I do not wish to spoil my argument by exaggerations. I have promised to make some qualifications and reservations of my free trade position, and I am now ready to do so.

My concessions concern the old-fashioned (one could almost say the "classical") "infant industry argument" for protection. It cannot be denied, I believe, that sometimes well chosen methods of moderate protection of particular industries can help to speed up economic development. This implies that free trade can to some extent retard the development of a country, not compared, of course, with a situation of *no* trade, but compared with a situation in which a certain moderate amount of protection is given to suitably selected industries. There is no presumption at all that the *development* and *growth* of the industrial countries will hurt the less developed countries. My argument that on the contrary, as a rule, the growth of the developed countries will spread to, and benefit, the less developed countries fully stands—although some peculiar constellation is always imaginable in which a particular less developed country (or, of course, developed country) may be hurt by the development of a developed (or underdeveloped) country. But this would be in the nature of a fluke and does not invalidate the general presumption of harmony of interests.

Let me now try to state as briefly and as concisely as possible the case for infant industry protection.

It is possible that the development of a particular manufacturing industry, or of manufacturing industries as a whole, will produce "external economies", that is to say, slow pervasive improvements benefiting many or all firms, which eventually will make those industries able to stand up to foreign competition without protection. But since these economies are slow in coming, difficult to foresee, and often of such a nature that private enterprise cannot well appropriate them, private initiative may not be enough to ensure their realization. Let me give what seems to me the most important example: The development of industry in less developed countries is often made difficult or held back by the lack of even moderately well trained, moderately reliable and skilled labor. It is the mistake of the theory of disguised unemployment to overlook or at any rate divert attention from, this important fact. But untrained, unskilled, unreliable labor can be trained and improved. This improvement is a slow and very costly process. It will usually require force and compulsion, which only the government can wield, to bring it about as quickly as it is desired. But even if its cost, in view of inherent uncertainty, is not such as to put it beyond the power of private business, the private enterprise cannot be sure that the workers, once they have been trained and once the productivity has increased, will not demand the fruits of these improvements for themselves in the form of higher wages. Hence private enterprise cannot always be relied upon to carry out this process, i.e., to produce for a while at a loss in the hope that after labor has become more efficient the enterprise will be able to stand up against foreign competition and recoup the initial losses—or expressed differently, get the rewards for the initial "investment"—investment in skill, training, enterprise.

Now in such a case the government can step in and make the necessary "investment". This can be done either directly in the form of educational and training programs or government-operated enterprise, or indirectly: One form of such indirect investment is to grant protection to the industry concerned thus assuring it a market and making it worthwhile to employ workers, even though they are inefficient and costly compared with better paid but more efficient foreign workers. One should not overlook the fact that this policy, even if eventually successful, throws a temporary burden upon the country in the form of higher prices of things that could be obtained cheaper by international trade. But it is the essence of any kind of investment that it causes a temporary hardship. The country foregoes present consumption and welfare in the hope of getting it back in the future. I think it is very important to recognise the operation for what it is—investment of capital, possibly a very profitable investment but involving a temporary burden. The mistake of the theory of disguised unemployment is precisely this that it pictures as a free gift of nature what in reality is an act of investment of capital, implying hardship in the form of postponed consumption.

Now capital is scarce and has therefore to be economized. For that reason it is so tremendously important that only worthwhile projects are undertaken. Applied to our case of investment in training, skill, education, by means of import restrictions, it means that a country should protect only those industries which really hold out hope that after a while they will be able to stand on their own feet.

Investment is always a gamble. There is always the danger of misjudging the chances intailing to the loss of all or part of the capital invested. In our case the danger is even greater than usual because the cost is concealed. Private investors, if they do not succeed, are automatically punished. If the private producer does not produce what people want, he will suffer losses. In the case of infant industry protection, the losses of failure are borne by the economy at large in the form of higher prices of commodities that could be provided more cheaply via international trade than by home production. Few people realize what is really going on and hardly anyone is able to figure out the real cost of the operation. Once a new industry has been established behind a high tariff wall it will be very difficult to get rid of the tariff, even if that were possible without endangering the whole industry or a large part of it. There will always be some marginal firms that would really get into trouble, and the other intra-marginal firms will not want to lose the extra profits which protection secures.

It would be nice if it were possible to lay down simple clearcut criteria which would permit the selection of the industries which are worth protecting and in addition would determine the height of the tariff needed to do the job. I suspect, however, that it will always be necessary to rely on judgment, taking into account the whole structure of the economy and all the measures of internal development policies which are being undertaken at the same time.

I cannot at the end of my lectures even begin to develop systematically my ideas on this matter. Let me simply state in greatest brevity, and hence somewhat dogmatically, my general position.

My preference would be for general measures. I mistrust detailed structural blueprints. These things never work, not even in developed countries where the statistical basis for input-output and similar planning devices is much better than in underdeveloped countries. A uniform import tariff on manufactured goods, or on broad categories of such goods, is probably the best method of infant industry protection. This system leaves the selection of the commodities actually produced to the forces of the market. Especially in countries which are well endowed with entrepreneurial talents this method would be much superior to governmental designation or actual operation of the industries to be developed.

As to the height of the uniform tariff, I would not want to be dogmatic. Let me mention, however, that List himself was of the opinion that an industry that does not grow to maturity with a longlasting protection of 20–30 per cent would not be worth protecting. In other words, it would have to be assumed that the country lacks basic comparative advantage in such an industry.

I am fully aware of the fact that practically all underdeveloped countries (and developed countries for that matter) pursue policies which are almost the exact opposite of those sketched above. They have highly differentiated tariffs and most of them have in addition severe exchange control which is equivalent to high supplementary tariffs, the structure and incidents of which are completely shrouded in administrative secrecy as far as outsiders are concerned, and I strongly suspect are known only in the dimmest outline to those insiders who are in charge of development policies.

It is my contention that this type of policy hurts the underdeveloped countries. In other words, that they could speed up their development by changing over to the system I have sketched. Let me emphasize once more that this advice does not add up to a counsel of extreme *laissez-faire*. It rather means that development policies should be such as to work through and with the help of the powerful forces of the price mechanism instead of opposing and counteracting the market forces. This holds for measures in the area of international trade as well as in the domestic field. I should like to repeat my conviction that the latter—action in the field of education, health, public overhead investment—are more important than the negative policy of import restriction. The latter is, of course, much easier than the former. For that reason, it is likely to be overdone, while the former is apt to be neglected.

Notes

1. English edition. Princeton, New Jersey, U.S.A., 1949, p. 286.

2. Needless to add that the growth of "tertiary" industries is a sign or symptom of development only when it comes "naturally". One cannot turn the argument around and assume that if the Government puts a large part of the people into tertiary occupations, say entertainment or even dentistry, by artificial means, it will automatically raise the level of economic development correspondingly.

3. Physical output may be lower than in some less developed countries owing to comparatively poor soil and climate. Value output may still be high, if import restrictions keep the price of agricultural products high.

4. Fear of blockade in case of war or fear of being at the mercy of unfriendly powers is, however, not so easy to dispel.

5. Germany did have some colonies before the first World War. But I don't think that any economist would argue that they were economically speaking of any consequence.

6. Needless to add that statistical problems of measurement remain. What I am speaking of is theoretical criteria.

7. It also goes without saying that in countries where the Government runs the economy—in the communist countries—is has also to conduct foreign trade. But socialist state trading, if it is efficient and rational and motivated by economic objectives, would be along the lines of comparative cost. I might add that socialist theoreticians fully agree to that, although many do deny that trade in capitalist countries is, in fact, conducted along these lines.

8. In many cases very expensive and poor substitutes can be produced. There is not much sense in contemplating extreme situations. But if I were pressed to guess, I would say that the developed countries as a group, and a few of them individually, could get along without trade a little easier (although still at a terrific loss) than the underdeveloped countries.

9. Williams: "The Theory of International Trade Reconsidered", *Economic Journal*, 1929. Myrdal: *Development and Underdevelopment*, National Bank of Egypt, 1956.

10. It is strange that Myrdal, who quotes copiously from earlier and contemporary writers (see especially the full dress presentation of his views in *The International Economy*, New York, 1956) fails to mention List, to whose theory his own bears a most striking similarity, notwithstanding the fact that List's policy recommendations are more moderate than Myrdal's.

11. The short run business cycle, on the other hand, is a type of problem of which a static explanation is rather useless. That is the reason why the *static* Keynesian system is so barren. In the short run, dynamic factors completely overshadow and distort the static Keynesian relationships—especially the liquidity preference and the investment function. Needless to add there are plenty of so-called "Keynesian type" dynamic models. But logically they have very little to do with the static Keynesian theory and nothing at all with the chapter on the "Trade Cycle" in *The General Theory*. This type of model building has been launched independently of Keynes by Frisch, Tinbergen and Lundberg. But nobody would deny that many others, who later became active in that field, thought they were merely dynamizing Keynes.

12. H. Myint. "The 'Classical Theory' of International Trade and the Underdeveloped Countries," *Economic Journal*, June 1958, pp. 317–337. A. Smith, *Wealth of Nations*, Vol. 1, Cannan ed., p. 413. J. S. Mill, *Principles*, Ashley ed., p. 581. Myint distinguishes from the dynamic "productivity" theory, the "vent-of-surplus" theory and distinguishes the latter also from the static comparative cost theory. This distinction I find unconvincing. The "vent-of-surplus" (if it is not part and parcel of the productivity theory) seems to me simply an extreme case of differences in comparative cost—a country exporting things for which it has no use. This case does not call, it seems to me, for a special theory. But Myint is, of course, quite right that if this extreme situation exists (in modern parlance it might be described as disguised unemployment in export industries) it makes trade appear doubly productive and desirable.

13. I am not speaking here of policies concerning international trade such as the imposition of import restrictions. Changes resulting from trade policy measures are trade induced and not autonomous changes.

14. This includes autonomously shifting.

15. In the neo-classical theory they have been somewhat neglected. The reason is perhaps that these factors do not lend themselves well to precise mathematical treatment.

16. This statement is made on the authority of Prof. John Jewkes of Oxford who has made a close study of sixty major industrial innovations (in the Schumpeterian sense) and comes to the following conclusion: "The cases taken as a whole reveal that no country has a monopoly of inventive power. The outstanding names and groups are widely spread over many industrial countries. One significant exception is that in none of sixty cases studied had contributions been made by Russian workers subsequent to the Revolution. Before that date numerous names of distinguished Russian contributors crop up." J. Jewkes. "The Sources of Invention," *Lloyd's Bank Review*, Jan. 1958, p. 23. The book that contains the material on which the quoted article is based was published under the same title by Macmillan, London, 1958. Note that what I say is that no industrial innovations have come from Russia to the West. That does not mean there are not any. Obviously, in the field of military technology they are

doing quite well and it would be surprising if they had not made any innovations elsewhere. But they are probably minor compared with Western achievements and at any rate none has come out.

17. *Principles of Political Economy.*

18. G. Myrdal in his Cairo lectures and elsewhere criticizes classical theory for teaching that free trade will equalize living standards internationally, while according to him, the opposite is the case. Myrdal's own views will be critically examined in the text.

19. With respect to the chances of the less developed countries to catch up with the advanced countries the old classical writers were too optimistic, because of their belief that, owing to the inexorable law of diminishing returns, there was an upper limit in the level of economic development which no country could ever pierce. Few economists would deny nowadays that the progress of science and technology may well stave off the dismal consequences of the law of diminishing returns indefinitely or at least for a long time to come.

20. *Manifesto of the Communist Party,* by Karl Marx and Friedrich Engels. Authorized English Translation, International Publishers, New York, 1932. See especially pages 11–14.

21. As a typical example of a staunch Marxist, let me quote an American, Paul Sweezy. In a paper "Marxism: A Talk to Students," (*Monthly Review,* New York, Oct. 1958) he admits that Marx was wrong in believing that workers in the advanced countries would get poorer all the time. Workers there have "a tolerable even if degraded (!) life." But the advanced countries "increasingly (!) impose the burdens on the peoples of the colonies and the raw material producing countries" (p. 221).

22. Myrdal, Cairo Lectures, p. 29.

23. Myrdal, *An International Economy,* p. 2.

24. The most important studies are C. P. Kindleberger's monumental book. *The Terms of Trade: A European Case Study,* New York, 1956: P. T. Ellsworth's, "The Terms of Trade between Primary Producing and Industrial Countries, "*Inter American Economic Affairs,* Summer 1956: T. Morgan's "The Long-Run Terms of Trade between Agriculture and Manufacturing," *Econometrica,* April 1957, p. 360. I myself have tried to sum up the case in a paper "The Terms of Trade and Economic Development," Round Table of International Economic Association, Rio de Janeiro, August 1957. This paper will be published in the proceedings of that conference by Macmillan, London. [Chapter 19 in this volume.] A German translation has appeared in the *Zeitschrift für Nationalökonomie,* Vienna, Austria, 1958. Another briefer summary of the discussions will be found in the excellent paper by G. M. Meier, "International Trade and International Inequality," in *Oxford Economic Papers,* October 1958.

25. See especially U.N. Economic Commission for Latin America, *The Development of Latin America and its Principle Problems,* New York, 1950. The original statistical basis is contained in the U.N. report *Relative Prices of Exports and Improts of Underdeveloped Countries, New York,* 1949. Myrdal makes reservations concerning the findings of these reports, but he accepts the Singer-Prebisch thesis nonetheless. See *The International Economy* p. 231–2.

26. "Convertibility and Triangular Trade," *Economic Journal,* Sept. 1955.

27. Care must also be taken when making long run comparison to place base year and given year at the same cycle phase.

28. W. Stanley Jevons in his gloomy book *The Coal Question. An Enquiry Concerning the Progress of the Nation, and the Probable Exhaustion of the Coal Mines.* (1st ed., London, 1865; 3rd ed. revised, edited by A. W. Flux, London, 1906) took up the theme. (See chapter XIII of the 3rd edition.) I have already mentioned that these British views were strongly echoed in Germany around the turn of the century.

29. Since what matters for welfare purposes is the single factoral terms of trade, it is well to remember that, unlike the commodity terms of trade (or the double factoral terms of trade) the single factoral terms are not a symmetrical concept. That is to say, the single factoral terms of trade may improve (or deteriorate) for two trading countries (or groups of countries) at the same time. Suppose, for example, the commodity terms of trade have remained unchanged, but each of two trading countries has been able to reduce the cost of its export products. Then each gets more commodities per unit of productive resources exported. This is what usually happens in a developing world.

30. See Dr. Köstner's "Comments on Professor Nurkse's Capital Accumulation in Underdeveloped Countries " (*L'Egypte Contemporaine*, No. 272, 1952) and his "Marginal Comments on the Problem of Underdeveloped Countries." (*Wirtschaftsdienst*, Hamburg, May 1954). Viner, "Some Reflections on the concept of Disguised Unemployment, in *Contribucoes a Analise do Desenvolvimento Econômico*. Essays in honor of Eugenio Gudin, Rio de Janeiro, 1957. T. W. Schultz, "The Role of Government in Promoting Economic Growth," in L. D. White, ed., *The State of the Social Sciences*, Chicago, 1956, and *The Economic Test in Latin America*, New York State School of Industrial and Labor Relations, Cornell University, Bulletin 35, 1956. Professor E. Gudin has told the writers many times that what underdeveloped countries are suffering from is not disguised unemployment, but low levels of productivity not only of manual labor, but managerial labor, engineering labor and so on. This, I believe, hits the nail on the head.

31. "Prospects for an International Economy," *World Politics*, April 1957, p. 466.

32. See the former of the publications mentioned, p. 375.

33. The second publication mentioned above, pp. 14–15. See also the previously cited article by G. M. Meier, who quotes Schultz and other sources.

34. Professor Nurkse was, of course, always aware of the fact that the cure for disguised unemployment was not that easy.

35. New Haven, U.S.A., 1958. I hope Professor Hirschman will accept my saying that he developed brilliantly an idea which the "old-fashioned" economist might have evolved, as a compliment, as in fact it is meant.

36. Myrdal. *Economic Theory and Underdeveloped Regions*, London, 1957, p. 23. This is a revised version of the author's Cairo lectures.

37. Every economist knows (or should know) that static equilibrium analysis has to be taken *cum grano salis*. After a change equilibrium must be thought of to be established not instantaneously, but usually through a dynamic process, possibly after some oscillations.

38. Modern growth theorists have elaborated on this well-known theme with great aplomb and much display of a pretentious terminology, "vicious circle of poverty", "minimum speed for successful take-off into sustained growth", and similar metaphors, which add little to our understanding.

39. Professor Hirschman (*op. cit.* and in *American Economic Review*, Sept. 19, 1957, pp. 559–570) speaks of "trickling down" and "polarization effects" instead of "spreading" and "backsetting". As compared with Myrdal, his perspective is broader, his treatment of the problem better balanced and his conclusions less dismal and pessimistic for the less developed countries.

40. The United States and other overseas countries have, of course, been benefited tremendously by the immigration of skilled workers, engineers, scientists and so on from the Old World—the last big wave having been set in motion by Nazi and Communist oppression. Some damage has undoubtedly been done by this migration to the countries of origin, but their economic development has not been seriously held up.

41. But even as far as the relations between regions of one country are concerned, two things ought to be remembered: The movement of labor and capital between the two regions is obviously in the interest of the resources that do more (although it damages the complementary factors of production, human as well as material, that are left behind in the stagnant region), and secondly, it is difficult to see how this whole movement could happen if conditions for development in the South were not less favorable than in the North. Hence the movement North may well be in the interest of the country as a whole.

42. The expert will recognize this as the Graham case or the typical infant industry situation. Lack of reference to the relevant theoretical concepts and literature makes it, however, difficult to pin down Myrdal's strictures. I try to give it the most reasonable interpretation possible.

V

**Money, Real Balance Effect,
and Other Essays**

22

Critical Notes on Schumpeter's Theory of Money—The Doctrine of the "Objective" Exchange Value of Money

1

Schumpeter's essay on the "Social Product and the Counting Chips" ("Das Sozialprodukt und die Rechenpfenninge," *Archiv für Sozialwissenschaften und Sozialpolitik*, vol. 44, 1918, pp. 627 seq.) centers on his "fundamental equation of the theory of money."

$$E = MU = p_1 m_1 + p_2 m_2 + \cdots + p_n m_n,$$

E = sum total of incomes, M = money stock, U = velocity of circulation, and m_1, m_2, etc., are the quantities of the various durable and nondurable consumer goods (goods of the first order) which are consumed during the economic period under consideration. For those (durable) goods which last beyond the period, the corresponding amortization, or—which comes to the same thing in a stationary economy—their new acquisitions, are included in the m's. The p_1, p_2, etc., are the money prices of the m_1, m_2, etc.

This equation, says Schumpeter, is self-evident, never denied and not deniable. "What may be debated is its explanatory value, in particular the question whether the equation is a mere tautology or identity or not, and above all, whether its terms can be separated into independent and dependent variables, so that it would reflect a causal relationship."

"A tautology in the strict sense of the word it is not. That would be the case if one side of the equation were only a different expression of the *same* quantity as the other. Then, a variation of the magnitude on one side would not only produce a variation of the magnitude of the other, but it would *ipso facto be* this variation, as is the case, e.g., with the price of a commodity and the reciprocal of the purchasing power of money vis-à-vis that commodity. This, however, is not the case here: E as

Zeitschrift für Volkswirtschaft u. Sozpolitik n.s., 4: 647–668 (1925). Translated from German. © 1925, Springer-Verlag. Reprinted with permission.

well as the products m_1p_1, m_2p_2, etc., are not only conceptionally but also practically distinguishable magnitudes, statistically obtainable from different sources." So states Schumpeter.

As against this, it is here asserted, and the proof is offered in what follows, that the equation is a tautology in the proper sense of the word. The one side of the equation is but a different arithmetic expression of the same quantities as on the other side. A change in the one magnitude not only brings with it a change in the other, but *ipso facto is* that change.

To anticipate the result: the equation $MU = m_1p_1 + m_2p_2 + \cdots + m_np_n$
(this is what matters primarily, because Schumpeter's further exposition is based on *this* part of the equation and his three propositions on the fundamental equation relate to it) comes to equating the *money price* of the goods sold to the *amounts of money* spent on exactly the same goods. That is clearly an identity (tautology), for the money price of a good is *by definition* equal to the amount of money received in exchange for that good. Thus, the second question—whether or not the elements of the equation can be separated into dependent and independent variables—also loses its substance. If the equation is a tautology it can naturally not represent a causal relation, and one cannot speak of any reciprocal interaction between its variables.

This should by no means be taken for a condemnation of the whole of Schumpeter's essay. "The Social Product and the Counting Chips" is certainly one of the most brilliant and instructive pieces of work written on the theory of money.

2

Consider first the right-hand side of the equation,

$m_1p_1 + m_2p_2 + \cdots + m_np_n$.

As indicated, m_1, m_2, etc., stand for the quantities of goods consumed or, respectively, the amortization quotas of the durable consumers' goods which outlast the period. p_1, p_2, etc., are the prices paid for them by the consumers. All goods of a higher order are excluded. The equation refers to *goods of the first order only*. To this corresponds, as we shall see, the concept of the velocity of circulation.

We can therefore define the *sum of the products* as the *expression in money of the goods consumed*.

The money expression of goods consumed is equated to the sum of incomes. To realize that this is a tautology, one need only consider Schumpeter's definition of the sum of incomes. On page 635 we read: "The concept of money income is here taken in Fisher's meaning, so that it includes neither sums saved nor tax payments, but does include also borrowings or part of capital spent on consumption—that is, simply as the *money expression of goods consumed*." [1] Note well! This says *defined* "as" the money expression, etc., *not equating*, "is equal to", the money expression, etc.

Insert this definition into the equation under review, and the result is: the money expression of goods consumed = the money expression of goods consumed. This equality is manifestly an identity. The right- and left-hand sides of the equation cover the same quantity, *viz.*, a series of purchases of goods of the first order. On the *right-hand* side the sum of these purchases is written explicitly; to each purchase corresponds one *mp*. On the *left-hand* side all those purchases whose *m* are attributable to *one* person are grouped together and then summed, and this sum is called the income of that person. The sum of these sums is then designated *E* and equated to the sum of the *mp* in which they originated by a purely arithmetical operation. As may be seen, we have here what Schumpeter characterizes as the criterium of a tautology, that "the one side is but another expression for the *same* quantity as the other."

3

The matter is very much the same, though a little less obvious, when it comes to equating of MU (i.e., quantity of money × circulation velocity of money) to the product sum $p_1 m_1 + p_2 m_2 + \cdots$

Schumpeter takes great care in defining M (p. 654). He enumerates six elements whose sum makes up M. There is, further, a whole series of deductions: for instance, hoarded money and idle sums (p. 666). Also left out is money which does not circulate in the sphere of consumption, but only in that of capital, e.g., in the real estate, mortgage and securities markets. We need not follow the author into all the details. For it will turn out that the precise demarcation of M does not matter, because a mistake which occurs here is offset by the manner in which Schumpeter defines U.

We understand by M simply the total of the means of exchange of the economy, regardless of whether these means of exchange exist in the markets of consumers' goods or of capital goods, whether they circulate or are hoarded.

That this simplified magnitude also satisfies the equation will become apparent presently when we now turn to the concept of the "circulation velocity of money." Schumpeter's exposition of this difficult subject is uncommonly instructive and puts our problem into the clearest possible light. This is true especially of the example on pp. 668 ff., which cannot, however, be repeated here. We limit ourselves to the result that Schumpeter obtains from his extensive discussion.

The definition of the velocity of circulation "is derived from the fact that one and the same quantity of money, in one and the same period of time, travels several times through the circuit from the sphere of consumption back to the sphere of consumption, or—which is the same thing—becomes several times an element of money income and is spent as such."

"From this follows directly what is the theoretically correct measure of the velocity of circulation of money, or its efficiency: precisely, the number of times that this happens in the economic period to which the sum of incomes refers" (p. 671).

Corresponding to Schumpeter's limitation of the m in the product sum to goods of the first order (i.e., consumers' goods), he *cannot* consider as a "satisfactory measure" of velocity circulation of "the average number of 'changes of hands' occurring in a period of time, or—expressed as its reverse—the average period of rest, i.e., the time during which a unit of money remains with an economic agent" (p. 671). For there are certainly many changes of hands of money—for example, in the securities markets—which do not serve to transfer goods of the first order to consumers. Where the production of a commodity from raw materials to the finished product is in *one* hand, e.g., in that of an oil trust, the sale of this commodity takes *one* change of hands. But where the production process is spread out such that every phase of production is handled by an independent enterprise which purchases the intermediate product, processes it and hands it on,—there clearly a large number of changes of hands of money is required. However, the velocity of circulation in the sense in which Schumpeter understands it, is the same in both cases. For its measurement takes into account only the *last* change of hands at the point, that is, where the commodity is transferred to the consumer.

Schumpeter explains this most graphically: "If, however, the consumer buys from a firm which controls only the last stage on the route of production, while behind it there are 99 other producers or wholesalers, then clearly only that part of the sum, which remains in the hands of this terminal firm must go through the same change of hands as in the earlier case (i.e., where the whole process of production is in one hand) in order to become an element of income. The remainder of that sum will, progressively diminishing, be delivered to more and more hands, and its elements will progressively pass through more and more hands until the last element which obviously must be transferred 100 times before its final distribution as individual income can take place" (pp. 671–672).

Up to there, the topic was always just velocity of circulation as such. Now we come to the decisive point. On p. 673 we read: "Naturally, to understand the efficiency of money ... one must pay attention to its differences in different social milieus.... The difference between peasant agriculture and capitalist industry is often too large ... and in such cases one will probably have to speak of *different*[2] velocities of circulation of money in the same country and at the same time. Equally, different types of money possess different efficiencies. Large-denomination bills have a different one from that of small change. Bills of exchange of limited circulation have another velocity than that of coin, etc. That we wish to disregard this and choose to speak of only *one* velocity of circulation, should be understood merely as a simplification of exposition...."

Thus Schumpeter himself concedes that one *cannot* speak of one *uniform* velocity of circulation of money. However, one will have to go further than he does; to be consistent, one must accept *a separate velocity of circulation for every separate coin or money token*. We must clearly take it as a mere accident if two or more pieces of money have the same velocity of circulation; that is not of the essence of the matter.

Our equation now takes the following form:

$$MU = g_1 u_1 + g_2 u_2 + g_3 u_3 + \cdots + g_k u_k = p_1 m_1 + p_2 m_2 + \cdots + p_n m_n,$$

where g_1, g_2, etc., are the individual pieces of money, $u_1, u_2, \ldots$, their velocities of circulation,[3] and k indicates the number of money tokens.

It is clear now why we have not paid special attention to the delimitation of M, and why we said that, to satisfy the equation, it would be unnecessary to exclude money which circulates in the capital sphere or is hoarded. For such money would simply have zero velocity of circulation and could thus not affect the expression MU—which is merely a symbol for the sum $g_1 u_1 + g_2 u_2 + \cdots$.

4

Consider, next, any single element of the left-hand side of our equation, now corrected, and what such a $g_x u_x$ means exactly. g_x is a money token, a means of exchange, be it a coin, a bill, a check, a promissory note or whatever else serves as means of exchange, expressed in currency units of the economy, that is equal to a certain multiple of this unit. u_x is the efficiency of this piece of money. Let it, as an example, be 10. What now does it mean to say that the velocity of circulation of a piece of currency is equal to 10? It means: this piece of currency has, in one economic period, made the run through the circuit from the sphere of consumption back again to that sphere ten times. It has become an element of the income of two or more persons ten times, or to put it still differently, it has intermediated 10 purchases of goods of the first order. A has used it to buy the commodity m_1 from B; with B or one of his predecessors it has become income. B has used it to buy the commodity m_2 from C, and so on, ten times. $g_x u_x$ is thus the symbol for u_x purchases; written out explicitly:

$$g_x + g_x + g_x + \cdots u_x \text{ times}$$

Now it becomes clear that to every $p_t m_t$ of the right-hand side, i.e., of the sum of products, there must correspond one element or a sum of elements of the left-hand side. *On the left-hand side we have the sum of money, the number of currency units (ignoring velocities) which was spent on commodity m_t:* $g_{t_1} + g_{t_2} + \cdots + g_{t_k}$, where t refers to commodity and its subscript to the money token. *On the right-hand side we have the money price of this commodity.* As demonstrated in the beginning: the equation means

that the money prices of the commodities equal the sums of money paid for identically these same commodities—which is obviously a tautology since the money
price of a commodity is by definition equal to the sum of money received for it in
exchange.

One might ask, how does one treat the cases when such purchases are handled
through accounting entries rather than through the transfer of currency? Schumpeter
has allowed for these cases as well. For he includes in the total of the quantity of
money "the amounts of all payments that are expenditures of income and settled
solely by the debiting (and crediting) of accounts." Thus, the creation of a quantity of
money is here invented *ad hoc*, equipped with a velocity of circulation of unity, and
inserted into the equation.[4]

From this it emerges that what is involved in Schumpeter's equation are not so
much technical, real means of exchange, but rather an ideal means of exchange and
measure of prices, a unit of calculation (a numéraire), the counting chip. But the two
one must keep separate.[5]

5

Schumpeter's first proposition on the fundamental equation is: "No change in the
magnitudes of which the sum of the products consists, can have a direct influence on
this sum, i.e., on $p_1m_1 + p_2m_2 + \cdots + p_nm_n$."

"This proposition does not preclude an indirect effect of changes in quantities
and prices of commodities on the sum of the products, such that they first change the
product of the quantity of money times efficiency, and that then this change affects
prices and quantities so that the sum of the products changes" (pp. 676–677).

We cannot agree with this proposition as it stands. We have shown that every
term on the right-hand side is by definition equal to one term, or a sum of terms, on
the left-hand side. One cannot therefore speak of an effect of these terms on one
another. If there is any change on the right-hand side—if, e.g., production increases
and more *m* appear on the market—this in itself means *eo ipso* an acceleration of
circulation or a new creation of money; if neither has happened, i.e., when this
increase has been financed by a change in book entries, then the appropriate quantity
of money is simply invented *ad hoc*.

Corrected, Schumpeter's proposition should run: *Every change in a term of the
product sum means a change in that sum—unless this change is offset by another change.*
Schumpeter puts it in reverse: *No change in a term of the sum can affect the sum* (because
each change is offset by another change)[6]—*unless at the same time MU changes.* Since
we have shown that *MU* is only another arithmetical expression for the same
magnitude as the sum of products, we can formulate the exception as follows: unless
the sum does in fact change (i.e., *no* compensation through an opposite change
occurs). This proposition is equivalent to our previous one. For it does not matter

that Schumpeter calls an exception what we call the rule, and considers to be the rule what we call an exception—that is, that a compensation occurs.

This proposition is no more than a truism clothed in a pretty play of words.

It would, however, indeed be interesting to know *when* a change of a term of the sum will *not* affect the sum because it is compensated. But about this we learn— nothing. We must therefore deny any analytical value to Schumpeter's first proposition on the fundamental equation.

The so-called "sum of products" is a theoretically and practically most uninteresting magnitude which is of no use for anything. In fact, Schumpeter soon proceeds to consider an essentially more interesting magnitude: the price level, the value of money. Value of money is for Schumpeter the same as purchasing power, that is, the reciprocal of the price level.[7] The distinction between "external" and "internal" objective exchange value of money he does not recognize. For him, there is only *one* value of money—and, so it seems to us, with good reason.

I may be permitted to spend a monent on this pair of notions, "internal" and "external" objective (collective) exchange value of money. This terminology is not only infelicitous, as Mises[8] thinks, but nonsensical. There is in truth only *one* objective exchange value of money[9]: its purchasing power, the reciprocal of the price level, the exchange ratio between money and commodities. This exchange ratio may change because of monetary developments or because of developments in the world of commodities. In *both* cases what changes is the *same* thing, namely, the exchange ratio between money and commodities, or in other words, the value of money, the purchasing power of money, the level of prices. Therefore, one cannot say that in the first case there was a change in the "internal" and in the second in the "external" objective exchange of value of money.

This has, by the way, been said by Mises with all the clarity one might wish for (p. 132), but he does not strictly adhere to it later on in his work. For instance, the sixth chapter is headed "The Accompaniments of Changes in the Internal Objective Exchange Value of Money". Does this mean that these social phenomena occur only when the value of money is changed by "monetary causes"? Are the effects of a devaluation of money different when they are caused by a contraction of output— —say, in consequence of a war—that is from the side of commodities rather than when the impulse lies with the "monetary side"? Can one, if one sticks to the proposition that there is no "internal" and no "external", but only *one* value of money—can one then speak of *two* problems of measuring, i.e., of one of measuring the "external" and another of measuring the "internal" objective exchange value of money? I believe one can meaningfully speak only of *one* measurement, of the measurement of the value of money pure and simple, of purchasing power, because there is in fact nothing else! Whether a change in the value of money started from the money side (problem of measuring the "internal" value of money) or from the commodity side ("external" value of money)—that one can find out, but not "measure"!

Let us return to Schumpeter who, as we saw, does not concur in this distinction between internal and external value of money. Since he does not know what to do with his "sum of products", he tries to apply his first proposition about the fundamental equation somehow to the price level, i.e., to the value of money. "Something similar applies to the price level. If one abstracts from the intervention of money, and considers the exchange relations which underlie money prices, then it is full clear that the rise of one of them does not produce, but *ipso facto* means the decline[10] of others. All of them cannot rise or fall together. . . . Prices are nothing but ratios of exchange expressed in money. If nevertheless all of them can rise or fall together, this cannot be explained from the causes which would explain the rise and fall of individual prices, but only from a relation between the world of commodities and the flow of money" (p. 679).

At bottom all this is quite obvious. One can only speak of the price level if one presupposes a general denominator of all prices (a price indicator), a unit of counting, in short, money; for the price level is a sum or an average; and summing and taking averages one can only do with magnitudes of the same denomination. Without such a common denomination, i.e., without money in Schumpeter's sense, there is no price level. It is therefore no miracle that a change in the price level can only be attributed to a change in the relationship between the world of commodities and the flow of money![11]

6

So far we have taken the concept of price level or its reciprocal, the value of money as self-explanatory. Submitting now this concept to a more detailed examination, a remarkable fact emerges: it seems quite impossible to find an exact mathematical expression for the concept.

Quite correctly, Schumpeter says: "The purchasing power of money can however be taken as a plain fact only vis-à-vis single commodities" (p. 653). "This (price level or purchasing power) is not given as a plain fact, but always only as an artificial entity,[12] which draws its justification from the purpose one pursues with its use. To each such purpose corresponds a different concept of price level and thus of its reciprocal, the general purchasing power of money . . ." (p. 653). Thus there is not *one* value of money as such, but there are as many different values of money as purposes which one pursues with them.

Since then, the value of money resists all exact conceptual determination—for nothing but this is hidden behind the impossibility to measure it—but since Schumpeter wants to present an exact theory, he calls on the sum of products which, however, has nothing whatever to do with price level or value of money. Among the terms of the sum of products there figure the single prices p_1, p_2, p_3, etc., but not an average price or a price level.[13] Later on, he attempts to find the way back to the value of money, in that he tries to apply statements about the sum of products to the price level. But here there opens a gap in the exposition for which the statement "something similar is true for the price level" cannot furnish a logical bridge; it merely pretends to be one.

We insist: a precise definition of what he understands by value of money—let alone a mathematical expression for the price level—Schumpeter is unable to provide.

Mises as well arrived at the result that none of the customary indexing methods meets its purpose. Indeed, he went further and has shown that a measurement of the value of money is impossible on principle.

Where the matter now rests is as follows: the theory of money works with the concept of the objective exchange value of money. It is the reciprocal of the price level and it should be statistically determinable. But this has been denied, and it is impossible in principle and not only for reasons which lie in the imperfection of statistical methods. This is a contradiction. How can it be resolved?

The answer is very simple. It sounds paradoxical, seems to contradict all monetary theory, and yet it is true. The problem of the value of money is a sham problem! The value of money is a hypostasis of complex economic phenomena, a symbol for certain price combinations. *Changes* in the value of money—and it is this which exclusively concerns monetary theory; nobody would be interested in the value of money in a static economy—dissolve into a sum of price changes. In reality, nothing in the real world corresponds to the concept of value of money. In a word, *there is no objective, global exchange value of money!*[14]

Before we examine this more extensively and furnish a proof for what has just been said, be it emphasized that it is in no way intended to reconstruct the theory of money on a completely new basis. This is not meant at all. The consequences of becoming aware that no objective value of money exists, that the expression value of money is but an abbreviation, a symbol for certain price phenomena, are altogether not too large. A corrected formulation of certain propositions of the theory of money, the solution or the disappearance of some false problems, follow directly from that insight. It may well be of some value for the study of the effects of changes in the "value of money" (one may retain the term if one is clear about what it means), and for their connection with the rate of interest and with crises.

Let us begin with the *subjective* value of money.[15] This is a special case of subjective value in general. We may tentatively define it, following Böhm-Bawerk, as the significance which may be attributed to money as the perceived recognition of a utility that would otherwise have to be done without, for the welfare purposes of a *single* individual.[16]

[The term] "subjective values" always refers to *one* economic agent. This appears, in pure economics, as a system of targets. The concept of value is a construction designed to explain the economic actions, the disposal of goods, by that particular economic agent. The concept draws its justification from this function in the structure of the science. If it is employed other than in this specifically single-economic context, it loses all meaning and explanatory value, as will be shown presently. (Whether the concept of value is altogether superfluous is not to be investigated here. In Böhm-Bawerk's system there is no place for value as something other than the notion of a dependent utility.)[17]

At any rate, subjective value is not an absolute but a relative magnitude. It is nothing absolute in the sense of a psychological reality in the psyche of the economic agent; rather it is the significance of one good in relation to another. A value judgement does not measure, as it would were value an absolute magnitude; rather it *scales*. Thus we propose to say: value is the significance which an economic agent attaches to one good in relation to another—or, to follow Strigl[18]: value is the measure of the substitutability of one good for another. For quantities of goods which have the same significance for the economic agent are for him substitutable one for the other.

The common basis of reference, i.e., that which—for *one* economic agent—makes the values of different goods comparable, and holds them intimately together, is the system, or the totality, of individual aims.

This, plus *rational action according to this system of aims*, are the indispensible conditions for being able to speak sensibly of economic value in the meaning or the theory of marginal utility. It follows that a *comparison of subjective value of a good to different persons, with different systems of aims, is meaningless precisely because value expresses only a relation of different goods to one person*.

Thus, one cannot say, as often happens: the subjective value of money is greater to the poor man than its subjective value to the rich man. It is also a mistake to defend progressive taxes "scientifically" with the lower value of money to recipients of higher incomes. Such assertions contain hidden value judgements,[19] of which we can easily convince ourselves.

If, to circumvent this difficulty, one were to construct a system of collective aims that would dominate the aims of lay individuals—which, of course, it is open to anyone to do—and if one were to relate to one another, according to such a system, the subjective values of *different* economic agents, then one would leave the terrain of theoretical economics. For such a supra-individual "social" system of aims has nothing but its name in common with the system of aims (system of wants) of the doctrine of marginal utility. For marginal utility theory,[20] the system of aims is not a scale of ideal values but *causa finalis*. This emerges when the theory explicitly or implicitly presupposes rational behavior. Where then is the power which behaves according to that "social-economic" system of aims that supercedes the individual? There is no such power! A social-economic system of aims can thus not be a *causa* but only an ideal standard of value. But this means that one no longer *explains*; one *values*. One no longer practices causal-explanatory economics, but one makes value judgements, one leaves the confines of being and enters the realm of ethics.

What then is the relation between subjective and objective—or, to follow Wieser, "national-economic"—value of money? Unfortunately, the two expressions have the word "value" in common. From this derives the considerable danger of believing that the two concepts are coordinate, that they have a common *genus proximum*: value is the common generic term. Values divide into the subjective and the objective (social-economic). Social-economic value plays in the economic system the same part that subjective value plays in the economy of the individual. What are we to think of this?

We need only keep before our mind what the assumptions are under which the theory of subjective value holds. We said: rational behavior according to a system of aims. To construe national-economic value analogously, one would have to make the same assumptions. But that will not work out. There is no national-economic system of aims according to which some super-individual with collective power would behave, whose members would consist of individuals. The national economy is not collective in the sense of a large individual economy. The economic value of money (called exchange value in the case of commodities) has nothing at all to do with subjective value. It is something totally different functions in the theory of the national economy from those of the subjective value of money in the theory of single, individual behavior. (That does not, however, preclude that prices originate from A to Z in subjective values, even though also this formulation of Böhm-Bawerk's is perhaps debatable[21]). There is a contrast between value and price also in that value is a *means* of explanation while prices are essential *objectives* of explanation in economics.

It is Ammon's merit[22] to have stressed the differences between subjective and objective value. For this is indeed what he means when he does not tire to repeat that national economics (= theory of prices) has nothing to do with economic analysis (= theory of individual economic behavior).

We now proceed to show that the postulate of a national-economic value of money—if one takes it seriously—implies the error of mixing value and price, individual and collective economic behavior.

We may mention in passing that this error is not infrequent also outside the theory of money. Wieser commits it where Böhm-Bawerk accuses him, in the polemic about the theory of imputation, of explaining in a "single step", i.e., by deducing the distribution (of incomes) directly from imputation. The doctrine of marginal productivity as presented by Clark, does not steer clear of it. Spann's universalist-teleological method raises this basic error to a principle. Finally, it may be mentioned that the same applies to the concept of the balance of trade. Wieser has shown this with unmatched clarity[23]).

7

We may divide the theories of money[24]—only those which are based on the modern doctrine of subjective value are relevant to us here—into two groups: (1) those which regard the value of money simply as the reciprocal of the level of prices (among others Schumpeter and Fisher) and (2) those which hold that the value of money is different from the price level.

It is very easy to show that this second group falls into the error of confusing value and price, individual and collective economic behavior. Had they not done so, their value of money would turn out to be most superfluous, a fifth wheel to the wagon, as Fisher said once, though in another connection.

In the German literature, Wieser[25] may be considered as a representative of this version. Wieser defines the value of money as "the *significance which money possesses for all participants in the national-economic process, by virtue of the general level of prices.* The value of money says more than the bare fact of the general level of prices. . . . It says that, in the national-economic process, money has this or that significance for *everyone, by virtue of* the general price level. We can therefore define the value of money more precisely by saying that it is the significance which is attributable *to the unit of money because of its relation to the unit of utility*" (p. 311). To this one must note that *a social unit of utility does not exist.* Social (collective) utility is useful as a principle of explanation only if one conceives of society as an acting person who proceeds to maximize utility—or, which is the same thing, which behaves rationally. This latter may be assumed in the case of an individual (the assumption is probably even here not fully self-evident, but as a method of ideal types one will probably have to accept it). But in the case of a social (collective) economy, there can of course be no question of accepting this assumption.

Now Wieser does not really do this; he does not conceive of society as a whole as a large individual economic agent (even if such a conception is the inevitable consequence of many of his assertions). He emphasizes explicitly that the social-economic value is nothing objective, but only something subjectively general. All the more transparent becomes the untenability and superflousness of his objective exchange value!

"If the price of a commodity is 100, all sellers without exception reckon the exchange value at 100 because all of them agree without exception that the exchange value will take its size from the expected price. In this regard, their evaluation possesses nothing personal; a personal element enters only when every one of them evaluates the price according to his concrete personal circumstances.

Here we encounter the fact of a national-economic exchange value. The national-economic exchange value is that first step, uniformly accepted by all participants, of their evaluation of the exchange value which precedes the individual evaluation of money. *Already this first step is not solely a statement on the fact of a price, it is rather a statement of value*[26]; by saying a commodity has the exchange value of 100, one wants not only to say that its market price is 100, but one wants to indicate the market significance which is attributable to it because it has the price 100" (p. 291). What does market significance mean? Obviously, no more than that one can get 100 for the commodity or that one has to spend 100 for it. "That all sellers (and buyers) are agreed to reckon with 100, because they all, without exception, agree that the exchange value is measured by the expected price" is but a transcription of the plain fact that nobody will sell this commodity for less than 100 (or that nobody will pay more than 100 for it), when its market price stands at 100, that is, that there is a chance to be able to buy or sell it for 100. That is self-evident. To make that clear, one need not postulate the existence of a mystical national-economic exchange value which is valid for everybody and yet is nothing objective, but a "commonly subjective step" and yet again is not common, "because it is never valid for those persons who do not wish to participate in the exchange" (p. 291).

Analysis can manage perfectly with two concepts: subjective value and price. Price originates, as Böhm-Bawerk puts it, from beginning to end from subjective valuations, and there is not the slightest need, nor is there any room, for a separately existing national-economic exchange value.

Wieser's attempt to prove such things therefore had to fail. The presupposition of a national-economic exchange value only ensnares him in contradictions and obscurities.

Let us now, very briefly, examine Anderson's book *The Value of Money*[27] as a representative of the Anglo-Saxon literature of this variant of the theory of money. It is of considerable interest for us because it expresses with ruthless clarity and precision what, implicitly and indistinctly, is at the base of many other theories: the presupposition of a social, national-economic value ("social value").

Anderson invokes Mises and Wieser. The invocation of Wieser is, as we have seen, altogether justified. That of Mises probably rests on a misunderstanding. To be sure, it is not to be denied that the distinction between inner and external objective exchange values of money can easily give rise to misunderstanding. About this Anderson says: "Mises, like Wieser, needs an absolute value of money in his thinking. He does not call the concept by that name, but, following Menger, speaks of the 'inner objective value of money' and the 'outer objective value of money'. The latter is the purchasing power of money, a relative concept, exactly expressed in the price level. The inner objective value of money ... performs the same logical function in the theory of money that the absolute social value concept of the present writer does, even though the psychological explanation lying behind it is very different" (pp. 109–110).

Anderson rejects energetically any view which sees in value something "relative": "it (value) is an absolute quantity not a relative one" (p. 7). "Many economists ... have defined value as a ratio of exchange. That is imprecise. An exchange ratio presumes *two* values which form the terms of the ratio" (p. 6). In this sentence the reference is not to the *subjective* value of money, as one might suspect, but to the national-economic value. Anderson is fully aware of the difference between subjective and national-economic value. "The subjective exchange value of money is the personal value of money, as distinct from its public economic value ..." (p. 88).[28] If, then, he goes on: "Values lie behind ratios of exchange and causally determine them" (p. 6), we have to think of the "public economic value".

What, then, is this mysterious something that is switched in between value and price, determines prices causally and is itself determined by subjective value? Value is the economic substance. It is that property which makes otherwise totally heterogeneous goods economically comparable. "Ratios of exchange are ratios between two quantities of value, the wealth of the units of the two kinds of wealth exchanged" (p. 16). From this it follows that a rise in prices (of the total level of prices) can have two causes: the fall of the value of money or the rise of the value of commodities (p. 57). That is a very remarkable thought which may be found also in Wieser and Mises. Here all we can say is that it is very likely that a general rise of prices has different effects in different circumstances. However, that certain (mostly adverse) effects follow a general rise of prices when, and only when, they originate in the money side—as Mises also seems to think—that is by no means obvious and would have to be shown. One thing is certain: there is no need to presuppose a national-economic exchange value in the sense of Wieser or Anderson, *different from* the phenomenon of prices.

Already now we may note that Anderson's theory of value operates on a very low level. Anderson's value much recalls the notion of an absolute substance in the natural sciences. Behind this economic quantity, this *qualitas occulta*, are hidden many important problems without being solved.[29]

Let us briefly consider the relation between objective value and price in Anderson. Anderson criticizes the Austrian theory. His criticism maintains that the marginal utility theory is individualist; it overlooks, he says, the social interdependence of men. "Individuality is a social product" (p. 17).

We need not expand on this. German literature surely does not lack such criticism. One need only recall Spann, who brands the explanation of price from individual values individualist-atomistic, and on his part conceives of prices as quantitative expressions of the performance of goods in the national economy.

Anderson's conception is similar. Moreover, he makes the additional distinction between price and social value (= public economic value). To him prices are not strictly expressions of social value. It may happen that a good has a high value but is unsaleable and thus possesses no price. "The Capitol in Washington cannot be exchanged, yet has value" (p. 401).

Two factors determine the size of a price: (1) the value, (2) the saleability (p. 10). And what, one must ask, determines saleability? About this, one learns—nothing. Still, it does happen that prices are precise expressions of values. "In the fluid market, prices correctly express values" (p. 11). the proof—is absent! We see the relation between value and price is rather obscure.

All these "organic", "social" theories of value and price suffer from a methodological opacity. They overlook that all "social stimuli"—as Anderson puts it—take effect only through individuals; they cannot directly affect prices. To be sure, Anderson admits this when he says "All mental processes play in the minds of men. There is no 'oversoul' which transcends the soul of individuals..." (p. 16). With this one can only agree. But with this everything is conceded which the Austrian school requires as justification. For it, aims and needs of the individuals are data. Where these data come from it does not investigate. On that one may formulate theories *ad lib* without touching the results of pure economics.

But he who maintains that prices are the realizations of social values, express a measure of performance, that prices measure the significance of commodities for society, or that they are symptoms for the spiritual structure of society—he would have to show all this through economic theory. He would have to show that the economic data are such and so, and the economic mechanism (or organism, if one will) as explained by economic theory, produces prices which correspond to the significance[30] of goods for society. Such an "organic" theory would thus have no reason to reject pure theory as individualist. On the contrary! It would have to employ it as an explanatory instrument, if it wants to present more than mere assertions.

It is another question whether economic data are really such that prices will result which correspond to the significance of commodities to the national economy. (From the point of view of pure economic theory this is perfectly possible; for it does depend on the data which theory accepts as given). To us it does indeed seem that this is not the case, that prices in no manner correspond to the significance for, to the extent of performance in, the national economy. We have, however, no reason to examine this question here; for the burden of proof is on him who would so argue. And of such proof—which would, in the manner indicated, have to be conducted as a "theory of economic data"—no trace can be found in either Spann or Anderson.

Spann's reference to the doctrine of imputation, his assertion that prices do not originate in subjective valuations but are imputed magnitudes, cannot be regarded as a proof. For imputation is possible only in reference to goods of higher order, not to consumers' goods. If Spann means by theory of imputation nothing than the theory of marginal utility—but one can hardly suppose so since he invokes Wieser—then one may counter, on Böhm-Bawerk's lines: to his dialectic antithesis between imputed value and subjective value there corresponds no real antithesis, for an imputed value is only a special case of subjective value in general.

* * *

In a second essay it will be demonstrated, first, that the concept of an objective value of money is superfluous and untenable as against theories which see in the value of money no more than purchasing power, the reciprocal of the price level. Eminent representatives of the theory of money must be considered in this connection, such as Fisher, Menger, Mises, Schumpeter, Walsh. Moreover, an examination of the diverse methods of index number calculation will be unavoidable; for each method of computing price index numbers contains implicitly a theory of money. In this context there will be an opportunity to investigate what function the concept of the value of money has to perform in general catallactics. From this it will be possible to deduce the essence of the value of money, that is, that in reality there is no value of money, that it is but an abbreviative turn of phrase, a linguistic symbol: for what? That will have to be shown in detail.

Postscript

In the last part of the preceding essay I promised a second paper on the concept of the "objective" value of money and the related concepts of the price level and price index numbers. This paper has not been written, but the problems of the value of money are the subject of my book *The Meaning of Index Numbers. An Enquiry in the Concept of the Price Level and the Methods of Its Measurement*[31] and of the article "The Objective Value of Money and the Price Index Numbers".[32] This article, a reply to a critic of my book, restates very briefly the basic message of the book and clarifies some points in the argument.

The basic message is that the theory of the objective value of money (generalized purchasing power) and the correlated concept of the general price level must be traced back to the value of money (purchasing power), and the correlated concept of the price level from the point of view of the individual (household). A change in the objective value of money (generalized purchasing power) must be conceived as some sort of an average of the changes of the individual values. The theory can thus be described as an early and radical version of what is now known as the micro foundation of macro theory.

The gist of the theory is developed in chapter 2 of Part II of the book (pp. 77–100). The theory provides an economic interpretation of the two index number formulas that have been recommended as the best in the literature on the subject, for example, in Irving Fisher's celebrated monograph *The Making of Index-Numbers* (2nd edition, Boston, 1922).

The data are the prices and quantities of n commodities consumed by an individual household in periods 1 and 2. The two formulas are the "Laspeyres" (L) formula $\Sigma p_2 q_1 / \Sigma p_1 q_1$ and the "Paasche" (P) formula $\Sigma p_2 q_2 / \Sigma p_1 q_2$. These are weighted averages, the first using the quantities of the first period as weights, the second those of the second period.

The two methods yield two alternative measures of the change in the price level from period 1 to period 2. The theory states that, under certain assumptions, the "true" change in the price level lies somewhere between the two measures. The true change in the price level is defined as the ratio of the money income in the first period to the money income in the second period that would leave the individual indifferent, in other words, would yield the same satisfaction. For example, the statement that the price level has risen by 10 percent means that in the second period a money income 10 percent larger than that in the first period yields the same satisfaction. The actual money income of the second period can then be compared to the one that yields the same satisfaction. This is what we mean by comparing real incomes. The statement that the real income in the second period is, say, 20 percent higher than in the first simply means that the actual money income is 20 percent higher than the one which yields the same satisfaction as the money income in the first period. It does not involve such vague nonoperational concepts as the absolute level of satisfaction or of utility.[33]

I now come to the main point. Suppose the L formula $\Sigma p_2 q_1 / \Sigma p_1 q_1 = 2\frac{1}{2}$. The price level has risen by 250 percent. The collection of goods that was bought in period 1 cost $2\frac{1}{2}$ as much at the prices of period 2. It follows that any income Y_2 in period 2 will yield *at least* as much satisfaction as Y_1 and the price level has *at the most* risen by 250 percent—at the most, because by rearranging its expenditures, buying less of commodities whose prices have risen relatively more, and buying more of commodities which have become relatively cheap, the individual can derive the same satisfaction from a Y_2 that is smaller than $2\frac{1}{2}$ of Y_1. This means the formula L yields the upper limit of the change of the true rise in the price level.

Now suppose that the P formula $p_2 q_2 / p_1 q_2 = 2$; the price level has gone up by 100 percent. That means that the goods consumed in the second period would have cost only half as much at the prices of the first period. Therefore, every Y_1 that is greater than $\frac{1}{2} Y_2$ yields a greater satisfaction than Y_2. It is tempting to conclude that every Y_2 that is smaller than $2Y_1$ will yield less satisfaction than Y_1, that, therefore, the price level has risen at least 100 percent, and that the true change of the price level must be somewhere between 2 and $2\frac{1}{2}$. Since experience has shown that the two measures practically always are close together, it is reasonable to say that any average between the two, for example, the geometric mean, is an acceptable approximation.[34]

Unfortunately, there is a flaw in this reasoning. From the fact that every Y_1 that is greater than $\frac{1}{2} Y_2$ we cannot conclude that every Y_2 that is smaller than $2Y_1$ will be inferior to Y_1. We know that this is true of the actual Y_1. Suppose $Y_2 = 1000$. Then we know that every Y_1 that is greater than 500 will be preferred. If this were true of every Y_2, if every Y_1 that is greater than 100 will be superior to a Y_2 of 200 and so on, then we can conclude that every Y_2 that is smaller than $2Y_1$ is inferior.

But this is not so. Suppose Y_2 is much larger, that the individual has moved into a much higher income bracket, then many commodities that he could not afford in period 1 will enter his budget. And it is possible that the prices of these goods have changed differently. In principle, the price level has changed differently for different individuals depending on their income, their tastes and their needs.

But there are reasons to believe that this complication does not preclude the conclusion that an average of the L and P indexes is, in practice, a reasonable approximation of the true change in the price level. Empirical studies have shown that price indexes based on budgets of different income levels do not diverge too much, except for extremes—the very rich and the very poor—and there are good *a priori* reasons why that should be so. Price level changes due to monetary forces, especially those of inflation, one would not expect to be biased one way or the other.

This is, in desperate brevity, the theory of the value (purchasing power) of money and the price level from the point of view of the individual market participants.

In chapter IV of Part II of the book the question is discussed which price level should be used as guide for monetary policy. Before tackling the main problem how this fits in with the postulate that the concepts of the value of money and the price level must be traced back to, and built up from, the concepts of the value of money relating to individual households, some preliminary questions are raised.

First, what should be "the subject of monetary stabilization, the foreign exchange value of money or the purchasing power of money" (the price level)? The answer is that small countries should stabilize the foreign exchange value; or, as we say now, should peg their currency to that of a large trade partner. Only "large" countries can "afford" to stabilize the price level "without regard to exchange rates". But exceptions to these rules are possible.

Then there is a brief critical discussion of the concepts of the "objective" value of money in the earlier literature, "esteem value", "real cost value", etc., in the Anglo-Saxon literature, and the so-called "internal" and "external" value of money as used by Austrian economists Carl Menger and Ludwig von Mises.

These distinctions are related to the question as to whether a change in the price level and the value of money is due to "monetary" causes, increases or decreases in the quantity of money (or changes in the velocity of circulation of money), or to "real" changes.

This distinction has played a great role in the earlier monetary literature. It was widely argued that for best results monetary policy should aim at letting the price level decline *pari passu* with the secular growth of output.[35] This view has gone out of fashion. The modern view is that the best we can hope to achieve is a stable price level. A declining price level is regarded as not feasible because of wage pressure.

The problem of whether a change in the price level, especially a decline of prices, is due to monetary or real causes, was also at the bottom of an interesting nineteenth century debate, namely, the bimetallist controversy of the 1870s and 1880s. There is a brief review of this episode in my book (pp. 104–107). The gold standard triumphed, but it should be mentioned that a galaxy of famous economists were ranged on the side of the double standard of gold and silver in the form of bimetallism or symmetallism against the monometallism of gold—F. Y. Edgeworth, Irving Fisher, Alfred Marshall, N. G. Pierson, and Leon Walras.

The problem of monetary stabilization is then linked up with what had been said earlier about the concept of the objective value of money (generalized purchasing power, general price level). It is argued that a change in the value of money should be defined as some sort of average individual values of money and price levels. The relevance of this definition derives from the fact that for the great bulk of the population changes in the value of money (or cost of living or price level) do not diverge very much.

This conception of the problem goes very well with the modern view which emphasizes the consumer price index (CPI) as the proper measure of the price level that should guide monetary policy.

A separate section (pp. 122–124) deals with "wholesale price level", roughly equivalent to producer prices in modern terminology, whose function is different from that of the CPI. It is important as a sort of indicator, a roughly coincident, or possibly a leading indicator, of the CPI from which its importance derives. This is further discussed in a final brief section on "The Price Index in the Theory of the Business Cycle" (pp. 125–127).

Notes

1. My emphasis.

2. My emphasis.

3. It is certainly permissible to group together all the g which have the same u, to factor out the common u: $u(g_1 + g_2 + g_3 + \ldots)$, and to call the sum in the bracket M_1. That is a purely

arithmetical operation which has no significance in itself, even should the M_1, M_2, etc., coincide approximately with the types of money in use by the different economic groups.

4. In similar fashion one could call drawings on credit money, as Schumpeter does, or one could consider them as an acceleration of the velocity of circulation, as Wicksell does. Which form of description one chooses is a matter of taste.

5. On this, see A. [Alfred] Ammon, *Objekte und Grundzüge der Theoretischen Nationalökonomie* (*Object and Principles of Theoretical Economics*), Vienna, 1911, p. 345; [Arthur Wolfgang] Cohn, *Kann das Geld Abgeschafft Werden?* (Can Money be Abolished), Jena, 1920.

6. He does not say so literally, but that is the sense of what he says: "If the economic agents spend out of their incomes—whose total remains unchanged—more or less on any one commodity, then they have less left to spend on the remaining commodities, and their prices ... and also their quantities must change exactly sufficiently to absorb the excess or to cover the deficiency ..." (p. 768). But velocity of circulation may change.

7. Thus, e.g., p. 653.

8. [Ludwig von Mises] *Theorie des Geldes und der Umlauffmittel* (*Theory of Money and the Means of Circulation*), 1st ed., 1912, p. 132.

9. This concept may be accepted for the time being, even though it is nothing but a hypostasis of complicated economic phenomena, as will be shown later on.

10. Strictly speaking, a *ratio* cannot rise or fall, but only change. Speaking of rises and declines already presupposes a common point of reference—money. If one has anything to say about the price level, one cannot therefore "abstract from the intervention of money".

11. The attempt to explain a general rise in prices of commodities from non-monetary causes has been made, e.g., by [Othmar] Spann in his book *Theorie der Preisverschiebung* (*Theory of Price Shifting*), Vienna, 1912.

12. We shall say: a symbol for a given combination of prices, for changes of money value, an abbreviation for complicated economic phenomena (price changes).

13. The same problem faces Fisher. How he circumvents it—he does not solve it because it is not solvable—remains to be considered.

14. This has, of course, nothing to do with the assertion, which has a similar sound, by the "nominalists" of the genre of Bendixen, that there is no value of money. Bendixen regards money as a unit of measuring, we, on the other hand, the real means of exchange (bank deposits are also a real means of exchange). Bendixen puts money into the sharpest contrast with commodities, we believe that it is subject to the same laws of value and price as goods. In this sense we may say with Ricardo: money is the most saleable good. This would be wrong only if one were to mean by that that it provides real satisfaction. But that need not be implied, and it is not meant to be implied.

15. To speak of the exchange value of money is really a pleonasm, at least if one defines money as a means of exchange, because then the concept of money says already that money value is exchange value.

16. The objection, especially suggestive in the case of money but appearing again and again also elsewhere in more recent analysis, that a value so defined cannot contribute anything to

the explanation of prices because it already presupposes prices, this objection cannot be examined here. Be it emphasized only that there is in reality no circle; for presupposed are the prices of *yesterday* and to be explained are the prices of today.

17. See [Eugen von] Böhm-Bawerk, *Positive Theories des Kapitals* (*Positive Theory of Capital*), vol. 2, Excursus VII.

18. [Richard von Strigl], *Die Ökonomischen Kategorien und die Organisation der Wirtschaft* (*Economic Categories and the Organization of the Economy*), Jena, 1923.

19. Here, "value" not in an economic sense.

20. Cp. Hans Meyer, "Zum Grundgesetz der Wirtschaftlichen Wertrechnung" ("On the Fundamental Law of the Economic Calculation of Value"), in *Zeitschrift für Volkswirtschaft und Sozialpolitik*, N.F. vol. I, p. 1.

21. Cp. the critique by [Oscar] Engländer in *Schmoller's Jahrbuch*, 1919 and 1920.

22. [Alfred Ammon], *Objekt und Grundbegriffe der Theoretischen Nationalökonomie* (*Object and Basic Concepts of Economics*), and his criticism of Cassel's theory in *Archiv für Sozialwissenschaft und Sozialpolitik*, vol. 51, p. 1.

23. [Othmar Spann], *Theorie der Gesellschaftlichen Wirtschaft* (*Theory of Social Economics*), in *Grundriss der Sozialökonomie*, Tübingen, 1914, p. 435.

24. Unless otherwise noted we always mean the objective national-economic value of money.

25. *Ibid.*

26. My emphasis.

27. [Benjamin McAlester Anderson], New York, 1917.

28. Public economic value is the translation of Wieser's national-economic exchange value.

29. This is not to deny other merits of the book. They lie, however, more in critical than in positive, constructive fields.

30. What one means by significance would have to be more closely specified: it will not do simply to speak of social value or of measure of performance.

31. *Der Sinn der Indexzahlen. Eine Untersuchung über den Begriff des Preisniveaus und die Methoden seiner Messung*, Verlag Von J. C. B. Mohr (Paul Siebeck), Tübingen, 1927. Available only in German.

32. "Der Volkswirtschaftliche Geldwert und die Preisindexziffern. Eine Erwiderung," in *Weltwirtschaftliches Archiv*, Institut für Weltwirtschaft, University of Kiel, vol. 30, July 1929, pp. 6–17. Available only in German. Unfortunately, there is no single English word for "volkswirtschaftlich". What it means is "objective" value of money in the sense of generalized purchasing power, as distinguished from the value of money from the point of view of an individual or household.

33. In the book an alternative application of the theory is discussed. Instead of intertemporal comparison of price levels, etc., territorial comparison can be made; that is to say, instead of two periods, two countries may be designated by 1 and 2. This is an instructive variation.

34. This would be the economic justification of Irving Fisher's "ideal" index formula:

$$\sqrt{\frac{\sum p_2 q_1}{\sum p_1 q_1} \times \frac{\sum p_2 q_2}{\sum p_1 q_2}}.$$

But Fisher's reasons for choosing his ideal formula are entirely different; they were purely formalistic and have no economic foundation.

35. Some writers make the further distinction between output growth due (a) to an increase in the labor force, and (b) to an increase due to productivity growth (output per man hour). There is a good theoretical reason for making that distinction. If prices decline because labor productivity increases, the average money wage rate need not decline. On the other hand, if output increases because the labor force grows, the average money wage has to decline. This obviously is not easy.

23

Mr. Keynes' Theory of the "Multiplier": A Methodological Criticism

1

According to Mr. Keynes, his analysis of the so-called "multiplier" is "an integral part" of his "General Theory of Employment" (p. 113). This multiplier, k, "establishes a precise relationship, given the propensity to consume, between aggregate employment and income and the rate of investment" (p. 113). "It tells us that, when there is an increment of aggregate investment, income will increase by an amount which is k times the increment of investment" (p. 115). "Before coming to the multiplier" Keynes introduces "the conception of marginal propensity to consume" (p. 114). He calls Y_w income in terms of wage units, C_w and I_w are consumption and investment respectively also in terms of wage units. For our purpose it is not necessary to go into the choice of the units—a matter which Keynes discusses carefully. He points out that changes in Y_w must not be identified with changes in income in terms of product and with changes in employment. "The fact that they always increase and decrease together," however, makes it, in certain contexts, possible "to regard income in terms of wage-units as an adequate working index of changes in real income" and in employment (p. 114). Since our argument is independent of the unit, we may accept Keynes' choice and in the following discussion use the symbols Y, C and I alone without the subscript w.

Keynes assumes that "when the real income of the community increases and decreases, its consumption will increase and decrease, but not so fast" (p. 114). That is to say, ΔC and ΔY have the same sign, but $\Delta Y > \Delta C$. The marginal propensity to consume is defined as $\Delta C / \Delta Y$. If, e.g., the marginal propensity to consume is $\frac{9}{10}$, that means that $\frac{9}{10}$ of a small increment of income will be consumed. If it is 1 the whole increment will be consumed, if it is zero the whole will be saved.

"This quantity (the marginal propensity to consume) is of considerable im-

Zeitschaift für Nationalökonomie, VII; 299–305 (1936). Reprinted in *Readings in Business Cycle Theory* (Philadelphia; The Blackiston Co., 1944), 193–203. © 1936, Springer-Verlag. Reprinted with permission.

portance, because it tells us how the next increment of output will have to be divided between consumption and investment" (p. 115). Now,

$$\Delta Y = \Delta C + \Delta I$$

$$= \frac{1}{1 - \dfrac{\Delta C}{\Delta Y}} \cdot \Delta I,$$

$1/[1 - (\Delta C/\Delta Y)]$ is, by definition, the multiplier, k.

Or $1 - (1/k)$ is, by definition, the marginal propensity to consume (p. 115).

It follows that if, e.g., the marginal propensity to consume is $\frac{9}{10}$ the multiplier is 10; "and the total employment caused (e.g.) by public works will be ten times the primary employment provided by the public works themselves, assuming no reduction of investment in other directions" (p. 116–117). This result is clearly implied by the assumption: if we assume that an increment in Y is divided in the proportion of $1:9$ between I and C, then we assume that an increase in I by X units will mean an increase of $9X$ in C and an increase of $10X$ in Y. If we assume the marginal propensity to consume to be zero, in other words that an increment in Y is wholly confined to I, then we assume that an increment in I increases Y by no more than its own amount. If the marginal propensity to consume is assumed to be 1, that is if we assume that "the next increment of output will have to be divided between consumption and investment" in the proportion 1 to 0, then, in order not to contradict this assumption, we must assume that any increase in I is accompanied by an infinite increase in C and Y—we assume the multiplier to be infinity.

2

We have now to ask, what is gained by this procedure? In reality nothing more than that a new name is given to the multiplier. The multiplier is defined in terms of marginal propensity to consume. Instead of the multiplier we can always say $1/[1 - \Delta C/\Delta Y)]$ and for marginal propensity to consume we can always substitute $1 - (1/k)$. One and the same thing has got two names.

Now, I do not question that sometimes it may serve a useful purpose to have two names for the same thing, but it seems that Mr. Keynes has fallen into the trap of treating such a relationship by definition as a causal or empirical relationship between investment and income and that thereby a large part of what he says about the multiplier and its probable magnitude is vitiated. By assuming something about the marginal propensity to consume he assumes something about the multiplier, but this is no more an explanation of the multiplier that pauvreté is an explanation of poverty.

Mr. Keynes has adopted exactly the same procedure in his Treatise on Money in respect to differences between savings and investment. As Professor Hayek and Mr. Hawtrey have emphasised, Mr. Keynes there defines savings and investments in such a way that an excess of savings over investments is identical with an equal amount of losses and an excess of investment over savings is identical with an equal amount of profits, so that for excess saving we can always substitute losses and for excess investment profits. But although he has identified these magnitudes by his definitions, he treats them on numerous occasions as cause and effect by saying that a certain event or measure or factor can cause losses or profits only if and in so far as it leads to excess saving or excess investment. If we insert the definition for these expressions this amounts to saying that certain events will cause losses or profits only if and in so far as they lead to losses or profits.

This mistake of treating relationships by definition as causal relationships occurs rather frequently in economics,[1] not only in Cambridge, so that it might be useful to analyse the multiplier case, which constitutes an interesting specimen of this fallacy, a little further.

3

The problem was originally to get a quantitative idea about the secondary effects of a certain piece of investment on employment and income. If the Government spends a hundred millions on road construction and employs thereby directly and indirectly a certain number of workers, how large will be the secondary effect? This is certainly a very important question and since it is impossible to estimate the secondary effect offhand, the problem must be closely analysed and various cases distinguished.[2]

Now Keynes approaches the problem by means of a terminological roundabout way, that is to say, by giving the magnitude in which we are interested another name. He expresses the multiplier in terms of marginal propensity to consume and treats the latter as if it were a thing in the real world which is independent from the former, whilst in fact the two are closely connected by definition—so closely indeed that the author himself on one occasion forgets that they are conceptually not the same and treats them by mistake as synonyms (p. 123 and erratum on p. 403).

I still believe in the superiority of longer over shorter roundabout ways of production of concrete goods, but I am highly suspicious of terminological roundabout ways in the construction of theories. They cannot always be avoided, but they are dangerous, and in the case under review the verbal roundabout method has led to a confusing terminological duplication.

This criticism will be contested. Probably it will be urged that the deprecated roundabout way proves to be fruitful, since it is possible to make, on the basis of psychological observations of a general nature, a number of statements about the approximate magnitude of the marginal propensity to consume—statements which cannot be made directly about the multiplier. To confirm this, chapters 8 and 9 may be pointed to, where Keynes discusses in detail the objective and subjective factors which influence the propensity to consume. I do not question either the validity or the usefulness of these observations, and I readily agree that these psychological considerations do not apply except very indirectly to the multiplier and that therefore, if they are to be used in determining the multiplier, a bridge must be constructed to link them to it. There is, however, this difficulty. If we really can, on the basis of psychological considerations, guess in what proportions an increment in Y, however brought about, will be divided between C and I, we do *ipso facto* estimate the proportion by which an increment in I will increase Y. If we say something about the marginal propensity to consume, we say thereby something about the multiplier. The premise that we can say something on the basis of such psychological considerations about the propensity to consume sounds very plausible: the inference that the multiplier too can be completely determined by such familiar psychological considerations is manifestly precarious. This strongly suggests that something is rotten in the State of Denmark! It is not very difficult to see what is wrong. Keynes has in fact two different concepts of propensity to consume. In his arithmetics he uses it in the formal sense which we have discussed; in this sense it is by definition directly related to, and is another aspect of, the multiplier. In the chapters 8 and 9 where he discusses on what circumstances depends the proportion of man's income which he spends on consumption, he speaks of the marginal propensity to consume in the ordinary or "psychological"[3] sense without realising that this is an entirely different thing. About the latter, we can, of course, make generalizations on the basis of our everyday experience derived from our own attitude towards increases in income and our observations of the behaviour of other people in this respect under various attendant circumstances. But from this the multiplier cannot be directly deduced. Keynes achieves this deduction only by substituting the propensity to consume in the formal sense for the propensity to consume in the ordinary sense. In other words, he now uses the same word for two entirely different things having previously bestowed two words upon the same thing. His terminology exemplifies the paradox of poverty in the midst of plenty.

It is easy to see that marginal propensity to consume in the formal sense, that is, $1 - (1/k)$, is not the same thing as marginal propensity to consume in the ordinary sense. Suppose the latter is unity, that is to say, people spend all their additional income on consumption. What, under this assumption, will be the secondary effects of public works? What will be the multiplier, that is $1/[1 - (\Delta C/\Delta Y)]$? Will the multiplier necessarily be infinite and the marginal propensity to consume in the formal sense unity? Not at all! How it works out, in the end, depends on many other circumstances, a number of which have been treated by Keynes himself and by Kahn, and especially by J. M. Clark, and E. R. Walker. It depends on the leakages discussed by Mr. Kahn[4]; on the time which is allowed to elapse; on the effects of the primary investment on other investment, that is, in the terminology of Mr. Keynes, on the marginal efficiency of capital[5]; on the velocity, especially the income velocity of money. If we say that according to our psychological experience people spend a certain proportion or the whole of their income on consumption, we do not mean that they spend it instantaneously, we mean that they spend it during the income period as fixed by the habits of payment. A multiplier of infinity, that is a propensity to consume, in the formal sense, of unity would involve a velocity of circulation of infinity—an absurd consequence which is not involved by the assumption that the propensity to consume in the ordinary sense is unity. For various reasons which I cannot discuss here, I am inclined to believe that usually the secondary effects of public works will be larger, if the marginal propensity to consume, in the ordinary sense, is larger than if it is smaller. There is, however, no close and unique relationship between the marginal propensity to consume in the ordinary sense (as determined by the objective and subjective factors discussed by Keynes in his chapters 8 and 9) on the one hand, and the multiplier (and the marginal propensity to consume in the formal sense) on the other hand.

It could conceivably be objected that even in chapters 8 and 9 Keynes does not mean marginal propensity to consume in the ordinary sense, but that in the formal sense, and this objection could be corroborated by pointing to the definition of marginal propensity to consume at the beginning of chapter 8 (p. 90). If, however, this were the case, then the analysis of the objective and subjective factors determining the marginal propensity to consume is simply beside the point because these factors have clearly no direct bearing on the marginal propensity to consume in the formal sense and, what comes to the same thing, on the multiplier. In that case it also follows that the guesses about the probable magnitude of the marginal propensity to consume (which are erroneously extended to the multiplier), which are based on the analysis of the objective and subjective factors just mentioned, are unsupported and unsubstantiated statements.

An interesting illustration of the state of confusion is afforded by the following statement on p. 117: "An increment of investment in terms of wage-units cannot occur unless the public are prepared to increase their savings in terms of wage units. Ordinarily speaking, the public will not do this unless their aggregate income in terms of wage-units is increasing. Thus their effort to consume a part of their increased incomes will stimulate output until the new level (and distribution) of incomes provides a margin of saving sufficient to correspond to the increased investment. The multiplier tells us by how much their employment has to be increased to yield an increase in real income sufficient to induce them to do the necessary extra saving, and is a function of their psychological propensities." It is not easy to interpret this statement, since we must remember that, according to Keynes' terminology, aggregate (net) saving is by definition equal to aggregate (net) investment. Suppose, e.g., that roads are being built by the Government with the value of 100 (wage units) and assume further that there are no repercussions whatsoever on other investment which is Keynes' own assumption (first line, p. 117). Then according to Keynes these 100 wage units constitute an addition to total income, investment and savings, all three are being increased by the same amount, whatever happens to consumption. For any net increase in investment constitutes by definition also saving. What is then the sense of saying that income must increase by so and so much in order to induce income-receivers to provide the necessary saving? If we adhere to all the definitions given, the meaning can be only this: On the basis of the objective and subjective factors metnioned above, certain assumptions are arrived at about the actual magnitude of the propensity to consume in the psychological sense. Then the propensity to consume in the formal sense is substituted for the propensity to consume in the psychological sense. The quantitative estimate about the latter is thereby extended to the multiplier. By now everything is assumed. An increase in investment cannot occur without an increase in aggregate income as determined by the multiplier, not, as Keynes says, because otherwise the public will not be prepared to provide the necessary savings,[6] but because we have assumed that it cannot occur otherwise. The quoted statement turns out to be not an empirical statement which tells us something interesting about the real world, but a purely analytical statement about the consistent use of an arbitrarily chosen terminology—a statement which does not explain anything about reality.

4

I do not deny that there are interesting observations and helpful hints in these pages on the multiplier. But they are thrown out incidentally as by-products and are, so to speak, not put in the right perspective. The consequences are rather serious. On p. 118, e.g., in application of the theory, the following statement is made[7]: "In actual fact the marginal propensity to consume seems to lie somewhere between the these two extremes, though much nearer to unity than to zero; with the result that we have, in a sense, the worst of both worlds, fluctuations in employment being considerable and, at the same time, the increment in investment required to produce full employment being too great to be easily handled."

I do not wish to discuss the truth or falsehood of the proposition that, as a rule, under certain circumstances, the secondary effects of increments in investment are such as Mr. Keynes says. It is perhaps possible to demonstrate that our economic world is so organised that the multiplier sometimes works out according to the quoted statement. But Mr. Keynes offers no adequate proof, only a number of rather disconnected observations (which could be used for the construction of an adequate theory). His central theoretical idea about the relationships between the propensity to consume and the multiplier, which is destined to give shape and strength to those observations, turns out to be not an empirical statement which tells us something about the real world, but a barren algebraic relation which no appeal to facts can either confirm or disprove.

Notes

1. The general aspects of methodology are discussed by F. Kaufmann, Methodenlehre der Sozialwissenschaften, Vienna, 1935, pp. 32, 43, 48, 257. See also his article "On the Subject-Matter and Method of Economic Science," in *Economica*, November 1933, p. 387 et seq.

2. Mr. Kahn stated the problem clearly in his well known article in the *Economic Journal*. For a theoretically correct and at the same time realistic discussion of the factors on which the result depends, see J. M. Clark, *Economics of Planning Public Works* (1935), p. 80 and seq., and E. R. Walker's illuminating article "Public Works as a Recovery Measure," in *The Economic Record*, Vol. XI, Dec. 1935. See also M. Mitnitzky, "The Effects of a Public Works Policy on Business Activity and Employment," *International Labour Review* XXX (1934), and H. Neisser, "Secondary Employment: Some Comments on R. F. Kahn's Formula," in *Review of Economic Statistics*, Vol. 18, 1936.

3. The words "formal" and "psychological" are not well chosen. It would be better to characterize the distinction as "aggregate," "*ex post*," relating to society as a whole *vs.* "individual," "*ex ante*," relating to individuals rather than to corporations and governments. Evidently behavior patterns derived from individual psychology cannot be confidently expected to hold of corporations, governments and government agencies. Individual propensities cannot even be applied to groups without paying attention to changes in income distribution. Moreover, in order to obtain *stable* individual propensities to consume, it would probably be better to define them in the Robertsonian sense, that is C_t/C_{t-1} where t and $t-1$ stand for successive time periods. (This footnote was added by the author in 1943. For further elaborations see Haberler, *Prosperity and Depression*, 2nd or later editions, Chapter 8, §4, especially p. 228 et seq.)

4. Some of these leakages, not all, involve the assumption that the propensity to consume in the ordinary sense is less than unity.

5. I am aware that Keynes speaks of net changes in aggregate investments in which these secondary investments are to be included. But to assume these secondary investments as given detracts considerably from the value of the theory. This reveals a significant change in the meaning of the multiplier. Originally it was defined as the ratio of the secondary to the primary employment, when the primary employment is that which is required by the production of a concrete piece of investment. Now that the meaning has been changed, we can no longer speak of primary and secondary. This alteration is symptomatic for the transformation of the theory of the multiplier from an empirical statement into a barren identity.

6. If there is an additional investment this is in itself, by Keynes' own definition, savings and nobody is called upon to provide savings.

7. It should be noted that after the theory has thus been applied to practical problems, Mr. Keynes finds it necessary to qualify his theory very severely. But these qualifications are not expressly extended to the applications. This procedure, which is adopted more than once, makes the book very dangerous for the unguarded reader.

24

Schumpeter's Theory of Interest

1

Schumpeter's theory of interest, which was fully expounded in the first edition of his *Theory of Economic Development* (1912) but had been clearly foreshadowed in his first book, *Das Wesen und Hauptinhalt der theoretischen Nationalökonomie* (1908), is fairly well known, although it has not baen widely discussed in English. Nor has it been widely accepted, but most critics recognize, explicitly or implicitly, that the extreme version of the theory of interest is not an essential part of Schumpeter's dynamic system.[1]

A thorough understanding of Schumpeter's views on the problem of the interest rate requires, I believe, that we distinguish between an extreme and a less extreme version of his theory.

The extreme version culminates in the proposition that in a stationary or quasi-stationary economy, in the *Kreislaufwirtschaft*, the rate of interest would be zero, and that the positive rate which we observe in reality is entirely the result of the well-known dynamic mechanism that Schumpeter has described and analyzed so brilliantly.

The less extreme version admits that there would exist a positive rate of interest in the stationary economy, but insists that dynamic forces not only are likely to raise the interest rate above its stationary level but add, qualitatively, entirely new features to the static picture.[2]

The extreme version of his theory is hardly acceptable. Although Schumpeter spent much time and effort in defending it (e.g., in his famous controversy with Böhm-Bawerk),[3] he frequently made remarks which indicate clearly that he was

The Review of Economics and Statistics, XXXIII (2): 122–128 (May 1951). Reprinted in *Schumpeter-Social Scientist*, S. E. Harris, ed. (Cambridge, Mass.: Harvard University Press, 1951), 72–78. Reprinted with permission.

aware of the fact that this version was by no means essential for his dynamic mechanism.

On the other hand, adherents of what might be called the ruling theory of interest—Böhm-Bawerkians, Fisherians, Knightians, etc. (the differences between them are minor, at any rate much less important than the fierce controversies in which they were or still are embroiled would suggest)—might well admit that there are few branches of static, equilibrium theory that require such drastic alterations, in order to preserve a semblance to reality under realistic dynamic conditions, as does the static, equilibrium theory of interest. Schumpeter was always keenly conscious of, and felt most uncomfortable with, the unreality of many assumptions underlying most static theorizing on the interest rate: existence of a uniform rate, absence of uncertainly, free capital market in the sense that everybody can borrow as much as he wants to at the ruling rate. These are, indeed, most unrealistic assumptions which have far-reaching implications.

2

The discussion of Schumpeter's theory has been concerned almost exclusively with the criticism of the extreme version. That is unfortunate, because in this way attention has been diverted from more fruitful problems connected with the less extreme version.

The extreme version follows from two assumptions which can be formulated as follows: (a) There is no systematic time preference. (b) In the absence of the dynamical mechanism which Schumpeter describes (i.e., the innovator-entrepreneur financed by inflationary bank credit), the marginal productivity of capital is zero, or, in Böhm-Bawerkian language which Schumpeter used, there is no room for more productive roundabout ways of production; it is impossible, in other words, to produce more than a dollar's worth of future income for each dollar's worth of present income that is saved and suitably invested.[4]

Both propositions are highly complex statements about facts which are easily misunderstood but not readily verified or refuted. But whether true or not, it is not difficult to derive their implications. If the two conditions obtain, the consequence is, indeed, a zero rate of interest. That is perhaps most easily seen, if we think in terms of the diagrams introduced by I. Fisher,[5] where present (real)income is measured on the vertical axis and future (real) income on the horizontal axis. Time preference is then defined in terms of the indifference map drawn in that diagram: If the slope of the indifference curves along a straight line from the origin bisecting the income plane is 45° to both axes (perpendicular to the bisecting line), if in other words the marginal rate of substitution of present for future income is unity *in case present and future incomes are equal*, we say that there is no time preference. If the indifference curves at the bisecting line are flatter, i.e., if the rate of substitution of future for present income is greater than unity, there is positive time preference. If the indifference curves are steeper, time preference is negative (the opposite of what is usually assumed).

If there is no time preference, the system cannot be in a stationary equilibrium (i.e., cannot come to rest on the bisecting line) except at a zero rate of interest. The equilibrium will, however, be a stationary one (i.e., the equilibrium point will be located on the bisecting line in our diagrams) only if the marginal productivity of capital is zero. The latter magnitude is represented in our diagram by a transformation curve which shows what combinations of present and future income can be produced. Let us assume that this curve has the usual shape, namely, that it is concave toward the origin ("decreasing returns of future income in terms of present income and vice versa"). The slope of this curve at any point is the marginal rate of transformation of present income into future income. If the slope is 45°, the marginal productivity of capital is zero: By giving up one unit of present income, only one unit can be obtained in the future. If the slope of the transformation curve at the point where it crosses the bisecting line is less than 45° (with respect to the horizontal axis), in other words, if the marginal productivity of capital is positive, the equilibrium point, that is the point where the transformation line touches an indifference curve, will be to the right of the bisecting line, i.e., future income will be greater than present income; in other words, the system is not a stationary one but is an investing and expanding one and the rate of interest (which in equilibrium is equal to the time preference and the marginal rate of transformation) is positive.

Schumpeter did not express his theory in those terms, but from conversations with him I got the impression that he was not unwilling to accept this transcription of his theory into the Fisherian model.[6]

How about the realism of the two basic assumptions? I shall say only a few words on the much discussed question as to whether there is a widespread typically positive time preference or, what is much the same thing, the motives of saving; how many people would save at a zero rate of interest, etc? I should like first to draw attention once more to the fact that I define time preference by the slope of the indifference curves along the bisecting line, that is to say, under the assumption that present and (expected) future incomes are about equal. Time preference is said to be absent, if the slope of the indifference curves *there* is 45°. There can be no question that, even without time preference in the defined sense, somewhere to the right of the bisecting line (not necessarily in the immediate neighborhood) the rate of substitution of future for present income becomes greater than unity, implying that it would require a positive rate of interest to induce an individual to make a further shift toward the future (i.e., to save).[7] But I personally do not doubt that the majority of people do have a positive time preference in the proper sense, at least for more distant periods.

The reason why this is so often denied is, I believe, that the implications of the assumption that there is absolutely no time preference, not even with respect to the remote future, are seldom fully realized. Let me briefly indicate what I mean: It has often been pointed out that a zero rate of interest would imply an infinite value of permanent or nearly indestructible instruments, such as land, railway tunnels, dams, and the like. Let us assume the value of land is not literally infinite, but very high. Would it then not be tempting to sell a little land and use the proceeds for having a good time? Essentially the same argument was used by L. Robbins (*op. cit.*) for other types of capital goods. Some people would consume some of their capital, and that would recreate a positive rate of interest. No good, replies the remorseless logician—the argument is circular, it implies time preference! Whoever has no time preference ought to forego present pleasures even if the reckoning comes only in infinite time! The logician is, of course, right; he has won a point, but has he not lost the argument? Does not the reasoning show that there is, in fact, always time preference? [8]

Turning now to the marginal productivity of capital, two questions must be distinguished: We have *first* the problem which has in recent years been much debated by Knight and the Keynesians as to whether investment opportunities would not quickly be exhausted, if technological knowledge ceased to advance, if no territorial discoveries were made and the population did not increase. The *second* question is whether in an individualistic economy investment can be achieved on the whole or in large part only by means of the Schumpeterian dynamic mechanism, the innovator-enterpreneur supported by inflationary bank credit. In other words, does every major investment scheme, every important lengthening of the period of production or new roundabout way of production require an entrepreneurial feat, or is there at any time or most of the time a large, if not inexhaustible, reservoir of "routine investments" available which are within the grasp of Schumpeter's "static production managers"?

On the first question, we have a group of optimists and of pessimists opposed to one another. The optimists are the Böhm-Bawerkians and Knightians who believe that there is always a practically inexhaustible stock of investment opportunities available even without new discoveries and inventions. The pessimists are, of course, those Keynesians who believe that investment opportunities would be quickly exhausted, if they were not constantly replenished by discoveries and inventions. Schumpeter took a middle position. [9] It seems to the present writer, however, that (for reasons which will presently become obvious) it would have been more consistent for Schumpeter to side definitely with the Keynesians on this issue. I personally am inclined to agree with the optimists, at least to the extent that at any time in modern history there were (and still are) plenty, though perhaps not a literally inexhaustible stock of investment opportunities available, even without new inventions. Let us, furthermore, not forget that, as Schumpeter points out, many inventions are in the long run capital saving. If the automobile had not been invented, who can tell whether investments in railroads and canals would not have absorbed more capital than was actually invested in automobiles, roads, garages, and so on?[10] It would be my guess that, if technological progress came to a halt today, there would be productive investment opportunities for many, many years to come.[11]

On the other question mentioned above, Schumpeter's opinion was that in an individualistic economy[12] large new investments are always made and can be made only by means of his dynamic mechanism. This theory seems to me difficult to uphold in an uncompromising form. But it is a type of proposition which can be partially true. If the optimistic view with respect to the availability of investment opportunities in the absence of technological progress is correct, if there are all the time (or most of the time and for a long time to come) investment opportunities available from past innovations, then it is difficult to accept that large new investments require again and again truly entrepreneurial acts in Schumpeter's sense. Once railroads have been built and electrified and tunnels and roads constructed by entrepreneurial geniuses, the static production managers can continue to copy these things for an indefinite period.[13]

Schumpeter was, however, not entirely uncompromising on this issue. (He never was in such matters; that was precluded by his empirico-positivist *epistemology*.) He envisaged the possibility that progress may be progressively "mechanized" (see *Business Cycles*, p. 1034 and Chapter III, and *Capitalism, Socialism and Democracy*), which would diminish the importance of the entrepreneurial role.

In my opinion, he could have made even greater concessions without damage to his main argument. He could have admitted that there are always practically unlimited investment opportunities of a routine character available which are well within the grasp of the static producer. He might have even conceded that occasionally, as a matter of exception, genuine innovations are introduced by others than by his dynamic entrepreneurs and may be "financed from the depreciation accounts" of old enterprises rather than by inflationary bank credit.

It is true the extreme version of his interest theory would be rendered untenable by these concessions. If they are made, the elimination of Schumpeter's dynamic mechanism would not result in the emergence of a stationary state with a zero rate of interest. The interest rate would not disappear but possibly, though not necessarily (see below), it would fall to a lower level and progress would be slowed down greatly but would not cease altogether. However, his theory that capitalist society as we know it could not long survive such a change (or would be drastically transformed) stands on its own feet and is not affected by the concessions mentioned above. The same is true of the less extreme version of his interest theory, to an examination of which I now turn.

3

The milder version of Schumpeter's interest theory can be set out most easily by stating briefly the "traditional" equilibrium theory and showing where Schumpeter's views deviate and what his theory adds to the classical picture.

By the classical or traditional theory, I mean the "pure," static, equilibrium theory of interest as developed by Böhm-Bawerk, Fisher, Wicksell, Knight, to mention only a few prominent writers on the subject,[14] as distinguished from monetary aberration and disturbances, Wicksell's discrepancies between natural or equilibrium rate, on the one hand, and money or market rate, on the other, and related complications.

According to the traditional theory, there are always investment opportunities available. There always exists the possibility of producing more by longer round-about ways, in other words, to obtain a larger future income for a given amount of present consumption or, in Knight's formulation, to exchange a segment of current consumption against a narrower infinite stream of income in perpetuity. These opportunities are successively utilized as savings become available. If new inventions and discoveries are made, the new investment opportunities either swell the stock of as yet unutilized outlets for saving, provided their expected rate of return is less than the current interest rate; or if this expected yield is greater than the going interest rate, they are utilized, the interest rate is pushed up, and some hitherto utilized methods become extramarginal. If new methods of production are discovered which require less capital than the old methods in use—"capital saving inventions"—they will replace the old methods, probably gradually as the existing equipment wears out, capital is set free, the rate of interest falls, and the margin of investment is pushed out.

In its less extreme interpretation, Schumpeter's theory would accept this picture in principle. It would admit that even in the absence of his dynamic mechanism some investments would be made and intramarginal improvements effected. It would concede that there would be a positive, though probably comparatively low, interest rate. But it would insist that in our world actually not much is being achieved in this smooth and orderly fashion. And it would emphatically deny that economic progress since the industrial revolution can be explained in this way. Not only did things not happen this way—few economists would deny that—but the economic and technological revolution of the nineteenth and twentieth centuries could never have been accomplished, if investment funds had been limited to voluntary savings and depreciation allowances, and if it had not been possible for "outsiders," for an ever-changing group of entrepreneur-innovators, to force themselves and their projects into the circular or quasi-circular flow by means of inflationary bank credit created *ad hoc.*

New ventures are always risky. There is, therefore, no guarantee—in fact there is no likelihood—that established producers or firms in possession of sufficient funds from depreciation quotas or from income will be willing, to any great extent, to finance such new ventures.

Even capital-saving inventions which enable the production of existing weli-known products with the use of less capital are not sure of being introduced by those producers who are already in the field although, ideally, they could be introduced smoothly, without any sacrifice in the form of postponement of consumption being required, by redirecting depreciation quotas.

These "frictions" will necessarily be greater in the case of all those innovations, probably the great majority, that do require new saving and especially of those which involve the introduction of new products, consumers' goods as well as capital goods that do not fit into the existing industrial pattern but require the creation of new industries.

Schumpeter's theory is in this respect in sharp contrast to the theories of Mises and Hayek, which also grew up on the basis of the Böhm-Bawerkian capital theory. While they are of the opinion that the capital stock of an economy could never be permanantly enriched by inflationary credit and forced saving, because what is constructed during the upswing of the cycle will necessarily be lost in the following depression, Schumpeter's theory emphatically asserts that such a permanent enrichment is not only possible but always occurs in prosperity periods. His theory was much more akin to that of, say, Spiethoff or Robertson than to those of his fellow Austrians.

There can be hardly a doubt that there is much truth in his theory and that his dynamic, "disequilibrium" approach to the problem of development and of the business cycle is much more realistic and fruitful than the excessively static "equilibrium theory" of Mises and Hayek. But surely a model like Schumpeter's has to be taken *cum grano salis;* it can be more or less true in the sense that it need not fit every period or every single cycle within a certain period. His mechanism can be disturbed or cease to function, and other forces can produce cyclical fluctuations of the same general nature. Schumpeter was not unaware of all that, although he often was emphatic in his claim of having fully and definitively explained economic fluctuations of different amplitude and length as well as long-run trend since the industrial revolution until our times. He was, however, fully conscious of his obligation as a scholar to substantiate and verify his theory by historical and statistical research, something one cannot say of all business-cycle theorists. Since everybody knows it, we need not dwell upon the fact that his effort in this direction is of truly imposing magnitude and scope and has not been surpassed by any other writer who had to work single-handed in that field.

4

Our discussion has strayed away from the subject of this paper, the rate of interest. This is, however, quite natural and proper because the rate of interest becomes a comparatively unimportant detail in the dynamic picture. But although it is a detail within a detail, a word might be said on whether it is generally true, arguing on the basis of the less extreme version of Schumpeter's theory, that in the dynamic economy—dynamic in the sense that the Schumpeter mechanism is at work—the rate of interest is always higher than in the stationary or quasi-stationary state.

If, as a consequence of Schumpeter's dynamic mechanism, many investment projects are undertaken which otherwise would remain unused, the interest rate will be driven above its stationary level. Increased uncertainty and rising prices will work in the same direction, at least as far as the money rate (as distinct from the "pure" or "equilibrium" rate) is concerned.

But there are countervailing forces at work. Inflationary bank credit supplements the supply of investible funds from voluntary saving and this, one should expect, will depress the interest rate. Morever, the dynamic process creates large incomes which become the most important source of voluntary saving.

Schumpeter's theory of saving is the complete anithesis of the current Keynesian view. He denied that saving is a function of income. In his first book in 1908, long before the appearance of the *General Theory*, he discussed the hypothesis that saving is an increasing function of income and came to the conclusion that "saving is undoubtedly no such [i.e., no 'simple'] function of income." [15] From this argument it appears that by "simple" he meant not an increasing function of income. He argued that consumption habits change with rising income in such a way that people in higher income brackets often save less percentagewise or even in absolute terms than those in lower income levels.

In *Capitalism, Socialism, and Democracy*, he argued that normally people save in order to invest. "It is not only that the bulk of individual savings—and, of course, practically all business savings which, in turn, constitute the greater part of total saving—is done with a specific investment purpose in view. The decision to invest precedes as a rule, and the act of investing precedes very often, the decision to save." [16]

In view of these conflicting tendencies, it is hardly possible to make a general statement with any confidence either that in a dynamic economy the rate of interest will be higher or lower than in a stationary or quasi-stationary state (both terms in Schumpeter's sense). Fortunately, however, this is an unimportant, indeed an idle, question. If it is true that during the capitalist epoch of the last two centuries not only the economies but the whole social structure of the Western World were continuously transformed and revolutionized in the manner which Schumpeter describes—and there can be hardly a doubt that this is true to a large extent—it does not matter whether the rate of interest was a few per cent higher or lower than it would have been if that dynamic mechanism had not existed.

Notes

1. L. Robbins' criticism in his article "On a Certain Ambiguity in the Conception of Stationary Equilibrium" (*Economic Journal*, June 1930) is typical. A more sympathetic treatment is to be found in Samuelson's paper, "Dynamics, Statics and the Stationary State" (this REVIEW, 1943). There is a considerable literature in German, which is, however, largely concerned with methodological questions and has not contributed much to the basic issues. Those German theorists who belong to the neo-classical school—Marshallian, Austrian, or Walrasian—and have concerned themselves with the theory of capital and interest, like Eucken, Schneider, and Stachelberg, have not accepted Schumpeter's theory.

2. It is more correct in the present context to speak of a stationary rather than static economy. In his later writings, Schumpeter sharply distinguished between the two. In the introduction to the Japanese translation of *The Theory of Economic Development* (1934), he says that he "discovered not only that [the Walrasian System] is rigorously static in character (this is self-evident and has been again and again stressed by Walras himself), but also that it is applicable only to a stationary process. The two things must not be confused. A static theory ... can be useful in the investigation of any kind of reality, however disequilibrated it may be. A stationary process, however, is a process which *actually* does not change of its own initiative. ... If it changes at all, it does so under the influence of events which are external to itself, such as national catastrophes, wars and so on." (p.2)

3. *Zeitschrift für Volkswirtschaft*, Vol. 22 (1913).
   In addition, we ought to say "*quasi*-stationary," because changes due to such catastrophes as well as to minor accidents to population growth and even to improvement of the production process are not excluded from the stationary state.

4. In Knight's formulation: It is not possible to exchange, by production, a finite segment of present income for an infinite stream of future income. Since Knight has admitted the possibility of physical disinvestment not only for an individual but for the economy as a whole, i.e., the possibility (within limits) of converting an infinite stream of future income into a finite segment of current income, there is only a verbal difference between his formulation and the formulation of those who, following Böhm-Bawerk (although not necessarily accepting the concept of an average period of production for the individual process or for the economy as a whole), speak of an exchange of a finite sum of present for a finite sum of future income or goods.

5. See his *Theory of Interest, passim*. Professor Fellner reminds me that a word should perhaps be said about the income concept. As is well known, Fisher defines income as consumption, not as consumption plus investment. In the present context, what is given up is, indeed, present consumption, not income. What is substituted is future consumption *or* income (since future income may again be invested). If we keep that in mind, we need not worry about the precise definition of income in the present connection.

6. In spite of his love for pure theory, he was always reluctant to encase his theories of economic development—and his interest theory he regarded as an integral part of it—in an abstract, mathematical model. For example, he was never quite happy with Professor Frisch's mechanical model of his theory. (See R. Frisch, "Propagation Problems and Impulse Problems in Dynamic Economics," in *Economic Essays in Honour of Gustav Cassel*, London, 1933, pp. 203–4). At least as far as his dynamic theory was concerned, he agreed with Keynes that "in ordinary discourse ... we can keep 'at the back of our heads' the necessary reserves and qualifications and the adjustments which we shall have to make later on, in a way in which we cannot keep complicated partial differentials 'at the back' of several pages of algebra ..." (Keynes, *General Theory*, p. 297). He often was torn by conflicting emotions: On the one hand, there was his love for precision and his enthusiasm and admiration for mathematical ingenuity; on the other hand, his impatience with the lack of judgment, ignorance about the complexity of the real world and with the irresponsibility which econometricians often display by the rash and premature application of their models to practical problems. He felt like Keynes that "too large a proportion of recent 'mathematical' economics are mere concoctions, as imprecise as the initial assumptions they rest on, which allow the author to lose sight of the complexities and interdependencies of the real world in a maze of pretentious and unhelpful symbols" (*General Theory*, p. 298). It was largely post-Keynesian writings which aroused such resentment in him. However, Keynes himself may well have shared in these feelings.

7. Absence of time preference cannot be defined as a rate of substitution of unity between present and future income irrespective of the time shape of the income stream, that is, as an indifference map consisting of straight lines at 45° angle. If it were so defined, we would have to say that time preference (positive or negative) always exists. See the excellent discussion in Hayek, *The Pure Theory of Capital*, Chapters 17 and 18.

Lack of precision in the definition of time preference has caused endless confusions in interest theories. Böhm-Bawerk's extensive controversies with L. v. Bortkiewicz and I. Fisher on the question whether his "third ground" (productivity of capital) by itself could explain a positive interest rate without the aid of the first two grounds (time preference), and also Wicksell's intervention into that dispute ("Zur Zinstheorie, Böhm-Bawerk's Dritter Grund," in *Die Wirtschaftstheorie der Gegenwart*, Vol. 3, pp. 199–210, Vienna, 1928, which was Wicksell's last work) suffered seriously from ambiguities in that matter, and Schumpeter's discussion of the problems is by no means impeccable in this respect.

8. In the above mentioned controversy between Böhm-Bawerk and Bortkiewicz and I. Fisher, the last two were right: They could demonstrate that Böhm-Bawerk, when he claimed independence for his third ground, tacitly introduced time preference by assuming that the planning period or time horizon is always limited, in other words that people do not plan for infinite periods. Böhm-Bawerk explained laboriously and inelegantly but conclusively in an appendix of almost a hundred pages to the third edition of his *Positive Theory* (*Exkurs*, XII, pp. 338–434), which hardly anybody ever read, that he assumed the finiteness of the time horizon as an indisputable fact and reserved the expression "time preference" for the subtle psychological myopia with respect to the future.

9. See, especially, Chapter XV, Section G, *Business Cycles*, Vol. II, pp. 1032 *et seq*. On Schumpeter's position on this issue, see D. McCord Wright's illuminating remarks in "Schumpeter and Keynes" (*Weltwirtschaftliches Archiv*, Vol. 65, 1950, pp. 188–90). Cf. also Wright's stimulating discussion of the problem in "The Prospects of Capitalism" (*A Survey of*

Contemporary Economics, 1948) and "Professor Knight on Limits to the Use of Capital" (*The Quarterly Journal of Economics*, Vol. 58, 1944, pp. 331 *et seq*).

10. It is another question, as Schumpeter also pointed out (cf. *Business Cycles*), whether at present many investment opportunities are not of such a nature that, given the existing political climate and current economic policies and regulations, they are effectively closed to *private* enterprise and fall into the domain of *public* investment.

11. Needless to say, Schumpeter had no sympathy whatsoever for the secular stagnation thesis. But the reason was not so much the belief that at any given moment there are inexhaustible investment opportunities in existence, but the confidence that in a free enterprise economy entrepreneurs would always find and create new investment outlets, and especially his conviction that by and large people save in order to invest and that, therefore, if investment opportunities should give out, saving would also vanish (see below).

He probably agreed with Knight ("Diminishing Returns from Investment," *Journal of Political Economy*, Vol. 52, March 1944, *passim*) that investment and advance of knowledge cannot be entirely separated, because investment, even along previously known lines, always teaches new lessons.

12. It would be somewhat question begging to say in a "capitalistic economy" because his definition of capitalism includes this particular feature. "Capitalism will be defined by three features of industrial society: private ownership of physical means of production; private profits and private responsibility for losses; and the creation of means of payments—bank notes or deposits—by private banks. The first two features suffice to define private enterprise. But no concept of capitalism can be satisfactory without including the set of typically capitalistic phenomena covered by the third." ("Capitalism in the Postwar World," in *Post-war Economic Problems*, ed. S. E. Harris, New York, 1943, p. 113.) As it stands the statement is, however, not tautological. For Schumpeter gives reasons why he thinks that an individualistic private enterprise economy would decay and "capitalist society cannot exist" (*Business Cycles*, p. 1033), if there were not a constant stream of innovations and the credit mechanism of introducing them were destroyed. This theory may be wrong or exaggerated, but it is not question begging.

13. This issue was debated by Taussig and Böhm-Bawerk. Taussig argued that the introduction of any "longer round-about-method of production" is a dynamical change which requires a change in technological knowledge and an entrepreneurial act ("Capital, Interest and Diminishing Returns," *Quarterly Journal of Economics*, May 1908), to which Böhm-Bawerk replied that there are always longer round-about ways known which could be undertaken, if only the capital were available (*Positive Theorie des Kapitals*, 3rd ed., Innsbruck, 1912, *Exkurs*, I, p. 17 *et seq.*).

14. As stated earlier, the difference between those authors seems to me not very great. There is at any rate a common core of propositions on which they all could agree.

It is interesting to observe that Walras' Theory of interest has certain similarities with that of Schumpeter. He too regards interest as originating in a progressive economy only. Wicksell criticized him on this point (*Wert, Kapital und Rente*, Jena, 1893, p. 142), while Hicks treats it, perhaps too generously, as a mere slip ("Léon Walras," *Econometrica*, Vol. 2, 1934, p. 346) which could be easily corrected by dropping the assumption made by Walras that "the reinvestment is technically given" and assuming instead that depreciation allowances are reinvested, or rather invested, according to the same principles as new savings.

15. *Wesen und Hauptinhalt*, p. 308.

16. P. 395. That seemed to him the basic argument against the secular stagnation thesis: If investment opportunities give out, saving too will vanish. He was careful, however, to stress that temporary hitches in the flow of saving into investment often occur in depression periods and that government deficit financing is the proper remedy for such conditions.

1

The Pigou effect continues to draw comments.[1] Much of the discussion seems, however, to suffer from an unfortunate mixing of different levels of abstraction and from an unnecessary and historically incorrect interpretation of the theorem as a more or less rigid and exclusive policy recommendation.[2]

I do not know of any modern writer among the adherents of the Pigou effect who has argued that antidepression policy should consist entirely or primarily of making wages and prices flexible by relying on the Pigou effect, that is, on the rise of the real value of cash balances brought about by falling prices to stimulate sufficient expenditure, to relieve a situation of general unemployment. Surely the author of *Industrial Fluctuations* himself is miles away from recommending such a policy.[3]

Let us not forget in what doctrinal situation and for what purposes Pigou enunciated the "wealth-saving relation" (to use Professor Metzler's apt description of the Pigou effect). It was designed as a refutation of the post-Keynesian secular stagnation thesis,[4] which is based on the Keynesian notion of an underemployment *equilibrium* under *competitive* conditions in the labor market, that is, with flexible wages. In the heydays of Keynesianism it was believed that the possibility of a competitive underemployment equilibrium can be proved for the static Keynesian model. This implies, as Pigou points out—referring to Professor Hansen's presentation of the theory in *Fiscal Policy and Business Cycles*—that the argument

is conducted on the level of abstraction where perfect homogeneity and mobility of labor are assumed, so that "full employment" signifies a state of things in which everybody seeking employment at the ruling (uniform) rate of wages is able to obtain it. It does not have the esoteric meaning, which is given to it in much current writing, where full employment is allowed to prevail alongside of large masses of "frictional unemployment." In this article also I shall stand on that level of abstraction.[5]

Journal of Political Economy, LX: 240–246 (June 1952). Reprinted with permission.

The ideal, static conditions under which the Pigou effect has been formulated, assuming away as they do disturbances caused by unfavorable expectations, immobility of labor, bottlenecks, the dead weight of fixed money contracts, are thus of the Keynesians' own choosing. Let us also remember that in the static, Keynesian world with competitive, flexible wages, full employment will be effectively maintained even without the operation of the Pigou effect, except in the extreme cases where either the liquidity preference is infinitely elastic at a positive interest rate or the marginal efficiency of capital is entirely inelastic with respect to the interest rate. Barring these extremes, full employment will be assured, as Keynes himself realized, by virtue of the "Keynes effect," that is, through a fall in the interest rate. The Pigou effect need be called upon to bring about full employment only in the extreme cases just mentioned whose actual occurrence in a static world is highly questionable. It thus effectively removes the narrow remaining basis of what has often been hailed as Keynes's greatest achievement, viz., the demonstration of the possibility of a static, competitive underemployment equilibrium. (This claim does, by the way, decidedly less than justice to Keynes. But any theory which throws doubt upon the feasibility of a well-functioning free-price system seems to be sure of enthusiastic welcome.)

It is not surprising, therefore, that the Keynesians find it advisable to leave the static Keynesian world, which in its simplicity and transparency hardly offers any hiding place, and to seek refuge in the jungle of institutional and dynamic complications in which the real world abounds.

2

Hansen calls attention to the fact that in the real world cyclical fluctuations in output and employment are closely paralleled by fluctuations in the price level. Hence the Pigou effect actually operates as an expansionary factor only during the downswing of the business cycle and possibly contributes something to stopping "the deflation and the decline in output and employment." But it "could never of itself restore the economy to full employment" because, as soon as employment and output pass the lower turning point, "prices and wages will cease falling, and the real value of [money] assets will cease rising."[6]

That prices do in fact move with the business cycle (apart from occasional short lags or leads at the turning points) is not open to doubt, and hence actual cyclical upswings cannot be explained in terms of a continuing upward shift of the expenditure function caused by a sustained rise in the real value of cash and government bonds. I do not know, however, of any economist who has put forward such a theory of cyclical expansion. It surely is completely alien to Pigou's thinking.

But in the static Keynesian model world, wages and prices would behave differently: If there was "thoroughgoing competition" (Pigou) among wage-earners, the (uniform) wage rate as well as prices would go on falling right up to the point of full employment.[7] Why does the real world not correspond to the Keynesian model? Evidently a combination of circumstances is responsible. First, wages (and certain prices) were never very flexible, even before the emergence of powerful trade-unions made wage rates almost completely rigid in the downward direction.[8] Moreover, unions not only make wages rigid downward but tend to push them up even if there is still a good deal of unemployment.

Second, even if wages were very flexible, immobility of labor, that is, the existence of noncompeting groups[9] as well as material and equipment shortages in particular fields, would result in the rise of certain prices as soon as aggregate effective demand expands. There is almost always the important agricultural bottleneck where employment is well maintained even in depressions and where, precisely because there is little slack in the form of unemployment, prices can be expected to rise soon after demand begins to increase. As the expansion proceeds, full employment is reached in other branches of the economy, and the number and importance of bottlenecks increases. But so long as there is unemployment elsewhere, under competitive conditions (flexible wages and prices), the price rise in the fully employed sectors (bottleneck areas) may be only relative to prices in those fields where there is still unemployment and where, hence, prices are still falling. In other words, the price *level* may still fall or remain unchanged.

Admittedly that is not the typical picture of a cyclical upswing. In the cycle of the real world the price *level* starts rising either when or soon after output and employment have turned upward. But that proves nothing against the Pigou effect and the proposition that a Keynesian underemployment equilibrium is impossible without rigidity. First, the price behavior which we observe in the real world is largely due to rigidities. Second, if the economy has passed the lower turning point and a cumulative process of expansion gets under way and proceeds in the familiar fashion financed by a more rapid turnover of money and by new bank loans, the Pigou effect is no longer needed "to restore the economy to full employment." Nobody claimed that it was needed except under the extreme conditions of the static Keynesian system. Third, even sectional (involuntary) unemployment (unemployment in "depressed areas" as distinguished from general or widespread unemployment) is incompatible with *competitive* equilibrium.[10]

If unemployment persists in isolated pockets, with demand for the products in question being inelastic and workers unable or unwilling to move elsewhere, wages may have to fall to intolerable levels, if full employment is to be restored. We could not rely, in that case, on the Pigou effect to eliminate unemployment; but an increase in aggregate money demand would not help either. The analytic equivalence of the two types of policy still exists.

3

Let us take a few more steps away irom the static model into the jungles of the real world. We have dropped the assumption of a homogeneous, mobile labor force. The real world is also complicated by the existence of fixed money contracts and by the fact that price declines may give rise to adverse expectations. For these two reasons it would be foolish to rely entirely on price and wage deflation to cure a depression through the Pigou effect. To repeat, I do not know of any writer who has recommended that kind of policy.

It does not follow, however, either that wage and price rigidity is unimportant or desirable or that the wealth-saving relationship is of no consequence in the real world.

Surely a certain flexibility of *relative* wages and prices is desirable. And in a general depression changes in relative wages and prices will mainly have to assume the form of differentiated wage and price reductions. If there is unemployment and excess capacity everywhere, one would hardly want to recommend that wage and price reductions in some lines must be compensated by wage and price increases elsewhere so as to keep the wage and price level unchanged. It should be easy, however, to prevent, by means of monetary and fiscal methods of expansion, an intensification of a general deflation resulting from such a policy of differentiated wage and price reductions.

Moreover, I find it hard to believe that there do not exist important cases in which investment in certain lines (e.g., in the building trade) or consumption of particular commodities can be significantly stimulated by cost and price reductions without offsetting changes elsewhere. Since it is clearly possible to cripple or damage an industry by excessive wage demands or choke demand for particular commodities by exorbitant prices, the opposite must be possible too. I conclude that flexibility of relative prices is desirable not only from the point of view of correct allocation of resources but also as a possible stimulant of aggregate expenditure.[11]

The importance of the wealth-saving relation goes beyond the case usually designated by the Pigou effect, viz., beyond the effect of an increase in the real value of cash balances and government bonds due to falling prices. Suppose the quantity of money is increased by tax reductions or government transfer payments, government expenditures remaining unchanged and the resulting deficit being financed by borrowing from the central bank or simply by printing money.[12] The wealth-saving theorem tells us that, apart from the operation of the Keynes effect (through the rate of interest), consumption and investment expenditure will increase when the quantity of money grows. I find it difficult to believe that this might not be so.

There is, furthermore, the possibility that the secular growth of real (per capita) wealth may gradually push up the consumption function and, thus, counteract the effect of rising income on the level of saving.

My guess is that the Pigou effect does not play an important role in the actual cycle mechanism. On this I entirely agree with Hansen. But it does dispose effectively of the secular stagnation hypothesis, also in a cycle-ridden world (not only within the static Keynesian model world). In the actual cycle-ridden world the secular stagnation thesis amounts to saying that even at the top of the boom there is no approach to full employment because of a secular insufficiency of effective demand.[13] Let me illustrate what I mean by applying it to Hicks's theory.[14] Hicks's "Equilibrium line" (the "E-line" in his Diagrams 12 and 13, pp. 97 and 121, *op. cit.*) cannot be an equilibrium line except with rigid wages and prices. If wages were flexible, the trend value of real cash balances would grow (prices would fall more in depressions and rise less in prosperity periods), and Hicks's equilibrium ("E-line") would be pushed up to the full-employment level ("F-line"). As far as I can see, the rest of Hicks's theory would not be affected in any way by this amendment. A similar argument applies to similar (nonlinear) models as, for example, those of Goodwin and Harrod.[15]

4

I should like to end my note with a few comments on Metzler's most interesting article. His thesis is this: A theory which accepts the wealth-saving relation differs from the orthodox classical position as exemplified by Ricardo, because the equilibrium rate of interest is no longer determined exclusively by "real" conditions. Metzler tries to show that, if the wealth-saving relation is accepted, certain types of changes in the quantity of money must be assumed to alter the rate of interest permanently. Specifically, if the quantity of money is increased by the central bank's buying securities in the open market, the equilibrium, full-employment rate of interest is reduced.

This somewhat unexpected conclusion follows from three premises: (1) open-market purchases of securities reduce the real value of privately held wealth; (2) this leads, according to the Pigou effect, to an increase in the supply of saving; while (3) there is no reason to believe that the demand for saving (investment) is affected. Hence saving and investment come into equilibrium at a lower rate of interest than before.[16]

Let us examine these three premises. Initially, open-market purchases cause a change in the composition of privately held wealth: the stock of securities (common stock which stands for real wealth) is reduced while the stock of money increases. But since the increase in the quantity of money drives up prices, the real value of money falls again, and the result is a reduction of total private wealth. Within the Metzlerian model there seems to me no reason to doubt that this is correctly deduced. The second premise is a clear consequence of the saving-wealth relation.

Professor Duesenberry has convinced me that the third premise, which I was at first inclined to question, is valid: Since Metzler evidently assumes that aggregate private income remains unchanged (the government, by lowering taxes or transfer payments, feeds back into the private income stream the dividends on the securities which it has acquired),[17] there seems to be no plausible reason why the inducement to invest should have changed one way or the other.

It thus seems that Metzler has proved his thesis: Certain monetary policies do, indeed, tend to affect the equilibrium rate of interest. I do not believe, however, that from a classical standpoint this should be regarded as a disturbing or heretical conclusion. For, as Metzler himself points out, even thoroughly "classical" writers found it necessary to qualify their contention that, broadly speaking, the rate of interest is determined by "real" conditions. For example, if credit inflation changes the income distribution in such a way that the community's propensity to save increases, the real equilibrium rate of interest will fall.[18] I imagine that Ricardo himself would have accepted that proposition.

Metzler's case seems to be exactly analogous. He assumes that open-market operations produce a change in the wealth distribution in favor of an economic unit, the government, which has a different behavior pattern than the rest (i.e., does not save less when its wealth increases). Hence the over-all propensity to consume is changed.

I am sure that Metzler will agree that his model, although undoubtedly an improvement over the original Keynesian model, is still much too drastically simplified a picture of the real world to warrant the deduction of practical conclusions with respect to such complex questions as the one under consideration. He surely does not wish to recommend inflationary open-market purchases (or a capital levy in kind which, as he points out, is strictly analogous to open-market purchases inasmuch as it too reduces private wealth—without inflation at that!) in order to stimulate saving, to bring down the rate of interest, and to accelerate economic growth.

I hasten to add that these remarks are not meant to cast aspersion on Metzler's essay. The great theoretical value of the article is beyond question, but it seems to lie in the most elegant method of analysis and the exemplary clarity of exposition rather than in its concrete results with respect to the influence of monetary or other policies on the rate of interest.

Notes

1. The latest comments are A. H. Hansen's interesting note, "The Pigovian Effect," this *Journal*, December, 1951, and L. A. Metzler's admirable article, "Wealth, Saving, and the Rate of Interest," this *Journal*, April, 1951. See also the revised version of Don Patinkin's well-known

paper, "Price Flexibility and Full Employment," in *Readings in Monetary Theory* (Philadelphia: Blakiston, 1951).

2. This criticism does not apply to the contribution of Professor Metzler, who remains throughout his paper within the confines of his abstract theoretical model.

3. See, especially, chap. xi on "Wage Policy" in Part II of *Industrial Fluctuations*. In the Preface to his *Lapses from Full Employment*, Professor Pigou goes out of his way "to say clearly" that he is *not* "in favour of attacking the problem of unemployment by manipulating wages rather than by manipulating demand" (p. v). The two essays, "The Classical Stationary State" (*Economic Journal*, LIII [1943], 343–51) and "Economic Progress in a Stable Environment" (*Economica*, XIV [new ser., 1947], 180–90, now reprinted in *Readings in Monetary Theory*), where the Pigou effect was formally introduced, are frankly and severely abstract and theoretical; the author eschews any direct policy implications and even disclaims, overmodestly in my opinion, any relevance of his model for the real world.

4. I say "post-Keynesian" because it is not quite clear whether Keynes himself really believed in the secular stagnation thesis as an actual condition rather than a future contingency. It would be easy to quote from *The General Theory* passages where he accepts it along with others which point in the opposite direction.

5. "The Classical Stationary State," *op. cit.*, p. 343.

6. *Op. cit.*, p. 535.

7. If we assume constant marginal cost, prices and wages would fall at the same rate, and the real wage remain constant. If marginal costs rise, prices would fall less fast than wages, and real wages would decline.

8. I cannot agree with Hansen when he denies that "frictions preventing further wage declines so long as any unemployment remains" have anything to do with the fact that prices rise during cyclical upswings, even if there still exists a lot of unemployment. Wage rigidity is not the whole story, but it is surely an important part of the story. Hansen says: "Improved expectations will raise prices and wages in the most perfectly flexible markets" (*op. cit.*, p. 535). I cannot see how expectations could raise wages in a perfect labor market so long as there is much involuntary unemployment.

9. I assume competition among the members of each noncompeting group.

10. Needless to say, I do not wish to minimize the seriousness of such conditions or to recommend that nothing except making wages flexible should be done about them.

11. That there are relations between relative prices and changes in relative prices, on the one hand, and changes in aggregate demand, on the other, has been increasingly recognized in recent years. But no comprehensive theory of this relation has yet been developed. See, however, the article by G. Ackley and Daniel B. Suits, "Relative Price Changes and Aggregate Consumer Demand" (*American Economic Review*, Vol. XL [December, 1950]), for a promising beginning and some references to the literature.

12. Open-market operations are different, because they result merely in a substitution of one type of asset for another; and public works (increase in government spending) result, of course, directly in increased demand for goods and services.

13. I do not think that it would be correct to represent the secular stagnation thesis as merely saying that the cycle plays around a less-than-full-employment trend. For the trend (average rate of output over the cycle) cannot help being below the full-employment level, because it is impossible to imagine that the overfull employment that may exist during part of the boom can be anywhere near the same order of magnitude as the unemployment during the depression. (By "overfull employment" I mean here a situation in which people work temporarily longer hours than they are really prepared to work, or take a job although they would rather stay at home, because, say, of patriotic appeals or because they are under a money illusion or something like that.) If I understand him right, Professor Higgins reaches the same conclusion in his interesting paper, "Concepts and Criteria of Secular Stagnation," in *Income, Employment, and Public Policy: Essays in Honor of Alvin H. Hansen* (New York, 1948).

14. *A Contribution to the Theory of the Trade Cycle* (London, 1950), *passim*.

15. I realize that serious difficulties remain, inasmuch as it is hard to reconcile even cyclical (short-run) unemployment with a fully flexible wage and price system. No adequate discussion of that problem is, of course, possible in this note. But it may be suggested that the simplest, though not the only, solution seems to be the assumption that wages and prices, although flexible in a somewhat longer run, are rigid in the short run. It must be emphasized, however, that this does not imply that cyclical (short-run) fluctuations in aggregate output could be eliminated (they may not even be reduced) simply by somehow making wages and prices flexible in the short run.

16. It is interesting to observe that after the long Keynesian interlude we are back at the old classical position which was so vehemently attacked by Keynes: saving and investment are again equated by the rate of interest. True, the mechanism is not exactly the same as it used to be, the argument has become more sophisticated, and the wealth-saving relation has been added. But let me repeat the reminder: The wealth-saving relation has to be called upon only in extreme cases which may rarely be realized in practice.

17. If he assumed that the government used the dividends for its own purposes and thus reduced private incomes, he could not be sure that private savings would increase; the reduction in private income would tend to reduce savings and thus offset the increase induced by the reduction of wealth.

18. Much more important, I am sure, are dynamic changes as envisaged by Schumpeter. If by inflationary credit expansion Schumpeterian innovators are enabled to carry out their projects and to squeeze out or force into action lethargic, static producers. profound and lasting changes may be wrought.

**The General Theory after
Ten Years and Sixteen
Years Later**

After Ten Years [1946]

1.   I shall confine myself in this essay to the purely scientific content of *The General Theory of Employment, Interest, and Money*, the most famous of Keynes' economic works, whose tenth anniversary unhappily coincided with the death of its author. In the light of ten years of intense and voluminous discussion, what remains of the Keynesian revolution, of the New Economics? What will be the verdict of a historian of economic thought one hundred years hence? There is no doubt Keynes stirred the stale economic frog pond to its depth. He has kept economists in a state of agitation for the last ten years, and probably for many years to come. The brilliance of his style, the versatility, flexibility, incredible quickness, and fecundity of his mind, the many-sidedness of his intellectual interests, the sharpness of his wit, in one word the fullness of his personality, was bound to fascinate scores of people in and outside the economic profession. Only a dullard or narrow-minded fanatic could fail to be moved to admiration by Keynes' genius. But the novelty and validity of the propositions which constitute his system are a different matter altogether—quite independent of the challenging way in which he pronounced them, of the psychological stimulus afforded by his bold attack on widely accepted modes of thought, of much needed change in emphasis which we owe to his book, and of the wisdom (or unwisdom) of his policy recommendations. Apart from a few observations on alleged policy implications of the *General Theory* at the end of this paper, we shall be concerned exclusively with the logical content of the system.

2.   The tremendous appeal of the *General Theory* to theoretically minded economists has been attributed by many to the (alleged) fact that it uses for the first time in the history of economic thought a general equilibrium approach in easily manage-

The New Economics: Keynes' Influence on Theory and *Public Policy*, Seymour E. Harris, ed. (New York: Alfred A. Knopf, Inc., 1947), chap. 14. Reprinted in *Keynes' General Theory, Reports of Three Decades*, Robert Lekachman, ed. (New York: St. Martin's Press, 1964), 269–296. Reprinted with permission of the Estate of Seymour E. Harris.

able, macroscopic (aggregative) terms. There is no doubt, in my opinion, that this made the theory very attractive, especially because such a system lends itself easily to refinement and dynamization. But we can safely assume that the concrete content and the policy recommendations which Keynes and others deduced from his system had even more to do with its persuasiveness (even for his theoretically minded followers) than its theoretical beauty and simplicity.

The use of aggregative systems of general equilibrium is by no means new. All business cycle theories run in macroscopic terms. It is true that most of the earlier business cycle theories are incompletely stated, the number of explicitly stated relations is frequently not equal to the number of unknowns, the structure of the system is such that it is unstable (or does not oscillate, which is bad for a business cycle theory). But even before the appearance of Keynes' *General Theory*, the work of econometricians, notably Frisch[1] and Tinbergen,[2] had done much to clarify these issues and had set higher standards of formal completeness and precision. In fact, these early models, or models of models, were superior to Keynes' system in scientific workmanship because they made a clear distinction between statics and dynamics, while Keynes' system is entirely static, as is well known (although it lends itself to dynamization).[3] Moreover, they were tentative, experimental, hypothetical, not yet frozen into a dogmatic pattern. This made them politically neutral, which, together with the fact that they were expressed in mathematical terms, made them decidedly less accessible and less attractive than the Keynesian system. But there is no doubt that Keynes gave a tremendous impetus to model building, static as well as dynamic.

3.   Let us look now into the content of the system. We shall first examine the individual relationships ("functions" or "propensities") of which it is composed, and then the working of the system as a whole.

Little need be said about the marginal efficiency of capital or demand schedule for capital, because here Keynes follows conventional lines. Investment is a decreasing function of the rate of interest. In the post-Keynesian, Keynes-inspired literature, it has been more and more questioned whether the rate of interest is really such an important factor; in other words, the view has gained ground that the demand curve for capital may be fairly inelastic with respect to the rate of interest. But this is not the position of the *General Theory*, at least not of its theoretical skeleton, although Keynes in *obiter dicta* and policy recommendations frequently accepted openly or by implication the theory of lacking investment opportunities.

The liquidity preference theory of the rate of interest appeared very unorthodox and novel in 1936. The ensuing discussion has made it clear, however, that the only innovation is the assumed relationship between the rate of interest and hoarding, i.e., money held for speculative purposes (M_2) or idle deposits. (Assuming that the velocity of circulation of money, of M_1, remains the same, or if it too varies with the rate of interest, the proposition implies that the velocity of the total money stock

$(M_1 + M_2)$ also is positively correlated with the rate of interest.)[4] The older monetary theory assumed (more or less explicitly) that the demand for hoards is inelastic with respect to the rate of interest. Keynes assumed it to be elastic. The reasons given for this are two: (1) Hoarding is the cheaper (i.e., its opportunity cost is the lower), the lower the rate of interest; (2) the lower the rate of interest, the smaller the likelihood that it will go still lower and the greater the chance that it will rise again.[5]

The older theory was probably more realistic on this point. At any rate, cyclical and other shifts of the liquidity preference schedule are undoubtedly much more significant than its alleged positive slope. A change in the rate of interest of a few per cent, *other things being equal*, is hardly an important factor in determining the volume of hoards. The latter is determined primarily by other factors such as price expectations, general pessimism, temporary lack of investment opportunities, and so on.[6] It is true that some writers, e.g., Kalecki and James Tobin, have managed to compute beautiful correlations between the rate of interest, on the one hand, and the volume of idle deposits, on the other. But the reason is that both are (or until now were) the joint effect of the same cause, of the business cycle. It is quite easy, however, to imagine future ups and downs of business without any significant changes in interest rates. I venture to predict that in such cases we shall still find idle deposits rising in the downswing and falling in the upswing, which would prove that the correlation between hoards and interest rates does not indicate a causal relationship in the sense that people hoard more when a fall in the rate of interest makes it cheaper and vice versa.

Other propositions frequently associated with Keynes' interest theory—e.g., those concerning the connection between short- and long-term rates and the alleged floor, well above zero, below which the rate of interest cannot fall—were frequently discussed in the pre-Keynesian literature.[7] But Keynes certainly improved the analysis and utilized those theorems effectively by putting them into the broader context of a general equilibrium system.

The theory of liquidity stands in great need of further elaboration. It will be necessary to distinguish a larger number of different types of assets than just money and real goods, or money, securities, and real goods. The different types of assets have to be arranged according to their liquidity, with cash on one end of the scale, certain types of finished goods on the other end, and loans, bonds, equities, raw materials, etc., in between. Much work had been done along that line before the appearance of the *General Theory*[8] (and more has been done since publication of the volume), and Keynes himself contributed important elements for a comprehensive theory, especially in his *Treatise on Money*. But these refinements, indispensable though they are for a useful application of the theory to reality, were not incorporated, and were not easy to incorporate, into the body of the *General Theory*—

a fact which should be kept well in mind by those who try to find empirical support for the liquidity prefernce theorem of the *General Theory.*[9]

We now turn to the consumption function. The idea that saving depends on the level of income—other things such as the rate of interest being equal—is an old one. Suffice to recall the fact that scores of writers made the point that inequality of the income distribution is necessary or desirable to guarantee a sufficient supply of capital, because the bulk of saving comes from the higher income brackets. Keynes' great contribution was that he strongly emphasized the income factor and used it much more systematically in the analysis of economic change than had ever been done before. It is true that the consumption function has often been overworked by Keynes and his followers; it has been too rigidly formulated and too inflexibly applied to short- as well as long-run problems without allowing for all the necessary qualifications, such as secular shifts, cyclical fluctuations, the influence of capital gains, and other factors. But on the whole the change in emphasis toward income was needed and beneficial. The strong and exceedingly fruitful accent on income effects, which has become more and more noticeable in recent years in all branches of economics, such as price and demand analysis, international trade, etc., is largely due to Keynes. The same is true of the multiplier technique, whose usefulness should not be doubted, despite the crudity with which it is often used.

4.   Let us turn now to the interaction of the various parts and the working of the system as a whole. Even if it were true that all the materials and tools used by Keynes had been known and used before and that he did not improve them—is it not true that with their help he constructed an entirely new theoretical structure?

His demonstration that unemployment is possible in equilibrium, and his analysis of the factors determining the size and changes of employment and unemployment, are generally regarded as Keynes' most important theoretical discovery. The originality and importance of this conclusion remains unimpaired, it will be said, even if it can be demonstrated that it is derived entirely from well-known premises, just as the work of a great artist remains great even if he uses well known tools and techniques.

According to a widely held view, which can be described as a sort of simplified, popular Keynesianism,[10] the possibility of underemployment equilibrium has been denied by the "classical" school and demonstrated by Keynes. The matter, however, is not so simple as that. This becomes quite clear if we reflect upon the intricate and crucial question concerning the role of wage (and price) rigidity in the Keynesian system. Keynes assumes that (money) wages are rigid downward. If this assumption, which is certainly not entirely unrealistic, is rigidly adhered to, most of his conclusions follow: Underemployment equilibrium is then possible; an increase in the propensity to consume will then reduce unemployment and a decrease in the propensity to consume will produce unemployment (except if, as many classical writers assumed, the demand for idle funds, the liquidity preference proper, is wholly inelastic with respect to the rate of interest). But all this is entirely in accord with pre-Keynesian theory, although these conclusions certainly had not been generally realized and sufficiently emphasized before the appearance of the *General Theory*.

If flexible wages—"thoroughgoing competition between wage earners" (in Pigou's words)—are assumed, the situation is radically changed.[11] Obviously, under-employment equilibrium with flexible wages is impossible—wages and prices must then fall continuously, which can hardly occur without further consequences and cannot well be described as an equilibrium position.[12] This is the weak spot of the Keynesian system which is usually slurred over by the Keynesians.

As in many other cases, two different attempts to deal with this problem can be found in the *General Theory*. The first one, which belongs to what I called the oversimplified, popular version of Keynesianism, is stated early in the book (p. 11 *et seq.*), and has been too readily accepted by friend and foe. It simply says that when money wages fall, prices too will fall to the same extent; therefore real wages will remain unchanged, and since "an increase in employment can only occur to the accompaniment of a decline in the real rate of wages"[13] (p. 17), employment and unemployment will remain the same.

This solution is obviously unsatisfactory and should not be regarded as Keynes' last word. This becomes clear if we consider the solution consistent with the system as a whole which can be found in Chapter 19. There it is pointed out that a reduction in money wages will usually influence employment, but in an indirect fashion, through its repercussions upon the propensity to consume, efficiency of capital, or the rate of interest. The last-mentioned route, via the interest rate, is the one most thoroughly explored by Keynes and the Keynesians. As wages and prices are allowed to fall, money is released from the transactions sphere, interest rates fall, and full employment is eventually restored by a stiumlation of investment. This amounts to giving up the idea of under-employment equilibrium under a regime of flexible prices and wages except in two limiting cases: Full employment may be prevented from being reached via this route, (a) if the liquidity trap prevents a fall in the rate of interest—that is to say, if the liquidity preference schedule is infinitely elastic, i.e., if people are willing to hoard unlimited amounts of money at a positive rate of interest—or (b) if investment is quite insensitive to a fall in the interest rate. Keynes himself regarded both these situations not as actually existing but as future possibilities. But what if we do regard them as actually existing—which as a short-run proposition, allowing for dynamic disturbances through unfavorable expectations, etc., would be by no means absurd? We would still not have established a stable underemployment equilibrium, for wages and prices would still continue to fall. The truth is that what would happen in this case cannot be told within the Keynesian framework, and Keynes himself would have been the last one to stick to it through thick and thin.[14] We must assume that some of the Keynesian schedules would shift.

The most obvious hypothesis would seem to be that the consumption function will shift upward, because of the accumulation of liquid reserves.[15] For we must assume, it seems to me, that consumption is not only a function of income but also of wealth (and liquid wealth in particular) and of other factors which we need not discuss here and which are in fact indicated in the *General Theory* (cf. Chs. 8 and 9). A similar argument would seem to hold for the investment function.

Such extensions and modifications of the Keynesian system are entirely in keeping with Keynes' own injunction aganist dogmatically treating any such system as rigid and sacrosanct. He warns us that the determinant relations and magnitudes of his own system (i.e., the three propensities, the quanitity of money, and the wage unit) are "complex, and that each is capable of being affected by prospective changes in the other"[16]; he says that only "sometimes" (meaning, obviously, in certain context and over limited ranges) can they be regarded as "ultimate independent variables."[17]

It should be clear, however, that even with these modifications the theory is still much too rough for direct application and must be further elaborated and supplemented before it can be used, even in a tentative fashion, for the explanation of reality. In the short run, dynamic repercussions (unfavorable expectations, disturbances caused by bankruptcies and credit crises, etc.) muct be taken into consideration. Pigou was probably right when he insisted that in a cyclical depression negative wages and prices frequently would be necessary to prevent unemployment altogether or to eliminate it quickly once it appeared.[18] The situation in the long run is radically different. Unfavorable expectations and credit crises do not last forever, disturbances caused by bankruptcies disappear, and the assumption of an infinitely elastic liquidity preference and entirely inelastic marginal efficiency of capital schedule is hardly tenable as a long-run proposition. But most economists will agree that it is not only politically easier but also economically more desirable, in the long run as well as in the short, to bring about the saturation of the economy with liquid funds (if required) by increasing the quantity of money rather than by raising its value through a fall in prices. The reasons for and against that proposition (such as rigidity of long-term money contracts, avoidance of industrial disputes, and unjust and undesirable changes in the income distribution, etc.) are the same ones that were discussed extensively in the literature on money throughout the nineteenth century and later in connection with the problem of whether in a progressive economy it is better to let prices fall or to keep them stable.[19] Therefore, the question ought not to constitute an issue between Keynesians and non-Keynesians.

One last word on this important subject. There is nothing in the Keynesian theory to exclude a more direct influence of wage reductions on employment. We stated above that according to Keynes this influence works via repercussions upon the consumption function, marginal efficiency of capital, and the liquidity preference (the rate of interest). In the preceding pages, we discussed the last route. But it is clearly possible that consumption and investment might be affected more directly by a reduction in wages. A reduction in the cost of certain consumption or investment goods may well stimulate demand for them, and for consumption and investment as a whole. Is it not possible that more roads, houses, hospitals, will be built when construction cost is reduced, or that the demand for certain private consumption goods will rise when their price falls.[20] Assume, to make it quite simple, that the elasticity of demand for some of those things, and therefore indirectly for labor, is unity.[21] Then the wage bill remains unchanged and there are no adverse effects through a fall in consumption demand of the workers. Then employment will clearly rise. In Keynesian language we shall have to say that the marginal efficiency of capital schedule or the consumption function has gone up (which one depending upon whether the newly produced goods or installations are regarded as consumption or investment goods), and that it is this shift which has brought about the increase in employment.

One may, of course, be more or less optimistic or pessimistic concerning such favorable direct influences.[22] Keynes' theory certainly does not exclude them.

5.   The gist of the foregoing discussion may be briefly restated from a different point of view or rather (for it amounts to nothing more) in terms of a different economic jargon. I take Paul Sweezy's brilliant obituary note on Keynes as my text.[23] Sweezy regards as the basis of the Keynesian system, and of Keynes' criticism of classical economics, the "flat rejection and denial of what has come to be known as Say's Law of Markets which, despite all assertions to the contrary by orthodox apologists, did run like a red thread through the entire body of classical and neoclassical theory. It is almost impossible to exaggerate either the hold which Say's Law exercised on professional economists or its importance as an obstacle to realistic analysis. The Keynesian attacks, though they appear to be directed against a variety of specific theories, all fall to the ground if the validity of Say's Law is assumed."[24]

What is the content of Say's Law? After the early statements of the Law by the old classical writers, the subject has become so confused by criticism and defense that neoclassical writers only rarely make use of, or allusion to, it. But I think that a careful perusal of Ricardo's formulation (which is quoted by Sweezy) should make it clear what the original meaning of Say's Law was. The passage reads as follows: "No man produces but with a view to consume or sell, and he never sells but with an intention to purchase some other commodity which may be useful to him, or which may contribute to future production. By producing then, he necessarily becomes either the consumer of his own goods, or the purchaser and consumer of the goods of some other person.... Productions are always bought by productions, or by services; money is only the medium by which the exchange is effected."[25]

The meaning of this original formulation of this law seems to me quite clear: It states that income received is always spent on consumption or investment; in other words, money is never hoarded, the money or expenditure stream, MV (in some sense), remains constant or, in still other terminology, money remains "neutral." (Note how clearly the last sentence in Ricardo's passage foreshadows what a hundred years later became known as "neutral money.")

If this straightforward, monetary meaning of the law is firmly kept in mind (which is not easy because of the hocus-pocus accumulated over the years in later classical and anticlassical writings on the subject) two conclusions are obvious. First, Say's Law does not hold in reality; every depression is a proof to the contrary. Second, hardly any neoclassical economist who ever wrote on money or the business cycle thought that Say's Law did hold in reality. The major theme of their theories of money, interest, and the business cycle, is to analyze the causes and consequences of changes in the "intrinsic" or "extrinsic" value of money, of deviations of the money rate of interest from the equilibrium rate, and of other "aberations from monetary neutrality," which are all different expressions for deviations of reality from the ideal state as postulated in Say's Law.

A few neoclassical writers, rather naively, attributed such deviations entirely to the wickedness or incompetence of those in charge of monetary policy, but many, and as time went on more and more, of them realized that these deviations are deeply rooted in the structure of the capitalist system and cannot be easily prevented or cured by slight changes in monetary policy. Some recent neoclassical writers like Hicks and Rosenstein[26] went so far as to deny the compatibility of money and static equilibrium altogether.

Our conclusion, thus, is that there is no place and no need for Say's Law in modern economic theory and that it has been completely abandoned by neoclassical economists in their actual theoretical and practical work on money and the business cycle. That should be clear to anyone who is interested in living science (theoretical as well as realistic) and knows how to distinguish it from verbal squabbles and historical reminiscences in which economists so often indulge. The question must still be asked, however, why Say's Law was more often silently dropped rather than openly repudiated. Why did some older writers (especially Say and J. S. Mill), after having been forced to emasculate the law and to make it tautological, still pay lip service to it?

Liberal prejudices, the inability to rid oneself entirely of the assumption of a pre-established harmony of interests, were undoubtedly a factor, but it would be a bit too crude and naive to rely on this factor.[27] There is a perfectly good scientific explanation (as against a superficial explanation in terms of ideological prejudices) for the lingering doubt concerning Say's Law, the reluctance of some to repudiate it openly and the occasional attempts to uphold it in some rarefied (nonmonetary) form.[28] The reason is the difficulty, upon which I commented above, of reconciling a competitive system with the existence of unemployment. This difficulty has, as we have shown, not been solved by Keynes.

Summing up, we may say there was no need for Keynes to rid neoclassical economics of Say's Law in the original, straightforward sense, for it had been completely abandoned long ago. Keynes was unable, on the other hand, to solve the riddle of how to reconcile competition and unemployment which is at the root of some remaining qualms about the matter in the mind of some writers.

6. We thus reach the conclusion that, as far as the logical content of Keynes' theory goes, i.e., apart from his judgment of the typical shape of the various functions and of concrete situations and apart from policy recommendations, no revolution has taken place; the *General Theory* marks a milestone, albeit a conspicuous one, but not a break or a new beginning in the development of economic theory. The impression to the contrary stems from two sources. The first is excessive and untenable claims made by Keynes and his followers (and accepted too readily at their face value by many of his critics)—claims which are based on an oversimplification of the Keynesian system itself[29] as well as misrepresentations and misinterpretations of the "classical" doctrine.[30]

The second source is differences in policy recommendations. However, if the preceding analysis is correct, differences about policy cannot logically be explained by basic theoretical disagreement but must be explained by different judgments concerning concrete situations, administrative efficiency, the possibility of rational policy making and, perhaps most important, by different attitudes concerning the broad issues of government intervention and central planning versus laissez faire. It follows from our analysis that specific policy recommendations derivable from the Keynesian system are not at all revolutionary. They are in fact very conservative. Laissez faire liberals, like Michael Polanyi,[31] who wish to conserve free enterprise and freedom of consumer choice, are entirely justified in their enthusiastic acceptance of the Keynesian doctrine.[32]

A few words of justification are needed, because fairly radical proposals for equalizing income distribution, and for direct control of investment and the location of industry, have been made under the Keynesian flag, by Beveridge and his group, for example.

In fact, as far as policy recommendations are concerned, we may distinguish two wings of the Keynesian School, a radical, interventionist or even socialistic one to which many of the younger Keynesians belong, and a liberal wing represented by John Jewkes, Polanyi, McCord Wright, and A. P. Lerner (and many others who do not count as Keynesians because, although acknowledging their debt to Keynes, they do not believe that the continuity of development of economic thought has been interrupted by the appearance of the *General Theory*). There are good reasons to believe that at the bottom of his heart Keynes himself belonged to the liberal wing of his school, especially in later years when, after what must have looked to him a victorious battle for the acceptance of his views, he regained some perspective. Even during the years immediately after the appearance of the *General Theory*, when he was carried away by his enthusiasm, he never went all the way in accepting socialism or even anything like Beveridge's radical proposal, although in the heat of the battle against hostile critics he said things that seem to give comfort to his radical followers.

But whatever his real attitude was, my point is that the radical schemes hitched to the Keynesian bandwagon have nothing to do, logically speaking, with the *General Theory*. From the point of view of the *General Theory*, what is needed to prevent mass unemployment is monetary policy and, at the most, a mild form of fiscal policy. Monetary policy would be sufficient, in most cases at least, if the monetary authorities were prepared to extend the scope of their operations, as Keynes proposed, to purchases and sales of long dated securities or possibly equities. If fiscal policy is required, it need not imply increased government expenditures and extended government activities; it could be of the milder, less interventionist form of varying revenues and thus, when necessary, creating a deficit by tax reduction instead of by public works.

I do not wish to say, nor did Keynes ever claim, that such policies would insure literally full employment all the time (much less that they would cure all economic ills and injustices). It can be argued, and I am sure Keynes would have agreed (perhaps he actually said so somewhere), that for quick results in a cyclical depression well-directed increases in government expenditure (public works) would be needed in addition to tax remissions. This does not follow, however, from the *General Theory* but from supplementary assumptions about labor mobility and the distribution of productive resources among industries and localities, compared with the distribution of aggregate expenditure among types of goods and services. Let us not forget that the *General Theory* runs in broad, aggregative terms and is therefore precluded from dealing, and is not designed to deal, with sectional unemployment, which is the result of faulty allocation of resources or of shifts in demand. It is meant to deal only with general mass unemployment resulting from a deficiency in *aggregate* effective demand (deflation). Its author clearly assumed that all other problems would take care of themselves, if only aggregate effective demand was kept on an even keel or raised when necessary, for example when the wage and price level is pushed up by monopolistic and restrictive policies of aggressive trade unions or other pressure groups.

This is certainly a much too optimistic view. Keynes and most Keynesians (especially Beveridge) underestimate, it seems to me, the possible magnitude of frictional unemployment (people on the way from one job to the other) and structural unemployment (unemployed workers in special depressed areas and industries) which, unlike general (i.e., well-dispersed) unemployment, cannot be cured by merely manipulating aggregate demand. They fail to realize, or at least to realize fully, the enormous difficulties, or almost impossibility in the kind of "free society" as we today know it in the western world, to restrain labor monopolies from pushing up wages and thus forcing a rise in prices whenever full employment is approached or even long before that point, in consequence of which unemployment becomes necessary to prevent inflation.[33] Socialist economists like Professors Myrdal[34] and Pigou[35] have seen this problem much more clearly than the Keynesians.

But all this is a matter of judgment about the operation of certain social forces. Although crucially important, it does not involve the principles of the *General Theory*.

7. What has been said in these pages is not intended to detract from Keynes' claim to subjective originality or to belittle his many genuine and ingenious innovations, both in substance and emphasis, or to play down the obvious fact that the *General Theory* has exerted a tremendously stimulating influence on economic thinking. Not only did Keynes inspire a large and growing group of enthusiastic and highly competent followers, especially among the younger generation of economists, but he also spurred on to clarifying and creative work many of those who at first received the *General Theory* with suspicion and skepticism. Keynes forced them to think through things which they used to leave in an ambiguous twilight, and to draw from accepted premises conclusions of which they were unaware or which they left discreetly unexpressed. A classical treatise like Pigou's monumental work, *Equilibrium and Employment* (which is so much more general than the *General Theory* that the latter by comparison appears as a very special case),[36] would never have been written without the Keynesian challenge, although it is not in contradiction to, but rather constitutes a clarification of, Pigou's own pre-Keynesian, "classical" position.

Sixteen Years Later [1962][37]

1. It is now 26 years since the appearance of the *General Theory* in 1936, and Keynes' ideas continue to influence strongly economic theory and policy. Not only does every book on money, business cycles, and related problems refer to and take issue with Keynes' views, but whole volumes and special articles still appear that are devoted to a restatement, appraisal or refutation of the New Economics. Sympathetic reappraisals have recently been attempted by Harry Johnson and D. McCord Wright.[38] Of recent critical works let me mention Henry Hazlitt's two massive volumes: *The Critics of Keynesian Economics*[39] and *The Failure of the New Economics: An Analysis of the Keynesian Fallacies*.[40] Of earlier books two stand out prominently: Pigou's magistral lectures, *Keynes's 'General Theory': A Retrospective View*, an eminently fair and generous reappraisal written with a warm personal touch,[41] and A. H. Hansen's equally incisive, very skillful and immensely popular *Guide to Keynes*.[42]

There can be no question, then, that Keynes' ideas still have a strong appeal and fascination, not only for those who are primarily interested in economic policy and social reform, but also for first-rate theoretical minds.[43] I must confess, however, that after rereading my article on the *General Theory* of sixteen years ago (see p. 581 above), I see no reason to change the views expressed there concerning both the subjective and objective originality and the limitations of the *General Theory*.

To explain my own view, I think I can do no better than to quote from Pigous's reappraisal. "The kernel of Keynes' contribution to economic thinking is to be found," Pigou says, "in a short passage on page 246 of the *General Theory*" (p. 65). This passage reads as follows:

Thus we can sometimes regard our ultimate independent variables as consisting of (1) the three fundamental psychological factors, namely, the psychological propensity to consume, the psychological attitude to liquidity and the psychological expectation of future yield from capital assets, (2) the wage-unit as determined by the bargains reached between employers and employed, and (3) the quantity of money as determined by the action of the central bank; so that, if we take as given the factors specified above, these variables determine the national income (or dividend) and the quantity of employment.

Pigou continues: "Nobody before him, so far as I know, had brought all the relevant factors, real and monetary at once, together in a single scheme, through which their interplay could be coherently investigated. His doing this does *not*, to my mind, constitute a revolution. Only if we accepted the myth—as I regard it—that earlier economists ignored the part played by money, and, even when discussing fluctuations in employment, tacitly assumed that there weren't any, would that word be appropriate. I should say rather, that, in setting out and developing his fundamental conception, Keynes made a very important, original and valuable addition to the armoury of economic analysis" (pp. 65–66).

In the Keynesian passage quoted above, one of the "ultimate and independent variables"—"exogenous variables" we would say today—is the wage unit. This is the assumption of rigid wages. Keynes' analytic contribution consists largely in working out the implications of that assumption. It is now almost generally recognized that the Keynesian theoretical system proper (apart from the discussions of related matters and of the hints and asides that can be found in profusion in the *General Theory*) depends on the assumption of wage rigidity. If that assumption is not made, the Keynesian system simply breaks down or, to put it differently, it loses its distinctive and differentiating quality which sets it apart from what is loosely called the "classical" system.[44]

It is true that later in the book (see Chs. 18 and 19) Keynes extensively discusses changes in money wages, especially what will happen if unemployment drives down money wages. In the earlier parts of the book the oversimplified theory is put forward that when money wages decline prices will fall exactly as much as wages and hence unemployment can not be cured by making money wages flexible, in other words by introducing competition in the labor market. In Chapter 19, in contrast, it is conceded that full employment would be restored via a fall in interest rates ("Keynes effect")—except in the unlikely case that the liquidity schedule was entirely elastic ("liquidity trap") or investment unresponsive to falling interest rates. From the comparative static point of view, the Pigou effect definitively disposes of the possibility that the liquidity trap or inelastic investment schedules prevent the attainment of full employment.

Needless to add that the Pigou effect was not meant to be an easy policy prescription[45] and that in the short run friction and expectational complications (vicious spirals of deflation, waves of pessimism, expectation of falling prices and wages) may confuse things and prevent the quick restoration of full employment. Some "classical" writers realized before Keynes that it was not easy to make wages flexible in the short run and that even if it could be done it would not immediately eliminate all cyclical unemployment. Let me recall that Pigou in his *Industrial Fluctuations* had said that in a depression it might require "negative wages" to restore full employment quickly.

There can be no doubt, however, that the theory of the "Keynes effect," the "Pigou effect," or more generally the "wealth-saving relation," constitute a permanent enrichment to our analytical apparatus: this we largely owe to the stimulus provided by the *General Theory*. Keynes forced the classical writers to rethink, restate and to refine their theories.[46]

It should be observed, however, that Keynes carefully qualified his theory (at least in the passage quoted above)[47] by saying that the variables mentioned can only "sometimes" be taken as independent. He clearly wanted to restrict his theory to short-term analysis and he surely would have strongly disapproved of using it for long-run analysis.

The sin of applying the short-run Keynesian theory to long-run problems has been flagrantly committed in the Harrod-Domar models of secular growth. Surely in the long run Keynes' "ultimate independent variables" can no longer be taken as independent. In fact, many of the growth models are even more restrictive than the Keynesian system because they postulate not only constant consumption and investment *functions*, but constant (or only exogenously changing) capital-output and consumption-income *ratios*. Growth models have been gradually purged of their unnatural and unrealistic rigidity and instability by Duesenberry, Kaldor, Smithies, Solow, and others. Growth theory has, thus, slowly and laboriously worked its way back to the "classical" position—a process which has reached its high point, so far, in Meade's *Neo-Classical Theory of Growth*.[48]

As far as money wages are concerned, even if they are completely rigid in the long run, prices need not be rigid, at least not in a progressive economy. Increasing productivity would permit a gradual lowering of the price level provided money wages rise less fast than output per worker. Only if to wage rigidity downward is added an inexorable wage push upward do we really get into a nasty dilemma, also in the long run.

But whatever one believes to be actually the case, one thing is clear and should have been clear from the beginning. As soon as we assume wage rigidity and wage push, in the short or long run, the main difference between Keynes and the classics disappears, and with it vanishes what many Keynesians regard as Keynes' greatest achievement—the demonstration of the possibility of an underemployment equilibrium. There is no difficulty in "classical theory" with any amount of involuntary unemployment, if wages are rigid and the rigid floor is pushed high enough.

What Lerner said in his brilliant contribution to the great debate on the "*General Theory* After 25 Years" at the A.E.A. meeting in 1960 is quite true: "almost all of the 'revisions' of Keynes [that have been proposed] are to be found as implications and hints in [the *General Theory*]." But is it not equally true that almost all of Keynes' innovations (insofar as they are valid) can be found as implications or hints (or sometimes quite explicitly) in pre-Keynesian and post-Keynesian "classical" writings?

I do not agree with Lerner that the *Gerneral Theory* would necessarily have become three times as long, if Keynes had "spelled out all hints and implications." After all, Pigou's *Employment and Equilibrium*,[49] a really general theory which comprises the *General Theory* as a special case, is much shorter than Keynes' great book. But Lerner is certainly right that the *General Theory* would have been much less influential if the hints had been fully worked out, if, in other words, the book had offered a really general theory. It surely would not have been as successful as it actually was had it been built on existing foundations and had it done justice to earlier writers; had its author refrained from setting up a caricature of "the classical economics" as a straw man to be knocked down; in other words, had he written a scholarly, well-balanced treatise instead of providing an *ad hoc*, makeshift theory serving as underpinning for a combination of a policy tract, a passionate call for economic reforms, and an impassioned indictment of orthodoxy.

2. Turning to the impact of the *General Theory* on economic policy, it is certainly true that economic policy everywhere is very different from what it was in the 1920's and 1930's; furthermore, it cannot be denied that the change that has taken place can be broadly described as a shift in the Keynesian direction. There is much more concern with employment, less hesitation to use deficit financing and little heed is paid to the canons of "sound finance." This is still true despite certain latter-day reactions—the "rediscovery of money and monetary policy" and what E. Lundberg has called the "anti-Keynesian counter-revolution."

I doubt very much, however, whether all that would have been much different if Keynes had never written the *General Theory*. My reasons are the following: A number of countries had already changed their policy in the "Keynesian" direction before the appearance of the *General Theory* and others changed it demonstrably without having been influenced by Keynes. Australia and Sweden are examples of the former and Nazi Germany of the latter category. In all these countries (including Germany) high-quality scientific rationalizations of expansionary policies had appeared which were not influenced by Keynes. No single one of these writings can compare with Keynes in breadth, originality, elegance, brilliance, and none had the sustained influence of the *General Theory*. But their cumulative impact has profoundly changed the climate of opinion and brought about the shift in economic policy. In all developed industrial countries policies of economic recovery, stabilization, and growth have been much more successful after the second World War than after the first. But it is difficult to attribute this to the spread of Keynesian thinking. It so happens that none of the economists and economic statesmen who were largely responsible for the assorted postwar economic miracles can be called a Keynesian: not Camille Gutt in Belgium, nor Luigi Einaudi in Italy, nor Ludwig Erhard in Germany, nor Reinhard Kamitz in Austria, nor Jacques Rueff in France. The greatest economic miracle of all, the Japanese, seems to have been performed by conservative Japanese governments and statesmen with the help of some ultraconservative American advisers, while the numerous Keynesians and Marxo-Keynesians had to look on in impotent opposition.

3.   I have argued that the Keynesians greatly exaggerate the originality and validity of the *General Theory* as well as the influence which Keynes has exerted on the great changes that have occurred in economic policy during the last twenty-five years. Let me emphasize again, as I did in 1946, that I do not wish in the least to belittle Keynes' claim to greatness and subjective originality. As I see it, what is true of other sciences, among them the queen of sciences, mathematics, is also true of economics, pure and applied: the accumulated mass of knowledge is so enormous that it has become impossible for any single man, however great a genius he may be, to bring about a real revolution. It does, of course, require men of genius to increase the stock of knowledge, but the contribution of any single one is small compared with the existing stock. Even the greatest stand on the shoulders of those who went before, and in mathematics[50] it has happened many times that great discoveries firmly associated with great names were later found to have been discovered earlier, but were then ignored because the time simply was not ripe. The time surely was overripe and the ground fully prepared for the message of the *General Theory*. Let us admire without stint the great genius but avoid untenable exaggerations. Hero worship is nowhere less appropriate than in science.

Notes

1. See his famous contribution to the Cassel *Festschrift*, "Propagation and Impulse Problems," 1933.

2. For example, in "Suggestions on Quantitative Bussiness Cycle Theory," in [*Econometrica*], 1935.

3. What is strictly static in the *General Theory* is the theoretical skeleton as precisely stated in several places in the book (e.g., p. 245 *et seq.*, or p. 280 *et seq.*) and later formalized by Lange, Meade, and others. The text surrounding the theoretical statements in the *General Theory* contains, of course, many dynamic considerations. The frequent use made of the expectation concept shows the dynamic intent. But the dynamic elements are not incorporated into the theory. All the functions stated are strictly static.

4. The proposition was clearly foreshadowed in the earlier ("classical") literature. See, e.g., Lavington, *English Capital Market* (1921), p. 30. "The quantity of resources which [an individual] holds in the form of money will be such that the unit of resources which is just, and only just, worth while holding in this form yields him a return of convenience and security equal to the yield of satisfaction derived from the marginal unit spent on consumables, and equal also to the net rate of interest."

See also Pigou, "The Exchange-Value of Legal-Tender Money," in *Essays in Applied Economics* (1922), pp. 179–81. In his later, post-Keynesian writings Pigou always makes a specific assumption with respect to the policy followed by the banking system. In what he calls the "normal" case the banks act in such a way as to allow the quantity of money to rise and fall with the rate of interest. (See, e.g., *Equilibrium and Employment*, p. 61.)

This latter-day Pigovian approach, institutional in nature, seems to me more realistic than the Keynesian liquidity preference theory. The latter is clearly a direct descendant of the penetratingly classical Cambridge type of quantity equation (as Hicks pointed out in his paper, "Mr. Keynes and the Classics," *Econometrica*, Vol. 5, 1937), and suffers from the same weakness as its parent concept, viz., excessive utilization of a marginalistic psychology in a field where a frankly institutionalistic analysis is much more fruitful.

5. We may, perhaps, say in Hicksian terminology: The lower the rate of interest, the smaller the elasticity of expectation of future rates.

6. I do not deny that hoarding and changes in the velocity of circulation have been much neglected in the literature, and that it is a mistake (of omission rather than commission) to regard these phenomena as data (or as occasional disturbances) instead of explaining them systematically. The point is that the level of the rate of interest as such is a comparatively unimportant factor.

Expectations of changes in interest rates are, however, a different matter. But the state of expectation is a complicated matter, and no simple formula, such as the one suggested in the preceding footnote, can do justice to its complexity.

Professor W. Fellner in his elaborate and searching investigation of the subject reaches the conclusion "that the elasticity of liquidity provisions with respect to interest rate is not likely to be high" (*Monetary Policy and Full Employment*, Berkeley, 1946, p. 200).

7. E.g., in I. Fisher, *The Theory of Interest* (in the third approximation of his theory), or Karin

Kock, *A Study of Interest Rates* (London, 1929). See, especially, Chapter VII, "Short and Long Rates of Interest."

8. Cf., for example, Hicks "Gleichgewicht und Konjunktur" in *Zeitschrift für Nationalökonomie*, Vol. 4, Vienna. 1933.

9. In all attempts at verification, the liquidity preference theory is applied to the choice between (a) cash (including bank notes and deposits) and (b) the next item on the scale, viz., shortest-term securities, in other words, between (a) money and (b) near-money (i.e., money's closest substitute). For that very limited choice (i.e., the decision whether to hold one's idle funds in cash or short-term securities) the short-term rate of interest may indeed be an important factor. But that choice is an unimportant detail as far as expenditures on goods and the volume of output and employment are concerned. And any empirical regularities found with respect to this detail cannot be regarded as a verification of the liquidity preference theorem in a rougher model which does not distinguish a whole scale of different assets with small gradations in liquidity, but only two or three types of assets.

10. Unfortunately, there is much of this oversimplified version in the *General Theory* itself, especially in the three summarizing chapters in Book I. A sociology of the formation of scientific schools will attribute much importance to this fact. It helped to crystallize a compact group of followers by repelling and annoying some readers and attracting others.

11. The crucial importance of wage rigidity in the Keynesian system has been emphasized by many critics, most systematically perhaps by Franco Modigliani in his remarkable article "Liquidity Preference and the Theory of Interest and Money," *Econometrica*, January, 1944.

12. A logical possibility would, of course, be that all money expressions (prices, wages, money values) fall continuously, while the real magnitudes including employment remain the same. That would be the implication of the assumption that the Keynesian relations remain unchanged in real terms in the face of such a situation. But this case is surely too unrealistic to be seriously contemplated.

13. Professor Hansen objects to my quoting this passage because it "fails to include the very important conditions which must be assumed to make the statement [as quoted from Keynes] true, namely, no change in 'organization, equipment and technique'; in other words, no change in productivity. Moreover, Keynes (March, 1939, [*Economic Journal*]) explicitly repudiated the notion that employment must increase *by or through* a lowering of real wages and a movement *along* a declining so-called general demand curve for labor. In his view "employment is increased by raising effective demand thereby causing an upward *shift* in the demand curve for labor." (*Review of Economic Statistics* Vol. 28, Nov., 1946, p. 185. See also Chap. XII.)

It is true Keynes did qualify his statement by the clause "with given organization, equipment, and technique" (p. 17). But in the present context the qualification is irrelevant. For in the short run (and the problem under discussion is essentially a short-run problem) Keynes always assumes "organization, equipment, and technique" constant. In *Economic Journal*, March, 1939, Keynes took issue with Dunlop's and Tarshis' criticism; he there was very reluctant to give up his generalization. "I still hold," he said, "to the main structure of the argument, and believe that it needs to be amended rather than discarded" (p. 40). He tried to reconcile Dunlop's and Tarshis' findings with his theory *without* dropping the assumption of constant organization, equipment, and technique.

It is, of course, true that according to Keynes "employment is increased by raising effective demand," but he thought (with certain tentative qualifications as enumerated in the quoted article) that, by a rise in effective demand, prices are necessarily raised more and faster than money wages, and that therefore a rise in effective demand is always associated (in the short run) with a fall in real wage rates.

Keynes' reluctance to drop his hypothesis is understandable because a change of view would have required far-reaching modifications of his whole theoretical structure. He, after all, had emphasized that he was "not disputing this vital fact which the classical economists have (rightly) asserted as indefeasible" (*General Theory*, p. 17). He had argued emphatically that, if workers could effectively bargain about real wages rather than merely about money wages, unemployment could always be eliminated by wage bargains at lower wages. The disputed proposition is, thus, deeply embedded in Keynes' theory.

I personally always felt that Keynes' dogmatic insistence on the proposition in question was due to the excessively static nature of his theory. If Keynes had incorporated swings of optimism and pessimism in his theory, he would have had no difficulties in admitting that an expansion can raise not only money but also real wages (even in the short run, i.e., with organization, equipment, and technique unchanged). The plain fact is that Keynes' theory is not only more static but in several respects also more "classical" than, for example, Pigou's *Industrial Fluctuations*, where it had been pointed out that "the upper halves of trade cycles have, on the whole, been associated with higher rates of real wages than the lower halves." (1929 edition, p. 238.)

14. See the following paragraph, and footnotes 16 and 17 below.

15. If wages and prices fall, the real value of the money stock will increase beyond all limits. I called attention to this fact and its probable effect on consumption in the first edition of my *Prosperity and Depression* (1937) without then using the term "propensity to consume." Pigou has since stressed it repeatedly. Kalecki in his brief note, "Professor Pigou on the Classical Stationary State—A Comment" *Economic Journal*, April, 1944, p. 131), in principle conceded the argument that a rise in the real value of the money stock will act as a stabilizer in a period of falling prices. He makes, however, the point that this argument applies only to gold and bank notes which are not issued by the banks through making loans or through purchases of private securities; for in the case of bank money issued against loans and private securities, the rise in the real value of money is canceled by the rise in the real value of the corresponding bank assets (loans and securities) which are liabilities of the public. (The net worth of the public is, therefore, not increased by the fall in the price level.)

However, as long as there is money which is not issued against private evidences of indebtedness, Kalecki's argument is invalid from the theoretical point of view, because *money* wages and prices (*note*: real wages need not fall) can always fall sufficiently to raise the real value of gold money to any level necessary, however small the (dollar) value of gold or gold certificates in circulation.

From a practical point of view, however (i.e., taking account of frictions, disturbances through expectations, etc., which are assumed away in the pure model), Kalecki's argument is important. But I need not go into that, because I believe (and I think this is also Pigou's view; cf. the Preface to his *Lapses from Full Employment*) that the model under consideration is much too simplified to be useful for practical application. (See next paragraph in the text.) It should be observed that the simplifications are essentially the Keynesian ones.

16. *General Theory*, p. 184. What is said of *prospective* changes naturally holds also of the *actual* level and *actual* changes.

17. *Ibid.*, pp. 246–47. Cf. also p. 297.

18. See, e.g., his *Industrial Fluctuations*, 2nd ed. 1929, p. 225.

19. The older literature which dealt with these questions under various guises and in outmoded terminologies is extensively reviewed in C. M. Walsh, *The Fundamental Problems of Monetary Science* (New York, 1903). In the present case the argument for increasing the quantity of money and holding the price level constant is, of course, much stronger than in the historical case mentioned, because in the present case all prices (including factor prices) would have to fall, while in the other case it was for the most part a question of keeping factor prices stable and letting product prices fall *vs.* keeping product prices stable and letting factor prices rise. But the point is that many of the arguments used there are relevant for the present case too.

20. It can hardly be denied that it is possible to raise construction cost of houses, etc. (to mention a much discussed case) to such an extent that the demand for houses is seriously restricted. It obviously follows from this proposition that a reduction of such cost (brought about by elimination of monopolistic and restrictive practices on the part of labor and contractors, etc.) may stimulate demand for homes (investment). It is generally assumed that cost reducing innovations (e.g., prefabrication of houses) can stimulate investment. Why should then a reduction of labor costs not be capable of bringing about the same result?

21. If the elasticity of demand is not unity, we get a much more complicated situation, which cannot be discussed here. But much of the argument could be adapted to fit that case.

22. It is true, Keynes calls such influences "roundabout repercussions" (p. 257) and criticizes older writers for assuming a "direct" effect of wage reductions on employment. But, as I pointed out in my *Prosperity and Depression* (2nd or later editions, p. 241), what to call direct or indirect is a purely terminological question. The most direct effect imaginable Keynes calls "roundabout" because, by definition of the terms, it must imply a change in the propensity to consume or in the marginal efficiency of capital.

23. *Science and Society*, Vol. X, 1946, pp. 396–406. See also Part One above.

24. *Ibid.*, pp. 400–1.

25. *Principles of Political Economy* (Gonner, ed.), pp. 273 and 275. The following quotation from Say clearly conveys the same meaning: " . . . a product is no sooner created than it, from that instant, affords a market for other products to the full extent of its own value. When the producer has put the finishing hand to his product, he is most anxious to sell it immediately, lest its value should vanish in his hands. Nor is he less anxious to dispose of the money he may get for it; for the value of the money is also perishable. But the only way of getting rid of money is in the purchase of some product or other. Thus the mere circumstance of the creation of one product immediately opens a vent for other products." Jean-B. Say, (*Treatise on Political Economy*, Prinsep edition, Boston, 1921.) In later editions, Say obscured and attenuated the original meaning more and more through his attempts to meet criticisms by Malthus and Sismondi. He was forced to redefine the terms until the whole proposition became an empty tautology. See, for a brief account, P. N. Rosenstein-Rodan, "A Co-ordination of the Theories of Money and Price," *Economica*, 1936, pp. 268–9; and H. Neisser, "General Overproduction:

A Study of Say's Law of Markets." *Journal of Political Economy*, Vol. 42, 1934, reprinted with revisions in *Readings in Business Cycle Theory* (1944), pp. 385 *et seq.*

26. Even Hayek should be mentioned here. This becomes clear if we reflect that the extremely complicated nature of a monetary system which is neutral in his sense makes the existence of neutral money in practice utterly impossible.

27. Very sophisticated writers whom it would be utterly absurd to accuse as capitalist or orthodox apologetics (especially inasmuch as they are often on the other side of the fence as far as their political convictions are concerned) have been attracted by the intricacies of the problem and have refrained from rejecting Say's Law out of hand. Cf., for example, the articles by Neisser and Rosenstein-Rodan mentioned above and some of the literature there quoted.

28. Something like the following formulation is probably in the back of the minds of many writers: Any amount of money expenditures, however small, can buy any volume of goods offered for sale, provided prices are flexible and are low enough. This is obviously an arithmetic truism which cannot be denied, but is not very useful.

29. For example, the proposition that in the Keynesian system the rate of interest is independent of the marginal efficiency of capital and the propensity to save. Or the misconceptions concerning the role of the assumption of rigid wages.

30. For example, the proposition, which is closely connected with the misconception of the role of wage rigidity in the Keynesian system, that there is no room for "involuntary" unemployment in the "classical" system. Another misconception is the view that classical economics assumed that an act of saving always brings about a corresponding act of investment, while in the Keynesian system the two types of decisions are independent of each other, although aggregate saving and investment are equalized ex-post by appropriate changes in income. In reality, the neo-classical literature, especially its Wicksellian branch, stressed the fact that new saving *may* fail to induce new investments, with a consequent fall in money income and usually also in real income.

31. See his *Full Employment and Free Trade* (Cambridge, 1945).

32. As a chemist, Mr. Polanyi can be pardoned for overlooking the fact that his conclusions could have been derived from economic principles widely accepted before the appearance of the *General Theory* (which, of course, does not mean that those conclusions were *generally* accepted before Keynes).

33. I do not say that historically all depressions have come about for this reason. I only say that if it were possible to stabilize aggregate demand and to prevent depressions arising from other causes, the factor mentioned in the text would make it very hard to maintain full employment for some length of time.

34. Cf. *Monetary Equilibrium* (1939), esp. pp. 143−147 and 155−156.

35. *Lapses from Full Employment (1945), passim.* See also the illuminating review of Pigou's book by Professor Hicks, *Economic Journal*, Dec., 1945, pp. 398−401. Professor Hicks seems substantially to accept Pigou's conclusions, although he finds them "sour."

36. The superiority of Pigou's great work has been recognized by so Keynesian a critic as N. Kaldor (*Economic Journal*, December, 1941). It is a pity that another work of outstanding

originality and scholarship which was stimulated by Keynes' challenge, viz. A. W. Marget's *The Theory of General Prices* (1938–42), has not yet exerted the influence which it should have.

37. Written in October 1962.

38. H. G. Johnson, "The 'General Theory' After 25 Years." *American Economic Review*, May 1961, pp. 1–17. D. McCord Wright, *The Keynesian System*, Fordham, New York, 1962.

39. Van Nostrand, New York, 1960. This is a very useful collection of old and new essays dealing critically with Keynesian issues. The contributions range from J. B. Say and J. S. Mill to Mises, Knight, Hayek and Röpke.

40. Van Nostrand, New York, 1959.

41. St Martin's, New York, 1953. It will be recalled that Pigou's first reaction to *The General Theory* was very negative (review article in *Economica*, London, 1936, pp. 115–132). He evidently was greatly annoyed by "what seemed to [him] misrepresentations of things that other people had written" (p. 1). In his reappraisal all bitterness is gone and Pigou confesses that in his original review article of the *General Theory* he had "failed to grasp its significance and did not assign to Keynes the credit due for it" (p. 65). See below what Pigou in his reappraisal regarded as the basic contribution of the *General Theory*.

42. McGraw-Hill, New York, 1953.

43. I do not know, however, of any theorist who has embraced Keynes' theory for its own sake—that is to say, a theorist who either takes no interest in questions of policy and reform (if there still exist such individuals), or one who lacks sympathy for the policies and reform measures Keynes stood for. Professor Jewkes, if he can be described as a Keynesian, could possibly be said to fall into the latter category and thus constitute an exception that proves the rule. I should perhaps add that in my opinion it is logically quite possible to deduce from Keynes' theory conservative and laissez faire policy conclusions if the appropriate assumptions are made about the concrete shape of some of Keynes' functions and about administrative and political feasibility, etc.

44. Following Hicks, many writers see the difference between the Keynesian and the "classical" system in the shape of the liquidity function—the "classical" writers assuming that it is inelastic with respect to the rate of interest; in other words, that the velocity of circulation of money is constant (or an exogenous variable). This does not seem to me a very important difference and it is not correct that nobody before Keynes had suspected that the velocity of circulation of money may be influenced, among other things, by the rate of interest.

45. See my "The Pigou Effect Once More," in *Journal of Political Economy*, June 1952, reprinted in my *Prosperity and Depression*, Harvard, Cambridge 1958, Appendix II. [Chap. 25, this vol.]

46. It should be clear, however, that quite possibly wage reductions influence employment directly (rather than via the Keynes or Pigou effect). This simple truth has been obscured by the fact that in the Keynesian system the most direct effect that can be imagined—e.g., a rise in demand for, and employment of, domestic servants when their wage falls—has to be described as being operative via a change in the propensity to consume (or via a change in the marginal efficiency of capital if the services in question were those of engineers and not those of houshold help).

47. The *General Theory* abounds, however, with unqualified statements—hence everybody can find what he wants.

48. The statement that this quasi-Hegelian process—thesis, antithesis, synthesis—has largely vindicated the "classical" thesis, because if properly understood it turns out to be substantially identical with the emerging synthesis, does not change the fact that the process has been very productive of clarification and refinement. The ways of the human mind are often devious and roundabout.

49. Pigou relates (*op. cit.* p. 65) that "when I wrote my *Employment and Equilibrium* in 1942 and again when I revised it recently, I had not read the *General Theory* for some time and did not realize how closely my systems of equations conform with the scheme of his analysis."

It is, however, quite safe to say, it seems to me, that Pigou would not have written his *Employment and Equilibrium* without the Keynesian challenge. But it is equally clear that the new book, far from contradicting classical theory, constitutes a clarification and elaboration of Pigou's own pre-Keynesian "classical" position—if I may repeat what I said in the earlier article.

50. Compare on all this N. A. Court, *Mathematics in Fun and in Earnest* (Mentor, New York, 1961). Especially Chapter 11, "Mathematics and Genius," pp. 75–84.

27 Notes on Rational and Irrational Expectations

1. Psychological Factors in Business Cycles

Like Pigou, Keynes and other earlier writers, Professor Jöhr has stressed in numerous writings the role of psychological factors, of what he has called "psychological infection", in the business cycle.[1]

Of modern business cycle theories the one by A. C. Pigou is generally associated with the psychological factor.[2] In fact, Pigou's theory is often described as a psychological theory. This is, however, an inappropriate description because Pigou attributes equal importance in explaining the amplitude of the cycle to "monetary and banking policy" and to "errors of optimism and pessimism"; he also attributes some importance to "harvest variations".[3] But waves of optimism and pessimism do play an important role. Pigou analyses them at great length and shows how "errors of optimism" once revealed breed "errors of pessimism". He guesses that "if all errors were removed, the normal range of industrial fluctuations would be reduced substantially, perhaps to the extent of one-half; but considerable industrial fluctuations would still remain" (p. 220), because there are the other factors mentioned above that produce cyclical swings.[4]

In his "Notes on the Trade Cycle" Keynes has essentially translated certain parts of the Pigovian theory into his own terminology.[5] The slump is due to, "a collapse of marginal efficiency of capital". The decline in investment, in turn, is a reaction to over-optimism during the boom, to "the uncontrollable and disobedient psychology of the business world" (p. 319). "It is an essential characteristic of the boom that investment which will in fact yield, say, 2 percent in conditions of full employment are made in the expectation of, say, 6 percent ... When the disillusion comes, this expectation is replaced by a contrary 'error of pessimism' with the result that the

Wandlungen in Wirtschaft und Gesellschaft: Die Wirtschaftsund die Sozialwissenschaften vor neuen Aufgaben, Enril Kung, ed., J. C. B. Mohr (Paul Siebeck), Tübingen, 1980. AEI Reprint no. 111 (Washington, D.C.: American Enterprise Institute, 1980). © 1980, American Enterprise Institute. Reprinted with permission.

investments, which would in fact yield 2 percent ... are expected to yield less than nothing." [6]

The Pigou–Keynes–Jöhr emphasis on errors of optimism and pessimism would seem to be a good example of a theory of irrational expectations. Thus, it is subject to the standard criticism by the rational expectations school to the effect that the rational "agents" in the market, firms and households, cannot be expected to make the same mistake again and again. Actually, everyone, not only economists but the public ("agents"), has become more and more cycle-conscious. The view became widely popular in the 1920s that the business cycle would all but disappear if and when it was properly understood and correctly forecast. This would forestall, it was thought, the emergence on a large scale of errors of optimism and pessimism and so at least drastically reduce the amplitude of cyclical swings. Over the years numerous forecasting institutes, public and private, have sprung up and many large firms acquired economic specialists to keep them informed about the cyclical situation. Yet the business cycle did not go away; it is still with us. The fact is that the cyclical swings are too irregular and the government's policy reactions too uncertain to warrant the conclusion that all market participants, or the great majority, are likely to draw the same—correct—conclusions for the future. Thus, errors of optimism and pessimism continue to be made. [7]

Economists themselves have been subject to waves of optimism and pessimism. Thus, the business cycle has been declared dead many times. For example, in the 1920s the fact that the price level remained fairly stable from 1921 to 1929 was widely regarded as an assurance that the cycle was finally on the way out. The same happened in the 1950s and 1960s, the heydays of Keynesian fine-tuning of the economy. Subsequent developments quickly disproved these claims and optimism was followed by pessimism. The Great Depression spread gloom and dejection and the euphoria of the 1950s and 1960s was followed by a general malaise in the 1970s. There has been much talk in recent years about a "new crisis of capitalism", a replay of the Great Depression or a prolonged stagnation. [8] If the economists are subject to waves of excessive optimism and pessimism, is it reasonable to assume that the actors in the market are immune?

The proponents of the psychological factor do not claim that waves of optimism and pessimism provide an independent causal explanation of the business cycle. They speak of an intensifying factor which enhances the self-reinforcing, cumulative nature of the process of cyclical expansion and contraction. [9] This leaves open the question of what starts those processes in the first place—a big question that cannot be tackled here. I confine myself to a few remarks about the monetary factor.

I would not go so far as to say, as some monetarists do, that all fluctuations in economic activity which the National Bureau of Economic Research lists as business cycles, including the mild ones (recessions or growth recessions), are caused by monetary expansions and contractions—that, as Irving Fisher once put it, the business cycle is merely "the dance of the unstable dollar." But there can be no doubt in my opinion that most, if not all, *major* booms and slumps can be traced to monetary mismanagement or have been greatly aggravated by monetary factors. I mention one example: The extraordinary severity of the Great Depression of the 1930s was due to monetary mismanagement, to acts of commission and omission by the Federal Reserve. If the stock of money had not been allowed to contract by about a third, the depression would never have become so long and deep. To that extent the analysis of Milton Friedman and Anna J. Schwartz is entirely convincing, although it does not exclude the possibility that the depression may have been started by some other, non-monetary factor.[10]

Elsewhere I have argued at some length that, given the extraordinary severity and cumulative force of the Great Depression, greatly enhanced as it was by psychological factors, the policy prescription for dealing with the slump put forward by Keynes and by monetarists can be reconciled.[11] In the last paragraph of their fascinating chapter on the Great Contraction, Friedman and Schwartz say: "Yet it is true that small events can have large consequences, that there are such things as chain reactions and cumulative forces.... Economic collapse often has the character of a cumulative process. Because no great strength would be required to hold back the rock that starts the landslide, it does not follow that the landslide will not be of major proportion."

The Great Depression surely was a landslide of major proportion. What Keynes recommended to halt the depression was deficit spending by the government.[12] I suggest that this prescription can be accepted by the monetarists. True, the landslide could have been prevented from becoming so large as it did by monetary measures. The rock which started the slide, or made the slide a major one, could have been held back without great difficulties by a better monetary policy. But after the slide had been allowed to gather momentum more drastic measures were indicated than monetary policy (open market operations). These drastic measures were direct injections of money into the expenditure-stream through government deficit spending, as Keynes recommended. True, monetary measures on a sufficient scale would have eventually overcome the depression. But it would have taken considerable time, for there is agreement that changes in the money supply affect the real economy with a substantial lag. Thus, a large pool of liquidity would have been created which would have led to an unhealthy inflationary boom after the economy had turned the corner.[13]

2. A Post-Keynesian Consensus

At least since Irving Fisher's celebrated paper *Appreciation and Interest* (1896)[14] economists have been familiar with the distinction between money or nominal interest and real interest, the latter defined as the nominal rate corrected for changes in the purchasing power of money (rising or falling prices). Fisher put forward the theory that rising prices (inflation) exert an upward pull on interest rates and falling prices a downward push. But he made it clear that changes in the price level have that effect only when they are foreseen. He thus introduced the important distinction between anticipated and unanticipated inflation and deflation. In addition, he ran statistical tests and found "that price changes do generally and perceptively, affect the [nominal] interest rate in the direction indicated by a priori theory. But since forethought is imperfect, the effects are smaller than the theory requires and lag behind price movements, in some periods very greatly." [15] It is safe to say that this lag can be observed also in the U.S. inflationary period of recent years. For long stretches real interest rates have been zero or even negative.

In his *General Theory* Keynes referred to Fisher's *Appreciation and Interest*.[16] But the vital distinction between nominal and real interest plays hardly any role in Keynesian thinking. The reason is that the *General Theory* is really a special theory; it is depression economics where money wages and prices are assumed to be substantially stable. Keynes himself was too much of a realist to stick to this assumption through thick and thin and he changed his tune a year later as we have been. But in the inflationary period after World War II the neglect of, or insufficient attention to, the public's changing expectations about an impending rise in the price level became a serious weakness in Keynesian policy discussions. As late as 1972 James Tobin extolled the virtues of inflation in adjusting "blindly, impartially and non-politically the inconsistent claims of different pressure groups on the national product." [17]

The Keynesian revolution demoted money and monetary policy from the center of macroeconomics to the backstage until money was resurrected by what Harry Johnson called the monetarist counterrevolution. The resurgence of money and monetary policy was largely, but by no means entirely, the work of the Chicago school and its offshoots in Rochester, Pittsburgh and elsewhere; it was broadly based. For example, there was Clark Warburton, the "pioneer monetarist", and the "rediscovery of money" had been independently proclaimed by Howard Ellis and Michael Heilperin.[18]

Thus, prior to the advent of the rational expectations theory whose numerous versions have filled many hundred pages in the learned journals in recent years, a broad consensus (excluding some die-hard Keynesians) has been reached which, very briefly, can be described as follows:

Money is essentially involved not only in the ups and downs of price level but also in the fluctuations of economic activity, the *real* business cycle. Specifically, there has never been a significant inflation, say, 5 percent or more over a significant period without a significant increase in the quantity of money. This does not mean that the velocity of circulation of money is constant or that it is not systematically related to the real business cycle and to movements in the price level (price inflation). But changes in velocity are as a rule an intensifying factor and only in exceptional cases a prime mover.[19] However, the fact that expansion in the money supply is the cause or indispensable condition of a cyclical expansion of output and employment, and the fact that a contraction of the money supply produces a contraction in real activity, do not imply that there exists a *permanent stable* trade-off between unemployment and inflation. Rejection of the Phillips curve as a long-run proposition is an essential feature of the consensus which I tried to describe. The consensus denies the possibility of fine-tuning the economy in the sense of eliminating even *minor* fluctuations of economic activity—mild recessions. But it does not exclude the possibility, and desirability, of counteracting major slumps—depressions.

The reasons that there is no permanent tradeoff are well-known: Inflationary expectations are bound to develop, interest rates adjust to the expected price rise, unions press for higher wages, market participants (households and firms) economize on money holdings, and thus the velocity of circulation of money increases. All this does not mean that every creeping inflation must become a trotting and galloping one, but rather that inflation loses its stimulating effect once it is expected and anticipated by the market.[20]

The consensus thus is that in the long run the Phillips curve tends to become vertical, or to put it differently, that the short run curve tends to shift up; the consensus accepts a trade-off for the short run. In other words, Keynesian policies are effective in the short run but tend to become less and less effective the longer the inflation lasts.

But how long is the short run and the long? Where is the line to be drawn between "major" booms and slumps that can or should be counteracted (or prevented) and minor ones that cannot be eliminated or "tuned out"? With respect to such questions, there is room for disagreement among those who subscribe to the broad consensus—and for compromise with some Keynesians.

3. Rational Expectations

Instead of trying to answer these last questions I shall now discuss how the rational expectations theory fits into the picture of the post-Keynesian consensus. This is not an easy task because the literature on rational expectations has proliferated enormously. There exist almost as many versions as there are members of the school, and later versions of the same author often are different from, and are more qualified than, earlier ones.[21]

The rational expectations school is an offshoot of Chicago-monetarism and can be described as the radical wing of monetarism. It is best known for the startling policy conclusions that are often attributed to it—to wit that macro-economic policies, both monetary and fiscal, are ineffective, *even in the short run*, to influence the real economy (output and employment); that these policies merely change the price level and the nominal interest rate. The adjustment in the nominal magnitudes (prices, interest rates) occurs without delay because the rational private agents correctly foresee and anticipate the outcome. This is indeed an amazing conclusion: the rational expectations theory is the extreme antithesis of orthodox Keynesianism with its assumption of rigid wages and prices, it contradicts what is sometimes called the Austrian theory of money and the business cycle (of Hayek and Mises) which asserts a basic *unneutrality* of money and it goes beyond Friedman's monetarism, which assumes a long lag, up to two years, of the effect of monetary measures on prices and does not exclude quick though transitory effects on output and employment.

In reality the results of the rational expectations theory are not quite as startling nor do they deviate so much from the consensus as stated above. The claim that monetary and fiscal measures influence only the nominal economic variables (prices) but not the real economy applies only to "systematic", "perceivable" and "predictable" policy measures of the government. In fact, Robert E. Lucas, a prominent member of the rational expectations school, has shown how, "unsystematic monetary-fiscal shocks" with the help of an "acceleration effect" (similar to the old-fashioned acceleration principle) can produce business cycles with the usual features of "pro-cyclical" price and investment movements and "in somewhat limited sense pro-cyclical movements in nominal interest rates." [22]

This leaves open serious questions some of which have not been faced squarely in the rational expectations literature, let alone satisfactorily answered. To begin with, it is not quite clear what the "systematic" policies are, and it must be questioned whether modern democratic governments are able to pursue truly systematic and consistent monetary-fiscal policies.[23] Be that as it may, as William Fellner has pointed out, systematic policies and unsystematic shocks usually come in a package and are difficult if not impossible to separate. In fact, the distinction between systematic and unsystematic government policies is essentially not a sharp but a fuzzy one. It is a drastic simplification to divide government actions into just two sharply distinct categories—systematic fully predictable policies and unsystematic entirely unpredictable shocks. In reality, government policies are spread out over the whole range between the two extremes. In other words, it is a question of more or less predictability and not one of either-or.

It follows, first, that it is impossible to determine whether the actual cycle is, as Lucas says, the result only of the unsystematic shocks and, second, that it is most unlikely that all, or the great majority of, private agents will interpret governmental policies or intentions identically and draw the same conclusions for the future course of events. As Arrow says, in "the rational expectations hypothesis, economic agents are required to be superior statisticians capable of analyzing the future general equilibrium of the economy" resulting from systematic government policies.[24] I would add that the economic agents are also assumed to be convinced monetarists who draw the same monetarist conclusions from identically perceived information. Actually, it would seem much more plausible to assume, as Arrow argues at some length, that, "the anticipations of the different agents are not only not based on the same general model but [that] they should in general differ considerably from each other."[25]

This criticism does not imply that the basic idea of the rational expectations theory is wrong, namely that people do not simply extrapolate the current rate of inflation (or its recent acceleration) and that they do try to form a judgment on what the government's policy is and how this policy is likely to change the course of events. What the criticism does mean is that the concrete rational expectations assumption—namely that all private agents (or the great majority) have the same perceptions of the government's policy and draw the same (that is to say, the correct monetarist) conclusion—is highly implausible.[26]

A worrisome feature of the rational expectations literature is the complete neglect of institutional rigidities, in particular rigidity of money wages and increasingly of real wages. Rational expectations theory is competitive theory in the strict sense of the word. What Lucas says of his business cycle model, "that prices and quantities at each point of time are determined in *competitive equilibrium*",[27] holds pretty much for the whole rational expectations literaure. Competitive theory has very important positive and normative uses.[28] But the unemployment problem, the business cycle, especially recession and depression, would be very different if all markets were competitive auction markets. Anti-inflation policy would become a much easier task if wages were less rigid. Arrow raises basically the same complaint when he says, "They [the rational expectations theorists] have put, for the most part at least, most exclusive stress on prices. Individuals are regarded as responding solely and exclusively to present and anticipated prices."[29] The neglect of institutional rigidities greatly impairs the relevance of the rational expectations theory for the real world. Institutional rigidities make it impossible for government monetary-fiscal policies, even if entirely systematic and correctly perceived by the public, to be neutral with respect to the *real* economy as the rational expectations school claims.

It is instructive to consider a concrete example where the total neglect of rigidity has led to questionable policy recommendations. In his very interesting paper, "Rational Expcetations and the Role of Monetary Policy",[30] Robert J. Barro discusses the oil price rise and the shortfall of agricultural harvests in 1973–1974. "These shocks can be represented by a downward movement in aggregate real supply.... It follows that output ... would fall while prices would rise. What is the proper role for monetary policy in this situation? The present analysis suggests that there is a substantive role only to the extent that the monetary authority has better information than the public about the disturbance, or, possibly, about their implications for the economy. Perhaps the most obvious observation about the oil and agricultural shocks is the extent to which they are perceived. Hence, this paper argues that there is no role for monetary policy in offsetting these real shifts. Adverse shifts like the oil and agricultural crises will reduce output and cause painful relative adjustments no matter what the reaction of the monetary authority. Added monetary noise would only complicate and lengthen the process of adjustment" (p. 26).

I suggest that by taking explicit account of the fact that in the present-day world money wages are almost completely rigid downward, one gets a better and more realistic picture of the consequences of the OPEC oil price rise and the shortfall of farm output. There is agreement that those changes constitute, as Barro says, a decline in aggregate real supply. This implies that if full employment is to be preserved, real wages (or more generally real incomes) must decline. In the ideal competitive world assumed by the rational expectations school this could be accomplished without a rise in the price level by reducing the money supply. Oil and food prices would go up, other prices would go down, and money wages would decline slightly. With money wages rigid downward, keeping the price level stable would create unemployment. It is, therefore, not unreasonable to argue that the authorities should increase the money supply so as to let the price level rise a little in order to bring about the unavoidable decline in *real* wages by higher prices rather than by lower money wage rates.[31]

This argument assumes, of course, that money illusion has not completely disappeared, while the rational expectations models are, without exception as far as I can see, "derived within a framework from which all forms of money illusion are rigorously excluded" and "all prices are market clearing."[32] True, money illusion tends to become progressively eroded in a long period of inflation. This is implicit in the consensus that I have described. It follows that money illusion cannot be used to justify a policy of permanent inflation. But money illusion is a fairly hardy plant.[33] In the short run, in the context of a single shock such as the oil price crisis in 1973–74, it was not illegitimate or unrealistic to proceed on the assumption that there was still some money illusion left.

Even the highly inflationary period of the last five years offers many examples of stepped-up monetary-fiscal expansions that have been quite effective *in the short or medium run* in bringing about a rapid expansion of the *real* economy, of output and employment. The U.S. cyclical expansion from March 1975 to 1979, which started with an inflation rate of almost 6 per cent, is one example. Britain and Italy with much higher inflation rates than the United States offer more striking examples. The upshot is that, contrary to what the rational expectation theory tells us, monetary-fiscal measures still are effective in the short run. The examples just cited suggest that the short run has been two years or so. But one would expect it to become shorter if the inflationary trend continues. In other words, there is still some money illusion left, which can be exploited by monetary policy and misused by politicans to win the next election.

4. Concluding Remarks

In section 3 the question was raised how the rational expectations theory, or rather theories, fit into the broad post-Keynesian consensus that was sketched in section 2.

The answer seems to be that the rational expectations theories have sharpened the concepts on which the consensus is based and increased our knowledge of the way expectations are formed. But the open questions formulated at the end of section 2 are still not fully answered. The radical answer suggested by the rational expectations school—that the assumption of rational behavior on the part of the "agents" in the market eliminates the gap between the short run and the long run and establishes long run equilibrium without delay—is not acceptable. It is true, the rational expectations theorists leave room for a compromise by admitting that "unsystematic" government actions influence the real economy. We have seen, however, that it is impossible to accept the assumption of the rational expectations school that all government actions can be classified under just two extreme categories—systematic wholly predictable policies which affect only nominal variables (prices and interest rates) but are neutral with respect to the real economy, on the one hand, and unsystematic entirely unpredictable shocks which affect not only nominal but also real magnitudes, on the other hand. Most government actions come in between the two extremes.

It was the problem of how to wind down inflation, the pressing problem of our times, that set on fire the rational expectations debate. As far as that problem is concerned, William Fellner's "credibility hypothesis" seems to capture what is valid in the rational expectations theory and a good deal that is not in the theory but still valid. In numerous writings, Fellner has developed the theory that if the government wants to maximize the chances of success of its anti-inflation policy, that is to say to subdue inflation without creating much unemployment, it must conduct its policy in such a way as to create favorable expectations of the market participants. That requires credibility and persistence. Market participants must be persuaded that the government will firmly stick to a policy of reducing money GNP growth to a noninflationary level within a reasonable period of time. The government must not give the impression that it will give up or interrupt the policy of disinflation as soon as unemployment rises somewhat. If the government succeeds in making its policy credible, there is a good chance, although no absolute certainty, that market participants, including labor unions and other pressure groups, in order not to price themselves out of the market, will moderate their wage and price demands to a noninflationary level.[34]

In a recent paper Fellner has discussed the relation between his credibility approach and the rational expectations theory.[35] The two approaches "overlap ... because both stress that the public is forming its expectations on the basis of ... information on the probable future actions of policy makers". But the overlap is merely partial.

An important difference between the two theories, according to Fellner, is that "the rational expectations hypothesis suggests that experience has in fact enabled the public to detect a system by which the authorities exert an influence on nominal demand, while the credibility hypothesis suggests that the public can detect such a system only if the authorities ... effectively ['condition' the expectations] of the market participants by behaving consistently in an understandable fashion". Thus the credibility approach does not accept the assumption made by the rational expectations school that government actions fall nearly into two extreme categories—systematic, wholly predictable policies and unsystematic, entirely unpredictable shocks. Especially after a long period of inflation, which has shaken the public's confidence that the government will carry out its anti-inflationary policy, a sustained and deliberate effort must be made to restore credibility.

Another important difference between the two approaches is that the credibility hypothesis pays attention to "institutional rigidities" which are ignored by the rational expectations school. "The list of institutional rigidities ... would have to include not only those that come most readily to mind for all real world economies [such as wage and price rigidities] but also such items as the inevitable imperfections of all tax indexation schemes." Another rigidity Fellner mentions is that the nominal rate of interest "cannot decline below approximately zero." However, this latter rigidity is likely to become operational only in periods of declining price level. But it is well to recall Irving Fisher's finding that in periods of falling as well as rising prices nominal interest rates adjust only imperfectly to the real situation—a statement that seems to hold true also for the recent inflationary years, which have exhibited zero or negative real interest rates over extended periods of time. These rigidities make it virtually impossible that, as the rational expectations school claims, "systematic" monetary-fiscal policies be "neutral" with respect to (do not affect) the real economy.

Let me repeat once more, the rational expectations theories have made important contributions and have enhanced our knowledge of how the economy works. But they have, unnecessarily, exaggerated their claims and have gone too far beyond the post-Keynesian consensus. This is a pity, because there is no better way to damage a good cause than overstate it. In summary, the post-Keynesian consensus still stands, fuzzy though it is on the edges like most concepts in the social sciences.

Notes

1. See especially his book, *Die Konjunkturschwankungen*, Tübingen–Zürich, 1952.

2. See Pigou, A.C.: *Industrial Fluctuations*, 2nd edition, London, 1929. The rudiments of his theory can be found in his earlier book, *Wealth and Welfare*, London, 1913, which was the forerunner of *The Economics of Welfare* and *Industrial Fluctuations*.

3. See the remarkable Chapter XXII, "The Comparative Importance of Various Factors in Determining the Amplitude of Industrial Fluctuations" (*Op. cit.* p. 207–226.) Pigou also stresses the role of "Rigidity in Wage-Rates" (Chapter XX). It is worth noting that he usually refers to the rigidity of *real* wages.

4. According to Pigou the various factors interact and reinforce each other so that the contributions of each factor, obtained by assuming the removal of the factor in question, add up to more than the total.

5. Keynes, J.M.: *The General Theory of Employment, Interest and Money* (London, 1936), Chapter 22, pp. 313–332.

6. p. 321. Keynes draws from this an extraordinary conclusion: "Thus the remedy of the boom is not a higher rate of interest but a lower rate of interest! For that may enable the so-called boom to last. The right remedy for the trade cycle is not to be found in abolishing the boom ... but in abolishing slumps and thus keeping us permanently in quasi-boom" (p. 322). This recipe for permanent accelerating inflation has been eagerly absorbed and consistently propagated by most of Keynes' desciples. But Keynes himself evidently had some misgivings about that statement which induced him to qualify it slightly (see footnote on p. 322 and p. 327); and one year later he changed his mind. In 1937 he became greatly concerned about inflation and recommended a change in policy, although at that time inflation was not high by our present-day standards and unemployment was still close to the 10 percent mark. For Keynes's 1937 shift see Hutchinson, T.W.: *Keynes versus "The Keynesians...?" An Essay on the Thinking of J. M. Keynes and the Accuracy of its Interpretations by his Followers* (Institute of Economic Affairs, London, 1977).

7. One recalls Oskar Morgenstern's radical criticism of economic forecasting. See Morgenstern, Oskar: *Wirtschaftsprognose, Eine Untersuchung ihrer Voraussetzungen und Möglichkeiten* (Wien 1928), repeated in Morgenstern, Oskar: *The Limits of Economics* (London, 1937).

8. See my paper, "The Present Economic Malaise" in *Contemporary Economic Problems 1979* (American Enterprise Institute, Washington, D.C., 1979).

9. Schumpeter accepts "waves of optimism" that "feeds upon itself" as an intensifying factor, provided the basic causes have been established independently. See Schumpeter, Joseph A.: *Business Cycles. A Theoretical, Historical, and Statistical Analysis of the Capitalist Process* (New York, 1939), Vol. I, pp. 140–141.

10. Friedman, Milton and Schwartz, Anna J.: *Monetary History of the United States 1867–1960* (New York, 1963), Chapter 7, "The Great Contraction, 1929–1933". This chapter is also available separately as a Princeton University Press paperback.

11. See Haberler, Gottfried: "Austria's Economic Development after the Two World Wars: A Mirror Picture of the World Economy," in a *Festschrift for Stephan Koren*, Werner Clement and

Karl Socher, eds. (Berlin: Duncker & Humbolt, 1979); AEI reprint 103. It would be interesting retrospectively to apply rational expectations reasoning to the situation in the 1930s. Would members of the school have argued that in the midst of mass unemployment the credible announcement of large government deficit spending would merely have driven up prices without any effect on the real economy? Hardly. True, the Keynesian notion that up to full employment any increase in aggregate monetary demand goes entirely into quantities, and then, from the point of full employment on, merely drives up prices, is too simple. Keynes himself was fully aware that the transition from unemployment to full employment is gradual, that the effects of successive increases in aggregate expenditures shift gradually from influencing primarily the real economy to influencing prices; in other words, becomes more and more inflationary. True, too, the Keynesians neglected taking account of rising inflationary expectations. But the rational expectations school neglects taking account of increasing downward rigidity of wages and prices. (See below.)

12. It must be stressed that, contrary to later statements by Keynes' disciples, Keynes was by no means the only British economist who recommended deficit spending and public works. He was joined in this recommendation by many economists, including A. C. Pigou, D. H. Robertson, and Hubert Henderson. For extensive references see Hutchison, T.W., *On Revolutions and Progress in Economic Knowledge*, Cambridge University Press, Cambridge, 1978, Chapter 6, "Demythologizing the Keynesian Revolution," pp. 175−199. In a letter to *The Times* (July 28, 1933) Keynes went out of his way to emphasize his agreement on policy with Pigou (See Hutchison, T.W., *op. cit.* p. 187).

13. In fact the accumulation of liquid funds in the downswing of the cycle which are then released during the upswing has been used by many theorists as part of a mechanism that can produce cyclical swings. On the basis of a rather different type of reasoning Axel Leijonhufvud reaches the conclusion that in "moderate displacements from the 'full coordination' timepath" of the economy "the presumption is in favor of 'monetarist' ... policy prescriptions." For large displacements Keynesians "fiscalist" policies are indicated. (See "Effective Demand Failures." Leijonhufvud, Axel. *The Swedish Journal of Economics*, Vol. 75, 1973, pp. 32−33.)

14. *Publications of the American Economic Association*, Third Series, Vol. XI, No. 4, August 1896, pp. 331−442. See also Fisher, I.: *The Theory of Interest*, New York, 1930, Chapter II, "Money Interest and Real Interest", and Chapter XIX, "The Relation of Interest to Money and Prices".

15. See Fisher, I.: *The Theory of Interest*, p. 451. He noted that at the end of the great German inflation of the 1920s the adjustment was almost instantaneous and complete.

16. p. 142.

17. See his brilliant presidential address, "Inflation and Unemployment". *American Economic Review, Vol. 62*, March 1972, p. 13. Tobin later admitted that he had "been over-optimistic about the trade-off [between unemployment and inflation] and too skeptical of accelerationist warnings". See James Tobin, "Comment of an Academic Scribbler", *Journal of Monetary Economics, Vol. 4*, 1978, p. 622.

18. See Bordo, Michael D. and Schwartz, Anna J.: "Clark Warburton, Pioneer Monetarist," *Journal of Monetary Economics, Vol. 8*, No. 1 (January 1978) pp. 43−65.

19. Exceptional cases are, for example, periods of high inflation. Thus, in the German hyperinflation after World War I the velocity of money ran to fantastic heights.

20. Moreover, expectations may well run ahead of the actual rise in prices that is in store, which clearly constitutes an unstable situation. This can be regarded as "an error of optimism" in the Pigou—Keynes—Jöhr sense.

All this is by no means a new discovery. Thus, in his first book Fritz Machlup pointed out that the foreign exchange market reacts quickly and often anticipates expected future developments which explains why the foreign exchange value of a currency may decline ahead of the drop of the dramatic purchasing power. (See Machlup, Fritz: *Die Goldkernwahrung*, Halberstadt, H. Meyer's Buchdruckerei, Abteilung Verlag, 1925, page 135.) There are in Machlup's book several statements to the effect that anticipation of future events ("speculation") can cause deviation of the exchange rate from the purchasing power parity and there is a reference to a remark by Wicksell which makes the same point. (See Wicksell, Knut: *Vorlesungen über Nationalökonomie. II. Geld und Kredit*, Jena, 1922, S. 114.)

21. There exist several attempts at summarizing the literature, with extensive bibliographies. See, for example, Poole, William: "Rational Expectations in the Macro Model," in *Brookings Papers in Economic Activity*, 1976, pp. 463—514; Santomero, A.M. and Seater. John J.: "The Inflation-Unemployment Trade-off: A Critique of the Literature", *Journal of Economic Literature, Vol. XVI*, No. 2, June 1978, pp. 499—544; and Shiller, Robert J.: "Rational Expectations and the Dynamic Structure of Macroeconomic Models, A Critical Review", *Journal of Monetary Economics, Vol. 4*, No. 1, January 1978, pp. 1—44. The latest macroeconomic textbooks have short references to the rational expectations theory. See, for example, Wonnacott, Paul: *Macroeconomics* (2 nd edition, Homewood, Illinois, 1978). and Dornbusch, Rüdiger and Fischer, Stanley: *Macro-Economics* (McGraw-Hill Book Co.), New York, 1978.

Paul Samuelson has announced that the 11th edition of his famous text *Economics* will present "an understandable survey" of the rational expectations theory which "offers a serious challenge to both monetarism and simple Keynesianism". The new edition will be published by McGraw-Hill, New York, early in 1980.

A good non-mathematical summary has been presented by Herschel I. Grossman, "Rational Expectations, Business Cycles and Government Behavior", Working Paper 78—25, National Bureau of Economic Research, New York, 1978 (Mimeographed, to be published in a conference volume). For a searching but not unsympathetic criticism see Arrow, Kenneth J.: "The Future and the Present in Economic Life", *Economic Inquiry, Vol. 16*, April, 1978, pp. 157—169.

For a good popular presentation of arguments for and against the rational expectations approach see," How Expectations Defeat Economic Policy", *Business Week*, November 8, 1976, and Guzzardi, W.: "The New Down-to-Earth Economics", *Fortune*, December, 1978.

22. Lucas, Robert E.: "An Equilibrium Model of the Business Cycle", *Journal of Political Economy, Vol. 83* (December 1975) p. 1113.

23. On the last point see the paper by H. Grossman quoted in note 21 above.

24. *Op. cit.*, p. 160.

25. *Op. cit.*, p. 165.

26. If one endows the private agents with so much foresight as the rational expectations theory does, should one not go one step further and assume that the private agents will take into consideration that their reaction to the government's policy will induce some policy reactions on the part of the government? Moreover, should one not concede some rationality even to the government? Perhaps the authorities, too, try to take into consideration the likely

reactions of the private agents to the government's actions. There is work to do for the model builders to incorporate these actions and reactions into their scheme! Something like Oskar Morgenstern's Sherlock Holmes-Moriarty impasse may emerge. See Morgenstern, Oskar: *Wirtschaftsprognose*, p. 98 and, "The Collaboration Between Oskar Morgenstern and John von Neumann on the Theory of Games" *The Journal of Economic Literature*, Vol. 14, Sept. 1976, p. 806. Attention should also be given to what Karl Popper calls the, "Oedipus effect", the effect that a prediction may have on the predicted events. In everyday language: A prophecy may be self-fulfilling—or self-frustrating. (See Popper, Karl, *The Poverty of Historicism*, 2nd ed., London, 1960.)

27. *Op. cit.*, p. 113. Italics in the original. Competitive, market-clearing prices effectively rule out involuntary unemployment.

28. The assumption of perfect competition greatly facilitates the mathematical analysis. It is comparatively easy to introduce minor qualifications (e.g., deviations from the pure model such as Chamberlin's monopolistic competition, oligopolistic pricing and sluggish price adjustments in certain parts of the economy) without changing the main results. (See, for example, McCallum's, Bennett T. interesting paper, "Monetarism, Rational Expectation, Oligopolistic Pricing and the MPS Econometric Model" *Journal of Political Economy*, Vol. 87 No. 1, 1979, pg. 57–73.) But the almost total downward rigidity of money wages and growing "real wage resistance" (Hicks) is a different matter that changes the picture profoundly.

29. *Op. cit.*, p. 167. Arrow adds that this is "very much in the spirit of textbook neoclassical theory". But when neoclassical writers turn their attention to unemployment, money and the business cycle, they usually do pay attention to rigidities, failure of markets to clear and similar complications. Pigou, the arch-neoclassicist, attributes about a third of the amplitude of industrial fluctuations to wage and price rigidities. Pigou, *op. cit.* Chapter XX.

30. *Journal of Monetary Economics*, No. 2 (1976). pp. 1–37.

31. This is how Arthur Burns argued when he was chairman of the Federal Reserve Board. He told a Congressional Committee that the Federal Reserve could have kept the price level steady, but it would have meant that prices other than those of oil would go down, which would have created much unemployment. I have analyzed the oil shock along similar lines in my paper. "Oil, Inflation, Recession and the International Monetary System" (*The Journal of Energy and Development*, Vol. 1, No. 2, Spring, 1976, available as American Enterprise Institute Reprint No. 45, Washington, D.C. 1976.) [Chapter 14 in this volume.]

In a footnote Barro says that if the monetary authority announced, "that there had been an oil crisis" and told "people that this crisis meant lower output and higher prices, [it] would be equivalent to the appropriate active response of money". (*op. cit.*, p. 26) Realistically, that would mean persuading the labor unions to accept a lower *real* wage either in the form of higher prices or of lower money wage rates. Appeals to unions to behave reasonably or rationally have rarely been successful. But the crucial problems posed by powerful labor unions, other pressure groups, government regulations, fixed contracts, etc., are completely ignored in the rational expectations literature and minimized by monetarists in general.

32. Lucas, Robert E.: "Expectations and Neutrality of Money", *Journal of Economic Theory*, Vol. 4, 1972, p. 103.

33. Moreover, it seems to be capable of being revived, at least to some extent, by spells of comparative price stability.

34. See especially Fellner, William: *Towards a Reconstruction of Macroeconomics, Problems of Theory and Policy* (American Enterprise Institute, Washington, D.C., 1976).

35. Fellner, William: "The Credibility Effect and Rational Expectations: Implications of the Gramlich Study", *Brookings Papers on Economic Activity 1979*, 1, pp. 167–189. (The Brookings Institution, Washington, D.C., 1979).

Bibliography: Writings of Gottfried Haberler

Articles and pamphlets marked with asterisks are included in the volume with cross references in brackets to the chapter numbers used in this collection.

The editor will be grateful for any additions and corrections. Professor Haberler does not possess copies of many of his writings or translations, and he has few, if any, of his book reviews. It has not been possible to produce a complete and accurate bibliography.

I Books and Pamphlets

1. *Der Sinn der Indexzahlen.* Eine Untersuchung über den Begriff des Preissniveaus und die Methoden seiner Messung. (Verlag von J. C. B. Mohr (Paul Siebeck), 1927), 134 pp.

2. *Der Internationale Handel. Theorie der Weltwirtschaftlichen Zusammenhänge sowie Darstellung and Analyse über Aussenhandelspolitik.* (Berlin: Verlag von Julius Springer, 1933), 298 pp. Spanish translation: *El Commercio International* (Barcelona: 1936); Japanese translation in two volumes.

3. *The Theory of International Trade with its Applications to Commercial Policy.* Translated from German (with numerous revisions) by Alfred Steiner and Frederic Benham. (Edinburgh: William Hodge; New York: The Macmillan Co., 1936, with later impressions), xv + 408 pp.

4. *Prosperity and Depression.* League of Nations. Original edition (English and French), Geneva, 1937; second impression (English and French), 1937; third impression (English only), 1938. New revised and enlarged edition (English and French), 1939; second impression (English only), 1940; third impression (English only), 1941. Third edition enlarged by Part III (English only), 1941, xxiv + 532 pp.; second impression (English only), 1942; third impression (English only), 1943; later impressions, United Nations, New York. New edition: London, George Allen & Unwin, Ltd.; Cambridge, Mass., Harvard University Press, 1958, 517 pp. (For Part III in third edition is substituted "Monetary and Real Factors Affecting Economic Stability: A Critique of Certain Tendencies in Modern Economic Theory;" reprinted from *Banca Nazionale del Lavoro*, no. 38, September 1956. New Appendix I, "Notes on the Present State of Business Cycle Theory," translated from German. First published in *Wirtschaftstheorie und Wirtschaftspolitik. Festschrift für Alfred Amonn*, 1953. New Appendix II, "The Pigou Effect Once More," reprinted from the *Journal of Political Economy*, vol. LX (June 1952), 240–246. Japanese translation, 1938; Swedish translation, 1940; Spanish translation with a new introduction (Mexico), 1942; Greek translation in Athens, 1943; German translation:

Prosperität und Depression (Bern: Verlag A. Francke, 1948), 536 pp. New appendix containing German translation of "The Place of the General Theory of Employment, Interest, and Money in the History of Economic Thought," in *The New Economics*, S. E. Harris (ed.), 1947, and in the *Review of Economics and Statistics*, 1946. Second German translation (Tübingen: J. C. B. Mohr (Paul Siebeck), 1955). New appendix containing German translation of the note on "The Pigou Effect Once More," 1952, and "Bemerkungen zum Gegenwartigen stand der Konjunkturtheorie," from *Festschrift für Professor Alfred Amonn*, 1953. Russian translation, Moscow 1960.

5. *Consumer Instalment Credit and Economic Fluctuations* (New York: National Bureau of Economic Research, 1942), xx + 236 pp.

6. *Problemas de Conjunctura e de Politica economica*, Fundacao Getulio Vargas (ed.) (Rio de Janeiro: 1948), 228 pp. (con sommari in inglese e francese).

7. *Liberale und Planwirtschaftliche Handelspolitik*, in collaboration with Stephen Verosta (Berlin: Junker und Dunnhaupt Verlag, 1934), 121 pp.

8. *Quantitative Trade Controls—Their Causes and Nature*, in collaboration with Martin Hill, (Geneva: League of Nations, 1943), 45 pp.

*9. *A Survey of International Trade Theory*, Special papers in International Economics, No. 1 (Princeton: September 1955), 68 pp.; seconda ristampa, 1956; terza ristampa, 1958. Revised and enlarged edition, 1961. [Chapter 4]

10. *Currency Convertibility* (Washington, D.C.: American Enterprise Association) 43 pp.; traduzione tedesca: "Konvertibilität der Währungen," in *Die Konvertibilität der Europäischen Währungen*, A. Hunold (ed.) (Zürich: 1954), pp. 15–59.

11. *Growth and Balance in World Trade*, The Galen L. Stone Inaugural Lecture delivered at Harvard University, Littauer Auditorium, on December 10, 1957. (Cambridge: Harvard University Press, 1958), pp. 3–21.

12. *Inflation: Its Causes and Cures*. Revised and enlarged edition (Washington, D.C.: American Enterprise Institute, 1966).

13. *Money in the International Economy* (London: The Institute of Economic Affairs Ltd., 1965), pp. 3–65. German translation: *Geld in des Internationalen Wirtschaft* (Gmbh-Hamburg: Verlag Weltarchiv, 1965), pp. 9–53.

14. *U.S. Balance-of-Payments Policies and International Monetary Reform: A Critical Analysis*, with Thomas D. Willett (Washington, D.C.: American Enterprise Institute, 1971).

*15. *A Strategy for U.S. Balance of Payments Policy*, with Thomas D. Willett, (Washington, D.C.: American Enterprise Institute, 1971). [Chapter 9]

16. *Incomes Policy and Inflation, An Analysis of Basic Principles*, Special Analysis No. 11 (Washington, D.C.: American Enterprise Institute for Public Policy Research, 1971), pp. 1–41.

*17. *Inflation and the Unions*, with Michael Parkin and Henry Smith (London: The Institute of Economic Affairs, 1972). [Chapter 12]

18. *Probleme der Wirtschaftlichen Integration Europas*, Bernhard-Harms-Vorlesungen, Heraugegeben von Hergert Giersch (Institut für Weltwirtschaft an der Universität Kiel, 1984), pp. 13–36.

19. *Economic Growth and Stability: An Analysis of Economic Change and Policies* (Los Angeles: 1974), xvii + 290 pp.; traduzione tedesca, 1975; edizione brasiliana, 1976.

*20. "The World Economy, Macroeconomic Theory and Policy—Sixty Years of Profound Change," paper prepared for the occasion of the award of the Antonio Feltrinelli Prize by the Academia Nazionale dei Licei (Italian Academy of Science) (Rome, Italy: 1982); AEI Occasional Reprints (Washington, D.C.: American Enterprise Institute, no date). [Chapter 18]

II Articles

1925

*"Kritische Bemerkungen zu Schumpeters Goldtheorie. Zur Lehre vom 'objektiven' Tauschwert des Goldes," *Zeitschrift für Volkswirschaft u. Sozpolitik N.F.*, vol. 4 (Wien, 1925), pp. 647–668. [Chapter 22]

1927

"Albert Hahns 'Volkswirtschäftliche Theorie des Bankkredits,'" *Archiv für Sozialwissenschaft u. Sozialpolitik*, vol. 57 (1927), pp. 803–819.

1928

"A New Index Number and Its Meaning," *The Quarterly Journal of Economics*, Vol. XLII (May 1928), pp. 434–449.

1929

"The Theory of Comparative Cost, Once More," *The Quarterly Journal of Economics*, vol. CLIII (February 1929), pp. 376–381.

"Die Kredittheorie der Cambridge Schule," *Archiv für Sozialwissenschaft u. Sozialpolitik*, Tübingen, vol. 62 (1929), pp. 251–270.

"Der volkswirtschaftliche Geldwert und die Preisindexziffern," *Weltwirtschaftliches Archiv*, vol. 30 (1929), pp. 6–14.

1930

"Wirtschaft als Leben Kritische Bemerkungen zu Gottls methodologischen Schriften," *Zeitschrift für Nationalökonomie*, Band 1930, pp. 28–50.

*"Transfer und Preisbewegung," *Zeitschrift für Nationalökonomie*, vol. I (January 1930), pp. 547–554. [Chapter 6]

"Internationale Kartelle und Handelspolitik," *Der Oesterreichische Volkswirt*, vol. 22 (July 5, 1930), pp. 1104–1108.

*"Die Theorie der komparativen Kosten und ihre Auswertung für die Bergründung des Freihandels," *Weltwirtschaftliches Archiv* (October 1930), pp. 349–370. [Chapter 1]

1931

*"Transfer und Preisbewegung," *Zeitschrift für Nationalökonomie*, Band II (1931), pp. 100–102. [Chapter 6]

"The Different Meanings Attached to the Term 'Fluctuations in the Purchasing Power of Gold' and the Best Instrument or Instruments for Measuring such Fluctuations," Memorandum for the Gold Delegation of the League of Nations (Geneva, 1931). German translation: "Die Kaufkraft des Goldes und die Stabilisierung der Wirtschaft," *Schmoller's Jahrbuch*, vol. 55 (1932).

"Irving Fisher's 'Theory of Interest,'" *The Quarterly Journal of Economics*, vol. XLV (1931), pp. 499–516.

1932

"Money and the Business Cycle," *Gold and Monetary Stabilization* (Harris Foundation Lectures), Chicago, pp. 43–74: reprinted in *The Austrian Theory of the Trade Cycle and Other Essays*, the Center for Libertarian Studies, occasional paper series no. 8, pp. 7–20.

"Die amerikanische Bankreform," *Der deutsche Volkswirt* (March 11, 1932), pp. 780–783.

"Some Remarks on Professor Hansen's View on Technological Unemployment," *The Quarterly Journal of Economics*, vol. 44 (May 1932), pp. 558–562.

"Mit oder ohne Inflation? Zu: 'Aufbau, Nicht Abbau,'" *Der Oesterreichische Volkswirt* (November 5, 1932), pp. 136–137.

"Aufbau, nicht Abbau!" Entgegung von Dr. Otto Deutsch und Ingenieur Alexander Vertes; Replik von Dr. Karl Polanyi und Dr. Gottfried Haberler, *Der Oesterreichische Volkswirt* (November 19, 1932), pp. 183–187.

1933

Contribution to *Der Stand und die nächste Zukunft der Konjunkturforschung*, Festschrift für Arthur Spiethoff, J. A. Schumpeter (ed.) (München: Duncker & Humblot, 1933), pp. 92–103.

1934

"Systematic Analysis of the Theories of the Business Cycle," League of Nations, Geneva. (Mimeographed, August 1934.) Polish translation: "Systematyozna analima teoryj cyklu gospodarozego," *Ekonomista*, vol. IV (Warsaw, 1935), pp. 4–41.

1935

"Koordination der Wirtschaftspolitik unter dem Gesichtspunkte der Konjunkturbeeinflussung," *Wirtschaftliche Nachrichten* (Vienna, January 10, 1935), pp. 46–47.

1936

"Monetary Equilibrium and the Price Level in a Progressive Economy: A Comment," with Karl Bode, *Economica* (February 1936), pp. 75–81.

*"'Mr. Keynes' Theory of the Multiplier': A Methodological Criticism," *Zeitschrift für Nationalökonomie*, vol. VII (1936), pp. 299–305. Reprinted with revisions in *Readings in Business Cycle Theory* (Philadelphia, 1944), pp. 193–203. [Chapter 23]

"Some Reflections on the Present Situation of Business Cycle Theory," *The Review of Economic statistics* (February 1936), pp. 1–7.

1938

"Some Comments on Mr. Kahn's Review of *Prosperity and Depression*," *The Economic Journal* (June 1938), pp. 322–333.

"Economic and Political Aspects of the Gold Problem," *Harvard Alumni Bulletin* (March 25, 1938), pp. 735–738.

1939

"The Interest Rate and Capital Formation," *Capital Formation and Its Elements*, a series of papers presented at a symposium conducted by the Conference Board (1939), pp. 119–133.

"Recovery Policies in Democratic Countries," paper read at Detroit Meeting of American Economic Association, December 1938, *Proceedings* (March 1939).

"National Income, Saving, and Investment" (and discussion), *National Bureau of Economic Research: Income Studies*, vol. II (1939), pp. 139–165 and 185–190.

"Some Factors Affecting the Future of International Trade and International Economic Policy," *Economic Reconstruction*, S. E. Harris (ed.), pp. 319–335. Reprinted with revisions and additions in *Readings in the Theory of International Trade*, H. S. Ellis and L. A. Metzler (eds.) (Philadelphia, 1939), pp. 530–554.

1943

"The Political Economy of Regional or Continental Blocs," *Postwar Economic Problems*, S. E. Harris, (ed.) (New York, 1943), pp. 325–344.

1945

"The Choice of Exchange Rates After the War," *American Economic Review*, vol. XXXV (June 1945), pp. 308–318.

Contribution to "Five Views on the Murray Full Employment Bill," *The Review of Economic Statistics*, vol. XXVII (August 1945), pp. 106–109.

1946

"The Place of *The General Theory of Employment, Interest and Money* in the History of Economic Thought," *Review of Economic Statistics*, vol. 28 (1946), pp. 187–194. Revised and enlarged version in *The New Economics. Keynes' Influence on Theory and Public Policy*, S. E. Harris (ed.) (New York, 1947), pp. 161–180. Reprinted in *John Maynard Keynes: Critical Assessment*, John Cunningham Wood (ed.) (Kent: Beckenham, 1984). German translation in *Prosperität und Depression*, (Bern, 1948), pp. 493–511. Also in second German edition (1955).

"Taxes, Government Expenditures, and National Income," G. Harberler and E. E. Hagen, *Studies in Income and Wealth*, vol. VIII, Conference on Research and Wealth (New York: National Bureau of Economic Research, 1946), pp. 1–31.

"Multiplier Effects Of A Balanced Budget," *Cowles Commission Papers*, New Series, No. 15, pp. 148–151. Reprinted from *Econometrica* (1946).

"Currency Depreciation and the International Monetary Fund," *Review of Economic Statistics* (1946). Reprinted with revisions in *Foreign Economic Policy for the United States*, S. E. Harris (ed.) (Cambridge: Harvard University Press, 1948), pp. 384–396.

1947

"Protecionismo Alfandegário," *Digesto Economico*, vol. 35 (São Paulo, Brazil, October 1947), pp. 35–89.

"Balanca de Pagamontos om Regime de Papel-Mocda," *Digesto Economico*, vol, 36 (São Paulo, Brazil, 1947), pp. 89–93.

"Haveré Depressão nos Estados Unidos?" *Revista Brasileira de Ecónomia*, vol. 1 (Rio de Janeiro, 1947), pp. 27–46.

"Comment on The Foreign Trade Multiplier by J. J. Polak," and "A Restatement," by J. J. Polak and G. Haberler, *American Economic Review*, Vol. XXXVII (1947), pp. 898–907.

"The Economic Systems of the Democracies and Totalitarian States," *Proceedings of the Academy of Political Science*, Vol. XXII (1947), pp. 304–311.

"Comments on 'National Central Banking and The International Economy,' by Robert Triffin," *Postwar Economic Studies*, no. 7 (Washington, D.C.: Federal Reserve Board, September 1947), pp. 82–102. Reprinted in *Economia Internationale*, vol. I, no. 4 (Geneva, 1948), 16 pp. and in *El Trimantre Economico*, vol. XIV (Mexico), pp. 618–645.

1948

"The Present Cyclical Situation of the American Economy in the Light of Business Cycle Theory," *Economie Internationale*, vol. I (Geneva, 1948), pp. 235–238.

"Causes and Cures of Inflation," *The Review of Economics and Statistics*, vol. XXX (February 1984), pp. 10–14. Reprinted in *Readings in Money and Banking*, Charles R. Whittlesey (ed.) (New York, 1952), pp. 317–325.

"Kommt es zu einer Wirtschaftskrise in den USA?" *Die Industrie*, vol. 48 (Vienna, July 17, 1948), pp. 4–6.

"Some Economic Problems of the European Recovery Program," *The American Economic Review*, vol. XXXVIII (September 1948), pp. 495–525.

"Dollar Shortage?" in *Foreign Economic Policy for the United States*, S. E. Harris (ed.) (Cambridge: Harvard University Press, 1948), pp. 426–445. Portuguese translation: "Escassez de Dólares?" *Revista Brasileira de Ecónomia*, no. 1 (March 1948), pp. 7–39.

Foreword to Full Employment and Free Trade by Michael Polanyi (Cambridge at the University Press, 1948 edition), pp. IX–XII.

1949

"Current Research in Business Cycles—Discussion," *American Economic Review*, vol. 39 (May 1949). Reprinted in *Cowles Commission Papers*, New Series, no. 35, pp. 84–88.

"Economic Aspects of a European Union," *World Politics*, vol. 1 (July 1949), pp. 431–441. German translation (1965). Reprinted in *International Economics Selected Readings*, R. N. Cooper (ed.) (London: Penguin Book, 1969), pp. 107–134.

"Further Comments on 'Professor Leontief on Lord Keynes,' by Ira O. Scott," *Quarterly Journal of Economics*, vol. LXIII (November 1949), pp. 569–571.

"Der Marshall-Plan für den wirtschaftlichen Wiederaufbau Europas und die Dollar-Knappheit," *Aussenwirtschaft*, vol. 4 (Bern, 1949), pp. 193–215.

*"The Market for Foreign Exchange and the Stability of the Balance of Payments. A Theoretical Analysis," *Kyklos*, vol. III (Bern, 1949), pp. 193–218. [Chapter 7]

1950

"European Unification and the Dollar Problem: A Comment," *The Quarterly Journal of Economics*, vol. LXIV (May 1950), pp. 306–310.

"Joseph Alois Schumpeter, 1883–1950," *The Quarterly Journal of Economics*, vol. LXIV (Aug. 1950), pp. 333–372. Reprinted in *Schumpeter Social Scientist*, S. E. Harris (ed.) (Cambridge, Mass.: Harvard University Press, 1951), pp. 24–44, and (abridged) in *The Development of Economic Thought. Great Economics in Perspective*, H. W. Spiegel (ed.) (New York: John Wiley and Sons, 1952), pp. 734–762.

"Schumpeter, Ministre des Finances, 15 Mars–17 Octobre 1919," *Economie Appliquée*, vol. III (Paris, Juillet-December 1951), pp. 427–439.

*"Some Problems in the Pure Theory of International Trade," *The Economic Journal*, vol. LX (June 1950), pp. 223–240. Reprinted in *Readings in International Economics*, R. E. Caves and H. G. Johnson (eds.) (Homewood: Richard D. Irwin, 1968), pp. 215–229. [Chapter 3]

1951

*"Schumpeter's Theory of Interest," *Review of Economics and Statistics*, Vol. XXXIII, no. 2 (May 1951), pp. 122–128. Reprinted in *Schumpeter Social Scientist*, S. E. Harris (ed.) (Cambridge, Mass.: Harvard University Press, 1951), pp. 72–78. [Chapter 24]

"Further Comment on 'European Unification and the Dollar Problem' by T. Balogh," *The Quarterly Journal of Economics*, vol. LXV (February 1951), pp. 122–129.

*"Real Cost, Money Cost and Comparative Advantage," and "Concluding Remarks," Proceedings of a Round Table Discussion held by the International Economic Association, Monaco, September 1950, *Extracts from UNESCO'S International Social Science Bulletin* (Spring 1951), pp. 48–52 and 85–93. German translation in *Zeitschrift für Nationalökonomie*, vol. XIII (Vienna, 1952), pp. 415–422 and 461–473. [Chapter 2]

"Wage Policy, Employment, and Economic Stability," in *The Impact of the Union* (New York: Harcourt, Brace and Company, 1951), pp. 34–62.

"Welfare and Freer Trade—A Rejoinder," *The Economic Journal*, vol. LXI (December 1951), pp. 777–784.

1952

*"The Pigou Effect Once More," *The Journal of Political Economy*, vol. LX (June 1952), pp. 240–246. Reprinted in 1958 edition of *Prosperity and Depression*. German translation in second German edition of *Prosperity and Depression* (1955). [Chapter 25]

"Quotas," *Encyclopedia Britannica*, vol. 18 (1952), pp. 857–858.

*"Currency Depreciation and the Terms of Trade," *Wirtschaftliche Entwicklung und soziale Ordnung*, Festschrift für Professor F. Degenfeld-Schönburg (Vienna, 1952), pp. 149–158. [Chapter 8]

1953

"Reflections on the Future of the Bretton Woods System," *Wirtschaftsdienst* (edited by Hamburgisches Welt-Wirtschafts-Archiv, Feburary 1958), pp. 1–7. German translation: "Betrachtunger aber die Zukunft des Bretton Woods System," *Wirtschaftsdienst*, vol. 33 (February 1953), pp. 83–91. Spanish translation: "Reflexionos sobre el Futuro del Sistema de Bretton Woods," *Boletin del Banco Central de Venezuala*, vol. XII (Julio–Deciembre 1952), pp. 9–18. An abridged versions appears in *The American Economic Review*, vol. XLIII (May 1953), pp. 81–95.

"Bemerkungen Zum Gegenwürtigen Stand Der Konjunkturtheorie," *Wirtschaftstheorie und Wirtschaftspolitik*, Festschrift für Alfred Amonn (Bern 1953), pp. 226–240. Reprinted in second German edition of *Prosperity and Depression* (1955). English translation in 1958 edition of *Prosperity and Depression*.

"The Foreign Trade of Western Europe: Accomplishments and Prospects," *Proceedings of the Academy of Political Science*, vol. XXV (May 1953), pp. 79–89.

"Die Konjunkturaussichten in den Vereinigten Staaten von Amerika," *Aussenwirtschaft* (Bern, September 1953), pp. 149–187.

1954

"The Relevance of Classical Theory of International Trade under Modern Conditions," *Papers and Proceedings* of the 66th Annual Meeting of the American Economic Association (Washington, D.C.: American Economic Association, December 1953). *American Economic Review*, vol. 54 (May 1954), pp. 543–551.

"Aussenhandel (Theorie)," *Handwörterbuch der Sozialwissenschaften*, vol. I (Tübingen, 1954), pp. 457–477. English enlarged and revised version, "Survey of International Trade Theory" (1955); 2nd edition, revised and enlarged, Special Papers in International Finance (Princeton, 1966).

"Die Ausgleichsgesetze der Amerikanischen Zahlungsbilanz," *Schweizerische Zeitschrift für Volkswirtschaft und Statistik*, 90, Jahrgang, Heft 4 (1954), pp. 506–509.

"Die Gleichgewichtstheorie des Internationalen Handels," in *Deutschland und die Weltwirtschaft, Schriften des Vereins für Sozialpolitik*, N.F. Ed. 10 (Berlin: Verlag von Dunck, 1954), pp. 35–63.

1955

"Some Aspects of Convertiblity," *Economie Internationale*, vol. VIII, no. 1 (Geneva, 1955), pp. 1–21.

"Defects in the Concept of Regionalism to Solve Trading Problems," in Hearings before the *Subcommittee on Foreign Economic Policy* of the *Joint Committee on the Economic Report*, 84th Congress (Washington, D.C.: Government Printing Office, 1958), pp. 505–508. Reprinted in *The Indian Journal of Economics*, vol. XXXVIII (Allahabad, India, July 1957), pp. 25–30.

1956

"Economic Consequences of a Divided World," *The Review of Politics*, vol. 18 (January 1956), pp. 3–22. Also in *From Disorder to World Order* (Series of Addresses delivered at Marquette University, Nov. 8–11, 1956), pp. 159–184, and in *The Fate of East Central Europe*, Stephen D. Kertesa (ed.) (South Bend, Indiana: University of Notre Dame Press, 1956), ch. 16, pp. 377–395.

"Montary and Real Factors Affecting Economic Stability," *Banco Nationale del Lavoro*, no. 38, (Rome, September 1956), p. 46. (An abridged and slightly altered version of a paper read at the First Congress of the International Economic Association held in Rome, Sept. 6–11, 1955. Full paper published 1958.) Reprinted in 1958 edition of *Prosperity and Depression*.

1957

"Critical Observations on Some Current Notions in the Theory of Economic Development," *L'industria*, no. 2 (Milan, 1957), pp. 373–383. (Written in honor of Guiseppe Ugo Papi.)

"Inflation and Economic Development," in *Contribuicoes a Analise de Desenvolvimento Economico*, Festschrift for Eugenio Gudin (Rio de Janeiro, 1957), pp. 178–187. Spanish translation: "Inflación y desarrollo económico," *Moneda y Credito* (December 1957), p. 11. Italian translation: "Inflazione e sviluppo economico," *Rassegna Economica*, No. 3 (July–Sept., 1957), pp. 383–393.

*"The Terms of Trade and Economic Development," Paper read at round table of International Economic Association (Rio de Janeiro, 1957). German translation: *Zeitschrift für*

Nationalökonomie, (1958). Reprinted in *Economic Development for Latin America*, Howard Ellis and H. C. Wallich (eds.) (New York: St. Martin Press, 1961), pp. 275–97. [Chapter 19]

"Die Wirtschaftliche Integration Europas," Festgabe rum 60. *Geburtstag von Bundeswirtschaftsminister Ludwig Erhard* (1957), pp. 521–530. Earlier version appeared in *Deutsche Zeitung und Wirtschafts Zeitung* (December 8, 1956). Italian translation: "L'integrasione migliere e la liberta di commercio," *Rassegna Economica*, no. 1 (January–March 1957), p. 15.

"Implications of the European Common Market and Free Trade Area Project for United States Foreign Economic Policy," and "The Use of Quotas in the Regulation of Imports," *Compendium of Papers on United States Foreign Trade Policy*, collected by the Staff for the Subcommittee on Foreign Trade Policy of the Committee on Ways and Means (Washington D.C.: Government Printing Office, 1957), pp. 477–481 and 639–642.

1958

"The Quest for Stability: The Monetary Factors," *Stability and Progress in the World Economy*, (The First Congress of the International Economic Association) (London: Macmillan, 1958), pp. 151–207. French translation: "Facteurs Monétaire et Stabilité Économique," *Économie Appliquée* (Paris, 1958), pp. 147–202. German translation: "Beeinflussung der Wirschaftsstabilität durch monetäre Kräfte," *Zeitschrift für Nationalökonomie*, Band XVIII, Heft 1–2 (Vienna, 1958), pp. 60–101. Abridged and slightly altered version appears under the title "Monetary and Real Factors Affecting Economic Stability," *Banca Nazionale del Lavoro*, no. 38, (Rome, September 1956). Reprinted in 1958 edition of *Prosperity and Depression*.

"Die Amerikanische Depression," *Deutsche Zeitung und Wirtschafts Zeitung*, no. 53 (July 5, 1958), p. 25. Revised and enlarged Italian translation in *Rassegna Economica* (1958). Spanish translation in *Moneda y Credito* (1958).

"Notes on Some Problems of Anti-inflation and Anti-depression Policy," *Investigation of the Financial Condition of the United States*, comments of economists, professors, and others in response to the questionnaire of the Committee on Finance, U.S. Senate, 85th Congress, 2nd Session, Chapter 5 (Washington, D.C.: Government Printing Office, 1958), pp. 617–628.

"Introduction" to *Problems in International Economics*, papers presented at a conference called by the National Bureau Committee for Economic Research. Reprinted in *Review of Economics and Statistics*, supplement, vol. XL (1958), pp. 3–9.

"The Case for Minimum Interventionism," *Foreign Aid Reexamined*, James W. Wiggins and Helmut Schoeck (eds.) (Washington, D.C.: Public Affairs Press, 1958), pp. 139–150. (Summary prepared by editors.)

"Methods of Harmonizing Resources and the Demand for Resources in the Western Countries," paper read at East–West Conference of the International Economic Association in Bursa, Turkey (1958). Mimeograph. *The Academia Economic Papers* (Academia Sinica, Taipei), vol. 13, no. 1 (1985), pp. 1–22.

"Brief Comments on the Recession," *The Review of Economics and Statistics*, vol. XL, no. 4 (1958), pp. 309–311.

Reply to CED Question, "The Most Important Economic Problem to be Faced by the United States in the Next 20 years," asked by the Committee on Economic Development (CED)

(New York, Autumn 1947). Published along with answers of many other economists to the same question in a book *Problems of U.S. Economic Development*, vol. I (1958). Italian translation: "L'inflatione subdola," *Rassogna Economica*, Banco di Napoli (1958), p. 14. Spanish translation in *Moneda y Credito*. Reprinted as "Creeping Inflation," *Ekonomi Politik Samhalle*, published in honour of Professor Bertil Ohlin's sixtieth birthday on 23 April 1959, (Stockholm, 1959), pp. 87–95.

1959

"Frank William Taussig," in *Handwörterbuch der Sozialwissenschaften*, vol. 10 (Gottingen: Vandenhoeck and Ruprecht, 1959), pp. 291–292.

*"International Trade and Economic Development," *National Bank of Egypt*, Fiftieth Anniversary Commemoration Lectures (Cairo, 1959), 36 pp. Reprinted in *Expansion of World Trade and the Growth of National Economies*, Richard S. Weckstein (ed.) (New York: Harper Torchbooks, 1968), pp. 97–136. [Chapter 21]

"Against the Stream and Against the Cycle!" *Freundesgabe zum 12. Oktober 1959 für Albert Hahn* (Frankfurt (Main): Fritz Knapp, 1959), pp. 26–29.

"Wage Policy and Inflation," *The Public Stake in Union Power*, Philip D. Bradley (ed.) (Charlottesville, Virginia: University of Virginia Press, 1959), pp. 63–85.

1960

"Gibt es noch einen Konjunkturzyklus?" *Der Volkswirt*, Doppelnummer 52/53 (December 24, 1960), pp. 69–73.

"Population Pressure and Economic Policy in Developed and Under-Developed Countries, "*Annales Nestlé*, Humanity and Subsistence Symposium in Vevey (Switzerland), April 21–23, 1960, pp. 1–14.

1961

"Bemerkungen zum Problem des wirtschaftlichen Regionalismus," *Wirtschaft, Gesellschaft und Kultur*, Franz Greiss and Fritz W. Meyer (eds.), Festgabe für Alfred Muller-Armack (Berlin: Duncker & Humblot, 1961), pp. 415–424.

"The Deficit in the American Balance of Payments and the U.S. Foreign Economic Policy: A View Early in 1960 and in 1961," *Public Policy*, vol. XI (Cambridge, Mass.: Harvard University Press, 1961), pp. 109–126.

"Why Depressions are Extinct," *Think* (New York: I.B.M., April 1961).

"The Economics of International Markets," *Meeting Foreign Competition at Home and Abroad*, Proceedings of the First 1961 Economic Institute (February 15, 1961), pp. 3–25.

"Amerika und die europäische Integration: Einige grundsätzliche Bemerkungen," *Aussenwirtschaft: Zeitschrift für Internationale Wirtschaftsbeziehungen* (St. Gallen, Sept.–Dec. 1961), pp. 49(233)–66(250).

"Um das Gleichgewicht in der Weltwirtschaft," *Die Aussprache*, Herausgeber: Arbeits-gemeinschaft Selbständiger Unternehmer e.V., 11. Jahrgang, (Bonn am Rhein, Juli 1961), pp. 204–211.

"Das Dollarproblem: Bemerkungen zur Frage des Gleichgewichts der internationalen Zah-lungsbilanzen," *Weltwirtschaftliches Archiv*, vol. 87, Heft 2 (1961), pp. 171–187.

"Domestic Economic Policies and the U.S. Balance of Payments," *The Dollar in Crisis*, Seymour Harris (ed.) (New York: Harcourt Brace, 1961), pp. 63–72.

1962

"Die Verschwendung als Wirtschafts-philosophil," *Verschwendung als Wirtschafts-Philosophie*? Sounderdruck aus der Schriftenreihe der Stiftung "Im Gruene," Ruschlikon/Zurich Band 23, pp. 47–54. (Dusseldorf u Wien: Econ-Verlag Werbeabteilung, 1962).

1963

"Sparen, Investition and Währungsstabilität—Vorbedingungen wirtschaftlichen Wach-stums," ("Saving, Investment and Monetary Stability as Preconditions of Economic Develop-ment and Growth"), Deutsche Übersetzung eines Vortrags in englischer Sprache gehalten am 7. *Internationalen Sparkassenkongress*, Wien, 21. Mai 1963. Amsterdam: Internationales Institut der Sparkassen, (1963), pp. 32–53.

"Monetary and Fiscal Policies in U.S. Strategy," *National Security: Political, Military, and Economic Strategies in the Decade Ahead*, David M. Abshire and Richard V. Allen (eds.) (New York: Praeger, 1963), pp. 895–917.

"The New Trade Policy, European Integration, and the Balance of Payments," *Current Problems in Political Economy*, 1962–1965 Dr. Paul L. Morrison Lectures in Political Economy, DePauw University, Greencastle, Indiana, pp. 35–56. Delivered at DePauw University, March 12, 1963.

1964

"Inflation," *The Conservative Papers*, (Garden City, New York: Anchor Books, Doubleday & Co., Inc., 1964), pp. 175–199.

"An Assessment of the Current Relevance of the Theory of Comparative Advantage to Agricultural Production and Trade," *International Journal of Agrarian Affairs*, vol. IV, no. 3 (May 1964), pp. 130–149. Reprinted in *Der Internationale Handel*, Gottfried Haberler, reprint (Berlin-Heidelberg-New York: Springer-Verlag, 1970), pp. 1–20.

*"The General Theory After Ten Years," and "Sixteen Years Later," *Keynes' General Theory. Reports of Three Decades*, Robert Lekachman (ed.) (New York: St. Martin's Press, 1964), pp. 269–296. [Chapter 26]

*"Integration and Growth of the World Economy in Historical Perspective," *The American Economic Review*, vol. LIV, no. 2, part I (March 1964), pp. 1–22. Presidential Address, American Economic Association. [Chapter 20]

1965

"Der Devisenmarkt und die Stabilität der Zahlungsbilanz. Eine theoretische Untersuchung," *Theorie der internationalen Wirtschaftsbeziehungen*, Klaus Rose (ed.) (1965), pp. 214–238. (German translation of "The Market for Foreign Exchange and the Stability of the Balance of Payments," *Kyklos*, Bd. 3 (1949), pp. 193–218.)

"The Present State of Economics and the New Tasks of Diplomacy," *Die modernen Wissenschaften und die Aufgaben der Diplomatie*, Karl Braunias and Peter Meraviglia (eds.), Veröffentlichungen der österreichischen Gesellschaft für Aubenpolitik und Internationale Beziehungen (Graz: Verlag Styria, 1965), pp. 177–188.

1966

"Marxian Economics in Retrospect and Prospect," *Marxist Ideology in the Contemporary World—Its Appeals and Paradoxes*, M. M. Drachkovich (ed.) (New York: Praeger Publishing Co., 1966), pp. 113–125. Reprinted in *Zeitschrift für Nationalökonomie*, vol. XXVI/1–3 (Vienna, 1966), pp. 69–82.

"The International Payments System: Postwar Trends and Prospects," *International Payments Problems*, A Symposium sponsored by the AEI (Washington, D.C.: American Enterprise Institute, 1966), pp. 1–20.

"Einige Bemerkungen zur gegenwärtigen Diskussion über das internationale Währungssystem," *ORDO, Jahrbuch für die Ordnung von Wirtschaft und Gesellschaft*, Band XVII (1966), pp. 57–73.

"Adjustment, Employment, and Growth," *Maintaining and Restoring Balance in International Payments*, (Princeton: Princeton University Press, 1966), pp. 123–135.

"Further Remarks on the Problem of Integration of Less Developed Countries," *Revista Brasileira de Economia*, ano. 20, nos. 2–3 (Rio de Janeiro, Jun/Set. 1966), pp. 201–212.

1967

"Monetary and Fiscal Policy for Economic Stability and Growth," *Il Politico*, vol. XXXII, no. 1 (University of Pavia, 1967), pp. 32–48.

"Comment" (on Otmar Emminger, "Practical Aspects of the Problem of Balance-of-Payments Adjustment," and Tibor Scitovsky, "The Theory of Balance-of-Payments Adjustment,"), *Journal of Political Economy*, vol. 75, no. 4, part II (August 1967), pp. 531–536.

1968

"Theoretical Reflections on the Trade of Socialist Economies," *International Trade and Central Planning: An Analysis of Economic Internations*, Alan A. Brown and Egon Neuberger (eds.) (Berkeley: University of California Press, 1968), pp. 29–54. Also published in *Geldtheorie und Geldpolitik, Günter Schmölders zum 65. Geburtstag*, C. A. Andreas, K. H. Hansmeyer, and G. Scherhorn (eds.) (Berlin: Duncker & Humblot), pp. 291–305.

1969

"Wage-Push Inflation Once More," *Roads to Freedom, Essays in Honour of Friedrich A. von Hayek*, Erich Streissler (ed.) (London: Routledge & Kegan Paul, 1969), pp. 65–73.

"The Future of Gold—Round Table," *American Economic Review*, vol. LIX, no. 2 (May 1969), pp. 357–360.

"Appendix: Taxes on Imports and Subsidies on Exports as a Tool of Adjustment," *Monetary Problems of the International Economy*, Robert A. Mundell and Alexander K. Swoboda (eds.) (Chicago: University of Chicago Press, 1969), pp. 173–179.

"The International Adjustment Mechanism," *The International Adjustment Mechanism*, The Federal Reserve Bank of Boston Monetary Conference, October 1969, pp. 27–33.

"Protectionism or Freer Trade in the Less Developed Countries," *Il Politico*, vol. XXXIV, no. 3 (University of Pavia, 1969), pp. 407–418.

"Internationale Währungsprobleme," *Schweizer Monatshefte*, 49. Jahr, Heft 3 (Juni 1969), pp. 268–284.

"Weitere Bemerkungen zum Internationalen Währungsproblem," *Schweizer Monatshefte*, 49. Jahr, Heft 6 (September 1969), pp. 551–553.

1970

"Import Border Taxes and Export-Tax Refunds Versus Exchange-Rate Changes," *Approaches to Greater Flexibility Exchange Rates, The Bürgenstock Papers*, George N. Halm (ed.) (Princeton: Princeton University Press, 1970), pp. 417–423.

"The International Monetary System: Some Recent Developments and Disscussions," *Approaches to Greater Flexibility of Exchange Rates, The Bürgenstock Papers*, George N. Halm (ed.) (Princeton: Princeton University Press, 1970), pp. 115–123.

"The U.S. Balance of Payments: Freedom or Controls," *Banca Nazionale del Lavoro Quarterly Review*, no. 92 (March 1970), pp. 3–9. Reprinted with a Postscript in *The Economics of Common Currencies*, H. G. Johnson and A. Swoboda (eds.) (London, 1973), pp. 221–228.

"The Balance of Payments Adjustment Mechanism from the American Standpoint," prepared statement submitted to the subcommittee on Foreign Economic Policy of the Joint Economic Committee, 91st Congress, 2nd session. Part 5, *U.S. Foreign Trade: The Internal and External Adjustment Mechanisms*, pp. 994–1003.

1971

Foreword to Juergen B. Donges, *Brazil's Trotting Peg: A New Approach to Greater Exchange Rate Flexibility in Less Developed Countries*, AEI Special Analysis, no. 7 (August 1971), pp. 1–5.

"Two Conflicting Views of the German Balance of Payments Predicament," *Kieler Diskussionsbeiträge zu aktuellen wirtschaftspolitischen Fragen*, Hubertus Müller-Groeling (ed.) (Kiel: Institut für Weltwirtschaft, June 1971), pp. 16–18.

"Reflections on the Economics of International Monetary Integration," *Verstehen und Gestalten der Wirtschaft*, Festgabe für Friedrich A. Lutz zum 70. Geburtstag am 29. Dezember 1971 (Tubingen: J. C. B. Mohr (Paul Siebeck), 1971), pp. 269–278.

"The Case Against the Link," *Banca Nazionale del Lavoro Quarterly Review*, no. 96 (Rome, March 1971), pp. 3–12.

"Income Policies and Inflation: An Analysis of Basic Principles," AEI Special Analysis, no. 11, (1971), pp. 1–41; Institute of Economic Affairs (London, 1972).

"Incomes Policy and Inflation: Some Further Reflections," Industrial Relations Research Association, *Proceedings* of the Twenty-Fourth Annual Winter Meeting, December 27–28, 1971 (October 1972), pp. 132–142. AEI Reprint no. 5.

1972

"Prospects for the Dollar Standard," *Lloyds Bank Review*, no. 105 (July 1972), pp. 1–17. AEI Reprint no. 3. Appeared also in Chapter 4 of *Leading Issues in International Economic Policy, Essays in Honor of George N. Halm*, C. Fred Bergsten and William G. Tyler (eds.) (Lexington, Mass.), pp. 63–80.

"General Economic and Monetary Policies for Technological Progress," Symposium aus Anlass des Nationalfeiertages 1972 Veranstaltet von der Österreichischen Bundesregierung, Die Zukunft von Wissenschaft und Technik in Österreich, Fachdiskussionsgruppe XII, pp. 320–323.

"Some Observations on Japanese-American Economic Relations," *Banca Nazionale del Lavoro Quarterly Review*, no. 102 (September 1972), pp. 3–15. AEI Reprint no. 11.

"U.S. Balance of Payments Policy and the International Monetary System," *Convertibility, Multilateralism and Freedom, World Economic Policy in the Seventies. Essays in Honor of Reinhard Kamitz*, (Vienna: Springer-Verlag, 1972), pp. 117–194. AEI Reprint no. 9.

"Income Policy and Inflation: Some Further Reflections," *American Economic Review*, vol. LXII, no. 2 (May 1972), pp. 234–241.

"The Balance of Payments Adjustment Mechanism from the American Standpoint," in *SEPARAT do livres "Ensaios Económicos Homenajen a Octario. Couvén de Bulhóes,"* editado plea APEC Editóra S.A. (Rio de Janeiro, 1972), pp. 281–292.

"The Theory of Business Cycles as a Part of Western Economic Theory," with Vaclar Holesovsky in *Marxism, Communism and Western Society. A Comparative Encyclopedia* (New York: Herder and Herder, 1972), pp. 347–364.

1973

*"International Aspects of U.S. Inflation," *A New Look at Inflation. Economic Policy in the Early 1970s*, AEI Domestic Affairs Study, no. 17 (September 1973), pp. 79–105. [Chapter 13]

"The Dollar–Mark–Yen Crisis, 1973," *SAIS Review*, vol. 7, no. 3 (Washington, D.C.: Spring 1973). AEI Reprint no. 16.

"The Future of the International Monetary System and the Convertibility of the Dollar," paper read at Universite du Quebec at Montreal, January 6, 1973; revised February 26, 1973.

Reprinted in *The 1973 Economic Report of the President*, Hearings before the Joint Economic Committee, U.S. Congress, 93rd Congress, 1st Session, Part 2. (Washington, D.C.: U.S. Government Printing Office, 1973), pp. 458–466.

"The Second Post-Smithsonian Currency Crisis," prepared statement in *The 1973 Economic Report of the President*, Hearings before the Joint Economic Committee, U.S. Congress, 93rd Congress, 1st Session, Part 2. (Washington, D.C.: U.S. Government Printing Office, 1973), pp. 455–458.

"Two Essays on the Future of the International Monetary Order," with a postscript on "The Impact of the Energy Crisis," revised version of "The International Monetary System After Nairobi," *Japan Economic Journal* (November 14, 1973) and revised version of a speech ("Prospects for the International Monetary Order") delivered on November 30, 1973, at a conference on the United States and international monetary reform sponsored by the University of Rochester, Graduate School of Management, Center for Research in Government Policy and Business and the Committee for Monetary Research and Education, Inc. AEI Reprint no. 21. Greek translation in *Spoudai*, Studies, University of Industry and Business, vol. 26, no. 4 (Pireus, Greece, October–December 1976), pp. 1002–1026.

"Comment on Arthur B. Laffer, 'Two Arguments for Fixed Rates,'" *The Economics of Common Currencies, Proceedings of the Madrid Conference on Optimum Currency Areas*, Harry G. Johnson and Alexander Swoboda (eds.) (London: George Allen & Unwin, 1973), pp. 35–39.

1974

"The Future of the International Monetary System," paper presented at the Western Economic Association, Las Vegas, June 10, 1974, *Zeitschrift für Nationlökonomie*, 34 (1974), pp. 387–396. AEI Reprint no. 30.

"Die Beschleunigung des Inflationsprozesses und ihre nationalen und internationalen Ursachen," *Das Inflationsproblem heute—Stabilisierung oder Anpassung*, Bericht über den wissenschaftlichen Teil der 37. Mitgliederversammlung der Arbeitsgemeinschaft deutscher wirtschaftswissenschaftlicher Forschungsinstitute e.V. in Bonn-Bad Godesberg am 9. und 10. Mai 1974. (Berlin: Duncker & Humblot, 1974), pp. 11–27.

"Probleme der wirtschaftlichen Integration Europas," *Bernhard-Harms-Vorlesungen*, 5/6, Herbert Giersch (ed.), Institute für Weltwirtschaft an der Universität Kiel (1974), pp. 13–36.

"Inflation as a Worldwide Phenomenon, an Overview," *The Phenomenon of Worldwide Inflation*, David I. Meiselman and Arthur B. Laffer (eds.) (Washington, D.C.: American Enterprise Institute, 1975), pp. 13–25. Also published in *Weltwirtschaftliches Archiv*, Heft 2 (Kiel, 1974), pp. 179–193.

"Comments on 'The Historical Setting,' by A. I. Bloomfield," *European Monetary Unification and its Meaning for the United States*, L. B. Krause and W. S. Salant (eds.) (Washington D.C.: The Brookings Institution, 1974), pp. 33–36.

1975

"The Challenge to the Free Market Economy," speech delivered in German at the International Management Symposium at the St. Gall Graduate School of Economics, Business and

Public Administration, Saint Gallen, Switzerland, May 6, 1975. German title: "*Marktwirtschaft als Aufgabe.*" AEI Reprint no. 38, 20 p. Separate de numero especial do Boletin da Faculdade de Direito de Coinbra 1978.

Introduction to "A Discussion With Friedrich von Hayek," AEI Domestic Affairs Study 39 (1975).

"Depression and Inflation on Spaceship Earth," *Economic Notes*, vol. IV, no. 1, Monte dei Paschi di Siena (Siena, Italy, 1975), pp. 7–24. AEI Reprint no. 53.

"Thoughts on Inflation: The Basic Forces," paper delivered at the September 23, 1974, Denver, Colorado, meeting of the National Association of Business Economists. *Business Economics*, vol. 10, no. 1 (January 1975), pp. 12–18. AEI Reprint no. 33.

1976

*"Die Weltwirtschaft und das internationale Währungssystem in der Zeit zwischen den beiden Weltkriegen," *Währung und Wirtschaft in Deutschland 1876–1975*, Deutsche Bundesbank (Frankfurt (Main): Fritz Knapp Verlag, 1976), pp. 205–248. English version: *The World Economy, Money and the Great Depression, 1919–1939*, AEI Foreign Affairs Study no. 30 (1976). Japanese translation, Tokyo Keizai Shinposha (1984). [Chapter 16]

*"Oil, Inflation, Recession and the International Monetary System," speech delivered at the Second International Conference on Energy, Surplus Funds and Absorptive Capacity, International Research Center for Energy and Economic Development. *The Journal of Energy and Development*, vol. 1, no. 2 (Spring 1976). German translation: "Erdol, Inflation, Rezession und das Internationale Währungssystem," *Heransforderungen der Marktwertschaft*, Institut für Wirtschaftspolitik an der Universität zu Köln, (1977), pp. 7–40. AEI Reprint no. 45. [Chapter 14]

"Some Currently Suggested Explanations and Cures for Inflation," *Institutional Arrangements and the Inflation Problem*, Karl Brunner and Allan H. Meltzer (eds.), Carnegie–Rochester Conference Series on Public Policy, vol. 3 (Amsterdam: North-Holland Publishing Co., 1976), pp. 143–177. AEI Reprint no. 55.

"The Case Against Capital Controls for Balance of Payments Reasons," *Capital Movements and Their Control*, Alexander K. Swoboda (ed.), Proceedings of the Second Conference of the International Center for Monetary and Banking Studies, (Leiden, Netherlands: A. W. Sijthoff); for the Institut Universitaire de Hautes Etudes Internationales (Geneva, Switzerland, 1976), pp. 63–82. AEI Reprint no. 62.

"Wenn der Staat die Monopole Schütz," *Frankfurter Allgemeine Zeitung*, no. 221 (October 2, 1976), p. 11.

*"The Problem of Stagflation," *Contemporary Economic Problems 1976*, William Fellner (project director and ed.) (Washington, D.C.: American Enterprise Institute, 1976), pp. 255–272. [Chapter 15]

"Importierte Inflation?" *Studien zur Stabilitaetspolitik*, Wolfgang Schmitz (ed.), Bundeskammer der gewerblichen Wirtschaft (Wien, 1976), pp. 34–40.

"Income Policies," *Grants and Exchange*, Martin Pfaff (ed.) (Amsterdam: North-Holland Publishing Company, 1976), pp. 260–267.

"Some Reminiscences on Alvin H. Hansen," *The Quarterly Journal of Economics*, vol. XC (no. 1, February 1976), pp. 9–13.

"Commentaries to 'The Eurocurrency Market, Exchange Rate Systems, and National Financial Policies,' by T. D. Willett," *Eurocurrencies and the International Monetary System*, C. H. Stern, J. H. Makin, and D. E. Logue (eds.) (Washington, D.C.: American Enterprise Institute, 1976), pp. 257–260; "Flexible Exchange Rates and the Recycling of Petrodollars," ibid, pp. 362–367.

1977

"Stagflation: An Analysis of Its Causes and Cures," *Economic Progress, Private Values, and Public Policy, Essays in Honor of William Fellner*, Bela Balassa and Richard Nelson (eds.), (Amsterdam: North-Holland Publishing Company, 1977), pp. 311–329. AEI Reprint no. 64. German Translation: "Stagflation—Eine Analyze ihrer Ursachen und ihrer Bekämpfung," *ORDO, Jahrbuch für die Ordnung von Wirtschaft und Gesellschaft*, Band 27 (Stuttgart and New York: Gustav Fischer Verlag, 1977), pp. 81–100. AEI Reprint no. 64.

"Das Floating als Inflationsmotor," *Neue Zürcher Zeitung*, no. 45 (February 23, 1977), p. 18.

*"How Important is Control Over International Reserve" and "Reply to Robert Triffin," *The New International Monetary System*, Robert A. Mundell and Jacques J. Polak (eds.) (New York: Columbia University Press, 1977), pp. 116–132 and 172–176. [Chapter 10]

"The International Monetary System after Jamaica and Manila," *Weltwirtschaftliches Archiv*, Band 113, Heft 1 (1977), pp. 1–27 and in *Contemporary Economic Problems*, William Fellner (project director and ed.), AEI (1977), pp. 239–288.

*"Survey of Circumstances Affecting the Location of Production and International Trade as Analyzed in the Theoretical Literature," *The International Allocation of Economic Activity*, Proceedings of a Nobel Symposium held at Stockholm, Bertil Ohlin, Per-Ove Hesselbom, and Per Magnus Wijkman (eds.) (New York: Holmes and Meier Publishers Inc. 1977), pp. 1–24. [Chapter 5]

1978

"Reflections on the U.S. Trade Deficit and the Floating Dollar," *Contemporary Economic Problems*, William Fellner (project director and ed.) (Washington, D.C.: American Enterprise Institute, 1978), pp. 221–243.

"The State of the World Economy and the International Monetary System," *Industry of Free China*, vol. L, no. 6 (December 25, 1978). AEI Reprint no. 92.

"Introduction and Summary," by Jacob S. Dreyer, Gottfried Haberler, and Thomas D. Willett, and "Commentaries," *Exchange Rate Flexibility*, Jacob S. Dreyer, G. Haberler, and T. D. Willett (eds.) (Washington, D.C.: American Enterprise Institute, 1978), pp. 1–5 and pp. 62–66. Conference sponsored by the AEI and the U.S. Department of Treasury, 1976.

"El orden Economico International Viejo Y nuevo," Dos Conferencias dictadas en la Facultad de Derecho y Ciencias Sociales de la Universidad Nacional de Buenos Aires, los dias 26 y 27 de Octubre de 1977 con los auspicios del Banco Nacional de Desarrollo (Buenos Aires, 1978), pp. 11–18.

"Less Developed Countries and the Liberal International Economic Order," *Zeitschrift für Nationalökonomie*, vol. 38, no. 1–2 (1978), pp. 145–160.

"Commemorations," *Essays on Economic Policy*, J. Marcus Fleming (New York: Columbia Press, 1978), pp. XIII–XIV.

1979

"The Present Economic Malaise," *Contemporary Economic Problems*, 1979, William Fellner (project director and ed.) (Washington, D.C.: American Enterprise Institute, 1979), pp. 261–290.

"Austria's Economic Development; A Mirror Picture of the World Economy," *Empirische Wirtschaftsforschung und monetare Ökonomik: Festschrift für Stephan Koren zum 60. Geburtstag*, Werner Clement and Karl Socher (eds.) (Berlin: Duncker & Humblot, 1979). AEI Reprint no. 103. Revised version in *The Political Economy of Austria*, Sven W. Arndt (ed.) (Washington, D.C.: American Enterprise Institute, 1982). German translation in *25 Jahre Staatsvertrag - Protokol des Wirtschaftssymposiums*, 14 mai 1980. Osterreichischer Bundesverlag (Vienna, 1981).

"Modernos atagues a un Sistema económico internacional liberal: una perspectiva Histórica," *Moneda y Credito Revista de Economia* (Marzo 1979), pp. 3–29. Earlier, shorter German version appeared in *Deutsche Zeitung und Wirtschafts Zeitung*, no. 53 (July 1958).

1980

*"Notes on Rational and Irrational Expectations," *Wandlungen in Wirtschaft und Gesellschaft: Die Wirtschafts- und die Sozialwissenschaften vor neuen Aufgaben*, Emil Kung (ed.) (Tübingen: J. C. B. Mohr (Paul Siebeck), 1980). AEI Reprint no. 111. [Chapter 27].

"Critical Notes on Rational Expections," *Journal of Money, Credit and Banking*, vol. 12, no. 4, Part 2 (November 1980), pp. 833–836.

"Schumpeter's Capitalism, Socialism, and Democracy," *Schumpeter's Vision*, Prager Special Studies, Arnold Heertje (ed.) (Prager Publishers, 1980), pp. 69–94. Reprinted in Japan with an introduction by Mutsumi Okada (Tokyo: Keibunsha, 1981).

"Flexible-Exchange-Rate Theories and Controversies Once Again," *Flexible Exchange Rate and the Balance of Payments*, John S. Chipman and Charles P. Kindleberg (eds.) (Amsterdam: North-Holland Publishing Co., 1980), pp. 29–48.

*"The Great Depression of the 1930s—Can It Happen Again?" in *The Business Cycle and Public Policy 1929–80*, 96th Congress, 2nd Session, A Compendium of Papers submitted to the Joint Economic Committee of the U.S. Congress, November 28, 1980, pp. 1–19. Hungarian translation, Kozgazdasagi Es Jogi Konyvkiado (Budapest, 1982); AEI Reprint Series no. 118. [Chapter 17]

"The Dollar in the World Economy: Recent Developments in Perspective," *Contemporary Economic Problems*, William Fellner (project director and ed.) (Washington, D.C.: American Enterprise Institute, 1980), pp. 135–165.

1981

"The Economic Malaise of the 1980s: A Positive Program for a Benevolent and Enlightened Dictator," *Essays in Contemporary Economic Problems: Demand, Productivity, and Production*, AEI for Public Policy Research (1981), pp. 215–244.

"Mises's Private Seminar," *Wirtschaftspolitische Blatter*, 4/1981 (Vienna, 1981), pp. 121–126.

"Inflation and Incomes Policy," Vorort des Schweizerischen Handel Sund Industrie-Vereins (Zurich, Switzerland, Dec. 1981), pp. 1–39; postscript, March, 1982, in English in *Economic Notes*, Monte dei Paschi di Siena (Italy, 1982).

"Alexander Gerschenkron," American Philosophical Society, 1980 Year Book (1981), pp. 579–586.

1982

"Reply to Questions Posed by the Honorable Roger W. Jepsen, Vice Chairman of Joint Economic Committee, Congress of the U.S.," *Monetarism and Federal Reserves' Conduct of Monetary Policy*, Compendium of views prepared for the Subcommittee on Monetary and Fiscal Policy of the Joint Economic Committee, 7th Congress, 2nd Session (Washington, D.C.: U.S. Government Printing Office, Dec. 30, 1982), pp. 83–86.

1983

"Fritz Machlup: In Memorian," *Cato Journal*, vol. 3, no. 1 (Spring 1983), pp. 11–14.

"A Comment on 'The Importance of Stable Money,'" *Cato Journal*, vol. 3, no. 1 (Spring, 1983), pp. 83–91.

"Comments" on *Trade Policy in the 1980s*, William R. Cline (ed.), (Washington, D.C.: Institute for International Economics, 1983), pp. 203–209.

"Theory as a Tool of Policy," *The AEI Economist*, Keynes issue (June 1983), pp. 2–4.

"Some Myths about Floating," in *A Monetary Agenda for World Growth*, The International Monetary Conference, Williamsburg, Virginia, May 17, 1983.

1984

"William Fellner in Memorian," *Essays in Contemporary Economic Problems—Disinflation*, 1983–1984 edition (Washington, D.C.: American Enterprise Institute, 1984), pp. 1–4.

William Fellner Memorial Pamphlet (AEI, 1983).

*"The International Monetary System in the World Recession," *Essays in Contemporary Economic Problems—Disinflation*, 1983–1984 Edition (Washington, D.C.: American Enterprise Institute, 1984), pp. 87–129. Reprinted in *Economic Impact*, 1984/3, United States Information Agency under the title "The State of World Economy," pp. 8–14. [Chapter 11]

"Floating Rates Buoy the World Money System," Letters to the Editor, *The Wall Street Journal*, July 25, 1984.

"Vera E. Friedrich Lutz una Famosa Coppia di Economisti dei Nostri Tempi," *Moneta, Dualisms e Pianificazione nel Pensiero di Vera C. Lutz* a cura dell'Ente per gli Studi Monetari, bancari e finanziari 'Luigi Einandi.' (Roma, Italy, 1984), pp. 47—53.

1985

"The Slowdown of the World Economy and the Problem of Stagflation—Some Alternative Explanations and Policy Implication," in *Stagflation, Savings, and the State*, Martin Wolf and Deepak Lai (eds.), World Development Report for 1984 (Washington, D.C.: The World Bank, 1985).

"The Problem of Stagflation—Reflections on the Micro Foundation of Macro Economic Theory and Policy," in *Political Business Cycles and the Political Economy of Stagflation*, Thomas D. Willett (ed.) (Pacific Institute for Public Policy Research, 1985). Also available as an American Enterprise Institute Study (Washington, D.C., 1985).

"Liberal and Illiberal Development—Free Trade Like Honesty Is Still the Best Policy," in *Pioneers in Development*, Gerald M. Meier and Dudley Seers (eds.) (Oxford University Press, published for the World Bank, 1985).

"International Issues Raised by Criticism of the U.S. Budget Deficit," in *Contemporary Economic Problems 1984–1985*, Philip Cagan (ed.) (Washington, D.C.: American Enterprise Institute, 1985), pp. 121–145.

III Book Reviews

1929

The Construction of Index Numbers, by Warran Milton Persons (Boston: Houghton Mifflin Co., 1928). In *Journal of Political Economy*, vol. 37, no. 6 (Dec. 1929), pp. 741–743.

1930

Ein kritscher Beitrag zur Theorie des Bankkredites, by Henrich Mannstaedt (86 S. Jena: G. Fiscner, 1927). In *Zeitschrift für Nationalökonomie*, Band I (1930), p. 177.

Amerikas Schutzzollpolitik und Europa, by Wilhelm Grotkopp (Berlin: Dr. Walther Rothschild, 1929). In *Zeitschrift für Nationalökonomie*, Band I (1930), pp. 779–781.

Die internationale Preisbildung: eine wirtschaftstheoretische Untersuchung über die Probleme der intenationalen Wirtschaftsbeziehungen, by E. Melchinger (Tübingen: Mohr. 1929), pp. iv, 1925. In *American Economic Review*, vol. 20, no. 1 (March, 1930), pp. 86–87.

De omloopssnelheid van het geld, by M. W. Holtrop (Amsterdam: H. J. Paris, 1928). In *Journal of Political Economy*, vol. 38, no. 2 (April 1930), pp. 234–236.

1931

Aussenhandel und Aussenhandelspolitik (Die internationalen Wirtschaftsbeziehungen), by Frank Eulenburg. Abteilung des "Grundriss der Sozialökonomik, vol. VIII (Tübingen: J. C. B. Mohr (Paul Siebeck), 1929). In *Journal of Political Economy*, vol. 39, no. 2 (April 1931), pp. 266–269.

Theorie der internationalen Wirtschaftsbeziehungen, by F. W. Taussig (Leipzig: G. A. Glöckner, 1929). In *Zeitschrift für Nationalökonomie*, Band II (1931), pp. 146–149.

Geldtheorie und Konjunkturtheorie, by Friedrick A. Hayek. Beiträge zur Konjunkturforschung herausgegeben vom Österreichischen Institut für Konjunkturforschung. I. Bd. (Wien-Leipzig: Holder-Pichler-Tempsky A. G., 1929). In *Journal of Political Economy*, vol. 39, no. 3 (June 1931), pp. 404–407.

1932

Die Gestaltung der Handelspolitik in der wichtigsten Ländern, by Heinrich Sieveking (Berlin: W. de Gruyter, 1930). In *Zeitschrift für Nationalökonomie*, Band III (1932), pp. 284–285.

Tariffs: The Case Examined, by a committee of economists under the chairmanship of Sir William Beveridge. Members of the Committee: Benham, Beveridge, Bowley, Gregory, Hicks, Layton, Plant, Robbins, Schwartz. (New York: Longmans Green and Co., 1931). In *Journal of Political Economy*, vol. 40, no. 6 (Dec. 1932), pp. 828–829.

1933

Weltwirtschaft und Aussenhandel Sonderabdrunck aus dem Werk: Die Beamten-Hochschule, by Wilhelm Röpke (Berlin-Wien: Spaeth & Linde, 1931). *Tariffs: The Case Examined by a Committee of Economists under the Chairmanship of Sir William Beveridge* (London: Longmans, Green and Co., 1931). 2 Verbesserte Auflage 1932. *Zölle: Lehrbuch des Internationalen Handels Under Mitarbeit hervorragender englischer Nationalökonomen herausgegeben von sir William Beveridge Aus dem Englischen übersetzt von Friedrich Thalmann Mit einer Einführung von Oskar Morgenstern* (Wien: J. Springer, 1932). In *Zeitschrift für Nationalökonomie*, Band IV (1933), pp. 428–429.

Principle of Economics, by Frederic B. Garver and Alvin H. Hansen (Boston: Ginn and Co., 1928). In *Zeitschrift für Nationalökonomie*, Band IV (1933), pp. 527–528.

Theorie des Dumpings (Problems der Weltwirtschaft herausgegeben von B. Harms 55 Bd.) by Ernst Döblin, IX und 128 (S. Jena: G. Fischer, 1931). In *Zeitschrift für Nationalökonomie*, Band IV (1933), pp. 538–539.

1934

Theorie des Aussenhandels Inwiefern ist das Freihandelsargument ungültig? by Otto von Mering (S. Jena: G. Fischer, 1933). In *Zeitsehrift für Nationalökonomie*, Band V (1934), pp. 397–401.

1935

Krisis der Zahlungsbilanzen (Veröffentlichungen der Handelshochschule St. Gallen), by Albert von Mühlenfels (12 S. St. Gallen, 1932). In *Zeitschrift für Nationalökonomie*, Band VI (1935), pp. 687–688.

1944

Mobilizing for Abundance, by Robert R. Nathan (New York: McGraw-Hill, 1944). In *American Economic Review*, vol. 34, no. 1 (Sept. 1944), pp. 604–606.

1946

America's Place in the World Economy, Addresses delivered at the Fourth Series of Conferences of the Institute on Postwar Reconstruction, Arnold J. Zurcher and Richmond Page (eds.) (New York: Institute on Postwar Reconstruction, New York University, 1945). In *American Economic Review*, vol. 36, no. 1 (March 1946), pp. 169–170.

1947

Grundsätze und Methoden zur Ermittlung der richtigen Währungsrelation zum Ausland, Vol. I, by Hans Bohi ("Untersuchungen des Instituts für Wirtschaftsforschung Zürich") (Bern, Switzerland: A. Francke A. G. Verlag, 1944). In *Journal of Political Economy*, vol. 55, no. 6 (December 1947), p. 586.

1951

The Life of John Maynard Keynes, by R. F. Harrod (New York: Harcourt Brace and Co., 1951). In *The Annals of the American Academy*, vol. 276 (July 1951), pp. 148–151.

1953

Problem of Economic Union, by James E. Meade (Chicago: University of Chicago Press, 1953). In *Journal of Political Economy*, vol. LXI, no. 4 (August, 1953), pp. 354–355.

1955

Foreign Exchange in the Postwar World, by Raymond F. Mikesell, with a Foreward by J. F. Dewhurst (New York: Twentieth Century Fund, 1954). In *Journal of Political Economy*, vol. LXIII, no. 1 (Februrary 1955), pp. 83–84.

1963

Money Growth and Methodology and Other Essays in Economics, in honor of Johan Akerman, March 31, 1961, Hugo Hegeland (ed.) (Lund, Sweden: CWK Gleerup, 1961). In *American Economic Review*, vol. 53 (March 1963), pp. 143–147.

1966

Money in the International Order, J. Carter Murphy (ed.) (Dallas: Southern Methodist University Press, 1964). In *American Economic Review*, vol. 56. no. 1 (March 1966), pp. 252–254.

1968

Theorie der Geldpolitik, by A. Bosch and R. Veit (Tübingen: J. C. B. Mohr (Paul Siebeck), 1966). In *Zeitschrift für Nationalökonomie*, Band XXVIII (1968), pp. 107–110.

1974

The World in Depression 1929–1939, by Charles P. Kindleberger. History of the World Economy in the Twentieth Century series, vol. 4 (Berkeley: University of California Press, 1973). In *Journal of Economic Literature*, vol. XII (June 1974), pp. 490–493.

1976

Economic Mobility and National Income Policy, by Richard N. Cooper, Wicksell Lectures 1973, (Stockholm, 1974). In *Journal of International Economics*, vol. 6, no. 1 (Feb. 1976), pp. 109–110.

The Monetary Approach to the Balance of Payments, Jacob Frankel and Harry G. Johnson (eds.) (Toronto and Buffalo: University of Toronto Press, 1976). In *Journal of Economic Literature*, vol. XIV, no. 4 (Dec. 1976), pp. 1324–1328.

1977

Jospeh A. Schumpeter: Leben und Werk eines Grossen Sozialökonomen (Life and Work of a Great Social Scientist), by Erich Schneider; translated and introduced by W. E. Kuhn (Lincoln: Bureau of Business Research, Univ. of Nebraska, 1975). In *Journal of Political Economy*, vol. 85, no. 3 (June 1977), p. 660.

1978

Inflation, Exchange Rates and the World Economy, by W. M. Corden (Chicago; University of Chicago Press, 1977). In *Journal of Money, Credit and Banking*, vol. 10, no. 3 (Aug. 1978), pp. 391–396.

1979

The International Monetary Fund, 1966–1971: The system Under Stress, vol. I: *Narrative*, by Margaret de Vries; Vol. II: *Documents*, edited by Margaret de Vries (Washington, D.C.: International Monetary Fund, 1976). In *Journal of International Economics*, vol. 9, no. 4 (November 1979), pp. 591–593.

Index

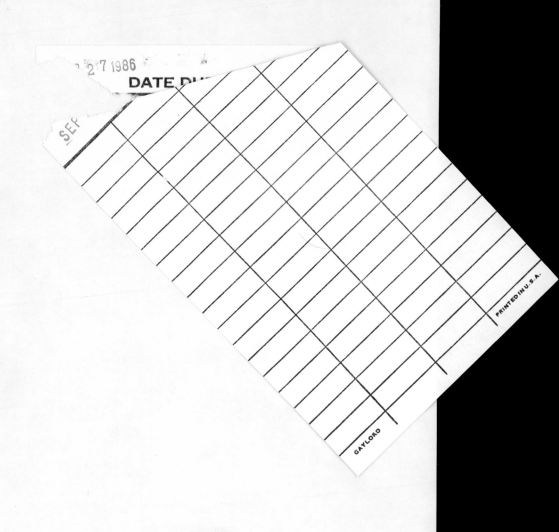